GLOBAL HUMAN SMUGGLING

THIRD EDITION

Global Human Smuggling

Buying Freedom in a Retreating World

edited by Luigi Achilli and David Kyle

Johns Hopkins University Press
BALTIMORE

© 2023 Johns Hopkins University Press
All rights reserved. Published 2023
Printed in the United States of America on acid-free paper

2 4 6 8 9 7 5 3 1

Johns Hopkins University Press
2715 North Charles Street
Baltimore, Maryland 21218
www.press.jhu.edu

Library of Congress Cataloging-in-Publication Data

Names: Achilli, Luigi, 1979– editor. | Kyle, David, 1960– editor.
Title: Global human smuggling : buying freedom in a retreating
world / edited by Luigi Achilli and David Kyle.
Description: Third edition. | Baltimore, Maryland : Johns Hopkins
University Press, [2023] | 1st edition: 2001. 2nd edition: 2011. |
Includes bibliographical references and index.
Identifiers: LCCN 2023003586 | ISBN 9781421447513 (paperback :
acid-free paper) | ISBN 9781421447520 (ebook)
Subjects: LCSH: Emigration and immigration. | Human smuggling. |
Transnational crime. | Organized crime.
Classification: LCC JV6201 .G56 2023 | DDC 364.1/372—dc23/eng/20230314
LC record available at https://lccn.loc.gov/2023003586

A catalog record for this book is available from the British Library.

Special discounts are available for bulk purchases of this book.
For more information, please contact Special Sales at specialsales@jh.edu.

CONTENTS

FOREWORD ix
Morgane Nicot

INTRODUCTION 1
Control, Complexity, and Creativity
David Kyle and Luigi Achilli

CHAPTER 1 37
Smuggling the State Back In: Agents of Human Smuggling Reconsidered
David Kyle and John Dale

CHAPTER 2 65
How the State Made Smuggling and Smuggling Made the State:
A History of Immigration Control and Evasion on the US-Mexico Line
Peter Andreas

CHAPTER 3 87
Multinational Initiatives against Global Trafficking
in Persons for Sexual Exploitation, 1899–1999
Eileen P. Scully

CHAPTER 4 106
Multilateral Protocols on Trafficking and Smuggling:
Divergent Paths of Cooperation and Disintegration since 2000
Sarah P. Lockhart

CHAPTER 5   127
Human Smuggling and Terrorism:
Complex Adaptive Systems and Special Operations
David C. Ellis

CHAPTER 6   152
Migrant Smuggling across the EU-Turkey Border:
Structural, Institutional, and Agency-Based Factors
Ahmet İçduygu

CHAPTER 7   174
The Double Duality of Migrant Smugglers:
An Analytical Framework
Jørgen Carling

CHAPTER 8   198
Financial Elements of Clandestine Journeys:
How You Pay Your Smuggler Matters
Kim Wilson

CHAPTER 9   220
The Burners: Smuggling Networks and Maghrebi Migrants
Matt Herbert

CHAPTER 10   249
Smuggling Migrants from Africa to Europe:
Threat, Resource, or Bargaining Chip?
Luca Raineri

CHAPTER 11   270
Irregular Migration and Human Smuggling Networks:
The Case of North Korea
Kyunghee Kook

CHAPTER 12   290
People Smuggling in Southeast Asia: Rohingya and Chin Stories
of Agency, Freedom, and Power in Cross-Border Movement
Gerhard Hoffstaedter

CHAPTER 13   308
What the Experiences of Women
Tell Us about the Facilitation of Irregular Migration
Gabriella E. Sanchez

CHAPTER 14   325
Enter the Boogeyman: Representations of Human Smuggling
in Mainstream Narratives of Migration
Luigi Achilli and Alice Massari

CHAPTER 15   345
Ecuadorean Migrant Smuggling: Contemporary Patterns and Dynamics
Soledad Álvarez Velasco

CHAPTER 16   371
Combatting People Smuggling with the Same Crime?
Australia's "Creative" Anti-smuggling Efforts in Indonesia
Antje Missbach and Wayne Palmer

CHAPTER 17   390
The Rise of "Border Security": Chaos, Clutter, and Complexity
in a Technological Arms Race
Victor Manjarrez Jr.

CHAPTER 18   410
Transnational Struggles and the "State": Biopower and Biopolitics
in the Case of a Nigerian Human Trafficking Ring
Gregory Feldman

CHAPTER 19   425
The Transformation of Mexican Migrant Smuggling Networks
during the Twenty-First Century
Simón Pedro Izcara Palacios

CHAPTER 20   448
In Search of Protection: Irregular Mobility among
Palestinian Youth in Gaza
Caitlin Procter

Contributors   467

Index   475

FOREWORD

Morgane Nicot

WHEN THE FIRST EDITION OF *Global Human Smuggling* was released in 2001, United Nations member states had just adopted the first-ever international law instrument on migrant smuggling. It would take another four years for the Protocol against the Smuggling of Migrants by Land, Sea and Air (Smuggling of Migrants Protocol), supplementing the UN Convention against Transnational Organized Crime (UNTOC), to enter into force (United Nations 2000a). The impact this new instrument would have on the phenomenon and how states would make use of its provisions was unknown and possibly yet unforeseeable.

The smuggling of migrants was defined in the context of the negotiation over a new convention against transnational crime, and it was quickly distinguished from trafficking in persons that was the subject of another protocol to the UNTOC (Trafficking in Persons Protocol; United Nations 2000b). The objectives of the drafters of this set of international legal instruments were clear: establish a common understanding of transnational organized crime in its various forms and prevent and prosecute this crime through enhanced cooperation. States came to an agreement to define migrant smuggling as the procurement of the illegal entry into a territory of another person with the aim of making a financial or other material profit (article 3, Smuggling of Migrants Protocol).

Three-quarters of UN member states have agreed to this definition by becoming parties to the Smuggling of Migrants Protocol.[1] Its objectives and provisions hence bind a fairly wide share of the international community. But what do we know about the measures adopted by states to address migrant smuggling and about their impact? Are we able to assess whether these actions contributed to reducing migrant smuggling in the last twenty years, whether it is less deadly for migrants and generates less profit for criminals, whether organized criminal groups have moved away from this business, and whether this is a result of states' increased capacity to cooperate among themselves? In other words, did the protocol serve to prevent smuggling? Did it support the prosecution of profit-seeking transnational organized crime groups and the freezing and confiscation of their criminal assets? Did it foster effective cooperation across borders (when implemented in conjunction with UNTOC), and were these actions conducive to upholding the rights of the smuggled persons?

Civil society, nongovernmental organizations (NGOs), and academics, among others, increasingly doubt that the protocol succeeded in addressing those challenges, as shown by many of the contributors to this book, and fear that its implementation has collateral effects, including on protecting the rights of people on the move. Their views are key to establishing the evidence base that is needed to adjust anti-smuggling measures to evolving realities and emerging challenges. Policymakers would benefit from considering the questions raised by the contributors to this book and the conclusions they draw from the critical analysis of anti-smuggling measures, not only from a legal perspective but also from a socioeconomic standpoint. This new edition of *Global Human Smuggling* captures thought-provoking reflections and offers innovative leads to be considered for a balanced approach that protects people and communities that engage with or are affected by smuggling.

A closer look at the Smuggling of Migrants Protocol is useful to understand the commitments states made by becoming parties. The protocol is primarily a criminal justice instrument that supplements UNTOC with provisions applying directly to organized migrant smuggling ventures. The presence and vigilance of human rights defenders (including UN agencies) during the negotiations (Gallagher and David 2014: 36–37) have ensured that the protocol contained reminders of states' obligation to respect international human rights and humanitarian and refugee law when implementing measures against migrant smuggling. The stated objectives of the protocol (article 2, Smuggling of Migrants Protocol) reflect this requirement of a balanced approach between prevention and prosecution of the crime, cooperation among states, and protection of the rights of the smuggled migrants. The articulation between the protocol and its mother convention, UNTOC, is also of essence for a coherent implementation of their provisions against migrant smuggling, especially for effective cooperation against cross-border crime (McAdam 2020). Yet the protocol often seems to be considered separate from UNTOC, which may explain common misunderstandings about its scope and purpose. Many, supporters and opponents, see it as a tool to curb irregular migration. This could be in part explained by a focus by many states on repression of the facilitation of irregular migration together with irregular migration.

Practice has shown that a large share of states have opted to address smuggling through the criminalization of irregular migration and its facilitation (UNODC 2017). In doing so, do they depart from the protocol's requirements and definition of migrant smuggling? This position implies that the migrant is considered an offender for breaching the laws regulating stay and entry in a territory. The protocol does not prohibit this practice,[2] although the UN at large does not support it. The criminalization of the facilitation of irregular migration (illegal entry or stay) in national legislation usually captures a large range of conducts and motivations of alleged offenders who may not be seeking to profit financially or materially, but if they were, they would face heavier sentences. Only situations where a financial or material benefit was sought would trigger the implementation of the Smuggling of Migrants Protocol and the UNTOC. The protocol also strictly prohibits smuggled migrants from being prosecuted for their own smuggling together with their smugglers, as accomplices, for example (article 5, Smuggling of Migrants Protocol).

Many states have favored this broader approach to criminalization,[3] and so has the European Union (EU) (also party to the protocol), whose legal framework to tackle irregular migration and its facilitation (the Facilitation Directive) does not require that the motivation for the facilitation of illegal entry be for the purpose of making a profit (European Union 2002). Binding on all EU member states,[4] this framework gives them the option to explicitly exclude humanitarian action from the application of the Facilitation Directive. This humanitarian exemption is mandatory for enabling the stay of a person but is only optional for facilitating the entry of a foreign national. As a result, states may decide to criminalize any form of assistance to migrants in relation to their illegal entry, whether provided as a service against payment or on charitable grounds.

While the protocol obliges states to treat more severely circumstances that endangered the life or safety of those smuggled, or that subjected migrants to inhuman or degrading treatment (article 6(3), Smuggling of Migrants Protocol); to uphold the migrants' right to life (article 16); and to respect the principle of non-refoulement (article 19), some jurisdictions still went on arresting and prosecuting NGOs and their personnel—for example, those engaging in search-and-rescue operations to save migrants' lives, including on the high seas—for smuggling or related charges.[5] With no requirement to bring evidence that these people's intention was to materially profit from transporting migrants across borders, and no humanitarian exemption included in the law, the consequence could be that less assistance will eventually be lent to migrants in distress, whose life and safety states have an obligation to protect. In the view of the independent expert on human rights and international solidarity, the "criminalization or suppression of the rendering of humanitarian assistance to irregular migrants and refugees significantly and unjustifiably impairs or harms many of their human rights and is thus illegal under international human rights law" (United Nations 2019: para. 48 [p.15]).

The drafters of the protocol did not consider the need to provide an exemption clause for humanitarian action, as they believed that including the purpose of obtaining a financial or other material benefit as an element both of the definition and of the criminalization of migrant smuggling made it clear that the conduct of family members and humanitarian workers was not within the ambit of the protocol:

> The reference to "a financial or other material benefit" as an element of the definition [of migrant smuggling] was included in order to emphasize that the intention was to include the activities of

organized criminal groups acting for profit, but to exclude the activities of those who provided support to migrants for humanitarian reasons or on the basis of close family ties. It was not the intention of the Protocol to criminalize the activities of family members or support groups such as religious or non-governmental organizations. (UNODC 2000: para. 88)

Anne Gallagher, a leading scholar on UNTOC and its protocols, has argued that "in implementing their legislative and regulatory responses, States have moved substantially away from the core tenets of the Protocol" (2017: 2). Indeed, the safeguards that existed for those providing assistance and protection measures in favor of migrants disappeared when the purpose (i.e., profit) element was left out of the core migrant smuggling offense in national legislation, unless a mandatory humanitarian exemption was introduced in the law. The consequences can be devastating for migrants' safety but could also engage states' responsibility. When examining deaths at sea, including in the hands of smugglers, the UN special rapporteur of the Human Rights Council on Extrajudicial, Summary or Arbitrary Executions reported that some states had a responsibility in the "unlawful killings of refugees and migrants, including through the excessive use of force and as a result of deterrence policies and practices which increase the risk of death" (United Nations 2017).

To avoid such disastrous consequences of states' anti-smuggling responses, a holistic approach that includes protection and prevention measures is thus essential to minimize the risk to the lives of migrants and refugees and the involvement of organized criminal networks in smuggling. The prevention measures contained in the protocol focus mostly on putting border-control measures in place, enhancing document security, training staff, and exchanging information. Indeed, beefing up borders is the most common preventive measure put in place by states, but when it is done in isolation, the problem is displaced, not suppressed (Achilli and Sanchez 2017). Journeys then become more expensive and dangerous for migrants while smuggling services become more professional and have a greater capacity to corrupt state officials. Opponents of such measures also stress that if there were no borders and the free movement of people were allowed, there would be no need for smugglers, there would be no illegal profits, and there would be no death and abuse of people in the hands of smugglers. What about other prevention measures such as addressing the root causes of smuggling—including poverty, insecurity, conflict, and the lack of economic opportunities or access to education—and investing in policies that provide accessible, legal, and safe channels of migration, as called for by many contributors in this book?

The discussions leading up to the New York Declaration and to the adoption of the Global Compact on Migration (United Nations 2018b, n.d.-b) confirmed the need for a strong, multidimensional prevention component to address migrant smuggling, and unsafe migration in general, in the long term. This requires a sustained and concerted dialogue among states that is directed at setting up agreeable objectives. Would the necessity to protect borders and the sovereignty of states offer common grounds for destination, transit, and origin countries altogether? Would it rather be the principle of shared humanity, in line with the UN Charter's spirit, that would reconcile all positions? Some believe that "in a political landscape dominated by economic and nationalist rhetoric, there is little space remaining for discussions around multiculturalism, global equality, and peacebuilding, all of which are aspirations that once lurked at the edges of migration analysis and perhaps form part of the long-term solutions to migrant smuggling and human trafficking" (Dandurand and Jahn 2019: 13). Although we can and should applaud the achievement that the (nonbinding) Global Compact on Migration represents, and the inclusion therein of a specific section addressing migrant smuggling, we can also regret that several states decided to opt out of the compact for fear of compromising their sovereign rights over their territory. Considering the section calling for the strengthening of the transnational response to migrant smuggling, it appears that the global compact did not create new obligations in this regard. So, whether in or out of the compact, states would still be bound by the same obligations.

Given these observations, it has thus become all the more essential that the international community strives to promote a balanced and comprehensive implementation of the four objectives of the protocol, in the context of UNTOC. This should be aligned with and be part of a holistic approach that aims at achieving the objectives of a safe, orderly, and regular migration identified in the global compact, in particular the following (United Nations 2018b):

- minimizing the adverse drivers and structural factors that compel people to leave their country of origin
- enhancing availability and flexibility of pathways for regular migration
- addressing and reducing vulnerabilities in migration including by "reviewing relevant policies and practices to ensure that they do not create, exacerbate or unintentionally increase vulnerabilities of migrants" (United Nations 2018b: para. 23)
- saving lives and establishing coordinated international efforts on missing migrants, including by "ensur[ing] that the provision of an exclusively humanitarian nature for migrants is not considered unlawful" and "review[ing the] impact of migration-related policies and law to ensure that these do not raise or create the risk of migrants going missing" (United Nations 2018b: para. 24)

Two decades after the adoption of the Smuggling of Migrants Protocol, the international community delivered a strong message for a safe, orderly, and regular migration that requires working hand in hand, and not on the basis of unilateral measures. On the twentieth anniversary of the protocol's adoption, the states parties to UNTOC also came to an agreement (after lengthy and difficult negotiations) to set up a review mechanism for the implementation of UNTOC and its supplementing protocols (United Nations 2018a). This mechanism offers an opportunity to observe the implementation of the protocol by its states parties. Based on a peer-review system among states parties, it offers two options for civil society to contribute to the consultations: either (1) at the national level, which is left to the individual state's discretion, or (2) through constructive dialogues that provide a space to exchange views and solutions from thematic rather than national perspectives. Considering that civil society organizations and actors are often the recipients of smuggled migrants' accounts of their contacts with smugglers and hence key witnesses to the whole process, and that their actions are often directly affected by anti-smuggling measures, they can be instrumental in better understanding the mechanics behind migration and organized crime and in initiating and accompanying a change of narrative on migrant smuggling and an adjustment of counter-smuggling policies. Hearing their voices and experiences, together with the views of researchers such as the contributors to *Global Human Smuggling*, is today more needed than ever to overcome practices that are detrimental to human life, security, safety, and dignity.

NOTES

The views expressed herein are those of the author and do not necessarily reflect the views of the United Nations.

1. The number was 151 states parties on April 4, 2023. For updates, see United Nations (n.d.-a).
2. See article 6(4) of the Smuggling of Migrants Protocol: "Nothing in this Protocol shall prevent a State Party from taking measures against a person whose conduct constitutes an offence under its domestic law."
3. For an overview of national anti-smuggling legislation, see UNODC (n.d.-c).
4. For a thorough analysis of the relevant legislation in the region, see European Agency for Fundamental Rights (2014).
5. See, for example, the case of Carola Rackete, captain of the NGO rescue vessel *Sea Watch*, in Italy in 2019 (UNODC, n.d.-a). Also see the French Constitutional Council Decision No. 2018-717/718 QPC of July 6, 2018, which repelled the provision of the French Code on the Entry and Residence of Foreign Nationals and the Right to Asylum that did not exempt humanitarian assistance without any material or financial benefit from criminal liability (UNODC, n.d.-b).

REFERENCES

Achilli, Luigi, and Gabriella Sanchez. 2017. *What Does It Mean to Disrupt the Business Models of People Smugglers?* Policy Brief Issue 2017/09, Migration Policy Centre, European University Institute.

Dandurand, Yvon, and Jessica Jahn. 2019. "The Failing International Legal Framework on Migrant Smuggling and Human Trafficking." In *The Palgrave International Handbook of Human Trafficking*, edited by John Winterdyk and Jackie Jones, 783–800. Cham: Springer Nature Switzerland.

European Agency for Fundamental Rights. 2014. "Criminalization of Migrants in an Irregular Situation and of Persons Engaging with Them." https://fra.europa.eu/en/publication/2014/criminalisation-migrants-irregular-situation-and-persons-engaging-them.

European Union. 2002. Council Directive 2002/90/EC of 28 November 2002 Defining the Facilitation of Unauthorized Entry, Transit and Residence. https://eur-lex.europa.eu/legal-content/EN/ALL/?uri=CELEX%3A32002L0090.

Gallagher, Anne. 2017. "Whatever Happened to the Migrant Smuggling Protocol?" In *Ideas to Inform International Cooperation on Safe, Orderly and Regular Migration*, convened by M. McAuliffe and M. Klein Solomon. Geneva: International Organization for Migration.

Gallagher, Anne T., and Fiona David. 2014. *The International Law of Migrant Smuggling*. Cambridge: Cambridge University Press.

McAdam, Marika. 2020. "There's No Human Trafficking or Migrant Smuggling without Organised Crime, the Law Says—and That Matters." openDemocracy, February 26, 2020. https://www.opendemocracy.net/en/beyond-trafficking-and-slavery/theres-no-human-trafficking-or-migrant-smuggling-without-organised-crime-the-law-says-and-that-matters/.

United Nations. 2000a. Protocol against the Smuggling of Migrants Supplementing the United Nations Convention against Transnational Organized Crime, UNGA 55/25 (November 15, 2000, entry into force on January 28, 2004). https://www.unodc.org/documents/treaties/UNTOC/Publications/TOC%20Convention/TOCebook-e.pdf.

———. 2000b. Protocol to Prevent, Suppress and Punish Trafficking in Persons, Especially Women and Children, supplementing the United Nations Convention against Transnational Organized Crime, UNGA 55/25 (November 15, 2000, entry into force on December 25, 2003). https://www.unodc.org/documents/treaties/UNTOC/Publications/TOC%20Convention/TOCebook-e.pdf.

———. 2017. A/72/335: Unlawful Death of Refugees and Migrants—Note by the Secretary-General—Report of the Special Rapporteur of the Human Rights Council on Extrajudicial, Summary or Arbitrary Executions. Press release, August 15, 2017. https://www.ohchr.org/en/documents/thematic-reports/a72335-unlawful-death-refugees-and-migrants-note-secretary-general.

———. 2018a. Conference of the Parties to the United Nations Convention against Transnational Organized Crime, Resolution 9/1, Establishment of the Mechanism for the Review of the Implementation of the United Nations Convention against Transnational Organized Crime and the Protocols Thereto. https://www.unodc.org/documents/treaties/UNTOC/Review%20Mechanism/Resolution/English.pdf.

———. 2018b. Global Compact for Safe, Orderly and Regular Migration—Resolution Adopted by the General Assembly, A/RES/73/195 (December 19, 2018). https://undocs.org/A/RES/73/195.

———. 2019. Human Rights and International Solidarity: Report of the Independent Expert on Human Rights and International Solidarity, A/HRC/41/44 (April 16, 2019). https://ap.ohchr.org/documents/dpage_e.aspx?si=A/HRC/41/44.

———. n.d.-a. "Chapter XVIII Penal Matters." Status of treaty, United Nations Treaty Collection. Accessed February 10, 2023. https://treaties.un.org/Pages/ViewDetails.aspx?src=TREATY&mtdsg_no=XVIII-12-b&chapter=18&clang=_en.

———. n.d.-b. "New York Declaration on Refugees and Migrants 2016." Accessed February 10, 2023. http://refugeesmigrants.un.org/declaration.

UNODC (United Nations Office on Drugs and Crime). 2000. Interpretive Notes for the Official Records (*Travaux préparatoires*) of the Negotiation of the United Nations

Convention against Transnational Organized Crime and the Protocols Thereto, A/55/383/Add. 1 (November 3, 2000). https://www.unodc.org/pdf/crime/final_instruments/383a1e.pdf.

———. 2017. *The Concept of "Financial or Other Material Benefit" in the Smuggling of Migrants Protocol*. Issue Paper. Vienna: UNODC. https://www.unodc.org/documents/human-trafficking/Migrant-Smuggling/Issue-Papers/UNODC_Issue_Paper_The_Profit_Element_in_the_Smuggling_of_Migrants_Protocol.pdf.

———. n.d.-a. "Carola Rackete/Sea Watch Case." Accessed February 10, 2023. https://sherloc.unodc.org/cld/case-law-doc/migrantsmugglingcrimetype/ita/2019/carola_racketesea_watch_case.html?lng=en&tmpl=sherloc.

———. n.d.-b. "No. 2018-717/718 QPC." Accessed February 10, 2023. https://sherloc.unodc.org/cld/case-law-doc/migrantsmugglingcrimetype/fra/2018/no._2018-717718_qpc.html?lng=en&tmpl=som.

———. n.d.-c. Smuggling of Migrants Knowledge Portal legislation database. Accessed Avril 4, 2023. https://sherloc.unodc.org/cld/v3/som/legdb/index.html?lng=en.

GLOBAL HUMAN SMUGGLING

INTRODUCTION

Control, Complexity, and Creativity

David Kyle and Luigi Achilli

WHY A THIRD EDITION?

Three decades ago, the topic of human smuggling was virtually nonexistent for academic researchers, though the practice itself is very old. Armed with organized collaborators, the means of transportation, and knowledge of the geographic and cultural terrains, people have for millennia facilitated the movement of others across physical and legal borders for reasons that range from the most sinister to the most altruistic. In the decades before the American Civil War, approximately one hundred thousand slaves were guided to northern states and Canada as "passengers" on the Underground Railroad, aided by a network of "conductors" who delivered them at great risk to a succession of safe houses or stations. Though slavery is nowhere legal today, extreme coercive control over people for profits is still ubiquitous globally and is associated with the broad, unevenly applied, rubric of "human trafficking." In contrast, at the center of human *smuggling* are migrants seeking opportunities for education and work unavailable to them for generations, to be reunited with loved ones living abroad, or refuge from persecution, war, and domestic abuse, among other motives described in this volume; the common feature is that they hire others to help them leave what they have come to believe is an untenable situation.

Given its extremely diverse global and clandestine nature, actions connected to the rubric of human smuggling can be abusive and violent, while routes and strategies regularly expose migrants to bullying and violence by others in transit. However, migrant smugglers are more akin to the conductors of the Underground Railroad, not the slave traders, with fees ranging from zero to tens of thousands of dollars or euros. Like previous editions, this volume focuses on the organization of the irregular journeys, where "smugglers"—a term that encompasses a diverse range of people engaging in some form of unauthorized or criminal(ized) activity—play a central role as facilitators or migration merchants. Most are engaged in actions consistent with a global culture of high mobility and nominally humanitarian ideals—they offer freedom and opportunity for those who believe they have few alternatives because they are hindered, exploited, or persecuted in ways inconsistent with the values shaping and justifying legal forms of social and physical mobility.

This book is about the enormous variety of people, facilitators, and contexts that contemporary human smuggling encompasses in every region of the world, the conditions for its recent evolution globally, the attempts to curtail or manage it by those with the means and motivation to intervene, and the impacts on or outcomes for all involved. Since the first edition of *Global Human Smuggling* was published in 2001, much has changed globally, directly affecting human mobility and attempts to manage it, which in turn has often catalyzed the social dimensions that lead to human or migrant smuggling.[1] Human smuggling is now more entrenched than ever, with laws and enforcement strategies to curtail it largely unsuccessful and frequently counterproductive. For the 2011 second edition of *Global Human Smuggling*, the introduction (with coeditor Rey Koslowski) began with these paragraphs, still relevant a dozen years later:

> United by powerful technologies, complex economic systems, and social institutions, the world is globalized for the first time in human history; it also now faces the truly global challenges of a transformative financial recession, the myriad effects of climate change, and the implications of an additional three billion people by midcentury. In sharp contrast, the ability for people to seek opportunities and escape serious problems of scarce resources, distributed unevenly within and among states, by resettling elsewhere is far from globalized....
>
> ... This second edition explores the historical context, social organization, and political ramifications of human smuggling across international borders as a global phenomenon.... More than a sub-

> category of international migration, the trade in migrants is a topic that intersects contemporary anxieties concerning the global political economy, ethnic and gender stratification, multiculturalism, population growth, political corruption, transnational crime, the Internet, human rights abuses, climate change, and the (in)ability of states and global agencies to manage any of these effectively. (Kyle and Koslowski 2011: 1–2)

Though the global recession has faded, climate-related crises have intensified and other events shaping mobility across borders have emerged: a once-in-a-century pandemic with myriad fallouts, a growing nationalist antidemocratic politics pulling up the welcome mat (to the extent it existed), a war between Russia and Ukraine on the doorsteps of the European Union, large-scale refugee movements from the Middle East, and the very recent development of a powerful artificial intelligence available to any smartphone, which will transform human physical and social mobility in ways we cannot yet imagine. These will continue to create the conditions for some to try to cross borders outside state laws and programs at great personal risk, compelled by an imagined better or safer future at a destination, typically very different from their own.

The three editions of this volume have a common theme across this uneven, dynamic landscape: the contributors reveal how politics, not just profits and criminality, shape migrant smuggling at the scale and complexity we are witnessing today. Because of its highly political nature, the coverage of human smuggling operates as a self-fulfilling prophecy, confirming preexisting beliefs about migrants and smugglers and reinforcing an impulse to simply demonize "the smugglers" rather than aid a clearly vulnerable population on the move. Primed by a polarizing media seeking to sell the most sensational story, and increasingly lacking the resources or attention span to fully delve into its many layers, there is no better example of confirmation bias globally than how migrant smuggling attracts attention to only those aspects we think we know as part of a morality tale of criminality, vulnerability, and regular tragedies on land or at sea.

With a desire to provide even greater context and understanding about those at the center of these stories, this new edition is much more than an update—a growing transnational research community at work on the topic, consistent with the insights of the first two editions, inspired the volume. While not entirely replacing the observations and insights of previous editions, this third edition reveals a novel research agenda of scholars from multiple academic disciplines, with research and writing that does not fit comfortably into either immigration or criminological subfields alone. This present volume represents the progress of human smuggling research on every continent, with nineteen new contributors and three updated critical chapters from previous editions. If space had allowed, we would have been able to triple the length of this volume given the growth of similar research in all regions of the world, much of it coordinated in local academic institutions based in sending and destination countries.

TWO DECADES OF HUMAN SMUGGLING RESEARCH

This volume comes at a critical time in migration studies, one in which the gap between empirically grounded scholarship and growing public attention to the most problematic, risky kinds of mobility is enormous. In recent years, there has been an explosion of popular and media interest in the various activities that loosely fall under the category of human smuggling (e.g., Gallien and Weigand 2022). Reflecting an assumption that the smuggling groups are taking advantage of their position of absolute domination, they are said to thrive in migration crises, creating in the process global syndicates of organized crime (e.g., GIN 2021; Miklaucic and Brewer 2013; Naim 2010; Shelley 2014). This view, which often invokes the "human cargo" trope, commonly folding into it coercive human trafficking for modern slavery, is buttressed by official state sources that claim that the systematic deception and exploitation of unauthorized movement across borders via human smuggling has become one of the fastest-growing criminal enterprises in the world (OECD 2016). For example, Europol (2016) estimated that in 2015 alone, criminal networks involved in facilitating irregular migration earned between EUR 3 and 6 billion, and the United Nations (UN) Office on Drugs and Crime reported that networks in Central America and along the US-Mexico border generate some US$7 billion, a figure that UN officials consider low (Blancas Madrigal 2017). The sense of impending doom communicated through mainstream academic and policy writing in this field has had considerable influence on public and political discourse, serving as a key legal, moral, and political justification for consolidating more intrusive and authoritarian forms of border security and migration policies (Bigo and Guild 2005; Pallister-Wilkins 2015).

Official narratives of smuggling point to complex, transnational criminal networks as responsible for the precarious and risky journeys migrants and refugees embark on—and for their economic, sexual, emotional, and physical suffering; exploitation; and sometimes violence. Depictions of irregular migrants from war-torn and economically deprived regions flooding refugee camps, riding atop trains, or drowning in vast seas have been effective at communicating notions of contemporary migration flows as constituting unprecedented, massive, and dangerous crises. Portrayed as stretching thin the resources of nation-states and undermining their security, irregular migration has incited anti-immigrant sentiment, prompted voters to support control regimes that favor strict migration policies, and secured support for increasing border surveillance and controls. The concerns over the ties of smuggling to varied forms of transnational crime have allowed Western governments to justify immigration enforcement actions in which counter-smuggling measures appear as the most important mechanism to stop or reduce the influx of irregular migrants. In February 2016, for example, Europol launched the European Migrant Smuggling Centre to "proactively support EU Member States and their operational partners in targeting and dismantling complex and sophisticated criminal networks involved in migrant smuggling" (Europol 2016: 14). The tragic images of capsized boats floating in the Mediterranean Sea, dead babies washed ashore, and women and children in tattered clothes crammed into refugee camps in hope of reaching countries in the Global North continue to fuel the official narratives. And the connection of their deaths to complex, organized networks has been fundamental in the emergence of crisis narratives, which, far from diminishing immigration flows, have resulted in an overabundance of short-sighted, piecemeal policy efforts that prioritize temporary solutions over the provision of sustainable and effective mechanisms of human protection and security.

Most news stories demonizing irregular migration, based on contemporary journalism with decreasing levels of support for in-depth reportage, regularly simplify the historical context of the phenomenon and the conflicting motives and difficult decisions leading to migrant journeys, and, similarly, why and how someone, often a return migrant, turns to smuggling or other forms of facilitation. Indeed, the facile consensus that smugglers are the predators par excellence of late modernity rarely leads to a consideration of motivations other than simply exploiting people for profit while putting them in grave danger. In the realm of human smuggling, it is not uncommon to find the simultaneous presence of violence and solidarity, as well as deception and trust. Contrary to popular perceptions, however, deception and exploitation can frequently be attributed to the sustained state of deprivation and irregularity without the protection of state agents experienced by migrants, rather than the criminal intent of mafia-like organizations.

Another variation on the tunnel vision marking this topic is a mirror image of the previous one, as the focus is more on the enforcers than the smugglers, with attention paid solely to individual migrants' mistreatment en route or in detention by enforcement agents of states, leaving those facilitating their crossing in the shadows or implicitly reproducing stories about who is deserving or most emblematic of the victimization in question. While it is true that many appalling things happen within the set of actions tied to government or law enforcement entities tasked with border security and control—many of them documented throughout this volume—scholars of authorized immigration, not only journalists, often unproblematically promote the meritocratic notion that some migrants are deserving of legal immigration pathways due to their "high-value" talents and have trouble recognizing how this merit-based system is, in part, a contributing factor undergirding state policies they find questionable or problematic in their execution. That is, as academic researchers we find it difficult to include our own unevenly meritocratic, highly bordered institutions within the frame of analysis. Who has "merit" has become a key criterion for all institutions and government agencies, though one that is itself rarely examined critically given the high propensity for humans to engage in self-regarding, self-dealing bias and tribal fear-mongering. For example, the ideal of only facilitating the legal immigration of those, typically wealthy or at least upper-middle-class, migrants with high levels of education or investment potential shapes the overall contours of policies that reinforce corrupt, dystopic educational systems in the origin country. The "highly skilled" feel they deserve the highest levels of freedom to resettle no matter the extreme elitism, nepotism, inherited wealth, and institutionalized social exclusion that marked their trajectories, while most in these same sending regions do not have an opportunity to prove, let alone improve, their talents. More importantly, the commonsensical mobility-of-merit consensus also implies and entrenches the central idea that even those experiencing some of the most heinous bullying and violence at home based on, for example, their ethnic or gender identities, religious beliefs, sexual preferences, or political views, did not fully, unambiguously earn their right to safety, freedom, or a chance to pursue the dream of finding and developing high-value talents in the first place.

This is the political cultural logic of what might be called meritocratic *talentism*, to give practical use to a word coined by economist Klaus Schwab of the World Economic Forum ("Talentism Is the New Capitalism," *Wall Street Journal*, July 17, 2014), as a core legitimizing ideology of *natural* inequality and elitist exclusivity within and across institutions and communities. The concept of a talent, originally the largest measure of wealth in the ancient world—about seventy pounds of gold—is today a metaphor for the gold between your ears, a kind of illusion that claims for itself the free-ranging prescient ability to predict a child's or young adult's future merits or demerits, aptitudes or limitations. In contrast to the established family-based forge of talent grooming and performativity, it is a talentism that is nearly always represented as the result of a highly individualistic, unbiased competition in creative excellence and educational achievement. In this sense, it is a kind of cultural laundering of familial financial talents (deposited in banks) into individual mental talents (deposited on résumés).

Many migrants engaging the services of professional facilitators or smugglers are attempting to bridge a meritocracy gap between the global, but highly fraught, ideal of following one's dream based in one's talents and the sobering reality of those born into a de facto caste system of rigid social identities and roles, and with it the lived experience of multigenerational social marginality and labor disposability. Talentism, as the core illusion of a highly individualistic ahistorical conception of cognitive power justifying a winner-take-all postdemocratic global order, can work hand in glove with racism, sexism, and any supposed natural hierarchy of brains or minds or essentializing characteristics, and yet do so through legal but meretricious institutional pathways and gatekeeping. We can observe how talentism provides an excuse for further excluding the most stigmatized classes from competitive educations as the game is largely won before adulthood, while provoking intense (social) mobility anxieties among middle classes. The bias of meritocratic talentism is important to note here, not only as an explanation of why some questions are not asked or pursued on the part of academic and government researchers but also as a preview and explanation of why many of the migrants and smugglers described in this volume are often not the "unskilled" poorest of the poor—many have comparatively high levels of education for their community, a record of informal entrepreneurial projects, property, and cultivated social resources. Without questioning our deepest assumptions about who might hire a smuggler—namely, migrants typically coded as cheap labor responding to the signals of global capitalism—we continue to overlook the more nuanced and subterranean social psychological forces of belonging, status, and the dire hope for their offspring's chances to develop their intellectual and creative potential, not because these are humanistic ideals but because these have been at the heart of their subjugation in a dystopic meritocracy.

An additional barrier to the kind of field research presented in this volume was noted in the introduction to previous editions: "Researchers wish to avoid areas of research that may link migrants with crime for fear of further stigmatizing immigrant minorities, or they perceive such research to be too risky, if not impossible" (Kyle and Koslowski 2011: 15). The past twenty years have proved this avoidant view incorrect. It is still the case that the general lack of critical academic research on human smuggling has led to a situation in which the cacophony of blogs, TV pundits, and influential politicians provides unfettered narratives of good versus evil as images of suffocated migrants in the backs of trucks or drownings at sea are projected across screens. It's important to note, however, that the myriad challenges of collecting original data among marginalized and hard-to-reach populations on the move may, in turn, produce considerable conceptual ambiguities (e.g., Aas 2013; Baird and van Liempt 2016) and are also open to interpretations fitting status quo political narratives. As we may also see in this volume, this conceptual ambiguity, which is at times a strategic feature of migration merchants operating both overt and covert businesses simultaneously, leads to theoretical innovations and radically different perspective taking by scholars of human smuggling, many of whom have an acute awareness of the marked diversity of the phenomenon globally, not simply the common feature that it may involve breaking immigration laws or getting creative with bureaucratic regulations.

Thus, despite the hypervisibility of the real tragedies and fear-mongering politics associated with human smuggling, this context of academic inertia, myopic meritocratic bias, and the very real challenges of the social research required has caused the migration-smuggling nexus to remain an understudied, undertheorized field of scientific inquiry. The way migrants interact with human smugglers, and the implications of these interactions at the level of both migratory trajectories and crime formation, remains a black box. This state of theoretical underdevelopment belies a recent modest but consequential increase in the number of empirical studies seeking to accurately describe the issue and offer conceptual or theoretical insights. The multidisciplinary contributors to the 2001 first edition laid the foundation for subsequent empirical scholarship, which has continued to describe and map migrant smuggling's organization, prevalence, and sociocultural dynamics (e.g., Bilger, Hofmann, and Jandl 2006; Koser 2008; Sanchez and Zhang 2018; Spener 2009). These studies provided insight on the community dimensions of smuggling, especially focusing on the relations between smugglers and their clients (Van Liempt and Doomernik 2006). Indeed, Kyle's original ethnographic and survey research in the early 1990s was part of a broader study focused on migrants' transnational communal solidarities and mobility strategies in two distinct regions of Ecuador rather than on migrant smuggling per se (Kyle 1995, 2000). They challenged the argument that smuggling was controlled by organized crime, and some even suggested that smuggling constitutes a form of resistance vis-à-vis the state, where migrants and smugglers work together and form strategic alliances toward the common goal of border crossings (Spener 2009). More recently, studies have pushed further this line of investigation by providing rich understandings of the lives, identities, and experiences of migrants (Mainwaring and Brigden 2016), smugglers (Zhang, Sanchez, and Achilli 2018), and other "criminal" actors of the so-called illicit global economy (Achilli and Sanchez 2021). One of the most important achievements of this scholarship has been to show how migrants, many refugees seeking asylum, can exert agency based on choices, even in situations characterized as exploitative and with an outwardly restricted range of options (cf. Bauman and May 2019). This body of literature has questioned the binary construction of smugglers as predators and migrants as victims and shown repeatedly how the interactions between migrants and smugglers across the world go beyond a simplistic cost-benefit rationale, with a complex set of motivations that include friendship and affective, spiritual, and even ideological elements (e.g., Achilli 2018; Achilli and Abu Samra 2019; Ayalew Mengiste 2018; Campana 2018; Galemba 2018; Khosravi 2010; Vogt 2018).

THE THREE CS: ADVANCING A CONCEPTUAL FRAMEWORK

By articulating a profound rethinking of the state-dominated narratives about smuggling and irregular migration, including not retreating from the dimensions of racism, sexism, and other deep historical ideologies and institutions of control and persecution these stories may conveniently leave out, we reveal that human smuggling is a grounded social and cultural practice spanning across countries (Sanchez 2017) and involving a myriad of roles and collaborative choices. Many previous studies often remained anchored to a micro-level analysis of nominally criminal phenomena, leaving us in need of a broader conceptual framework more apt to bring these findings together in an explanatory system. Still, the lack of systematic theorizing has hampered our ability to meaningfully interpret empirical "facts" (Bakewell 2010; de Haas 2021). The first and most immediate consequence is the failure of many of these studies to go beyond their rich empirical findings. When we try to scale up and draw broader conclusions about the evolution of the interactions of irregular migration and transnational crime, we remain trapped in overly deterministic and top-down causal explanations (see, e.g., Raineri, this volume, chap. 10). Contributions to previous editions also included a mix of conceptual, historical, and empirical data from field research, but the field at that time had little else to work with, and some contributors were recruited to the topic for that first volume. This volume, now with many more cases to draw on, addresses this gap by advancing a common conceptual framework based on the dialectic and overlapping relationships among three constitutive dimensions or features of the phenomenon known as "human smuggling": *control*, *complexity*, and *creativity*. Though the critical scholarship on human smuggling that has emerged since the first edition varies in its level of conceptualization and development of theory using empirical studies, we believe that these rich findings can be brought together in this explanatory framework.

The chapters in this book engage these themes, which are counterintuitive or less obvious dimensions of human smuggling, though ones that nearly all of our contributors witness in their research. Unlike in most accounts that place the origin of human smuggling in the psychopathic greed of a few criminal entrepreneurs or syndicates, in this volume, the theme of control is the starting point and a constant, ever-evolving feature of human smuggling. The nation-state control framework is not only strictly intertwined with the facilitation of irregular migration, it is the "alpha" event, as smuggling would not exist without states controlling, or managing, human mobility, sometimes for powerful domestic interests with much older ties to past coercive colonizing events that either moved people or moved borders, or both. This volume focuses on state origins and the complications of "blaming" the smugglers. In general, it complicates the picture of human smuggling as simply criminality posing a core threat to the security of the nation-state, as well as the presumed business- and market-based nature of it in all cases.

Because much of the activity is shaped by regional features of state control and other institutions of mobility management and law enforcement, which encompass an extremely diverse collection of regulations, cultural norms, and historical repertoires of extralegal or black-market problem-solving, there is an enormous overall complexity that continually surprises those attempting to intervene or curtail human smuggling framed as a universal scourge. *Complexity* most aptly describes the gray areas and blurry lines of legality, morality, and origin stories underscoring the diverse lived experiences of those involved, even within the same family, let alone community or region. This state of affairs complicates any easy definition or categorization—from whose perspective, to what end or purpose? The primary aspects developed here are the political, humanitarian, and ethical. This volume seeks to untangle the smuggling practice as a grounded social and cultural practice with actual humans in all of their talents and limitations, not highly stylized versions of them, while remapping its social and political trajectory amid global border and immigration enforcement and control. By doing so, we will look at the consequences of both smuggling and anti-smuggling programs for a range of people and institutions, including, but not limited to, smugglers and migrants. For many, if not most, migrants, leaving home to travel to a destination outside state laws—and protections—often entails a moral and social complexity with greatly varying degrees of knowledge about the journey, and armed with the uneasy comfort that their family and neighbors, or perhaps other compatriots, have successfully "crossed over" with this strategy or with those offering to take them.

Finally, and building on both of these, the creativity of all involved, the ability to continually develop novel responses to changing circumstances, is often not expected given the fact that migrants and smugglers are viewed as lacking education, talents, or creativity. These attributes are reserved for the "highly skilled" or "high-value" migrants, often dual nationals, believed to add value universally to an economy and society no matter the disruptions they may also bring. This dimension of creativity builds on the first two, as we have established that migrant smuggling reflects a wide range of social institutions, beliefs, and actions within a dynamic environment, but it emphasizes the process of strategic and tactical creative improvisations and transformations by all—smugglers, migrants, state agencies, political entrepreneurs, nonprofit aid organizations, corporate or family-based employers, and media, among others.

As a sensitizing conceptual framework, all three dimensions of control, complexity, and creativity can be found in nearly every aspect of migrant smuggling and among nearly all actors involved in it, even peripherally. The energizing force of the action globally is about overcoming control or reasserting it, always as an expression and deepening of complex cross-cutting conditions and opportunities embedded in very diverse regions, and marked by a creative dynamism, one matching the creativity of other global service and transportation industries. We next examine each of these three dimensions and how chapters in the volume represent or emphasize one or more of them.

CONTROL: A CREATION OF STATE REGULATIONS

Human smuggling can hardly be disentangled from the nation-state security framework. The chapters in this volume explore the multiple facets through which the human smuggling–state control nexus unfolds.

With its systematic transgression of borders and national sovereignties (Feldman 2019), human smuggling at first sight seems to constitute an overt threat to state monopolies over human mobility, a threat that needs to be contained and controlled not only to protect states but also, ideally, to guarantee the rights of migrants. In the fight against human smuggling, an important step for states has been to agree on a common definition of human smuggling. The UN Protocol against the Smuggling of Migrants was a decisive move in this direction (United Nations 2000). The document, the first global international instrument to contain such a definition, states that human smuggling is "the procurement, in order to obtain, directly or indirectly, a financial or other material benefit, of the illegal entry of a person into a State Party of which the person is not a national or a permanent resident." It must be noted that the protocol also explicitly underscores the protection obligations, responsibilities, and considerations that states have toward smuggled migrants. The inclusion of the phrase "financial or other material benefit" serves precisely, for the drafters, the goal of not criminalizing the facilitation of irregular migration for humanitarian reasons—for example, the family reunification of parents and children (see Nicot, this volume, foreword).

The definition was introduced, among other things, to put an end to the general confusion between human smuggling and human trafficking—that is, the recruitment, transportation, transfer, harboring, or receipt of people through force, fraud, or deception, with the aim of exploiting them for profit. The two terms had long been conflated in public and, sometimes, scholarly discourse. The trafficking and smuggling protocols—more commonly known as the Palermo Protocols—were ratified by 140 countries in 2003 precisely with the intention of distinguishing smuggling from trafficking. And yet these definitions do not seem to have worked out as per the intentions of their proponents. Human smuggling remains hard to define—and it is even more difficult to set it clearly apart from human trafficking. Most importantly, what emerges is the difficulty to address the tension between humanitarian and security-based goals: defending national borders and protecting vulnerable migrants appear less as complementary goals and increasingly as opposing sides in an entrenched battle.

The tension between humanitarian goals and security priorities, often resolved in favor of the latter, is clearly shown in two chapters of this volume. In chapter 4, Sarah P. Lockhart focuses on the development of the two protocols. She shows how, by embedding these multilateral agreements in the transnational crime regime, anti-trafficking and anti-smuggling policy entrepreneurs were able to muster broad state support, masking serious disagreements between states as well as nonstate actors, particularly around smuggling. This—the author concludes—has resulted in a policy paradox where the criminal phenomena the protocols were intended to fight are exacerbated by the policies meant to address them. If Lockhart remains skeptical about the capacity of the transnational crime framework to accommodate humanitarian considerations, in chapter 3, Eileen P. Scully shows the actual application of this framework. In her historical excursus into the evolution of the transnational trafficking of women for prostitution from 1850 to the end of the Cold War, the author demonstrates how the issue of trafficking—as for the case of human smuggling—is neither a new one nor one that can be easily disentangled from global mobility trends. Interestingly, the measures for combatting trafficking a century ago could just as easily describe the features of today's policy approach: prohibitionists, pragmatists, and enforcement agencies looked to the symptoms, through heightened scrutiny of travelers, stricter immigration laws, and beefed-up policing resources.

If the smuggling protocol marks the framing of human smuggling as a global "crime against the state," recent studies and reports have argued that it seems to be on the rise. Globalization—we were told until recently—empowered not just multinational corporations but also increasingly sophisticated human smuggling rings. Capitalizing on transportation and communication changes, smugglers have swiftly bypassed and subverted state control and authorities along the way. Slowed down by bulky bureaucracies and jurisdictional infighting, state actors cannot confront these slick actors of late modernity. Most worryingly, smuggling networks are growing into a veritable industry, which is running the facilitation of irregular migration alongside other illicit businesses, such as kidnapping for ransom, drug trafficking, human trafficking, and so on. This market convergence has increased the legitimacy and urgency of the fight against illegal immigration in the United States, Australia, and Europe as elsewhere.

It is difficult to say whether human smuggling is actually on the rise or, on the contrary, what is rising is simply its media coverage. What matters here is how the potency of this belief in human smuggling's rise has been effective in igniting the public's moral outrage against human smuggling and support for security-based policies and, concomitantly, the progressive criminalization of irregular migration across much of the so-called Global North. In fact, the official narrative blames transnational criminal networks for the precarious journeys migrants and refugees undertake and the exploitation they suffer. Within this context, counter-smuggling measures appear as the most important mechanism to guarantee both states' security and irregular migrants' safety (see, for example, İçduygu 2007). The extent to which this approach is entrenched within policy and political discourse in much of the Global North is clearly demonstrated by Ahmet İçduygu in chapter 6, on Europe's cooperation with Turkey in the fight to end human smuggling. Drawing on findings from fieldwork conducted in Turkey and its region over the last twenty-five years, the author unveils the interplay between the three main actors in unauthorized border crossings—that is, migrants, smugglers, and state (agents). In doing so, İçduygu shows with clarity the role of irregular migration and migrant smuggling in the bargaining process between the EU and Turkey, as Turkey relies on leveraging power vis-à-vis Europe through its role as "gatekeeper."

Media and policy attention on the brutality of smugglers and the plight of migrants is at times well placed. However, while successful at galvanizing public opinion and policymakers, media coverage overly focused on smugglers' legal and moral transgressions, and rarely the punctuated brutality of states' border enforcement units decoupled from the guard rails of domestic policing, fails to acknowledge the ability of these facilitators to help people navigate the bordered geographies of social mobility. The assumption of the smuggler as free-ranging criminal is hardly surprising as empirical data on the murky entanglements between human smuggling and other non-mobility criminal activities are scarce. The little available evidence comes almost exclusively from the experiences of government or law enforcement entities, or from migrants who have been victims of exploitation along the way. These narratives have not only obscured the perspectives of important actors—such as the migrants and the smugglers themselves—but they have also contributed to concealing the role played by the increasing precariousness of labor and life amid neoliberal restructuring in shaping human smuggling. An effective understanding of the purported convergence of illicit markets requires a theoretical and ethnographic engagement with the social and community dimensions of smuggling; without it, any policy measure intended to curb the "smuggling industry" may prove impossible as smuggling groups are profoundly enmeshed within complex social and cultural dynamics. It is thus hardly surprising that current immigration policies in the Global North have neither undermined the scaling-up of smuggling operations nor curbed the escalation of interactions between smuggling and other illicit trades.

To begin with, human smuggling groups have a structure and modus operandi that often escape law enforcement actions and control. This is clearly demonstrated by David C. Ellis in chapter 5. By examining the role of US Special Operations Command North in the fight against terrorist networks that can infiltrate US sovereign territory through smuggling groups, Ellis's chapter explores the limits of the current approach to the alleged smuggling-based terrorist threat. The author argues that human smuggling is an intricate adaptive system that requires a holistic policy approach. Rather than heavily relying on enforcement and control, it should concentrate also on diminishing the demand for smuggling services through the decriminalization of some aspects of the system while incentivizing migrant self-reporting.

The available evidence rules out the existence of major crime syndicates controlling a market devoted to the systematic enslavement of vulnerable migrants. Even though authorities have at times reported an overlap between the people engaged in drugs, arms, and human trafficking, the empirical evidence indicates that these groups do not generally run all these different "enterprises" together (Achilli and Sanchez 2021). The considerable instability of the current irregular migratory flows explains the nature of the business. Human smuggling involves flexible and adaptive networks that can deal with a market characterized by fast-changing scenarios and great insecurity. Smuggling networks active in the area consist of a system of organizations that can adapt and quickly respond to law enforcement operations. These groups can enter into partnerships with one another, but they generally do this only for short periods. A recent study by Paolo Campana suggests that there are structured hierarchies characterized by a division of labor and "a very small number of high-centrality actors operating at various stages along the smuggling route" (2017: 16). It is worth pointing out, however, that even wider-ranging networks do not have the rigid hierarchical structure observed within military or mafia-like organizations. Rather, smuggling networks tend to operate as a chain of independent but nevertheless closely interacting "stage coordinators," who organize the migration process by outsourcing certain smuggling activities to local coordinators—often individuals with solid ties in the local communities of the transit countries. The latter, in turn, subcontract the actual border crossing to local service providers (Campana 2018; Neske 2006).

Second, a growing number of studies have demonstrated that many of the current policies' efforts to curb human smuggling might be not only ineffective but also counterproductive. A large body of literature now exists on the role of powerful policy and border regimes in creating their "own enemy" (e.g., Andreas and Snyder 2000; Bigo and Guild 2005). A strand of this scholarship has established the new subfield known as the "criminology of mobility," which investigates states' construction of irregular migration as a crime and a security problem by mobilizing ideological and coercive powers usually reserved for criminal or military threats (Aliverti 2013; Pickering, Bosworth, and Aas 2015). Studies have focused on the production of criminality—including human smuggling—through the biopolitics of border controls (e.g., De Genova 2010; Fassin 2001) and the impact of this criminalization on the modus operandi of smuggling groups at sea (Basaran 2008) and in the desert (De León 2015). The process of "making illegality" has been charted in several seminal contributions that have shed light on the productive dimension of immigration enforcement in what has been called the "illegality industry" (Andersson 2014). These and many other studies have provided invaluable insights into the gender, class, and racial dynamics of crime and how state actions influence the development of human smuggling (see, e.g., Fradejas-García, Polese, and Bhimji 2021).

The contributors to this volume reject the idea that the alleged rise of human smuggling is a case of top-down market convergence in a highly globalized context marked by the rise of increasingly sophisticated transnational criminal organizations and the demise of the state. On the contrary, they move under the assumption that the facilitation of irregular migration and states' sovereign power are deeply entwined. This is clearly documented by Antje Missbach and Wayne Palmer in chapter 16, on state-sanctioned forms of human smuggling between Indonesia and Australia. In May 2015, members of the Australian Navy and Border Force intercepted an Indonesian boat with sixty-five asylum seekers on board and allegedly paid the crew US$32,000 to take the asylum seekers back to Indonesia. Through interviews with crew members and other key actors, Missbach and Palmer reconstruct what happened at sea that day and examine the accusation against the Australian government that it engaged in forms of "state-sanctioned" or "state-commissioned" reversed human smuggling. By putting this event within the larger context of Australia's anti-human-smuggling policies, they show the limitations and obstacles that this approach poses to regional cooperation.

If national border and state policies create human smuggling (if not only the need for smugglers), the illegal facilitation of human mobility plays an important role in the process of state building. In chapter 2, Peter Andreas demonstrates how states make smuggling and smuggling (re)makes states. By focusing on the transformation of migrant smuggling across the US-Mexico border, the author describes the development of a state-smuggler symbiosis and the unintended downhill cycles in which state control actions drive would-be migrants into the arms of smugglers, which in turn is used to justify even greater levels of border controls and "hardening." If US state policies have transformed the nature of smuggling itself from an informal affair to a big business attracting criminal organizations, more organized and sophisticated smuggling networks have prompted more expansive and intensive border policing. Likewise, David Kyle and John Dale, in chapter 1—a chapter that has anchored all three editions since 2001—develop an empirically grounded comparative framework that distinguishes migrant smuggling from human trafficking in ways that neither re-create state definitions nor a priori define them as entirely distinct. They are nonetheless starkly different in that the business model of the facilitators in human smuggling is one of "migrant exporting schemes," emphasizing that the primary goal of those profiting from this is to safely and successfully guide or deliver the migrant to a destination, with opportunities to do so shaped by the conditions that states have created.

In sum, our volume acknowledges the increasing interaction between smuggling and states, but it invites a more nuanced understanding of the role of migrants in this "age of involuntary immobility"—a period in which unprecedented numbers of people wish or feel compelled to live elsewhere but face increasing constraints to do so.

COMPLEXITY: COMPLICATING STORIES OF MORALITY AND POLITICS

Human smuggling is a complex phenomenon. An indication of this complexity lies in the ontological difficulty of defining what human smuggling ultimately is. International law attempts to provide clarity through a protocol with the first universally accepted definition of migrant smuggling, yet there are clear discrepancies in how human smuggling is criminalized in each state. States apply very different concepts and criteria in their efforts to combat the smuggling of migrants. While some common denominators are identifiable, there is no shared legal understanding about what constitutes the smuggling of migrants and what does not. For example, the "financial or other material benefit" element, which is a central dimension of the definition of smuggling in international law, is not a defining feature of what constitutes smuggling for the majority of the EU's member states. A case in point is the story of Salam Aldeen, cofounder of a volunteer rescue organization operating off the coast of Greece. Between 2015 and 2016, Aldeen, seeking to uphold the duty to rescue at sea, had responded to distress calls from approximately two hundred boats with a total of roughly ten thousand refugees on board. On January 14, 2016, he and his crew were arrested by Greek authorities and charged with attempted smuggling.

To complicate things even further, *human smuggling* does not mean, for most people, what international and domestic laws say it means. The discourses around smuggling and smugglers are more about moral judgments than the real-life people involved in everyday practices of irregular migration. Media and political discourses have placed more emphasis on the moral dimension of smugglers than on their logistical skills. Human smugglers have earned notoriety especially in western Europe and North America as greedy males from the Global South, orchestrators of human massacres, evil geniuses behind criminal trades, amassers of untold riches made at the expense of their victims. A profusion of photos and narrative accounts of migrants crammed into wretched boats or trucks in the media worldwide sketches out the moral traits of one of the cruelest figures of our time, an individual who preys on migrants' "need for assistance and their dreams for a better life" (Europol 2016: 3). "The smugglers," flattened into an interchangeable stick-figure, bad-guy role, are blamed for the countless deaths of migrants and the alleged invasion of Europe, the United States, and Australia in mainstream media.

The idea that human smuggling is intrinsically brutal and inhumane also circulates widely among migrants themselves. When called to speak generally of human smuggling, migrants and smugglers themselves often describe it as a very abusive and evil practice (Achilli 2019). Certainly, differences emerge in the way the figure of the smuggler is sketched out in people's accounts, and how people position themselves differently in relation to human smuggling. However, there seems to be a certain degree of consensus: *human smuggling is fundamentally evil*. Not surprisingly, the predatory-criminal dimension of human smuggling finds confirmation in the terminology used for referring to human smugglers and their clients around the world (Papadopoulos and Tsianos 2008)—if smugglers are referred to as coyotes or wolves and migrants are referred to as *pollos* (chicken) or sheep in Mexico (Spener 2009) and Morocco (Driessen 1998), Iranian migrants speak of themselves as being *gosfand* (sheep) or *darposte gosfand* (in the skin of sheep) (Khosravi 2010), while smugglers are called *shetou* (snakehead) by their fellow nationals in China.

Nonetheless, human smuggling appears to be rooted in patterns of cooperation, protection, and support. While the dominant narrative has continued to favor the smuggler-as-criminal line, the last twelve years have seen the advent of scholarly work that has showcased the strong bonds of trust and care that often tie smugglers and migrants together. As early as 2004, Jeroen Doomernik and David Kyle summarized the complex relationship between smugglers and migrants as a spectrum ranging from the altruistic assistance provided by family members or friends to the exploitative and abusive practices carried out by hardened criminals (see also Kyle 2000). Since their work, empirical research has shown that, despite assumptions of violence and deception, trust and cooperation seem to be more the rule than the exception in the interaction between smugglers and migrants (e.g., Bilger, Hofmann, and Jandl 2006; Koser 2008; Spener 2009; cf. Díaz de León 2020). Most smugglers operate by helping members of their immediate circles to reach the destinations that would be closed to them through legal channels.

As the relevant literature grew, a more nuanced picture emerged. Studies across different countries reveal that smuggling is often based on preexisting kinship and friendship connections that extend beyond the client-customer relationship (Zhang Sanchez, and Achilli 2018). Shared geographical proximity and kinship ties are not the only factors behind these relationships of solidarity and reciprocity. Ethnographic research has revealed that contacts and eventually support from smugglers can also be based on humanitarian principles, political self-identification, or allegiance to a shared national predicament (Achilli and Abu Samra 2019; Kook 2018). Often, the period before departure provides migrants and smugglers with ample opportunity to engage with one another in ways that extend beyond simple working relationships, sometimes involving friendship and even love affairs (Achilli 2018; Vogt 2018).

So why this inconsistency between what smuggling evokes and how it is actually accomplished? The existence of mechanisms of protection and solidarity between smugglers and migrants amid the proliferation of accounts about the brutality of human smuggling points to the complex nature of human smuggling (Aziani 2021), which escapes easy categorizations. This complexity is most immediately exemplified by the financial dimension of human smuggling, with its intricate mechanics of informal payment and financing systems. If one were to imagine the clandestine journeys of migrants and refugees, the image would most likely involve smuggling kingpins amassing fortunes by preying on vulnerable migrants. However, it is difficult to pinpoint precisely how much money flows into the pockets of smugglers, as many other actors also benefit from the revenues generated by this business. Not only does smuggling often spawn tangential criminal markets and illicit activities (document counterfeiting, border bribes and tolls, etc.), the flow of money also streams into the licit economy. Border towns and other cities located along key nodes of the smuggling trail survive—and in some cases even thrive—as a direct result of the presence of irregular migrants and their facilitators. All this is well documented by Kim Wilson in chapter 8, on the financial complexity of human smuggling. Taking up the refugee's or migrant's perspective, the author shows the different ways in which clandestine travelers finance their journeys from the planning stage and throughout the stages of their travel. She addresses the diverse payment and guarantee schemes that smugglers use, with illustrative routes and costs, disclosing the intricate system of licit and illicit financial intermediaries that characterize the financial ecosystems of human smuggling.

In this context, the complexity of the phenomenon springs from the encounter of migrants' determination to move, smugglers' ability to navigate unequal geographies of mobility, and states' efforts to enforce border controls and contain migration flows. Migrants' experience of human smuggling can hardly be disentangled from this triangular relationship. In chapter 12, Gerhard Hoffstaedter argues for a more holistic understanding of human smuggling and the process of movement across modern national borders. His chapter details how Malaysian Chin and Rohingya refugees' journeys have changed over time and how modern mass smuggling across the Thai-Malaysian border depends on the active participation of law enforcement to facilitate this movement. In so doing, the author demonstrates the difference between small-scale relief smuggling operations, run by individuals and small groups, which help a few refugees cross the border at a time, and large-scale trafficking operations made most visible in the 2015 refugee crisis in the region.

In this regard, several studies have demonstrated that smuggled people should not be considered victims of their smugglers, a point emphasized in all three editions of this volume (see Kyle and Dale, this volume, chap. 1). Recent studies show how different smuggling groups operating in southern Turkey take considerable care to establish and maintain a trusting relationship with their "clients," by behaving properly, keeping their "word," and being well mannered (Achilli 2018). Along the central Mediterranean route, Campana (2018) shows how Yusef, a top-level smuggler based in Sudan, reproaches his associate for sending out an overcrowded boat and urges him to pay compensation to the families of the victims of the October 2013 shipwreck.

Interestingly, however, smuggling also constitutes a resource not only for migrants but also for those very actors that seek to control migration: the states. In chapter 7, Jørgen Carling shows the dual roles of smugglers as a threat and a resource vis-à-vis both migrants and states. For prospective migrants, smugglers are a means to overcoming obstacles to migration; yet, during the journey, migrants are often at the mercy of smugglers. With respect to the relationship between smugglers and states, the author demonstrates how the former undermine the dominant migration regime in Europe, which is based on restricting people's access to asylum application policies. However, the threat is quickly commuted into a resource for states, which issue policies that effectively diminish migrants' mobility under the assumption that these would protect them from the smugglers.

The interactions between state actors and human smugglers are also documented by Gregory Feldman in chapter 18. His contribution affords us a close look at how state security actors, human smugglers, and migrants engage each other in a relational field that largely (though not entirely) takes place outside the state's legal purview. This chapter untangles the complexity of that interaction by distinguishing three analytical concepts to help us better examine human smuggling and trafficking more broadly: action, agency, and the state. To do so, it relies ethnographically on the investigative case of a Nigerian trafficking ring that operated through an unnamed southern EU member state and included a loose affiliation of actors stretching from West Africa to multiple points in the EU.

If we want to understand human smuggling, we need to account for its capacity to defy fixed dichotomies such as legal versus illegal or good versus evil. In this sense, particularly poignant is Kyunghee Kook's contribution, chapter 11. Through her ethnography of North Koreans fleeing their country, the author problematizes mainstream understandings of human smuggling. In the North Korean case, migrants' journeys have been traditionally depicted as a perilous trip operated either though greedy and selfish smuggling networks or, conversely, by altruistic and heroic missionaries. Kook found that there is not a rigid dichotomy between these two groups. While the relationship between the smugglers and the migrants might be rich in solidarity and reciprocity, at times the migrants had abusive and violent experiences with the underground railroad operated by the missionaries.

Exploitation and protection, deception and trust, threat and resource amalgamate to define the moral contours of human smuggling. None of these terms points to the demise of its opposite; on the contrary, together they define the complexity of the phenomenon in the context of an increasingly divided global order. This complexity also unsettles gender stereotypes. In chapter 13 Gabriella Sanchez, for example, problematizes the widespread idea that smuggling generally involves male perpetrators and female victims. She unpacks the mechanisms through which human smuggling is constructed by courts and criminal statutes in Latin America, Europe, and the United

States as an inherently male activity. In so doing, the author explores the experiences of women who have remained largely invisible in the way we talk about the facilitation of migrants' journeys.

CREATIVITY: INNOVATIVE SOCIAL AND SYMBOLIC WORLDS

This volume's rationale rests on a central premise: human or migrant smuggling is an ongoing process of daily adaptation to ongoing, relentless change in the social, legal, and enforcement worlds they inhabit with the singular goal of facilitating some aspect of the migrant's desired crossing. This feature might be lost if we only emphasized control and complexity, as those themes concern how the regulations and institutions of multiple states—from sending to transit to destination—produce the origins and defining features of the phenomenon in mostly stable terms. Thus, the third organizing theme is *creativity*, which may be thought of in two modes relevant to the topic, the obvious and the oppressive. First, smuggler-migrant activities offer many empirical instances of creative problem-solving, imaginative foresight, technological innovation, and flexible organizational forms with an improvisational ethos. Second, "creativity" has become a sacred totem at the center of the global meritocracy of talent leveraged to justify exclusionary educational practices and immigration policies, with its natural home in an elite creativity of patents, institutional power, and corporate profits that discounts, naturally and unthinkingly, smugglers and migrants as existing outside its elite creativity-as-progress frame. That is, the idea of creativity, typically defined very broadly as producing something novel and of value, does not often come to mind when considering migrant smuggling, as the concept is much more associated with the gentry of creative professionals or entrepreneurs than with those considered "at the margins" of technological, scientific, and cultural progress.

Creativity, when used casually and ubiquitously, often does not need further context or explanation, as it operates as both a mundane buzzword and the highest human ideal of genius—it is a broad, secular deity of the global political and economic self-styled creative geniuses managing the labor mobility of others, from the "unskilled" to the merely "talented" (McMahon 2013; see also Grosglik and Kyle 2022). If "talentism is the new capitalism" because "creativity is the driver of the global economy," as claimed by Klaus Schwab ("Talentism Is the New Capitalism," *Wall Street Journal*, July 17, 2014), then migrants are not so much trying to simply succeed under capitalism but rather not to be relegated to the margins of a meritocratic talentism (with an uncanny affinity to social Darwinism) as simply the result of a natural competition of natural talents. In some ways, the less political and more psychological *creativity* has come to replace the role *globalization* played in breathlessly describing the (creative) progress of technology and innovative institutions two decades ago at its peak. And yet, as with good and bad globalization (Kyle and Dale, this volume, chap. 1), today we have good and bad creativity.

Creativity, if at all, is negatively associated with human smuggling in very narrow and uninformed ways in the trope of the smuggler as evil genius or creative mastermind of a transnational syndicate. The bad creativity of smugglers seems to be on display with every news report of migrant deaths in transit. In contrast, migrants are most typically presented as "human cargo." As in most areas of their lives, they are the objects, not subjects, of creativity. Under an emerging meritocratic talentism, this perception reinforces the view that marginal travelers lack valuable or useful talents, while smugglers are using their talents to take advantage of their less worldly or skilled clients. The paradox for migrants is that they are believed to lack creativity of the kind that would validate their practical talents said to be of use in the destination labor market, but at the same time, it is their creative strategies and collective innovations that are getting them into even hotter waters.

One of the ways that the creative agency of smugglers is easily funneled into narratives of smugglers as ruthless evil geniuses duping their "human cargo" is through specific representational patterns. In chapter 14, Achilli and Alice Massari's study focuses on the visual depiction of smugglers in the two main Italian newspapers between 2015 and 2016—a key destination and transit country during the so-called migrant crisis. What they show is that against a general hysteria about the smuggler in narratives of human and national security, the subject is rather absent at the visual level. According to the authors, this divergence feeds into the representation of migrants as passive victims with no agency at the mercy of evil criminals—a representational pattern that ultimately contributes to justifying punitive migration regimes in Italy and the European Union at large (Arrouche, Fallone, and Vosyliūtė 2021).

Beyond this stereotype of the creative, but criminal, smuggler and uncreative migrant client along for the ride, the work of our contributors suggests a wider field of creative collective, even collaborative, action on the part of all. We make two observations. First, a closer look reveals a collective form of social creativity responsive to migrant clients' own creative strategies and desires, within a system of diverse individuals and institutions using many of the same technologies of the formal economy, including social media platforms, forming a transnational field of creative action. Second, we also observe, though with more difficulty, how the ideal of creativity is an important cultural and political ideology driving human smuggling, as it is closely associated with notions of meritocracy in which anyone can make it with talent, effort, and perseverance. The side effect of an individualistic creativity as the centerpiece of a global meritocratic talentism is that, if it were true or believed to be true, then one's failure would be deserved, as it would simply indicate a lack of natural talent and effort.

If one looks for the creativity of smugglers, it can be found in nearly all of the cases described in the three editions of this volume. For example, there is a plurality of different techniques that human smugglers employ to move migrants across the Eastern and Central Mediterranean routes. The recent crackdown on smuggling activities initiated by EU member states and local partners across both routes has not meant the demise of the practice across the Mediterranean Sea; rather it has led to a change in smugglers' modus operandi. To minimize the chances of apprehension, smugglers operate remotely and generally maintain contact by phone with the migrants who pilot the boats (UNODC 2018). With respect to both sea corridors, there is ample evidence that smugglers have minimized their costs by using disposable rubber dinghies instead of steadier and thus safer boats. This strategy, devised to escape detection and arrest, makes the journey far riskier for migrants, who are now more likely to capsize and perish at sea (UNODC 2018).

However, although these practices may seriously encroach on migrants' safety, we must recognize the creativity of those who have found temporary solutions to their mobility challenges and their frustrations around the conflicting globalized messages of "Don't come" versus "Never take no for an answer when pursuing your dreams." In a deeply divided global order, migrants are often caught up in what scholars have called "regimes of mobility," produced at the nexus of exclusionary state policies and increased circulation around the globe (Glick Schiller and Salazar 2013). En route, migrants live in a liminal state of transit for weeks, months, or even years as they attempt to cross land and sea borders, earn enough to live on, hire smugglers, secure food and shelter, find protection, or decide to stay where they are. This liminality and disconnection from core familial, spatial, and social networks open the door not only to new types of exploitation but also to novel avenues of opportunity associated with mainstream conceptions of creativity in the formal economy (e.g., Ehrkamp and Leitner 2006; Parreñas 2009). It is in this context of the protracted precarity and shrinking possibilities of legal migration that migrants develop strategies and social relationships that help them navigate their situation (see, e.g., Puga and Espinosa 2020). A striking feature of the countless interviews conducted across the studies in this volume is how many are propelled by the desire to one day have the freedom to develop or validate their creative or productive talents far away from dominant narratives and measures that precluded them from having any, the very reason formal legal routes to immigration are not readily available to them.

What we emphasize here is also the social dimension of this creativity. Studies have noted that the label or concept of human smuggling is too narrow and misleading, as it does not fully encompass the plurality of actors and long-standing local and regional practices that play an active role in the facilitation of irregular migration among Asian migrants (e.g., Majidi 2018; Missbach 2016), Central American migrants (e.g., Brigden 2018; Vogt 2018), and African migrants (e.g., Amigoni, Molinero, and Vergnano 2021; Brachet 2018; Scheele 2012). We should be cautious not to be lured by the growing fascination with the issues of borders and their crossing and, in so doing, neglect all those practices and roles that are ultimately conducive to the actual crossing of borders. For example, a considerable number of people—often locals—gravitate toward work as freelancers for relatively loose and small organizations, providing peripheral services that must shape-shift and change course as conditions warrant, though these services provide a foundation for smuggling networks to operate (Kyle and Koslowski 2011; Pastore, Monzini, and Sciortino 2006; Triandafyllidou and McAuliffe 2018). These freelance activities include working as lookouts and using lights to signal the presence of police forces patrolling the shores or the border, operating as costly taxi drivers who take migrants to the crossing points, or leveraging their resources as landowners if they have land near the shore or border that they can rent out to smugglers as embarkation zones or safe houses.

Human smuggling is the outcome of a multiplicity of micro-practices and associations that, "while often illegal in a formal sense, are not driven by a structural logic of organization and unified purpose" (Van Schendel and Abraham 2005: 4). All of this suggests that the best way to describe this important creative feature of migrant smuggling is as a collective *social* creativity in the shadows of the talented or creative geniuses whom most states compete to attract, rather than fight to repel through physical and legal barriers. And perhaps nothing exemplifies better the creative dimension of this phenomenon than smuggling groups' capacity to use the policy measures established to repel irregular migrants and the very narratives of anti-human smuggling and trafficking to their own benefit. In chapter 10 Luca Raineri explores how smuggling networks have tried to perpetuate their political salience by capturing the resources, both material and symbolic, connected with the fight against human smuggling. By building on extensive field research in the region, the author unveils the agency of human smuggling networks and their creative adaptation to changing circumstances, incentive structures, and authority claims.

Two contributions to this volume describe the several dynamic and creative changes in smuggling practices on both sides of the US-Mexico border. In chapter 17 Victor Manjarrez examines the evolution of border security efforts across the US-Mexico border. He argues that as the US government places greater emphasis on border security through the growth of trained personnel, border infrastructure, and technology, so have human smugglers: in the processes of tightening security and smuggling, technology has been at the center of a cyclical race to defeat each other. The chapter examines the evolution and use of technology by both border security personnel and smugglers. In chapter 19 Simón Pedro Izcara Palacios shows the evolution of migrant smuggling across the US-Mexico border during the twenty-first century as a result of the Mexican war on drugs, the tightening of border controls in the United States, and the decline of Mexicans' willingness to cross the border surreptitiously. Based on interviews with 185 Mexican migrant smugglers, the author demonstrates how Mexican migrant smuggling networks have adapted to a riskier and less profitable environment. In so doing, he puts the emphasis on two general trends: on the one hand, the development of smuggling groups into moderately larger organizations; on the other, their loss of autonomy.

It is critical to recognize that millions of people around the world are born into stateless or liminal spaces in which their very identities and nationalities are a creative space defined by limitations but not resigned to them. In chapter 20 Caitlin Procter focuses on the role that human smuggling plays among Palestinians in Gaza. The Israeli-Egyptian blockade of the Gaza strip since 2007 has led to the popular description of the territory as "the largest open-air prison in the world." Procter draws on ethnographic research conducted over ten months in Gaza in 2019 and prioritizes the perspectives and experiences of refugee youth who are engaged in processes of irregular mobility. She argues that despite an acute awareness of the dangers of trying to leave Gaza, young people see this as a way of seeking protection in a context of protracted occupation, siege, and violence. Similarly, in chapter 9 Matt Herbert describes and analyzes the creativity of smuggling groups utilized by Maghrebi irregular migrants. Drawing on a large number of interviews and a dataset of Arabic- and French-language materials, his chapter illustrates how migrant smuggling networks develop, their composition and structure, the process of smuggling, and the complicated interactions between state agents and smugglers. The utility of migrant smuggling for the state, smugglers' creativity, and the deep demand for the migrants themselves, which presents opportunities unavailable at home, suggest that Maghrebi migrant smuggling from Morocco, Algeria, and Tunisia is unlikely to abate.

Lastly, in chapter 15 Soledad Álvarez Velasco gives insight into the historical and contemporary dynamics of migrant smuggling taking place in Ecuador. For this purpose, her analysis focuses on three interlinked aspects: the causes that explain its endurance and current diversity; the new patterns of Ecuadorean migrant smuggling and of international migrant smuggling, or the use of Ecuador as a transit country by international migrants to reach other destinations with the aid of coyotes; and the role that technology, particularly in the digital space, has recently played in triggering autonomous irregular mobilities that increasingly challenge the traditional role of smugglers.

CONCLUSION: WHAT'S NEXT?

Paraphrasing Karl Marx, we might say that a specter is haunting Europe (and other wealthy destinations)—the specter of human smuggling and the resulting in-migration of unmanaged people without authorized permission. Human smuggling seems to be a ghostlike presence, ephemeral yet everywhere, in turns inspiring and horrifying, with weekly reports of migrants dying en route, sometimes due to the actions of smugglers and sometimes in spite of their efforts to save them. The last two decades have seen a deepening of the narrative of unauthorized migrants aided by smugglers as a threat to the body politic or to the well-being of citizens, many benefiting from their labor; it is a worrying analogy between migrants and pathogens that states and political entrepreneurs increasingly traffic in three years after the outbreak of the COVID-19 pandemic. This volume is not meant to provide an analysis of the impact of human smuggling on destination regions after arrival, or on the sending and transit countries per se, though we may get glimpses of this here or there; it does reveal diverse and creative collective actions overcoming the best-laid plans meant to prevent unauthorized mobility across state borders in every region of the world. When presented to us daily as a monolithic story of criminals trafficking in human cargo, it is not surprising that it can be difficult to systematically investigate and reconceptualize something so commonsensical and at the same time politically divisive. The following chapters of this volume demonstrate that this can be done and worth the effort.

We have two final observations about the emerging state of this global phenomenon. First, the ability and willingness of people to involve themselves in alternative routes out of, through, and into other states without bureaucratic and legal authorizations will continue globally as the very control over their mobility, with uneven and ever-changing measures, often contains the seeds of its regeneration and creative work-arounds. Second, we therefore may imagine, as in past volumes, that it will be other global secular trends and regional contexts that will continue to shape the contours and overall breadth, even the interpretive meaning, of organized migrant smuggling. For instance, as climate crises worsen, any of us could potentially become refugees due to uncertain future conditions in almost every locale on earth. This increasingly lived experience is prompting many more people to imagine the future necessity of moving to new faraway places—a cognitive migration—though they may not currently have permission to realize a physical resettlement (Koikkalainen and Kyle 2016). Meanwhile, this same situation leads others to consider how to maintain stability or guard resources by attempting to assert more control over others' resettlement plans with ever greater and more complex "borders crossing people" (Dutta Gupta 2022).

Contributing to and facilitating both cognitive and actual migrations are social media apps that allow an unprecedented sharing of information; as we finish this chapter, a current Reuters news story describes how several thousand Chinese nationals, some with small children, are using the Chinese version of TikTok to learn about and navigate a circuitous route through Ecuador to the US-Mexico border ("Migrants Find Tips on Chinese Version of TikTok for Long Trek to U.S.-Mexico Border," Reuters, April 28, 2023). The revolutionary role of widely available artificial intelligence (e.g., ChatGPT-4) will also shape the next decade of unauthorized mobility in ways that are truly unimaginable, radically altering the future of work and reframing the comparative merits of human creative talents. Will artificial intelligence be pressed into the role of machine smuggler via its powerful planning capabilities and its ability to mimic or alter anything that can be digitized? This technology of machine talent, combined with the more mature phase of social media and cloud computing, will continue to enhance military and law enforcement capabilities but will also allow for a real-time collaboration among smugglers and migrants well beyond an app like TikTok. This rapid and even shocking technological revolution remapping who or what has merit will continue to make the dimensions of control, complexity, and creativity even more salient in the coming decade.

Taken together, these chapters reveal a planet struggling to get along and how the choice between prosecuting and protecting vulnerable populations on the move is a central line of domestic and international political affinities and conflicts. While the covert actions by individuals or groups taking mobility matters into their own hands are not always easily placed into existing moral, legal, and social scientific frames, they nearly always tell us something about the state of the first truly globalized social world. Our era, like all eras, will be known for the kinds of criteria believed to justly determine the degrees of freedom and care we afford each other; we may also be known for the irony of a talentism that worships a relatively few human and digital brains ensconced in institutions of merit more than the collective fate of a planet, now increasingly on the move and sorely in need of a more social creativity.

NOTE

1. We fully agree with a growing literature that has warned against the danger of taking at face value categories such as "human smuggling" or "migrant smuggling." These categories obscure the social and cultural dynamics inherent in the practice and lead often to the development of counterproductive solutions. However, we also believe that disregarding the impact of the classification of this phenomenon on people's lives simply because certain categories do not sit well with preexisting local realities may be just as problematic as taking these categories at face value. The risk is to underestimate the influence that state-imposed categories have on the individuals and communities affected (Achilli 2019). For this reason, we choose to retain "human smuggling" throughout the text, though labeling is part of the subject of some chapters.

REFERENCES

Aas, Katja Franko. 2013. *Globalization and Crime*. Los Angeles: SAGE.

Achilli, Luigi. 2018. "The 'Good' Smuggler: The Ethics and Morals of Human Smuggling among Syrians." *ANNALS of the American Academy of Political and Social Science* 676 (1): 77–96.

———. 2019. "Waiting for the Smuggler: Tales across the Border'." *Public Anthropologist* 1 (2): 194–207.

Achilli, Luigi, and Mjriam Abu Samra. 2019. "Beyond Legality and Illegality: Palestinian Informal Networks and the Ethno-political Facilitation of Irregular Migration from Syria." *Journal of Ethnic and Migration Studies* 47 (15): 3345–3366. https://doi.org/10.1080/1369183X.2019.1671181.

Achilli, Luigi, and Gabriella Sanchez, eds. 2021. "Migration, Smuggling and the Illicit Global Economy." *Public Anthropologist* 3 (1).

Aliverti, Ana. 2013. *Crimes of Mobility: Criminal Law and the Regulation of Immigration*. London: Routledge.

Amigoni, Livio, Chiara Molinero, and Cecilia Vergnano. 2021. "Smugglers and Smuggled Migrants: Amid Sudanese Passeurs in the Border Regime of Ventimiglia." In *Debordering Europe: Migration and Control across the Ventimiglia Region*, edited by Livio Amigoni,

Silvia Aru, Ivan Bonnin, Gabriele Proglio, and Cecilia Vergnano, 137–158. Cham, Switzerland: Palgrave Macmillan.
Andersson, Ruben. 2014. *Illegality, Inc.: Clandestine Migration and the Business of Bordering Europe*. Oakland: University of California Press.
Andreas, Peter, and Timothy Snyder, eds. 2000. *The Wall around the West: State Borders and Immigration Controls in North America and Europe*. Oxford: Rowman and Littlefield.
Arrouche, Kheira, Andrew Fallone, and Lina Vosyliūtė. 2021. *Between Politics and Inconvenient Evidence: Assessing the Renewed EU Action Plan against Migrant Smuggling*. CEPS Policy Brief No. 2021-01. Brussels: Center for European Policy Studies.
Ayalew Mengiste, Tekalign. 2018. "Refugee Protections from Below: Smuggling in the Eritrea-Ethiopia Context." *ANNALS of the American Academy of Political and Social Science* 676 (1): 57–76.
Aziani, Alberto. 2021. "The Heterogeneity of Human Smugglers: A Reflection on the Use of Concepts in Studies on the Smuggling of Migrants." *Trends in Organized Crime* (2021): 1–27.
Baird, Theodore, and Ilse van Liempt. 2016. "Scrutinising the Double Disadvantage: Knowledge Production in the Messy Field of Migrant Smuggling." *Journal of Ethnic and Migration Studies* 42 (3): 400–417.
Bakewell, Oliver. 2010. "Some Reflections on Structure and Agency in Migration Theory.'" *Journal of Ethnic and Migration Studies* 36 (10): 1689–1708.
Basaran, Tugba. 2008. "Security, Law, Borders: Spaces of Exclusion." *International Political Sociology* 2 (4): 339–354.
Bauman, Zygmunt, and Tim May. 2019. *Thinking Sociologically*. 3rd ed. Hoboken, NJ: John Wiley and Sons.
Bigo, Didier, and Elspeth Guild. 2005. "Introduction: Policing in the Name of Freedom." In *Controlling Frontiers: Free Movement into and within Europe*, edited by Didier Bigo and Elspeth Guild, 1–13. Aldershot, UK: Ashgate.
Bilger, Veronika, Martin Hofmann, and Michael Jandl. 2006. "Human Smuggling as a Transnational Service Industry: Evidence from Austria." *International Migration* 44 (4): 59–93.
Blancas Madrigal, Daniel. 2017. "Tráfico ilegal de migrantes en AL genera 7 mil mdd a la mafia: ONU." *Cronica*, February 5, 2017. https://www.cronica.com.mx/notas-trafico_ilegal_de_migrantes_en_al_genera_7_mil_mdd_a_la_mafia_onu-1021584-2017.html.
Brachet, Julien. 2018. "Manufacturing Smugglers: From Irregular to Clandestine Mobility in the Sahara." *ANNALS of the American Academy of Political and Social Science* 676 (1): 16–35.
Brigden, Noelle Kateri. 2018. *The Migrant Passage: Clandestine Journeys from Central America*. Ithaca, NY: Cornell University Press.
Campana, Paolo. 2017. "Out of Africa: The Organization of Migrant Smuggling across the Mediterranean." *European Journal of Criminology* 15 (4): 1–22.
De Genova, Nicholas. 2010. "The Deportation Regime: Sovereignty, Space, and the Freedom of Movement." In *The Deportation Regime: Sovereignty, Space, and the*

Freedom of Movement, edited by Nicholas De Genova and Nathalie Peutz, 33–65. Durham, NC: Duke University Press.

de Haas, Hein. 2021. "A Theory of Migration: The Aspirations-Capabilities Framework." *Comparative Migration Studies* 9 (1): 1–35.

De León, Jason. 2015. *The Land of Open Graves: Living and Dying on the Migrant Trail*. Oakland: University of California Press.

Díaz de León, Alejandra. 2020. "'Transient Communities': How Central American Transit Migrants Form Solidarity without Trust." *Journal of Borderlands Studies*, online ahead of print, October 7, 2020. https://doi.org/10.1080/08865655.2020.1824683.

Doomernik, Jeroen, and David Kyle. 2004. "Introduction." *Journal of International Migration and Integration / Revue de l'integration et de la migration internationale* 5 (3): 265–272.

Driessen, Henk. 1998. "The 'New Immigration' and the Transformation of the European-African Frontier." In *Border Identities: Nation and State at International Frontiers*, edited by Thomas M. Wilson and Hastings Donnan, 96–116. Cambridge: Cambridge University Press.

Dutta Gupta, Tanaya. 2022. "Crossings: *Borderizing* and *Borderized* Mobilities in an Era of Converging Crises." PhD diss., University of California at Davis.

Ehrkamp, Patricia, and Helga Leitner. 2006. "Rethinking Immigration and Citizenship: New Spaces of Migrant Transnationalism and Belonging." *Environment and Planning A* 38:1591–1597.

Europol. 2016. *Migrant Smuggling in the EU*. European Police Office. https://www.europol.europa.eu/cms/sites/default/files/documents/migrant_smuggling__europol_report_2016.pdf.

Fassin, Didier. 2001. "The Biopolitics of Otherness: Undocumented Foreigners and Racial Discrimination in French Public Debate." *Anthropology Today* 17 (1): 3–7.

Feldman, Gregory. 2019. *The Gray Zone: Sovereignty, Human Smuggling, and Undercover Police Investigation in Europe*. Stanford, CA: Stanford University Press.

Fradejas-García, Ignacio, Abel Polese, and Fazila Bhimji. 2021. "Transnational (Im)mobilities and Informality in Europe." *Migration Letters* 18 (2): 121–133.

Galemba, Rebecca B. 2018. "'He Used to Be a Pollero': The Securitisation of Migration and the Smuggler/Migrant Nexus at the Mexico-Guatemala Border." *Journal of Ethnic and Migration Studies* 44 (5): 870–886.

Gallien, Max, and Florian Weigand, eds. 2022. *The Routledge Handbook of Smuggling*. Abingdon, UK: Routledge.

GIN (Global Initiative against Transnational Organized Crime). 2021. *The Global Illicit Economy: Trajectories of Transnational Organized Crime*. Geneva: GIN.

Glick Schiller, Nina, and Noel B. Salazar. 2013. "Regimes of Mobility across the Globe." *Journal of Ethnic and Migration Studies* 39 (2): 183–200.

Grosglik, Rafi, and David Kyle. 2022. "The Recipes of Genius on *Chef's Table*." In *A Philosophy of Recipes: Making, Experiencing, and Valuing*, edited by Andrea Borghini and Patrik Engisch, 185–198. London: Bloomsbury Academic.

İçduygu, Ahmet. 2007. "The Politics of Irregular Migratory Flows in the Mediterranean Basin: Economy, Mobility and 'Illegality.'" *Mediterranean Politics* 12 (2): 141–161.

Khosravi, Shahram. 2010. *"Illegal" Traveller: An Auto-ethnography of Borders*. New York: Palgrave Macmillan.
Koikkalainen, Saara, and David Kyle. 2016. "Imagining Mobility: The Prospective Cognition Question in Migration Research." *Journal of Ethnic and Migration Studies* 42 (5): 759–776.
Kook, Kyunghee. 2018. "'I Want to Be Trafficked So I Can Migrate!': Cross-Border Movement of North Koreans into China through Brokerage and Smuggling Networks." *ANNALS of the American Academy of Political and Social Science* 676 (1): 114–134.
Koser, Khalid. 2008. "Why Migrant Smuggling Pays." *International Migration* 46 (2): 3–26.
Kyle, David. 1995. "The Transnational Peasant: The Social Construction of International Economic Migration and Transcommunities from the Ecuadoran Andes." PhD diss., Johns Hopkins University.
———. 2000. *Transnational Peasants: Ethnicity, Networks, and Migrations in Andean Ecuador*. Baltimore: Johns Hopkins University Press.
Kyle, David, and Rey Koslowski. 2011. Introduction to *Global Human Smuggling: Comparative Perspectives*, 2nd ed., edited by David Kyle and Rey Koslowski, 1–30. Baltimore: Johns Hopkins University Press.
Mainwaring, Ċetta, and Noelle Brigden. 2016. "Beyond the Border: Clandestine Migration Journeys." *Geopolitics* 21 (2): 243–262.
Majidi, Nassim. 2018. "Community Dimensions of Smuggling: The Case of Afghanistan and Somalia." *ANNALS of the American Academy of Political and Social Science* 676 (1): 97–113.
McMahon, Darrin M. 2013. *Divine Fury: A History of Genius*. New York: Basic Books.
Miklaucic, Michael, and Jacqueline Brewer, eds. 2013. *Convergence: Illicit Networks and National Security in the Age of Globalization*. Washington, DC: National Defense University Press.
Missbach, Antje. 2016. "Perilous Waters: People Smuggling, Fishermen, and Hyperprecarious Livelihoods on Rote Island, Eastern Indonesia." *Pacific Affairs* 89 (4): 749–470.
Naim, Moises. 2010. *Illicit: How Smugglers, Traffickers and Copycats Are Hijacking the Global Economy*. New York: Random House.
Neske, Matthias. 2006. "Human Smuggling to and through Germany." *International Migration* 44 (4): 121–163.
OECD (Organisation for Economic Co-operation and Development). 2016. *Illicit Trade: Converging Criminal Networks*. Reviews of Risk Management Policies. Paris: OECD.
Pallister-Wilkins, Polly. 2015. "The Humanitarian Politics of European Border Policing: Frontex and Border Police in Evros." *International Political Sociology* 9 (1): 53–69.
Papadopoulos, Dimitris, and Vassilis Tsianos. 2008. "The Autonomy of Migration: The Animals of Undocumented Mobility." In *Deleuzian Encounters: Studies in Contemporary Social Issues*, edited by Anna Hickey-Moody and Peta Malins, 223–235. London: Palgrave Macmillan.

Parreñas, Rhacel Salazar. 2009. "Transgressing the Nation-State: The Partial Citizenship and 'Imagined (Global) Community' of Migrant Filipina Domestic Workers." In *Gendered Citizenships: Transnational Perspectives on Knowledge Production, Political Activism, and Culture*, edited by Kia Lilly Caldwell, Kathleen Coll, Tracy Fisher, Renya K. Ramirez, and Lok Siu, 89–107. New York: Palgrave Macmillan.

Pastore, Ferruccio, Paola Monzini, and Giuseppe Sciortino. 2006. "Schengen's Soft Underbelly? Irregular Migration and Human Smuggling across Land and Sea Borders to Italy." *International Migration* 44 (4): 95–119.

Pickering, Sharon, Mary Bosworth, and Katja Franko Aas. 2015. "The Criminology of Mobility." In *The Routledge Handbook on Crime and International Migration*, edited by Sharon Pickering and Julie Ham, 382–395. Abingdon, UK: Routledge.

Puga, Ana Elena, and Víctor M. Espinosa. 2020. *Performances of Suffering in Latin American Migration*. Cham, Switzerland: Springer International.

Sanchez, Gabriella. 2017. "Beyond the Matrix of Oppression: Reframing Human Smuggling through Intersectionality-Informed Approaches." *Theoretical Criminology* 21 (1): 46–56.

Sanchez, Gabriella, and Sheldon Zhang. 2018. "Rumors, Encounters, Collaborations, and Survival: The Migrant Smuggling–Drug Trafficking Nexus in the US Southwest." *ANNALS of the American Academy of Political and Social Science* 676 (1): 135–151.

Scheele, Judith. 2012. *Smugglers and Saints of the Sahara: Regional Connectivity in the Twentieth Century*. Cambridge: Cambridge University Press.

Shelley, Louise I. 2014. *Dirty Entanglements: Corruption, Crime, and Terrorism*. Cambridge: Cambridge University Press.

Spener, David. 2009. *Clandestine Crossings: Migrants and Coyotes on the Texas-Mexico Border*. Ithaca, NY: Cornell University Press.

Triandafyllidou, Anna, and Marie McAuliffe, eds. 2018. *Migrant Smuggling Data and Research: A Global Review of the Emerging Evidence Base*. Vol. 2. Geneva: International Organization for Migration.

United Nations. 2000. United Nations Convention against Transnational Organized Crime and the Protocols Thereto. https://www.unodc.org/documents/treaties/UNTOC/Publications/TOC%20Convention/TOCebook-e.pdf.

UNODC (United Nations Office on Drugs and Crime). 2018. *Global Study on Smuggling of Migrants 2018*. Vienna: UNODC.

Van Liempt, Ilse, and Jeroen Doomernik. 2006. "Migrant's Agency in the Smuggling Process: The Perspectives of Smuggled Migrants in the Netherlands." *International Migration* 44 (4): 165–190.

Van Schendel, Willem, and Itty Abraham. 2005. *Illicit Flows and Criminal Things: States, Borders, and the Other Side of Globalization*. Bloomington: Indiana University Press.

Vogt, Wendy A. 2018. *Lives in Transit: Violence and Intimacy on the Migrant Journey*. Oakland: University of California Press.

Zhang, Sheldon, Gabriella Sanchez, and Luigi Achilli. 2018. "Crimes of Solidarity in Mobility: Alternative Views on Migrant Smuggling." *ANNALS of the American Academy of Political and Social Science* 676 (1): 6–15.

CHAPTER 1

Smuggling the State Back In

AGENTS OF HUMAN SMUGGLING RECONSIDERED

David Kyle and John Dale

GIVEN THE IMMEDIATE POLICY and enforcement concerns of state agencies, it is unlikely that state representatives and others concerned with developing policies to reduce or manage human smuggling will reflect on either states' own role in creating and sustaining human smuggling or the nuances of its historical and sociological foundations. This chapter was written over twenty years ago for the first edition and updated for the second, and we include it yet again as news coverage of migrant smuggling and human trafficking continues to lump these two rubrics, based on legal distinctions, together into stories of human cargo and the dangers that those leading the journey placed them in. When a causal story is offered by state agencies or media, whether now or two decades ago, it usually takes the form of either of two conceptual extremes, one global and the other highly individualistic: first, global forces created the conditions for greater transnational crime of all sorts, of which trafficking in humans is the most recent illicit global activity; or second, some very ruthless and greedy professional criminals (above all, organized crime) are exploiting the weak and mostly innocent migrants who are either duped or coerced into a clandestine journey. Although there is an important element of truth to these statements regarding some smuggling operations, unfortunately they cover up more than they reveal, simplify more than they illuminate.

We take issue with these two general axioms in this chapter through an examination of two very different cases of human smuggling from the 1990s:

migrants contracting migration merchants in Ecuador to facilitate a journey to the United States, and young girls and women trafficked from northern Myanmar to Thailand and held in slavery. These two cases demonstrate the antithesis of the two axioms just stated; first, specific historical actions by politicians and other state actors in both sending and receiving states are largely responsible for the increase in global human smuggling, and second, we need to recognize the extreme diversity of smuggling operations and activities, both among and within sending regions, and how they are integrated into wider regional social structures.

If reporting on human smuggling is rife with the two aforementioned axioms, there is also a well-recognized paradox that academic researchers were quick to point out: state aggressiveness in combatting human smuggling, in the form of tighter border controls and asylum policies, sometimes prompts more people to seek smugglers and others to enter the migrant smuggling business, including ongoing transnational criminal enterprises attracted by the higher fees and relatively low risks of this activity. The rapid increase in US border enforcement activities in the mid-1990s (see Andreas, this volume, chap. 2) drove up the costs of illegal migration and increased the profits of human smuggling, thereby attracting the attention of criminal enterprises already engaged in other types of transnational smuggling, such as the drug trade. For would-be migrants, what had been a relatively low-cost, informal affair of crossing the Rio Grande now required great risks and resources and was less likely to be attempted without some type of professional smuggler. Of course, for those coming from more distant countries, this had been the case for some time (Kyle 2000).

What was telling about the positive correlation between the United States' enforcement actions along the border and the recent increase in the scope and profitability of professional smuggling was that US government representatives, especially from the Immigration and Naturalization Service (as it was called at that time), not only agreed with this assessment but hinted that this was the plan all along. However, unlike in Peter Andreas's detailed account of the unintended consequences of US domestic politics leading to the militarization of the US-Mexico border, suggesting a less than rational policy-making process, the specter of foreign terrorist threats is now consistently mentioned as a significant part of the border deterrence strategies of the 1990s. For example, a US General Accounting Office report began with these two sentences: "Alien smuggling is a significant and growing problem. Although it is likely that most smuggled aliens are brought into the United States to pursue employment opportunities, some are smuggled as part of a criminal or terrorist enterprise that can pose a serious threat to U.S. national security" (2000: 1). Hence, according to this interpretation, it was not the *Golden Venture* smuggling ship that ran aground in 1993 as much as the first World Trade Center bombing a few months earlier that prompted US government officials to reevaluate border security and strategy. In this scenario, it was desirable for the United States' security interests to diminish the chaos of small-scale mom-and-pop smuggling operations along the border in favor of larger, full-time criminal enterprises. Professional law enforcement techniques rely heavily on infiltration and disruption of stable and quite large criminal organizations rather than small-scale opportunists; in a nutshell, an ongoing professional criminal syndicate presents a much larger and weaker target than two cousins and an uncle moonlighting as migrant smugglers, as they saw it. Thus, by raising the physical and financial costs of a clandestine crossing, it was more likely that smaller operations would be driven out of business and migrants would be funneled through (monitored) criminal syndicates.

Interestingly, both of these alternative theories of the United States constructing institutional human smuggling along its border called into question the two axioms of human smuggling reportage, that unfettered globalization, the preferred catchall zeitgeist at the time, is the root cause and that those being smuggled are uniformly the victims of evil smugglers. In the first instance, the concept of technological globalization is much too nebulous and macrosociological to capture the specific actions and political and economic conditions in some regions that have led to increased human smuggling of the type we see today. In the US case, given state complicity in driving would-be migrants into more onerous smuggling operations run by professional criminals who routinely use violent coercion, apportioning all the blame to the smuggler conveniently avoids the legal and moral complexity of a range of actors that is a near-universal trait of actual smuggling activities. When such complexities do emerge from actual human smuggling situations, such as the prominent case of the Cuban boy Elián Gonzalez seeking refuge in Florida, depending on one's political agenda the story can be shoe-horned to fit within a preexisting morality story. In the Gonzalez case, it was striking that many who would otherwise be on the side of illegal migration control viewed the mother of Elián, who died in a smuggling operation, not as a victim but as someone who willingly risked her life in order to reach the United States and offer her son a better life. Thus, while the Mexican smuggler helping other Mexicans—many of whom Indigenous minorities persecuted by Mexican authorities—to find a better economic and political environment in the United States is described as exploitative and cruel when a smuggling operation ends in a death, his Cuban counterparts risking choppy seas in little more than rafts are almost never so described. Once again, the many paradoxes one encounters in the uneven and unbalanced control of people across state borders need to be viewed within the larger political context of conflicting strategic policy goals, of which controlling undocumented labor is only one consideration.

MIGRANT EXPORTING SCHEMES VERSUS SLAVE IMPORTING OPERATIONS

If the case of the US-Mexico border buildup demonstrates how state policies engender professional human smuggling, it is insufficient to explain its more complex sociological and political foundations found in various regions around the world. However, it demonstrates an important point: a narrow focus on the criminal smuggler overlooks a range of people implicated and benefiting from the politics and business of human smuggling. In order to bring some conceptual clarity to the complex social phenomenon of human smuggling, we distinguish between two ideal types: *migrant exporting schemes* and *slave importing operations*, which are exemplified in two cases from Ecuador and Myanmar, discussed shortly. One or the other usually predominates in a sending region, though sometimes both together. These conceptual categories draw attention to the entire range of activities at both ends and not simply under what immediate conditions a person is smuggled across a border. The idea is to understand two different kinds of smuggling activities that are profitable, but under different circumstances and with distinct kinds of transnational social organizations.

The primary goal of a migrant exporting scheme is to provide a limited or "package" migration service out of a sending region (see Salt and Stein 1997). Most of the organizational activity takes place on the sending side, and the contract is terminated once the migrant has arrived at the destination. In some cases, however, financial loans for the smuggling fees become an important source of income after arrival, but the terms of interest and payment and the division of labor vary greatly; the smuggler is not necessarily the loan shark. It is quite common for family members already abroad to lend the smuggling fee for a reduced rate. Such migrant exporting schemes are often characterized by highly irregular, often short-lived criminality, much of it opportunistic. Since many are part-timers, it is not simply a matter of breaking up a stable ring or criminal organization, though there is some evidence that larger criminal syndicates have moved into the migrant exporting business. It may or may not involve high levels of state corruption. Sending states typically find little political will to disrupt such migrant export projects owing to both a lack of criminal law for most related activities and the large sums of migrant remittances. Within such schemes, migrants are often driven to professional smugglers by blocked social mobility, preexisting corruption, and uneven development—not absolute poverty. Racism and sexism are common reasons for perceived ceilings in mobility, though many would be considered middle class within their home communities.

Migrant exporting is more like money laundering than drug smuggling. The type of flow is not intrinsically illicit—unlike heroin. The principal investors do not have to accompany the commodity physically across the border. The layering process of identity laundering is built into all transactions along the way; once the migrant is integrated by crossing the border, the activity is complete—in contrast, getting heroin across the border is only the beginning because the criminal organization still needs to distribute and sell it in order to reap the bulk of profits. And this is exactly the crucial distinction between a migrant exporting scheme and a slave importing operation.

In a slave importing operation, the goal is to import weak labor, typically vulnerable women, though not always so, for *ongoing* enterprises by relatively stable criminal organizations or even semilegitimate businesses in the destination country. Needless to say, a slave—held in bondage for economic profit—is extremely profitable (Bales 1999). Unlike a migrant exporting scheme, a slave importing operation nearly always involves corruption of state officials in all countries involved. In most cases, victims of such operations are duped into believing that it is a migrant exporting scheme on which they are about to embark. Contemporary slave traders are able to pretend to be migration exporters precisely because the latter do exist. As with many confidence schemes, it is the victim's own complicity in a relatively minor crime (an illegal border crossing) that leads to the final snare of the con and the reveal of the true price. Tragically, in this case, the migrant (now an "illegal alien") is stripped of all legal rights and personal dignity and made to pay off a rolling debt through coerced labor, typically prostitution. Migrants may be held for weeks, months, or years in such conditions, paying off the new debt incurred each time they change hands. Given the nature of this enterprise, unlike in a migrant exporting scheme, often the victims come from much more dire economic and social situations; it is a combination of their desperateness, political weakness, and lack of strong social networks that leads them to believe the false promises offering a way out. Such operations are sophisticated enough to have the initial contact person be a seemingly wealthy woman from the same ethnic group as the victim—the primary feature is that the victim or mark is targeted and presented with a façade that is sure to hook them. The recruiter's claims are buttressed by the ubiquitous images of idealized lifestyles of the most developed countries now beamed by satellite around the world through the global media industry.

There is a legal, political, moral, and sociological difference between the two types of smuggling activities we have outlined here. Slaves are slaves; it does not matter what unfortunate decisions were made to place them in the hands of slaveholders seeking to profit from coerced labor. By focusing on the nature of the economic enterprise spanning multiple countries, and not the degree to which a migrant agreed to be smuggled (few are actually kidnapped), we gain a better understanding of what is at stake for those at multiple levels of society who are benefiting from smuggling operations, whether directly or indirectly, and a deeper understanding of the different economic logics of human smuggling and trafficking. We next turn to two examples of a migrant exporting scheme and a slave importing operation in order to move from an ideal type to the historical complexities of actual cases.

ECUADOR: MIGRANT EXPORTING SCHEMES

Most Ecuadorians abroad until the end of the 1990s were from a single region of Ecuador, the southern province of Azuay, where the most recent development project in a long history of entrepreneurial efforts has come to include migrant exporting. Located approximately three hundred kilometers south of Quito over mountainous terrain, the province of Azuay includes Ecuador's third-largest city, Cuenca (population 330,000), and shares a common social and political history with the neighboring province of Cañar.

Unlike neighboring regions, Azuay is characterized by an early integration with, and dependence on, the capitalist world economy. Azuayans exported cloth during the colonial period. The Azuayan elite relied on ideological control of its nominally independent peasantry, which included unusually large numbers of Spaniards and mestizos compared with the Indigenous population. Unlike the rest of Ecuador, Azuay largely avoided the extremes of the colonial *encomienda* system of debt peonage but did not escape it altogether. Throughout the colonial period, policies restricting peasants to *reduciones*, or bounded communities, severely limited their social mobility.

After independence from Spain, the lack of royal authority and Azuay's general isolation meant that local elites could consolidate their political dominance and increase their ideological claims to the region's resources and surplus labor. For example, when the cloth trade in Azuay collapsed in the early 1800s owing to cheap British imports, Azuayan elites actively searched for economic solutions to the crisis that would not fundamentally alter the social status quo. The challenge for elites was straightforward: after several decades of placing little pressure on the Azuayan and Cañari peasantry following the decline of the cloth trade, they needed a peasant cottage industry that furthered the elite's role as intermediaries and could fill a market niche using preindustrial technology and inexpensive raw materials. Thus, local elites deliberately introduced to the region a productive activity—the weaving of straw hats—that would not upset but reinforce the existing Azuayan social structure.

In promoting the new industry, local officials noted the low cost of the straw and other materials needed and also that it was an occupation in which "all hands [could] be put to work, including men and women, elderly and children" (Dominguez 1991: 36). With such a concerted push by the elite and the quick popularity of the hats in sunny Azuay itself, the introduction was a huge success—to the extent that peasants and urban poor were soon weaving hats in nearly every corner of Azuay and Cañar. Once the internal demand was satisfied, the hats began to be exported for gold miners passing through Panama during the California gold rush of the 1850s (hence the name "Panama hat"); the value of straw hat exports from Ecuador jumped from 117,008 pesos in 1843 to 830,040 in 1855 (Palomeque 1990).

The weaving of straw hats—planned and instituted by local elites—began a radical transformation that would soon articulate the region into a labor-intensive, industrial bureaucracy, closely linked to the world economy. Though the cottage industry of hat weaving was similar to that of cloth weaving, whereby both raw material and woven product were brokered to the peasantry by middlemen who were, directly or indirectly, employed by urban export "houses," the production and marketing process entailed a greater division of labor on a much larger scale with (as city officials predicted) the participation of both men and women, young and old, each finding his or her production niche. The brokering system itself employs a hierarchy of *comisionistas*, who broker for the export houses, and independent *perros* (dogs), who sell to the *comisionistas* after paying the weaver slightly less for the hat than what the *comisionista* would have paid. Dominguez (1991) estimates that at the height of the hat trade in the 1940s, as many as 250,000 children and adults from the provinces of Azuay and Cañar were engaged in some activity directly related to making and marketing Panama hats.

Although the peasant weavers of Azuay enjoyed an unprecedented freedom in comparison with their counterparts living on haciendas or working in urban sweatshops, their ambiguous class position prevented the achievement of any significant economic or social gains through group mobilization; though thousands were and continue to be exploited at piece rates below subsistence level, this common exploitation as a potential source of group action is outweighed by their conservative position as landowners in direct economic competition with their neighbors—a fact fully exploited by the *comisionistas* and *perros*.

A "long decade" of economic depression in Azuay began with the precipitous drop in Panama hat exports in 1947 and their continuous decline every year until the mid-1960s. Cuenca's principal importer of Panama hats, the United States, began to import cheaper synthetic straw hats from Asia after World War II.

The impact of the hat industry's decline on Azuay and Cañar was immediate and severe, initiating a quiet revolution of economic disarticulation and social disintegration. For many members of the urban elite not directly connected to the hat trade, any financial losses were compensated by their ability to exploit the new vulnerability of the rural and urban labor force. It was, instead, those diverse groups engaged in some activity related to the hat trade (which at its height included over a quarter of the population) that had to seek external remedies to the immediate economic crisis they were experiencing. While the local and national elite did little to respond effectively to the Azuayan crisis of the 1950s, two groups—the white-mestizo exporters and the rural peasant weavers—began two different types of migration that together would set the stage for a mass exodus in the 1980s and 1990s. It is during the 1950s that the first Cuencanos arrived in New York City, mostly young men of wealthy white and mestizo families directly connected to urban hat export houses. They were looking for ways to capitalize financially on their long-standing connections with US importers—and for adventure (Astudillo and Cordero 1990). It is also during the late 1950s that regular jet airline service connected Cuenca to New York City via Guayaquil: it was now just as easy for a Cuencano to travel to New York City as to Quito, Ecuador's capital.

These pioneering migration networks notwithstanding, the mass regionwide phenomenon of international migration from Azuay, Cañar, and Morona Santiago (largely populated by Azuayans) that developed during the 1980s cannot be completely accounted for by a geometric increase—that is, a simple "snowball" effect—of migrants helping family and neighbors to make the multiple border crossings, especially the high number of peasants migrating to New York City directly from the most rural areas. Unlike other historical international flows of documented and undocumented immigrants, there is no evidence of direct recruitment by North American employers to facilitate the considerable financial and legal obstacles of the journey. Yet in just ten years, the modest international migrations of the 1970s turned into a mass exodus, making it one of the largest groups of undocumented immigrants in the New York City metro area.

This sharp increase in international migration, especially from rural, isolated areas, can be explained only by the reemergence of a centuries-old institution in the region—the usurious middleman, who profits from the economic and political space afforded by a complacent elite and a captive peasantry, in this case an integrated network of *tramitadores* (facilitators), who provide the range of legal and illegal services needed to make a clandestine trip to the United States. Instead of mediating the hat procurement for export houses as in the hat trade, tramitadores work, directly or indirectly, for unscrupulous travel agencies, which are themselves participants in larger formal and underground networks of migration merchants, or those who profit from some aspect of the migrant exporting business.

Although these facilitating networks are international in scope, they begin with a tramitador's sales pitch to the would-be migrant in his or her home village, not unlike the role played by the *perros* in the straw hat trade. The tramitador offers to arrange all the national documents needed to leave Ecuador, visas for intermediary countries, all the physical travel arrangements, and, depending on the type of trip, a falsified US visa or passport. To pay for all these services, which run from US$6,000 to US$10,000, an amount even the wealthiest of Ecuadorians would balk at, the tramitador arranges to have the money lent to the ingenuous peasant by a *chulquero* (smuggler/moneylender), at usurious interest rates of 10–12 percent, compounded monthly, with all land, animals, and possessions of the migrant held as collateral. In addition, numerous local banks and money exchange houses provide the needed financial infrastructure and legal cover for such operations. Local community-based networks of tramitadores and chulqueros typically are closely related by kinship, relying on social ties with a high degree of trust and loyalty, thus allowing for clandestine capitalism to operate with fewer costs (both monetary and psychological) related to maintaining the financial and legal security of the covert economic activity. For example, in one medium-sized Azuayan town with high levels of international migration, all the moneylenders are members of just five families, and each of these families is further interlocked through marital ties.

It should be emphasized that moneylending as an economic institution with a set of rules and customs had been a historical feature of the region even before the rural economy was completely monetized. The vicissitudes of small-scale and subsistence farming among the peasantry, along with the periodic burden of financing an annual religious festival, have traditionally required the services of moneylenders, who are either coethnic villagers or white-mestizo outsiders and whose rates are officially controlled by the state. For example, in times of crop failure, a loan enabled households not only to buy the few necessary household goods but also, most important, to continue the production cycle, which could include temporary coastal migrations and handicraft production. In times of regional scarcity, loans from "outside" the village from one of the urban-based "patrons" often involved usurious practices made possible by the peasant's ignorance and general position of weakness vis-à-vis the patron.

With corrupt local officials and a network of professional forgers, the necessary local and national documents are bought by the tramitador. Often the forger's work is so good that US embassy personnel in Quito cannot figure out how the documents can circumvent infrared detectors and laminate safeguards developed by the 3M company (personal communication). Next, working with legitimate travel agents, the tramitador makes the travel arrangements, which, broadly speaking, fall into either of two categories: (1) the direct route to New York City, using a "borrowed" passport or forged visa, which also entails a significant amount of cultural coaching on how to look and act like a *residente* (green-card holder); or (2) the tortuous overland route that includes a sophisticated network of Central American and Mexican contacts, "safe houses," and "coyotes" (those who actually lead the migrant across the Rio Grande). Since the Mexican government has made attaining a visa to its country more difficult, sometimes coyotes are also used to get into Mexico through a Guatemalan farm or by boat. At every step of the way, from the financing of the trip in Ecuador to the dependence on a nefarious international network spanning half a dozen countries, the migrant risks being swindled, ailed, deported, robbed, or violently abused, including rape and murder. Not surprisingly, the main task of the tramitador is to gain the confidence, whether founded or unfounded, of the potential "client." The price of land in Ecuador is so inflated owing to competition by return migrants in both urban and rural areas that only those who have a US dollar income can hope to purchase a new plot, lending support to the recruiter's sales pitch.

The particular configuration of financial and human resources brought to bear by each migrant on the problem of getting him or her across a border is often as unique as the Azuayan villages and barrios. The financing of the trip usually involves a combination of personal savings, free loans by relatives, interest loans by friends, and usurious loans by chulqueros. Similarly, a catalog of the techniques used to get across the US border or obtain a tourist visa could fill a medium-sized book. Kin- and community-based migration networks make use of the information and resources circulating within them, thereby making migration paths fairly consistent within a given social network. In this way, the path taken by a successful migrant pioneer gets repeated and revised within his or her network. Sometimes this evolutionary process may induce a pioneer, who has already made several trips and may be a *residente*, to become an in-network tramitador, coyote, or chulquero whose services are provided for a lower fee or even freely (that is, monetarily speaking, though reciprocity of some sort is assumed). Conversely, it is also common for return migrants to lend money to regional intermediaries (of the *perro* mold), who in turn lend at higher rates to professional chulqueros, who in turn lend to new migrants at the highest rate, thus forming a pyramid scheme that requires a constant influx of new migrants to keep capital circulating to the top.

The impact of mass international migration was nothing short of an economic and social transformation for the province of Azuay. These individual, community, and regional transformations leading to one of the most important mass international migrations from South America were built not on the foundation of either individual decisions or the snowball effect of social networks but rather on a regionwide migrant exporting industry in which a wide range of people played direct and indirect roles, from the recruiter to the local banker. At the time, the explosive construction of new concrete homes in some rural villages near Cuenca, often with a new SUV in the garage and chickens on the upper floors, provided testimony to the general success of the migrant exporting schemes in this region. The sustainability and future changes in the social organization of these schemes are topics for future research.

MYANMAR AND THAILAND: SLAVE IMPORTING OPERATIONS

In the mid-1990s, a guest staying in one of the finest hotels in Myanmar (Burma) may have been surprised to learn through an official tourist brochure that Myanmar had a unique natural resource that it would like to offer: its own female virgins (Knowles 1997; Kyaa Nyo 1997). A male tourist may therefore have been able to experience not only the virgin quality of a mysterious country dotted with hundreds of ancient pagodas, only recently opened to tourism, but also a night with a virgin girl from a rural village who may have been as young as twelve years old. If the Myanmar government helped promote its virgins as a local resource for sale, it is not surprising that virgins were also an exportable and highly profitable commodity. The primary destination for young women trafficked out of Myanmar was Thailand, with some eventually continuing on to other destinations.

The transnational trafficking of women and girls between Myanmar and Thailand, while perhaps increasing in overall numbers, was not a new development. By the 1890s, such networks of trafficked women were evident throughout Southeast Asia. Already, as is still the case today, sexual service to foreigners had been commoditized and stigmatized, the fate of low-born and marginal women (see Scully, this volume, chap. 3). What was novel about the flow of women from Myanmar to Thailand's sex-work industry at the time was that ethnic minority women from the countryside of Myanmar were in demand by foreign tourists and business travelers (particularly from China) in Thailand. This emerging, exoticizing preference for Burmese prostitutes was refined by one further criterion: these women (girls, really) must be virgins. At least, it was Burmese (ethnic Shan) virgins for whom foreign customers traveling in Thailand were willing to pay the most money. Moreover, the states of both Myanmar and Thailand were playing the most proactive role in constituting this demand. H. Richard Friman (2011) explains how the state (Japan) played a constitutive role in the ideological construction of the "snakehead" threat as "foreign" and how the state benefited from this construction both politically and economically. Myanmar and Thailand, however, profited by playing a more direct role in constructing the markets of transnational organized crime that we are describing here. Before turning to Myanmar, to understand the regional and international market for Burmese virgins, we must examine recent economic and demographic changes in Thailand.

In the minds of many Thai citizens, globalization came to mean currency crisis and unemployment. Joining the prescriptive belt-tightening fiscal austerity discourse provided by the International Monetary Fund had translated into a more indigenous, nationalist discourse targeting illegal immigration. Curiously absent from the Thai state's remedial discussion of the causes of illegal immigration was the state's own role in promoting it. In the summer of 1996, when financial analysts worldwide still perceived the Southeast Asian "tiger" economies as roaring, the Thai state issued a cabinet resolution allowing employers in forty-three provinces to register illegal Burmese,

Laotians, and Cambodians already living in Thailand to work for two years. The purpose of the resolution was to ease the burden of Thailand's labor shortage. The unanticipated currency crisis, however, engendered a new official policy toward illegal immigration: repatriation of the approximately one million illegal alien workers in an attempt to ease the sharp increase of unemployment among Thai nationals. Most illegal alien workers in Thailand are from Myanmar.

In the early 1990s, about twenty thousand young girls and boys (age ten to fifteen) were smuggled from Myanmar each year to work in Thailand's sex industry (Mirkinson 1994: 4). This represented about 10 percent of all prostitutes working in Thailand (Chaipipat 1997). Most of these youths came from Shan state in the northeastern region of Myanmar, bordering Thailand. According to research presented in Bangkok at a 1997 regional conference on the prevention of human trafficking, the annual illegal income generated by sex workers (of all ages) in Thailand was between 450 billion and 540 billion baht (or roughly US$10 billion).[1] To put these numbers in perspective, this is more money than is generated from drug trafficking. Moreover, Thailand's total state budget was only 1 trillion baht in 1995, before the currency crisis (Chaipipat 1997). Complicating Thailand's repatriation policy objective, Myanmar insisted that it would not accept illegal workers from its ethnic minority groups employed in Thailand.

In 1988, a statewide prodemocracy movement emerged in Myanmar to challenge twenty-six years of political repression and economic mismanagement under the military regime that usurped control of the state in a 1962 coup. The military state's crackdown was more dramatic and bloodier than that witnessed the following year in Beijing's Tiananmen Square. Western democratic states responded initially to what they identified as human rights abuses by passing economic sanctions against Myanmar. Sorely in need of foreign investment, the military state regime began to privatize its state-managed natural resources (teak, jade, and oil), abandoning its isolationist economic policy known as the "Burmese way to Socialism." The state also consented to the demands of the major opposition party, the National League for Democracy, led by Aung San Suu Kyi. Suu Kyi, who has since been awarded the Nobel Peace Prize for her efforts, is the daughter of the national hero Aung San, who was assassinated by the associates of Myanmar's current dictator shortly after he successfully led the country to democratic independence from the British and Japanese in the wake of World War II. Suu Kyi demanded successfully that the military regime hold fair and democratic elections, and in a 1990 landslide victory she was elected with 82 percent of the vote. The military, however, refusing to honor the results, instead responded by placing Suu Kyi under house arrest and systematically arresting or assassinating the newly elected members of her party in each township throughout the state.

As prodemocracy activists from the urban centers of Rangoon and Mandalay fled to the rural Thai-Myanmar border regions to join forces with ethnic minority rebels who had been fighting the state for national autonomy since the initial coup, the Burmese military launched a new campaign to eradicate these rebel strongholds. The military resorted to a systematic policy of burning local villages along the border; raping and torturing ethnic minority women; forcibly conscripting villagers to serve the military as porters, minesweepers, and human shields in its campaigns to exterminate oppositional groups; and coercively enslaving villagers to work on the military state's infrastructural projects. Some of these projects, like the oil pipeline being constructed through Myanmar to Thailand, were financed by transnational corporations like Unocal (based in the United States) and Total (based in France). Such military campaigns and development projects generated a dramatic increase in Thailand's refugee camps situated along the Thai-Myanmar border in this period.

In contrast to the Western democratic states that initiated economic sanctions (and encouraged by Suu Kyi's National League for Democracy), member states of the Association of Southeast Asian Nations (ASEAN), along with China and transnational corporations with high levels of investment in partnerships with the state-owned Myanmar Holdings Company, continued trading with Myanmar under a policy of constructive engagement. Proponents of this policy argued that reviving official development assistance, promoting more investment, and even encouraging nongovernmental organizations to provide humanitarian assistance would bring about much-needed social and political change in Myanmar. They maintained that isolating the military state regime through economic sanctions was ineffective. In 1997, ASEAN inducted Myanmar as a new member of its economic regional trading bloc. Myanmar's ruling party celebrated its induction into ASEAN as a solution to its flagging attraction as a site of foreign investment.

However, Myanmar was unable to cash in on this opportunity owing to the simultaneous onset of what became dubbed in the international financial press the "Southeast Asian currency crisis." Myanmar's potential trading allies, such as Indonesia and Thailand, were suddenly subjected to strict lending criteria imposed by the International Monetary Fund. Overt investment in Myanmar was no longer politically feasible. Yet Myanmar pursued other sources of unofficial revenue in more clandestine transnational markets of Southeast Asia (and beyond), as illustrated in some of its official tourist brochures promoting another of its putative natural resources: Burmese virgins.

Both men and women from Myanmar concentrated in Thai refugee camps along the border reported in interviews with humanitarian nongovernmental organization workers that local Thai officials forced them upon threat of being repatriated to serve as recruiters for organized human smuggling groups engaged in the trafficking of young girls from Myanmar into Thailand's sex industry.[2] The local Thai officials, typically immigration border patrol officers, then received a bounty from one of the agents of the human smuggling groups. Sometimes the process worked the other way around, whereby the agents approached the Thai officials and paid them bribe money to pass without complication through the border checkpoints. These refugee recruiters led the agents to their home villages in Myanmar. Along the way (and back), the agents paid bribes whenever necessary to Myanmar's military state personnel. The refugees were needed for their skills in speaking Burmese as well as the local ethnic minority language of the target village in Myanmar. Perhaps most important, the refugees were used to establish the trust necessary for persuading the young girls' families to relinquish custody of their daughters (usually with some form of material compensation) to the Thai officials.

While some girls had a vague idea of the nature of the work they would be doing, they were not aware of the working conditions (particularly the debt peonage) that awaited them. Upon returning, the local official typically charged 5,000 baht per person brought by agents of the human smuggling operation into Thailand. Brothel owners in Thailand paid the agents, who paid the state authorities, but ultimately the brothel owner charged this same amount to the young girl's debt. As a "virgin," she earned up to 15,000 baht from one customer. Virgins—particularly Burmese or Shan virgins—

commanded top dollar in many areas of Thailand at the time. Most of the demand seemed to be coming from Chinese tourists and businessmen. A young girl's "loss of virginity" could be sold several times, until she could no longer pass as a virgin in the eyes of her potential customers. Through a surgical procedure, a girl could also be "revirginized." Thus, the loss of virginity was viewed not so much as an event but rather as a gradual process. Many of these young girls from Myanmar, even before entering the sex trade in Thailand, could recount stories of being raped by the Myanmar military. Virgins were highly valued not only for the reduced risk of their having HIV but also because in many Asian cultures deflowering a virgin is considered to bestow on the perpetrator youthful potency and healthful benefits. Burmese and Shan girls were exoticized as special virgins, partly because of the relative isolation of Myanmar for several decades.

The money earned from the commodification of these young girls' virginity was significantly more than that earned by nonvirgins—a status the former were, of course, quickly on their way to assuming. Yet the percentage they actually received was not even enough to cover their initial smuggling debt. Moreover, the local police regularly raided these brothels (typically consisting of several rooms above a karaoke bar or coffee shop) in order to collect bribe money from the brothel owners, whose business in Thailand was illegal. The cost of these bribes was added to the young girls' debt, along with the cost of their food, clothing, cosmetics, toiletries, occasional health checks, and "rent" (although they typically slept in the same room, just big enough for a bed and sink, where they serviced their customers). A "Burmese virgin" could have expected to spend an average of eighteen months working simply to pay off her debt to her original brothel owner, or to any subsequent owner who purchased her (and her debt) from that original owner.

It is important to understand that it was not the girl who paid bribes to the police all along but rather the brothel owner. This money was not paid simply to prevent the girls from being arrested and deported; it was an informally institutionalized source of income for the police in exchange for their protecting the brothel owner. Sometimes brothel owners or agents would ask the police to arrest certain girls working in their brothel when the owners or agents did not want to give the sex workers the money they owed them. The more recent Thai policy of repatriating illegal alien workers did not diminish demand for the employment of these girls. It did, however, make it much more difficult for them to move into other areas of work and thus to remain in Thailand, once (or if) they had managed to buy back their freedom. Moreover, Thai immigration policy changes did not slow trafficking into slavery but rather made it easier for the brothel owners and police to threaten victims with repatriation.

Thailand's immigration policy proposal at the time appeared destined for failure (in terms of its alleged intent to curb migrant trafficking), but a careful reading between the lines suggested that, in practice, it served the state's interests. Thailand's immigration police announced in February 1998 that they had come up with a new strategy to encourage legal and illegal immigrants working in the country to return to their homelands voluntarily: instead of launching crackdowns on illegal workers, immigration police were being instructed to provide travel expenses and free meals to alien workers wishing to return home (Charoenpho 1998). They argued that this "psychological approach," which focuses only on illegal workers, would be more cost effective than crackdowns, whereby arrested illegal workers are sent directly to detention centers for months (of free meals). Under the new strategy, authorities would be required to pay only travel expenses and free meals on the day that the workers leave for their countries. In addition, the Thai immigration police, according to the national press, cited their concern for curbing the activities of human smugglers: "To prevent other Burmese immigrants from sneaking through the country [Thailand], Police Lieutenant-General Chidchai said he has liased with non-governmental organizations, the army and concerned agencies to help keep close watch on the movement of human smuggling gangs" (Charoenpho 1998: 2).

In a move that was meant to be interpreted as "putting their money where their mouth is," the immigration police, in the same report, assured Thai nationals that they had asked Police Region 7 (which is responsible for the western provinces bordering Myanmar) to deploy more officials at border passes to prevent the influx of Burmese into the country. This move addressed the common rebuttal promoted in the press that the rate of illegal immigration influx (particularly owing to internal conflict in Myanmar) outpaced that of repatriation. As a solution to preventing illegal Burmese immigration, however, the deployment of more officials at border passes, as we have seen, may serve only to exacerbate the problem. It was precisely such corrupt officials who had been making possible illegal migration from Myanmar through their complicity in human smuggling activities. In fairness to the government of Thailand, its historical and geographical location within one of the world's most volatile regions made its triple challenges of political stability, economic development, and migration control especially severe. Similarly, few countries in the world are untouched by some degree of official corruption. Nonetheless, the evidence suggests that while Thailand passed laws increasing the penalties for sexual relations with children, the ubiquitous sex industry—organized mostly for local consumption—and the enormous profits to be gained by investors in the sex trade called into question the notion that women and children trafficked into Thailand and held in bondage were simply the result of some criminal miscreants.

AGENTS OF HUMAN SMUGGLING RECONSIDERED

What do these cases have in common? First, in comparing these two differing cases of human smuggling from Ecuador and Myanmar, what is most striking is what is largely missing: "transnational gangsters." Although many point to "transnational organized crime" as the driving social force behind the global increase in human smuggling (see, e.g., Godson and Olson 1995), it plays only a support role, if any, in these two cases. Given the nature of the human commodity being smuggled, it is predictable that some human smugglers are members of traditional crime organizations, though by some definitions even corrupt police could be segregated conceptually into the organized crime camp. In the 1990s, there was much evidence that most smugglers of migrants around the world simply participated in what James O. Finckenauer (2011) called "crime that is organized" but not "organized crime." An additional element to this crime that is organized recalls earlier forms of widespread smuggling; for many around the world, participating in migrant exporting and even slave importing is not perceived, as a result of long-standing sociocultural norms, as a "real crime" in the region of origin.

Some migrant smugglers are more akin to the historical "free traders" of an earlier era when important commodities, in this case labor, were highly regulated and usuriously taxed. Migrant smugglers from the region of Azuay are not members of transnational organized crime in any traditional meaning of the term. Most are helping family and neighbors get to New York City.

This is a case that illustrates that mass undocumented migration can rapidly increase without organized crime. In contrast, Myanmar presents a case of "state-organized crime" (Chambliss 1989), entailing the smuggling of an illicit and, to be sure, morally bankrupt commodity. There is all too often a belief that a victim must somehow have deserved her or his fate. Especially on the migrant exporting end of the business, smugglers and moneylenders advertise in newspapers and do little to cover the nature of their business. Moreover, we have seen in the case of Myanmar that even states may subtly advertise to tourists the availability of commodities, the consumption of which is officially designated illicit, such as virgin prostitution. Similarly, it was the parents of young girls who sometimes sold a daughter for a sum equal to one year's income.

Apart from problematizing the role of organized crime, our two cases implicate other, unusual suspects in the social organization of migrant smuggling: (a) regional elites; (b) states pursuing their official interests and corrupt state officials pursuing self-aggrandizement; and (c) employers at the destination.

REGIONAL ELITES
For many developing countries, local economic and political power is concentrated in relatively few regional elite families (Walton 1977). This is especially striking in the case of Azuay, where such families were still referred to as "the nobles" in the 1990s. Since the early 1960s, many elites have adopted the discourse, if not also the strategies, of successive waves of development experts from North America and Europe, especially as foreigners have brought financial and technological aid. Yet the results of the previous modernization period were mixed at best, in large part owing to the unwillingness of regional elites to give up real power and the ideologies of social stratification that legitimize privilege. Hence, we had a common local "development" situation in the 1990s in many parts of the world: great strides in isolated areas that raised expectations for a better life but that did not live up to their promise.

Mass emigration may seem to be the ultimate measure of failure of a regional economy. However, mass *transnational* migration through an efficient, even rationalized, system of migration services commodification and smuggling overcame the two most important concerns for regional elites in the 1990s: migrant smuggling continued to extract profit from lower-status workers through financing, remittances, and other services and dampened potential political upheaval associated with the broken promises of failed "development" projects.

Not only does the export of people have some of the advantages of other traditional exports, such as backward linkages (e.g., financial services) and forward linkages (e.g., construction), but it also does not have the most significant disadvantage—competition from other regions around the world; migrants represent a global export paradoxically contained within a locally controlled market. Hence, transnational undocumented migration is an unintended consequence of development through modernization—a sort of grassroots development project itself from which many regional elites continue to profit (see Kyle 1995, 2000).

STATES AND CORRUPT STATE OFFICIALS

The commodification of migration affects sending and receiving states very differently, a fact that points to the real nature of human smuggling and undocumented migration vis-à-vis the saliency of the modern state system. State boundaries add to the value of any commodity needed across borders. Indeed, they are dependent on each other. In the case of human smuggling, sending states have generally viewed migration, whether legal or not, as a positive benefit. Remittances now rival many traditional sources of state revenue. Sending states have even reached out to include migrants abroad in domestic politics and have taken an active role in how undocumented conationals are treated in the United States and Europe. The Mexican ambassador Silva Herzog, speaking at the national convention of the League of United Latin American Citizens in Anaheim, California, observed, "It is particularly surprising that at a time of almost unprecedented success in the United States economy . . . the anti-immigration voices have once again taken the high ground. . . . Make no mistake about it, this is racism and xenophobia, and it has a negative impact on every person of Hispanic origin living in this country, regardless of their migratory status" (*Los Angeles Times*, June 26, 1997). Such aggressive campaigning for lessening immigration controls by a Mexican official in the United States is grounded not only in humanitarian concerns but also in the fear that the more than US$4.5 billion remittances (per the same *Los Angeles Times* article) to families in Mexico every year will recede during a grave economic crisis at home.

Similarly, in Myanmar, the military government cried foul because Thailand wanted to repatriate Burmese nationals in response to backlash against foreigners during a period of economic hardship. Illegal aliens from Myanmar working in Thailand managed to send home substantial amounts of money to their families (substantial, at least, to families living in a country where the annual per capita income was about US$150). However, Myanmar's military tended to collect this remitted money through various forms of violence, bribery, and "taxation," paid in cash, labor, social capital, or favors owed.

Highly publicized in the international media were the Myanmar military's violent campaigns and practices of coerced labor, extortion, "ethnic cleansing" (rape and murder), and crop burning against its rural ethnic minority communities living in the border regions of the state. We have also noted how less publicized practices of bribery, or the payment of "tea money" to state employees, became informally institutionalized.

However, the military also collected "taxes" from locals, which were typically imposed suddenly, as circumstances dictated. Taxes were imposed on particular villages for "beautification projects" (such as patching up ditches in the villages' dirt roads) purportedly designed to enhance tourism. Those who could not pay the tax in cash paid it in labor, helping to patch up the roads. The state also collected taxes from local villages that did not produce the quota of rice required by the state—even in cases when the state's military campaigns destroyed the rice crops, making it impossible for the villagers to meet such quotas.

When a family within the village had no money to pay these taxes, the state required that family to offer a male member of the household to serve either as a porter (without pay) in the military to fight in campaigns against rebel ethnic minority armies or in state construction projects. Few of these conscripts returned to see their families. It was not uncommon to learn that they had been literally worked to death. If a poor family had neither the money nor a male member of the family to serve in the military, it may have been able to borrow the money either from a wealthier family in the village or from the state in order to hire a neighbor's son to serve in the military for them. In this sense, the state "taxed" the villagers' social capital, a concept salient at this time.

In short, if the economically poor military state of Myanmar suspected that there were sources of wealth to be tapped within these villages, it could and did construct a justification for usurping that wealth. The state understood that a significant portion of that wealth was sustained through remittances from migrant members of the village working abroad. Thus it is not surprising that a proposal by Thailand's House Committee on Labor and Social Welfare met with protest from the state of Myanmar. In its effort to alleviate the burden of continuing to employ illegal workers from Myanmar, Thailand proposed to tax them all (including ethnic minorities) and remit the money directly to the state of Myanmar. If Myanmar had accepted these conditions, it then would have meant that it had also accepted the status of its minority workers in Thailand—an acknowledgment Myanmar was unwilling to provide. After all, there was little to gain in doing so: Myanmar already received at least as much in remittances by "taxing" local minorities who remained in Myanmar.

In regard to the receiving states, such as the United States, it would seem that the commodification of migration and the increasing use of smugglers would be uniformly negative. After all, some US policymakers have even considered the elimination of birthright citizenship for "illegal aliens." Although employers benefit from falsely documented labor, such benefits cannot be collapsed into the interests of the state. In addition, the economic benefit of both documented and undocumented migration to the US economy on the whole is an area of hot debate.

Unlike private employers, US leaders and policymakers have a variety of pro-immigrant, anti-immigrant, and ethnic communities to contend with and placate (see Freeman 1994; Joppke 1998). Although immigration laws must be upheld by the state, and although anti-immigrant voices include some demographic and economic rationales that cannot simply be reduced to racism, there is also a political price for "bashing immigrants." High-profile state agencies can diminish the political fallout of migration controls through a diffusing strategy that relies on a variety of third-party actors such as airlines and privatized detention centers. In a similar manner, a more commodified migration process, also using third parties (i.e., smugglers), allows states to develop a discourse that emphasizes the criminality and evil of alien smuggling rings, which can then be contrasted with hardworking immigrants.

EMPLOYERS AND SLAVEHOLDERS

North American employers of unskilled urban and farm labor directly benefit from an efficient underground source of labor. Were migrants dependent on their own social networks to cross borders under conditions of heightened state monitoring, immigrant labor flow might subside. Thus, smugglers might be conceptualized as an extension of, and in some cases a replacement for, labor recruiters. In some undocumented smuggling networks, the migrant, and even the individual smuggler for that matter, becomes a sort of indentured servant working for the syndicate or a collaborator (see Kyle and Dale 1999). In extreme cases, slavery returned in the form of garment and sex workers held captive in Los Angeles and New York City. Contemporary slavery, as Kevin Bales (1999: 14) pointed out, is not about slave owning but about "slave-holding," or complete control over people for economic profit. While this is a useful distinction between older and more contemporary forms of slavery, it is also one that is more disconcerting, since the organization of work around the world under the globalization project has led to greater levels of labor control, practices that are increasingly legitimized as necessary for survival within a competitive global arena. Even when free to find employment on their own terms, illegal immigrants with large usurious debts make an especially docile and hardworking labor force—a point not overlooked by employers or states in receiving countries.

Thus, beyond conceptualizing contemporary slaves as "disposable people," the title of Bales's book, we might also view them as an example of the growing process by which labor is forced underground into invisibility as well as disposability. One could argue that the concept of disposable people per se is not particularly novel to the current era. What is novel is the growing levels of work that is purposively hidden or obscured from consumers by employers, from the small restaurant to large transnational corporations. Tellingly, all the actors highlighted in this section—local elites, states, and employers—justify their less than honorable actions by invoking some form of the argument "globalization made me do it." Though the label has fallen out of favor, globalization *as an ideology* continues to blur the boundaries of what should be considered exploitative economic behavior first and foremost in the area of labor relations.

CONCLUSION

Accounts of transnational human smuggling, its organization, and the actors that sustain this practice are typically shaped by a particularly ahistorical conception of "organized crime"—one that allows no conceptual space for analyzing the organizational sources of transnational smuggling provided by, and thus implicating, regional elites, states, and employers (and hence consumers). Proceeding deductively from the common assumption that only large-scale transnational criminal organizations are driving increases in the levels of human smuggling fails to elucidate the central, proactive roles played by noncriminal migrants and criminal nonmigrants, including corrupt state representatives, in sustaining and transforming the practice of professional human smuggling. Other studies also suggest that even the premise of the deductive analysis of complex groups of transnational organized crime as necessary to the clandestine activities associated with human smuggling is faulty, especially in cases in which a previous legal activity has been converted to an illegal, heavily penalized one (see Reuter 1985).

We have taken a historical comparative approach in an attempt to understand the social organization, political benefits, and economic profitability of contemporary human smuggling as a diverse bundle of activities and participants. Our findings suggest that comparing processes of transnational migrant smuggling across different times and places reveals a wide range of social formations implicating diverse configurations of actors. Yet we have conceptualized some significant differences between two fundamental types of smuggling enterprises: migrant exporting schemes and slave importing operations. Both can be just as deadly for the movers and place them at a great legal and physical risk, but we believe that effective, humane policies still need to distinguish among a range of smuggling operations, some which are aiding people to leave situations of political persecution and economic hopelessness and others that deliver them into precisely such circumstances. In broad terms, three themes emerge from this comparison of a migrant exporting scheme and a slave importing operation: global diversity, internal organizational complexity, and contradictory state involvement in human smuggling activities and human rights.

The central argument of this chapter—that the role of criminal syndicates must be balanced with other state and commercial actors with domestic and global interests—was buttressed by the transformation of out-migration from Ecuador just as the first edition of this volume was being sent to the printers in 2000. Following the dollarization of its economy in that year, a mass irregular migration to Spain from every region of Ecuador, representing 10 percent of its population, unfolded so quickly that Ecuadorians became the largest immigrant community in Spain by 2004. Strikingly, this irregular mobility arriving by plane did not feature stereotypical smugglers but rather was facilitated by backroom deals by travel agencies and migration merchants lending migrants funds at high interest rates for the cost of the ticket and the approximately US$2,000 needed to demonstrate that they were "tourists" (see Kyle and Siracusa 2005). This was also made possible with complicit Ecuadorian and Spanish state involvement in the conditions and terms of Ecuadorian immigrant labor in Spain, though most were in violation of Spanish labor laws. Indeed, both Myanmar and Ecuador have continued to see changes to mobility patterns due to several political and economic crises and the global pandemic that began in late 2019 (see Alvarez Velasco, this volume, chap. 15).

In contrast, smuggling routes through Mexico have seen an increase in criminal syndicates involved in drug smuggling with high levels of violence threatening transiting migrants for purposes of kidnapping and extortion (Kyle and Scarcelli 2009). The most horrifying example was the 2010 massacre of seventy-two Central American and South American migrants, many Ecuadorian, in Tamaulipas State after the migrants allegedly refused to pay their captors. However, even in these cases, there was no evidence of complicity by the group's smugglers or coyotes. Other chapters in this volume that examine Mexico as a source or transit country give us a more recent account of changes in the diverse strategies, types of facilitation, and the roles played by migrants and their smugglers (see chapters 2, 13, 17, 19). We find that regardless of changes in the specific countries we first highlighted in this chapter, it remains useful to go beyond the superficial similarities of those moving via irregular, often clandestine, routes and the harms that may befall them but also to consider the distinct logics of two very different kinds of phenomena, migrant exporting schemes and slave importing operations.

NOTES

We wish to thank Daniela Kraiem and John Walton for their editorial scrutiny of an earlier version of this chapter, which was first presented to the annual meetings of the Society for the Study of Social Problems, August 1999, Chicago.

1. These data were presented by the Coalition to Fight Child Exploitation, the Thai Red Cross Society, and Mahidol University's Institute for Population and Social Research.
2. Fieldnotes and audio-taped interviews, February 1998, Thailand. These informants must remain anonymous. The information they provided JD is not the kind of information that their organizations are mandated to collect. These informants—they know who they are—have taken a great personal risk in providing this information, and JD offers them special thanks.

REFERENCES

Astudillo, Jaime, and Claudio Cordero. 1990. *Huayrapamushcas en USA: Flujos migratorios de la region centro-sur del Ecuador*. Quito: Editorial El Conejo.

Bales, Kevin. 1999. *Disposable People: New Slavery in the Global Economy*. Berkeley: University of California Press.

Chaipipat, Kulachada. 1997. "New Law Targets Human Trafficking." *Nation* [Bangkok], November 30, 1997.

Chambliss, William J. 1989. "State-Organized Crime." *Criminology* 27:2.

Charoenpho, Annucha. 1998. "New Way to Repatriate Immigrants: Illegal Workers Lured through Incentives." *Bangkok Post*, February 2, 1998, p. 2, col. 1.

Dominguez, Miguel E. 1991. *El sombrero de paja toquilla: Historia y economía*. Cuenca: Banco Central del Ecuador.

Finckenauer, James O. 2011. "Russian Transnational Organized Crime and Human Trafficking." In *Global Human Smuggling: Comparative Perspectives*, 2nd ed., edited by David Kyle and Rey Koslowski, 305-324. Baltimore: Johns Hopkins University Press.

Freeman, Gary. 1994. "Can Liberal States Control Unwanted Migration?" *ANNALS of the American Academy of Political and Social Science* 534:17-30.

Friman, H. Richard. 2011. "Migrant Smuggling and Threats to Social Order in Japan." In *Global Human Smuggling: Comparative Perspectives*, 2nd ed., edited by David Kyle and Rey Koslowski, 325-351. Baltimore: Johns Hopkins University Press.

Godson, Roy, and William J. Olson. 1995. "International Organized Crime." *Society* 32 (January/February): 18-29.

Joppke, Christian. 1998. "Why Liberal States Accept Unwanted Migration." *World Politics* 50 (2): 266-293.

Knowles, Joe. 1997. "Come for the Pagodas, Stay for the Virgins." *Might* 15 (March/April): 19.

Kyaa Nyo, Maung. 1997. "Myanmar Women." *Today* 4 (December 16–31): 82–84.

Kyle, David. 1995. "The Transnational Peasant: The Social Construction of International Economic Migration and Transcommunities from the Ecuadoran Andes." PhD diss., Johns Hopkins University.

Kyle, David. 2000. *Transnational Peasants: Migration, Networks, and Ethnicity in Andean Ecuador*. Baltimore: Johns Hopkins University Press.

Kyle, David, and John Dale. 1999. "The Social Construction of a 'New' Social Problem: Global Human Smuggling." Presented at the Society for the Study of Social Problem meetings "Legislating the Boundaries of Inclusion: Immigration, Citizenship, and the Law," August 6, Chicago.

Kyle, David, and Marc Scarcelli. 2009. "Migrant Smuggling and the Violence Question: Evolving Illicit Migration Industries for Cuban and Haitian Refugees." *Journal of Crime, Law, and Social Change* 52 (3): 297–311.

Kyle, David, and Christina A. Siracusa. 2005. "Seeing the State like a Migrant: Why So Many Non-criminals Break Immigration Laws." In *Illicit Flows and Criminal Things: States, Borders, and the Other Side of Globalization*, edited by Willem van Schendel and Itty Abraham, 153–176. Bloomington: Indiana University Press.

Mirkinson, Judith. 1994. "Red Light, Green Light: The Global Trafficking of Women." Accessed December 1, 2000. deepthought.armory.com/~leavitt/women.html.

Palomeque, Silvia. 1990. *Cuenca en el siglo XIX: La articulacion de una region*. Quito: Ediciones Abya-Yala.

Reuter, Peter. 1985. *The Organization of Illegal Markets: An Economic Analysis*. Research report, US Department of Justice, National Institute of Justice. Washington, DC: Government Printing Office, February.

Salt, John, and Jeremy Stein. 1997. "Migration as a Business: The Case of Trafficking." *International Migration* 35 (4): 467–494.

US General Accounting Office. 2000. GAO/GGD-00-103. 2000. "Alien Smuggling: Management and Operational Improvements." May 1. https://www.govinfo.gov/app/details/GAOREPORTS-GGD-00-103.

Walton, John. 1977. *Elites and Economic Development: Comparative Studies on the Political Economy of Latin American Cities*. Austin, TX: Institute of Latin American Studies.

CHAPTER 2

How the State Made Smuggling and Smuggling Made the State

A HISTORY OF IMMIGRATION CONTROL AND EVASION ON THE US-MEXICO LINE

Peter Andreas

MANY OF THE DYNAMICS of immigration law enforcement and evasion along the nearly two-thousand-mile-long US-Mexico border we have seen in recent years can be viewed as the latest chapter in an old story that dates back to the nineteenth century—a story that does not repeat itself, yet has a consistent underlying theme: through their interaction, immigration control and evasion have stimulated and reinforced each other. In this chapter I trace how the interaction between law enforcement and clandestine migration along the US-Mexico line has perversely generated a more organized and sophisticated migrant smuggling business and how this, in turn, has helped to propel more expansive and intensive border policing. I emphasize that while the relationship between law-evading smugglers and law-enforcing state actors has been conflictive, in practice it has in many ways also been unintentionally symbiotic. This dynamic along the border—an example of what the sociologist Gary Marx (1981) calls the interdependence between rule enforcers and rule breakers—is ultimately part of a much larger story about how the state makes smuggling and how smuggling (re)makes the policing apparatus of the state (Andreas 2013).

I first provide an overview of the emergence and evolution of migrant smuggling across the border and how this has intersected with various state practices over time. I then focus on the last years of the twentieth century, defined by a boom in both immigration control efforts and organized migrant smuggling activity in the US-Mexico borderlands. I conclude with a brief look at the continued escalation of border enforcement and evasion in the first decades of the twenty-first century.[1]

ORIGINS OF MIGRANT SMUGGLING ACROSS THE US-MEXICO BORDER

If smuggling can be defined as the practice of bringing in or taking out without state authorization, then all population flows involving a clandestine border crossing are by definition a form of smuggling. What has varied across time and place is the degree, nature, methods, and organization of such smuggling. In the case of crossing the US-Mexico border, this has ranged from self-smuggling (i.e., migrants clandestinely crossing the border without hiring the services of a professional smuggler), to local-level individual smuggling entrepreneurs (the traditional "coyotes"), to highly organized and sophisticated transnational smuggling networks (often specializing in the smuggling of non-Mexicans across the border).

The first wave of unauthorized immigration involved self-smuggling from the United States to Mexico. More than a century and a half ago, Mexico unsuccessfully tried to curb unauthorized American immigration to its northern regions. To a significant extent, the Mexican War was a conflict over immigration and immigration control. After the Treaty of Guadalupe Hidalgo of 1848 and the Gadsden Purchase of 1853, these territories formally became part of the United States. Large numbers of white settlers, many of them recent European immigrants, moved west to these sparsely populated lands. But while the political boundaries that were redrawn through war remain, the migratory movement has been turned around, with millions of people of Mexican origin populating these areas.

The movement of people across the border remained largely unregulated throughout the nineteenth century. The first real US initiative to restrict migration flows in the Southwest actually targeted Chinese. Efforts to prohibit Chinese immigration in the late nineteenth century mark the beginning of the federal government's long and tumultuous history of trying to keep out "undesirables." The Chinese Exclusion Act of 1882 barred the entry of Chinese laborers, who until then were mostly coming in by steamship to San Francisco. But while this front-door entry was closed, back doors were opening, especially via the US-Canadian and the US-Mexico borders. The federal government had no stand-alone immigration control apparatus when the Chinese Exclusion Act was passed, but enforcement of the law would stimulate the creation of entirely new federal administrative capacities.

The US-Mexico border, long a gateway for smuggled goods, was now also becoming a gateway for smuggled people. In 1900 there were just a few thousand Chinese in Mexico, but less than a decade later nearly sixty thousand Chinese migrants had departed to Mexico. Some stayed, but the United States was a far more attractive destination (Ettinger 2009: 99). In his investigations, US immigration inspector Marcus Braun witnessed Chinese arriving in Mexico and reported, "On their arrival in Mexico, I found them to be provided with United States money, not Mexican coins; they had in their possession Chinese-English dictionaries; I found them in possession of Chinese-American newspapers and of American railroad maps" (quoted in Ettinger 2009: 100). Boats of Chinese migrants would land south of the California-Mexico border at Ensenada, Guaymas, or Mazatlan. The migrants paid five dollars for the trip to the border and then up to forty dollars to be smuggled into California (Metz 1989: 365). The migrants also traveled deeper into the Mexican interior and were then smuggled across the border between Juárez and El Paso (Stoddard 1976: 180). Federal law enforcement officials (called "Chinese inspectors") were deployed to the border area to curb the smuggling of Chinese (McDonald 1997: 74).

In 1907, a US government investigator observed that between twenty and fifty Chinese arrived daily in the Mexican border town of Juarez by train, but that the Chinese community in the town never grew. As he put it, "Chinamen coming to Ciudad Juarez either vanish into thin air or cross the border line" (quoted in Lee 2003: 159). Foreshadowing future developments, a January 1904 editorial in the El Paso *Herald-Post* warned, "If this Chinese immigration to Mexico continues it will be necessary to run a barb wire fence along our side of the Rio Grande." The El Paso immigration inspector stated in his 1905 annual report that migrant smuggling is the sole business of "perhaps one-third of the Chinese population of El Paso" (quoted in Reynolds 1909: 148).

Some historians note that border smuggling operations involved cross-racial business collaborations, with white male smugglers often working with Chinese organizers and Mexicans serving as local border guides. A 1906 law enforcement report on Chinese smuggling noted, "All through northern Mexico, along the lines of the railroad, are located so-called boarding houses and restaurants, which are the rendezvous of the Chinese and their smugglers, and the small towns and villages throughout this section are filled with Chinese coolies, whose only occupation seems to be lying in wait until arrangements can be perfected for carrying them across the border" (quoted in Ettinger 2009: 60).

As US authorities tightened enforcement at urban entry points along the California-Mexico border, smugglers shifted to more remote parts of the border farther east in Arizona, New Mexico, and Texas. This provided the rationale to deploy more agents to these border areas (this dynamic would repeat itself again at the end of the century). In addition to hiring more port inspectors, a force of mounted inspectors was set up to patrol the borderline by horseback. As smugglers in later years turned to new technologies such as automobiles, officials also pushed for the use of the same technologies for border control (Lee 2003: 57–58).

Chinese migrants were not the only ones coming through the back door; they were simply at the top of a growing list of "undesirables" that included paupers, criminals, prostitutes, "lunatics," "idiots," polygamists, anarchists, "imbeciles," and contract workers in general. Japanese laborers were banned in 1907. Illiterates were banned from entry in 1917. As seaports became more tightly regulated and policed, immigrants who feared being placed in one of these excludable categories increasingly turned to the back door. Those groups that were disproportionately being turned away at the front-door ports of entry—among them Lebanese, Greeks, Italians, Slavs from the Balkans, and Jews—found Mexico to be a convenient backdoor alternative (Ettinger 2009: 105).

The popularity of the Mexican back door received a major boost by new US restrictions on European immigration through the national origins quotas in 1921 and 1924. Passport rules left over from World War I formalized in the Passport Act of 1918 also now required immigrants to secure visas at

US consulates abroad. The Mexico smuggling route offered a way to sidestep these new numerical restrictions and documentation requirements. This sparked alarm in Washington and provided political ammunition for calls for more border enforcement. The commissioner-general of immigration reported in 1923 that each new entry restriction "promoted the alien smuggling industry and furnished new and multiplied incentives to illegal entry" (quoted in Siener 2008: 60). The commissioner's report the following year predicted that the Immigration Law of 1924 "will result in a further influx of undesirable European aliens to Mexico with the sole object in view of affecting illegal entry into the United States over the Rio Grande" (quoted in McCullough 1992: 51–52).

Local media reports reinforced these concerns. A December 22, 1924, article in El Paso's Spanish-language newspaper *La Patria* pointed to the booming cross-border business for "contrabandistas de carne humana" (smugglers of human meat) in the wake of the new US immigration restrictions (quoted in McCullough 1992: 6). The article (with the headline, "Foreigners Who Want to Cross Over to the United States Have Invaded the City of Juarez") described Juarez as a depot for foreigners waiting to enter the United States (McCullough 1992: 230–231). Congress greatly expanded the immigration bureau's personnel powers to search and arrest along and near the borderline. In a country otherwise wary of increasing the power and reach of government, border control was one realm where there was a push to bolster federal authority.

Political pressure had been building up for a number of years to create a uniformed border patrol force. The US Border Patrol was formed in 1924 with a $1 million budget and a total force of some 450 officers. The primary mission was to keep out unauthorized immigrants, especially the smuggling of Europeans. Wesley Stile, one of the first border patrol agents hired in the summer of 1924, later recalled, "The thing that established the Border Patrol was the influx of European aliens." Border patrolmen "didn't pay much attention to the Mexicans" because they were considered merely cheap seasonal farm labor that returned to Mexico when no longer needed (quoted in Ettinger 2009: 162). This meant that the growing influx of unauthorized Mexican workers was largely tolerated and overlooked, at least for the time being.

As a substitute for European and Asian workers, employers considered Mexicans an ideal labor force: flexible, compliant, and temporary—or so it seemed at the time. Millions of unauthorized Mexican migrants would eventually settle in the United States, becoming a vital source of labor for agriculture and other sectors of the economy but also the main rationale for more intensive border enforcement. It was not until 1929 that US border inspectors even made any real effort to regulate the entry of Mexican nationals. Many Mexicans were informally recruited by US employers to work in southwestern agriculture. Whereas legal entry was cumbersome, crossing the border illegally was relatively simple. There was a growing disconnect between the formal entry rules handed down from a distant capital and the realities, needs, and practices along the border.

The Mexican Revolution, US labor shortages during World War I, and the expansion of southwestern agriculture fueled a further influx of Mexican workers across the border. An estimated half a million Mexicans entered the United States during the 1920s (Calavita 1994). When they were no longer needed during the Depression era, hundreds of thousands were deported. And when the demand for cheap labor increased again in the 1940s (as a result of labor shortages during World War II), Mexican workers were encouraged to come back. This time the state played a more formal role in the labor recruitment process. The Bracero Program, a guest-worker arrangement in place between 1942 and 1964, was created to provide a cheap source of labor for agribusiness.

The long-term consequence of the Bracero Program was to institutionalize mass labor migration from Mexico to the United States. As one immigration scholar has observed, "By the time the Bracero Program ended, a relationship of symbiosis between Mexican immigrants and U.S. employers had become well-entrenched, facilitated and nurtured by more than 50 years of U.S. policymaking. With the end of the program, employment of Mexican labor went underground as the guest workers of one era became the illegal immigrants of the next" (Calavita 1996: 289). After the Bracero Program was terminated in the 1960s, Mexican workers continued to be welcomed by employers. Legal sanctions did not worry employers, since the hiring of unauthorized workers was not a felony. In 1952, Congress had passed an act that made it illegal to "harbor, transport, or conceal illegal entrants." But employment was not considered harboring. This was the result of an amendment to the provision (called the Texas proviso), which was a concession to agribusiness interests (Calavita 1994: 60).

While unauthorized immigration increased rapidly during the 1960s and 1970s, the enforcement capacity of the then Immigration and Naturalization Service (INS) remained limited. Interior enforcement was largely nonexistent, while border controls were minimal. Even as the number of border apprehensions increased from approximately seventy-one thousand in 1960 to more than one million in 1978, the budget of the border patrol remained less than the budget of many city police departments (Teitelbaum 1980).

The limited presence and effectiveness of law enforcement meant that migrant smuggling was a fairly simple and inexpensive practice; migrants either smuggled themselves across the border or hired a local border guide. However, the sheer magnitude of the migration flow, competition between smugglers to service this flow, and the dispersion of the flow from agricultural to urban areas meant that smuggling gradually became more organized. As Peter Reuter and David Ronfeldt have noted, "After the termination of the Bracero program in 1965, smuggling of aliens into the United States was conducted by adventurous loners who had little concern for security and by small family-based operations. But the growth and competition for new business, the increased importance of operational skill and security, and the shift from agricultural areas to cities as the destination of many aliens created a need for larger, better organized operations" (1991: 14). Government reports suggest that smuggling organizations had grown substantially in size and complexity by the mid-1970s (Comptroller General of the United States 1976).

Still, hiring a professional smuggler remained more of a convenience than a necessity. In fiscal year (FY) 1970, only 8.4 percent of the unauthorized migrants caught by the border patrol in the southwestern region had attempted entry with the use of a smuggler. This increased to 13.5 percent in FY 1975 (Comptroller General of the United States 1976: 5–6). These statistics probably understate the amount of professional smuggling, since those migrants who hired the services of a smuggler were more likely to evade detection and arrest. Penalties against smugglers remained minimal: fewer than 50 percent of the smugglers caught between 1973 and 1975 were prosecuted, most on a misdemeanor charge (Comptroller General of the United States 1976: 18).

In one study, smugglers report that there was little demand for their services in the 1970s because migrants could easily enter the United States on their own. Smugglers were often hired for special needs, such as the smuggling of women, children, the elderly, and non-Mexican nationals (López Castro 1998: 970). Using a smuggler to cross the border generally meant a faster and safer trip. This involved some personal risks, but attempting the crossing without a smuggler heightened the possibility of assault by bandits and abuse by the authorities.

Failing as a meaningful barrier, INS control efforts remained largely symbolic (Heyman 1995). The border patrol could cover only a small portion of the borderline. While the INS insisted that "prompt apprehension and return to country of origin is a positive deterrent to illegal reentry and related violations" (INS Annual Report 1978, cited in Kossoudji 1992: 161), in practice migrants simply kept trying to cross until they succeeded. Repeated arrests did little more than postpone entry.

As migrants flowed north across the border for work, the Mexican government largely sat on the sidelines. Freedom of exit is guaranteed in the constitution, and the export of excess labor has long been an economic safety valve. Nevertheless, in the late 1970s Mexico, while not blocking the exit of Mexican citizens, began to cooperate with the United States in targeting professional smugglers. This was partly due to the Mexican government's rising concerns over the smuggling of Central Americans to the United States through Mexican territory. During the Carter years, the INS created a special unit called the National Anti-smuggling Program, which generated increased arrests and prosecutions of smugglers operating on the US side of the border. Mexico, in turn, collaborated by arresting hundreds of smugglers on its side of the line. During the 1980s, cross-border immigration control cooperation continued to focus primarily on the smuggling of third-country nationals through Mexico, especially Central Americans. Nevertheless, smugglers and those being smuggled remained largely undeterred (Nevins 1998: 326–328).

The most significant US policy response to unauthorized immigration was the passage of the Immigration Reform and Control Act of 1986 (IRCA). IRCA introduced employer sanctions, authorized an expansion of the border patrol, and offered a general legalization program (as well as a special legalization program for agricultural workers). Some two million Mexicans were eventually legalized. IRCA's proponents argued that this supply of newly legalized workers would satisfy the US demand for cheap imported labor, while the employer sanctions would inhibit the hiring of illegal workers. This, at least theoretically, would curb future unauthorized migration.

IRCA, however, reinforced the very problem the law was promoted to rectify. As one immigration researcher notes, "IRCA stimulated interest in coming to the U.S., and the possibility of obtaining a green card via the legalization programs led to a huge increase in the demand for coyote [smuggler] services" (López Castro 1998: 970). Those who were legalized under IRCA provided a stronger base for the arrival of new unauthorized immigrants. "By handing out more than 2 million green cards to former undocumented migrants," observes Douglas Massey, "Congress dramatically raised the odds that millions of other family members still in Mexico would themselves enter the United States as undocumented migrants" (1997: 26–27).

The employer sanctions law, meanwhile, provided no effective document verification system. The perverse impact of the law was to generate an enormous business in fake documents. Since IRCA did not require employers to check the authenticity of documents, they could simply continue to hire illegal workers at minimal risk—as long as the documents looked genuine and they made sure to fill out the proper forms. In the short term, IRCA helped to defuse some of the domestic pressure to "do something" about unauthorized immigration. But the law's failures would help make immigration control an even more daunting task in years to come.

THE INTENSIFIED BORDER ENFORCEMENT CAMPAIGN

The 1990s experienced a growing domestic anti-immigrant backlash, with California—home to an estimated half of the nation's unauthorized migrant population—at the epicenter. Just as the late nineteenth-century backlash against Chinese immigrants began in California, so too did the backlash against Mexican immigrants in the late twentieth century, with the fallout spreading along the entire border. Immigration control at the US-Mexico border was transformed in the early 1990s from a low-profile and politically marginalized activity into a high-intensity campaign attracting enormous policy and media attention. "The border build up," as one journalist observed, "represents by far the most expensive and prolonged budgetary initiative ever undertaken to reduce illegal immigration" (Suro 1998: 1).

Policymakers from across the political spectrum rushed to outdo one another in proposing tougher control measures. In this heated political context, President Bill Clinton launched an aggressive new campaign to "regain control" of the southwestern border. Noticeably less attention was given to the enormous employer demand for cheap migrant labor or the fact that as much as half of the unauthorized immigrant population in the country had entered legally (as students or tourists, for example) and then overstayed their visas.

The heightened political status of immigration control was reflected in the dramatic expansion of the INS. The INS budget grew from $1.5 billion in FY 1993 to $4 billion in FY 1999—making it one of the fastest- (and one of the only) growing federal agencies. The single most important growth area was border enforcement. In FY 1998, the INS spent $877 million on border enforcement, up from about $400 million in FY 1993. More than half of the $413 million increase in INS funding from FY 1998 to FY 1999 was allocated for border control.

As a result of its hiring spree, by the late 1990s the INS had more officers authorized to carry a gun and make arrests than any other federal law enforcement agency (*Migration News*, February 1998). Between FY 1993 and the end of FY 1998, the size of the border patrol along the southwestern border more than doubled—from 3,389 agents to 7,231 agents. Reflecting the intensified monitoring of the border, total line watch hours for the border patrol increased from 2,386,888 in FY 1993 to 4,807,669 in FY 1997 (Bean, Capps, and Haynes 1999). In addition, as of March 1997, the INS had about 1,300 inspectors at thirty-six ports of entry on the southwestern border. The inspections' appropriations totaled $151 million for FY 1997—a 78 percent increase from FY 1994 levels.

The new border enforcement campaign also involved a massive influx of new equipment, such as infrared night-vision scopes, low-light TV cameras, ground sensors, helicopters, and all-terrain vehicles. The increasingly high-tech nature of border enforcement included a new electronic identification system called IDENT, which stored the fingerprints and photographs of those apprehended at the border. The military also played a supporting role by assisting with the operation of night scopes, motion sensors, and communications equipment, as well as building and maintaining roads and fences. Along the border south of San Diego, for example, army reservists built a ten-foot-high steel wall that extends for fourteen miles. Similarly, in Nogales, army engineers constructed a fifteen-foot-tall fence that was nearly five miles long.

Congress ensured that the border buildup would continue by passing the Illegal Immigration Reform and Immigration Responsibility Act of 1996. The sweeping immigration law authorized the hiring of one thousand border patrol agents a year, reaching a total force of more than ten thousand by the year 2001. The 1996 law promoted other measures to secure the border, including a sharp increase in the penalties against migrant smugglers. The new sentencing guidelines in some cases called for a doubling of penalties and mandatory minimum sentencing for smuggling aliens for commercial gain.

The border control offensive was based on a strategy designed by the INS in 1993-1994 called "prevention through deterrence." By using more physical barriers, surveillance equipment, legal sanctions, and law enforcement agents, the objective was to inhibit illegal entry rather than trying to catch entrants once they have entered the country. The infusion of law enforcement resources at the most popular entry points was designed to disrupt traditional border-crossing methods and routes, forcing migrants to give up or attempt entry in more difficult and remote areas and at official ports of entry.

The deterrence strategy had its origins in Operation Blockade (later renamed Hold-the-Line), which was launched in El Paso on September 19, 1993. Some 450 agents were paid overtime to cover a twenty-mile stretch of the borderline. The sudden show of force led to a sharp drop in attempted illegal entries in the area. Before the operation, there were up to ten thousand illegal border crossings per day, and only one person out of eight who made the attempt was apprehended (Ekstrand 1995). The high-profile operation drew the applause of Washington, the media, and local residents. Importantly, it also attracted the attention of political leaders in California, who pushed to reproduce the El Paso "success story" along their portion of the border.

Impressed by the El Paso experience and the domestic support it generated, in 1994 the INS announced a comprehensive plan to apply the "prevention through deterrence" strategy across the entire southwestern border. The strategy would first target the busiest entry points—the El Paso and San

Diego sectors, which in FY 1993 accounted for 68 percent of all southwestern border apprehensions. Thus, El Paso's Operation Hold-the-Line was matched by Operation Gatekeeper south of San Diego in October 1994, which targeted the fourteen westernmost miles of the border (traditionally the location of 25 percent of all border apprehensions). The strategy would then be expanded to the Tucson sector and South Texas, where migrants were expected to move after the El Paso and San Diego sectors had been secured. As envisioned by the border patrol, the strategy would eventually be applied along the entire border (US Border Patrol 1994).

As predicted, the tightening of border controls in El Paso and San Diego pushed migrants to attempt entry elsewhere along the border. Thus, apprehensions in the El Paso sector remained far below the levels before Operation Hold-the-Line but skyrocketed to the west in New Mexico and Arizona. Similarly, apprehensions in the Imperial Beach sector south of San Diego (traditionally the single most important gateway for illegal entry) declined sharply after Gatekeeper began, but arrests jumped in the more remote areas of east San Diego County.

These shifts in human traffic provided a further political and bureaucratic justification to expand the border-policing campaign geographically. Thus, Operation Safeguard was launched in Nogales, Arizona, and Operation Gatekeeper, which first concentrated on the fourteen westernmost miles of the border, was extended in October 1996 to cover sixty-six miles. Similarly, in January 1997 Operation Hold-the-Line was extended ten miles west into New Mexico. And in late August 1997 the INS announced Operation Rio Grande in Southeast Texas, which included setting up portable floodlights, twenty-foot watchtowers, low-light video cameras, and high-powered infrared vision scopes along the Rio Grande.

Meanwhile, the heightened border patrol presence between the official ports of entry created more pressure at the ports of entry. Operations such as Gatekeeper prompted attempted illegal entries through the ports of entry, and the INS responded by deploying new port inspectors. Between FY 1994 and FY 1997, the number of INS port inspectors increased from 1,117 to 1,865, representing a 67 percent rise. The added personnel were reinforced by higher penalties for those who attempt entry through fraudulent document use (*Migration News*, February 1997).

THE BOOM IN MIGRANT SMUGGLING

Breaking up the traditional routes and methods of clandestine entry turned the once relatively simple illegal practice of entry without inspection into a more complex underground web of illegality. Past entry methods primarily involved either self-smuggling or limited use of a local smuggler. But with the buildup of border policing, the use of a professional smuggler became more of a necessity. The growing reliance on smugglers, a 1997 report of the Binational Study on Migration concluded, "helps to explain why most migrants attempting unauthorized entry succeed despite significantly more U.S. Border Patrol agents and technology on the border" (1997: 28).

Not surprisingly, as the demand for smuggling services and the risks of crossing the border grew, so too did the price of being smuggled. Prices along some parts of the border doubled and in some cases more than tripled. The smuggling fee could exceed $1,000. The trip from Agua Prieta to Phoenix, for example, cost as little as $200 in 1994 but reached as high as $1,500 in early 1999 (*Arizona Daily Star*, July 11, 1999). The exact price varied depending on location, the quality of service, and the set of services being purchased. As one border patrol agent explained, "It's much like a full-service travel agency, all depending on how much you're willing to spend" (*Los Angeles Times*, April 7, 1996). According to the INS, the increase in prices was an indicator that the deterrence effort was effective. Yet, higher prices were not necessarily a substantial deterrent, given that smuggling fees tended to be paid for by relatives and friends in the United States rather than by the immigrants themselves (López Castro 1998: 971). Alternatively, some immigrants may have been given the option of paying off the fee by working in a job arranged or provided by the smuggler (Binational Study on Migration 1997). Although the amount paid to be smuggled across the border was not insignificant, it could be earned back in a relatively short period of time working in the United States.

The most consequential impact of higher prices was to enhance the wealth and power of smuggling groups. As Miguel Vallina, the assistant chief of the border patrol in San Diego, noted, "The more difficult the crossing, the better the business for the smugglers" (*Los Angeles Times*, February 5, 1995). INS commissioner Doris Meissner explained in January 1996 that "as we improve our enforcement, we increase the smuggling of aliens that occurs, because it is harder to cross and so therefore people turn more and more to smugglers" (Federal News Service 1996). But at the same time that Meissner recognized that the border patrol had created more business for smugglers, she also emphasized that we are "moving as aggressively as we can ... so that we can put them [the smugglers] out of business" (Meissner 1996). The president's International Crime Control Strategy similarly emphasized the need to target organized smuggling, calling for "aggressive efforts to protect U.S. borders by attacking and decreasing smuggling and smuggling-related crimes" (quoted in Bach 1999).

Beefed-up policing removed some smugglers but also increased the market position of others. Moreover, many of those arrested were the lowest-level and most expendable members of migrant smuggling organizations—the border guides and drivers who were the "foot soldiers" of the business. Smugglers were first and foremost travel service specialists. And as long as there continued to be a strong demand for their services—which the tightening of border controls and the strong domestic employer demand for migrant labor guaranteed—smuggling would persist. The high profits from smuggling—inflated by law enforcement pressure—ensured that there would be smugglers willing to accept the occupational hazards. As one smuggler explained, "Figure it this way. If I work in a factory five days, I make $125 a week. If I take one person across the border, I get $300" (*Los Angeles Times*, May 2, 1992). A good guide could reportedly make $60,000 a year along the border (*San Diego Union-Tribune*, April 28, 1996).

US officials went to great lengths to portray migrants as the victims of smugglers, and they used this both to deflect criticism and to provide a further rationale to crack down on smuggling. Assistant US Attorney Michael Wheat, for example, suggested that "basically, alien smuggling is modern-day slavery. The whole idea behind slavery was moving humans to perform labor. The way the aliens are moved, the way they are treated, this is just a sophisticated form of slavery" (*Los Angeles Times*, February 5, 1995). Migrants, however, generally viewed smugglers as simply a "necessary evil," a clandestine business transaction that they willingly engaged in to evade the expanding border enforcement net. Within Mexico, migrant smuggling was considered a shady business, but one that was relatively harmless (López Castro 1998: 970). Smugglers, after all, had a clear economic motivation to deliver their "clients" unharmed across the border, since most of the payment was generally made only upon delivery. Of course, as documented in media reporting, smugglers could be abusive and reckless, and their efforts to bypass law enforcement could place migrants at great risk. Yet smugglers were hired precisely because they generally provided a safer and faster border-crossing experience. Indeed, many smugglers depended on customer satisfaction for future business, since migrants who had a successful experience were likely to recommend their smuggler to other friends and relatives. A smuggler's reputation could matter a great deal.

Smugglers became more skilled as border enforcement became more intensive. As one senior INS official noted, "Alien smugglers have developed a sophisticated infrastructure to successfully counteract U.S. Border Patrol operations along the Southwest Border" (Regan 1997). Those smuggling operations that had the greatest transportation and communication capabilities were the ones most capable of evading arrest, which left small-time smugglers at a competitive disadvantage. Pressured by law enforcement, some smugglers even turned to using commercial trucks to move migrants across the border, blending in with the massive boom in cross-border trucking brought on by the liberalization of trade and transportation. Northbound truck crossings doubled between 1993 and the end of the decade. Overwhelmed by the high volume of cross-border traffic, US port inspectors could realistically search only a small percentage of the trucks crossing the border. Enhanced border policing also prompted smugglers to become more technologically sophisticated. Peter Skerry and Stephen Rockwell noted that "as the Border Patrol pours more resources into night-vision scopes, weight sensors and giant X-ray machines for seeing into trucks, smuggling rings counter with their own state-of-the-art equipment paid for by increased [smuggling] fees" (1998).

Although many of the local freelance entrepreneurs who once dominated much of the migrant smuggling along the border were being squeezed out by intensified enforcement, they were being replaced by better-organized and more-skilled smuggling organizations. One INS intelligence report suggested that many smuggling groups once based in the United States had relocated to the Mexican side, helping to insulate principal leaders from the grasp of American law enforcement (cited in US General Accounting Office 1997: 42). A federal task force estimated that up to twelve family-based smuggling organizations came to dominate the trafficking of migrants across the border (*Migration News*, June 1998). Of course, it was easy to overstate these claims for political gain. One INS agent even went so far as to say that the border smugglers had become "huge, inter-locked cartels." Such threat inflation made effective media sound bites even if the empirical evidence was thin (*Arizona Daily Star*, July 11, 1999).

As migrant smuggling became a more organized and sophisticated enterprise in reaction to tighter controls, this served to justify tougher laws and tougher enforcement. For example, Operation Disruption was initiated in May 1995 to target drop houses used by migrant smugglers in the San Diego area. The operation produced 120 arrests of smugglers and the uncovering of 117 drop houses (*Migration News*, February 2, 1996). The crackdown in San Diego displaced much of the smuggling farther east to the Imperial Valley, as well as to Arizona. The border patrol, in turn, responded with a nearly tenfold increase in the number of agents assigned to combat smuggling rings in the area (*Los Angeles Times*, May 10, 1998). Other federal agencies, such as the FBI, also deployed new agents to the border in response to the increase in organized migrant smuggling (*Los Angeles Times*, May 29, 1996).

The enforcement crackdown, however, failed to cause a shortage of smugglers. One senior official from the border patrol's anti-smuggling unit commented that the smugglers "just get paid more for taking more risks" (interview with author, US Border Patrol, San Diego Sector Headquarters, April 8, 1997). And as the risks for smuggling rose, so too did the incentive for smugglers to use more dangerous methods to avoid law enforcement. This partly explained the increase in high-speed chases and accidents that resulted when smugglers try to circumvent INS checkpoints along the highways leading north from the border.

Border corruption also became a more serious problem. Increased enforcement increased the need for smugglers to bribe or buy entry documents from those doing the enforcing. And as smuggling groups became more sophisticated and profitable—as a consequence of the higher demand and cost for their services and the heightened risks involved in providing these services—the capacity and means to corrupt also grew. In one well-known case at the San Ysidro port of entry south of San Diego, US Customs inspector Guy Henry Kmett was arrested for helping a major smuggling ring move migrants through his inspection lane. The three vans busted in Kmett's lane carried Salvadorans, Guatemalans, Dominicans, and an Egyptian. Law enforcement officials estimated that the Peraltas smuggling organization, which was trying to transport migrants through Kmett's lane, earned $1 million per month for smuggling one thousand migrants across the border (*Los Angeles Times*, February 5, 1995).

On the Mexican side of the border, there were numerous cases of official corruption involving migrant smuggling (Rotella 1998). In one high-profile case, the Mexican migration service's regional head in Tijuana, his deputy, and his chief inspector were all fired and charged with assisting the smuggling of non-Mexican migrants. The Tijuana office reportedly brought in as much as $70,000 weekly from the proceeds of migrant trafficking (*San Francisco Chronicle*, July 11, 1994). It was also reported that Tijuana police took bribes that amounted to as much as $40,000 a month to permit the operation of safe houses where migrants stayed before attempting to cross into the United States (*Los Angeles Times*, February 5, 1995).

CONTINUED ESCALATION IN THE TWENTY-FIRST CENTURY

As we have seen, the business of migrant smuggling and the business of policing migrant smuggling along the US-Mexico border grew up together and expanded through their interaction. Each law enforcement move provoked a law evasion countermove, which in turn was matched by more enforcement. By the beginning of the twenty-first century, there was little indication that this escalating enforcement-evasion dynamic would end anytime soon. Indeed, after the terrorist attacks on September 11, 2001, this dynamic was not only reinforced but further intensified. The security stakes suddenly seemed much higher: US border officials sounded the alarm bells by claiming that the same groups, methods, and routes employed to smuggle migrants across the border could now potentially be used to smuggle terrorists and weapons of mass destruction. Similarly, they warned that the same fraudulent document industry that had long provided identification cards for unauthorized migrants could also potentially provide these services to terrorists.

The suddenly heightened importance of border security (Andreas and Biersteker 2003) was reflected not only in an infusion of more border control resources but also in the reorganization of multiple agencies (including the INS and the Customs Service) under the newly formed Department of Homeland Security—the largest restructuring of the federal government in half a century. The post–September 11 security environment also opened more space for a further militarization of immigration law enforcement on the border. In the past, military units operating along the border were formally limited to assisting antidrug work, but after September 11 the expanded mission could include targeting unauthorized immigration. Major military contractors, such as Lockheed Martin, Raytheon, and Northrop Grumman, were also recruited to play a larger role in border control—as one press report put it, "using some of the same high-priced, high-tech tools these companies have already put to work in Iraq and Afghanistan" (*New York Times*, May 18, 2006). For example, in September 2005, border officials in Arizona (which had become the leading entry point for smuggled migrants) unveiled a new unmanned aerial surveillance system based on the satellite-controlled Predator-B spy drone used for military operations in the Middle East and elsewhere. These developments were part of the larger securitization of immigration control issues in the post–September 11 era. Reflecting the shifting priorities, federal prosecutions for immigration law violations more than doubled from 2001 to 2005, replacing drug law violations as the most frequently enforced federal crime.

As part of this new push to secure the border, in 2006 the US Congress also approved the Secure Fence Act, which called for building seven hundred miles of border fencing and hiring thousands of additional border patrol agents. The size of the border patrol had reached some twenty thousand agents by the end of the decade—roughly twice its size before September 11 (and the force had already doubled in size in the 1990s). Nevertheless, the deterrent effect was not at all clear. Many migrants and their smuggler guides continued to be redirected more than deterred. This included providing more "express service" for migrants through ports of entry (hidden in vehicles or through fraudulent use of documents, or simply paying compromised inspectors to look the other way) rather than braving the harsh desert and mountain terrain. There was also a surge in the landing of migrants on California beaches by speedboat and other low-profile, radar-evading marine craft. Smugglers charged a premium for these faster and more convenient modes of clandestine entry (*Los Angeles Times*, March 24, 2011).

The continued escalation of enforcement certainly made the border a much more challenging and dangerous obstacle, with hundreds of migrants dying each year while attempting the crossing. Indeed, the border was far harder to cross than ever before in the nation's history. It was also increasingly difficult to even reach the border, with more and more US-bound migrants—especially Central Americans and other non-Mexicans transiting through Mexican territory—facing a gauntlet of extortionist criminals and corrupt cops along their northward journey (Brigden and Andreas 2018). It could then cost them more than $5,000 to hire a local smuggler to squeeze through the tightening U.S. border enforcement net (*New York Times*, January 6, 2019).

Thus, when Donald Trump promised an unprecedented border crackdown as part of his platform in his successful bid for the presidency, he was actually building on the massive enforcement buildup by his predecessors, Democrats and Republicans alike. By calling for a border wall and deploying thousands of troops—with the COVID-19 coronavirus pandemic later providing a convenient additional public health rationale to block border crossings—Trump was simply taking it to the next level. After all, much of his "big, beautiful wall" had already been built by the time he took office, even if not officially called a "wall." Indeed, most of the Trump administration's subsequent wall-building efforts, many with funds diverted from the military and rationalized as a national emergency, actually involved reinforcing or replacing existing physical barriers along the border. Trump's Democratic opponents were quick to denounce the "Trump wall" as inhumane, immoral, and wasteful, yet they had been energetic supporters of building more formidable border barriers for decades (in the form of more agents, surveillance technologies, fencing, and so on). Nevertheless, if the past is any guide to the future, bigger and better border barriers are unlikely to stop determined migrants from entering the country without authorization—going over, under, or around them—risking their lives in the process while sustaining a thriving business for the smugglers on whom they are forced to rely. The business of border enforcement and the business of border evasion, it seems, both have a bright future.

NOTE

1. For a more detailed analysis, see Andreas (2013, 2022), on which this chapter partly draws.

REFERENCES

Andreas, Peter. 2022. *Border Games: Policing the U.S.-Mexico Divide*. 3rd ed. Ithaca, NY: Cornell University Press.

———. 2013. *Smuggler Nation: How Illicit Trade Made America*. New York: Oxford University Press.

Andreas, Peter, and Thomas Biersteker, eds. 2003. *The Rebordering of North America: Integration and Exclusion in a New Security Context*. New York: Routledge.

Bach, Robert. 1999. Testimony before the House Judiciary Committee, Immigration and Claims Subcommittee, July 1.

Bean, Frank D., Randy Capps, and Charles W. Haynes. 1999. Testimony for the Hearings of the Subcommittee on Immigration and Claims, Committee on the Judiciary, US House of Representatives, February 25.

Binational Study on Migration. 1997. *Migration between Mexico and the United States: Binational Study*. Mexico City: Mexican Foreign Ministry; Washington, DC: US Commission on Immigration Reform.

Brigden, Noelle, and Peter Andreas. 2018. "Border Collision: Power Dynamics of Enforcement and Evasion across the U.S.-Mexico Line." In *Protean Power: Exploring the Uncertain and Unexpected in World Politics*, edited by Peter J. Katzenstein and Lucia A. Seybert, 100–123. New York: Cambridge University Press.

Calavita, Kitty. 1994. "U.S. Immigration and Policy Responses: The Limits of Legislation." In *Controlling Immigration: A Global Perspective*, edited by Wayne A. Cornelius, Philip L. Martin, and James Hollifield, 55–82. Stanford, CA: Stanford University Press.

———. 1996. "The New Politics of Immigration: 'Balanced Budget Conservatism' and the Symbolism of Proposition 187." *Social Problems* 43 (3): 284–305.

Comptroller General of the United States. 1976. *Smugglers, Illicit Documents, and Schemes Are Undermining U.S. Controls over Immigration: Report to the Congress by the Comptroller General of the United States*. Washington, DC, August 30.

Ekstrand, Laurie E. 1995. Testimony before the Subcommittee on Immigration and Claims, Committee on the Judiciary, US House of Representatives, March 10.

Ettinger, Patrick. 2009. *Imaginary Lines: Border Enforcement and the Origins of Undocumented Immigration, 1882–1930*. Austin: University of Texas Press.

Federal News Service. 1996. News conference with Janet Reno and Doris Meissner, Washington, DC, January 12.

Heyman, Josiah McC. 1995. "Putting Power into the Anthropology of Bureaucracy: The Immigration and Naturalization Service at the Mexico-United States Border." *Current Anthropology* 36 (2): 261–287.

Kossoudji, Sherrie A. 1992. "Playing Cat and Mouse at the U.S.-Mexican Border." *Demography* 29 (2): 159–190.

Lee, Erika. 2003. *At America's Gates: Chinese Immigration during the Exclusion Era, 1882–1943.* Chapel Hill: University of North Carolina Press.

López Castro, Gustavo. 1998. "Coyotes and Alien Smuggling." In *Migration between Mexico and the United States: Binational Study*, 965–974. Research Reports and Background Materials, vol. 3. Mexico City: Mexican Ministry of Foreign Affairs; Washington, DC: US Commission on Immigration Reform.

Marx, Gary T. 1981. "Ironies of Social Control: Authorities as Contributors to Deviance through Escalation, Nonenforcement, and Covert Facilitation." *Social Problems* 28 (3): 221–246.

Massey, Douglas S. 1997. "March of Folly: U.S. Immigration Policy under NAFTA." Paper presented at the Meetings of the American Sociological Association, Toronto, Canada, August 8–13.

McCullough, K. B. 1992. "America's Back Door: Indirect International Immigration via Mexico to the United States from 1875 to 1940." PhD diss., Texas A&M University, College Station.

McDonald, William F. 1997. "Illegal Immigration: Crime, Ramifications, and Control (the American Experience)." In *Crime and Law Enforcement in the Global Village*, edited by William F. McDonald, 65–86. Cincinnati: Anderson.

Meissner, Doris. 1996. Testimony before the Commerce, Justice, State, and Judiciary Subcommittee of the Appropriations Committee, US House of Representatives, May 8.

Metz, Leon C. 1989. *Border: The U.S.-Mexico Line.* El Paso, TX: Mangan Books.

Nevins, Joseph. 1998. "California Dreaming: Operation Gatekeeper and the Social Geographical Construction of the 'Illegal Alien' along the U.S.-Mexico Boundary." PhD diss., University of California at Los Angeles.

Regan, George. 1997. Testimony before the Subcommittee on Immigration Claims, Committee on the Judiciary, US House of Representatives, April 23.

Reuter, Peter, and David Ronfeldt. 1991. *Quest for Integrity: The Mexican-U.S. Drug Issue in the 1980s.* Santa Monica, CA: RAND.

Reynolds, James Branson. 1909. "Enforcement of the Chinese Exclusion Law." *Annals of the American Academy of Political and Social Science* 34 (2): 143–154.

Rotella, Sebastian. 1998. *Twilight on the Line: Underworlds and Politics at the U.S.-Mexico Border.* New York: Norton.

Siener, William H. 2008. "Through the Back Door: Evading the Chinese Exclusion Act along the Niagara Frontier, 1900–1924." *Journal of American Ethnic History* 27 (4): 34–70.

Skerry, Peter, and Stephen Rockwell. 1998. "The Cost of a Tighter Border: People-Smuggling Networks." *Los Angeles Times*, May 3, 1998.

Stoddard, Ellwyn. 1976. "Illegal Mexican Labor in the Borderlands: Institutionalized Support for an Unlawful Practice." *Pacific Sociological Review* 19 (2): 175–210.

Suro, Robert. 1998. "Tightened Controls and Changing Flows: Evaluating the INS Border Enforcement Strategy." *Research Perspectives on Migration* 2 (1).

Teitelbaum, Michael. 1980. "Right versus Right: Immigration and Refugee Policy—the United States." *Foreign Affairs* 59 (1): 21–59.

US Border Patrol. 1994. *Border Patrol Strategic Plan 1994 and Beyond: National Strategy*. Washington, DC: US Border Patrol, July.

US General Accounting Office. 1997. *Illegal Immigration: Southwest Border Strategy Results Inconclusive; More Evaluation Needed*. Washington, DC: US Government Printing Office, December.

CHAPTER 3

Multinational Initiatives against Global Trafficking in Persons for Sexual Exploitation, 1899–1999

Eileen P. Scully

TWENTIETH-CENTURY MULTILATERAL RESPONSES to global trafficking in persons for sexual exploitation passed through three distinct eras: (1) 1899–1919, when momentum came primarily from faith-based and secular associations; (2) 1920–1945, when energies shifted to the League of Nations; and (3) 1946–1999, when the United Nations (UN) took center stage. Across the century from 1899 to 1999, there was remarkable continuity in defining *trafficking* and formulating responses. Discussions at the 1899 London Congress on the White Slave Trade formulated a strategy repeatedly used thereafter: highly motivated advocacy groups harnessed state power through international agreements that obligated and empowered participating governments to enact sweeping controls over borders, resident nonnationals, and commercialized sex broadly construed. Decade after decade, these "transnational moral entrepreneurs" skillfully shepherded one anti-trafficking treaty into the next, including the 1904 international agreement and the conventions of 1910, 1921, 1933, 1937 (draft), and 1949 (Nadelmann 1990: 482). As anti-trafficking ranks grew, so too did disagreements and contending paradigms. Feminists and sociologically oriented humanitarians fought for long-term solutions and attention to cognate problems, such as the legal status of women, employment opportunities, punishment of clients and procurers, abolition of licensed prostitution, and so on. Prohibitionists, pragmatists, and enforcement agencies looked to the symptoms, through heightened scrutiny of travelers, stricter immigration laws, and beefed-up policing resources.

Remedial efforts were continually undermined by conflicting imperatives, vested interests, the untenable predicament of victims, the entrepreneurial opportunism of traffickers, and the ingenuity with which states leveraged treaty obligations to advance repressive social agendas and immigration controls. Trafficking polarized politics, creating unlikely alliances of "strange bedfellows." Public discourse on "sex trafficking" became entangled with issues of class, gender, race, and nationality. "Moral panic" might be a fair diagnosis in some instances. For many, though, it was closer to "rational moral distress," as populations felt alarmed and overwhelmed by complex public policy dilemmas that local and national governments seemed unwilling or unable to manage (Rivera-López 2006; Scully 2015: 13). Historically, trafficking surged when increased migration lowered operating costs and risks. Freer movement of labor generated employer demand for vulnerable individuals maneuvered into unfamiliar settings for purposes of gross exploitation not otherwise and elsewhere obtainable. Concomitantly, migration restrictions increased internal trafficking, while simultaneous surges in cross-border human smuggling provided a ready supply of potential victims.

FROM THE "WHITE SLAVE TRADE" TO THE "TRAFFIC IN WOMEN AND CHILDREN" (1899–1919)

The geography and animating forces of modern migratory prostitution took hold in the 1850s and continued to grow and complexify thereafter, driven and shaped by three overlapping developments. First was the deployment of Asian, West Indian, and African indentured labor as a "substitute for slavery," to prop up plantation economies, fuel extractive industries, and support monumental construction projects such as railroads and canals (Tomich 2018). Second, increased mobility among white males from Europe and the

Americas brought a global proliferation of frontier boomtowns and military garrisons. Third, expanding colonial empires drew Indigenous elites into imperial enclaves such as Hong Kong, while monetized economies pushed proletarianized peasants into cities, colonial armies, and migratory labor flows. These intertwining factors generated regional and international markets for gendered services, from prostitution to domestic chores. Women entered this market under a variety of circumstances, ranging from astute entrepreneurial calculation to unwitting entrapment. They operated along a spectrum of autonomy, from full control over their labor to virtual enslavement in locked brothels.

The expansion and entrenchment of international migratory sex work as a sprawling, resilient, and lucrative traffic with many stakeholders sparked ever-growing concerns about a worldwide "white slave trade." Circa 1850, the term *white slave trade* referred to the centuries-old traffic in forced labor that took women, girls, boys, and men from Eastern Europe and southern Russia across the Black Sea into the Ottoman Empire—along with a subsidiary branch operated by the Barbary States of North Africa. A constituent element of this traffic was the "harem trade" in females selected for sale as servants and concubines. Representative headlines during the Crimean War (1853–1856) document this connection: "The White Slave Traffic" (*New York Times*, August 27, 1856, 4) and "The White Slave Trade of the Circassians" (*Daily Placer Times* [CA], September 5, 1854, 1). Over time, "white slavery" expanded to include involuntary emigration, factory work, indentured labor, and migratory prostitution. Political and courtroom battles over the meaning of *servitude* and *consent* encouraged greater precision and distinctions. By the 1890s, *traite des blanches* carried a narrower "feminized" construction, one that framed prostitution as a "social evil" rather than forced labor (Peck 2011).

This was the context of the 1899 International Congress on the White Slave Trade, convened in London by the National Vigilance Association (NVA). Created in the late 1880s, the NVA operated as a watchdog to ensure rigorous enforcement of anti-procuration legislation Parliament had reluctantly enacted in hope of ending battles over the Contagious Diseases Acts (1864–1869) (Attwood 2015: 326–327). In the years following, the NVA extended its brief into "repression of criminal vice and public immorality," giving it a reputation as "the puritanical element," its self-constituted associations nothing more than "small knots of obscure and often mischievous busy-bodies" presumptuously claiming to be "national, and such" (NVA 1899; "The National Vigilance Association," *Times* [London], June 14, 1901, 14; "Licensing Committee," *Times* [London], October 9, 1890, 9). These shifts ruptured the original anti–Contagious Diseases Acts coalition, as indicated in the 1897 warning from Josephine Butler, the principal creator of that alliance: "Beware of 'purity workers' as allies," and all others who are "ready to accept and endorse any amount of coercive and degrading treatment of certain classes of their fellow creatures, in the fatuous belief that you can oblige human beings to be moral by force, and in so doing that you may in some way promote social purity" (Butler 1897: 7–8).

Butler's warning clarified the enduring battle lines of abolitionism. All agreed that state-regulated prostitution (regulationism) made large-scale trafficking possible and highly profitable. It allowed market niches to be identified, encouraged, and filled. It blurred lines between coercion and consent. However, the NVA advocated prohibitionism, meaning the comprehensive criminalization of commercialized sex and prosecution of all those involved. They viewed government and law enforcement as potential allies, and they leveraged state power for greater influence and legitimacy. By contrast, the International Abolitionist Federation, founded by Butler in 1875, had an abiding mistrust of "government by police" and fought regulationism as part of a larger campaign for women's rights (Butler 1879; Lammasniemi 2019: 70; Pliley 2010: 96–98). By the 1890s, anti-trafficking groups on all sides were seeing firsthand that cross-border trafficking required something beyond the power of national law enforcement. Trafficking proceeded through sequential transactions within and across states, some steps in the process being quite legal and even mundane; only the consummation of the entire transaction revealed—belatedly—the meaning and intention of all prior acts. Even when suspicions were aroused, or individuals were caught and prosecuted for a constituent offense, such as corrupting a minor, authorities in one nation lacked the inclination or wherewithal to communicate and act in concert across borders (Reinsch 1907: 615). Abolitionists' pivot into multilateralism was also a preemptive move against the ongoing campaign among public health officials to entrench legalized prostitution worldwide through international agreements on sanitation and contagious diseases (Nadelmann 1990: 514).

Delegates from ten European countries and the United States convened in London on June 21–23, 1899, and created the International Union for the Suppression of the White Slave Trade and an international bureau (IB) as its permanent secretariat. News coverage emphasized the precedent-setting and ambitious agenda of the congress. However, elemental disagreements over regulationism, and indeed about prostitution as potentially consensual or inherently coercive, limited horizons to "a minimum proposal on which all the Governments will be willing to act" (NVA 1899: 11). Closing resolutions charged national committees and the new IB to initiate outreach and groundwork for a diplomatic conference ("The National Vigilance Association," *Times* [London], June 14, 1901, 14). Largely driven by the IB and national affiliates of the NVA, European governments convened a 1902 diplomatic conference in Paris. This gathering produced a two-part instrument: a draft convention and a draft arrangement. The draft arrangement called on state parties to establish an infrastructure for internal enforcement and cross-border cooperation. It anticipated administrative measures that could be expeditiously put in place through executive and regulatory authority—bypassing legislatures and courts. A "central authority" in each state would communicate with counterparts abroad, gather information, track cases, help organize victim assistance, and engage with nongovernmental organizations such as the NVA. The draft convention pledged signatories to enact and harmonize criminal statutes and extradition treaties. A follow-up conference finalized the 1902 draft arrangement as the 1904 international agreement but postponed further work on the draft convention because of disagreements on the age of consent and proposed links between consular services and domestic courts (Reinsch 1907: 582–583; Reinsch 1909: 30; Reinsch 1911: 36). The 1902 draft convention was finalized on May 4, 1910, as the International Convention for the Suppression of the White Slave Traffic.

Intensive lobbying to involve the United States in these initiatives was led by the American Purity Alliance, which in 1906 became the American National Vigilance Committee. Although declining invitations to various anti-trafficking diplomatic conferences, President Theodore Roosevelt (1901–1909) took an active interest in those proceedings. He submitted the 1902 interlocking draft arrangement-convention for Senate approval in late 1902, and again in 1903; senators acquiesced in early 1905 ("Against White

Slave Trade. Senate Ratifies Treaty—All Countries to Enact Repressive Laws," *New York Times* [hereafter *NYT*], March 2, 1905, 5). Using this endorsement of the original two-part draft from 1902, without resubmitting for Senate review the final hived-off 1904 international agreement, Roosevelt proclaimed US adhesion to that agreement in June 1908 (Abbott 1933; Scully 2015). Commissioner-General of Immigration Daniel Keefe was named America's "central authority" under the international agreement. Relying on this agreement and the 1907 Immigration Act, Keefe ordered specially deputed officials to undertake "active, concentrated, and simultaneous action all over the country" to "make the importation of alien women for immoral purposes so dangerous and costly as to deal it a mortal blow, or to completely break it up so far as the U.S. is concerned," taking care, though, "not to act as an inquisitor, or to resort to any persecutory methods" (US Senate 1910: 25–26). However, this project ran aground in the Supreme Court's ruling in *Keller v. United States* (1909), which voided the 1907 Immigration Act's controversial anti-harboring provisions.

President William Howard Taft (1909–1913) opted not to move ahead on the 1910 convention, explaining to Congress that the United States was finding minimal cooperation from European governments, which were "out of sympathy" with "our immigration laws" ("White Slave Treaty Fails," *NYT*, February 1, 1910, 3). Congress agreed and that same year passed a revised Immigration Act, along with the White Slave Traffic Act (Mann Act). Those two statutes then became the enabling legislation for US adherence to the 1904 international agreement, with responsibilities shared between immigration officials and the new Department of Justice section later known as the Federal Bureau of Investigation. Article 6 of the Mann Act is a dubious interpretation of the international agreement: all persons "harboring an alien woman for the purpose of prostitution within three years after entry from any country party to the ... [international] agreement shall file a statement of facts with the Commissioner General of Immigration" (White-Slave Traffic [Mann] Act 1910). Whereas the Supreme Court had voided similar provisions in the *Keller* decision, justices put aside those concerns in the 1914 test case *United States v. Portale*, because "the statute ... was enacted in pursuance of an international agreement which requires every person to perform an act which may be assistance to the governments, it is construed literally, as reading it otherwise would deprive the government of such assistance to no good end."

The 1904 agreement is frequently criticized for not criminalizing procurement, and the 1910 convention is criticized for omitting victim protections and support. A different perspective emerges when the two are reunited as originally envisioned. Together, they (1) normalized cross-border government coordination and legislative harmonization; (2) defined trafficking around three core elements—the act, means, and purpose; (3) laid down fundamental distinctions between adult and underage victims; (4) sidelined conversations about victim consent; (5) legitimized voluntary associations and international nongovernmental organizations as stakeholders, investigators, and human rights watchdogs; (6) established victim assistance as a treaty obligation; and (7) opened the way for unprecedented government border regulation, as well as surveillance over populations on the move (Gallagher 2010: 57; Lammasniemi 2019: 69–73; Siller 2017). Resurrecting the original combined draft arrangement-convention also illuminates what the prime movers of these initiatives likely had in mind: a new type of intergovernmental union, where nongovernmental organizations (such as the NVA and IB) would become part of the treaty machinery, constantly engaging with the designated "central authorities" in signatory states to generate "international legislation," monitor compliance, disseminate information, invite new signatories, and organize periodic diplomatic conferences. Although this original vision was not formalized, the IB and anti-trafficking associations performed many of these functions. On the multilateral front, from 1900 to 1914, the IB adeptly coordinated national affiliates to keep a prod on governments and generate shared agendas through frequent gatherings, all very well attended by prominent officials, politicians, clergy, and law-enforcement representatives. They worked—unsuccessfully—to agree on the elusive meaning of *traite des blanches*, to settle definitively whether prostitution could be consensual, and to disentangle migration from trafficking.

FROM THE LEAGUE OF NATIONS TO THE UNITED NATIONS (1920–1945)

In 1920, the new League of Nations took primary responsibility for combatting human trafficking. Arrangements began for a 1921 international conference in Geneva, with invitations to include both league members and nonmembers. At that gathering of representatives from thirty-three countries, speakers declared that the "feebleness" of earlier arrangements was "to-day visible to every eye" (League of Nations 1921: 10). Delegates envisioned a comprehensive, multilateral attack on public and private fronts, "so that we can vanquish this powerful evil from which the world is suffering" (11). Prewar divides quickly resurged around polarized issues including regulationism, victim consent, repressive "purity campaigns," and punitive immigration laws. Three distinct paths forward were advocated: (1) better-regulated regulationism, with safeguards against coercion and underage victims; (2) total abolition of prostitution, enforced through repressive control over female mobility; and (3) "feminist abolitionism," ending regulationism without recourse to unequal moral standards or special—otherwise unconstitutional—legislation targeting women (Pliley 2010: 96).

Closing recommendations that emerged from these competing agendas included a new convention incorporating (1) more effective prosecution of procurers; (2) more rigorous extradition obligations; (3) cross-border harmonized legislation for oversight of employment agencies; (4) protections for female emigrants during voyages; (5) twenty-one years as a universal age of consent; (6) prohibitions on trafficking underage girls and boys and unsuspecting, unwilling adult women; and (7) the application of these provisions to all colonies and dependencies of signatory states. Many of these recommendations were incorporated into the 1921 International Convention for the Suppression of the Traffic in Women and Children. The racialized, sensationalist "white slave trade" was abandoned in favor of the "traffic in women and children." However, League of Nations proceedings and reports make clear the malignant persistence of race-based perspectives and projects throughout the interwar period (Faulkner 2019: 85–86). The 1921 convention also indirectly brought into the league's orbit those countries that had signed either or both the 1904 international agreement and 1910 convention—regardless of whether they had signed the League of Nations Covenant. Article 14 of the 1921 convention allowed each signatory state to exclude "any or all of its colonies, overseas possessions, protectorates or territories." Two decades later, Soviet delegates successfully made deletion of this article a condition for the 1921 convention's transfer to UN auspices ("Soviet Wins Point on White Slavery," *NYT*, October 21, 1947).

Covenant Article 23 gave the league "general supervision over the execution of agreements with regard to the traffic in women and children." This oversight was exercised principally through the Advisory Committee on the Trafficking of Women and Children (CTW, 1922–1936), which convened annually to discuss issues and state fulfillment of treaty obligations. To offset the shortcomings of government self-reporting, proceedings included input from nongovernmental organizations (assessors), such as the IB, the International Association for the Promotion of Child Welfare, and the International Alliance of Women for Suffrage and Equal Citizenship. During its first decade, the CTW favored a feminist abolitionist perspective, targeting state-sanctioned prostitution and supporting initiatives for women's equality, unfettered mobility, and economic rights (Limoncelli 2011; Pliley 2010). By the late 1920s, though, chief of the Social Section (1919–1931) Dame Rachel Crowdy was dismayed by continuing claims that "this traffic exists only in the mind of the crusader" (Crowdy 1927: 156). To document the reality and human costs of trafficking, the CTW worked with the secretary general to organize traveling inquiry commissions led by highly regarded experts, whose activities and findings were amplified through strategic publicity and information campaigns (Gorman 2008; Gorman 2012; Knepper 2016: 64; Legg 2012).

Much of the funding for these commissions came from the Social Hygiene Bureau of the Rockefeller Foundation. Cumulative reports give a general portrait of interwar trafficking for sexual exploitation, albeit one infused with presumptions about race, class, and sex work. Information from fifteen European nations undercut defenses of regulationism as a necessary guard against sexually transmitted diseases (Pliley 2010: 99). Reports from the late 1920s about Latin America described "a traffic in women from one country to another for the purpose of commercialised prostitution," with a heavy preponderance of women arriving from abroad (Crowdy 1927: 157). Demand was shaped by "a natural and psychological reason—people would not ask of women of their own country the kind of thing that they would ask of foreign women" (Crowdy 1927: 158). Investigations consistently showed that "a large number of foreign women were prostitutes before they went abroad" (League of Nations 1937: 18) but would not have consented to their current situation "had they known the conditions to which they were going and the life" that awaited them (Crowdy 1927: 159). Suggested remedies included enlightened public opinion, education of the young, greater cooperation between governments, stricter supervision of employment agencies, and a higher age of consent and legal marriage (Crowdy 1927: 161).

An early 1930s Commission of Enquiry into Traffic in Women and Children in the East found that "the bulk of this traffic was in Asiatic women from one country in Asia to another" (League of Nations 1934: 21; Metzger 2007: 72). With few exceptions, White Russian women were under the control of traffickers. Their stateless status and utter destitution pushed them to capitalize on their sexuality, with varying degrees of degradation, and they were found in China, the Philippines, Thailand, and Malaysia (League of Nations 1934, 1935). As had long been the case, demand came from large overseas settlements of males, seasonal movement of male labor, and tourism and troop deployments (League of Nations 1937: 12–14). Opponents of state-sanctioned prostitution found ample confirmation that "the principal factor in promotion of international traffic in women in the East is the brothel and, in the chain of brothels which are at the disposal of the trafficker" (League of Nations 1934: 96).

In combatting human trafficking, various groups—the IB in particular—suggested a range of repressive measures, including special passport requirements for females, curbs on women traveling alone, registration of females with local police when working abroad, and forced repatriation of foreign women employed in local regulated brothels (Limoncelli 2011; Pliley 2010: 95–96). Countervailing opinion was succinctly conveyed by French suffragist Marguerite de Witt-Schlumberger (1853–1924): "Protection sometimes comes to be a hidden form of slavery, a masked tyranny inspired by the best of intentions. . . . When the protection which is afforded affects the dignity or the freedom of the individual, the remedy is worse than the evil" (League of Nations 1922: 80). Women's rights groups opposed targeting victims rather than victimizers (Pliley 2010: 91–92). Others noted that as most countries still tolerated prostitution, extradition was not practical or likely; repatriated women tended to return to foreign brothels, thus making the proposition a costly one for governments and private organizations.

The post–Cold War proliferation of nonstate actors and civil society groups illuminates subtleties earlier missed in these league-era projects, such as the "soft law" power of vague and unenforceable interwar antislavery conventions (Cole 2005). Reports from the CTW reflect members' situational awareness of concurrent projects and their entrepreneurial energy. There are frequent references to groups working on "cognate problems," including labor protections, gender equality, children's welfare, prison conditions, and human rights. The CTW included liaison officers from the International Labor Organization and the League Health Organization. League absorption of the Brussels-based International Association for the Promotion of Child Welfare further expanded the committee's brief, which eventually included comparative laws on protection of life and health in early infancy, age of consent, age of marriage, preparation of an international convention for the assistance or repatriation of unaccompanied refugee minors, education, child labor, and others.

Anti-trafficking initiatives in the 1930s ran alongside projects lobbying for gender equality, efforts that finally produced the League of Nations Committee of Equal Status for Women (Pliley 2010: 105–106; "Surveys Women's Rights," *NYT*, September 23, 1937, 14). At the same time, the 1930s also brought a distinct shift from feminist abolitionism to prohibitionism (Limoncelli 2011; Pliley 2010: 99). Indeed, prohibitionist abolitionism took hold in league proceedings as "the proper humanitarian perspective" (Pliley 2010: 99). This shift is evident in Article 1 of the 1933 International Convention for the Suppression of the Traffic in Women of Full Age, calling for punishment of "whoever, in order to gratify the passions of another person, has procured, enticed or led away even with her consent, a woman or girl of full age for immoral purposes to be carried out in another country," regardless of whether those actions "may have been committed in different countries." Removing the requirement that international borders must be crossed "with respect to the offenses of procurement, enticement, or leading away . . . [subjects] certain domestic activities, particularly in the country of origin, to the Convention's provisions" (Gallagher 2010: 58). For some current commentators, the league's reach into domestic policing signals a "general authoritarian and conservative turn in politics worldwide" (Petruccelli 2020: 127–128), whereas others see it as "a milestone widening the scope of existing international law" in support of human rights (Metzger 2007: 74).

Although the United States did not join the League of Nations, American informal participation increased when Secretary of State Frank Kellogg, best known for the 1927 Kellogg-Briand Pact "outlawing war," shifted official rhetoric from the United States "helping" others to the United States being helped through cooperation (Hudson 1929: 21). In addition to significant Rockefeller Foundation funding, the United States sent unofficial consultants to gatherings on trade, currency, disarmament, emigration, narcotics, obscene publications, and human trafficking (Hudson 1929: 18). While not signing any of the league's anti-trafficking conventions, as a party to the 1904 international agreement, the United States provided annual reports to the CTW. This continuing connection opened the way to US "observer" status on that committee from 1922 to 1935, a role typically filled by an officer from the Children's Bureau in the Department of Labor (Knepper 2016: 54). In the late 1930s, the CTW was superseded by the Advisory Committee on Social Questions, and the United States was made a "full member" of that group (Norlin 1938: 259; Pliley 2010: 103–104).

These late 1930s organizational changes sought to make the League of Nations "essentially a governmental organization" (Petruccelli 2020: 126; Pliley 2010: 104–105). Voluntary groups closely associated with anti-trafficking since 1899 were sidelined in favor of more state-friendly organizations, such as the International Criminal Police Commission (later known as Interpol) and the International Bureau for the Unification of Penal Law (Petruccelli 2020: 128–130). Their understanding of human trafficking as part of transnational organized crime shaped the 1937 Draft Convention for the Suppression of the Exploitation of the Prostitution of Others. This draft was later folded into the 1949 UN Convention, signaling a melding of human rights and transnational criminal law (Petruccelli 2020: 126–127, 134; Pliley 2010: 105–106).

POST-WORLD WAR II TO THE CLOSE OF THE TWENTIETH CENTURY (1946–1999)

Postwar travel, tourism, and troop deployments expanded and intensified local, regional, and international markets in sexual services (IBSTP 1949: 47). The centerpiece of early postwar anti-trafficking cooperation was the consolidation of prewar instruments into the 1949 UN Convention for the Suppression of the Traffic in Persons and of the Exploitation of the Prostitution of Others (Gallagher 2010: 58; Petruccelli 2020: 134). Thoughtful critiques correctly point out that the 1949 convention retains an abolitionist focus on prostitution, fails to define "trafficking in persons," relies on state self-reporting, and lacks effective enforcement measures (Cole 2005; Gallagher

2010: 61; Lehti and Aromaa 2006; Scarpa 2006). Critics further note that the convention's nonbinding provisions and reliance on self-reporting by states effectively allow countries to "gain the moral highground by loudly proclaiming that they have signed a document condemning the buying and selling of women's bodies, when in reality prostitution continues unchecked in their own countries" (Toepfer and Wells 1994: 92). For some, the convention did not go far enough, while for others—including the United States—its provisions reached too far into domestic affairs ("U.S. Set to Abstain in Prostitution Ban," *NYT*, May 12, 1959, 5). Dissatisfaction on both sides helps explain why the 1949 convention has not been widely ratified, though it remains open for signature (Lammasniemi 2019: 76).

It is illuminating to consider how contemporaries were seeing things, what the universe of possibilities and probabilities looked like to them, as suggested by this late 1947 headline in the *New York Times*: "Europe's Collapse Called Complete" (November 1, 1947, 7). When surveying the early postwar years, recovering simultaneity is as important as reconstructing sequence. In May 1946, pending completion of the new UN headquarters, four subsidiary bodies of the UN Economic and Social Council convened at New York's Hunter College. The Temporary Social Committee set its sights beyond "theoretical studies" to consider "practical results in social welfare," such as model corrective schools for juvenile offenders and rehabilitation centers for prostitutes. Sidney Harris, a longtime British delegate on the anti-trafficking advisory committee, was instrumental in bringing forward League of Nations–era perspectives and priorities. He urged continuation and expansion of the practice of annual reports from states, leavened with information from nongovernmental organizations. Harris reiterated the long-standing abolitionist conclusion that state-sanctioned prostitution was a constant driver of both supply and demand ("U.N. Body Plans Aid in Social Welfare," *NYT*, May 4, 1946, 4).

Concurrent sessions of the Temporary Subcommission on the Status of Women drew up a "four-fold attack" on prostitution and sex trafficking, calling for states to (1) abolish prostitution by removing its legal and customary protections; (2) implement strong measures to put down the traffic in women and children; (3) preempt the growth of post-abolition clandestine prostitution by providing economic, educational, and health support for women in need; and (4) assist women to leave prostitution without stigma by providing them with employment assistance and access to education. Bridging back to projects undertaken by League of Nations committees and various women's organizations in the 1930s, the commission also advocated worldwide recognition of the need for "an effective scheme of health and social insurance legislation which [would] provide equal preventative and remedial opportunities for women and . . . include special provisions for maternal and child care." It called for a worldwide, up-to-date, and reliable survey of laws relating to the status of women and information about their actual treatment, to be gathered from governments, specialized agencies, academic institutes, and trade unions, supplemented by public opinion polls in various regions on relevant matters (Pliley 2010: 105–106; "Prostitution Fight Is Mapped in UN. Mrs. Roosevelt Chides Groups for Too Much Detail—Split Develops in Social Unit," *NYT*, May 10, 1946: 10).

Meanwhile, activist groups in Britain—the Antislavery and Aborigines Protection Society most especially—were pushing for a hard line at the UN on slavery-related practices and trafficking in forced labor in the Soviet bloc, the Middle East, and Africa. However, they were met by a Soviet-Arab-African coalition, which skillfully enlarged and reframed these same questions to encompass apartheid and colonialism. Along similar lines, the US government was neutralized by Soviet charges that America "condoned slavery" through segregation, peonage, and "lynch law," and, on the other hand, by mobilization among domestic coalitions such as the Workers Defense League ("Russian Says U.S. Condones Slavery. Mrs. Roosevelt Denies Charges in Geneva Session of Human Rights Commission," *NYT*, December 8, 1947, 13). Supplements to the 1926 Slavery Convention in 1953 and 1956 served only to fuel interminable debates over definitions of "slavery" and "slave labor." UN sessions henceforth brought seasonal headlines announcing the persistence and growth of slavery—including raiding, capture, transport, and sale—in Africa, Latin America, the Middle East, Eastern Europe, the Soviet Union, North America, Central America, South America, China, India, and the Pacific Islands.

The language and rationale of the 1949 convention thus emerged in a swirl of concurrent debates about slavery, forced labor, and universal human rights, including health benefits, pensions, insurance, education, a "decent living," and equal work for equal pay ("World Rights Bill Proposed by U.S. U.N. Body in Geneva to Study Draft Seeking 'Decent Living,' Security,

Freedom for All," *NYT*, December 1, 1947, 10). In the UN General Assembly, negotiations followed familiar battle lines of prostitution as an irrepressible "necessary evil" and as an irreplaceable "last resort" for women in economic distress. Insistence that prostitution-related trafficking should not be singled out from other forms of trafficking and exploitation threatened to mire deliberations in the same quicksand that was—at that very moment—stalemating debates on the future Universal Declaration of Human Rights ("U.N. Bill of Rights with Teeth Urged," *NYT*, May 14, 1946, 10). Those discussing trafficking in women and children were within hearing range of US-Soviet shouting matches about individuals, collectivities, and "true" equality. They were wise to the political perils of overstepping their authorized purview and justifiably cautious about jumping into divisive East-West, North-South polarities on "exploitation," "forced labor," "cultural exceptions," and "consensual prostitution" (Gallagher 2010: 58).

The 1949 convention looked to bridge the persistent divide in abolitionism between prohibitionists and feminists. Its preamble meshes with the 1948 Universal Declaration of Human Rights: "Prostitution and the accompanying evil of the traffic in persons for the purpose of prostitution are incompatible with the dignity and worth of the human person and endanger the welfare of the individual, the family and the community." Recalling the larger context of contemporaneous confrontations over what states owe the "human person," and what "slavery" and "forced labor" include, it becomes clear that the impatient, peremptory tone of this sweeping, unequivocal language is directed at governments, not at women. This same message was delivered in the collective rebuff to Britain on its continued toleration of colonial prostitution under the banner of cultural relativism ("Prostitution Curb Voted: U.N. Backs Draft Convention, Overrides British Objection," *NYT*, December 3, 1949, 6).

Over the next several decades, UN anti-trafficking initiatives took a more sociological turn, with a growing consensus that prostitution's roots lie in the structure and organization of society. Question arose around long-standing assumptions, such as whether trafficking necessarily required international transport of victims, whether victims are obliged to cooperate with authorities, whether rehabilitation was more likely when not compulsory, and indeed what purposes such rehabilitation should serve (United Nations 1959: 29–34). Preventive measures discussed included improved living conditions, education, social security, and legal and de facto equality of women. In the mid-1970s, reports began circulating about renewed large-scale, highly exploitative regional and international trafficking ("U.N. Aide Asks Inquiry on Forced Prostitution," *NYT*, June 27, 1975, 2). By the 1980s, trafficking had dramatically surged, driven by increased tourism and migration. American downsizing of troops abroad, combined with global economic trends, led countries most affected to turn to "sex tourism." This sector continued to expand into the 1990s, fueled by the "global restructuring of capitalist production and investment" (Kempadoo 1998: 15). Rural displacement, urban unemployment, the spread of AIDS, and rising demand for consumer goods cumulatively fueled an irreversible traffic in children for sexual exploitation (Kempadoo 1998: 7). Free-market reforms expanded commercial prostitution in the former Soviet bloc, Cuba, Vietnam, and China. Traffickers typically accumulated a diverse portfolio, often including narcotics, credit card fraud, money laundering, and a lucrative illegal market in human organs.

Campaigns to awaken public opinion and mobilize governments also sharpened debates about elements of consent and coercion in sex work. These developments brought a shift from abolitionist strategies toward a framework of human rights and gender equality (Cole 2005: 100–101). Advocates mobilized the growing canon of UN human rights instruments, weaving anti-trafficking protections into their provisions. For example, the 1979 Convention on the Elimination of All Forms of Discrimination against Women combines anti-trafficking measures with a UN oversight committee and an optional protocol opening the way to direct claims by individuals and nongovernmental organizations (Scarpa 2006: 439). Gatherings in Vienna (1993) and Beijing (1995) forged tighter connections between trafficking, human rights, and gender-based violence (Cole 2005: 108–110). These energies culminated in the 2000 Protocol to Prevent, Suppress and Punish Trafficking in Persons, Especially Women and Children, supplementing the UN Convention against Transnational Organized Crime. This "Palermo Protocol" is "a multifaceted instrument aimed at preventing human trafficking, protecting victims' human rights, and prosecuting traffickers" (Scarpa 2006: 437).

REFERENCES

Abbott, Grace. 1933. Memorandum to Secretary of Labor, on Draft Protocol for the Suppression of the Traffic in Women of Full Age. Records of Immigration and Naturalization Service, Reel 2: October 23.

Attwood, Rachael. 2015. "Stopping the Traffic: The National Vigilance Association and the International Fight against the 'White Slave' Trade (1899–1909)." *Women's History Review* 24:325–350.

Butler, Josephine E. 1879. *Government by Police*. London: Dyer Brothers.

———. 1897. *Truth before Everything*. Liverpool: Pewtress.

Cole, Alison. 2005. "Reconceptualising Female Trafficking: The Inhuman Trade in Women." *Women's Rights Law Reporter* 26 (97): 97–120.

Crowdy, Rachel E. 1927. "The Humanitarian Activities of the League of Nations." *Journal of the Royal Institute of International Affairs* 6 (3): 153–169.

Faulkner, Elizabeth A. 2019. "Historical Evolution of the International Legal Responses to the Trafficking of Children: A Critique." In *The Palgrave International Handbook of Human Trafficking*, edited by John Winterdyk and Jackie Jones, 79–95. Cham, Switzerland: Palgrave Macmillan.

Gallagher, Anne T. 2010. *The International Law of Human Trafficking*. Cambridge: Cambridge University Press.

Gorman, Daniel. 2008. "Empire, Internationalism, and the Campaign against the Traffic in Women and Children in the 1920s." *Twentieth Century British History* 19 (2): 186–216.

———. 2012. *The Emergence of International Society in the 1920s*. New York: Cambridge University Press.

Hudson, Manley O. 1929. "America's Role in the League of Nations." *American Political Science Review* 23 (1): 17–31.

IBSTP (International Bureau for Suppression of Traffic in Persons). 1949. "Post-war Europe as a Field for the Traffic in Women and Children." Box 193/6, IBSTP Papers, Fawcett Library, London.

Keller v. United States, 213 U.S. 138 (1909). https://supreme.justia.com/cases/federal/us/213/138/.

Kempadoo, Kamala. 1998. "Globalizing Sex Workers' Rights." In *Global Sex Rights, Resistance, and Redefinition*, edited by Kamala Kempadoo and Joe Doezema, 1–28. New York: Routledge.

Knepper, Paul. 2016. "The Investigation into the Traffic in Women by the League of Nations: Sociological Jurisprudence as an International Social Project." *Law and History Review* 34 (1): 45–73.

Lammasniemi, Laura. 2019. "International Legislation on White Slavery and Anti-trafficking in the Early 20th Century." In *The Palgrave International Handbook of Human Trafficking*, edited by John Winterdyk and Jackie Jones, 67–78. Cham, Switzerland: Palgrave Macmillan.

League of Nations. 1921. *Records of the International Conference on Traffic in Women and Children, June 30–July 5*. No. C.484.M.339.1921.IV. Geneva: League of Nations.

———. 1922. *Advisory Committee on the Traffic in Women and Children: Minutes of the First Session*. No. C.445.M.265.1922.IV. Geneva: League of Nations.

———. 1934. *Commission of Enquiry into Traffic in Women and Children in the East.* Summary of the Report to the Council. IV.Social.1934.IV. Geneva: League of Nations.

———. 1935. *Position of Women of Russian Origin in the Far East*. A.12.1935.IV.3. Geneva: League of Nations.

———. 1937. *Traffic in Women and Children: Conference of Central Authorities in Eastern Countries, Bandung, Indonesia*. C.228.M.164. Geneva: League of Nations.

Legg, Stephen. 2012. "'The Life of Individuals as Well as Nations': International Law and the League of Nations Anti-trafficking Governmentalities." *Leiden Journal of International Law* 25 (3): 647–664.

Lehti, Martii, and Kauko Aromaa. 2006. "Trafficking for Sexual Exploitation." *Crime and Justice* 341 (1): 133–223.

Limoncelli, Stephanie A. 2011. *The Politics of Trafficking: The First International Movement to Combat the Sexual Exploitation of Women*. Stanford, CA: Stanford University Press.

Metzger, Barbara. 2007. "Towards an International Human Rights Regime during the Inter-war Years: The League of Nations' Combat of Traffic in Women and Children." In *Beyond Sovereignty: Britain, Empire and Transnationalism, c. 1880–1950*, edited by Kevin Grant, Philippa Levine, and Frank Trentmann, 54–79. New York: Palgrave Macmillan.

Nadelmann, Ethan. 1990. "Global Prohibition Regimes: The Evolution of Norms in International Society." *International Organization* 44 (4): 479–526.

Norlin, George. 1938. "The United States and World Organization during 1937, Our National Defenses." *International Conciliation*, June, 221–294.

NVA (National Vigilance Association). 1899. *The White Slave Trade: Transactions of the International Congress on the White Slave Trade, Held in London, on the 21st, 22nd and 23rd of June, 1899*. London: NVA.

Peck, Gunther. 2011. "Feminizing White Slavery in the United States: Marcus Braun and the Transnational Traffic in White Bodies, 1890–1910." In *Workers across the Americas: The Transnational Turn in Labor History*, edited by Leon Fink, 222–241. New York: Oxford University Press.

Petruccelli, David. 2020. "The Crisis of Liberal Internationalism: The Legacies of the League of Nations Reconsidered." *Journal of World History* 31 (1): 111–136.

Pliley, Jessica. 2010. "Claims to Protection: The Rise and Fall of Feminist Abolitionism in the League of Nations' Committee on the Traffic in Women and Children, 1919–1936." *Journal of Women's History* 22 (4): 90–113.

Reinsch, Paul. 1907. "International Unions and Their Administration." *American Journal of International Law* 1 (3): 579–623.

———. 1909. "International Administrative Law and National Sovereignty." *American Journal of International Law* 3 (1): 1–45.

———. 1911. "Diplomatic Affairs and International Law, 1910." *American Political Science Review* 5 (1): 12–37.

Rivera-López, Eduardo. 2006. "Organ Sales and Moral Distress." *Journal of Applied Philosophy* 23 (1): 41–52.

Scarpa, Silvia. 2006. "Child Trafficking: International Instruments to Protect the Most Vulnerable Victims." *Family Court Review* 44 (3): 429–447.

Scully, Eileen. 2015. "Repressed Memories: Historical Perspectives on Trafficking and Anti-trafficking." *Slavery Today Journal* 2 (2): 1–19.

Siller, Nicole J. 2017. "Human Trafficking in International Law before the Palermo Protocol." *Netherlands International Law Review* 64 (3): 407–452.

Toepfer, Susan J., and Bryan S. Wells. 1994. "The Worldwide Market for Sex: A Review of International and Regional Legal Prohibitions regarding Trafficking in Women." *Michigan Journal of Gender and Law* 2 (1): 83–128.

Tomich, Dale. 2018. "The Second Slavery and World Capitalism: A Perspective for Historical Inquiry." *International Review of Social History* 63 (3): 477–501.

United Nations. 1959. *Study on Traffic in Persons and Prostitution*. 59.IV.5. New York: United Nations.

US Senate. 1910. Suppression of the White-Slave Traffic. Message from the President of the United States. 61.2. Document 214, Part 2, January 1.

United States v. Portale, 235 U.S. 27 (1914). https://supreme.justia.com/cases/federal/us/235/27/.

White-Slave Traffic (Mann) Act, ch. 395, 36 Stat. 825 (1910) (codified as amended at 18 U.S.C. § 2421 (2000)).

CHAPTER 4

Multilateral Protocols on Trafficking and Smuggling
DIVERGENT PATHS OF COOPERATION AND DISINTEGRATION SINCE 2000

Sarah P. Lockhart

IN 2000, THE UNITED NATIONS ADOPTED two protocols to the UN Convention against Transnational Organized Crime (UNTOC) specifically addressing human trafficking and smuggling: the Protocol to Prevent, Suppress and Punish Trafficking in Persons, Especially Women and Children, and the Protocol against the Smuggling of Migrants by Land, Sea and Air. Collectively known as the Palermo Protocols,[1] these supplements to the UNTOC are rare examples of widely ratified, multilateral agreements on migration-related issues. It is striking, then, that these protocols emerged under the auspices of the transnational crime regime, not the migration, refugee, or human rights regimes. The location of the anti-trafficking and anti-smuggling agreements within the UNTOC ensured their widespread adoption by capitalizing on the shared interests of both migrant-sending and migrant-receiving states: combatting criminality (Charnysh, Lloyd, and Simmons 2015; Simmons, Lloyd, and Stewart 2018). But there is a fundamental tension between criminal justice and human rights in terms of migrant trafficking and smuggling, since those victimized are also breaking the law by attempting to illicitly cross international borders. This creates a policy paradox that has hampered attempts to reduce both trafficking and smuggling, in which policy meant to reduce trafficking and smuggling has frequently exacerbated it.

The history of the Palermo Protocols is a case study in both the potential and limitations of creativity and human agency in the face of structural constraints. Anti-smuggling and anti-trafficking policy entrepreneurs—within state governments, from human rights organizations, and elsewhere—creatively found an institutional venue in which they could construct a majority in support of international treaty mechanisms to combat trafficking and smuggling. But the fact that the agreements were quickly signed and ratified by most states in the international system masked substantial differences in states' underlying interests and how they wanted to address trafficking and smuggling. The ways in which the anti-trafficking and anti-smuggling regimes have—or have not—developed subsequently reflect this underlying structural reality.

At first glance, it appears that the trafficking protocol is now embedded in a more robust regime, buoyed by greater international consensus, domestic adoption of model legislation, and leadership from states like the United States, which unilaterally "names and shames" states that fail to address human trafficking (Gallagher 2017). Anti-smuggling never generated the same type of consensus, especially around the identity of the victims and the perpetrators, and regime development remains weak. Nevertheless, the choice to link multilateral anti-trafficking and anti-smuggling efforts to the UNTOC as opposed to migration or human rights agreements legitimizes law enforcement approaches for both policy challenges, even when states actually violate the protocols themselves, as in the case of criminalizing humanitarian smuggling (McAdam 2020).

The criminalization of smuggling and increasing reliance on law enforcement to deter and punish illicit migration have reshaped the incentive structures for individual migrants and those who might help them cross borders. This binds trafficking and smuggling together, as enforcement both increases the demand for smuggling and makes it more costly, elevating the risk that a migrant may become trafficked. So while trafficking and smuggling have different legal meanings, policies to address one can affect the other, and the same migrant can experience both. As always, migrants continue to exercise their agency and look for new ways to overcome immigration barriers even as they are simultaneously made more vulnerable by structural forces, sometimes starting out as smuggled and then finding themselves trafficked along the way. The criminalization of smuggling thus has serious consequences for the human rights and freedom of migrants seeking to build better lives for themselves.

In this chapter, I show how an increase in illicit migration in the 1990s was fueled by increasing restrictions on legal immigration and migration enforcement in popular destination states, the collapse of the Communist bloc and its exit controls, and the increased ease of travel due to globalization and technological advances (Money and Lockhart 2018). The combination of growing numbers of people who wanted to migrate and fewer legal avenues to do so created a market incentive for traffickers and smugglers to facilitate illicit immigration. A wide range of states and nonstate actors were alarmed by these developments, but their viewpoints, interests and motivations, and ability to effect change varied. While they managed to find some common ground under the auspices of the UNTOC, the underlying disagreements about the nature of trafficking and smuggling and the proper policy responses have shaped their subsequent development. The chapter concludes with suggestions for ways forward that focus less on promoting a more robust anti-smuggling regime[2] and more on expanding avenues for legal migration and upholding obligations under the refugee regime.

THE DEVELOPMENT OF THE PALERMO PROTOCOLS

National legislation against the facilitation of illicit entry has long existed in countries around the world, and the earliest international instruments against what we would now call human trafficking date back to 1904.[3] But it was not until the late 1990s that states sought to adopt a multilateral treaty to address both of these phenomena in a comprehensive and uniform manner, under the auspices of the transnational crime regime (Gallagher 2015). The treaty was a response to changes more than two decades in the making.

By the 1970s, many of the highly developed states in North America and Europe, along with Australia, saw economic growth slow and political pressure build to both restrict immigration and actually *enforce* these restrictions. Thus, in places like the United States, the size of the undocumented population grew dramatically in the 1980s and 1990s, even though the overall number of immigrants arriving stayed fairly steady; their legal status changed, not their presence (Massey, Durand, and Pren 2016). Increased enforcement made entering destination states more difficult, necessitating the use of smugglers who could navigate new barriers and making migrants more vulnerable to traffickers.

Changes in migrant-sending states also fueled concern about smuggling and trafficking. The political and economic collapse of the Soviet Union and Eastern Bloc states generated a large pool of new potential migrants seeking entrance into Western Europe and developed countries more broadly (Outshoorn 2004). Without the authoritarian regimes that had maintained strict exit controls for decades, the fledgling states of the former Communist bloc did not have the capacity to manage the flow of their own citizens leaving for Western Europe, nor were they able to manage the flow of individuals from other countries, particularly in Asia, looking for backdoor access to Western Europe (Laczko 2003). As a result, Western European receiving states faced challenges to regulating their borders and controlling migration that simply had not existed before. In North America, traffickers and smugglers increasingly exploited the relative weakness of Mexican authorities to use Mexico as a transit route to the United States. Illegal migrants from China, Southeast Asia, and Central and South America smuggled and trafficked to the United States often came through Mexico, and sometimes through Canada (Finckenauer and Schrock 2000). There was also a spike in the number of undocumented Mexican migrants following the 1994 Mexican financial crisis (Monras 2018). Many of the migrants also employed smugglers, as the Clinton administration tightened border security and pushed illicit crossings into the desert, making the journey far more treacherous (Hagan and Phillips 2008).

Lastly, the processes of globalization and technological advance, which reduced the relative costs of transportation and communication more broadly, meant that far more people were traveling internationally. Forged travel documents and visa overstays became a significant challenge for states, and the ease of communication reduced the costs of coordination for transnational smuggling and trafficking operations, many of which behaved more like traditional businesses capitalizing on the opportunities of globalization than criminal syndicates by providing their "customers" with documents, information about routes, and logistical support (Koslowski 2011).

But increasing state enforcement made illicit migration ever more difficult and risky, driving up the price and drawing the attention of more traditional criminals. In the 1990s, states were alarmed by the participation of large-scale organized crime, which helps explain why they chose to address the trafficking and smuggling problem under the auspices of the UNTOC, along with drugs and firearms. However, in the decades since then, new communication technologies have also facilitated the fragmentation of trafficking and smuggling operations, and there is scholarly dispute about the degree to which organized crime is actually involved (Vermeulen, Van Damme, and De Bondt 2010). Today, migrants can find, vet, communicate with, and hire a smuggler via a social media app such as WhatsApp (Diba, Papanicolaou, and Antonopoulous 2019). Of course, this future was unknown during the dial-up days of the internet, in which the Palermo Protocols were conceived.

By the mid-1990s, both sending states and receiving states, along with human rights activists within those states, were putting trafficking and smuggling on the agenda in a number of international forums. This suggests that policymakers were engaging in "venue shopping," or looking for an institutional venue in which they could effectively gain traction in addressing this policy problem (Baumgartner and Jones 1993; Pralle 2003). Trafficking and smuggling came up in numerous regional consultative processes hosted by the International Organization for Migration, but none of the outcomes of these processes were binding. The issues were also debated in the drafting of the International Convention on the Protection of the Rights of All Migrant Workers and Members of Their Families. In fact, trafficking and smuggling are explicitly addressed in the treaty's preamble, which links migrant victimization by both traffickers and employers in the destination state to their irregular status. But the international convention went into force without the support of any major destination state.

The initial idea for incorporating trafficking and smuggling into the UNTOC stemmed from another failed effort elsewhere. At the April 1997 session of the UN Commission on Crime Prevention and Criminal Justice (CCPCJ 1997), Argentina proposed a new convention against the trafficking of children as part of a program to address transnational organized crime, in part because efforts to incorporate this into the UN Convention on the Rights of the Child had been inadequate (Gallagher 2001). At a meeting in

September, Austria suggested a partner protocol focusing on smuggling. These suggestions were embraced by the United States and a number of Western European states, which had also begun to unilaterally implement anti-trafficking and anti-smuggling policies of their own. An ad hoc committee was formed, and negotiations over the language of the new protocols ensued. Finally, states had found an institutional venue and a policy frame that appealed to both sending and receiving states.

The introduction of trafficking and smuggling to the UNTOC illustrates both the potential and limitations to the agency of international actors. Both states and nonstate actors can creatively and strategically look for venues in which they can put important issues on the agenda, framing them in ways that will garner widespread support for an agreement. But meaningful action will depend on the support of powerful states, guided by their own interests. The UNTOC provided a venue that allowed actors with divergent interests to rally against the criminality of trafficking and smuggling, and the victimization of trafficked migrants, while failing to address the ways in which restrictive migration policies and robust enforcement contributed to the problem.

The idea of the protocols enjoyed widespread state support, but the debate within the committee quickly turned contentious (Money and Lockhart 2018). The committee comprised state delegates from the UN crime control regime, but the UN High Commissioner for Refugees and the UN High Commissioner for Human Rights mobilized human and migrant rights nongovernmental organizations (NGOs) in order to influence a series of ad hoc committee meetings to prioritize the rights of trafficked and smuggled migrants, which came to be known as the Vienna Process (Fitzpatrick 2003). The debates centered on two issues: (1) whether the trafficking and smuggling problem should be approached as a crime and border control issue, or as a matter of state obligation to safeguard the human rights of trafficked and smuggled people; and (2) whether the definition of trafficking should include migrants involved in "voluntary" prostitution (Chuang 2006). Sending states and their allies in the human rights and immigrant rights policy communities advocated for emphasizing human rights in the protocols, but their efforts had limited success. Receiving states were receptive to the trafficking and smuggling protocols in the context of the UNTOC precisely because this allowed them to maintain a focus on law enforcement solutions rather than the obligations of receiving states to protect trafficked and smuggled migrants. The receiving states had no intention of signing anything that imposed new obligations, or expanded existing obligations, under international law. So while debate and discussion about the human rights aspects of trafficking and smuggling were plentiful during the Vienna Process, there was little hope that they would become part of the final agreement in any meaningful way (Money and Lockhart 2018).

The final versions of the trafficking and smuggling protocols said little of substance about human rights, beyond recognizing that states already have obligations to trafficked and smuggled migrants under existing human rights treaties and general legal principles that are not nullified by the Palermo Protocols (Fitzpatrick 2003). One concession that the sending states and human rights activists did achieve is the inclusion of the protection of human rights as one of the three "purposes" of the trafficking protocol. States, however, are not obligated to do much to actually protect the rights of trafficking victims; they must only "endeavor" to provide for their safety, "ensure" that their domestic legal systems provide privacy for victims and the possibility for victims to seek compensation, "consider" cooperation with NGOs to provide services for trafficking victims, and "consider" measures to allow trafficking victims to remain in the country. At the same time, receiving states are also free to arrest, prosecute, and deport trafficked or smuggled individuals. Sending states, however, do face obligations under the Palermo Protocols to accept the return of any trafficked or smuggled citizen or permanent resident; these obligations are stated in much more forceful language (Fitzpatrick 2003). Every section of Article 8 of the trafficking protocol, for example, asserts definitively that sending states "shall" carry out special obligations, including accepting the return of trafficked individuals, showing due regard for their safety, providing travel documents to the requesting receiving state without delay, and so on.

The smuggling protocol pays tribute to the human rights of smuggled migrants in both the preamble and Article 16, entitled "Protection and Assistance Measures." However, the five clauses of this article only serve to remind states that they have existing obligations under international law to protect the rights of those who have been "the object of conduct" covered by the protocol. In particular, states are reminded that smuggled migrants have the "right to life and the right not to be subject to torture," which is not exactly a high bar to clear (although states do fail to clear it). The substance of the protocol is focused on enforcement, going into particular detail about interdiction at sea, and it does not call on states to grant smuggled migrants any new rights.

On the issue of "voluntary" prostitution, the human rights community was deeply divided. One NGO bloc, called the Human Rights Caucus and led by the International Human Rights Law Group and the Global Alliance Against Trafficking in Women, brought together human rights, anti-trafficking, and sex worker rights activists to advocate for a distinction between trafficking and prostitution. The opposing bloc, led by the American-based Coalition Against Trafficking in Persons, argued that all prostitution was inherently coercive and thus all sex work should be considered trafficking in the protocol. Initially, this bloc enjoyed state support from Argentina and the Philippines, while the United States vocally opposed it. But, responding to public pressure from domestic interest groups, particularly from evangelical Christian anti-trafficking activists, the United States backed away from this position, while quietly working behind the scenes to eliminate language that would lead to burdensome international obligations to all immigrants engaged in prostitution (Bennett and Colson 2000; Gallagher 2001). Ultimately, the trafficking protocol excluded consensual prostitution and cleverly avoided defining prostitution altogether, instead referring to "exploitation of prostitution of others" and "other forms of sexual exploitation," leaving the interpretation of these terms to domestic legal systems (Chuang 2006). Ultimately, the prostitution debate so occupied the representatives of the various NGOs and intergovernmental organizations at the Vienna Process that they neglected to speak with a united voice about other rights issues, particularly in relation to smuggled migrants (Ditmore and Wijers 2003; Money and Lockhart 2018). In fact, the debate legitimized the idea that there should be fundamentally different rights for "voluntary" smuggled migrants and "victimized" trafficked migrants by focusing so heavily on whether prostitution alone could flip a migrant from one category to the other. If activists had focused on securing rights for all irregular migrants, instead of parsing the categorization implications of sex work, they may have secured stronger protections for all.

Despite the prostitution controversy, the Vienna Process made clear that there was a broad consensus that human trafficking produces victims to whom the state has some obligation, and that traffickers are criminals who should be prosecuted. In sharp contrast, the smuggling debate did not end with a similar consensus. First, while some smugglers are hardened criminals who present a danger to society, many are part of smaller operations at least partially driven by altruistic motives and embedded in social networks, even when money changes hands (International Council on Human Rights Policy 2010). Sending states may thus be less enthusiastic about cracking down on migrant smugglers, particularly if irregular migration provides an outlet for surplus labor and a source of remittances (Money and Lockhart 2018). Second, there is less consensus on the degree to which smuggled migrants are victims compared with trafficked migrants. In practice, the line between smuggling and trafficking is frequently unclear. Migrants sometimes seek to be smuggled but then find themselves trafficked as they struggle to pay off smuggling debts, or they become vulnerable to traffickers en route. In both trafficking and smuggling, there can be elements of free choice and coercion, despite the fact that coercion is one of the crucial legal distinctions between the two phenomena (Bouteillet-Paquet 2011).

The smuggling protocol articulated a compromise position on these issues rather than a consensus. It called for the criminalization of the smuggler, but it made clear that the migrants themselves are not criminals. It also recognized that states should seek to address the dire circumstances that lead migrants to seek out the services of smugglers, but it did not enforce any specific obligations toward smuggled migrants. By contrast, the trafficking protocol received a great deal of attention and provoked greater debate, but the basis for consensus (on both the criminalization of traffickers and the victimization of the trafficked) was stronger (Money and Lockhart 2018). An examination of the states that have signed, ratified, or acceded to the Palermo Protocols demonstrates the slightly greater consensus that the trafficking protocol generated versus the smuggling protocol. Overall, both received widespread support; 80 states promptly signed the trafficking protocol, and 77 states signed the smuggling protocol, in December 2000. As of 2019, the trafficking protocol has 117 signatories and 175 states are party to it; the smuggling protocol has 112 signatories and 149 parties (parties to the treaty may have accepted the treaty as legally binding while neither signing nor ratifying it). While most states signed and ratified the protocols at the same time, there were significant differences in nearly 50 cases. In only 5 of these did it take longer for the state to sign, ratify, or accede to the trafficking protocol; in every other case, it took states anywhere from a few months to nearly five years longer to become a party to the smuggling protocol, if they ever did. Fifteen states that signed or acceded to the trafficking protocol refused to sign, ratify, or accede to the smuggling protocol; most of these are countries of origin.

Some states registered reservations regarding the protocols, providing insight into their concerns at the time. The majority for both protocols concerned the requirement that interstate disputes be brought to the International Court of Justice, reflecting broader concerns about the court not specific to the protocols. There were also reservations by some Middle Eastern countries about parts of the trafficking protocol that call for opportunities for trafficking victims, particularly to housing and employment, reflecting the poor commitment to women's rights in these states. But Ecuador's reservation regarding the smuggling protocol stands out; it asserts that smuggled migrants are victims of smugglers and that the Palermo Protocols can be understood only in conjunction with the International Convention on the Protection of the Rights of All Migrant Workers and Members of Their Families and other human rights instruments. The reservation challenges the idea that irregular migration is criminal itself, stating that "the Government of Ecuador declares that migrants are the victims of illicit trafficking in persons on the part of criminal organizations whose only goal is unjust and undue enrichment at the expense of persons wishing to perform honest work abroad" (Protocol against the Smuggling of Migrants by Land, Sea and Air 2000).

Ecuador's reservation voiced the concern of many source and transit countries that resisted signing, ratifying, or acceding to the smuggling protocol; the protocol did not go far enough in recognizing the victimization of smuggled migrants and receiving states' obligations to them while putting undue burden on sending states to stop irregular migration (Schloenhardt and MacDonald 2017).

REGIME DEVELOPMENT AND THE PALERMO PROTOCOLS TODAY

Given the greater international consensus that surrounded the trafficking protocol in 2000, it is not particularly surprising that there has been greater regime development (or the generation of reinforcing norms, rules, and institutions) around trafficking than there has been around smuggling, despite the fact that smuggling became a headline-grabbing crisis in 2015, as smuggled migrants washed up on the shores of Europe's Mediterranean coastline on overloaded and capsizing boats. But developments since 2000 have only exacerbated the divergence between the trafficking protocol and the smuggling protocol. Although implementation of the trafficking protocol has been far from perfect, three factors explain its relative success: strong unilateral action, particularly by the United States; a global network of activist organizations, which have maintained public pressure on governments to address trafficking; and a clear, categorical definition of victimhood in this context.

The smuggling protocol enjoys absolutely none of these advantages for gaining support. First, at the same time that the United States was participating in the negotiations over the Palermo Protocols, it was drafting its own domestic legislation: the Trafficking Victims Protection Act of 2000. This law, and its reauthorization under three subsequent administrations, did two important things: it created the "T-Visa," a new category of visa that trafficking victims could get if they cooperated in the prosecution of their traffickers, and it established the Office to Monitor and Combat Trafficking in Persons within the Department of State to coordinate anti-trafficking initiatives with other countries, as well as monitor, evaluate, and rate their efforts. At the time, some criticized the United States for unilaterally enforcing its own definitions of trafficking and prescriptions for addressing it, seeing this as undermining the multilateral efforts embodied by the Palermo Protocols (Chuang 2006). And in the years since, the Trafficking Victims Protection Act has faced harsh criticism in its implementation for prioritizing the prosecution of traffickers over the protection of victims (Chacón 2006, 2010). But these unilateral actions advanced the anti-trafficking regime by going further than the trafficking protocol could, creating a model for how trafficking victims could be protected through domestic legislation, and naming and shaming states that fell short.

Second, public awareness and concern about human trafficking have only grown since 2000, in large part because of the work of activist groups that keep public pressure on governments to address trafficking. While some organizations, like Anti-Slavery International, have existed for decades, dozens more have emerged since 2000 to become actively engaged in anti-human trafficking advocacy and direct assistance to victims: the Polaris Project, Not For Sale, A21, Stop the Traffik, Free the Slaves, and many more. Some have criticized anti-trafficking activists for circulating misleading data that exaggerate the problem of trafficking, conflate prostitution with trafficking, and emphasize sex trafficking (particularly of women and girls) at the expense of labor trafficking, which is far more common (see Scully, this volume, chap. 3; as well as Brown 2015; Dandurand 2017; Farrell, Owens, and McDevitt 2014; Pearce, Hynes, and Bovarnick 2013; Zhang 2009). Regardless, it is clear that these groups are influential; in the United States, for example, material from anti-trafficking organizations is cited routinely by legislators and bureaucrats alike, as they draft and implement policies around trafficking (Kessler 2015).

Third, the anti-trafficking regime benefits from a clear category of victim: the trafficked individual. Even states that have failed to adequately address victims' needs do not actively dispute the premise of their victimhood. The number of states that criminalize trafficking in domestic law rose from 33 in 2003 to 158 by 2016. Most developed states have, since 2000, implemented some sort of national referral mechanism for responding to victims' needs and coordinating between governmental authorities, international organizations, and civil society groups (Liu 2018). The degree to which states have successfully implemented applicable law and national referral mechanisms varies, largely depending on the more general governance capacity of the state, but there is now a normative and legal framework that did not exist in the past.

The smuggling protocol has followed a very different trajectory from the trafficking protocol. Whereas the trafficking protocol has been strengthened by a robust growth in domestic legislation, grassroots activism, and normative development, states have actually challenged the very foundations of the smuggling protocol in two important ways. First, over the past two decades, states have defined *smuggler* more broadly than the protocol does (Gallagher 2017). Whereas the protocol explicitly exempted those who facilitated illicit entry for altruistic or humanitarian purposes, only criminalizing those who did so for pay, most countries have retained or adopted a broader definition of smuggling that includes facilitation of illicit entry for any reason. In fact, a survey conducted by the United Nations Office on Drugs and Crime of a representative sample of countries found that fully 85 percent of surveyed states retained the ability to prosecute people who facilitate illicit entry for free, in contradiction to the smuggling protocol (UNODC 2017). In the United States, for example, "alien smuggling" is an aggravated felony, regardless of whether the smuggled person is a family member or it is done for monetary gain (Kamhi and Prandini 2017).

Second, states' anti-smuggling efforts have increasingly criminalized smuggled migrants themselves and infringed on their right to asylum and non-refoulement, explicitly contradicting the smuggling protocol's prohibition against prosecuting smuggled migrants and its clear assertion that anti-smuggling efforts may not be used to violate either the spirit or the letter of international humanitarian law (Gallagher 2017). For example, nearly every European Union state has criminalized irregular entry, with sentences often including jail time (European Union Agency for Fundamental Rights 2014). The United States has also increased its use of the criminal justice system over the past twenty years, vigorously prosecuting tens of thousands of migrants every year for "entry related offenses" (American Immigration Council 2018). From 1997 to 2013, the number of entry-related prosecutions soared 500 percent, from just over fifteen thousand to more than ninety thousand in the United States, even as apprehensions declined (Rosenblum and Meissner 2014). Many of these migrants are subject to federal prison sentences, and an entry-related conviction can impede an asylum claim (American Immigration Council 2018).

In short, domestic policy over the past twenty years has increasingly violated the smuggling protocol by focusing solely on migration enforcement, ignoring the rights of migrants, and criminalizing anyone who helps them on their journeys. But by pursuing separate protocols for trafficking and smuggling in the first place, states were able to make a distinction between trafficked migrants who are victims clearly in need of state protection and smuggled migrants who are perpetrators of a crime against the state (Gallagher 2017). This distinction is salient for public opinion as well, explaining why popular campaigns against human trafficking have grown over the last twenty years while groups that advocate for irregular migrants fail to attract the same type of public support. Across destination states, large majorities support the deportation of immigrants in their countries illegally (the United States is a rare exception, where 46 percent support deportation and 47 percent oppose it) (Gonzalez-Barrera and Connor 2019). At the same time, the state makes for a less compelling victim than a trafficked person, and some scholars have even made a moral case *in favor* of smuggling (Achilli 2018; Aloyo and Cusumano 2018). In order to elicit cooperation on the enforcement components of the smuggling protocol in sending states, receiving states have had to provide economic incentives, and where those fail, some receiving states have resorted to economic threats; US president Donald Trump went so far as to threaten Mexico with tariffs for not doing enough to stem the flow of transit migrants from Central America (Haberman and Fandos 2019). The smuggling protocol has not developed into an anti-smuggling regime with a shared normative framework; instead, states have pursued unilateral anti-smuggling enforcement with some quid pro quo cooperation with key sending and transit states, at great expense.

THE INEFFECTIVENESS OF ANTI-SMUGGLING EFFORTS

If the multilateral regime to combat smuggling is little more than quid pro quo cooperation on migration enforcement, it is also ineffective. Anti-smuggling efforts suffer from three vexing challenges. First, given constant demand from migrants wanting to enter destination states, increased border enforcement or restrictions on legal immigration will only increase the demand for smugglers. As crossing borders becomes more dangerous or difficult, more migrants will turn to smugglers. Second, as the penalty for smuggling increases, fewer "regular people" will be willing to help migrants along their journeys. On the trans-Sahel route, for example, truckers who used to be willing to transport migrants along their routes are no longer willing to do so for fear of legal consequences; the reward does not justify the risk (Brachet 2018). Thus, smuggling is increasingly dominated by criminal networks; even if the characterization of human smuggling as transnational organized crime was inaccurate when the Palermo Protocols were drafted, enforcement efforts since then have actively transformed the industry to reflect better this characterization. This makes smuggling both more expensive and more dangerous for migrants (Reitano and Tinti 2015). Both of these factors also make it more likely that smuggled migrants may find themselves trafficked at some point on their journey, either because they must work off their debts to their smugglers or because they are more likely to come in contact with hardened criminal actors, corrupt officials, bandits, or militias. This danger is especially acute when migrants are transiting through unstable states, such as Libya (Aziz, Monzini, and Pastore 2015).

The third challenge is perhaps the most disheartening. When policymakers try to address the humanitarian catastrophes along smuggling routes, they may inadvertently worsen them. One notable example of this is what happened after Italy deployed Operation Mare Nostrum, a search-and-rescue anti-smuggling naval operation, in response to the shipwreck of a smuggling vessel in the Mediterranean that killed over three hundred migrants in 2013. While a laudable humanitarian effort, it led smugglers to take even more risks in the pursuit of higher profits. Instead of aiming to get boats loaded with migrants all the way from Libya to Italy, a 160-nautical-mile journey, smugglers aimed simply to get migrants into international waters, just 12 nautical miles from the Libyan shore, where they would be picked up by the Italians. This meant migrants were overloaded into even less seaworthy vessels, increasing danger for even greater numbers (Reitano and Tinti 2015).

These three challenges are compounded by security crises and economic deprivation in sending states, which push more people to migrate. The largest flows of migrants are often refugees fleeing violent conflict, but other migrants, with a variety of motivations, may join the flow along newly established or expanded routes. Distinguishing between those with legally valid claims to asylum and those with other compelling reasons for migration is exceedingly difficult (Trilling 2018). Anti-smuggling efforts, however, ensnare everyone and make it more difficult for asylum seekers to plead their cases, undermining their legal rights under the refugee regime.

In sum, the prospects for effectively reducing smuggling directly through law enforcement techniques are slim, and it is especially difficult to do so without violating human rights and exacerbating humanitarian crises.

THE WAY FORWARD

Jørgen Carling, in developing his taxonomy of strategies for countering migrant smuggling, writes, "The prospect of united and assertive action makes the fight against migrant smuggling a *seductive focal point* in a policy field that is often fraught with disagreement and incapacity" (Carling 2017: 102). I agree, and I argue that the Palermo Protocols to the UNTOC, in particular, are a manifestation of this "seductive focal point." By embedding these multilateral agreements in the transnational crime regime, anti-trafficking and anti-smuggling policy entrepreneurs were able to muster broad state support, masking serious disagreements between states as well as nonstate actors, particularly around smuggling. As Carling explains, this obscures the variety of motivations for opposing smuggling, claiming common ground for those who seek to protect migrants and those who seek to minimize states' humanitarian obligations, and between those who seek to channel migrants through legal mechanisms for entry and those who want to shut those down as well. Before policymakers can design and then cooperate on effective policy, there must be some clarity about both desired means and ends. Without this, the result is the policy paradox presented by the Palermo Protocols, where the problems are only made worse by the policies meant to address them.

I remain skeptical that there are effective ways to reduce smuggling through the transnational crime framework, especially without severe humanitarian consequences for migrants. The human rights organizations that participated in the negotiations of the smuggling protocol did a good job in ensuring that human rights language became part of the protocol, but this has been ineffectively enforced. At this point, organizations, agencies, and other actors concerned with the human rights of migrants should reject the dominant law enforcement framework and advocate for a policy framework that looks to mitigate the humanitarian consequences of smuggling rather than eliminate smuggling altogether (Carling 2017). Although politically unpopular in many places, expanding pathways for legal migration and facilitating asylum claims rather than evading them would likely be effective ways to undercut smugglers (Achilli and Sanchez 2017). To build political will for such policies, migrant rights activists need to make a concerted effort to rehabilitate the image of the smuggled migrant in the public imagination, shifting blame away from migrants and back toward the states (sending, receiving, and transit) that create the conditions compelling migrants to leave home in the first place and seek the help of smugglers.

There have been particular events that have triggered deep empathy and human concern for migrants, forcing the public to see individual human beings instead of numbers. The drowning death of three-year-old Alan Kurdi, who was found on a Greek beach after the inflatable boat in which he was traveling capsized in 2015, for example, triggered outrage and concern for Syrian refugees. Similarly, the policy of child separation at the US-Mexico border in 2018 galvanized opposition and led to a flood of donations to NGOs working on behalf of migrant rights; one small legal aid organization in Texas took in US$21 million in donations after a Facebook fundraiser went viral (Salmon 2018). To be sure, translating these moments into a sustained campaign for policy change is very difficult, but the best chance of doing this is to focus on domestic policies, not new international obligations. One small place to start, for example, would be to ensure that states are in compliance with the smuggling protocol's provision to decriminalize the smuggling of refugees for humanitarian purposes. While coordinating campaigns across countries can be a useful strategy, the real change will take place within domestic immigration laws. It has been twenty years since the Palermo Protocols were signed; this is the task for the next twenty years.

NOTES

1. There was also a third protocol: the Protocol against the Illicit Manufacturing and Trafficking in Firearms.
2. A regime is a set of rules, norms, and institutions that affect the behavior of states and other actors.
3. The International Agreement for the Suppression of the White Slave Trade was adopted in 1904, ratified by seventy-eight states, and amended in 1947 and 1949.

REFERENCES

Achilli, Luigi. 2018. "The 'Good' Smuggler: The Ethics and Morals of Human Smuggling among Syrians." *ANNALS of the American Academy of Political and Social Science* 676 (March): 77–96.
Achilli, Luigi, and Gabriella Sanchez. 2017. *What Does It Mean to Disrupt the Business Models of People Smugglers?* Policy Brief Issue 2017/9, Migration Policy Centre. http://cadmus.eui.eu/bitstream/handle/1814/46165/PB_2017_09_MPC.pdf?sequence=1.
Aloyo, Eamon, and Eugenio Cusumano. 2018. "Morally Evaluating Human Smuggling: The Case of Migration to Europe." *Critical Review of International Social and Political Philosophy*, online ahead of print, September 28, 2018. https://doi.org/10.1080/13698230.2018.1525118.
American Immigration Council. 2018. *Fact Sheet: Prosecuting Migrants for Coming to the United States.* Washington, DC: American Immigration Council.
Aziz, Nourhan Abdel, Paola Monzini, and Ferruccio Pastore. 2015. *The Changing Dynamics of Cross-Border Human Smuggling and Trafficking in Mediterranean.* Rome: Instituto Affari Internazionali.

Baumgartner, Frank R., and Bryan D. Jones. 1993. *Agendas and Instability in American Politics*. Chicago: University of Chicago Press.

Bennett, William J., and Charles W. Colson. 2000. "The Clintons Shrug at Sex Trafficking." *Wall Street Journal*, January 10, 2000.

Bouteillet-Paquet, Daphné. 2011. *Smuggling of Migrants: A Global Review and Annotated Bibliography of Recent Publications*. New York: United Nations Office on Drugs and Crime.

Brachet, Julien. 2018. "Manufacturing Smugglers: From Irregular to Clandestine Mobility in the Sahara." *ANNALS of the American Academy of Political and Social Science* 676 (March): 16–35.

Brown, Elizabeth Nolan. 2015. "The War on Sex Trafficking Is the New War on Drugs." *Reason*, November 2015. https://reason.com/2015/09/30/the-war-on-sex-trafficking-is/.

Carling, Jørgen. 2017. "How Should Migrant Smuggling Be Confronted?" In *Migration Research Leaders' Syndicate: Ideas to Inform International Cooperation on Safe, Orderly and Regular Migration*, edited by Marie McAuliffe and Michael Klein Solomon, 97–103. Geneva: International Organization for Migration.

CCPCJ (Commission on Crime Prevention and Criminal Justice). 1997. "Report of the Secretary General: Measures to Prevent Trafficking in Children." Doc. e/cn.15/1997/12.

Chacón, Jennifer M. 2006. "Misery and Myopia: Understanding the Failures of U.S. Efforts to Stop Human Trafficking." *Fordham Law Review* 74 (6): 2977–3040.

———. 2010. "Tensions and Trade-Offs: Protecting Trafficking Victims in the Era of Immigration Enforcement." *University of Pennsylvania Law Review* 158 (6): 1609–1653.

Charnysh, Volha, Paulette Lloyd, and Beth A. Simmons. 2015. "Frames and Consensus Formation in International Relations: The Case of Trafficking in Persons." *European Journal of International Relations* 21 (2): 323–351.

Chuang, Janie. 2006. "The United States as Global Sheriff: Using Unilateral Sanctions to Combat Human Trafficking." *Michigan Journal of International Law* 27 (2): 437–494.

Dandurand, Yvon. 2017. "Human Trafficking and Police Governance." *Police Practice and Research* 18 (3): 322–336.

Diba, Parisa, Georgios Papanicolaou, and Georgios A. Antonopoulous. 2019. "The Digital Routes of Human Smuggling? Evidence from the U.K." *Crime Prevention and Community Safety* 21 (2): 159–175.

Ditmore, Melissa, and Marjan Wijers. 2003. "The Negotiations on the UN Protocol on Trafficking in Persons." *Nemesis* 4:79–88.

European Union Agency for Fundamental Rights. 2014. *Criminalisation of Migrants in an Irregular Situation and of Persons Engaging with Them*. Vienna: European Union Agency for Fundamental Rights. https://fra.europa.eu/en/publication/2014/criminalisation-migrants-irregular-situation-and-persons-engaging-them.

Farrell, Amy, Colleen Owens, and Jack McDevitt. 2014. "New Laws but Few Cases: Understanding the Challenges to the Investigation and Prosecution of Human Trafficking Cases." *Crime, Law, and Social Change* 61 (2): 139–168.

Finckenauer, James O., and Jennifer Schrock. 2000. "Human Trafficking: A Growing Criminal Market in the U.S." *Human Trafficking: Data and Documents* 14. http://digitalcommons.unl.edu/humtraffdata/14.

Fitzpatrick, Joan. 2003. "Trafficking as a Human Rights Violation: The Complex Intersection of Legal Frameworks for Conceptualizing and Combatting Trafficking." *Michigan Journal of International Law* 24 (4): 1143–1168.

Gallagher, Anne. 2001. "Human Rights and the New UN Protocols on Trafficking and Migrant Smuggling: A Preliminary Analysis." *Human Rights Quarterly* 23 (4): 975–1004.

———. 2015. "Migrant Smuggling." In *Routledge Handbook on Transnational Criminal Law*, edited by Neil Boister and Robert J. Currie, 187–209. New York: Routledge.

———. 2017. "Whatever Happened to the Migrant Smuggling Protocol?" In *Migration Research Leaders' Syndicate: Ideas to Inform International Cooperation on Safe, Orderly and Regular Migration*, edited by Marie McAuliffe and Michael Klein Solomon, 105–109. Geneva: International Organization for Migration.

Gonzalez-Barrera, Ana, and Phillip Connor. 2019. "Around the World, More Say Immigrants Are a Strength Than a Burden." Pew Research Center, March 14, 2019. https://www.pewresearch.org/global/2019/03/14/around-the-world-more-say-immigrants-are-a-strength-than-a-burden/.

Haberman, Maggie, and Nicholas Fandos. 2019. "Mexico Will Face Tariffs Next Week, Trump Vows." *New York Times*, June 4, 2019. https://www.nytimes.com/2019/06/04/us/politics/mexico-tariffs.html.

Hagan, Jacqueline, and Scott Phillips. 2008. "Border Blunders: The Unanticipated Human and Economic Costs of the U.S. Approach to Immigration Control, 1986–2007." *Criminology and Public Policy* 7 (1): 83–94.

International Council on Human Rights Policy. 2010. *Irregular Migration, Migrant Smuggling and Human Rights: Towards Coherence*. Geneva: International Council on Human Rights Policy. http://lastradainternational.org/doc-center/2819/irregular-migration-migrant-smuggling-and-human-rights-towards-coherence.

Kamhi, Alison, and Rachel Prandini. 2017. "Alien Smuggling: What It Is and How It Can Affect Immigrants." Immigrant Legal Resource Center. https://www.ilrc.org/sites/default/files/resources/alien_smuggling_practice_advisory-20170728.pdf.

Kessler, Glenn. 2015. "The False Claim That Human Trafficking Is a '$9.5 Billion Business' in the United States." *Washington Post*, June 2, 2015.

Koslowski, Rey. 2011. "Economic Globalization, Human Smuggling, and Global Governance." In *Global Human Smuggling: Comparative Perspectives*, 2nd ed., edited by David Kyle and Rey Koslowski, 60–84. Baltimore: Johns Hopkins University Press.

Laczko, Frank. 2003. "Europe Attracts More Migrants from China." *Migration Information Source*, July 2003. https://www.migrationpolicy.org/article/europe-attracts-more-migrants-china.

Liu, Min. 2018. *Migration, Prostitution and Human Trafficking: The Voice of Chinese Women*. New York: Routledge.

Massey, Douglas S., Jorge Durand, and Karen A. Pren. 2016. "Why Border Enforcement Backfired." *American Journal of Sociology* 121 (5): 1557–1600.

McAdam, Marika. 2020. "There's No Human Trafficking or Migrant Smuggling without Organised Crime, the Law Says—and That Matters." openDemocracy, February 26,

2020. https://www.opendemocracy.net/en/beyond-trafficking-and-slavery/theres-no-human-trafficking-or-migrant-smuggling-without-organised-crime-the-law-says-and-that-matters/.

Money, Jeannette, and Sarah P. Lockhart. 2018. *Migration Crises and the Structure of International Cooperation*. Athens: University of Georgia Press.

Monras, Joan. 2018. "Immigration and Wage Dynamics: Evidence from the Mexican Peso Crisis." CEPR Discussion Paper No. DP13394, Centre for Economic Policy Research. https://papers.ssrn.com/sol3/papers.cfm?abstract_id=3302644.

Outshoorn, Joyce, ed. 2004. *The Politics of Prostitution: Women's Movements, Democratic States, and the Globalisation of Sex Commerce*. Cambridge: Cambridge University Press.

Pearce, Jenny J., Patricia Hynes, and Silvie Bovarnick. 2013. *Trafficked Young People: Breaking the Wall of Silence*. London: Routledge.

Pralle, Sarah B. 2003. "Venue Shopping, Political Strategy, and Policy Change: The Internationalization of Canadian Forest Advocacy." *Journal of Public Policy* 23 (3): 233–260.

Protocol against the Smuggling of Migrants by Land, Sea and Air, supplementing the United Nations Convention against Transnational Organized Crime. 2000. New York: United Nations. https://treaties.un.org/pages/ViewDetails.aspx?src=TREATY&mtdsg_no=XVIII-12-b&chapter=18#EndDec.

Reitano, Tuesday, and Peter Tinti. 2015. "Survive and Advance: The Economics of Smuggling Refugees and Migrants into Europe." Institute for Security Studies Paper 289. https://issafrica.org/research/papers/survive-and-advance-the-economics-of-smuggling-refugees-and-migrants-into-europe.

Rosenblum, Marc R., and Doris Meissner. 2014. *The Deportation Dilemma: Reconciling Tough and Humane Enforcement*. Washington, DC: Migration Policy Institute. https://www.migrationpolicy.org/research/deportation-dilemma-reconciling-tough-humane-enforcement.

Salmon, Felix. 2018. "How Is RAICES Handling Its $30 Million Windfall?" *Slate*, July 23, 2018. https://slate.com/business/2018/07/immigration-nonprofit-raices-took-in-usd20-million-from-a-facebook-donation-drive-what-now.html.

Sánchez-Montijano, Elena, and Albert F. Arcarons. 2018. "Southern Europe." In *Migrant Smuggling Data and Research: A Global Review of the Emerging Evidence Base*, edited by Anna Triandafyllidou and Marie McAuliffe, 2:99–122. Geneva: International Organization for Migration.

Schloenhardt, Andreas, and Hamish MacDonald. 2017. "Barriers to the Ratification of the United Nations Protocol against the Smuggling of Migrants." *Asian Journal of International Law* 7 (1): 13–38.

Simmons, Beth, Paulette Lloyd, and Brandon M. Stewart. 2018. "The Global Diffusion of Law: Transnational Crime and the Case of Human Trafficking." *International Organization* 72 (2): 249–281.

Smith, Helena. 2015. "Shocking Images of Drowned Syrian Boy Show Tragic Plight of Refugees." *Guardian*, September 2, 2015. https://www.theguardian.com/world/2015/sep/02/shocking-image-of-drowned-syrian-boy-shows-tragic-plight-of-refugees.

Triandafyllidou, Anna, and Marie McAuliffe. 2018. *Migrant Smuggling Data and Research: A Global Review of the Emerging Evidence Base, Volume 2*. Geneva: International Organization for Migration. https://publications.iom.int/books/migrant-smuggling-data-and-research-global-review-emerging-evidence-base-volume-2.

Trilling, Daniel. 2018. "Five Myths about the Refugee Crisis." *Guardian*, June 5, 2018. https://www.theguardian.com/news/2018/jun/05/five-myths-about-the-refugee-crisis.

UNODC (United Nations Office on Drugs and Crime). 2017. *The Concept of "Financial or Other Material Benefit" in the Smuggling of Migrants Protocol: Issue Paper*. New York: UNODC.

———. 2018. *Global Study on Smuggling Migrants*. United Nations Publication, Sales No. E.18.IV.9. Vienna: UNODC.

Vermeulen, G., Y. Van Damme, and Wendy De Bondt. 2010. "Perceived Involvement of 'Organised Crime' in Human Trafficking and Smuggling." *International Review of Penal Law* 81 (1): 247–173.

Zhang, Sheldon X. 2009. "Beyond the 'Natasha' Story—a Review and Critique of Current Research on Sex Trafficking." *Global Crime* 10 (3): 178–195.

CHAPTER 5

Human Smuggling and Terrorism
COMPLEX ADAPTIVE SYSTEMS AND SPECIAL OPERATIONS

David C. Ellis

FOLLOWING SEPTEMBER 11, 2001, US Special Operations Forces (SOF) were charged by the Department of Defense with leading its counterterrorism and counternetwork missions to protect the homeland against a potential weapons of mass destruction attack by terrorists, with obvious implications for working with US domestic law enforcement agencies on human smuggling. As with law enforcement, SOF have been unable to eliminate human smuggling networks and have embarked on a process to discover why. This chapter asserts that a counternetwork approach to human smuggling prevents SOF from being able to differentiate between actors with nefarious intent and those without, resulting in a dilution of capability and resources. Instead, human smuggling dynamics can be better appreciated and interpreted if perceived from a complex adaptive systems perspective, which reorients the analysis on the relationships between different kinds of actors and the structural incentives driving nonnefarious and nefarious actors together. Doing so enables SOF to concentrate their resources and capabilities on actual threat actors and contribute to devising potential interventions in other areas of the system to diminish the structural incentives for human smuggling and dangerous criminal groups to work together. Although nascent, SOF are beginning to adopt a complex adaptive systems perspective of counternetwork operations, and human smuggling represents an important case for changing its approach.

According to the existing joint publications *Counterterrorism* and *Countering Threat Networks* (counternetwork), the challenges for SOF are to (a) determine which networks of human smugglers are likely to enable or directly support terrorist operations and (b) eliminate the networks to remove the threat to the homeland, defined here as any citizen or property residing in the country's fifty states. US Special Operations Command was assigned coordinating authority for the military's counterterrorism operations in 2016 and provides the main operational-level support for this challenge (Congressional Research Service 2018). Due to statutory restrictions, SOF do not engage in operations in the homeland or send troops to patrol the border but can provide materiel, higher-level analysis, and information on potential threats to law enforcement at multiple levels of government. A key problem is that SOF are trained to think in linear terms and plan around decisive operations based on doctrine in joint publications. Complex adaptive systems, on the other hand, frustrate traditional military planning and doctrine because the agents and organizations constituting them have the freedom of maneuver, agency, and creativity to change how the systems as a whole behave.

The chapter proceeds in four sections. First, it describes why the joint publications *Counterterrorism* and *Countering Threat Networks* orient SOF human smuggling analysis on disrupting, degrading, and destroying networks at the expense of first recognizing the system-level dynamics at play. Second, it explores the literature on human smuggling, which suggests that perceiving it as a complex adaptive system could result in a more productive mindset for counterterrorism and counternetwork activities since human smuggling networks demonstrate extraordinary creativity and agency in the face of opposition. Third, the chapter describes how border securitization efforts without concomitant immigration reforms have made criminal networks "antifragile"—that is, resilient against pressure—and contributed to SOF's difficulties in analyzing how suspected terrorists, or special interest aliens (SIAs), might leverage human smuggling networks. Finally, it illustrates how SOF are creatively adapting to complex adaptive system dynamics and using institutional influence and agency to reimagine how they can most effectively intervene in social systems.

Readers will note the use of the terms *nonnefarious* and *nefarious networks* in this chapter. While many US federal agencies are charged with securing the border against these organizations as part of the government's exercise of sovereign control (US Immigration and Customs Enforcement 2017), SOF are only interested in human smuggling to the extent that individuals and organizations have the desire to conduct attacks against the homeland. Economically motivated individuals, asylum seekers, and refugees are here described as nonnefarious and are not a concern to SOF, *unless they are implicated in plots against the homeland.* There is robust scholarship indicating that many individuals involved in human smuggling, if not the majority, consider themselves, and their clients, to be community-oriented, helpful, and otherwise rule-abiding people whose limited labor opportunities, on the one hand, and limited legal mobility opportunities, on the other, require resorting to illegal activity (Achilli 2018: 79–83, 85; Kyle and Dale 2001: 47; Sanchez 2015: 3–4, 6, 52; Triandafyllidou 2018: 217–218; Zhang 2008: 4, 34; Zhang, Sanchez, and Achilli 2018: 13–14; Zhao 2013: 52). Many are asylum seekers facing grave risk by remaining in their home regions. In a number of ethnographic studies, kin-based human smugglers often specifically reject the amoral, pejorative terms associated with human smuggling, such as the Mexican *coyote*, Chinese *triad*, or Italian *mafioso*, as do their clients (Maher 2018: 41, 44; Sanchez 2015: 14–15, 53; Zhang 2008: 41).

Nefarious actors include drug smugglers, violent syndicates, human traffickers intending to enslave migrants, criminal gangs, their witting enablers, and, of course, terrorists. Official government and international organization discourses on human smuggling networks often conflate them with these more structured organizations (Finckenauer 2001: 145; Kook 2018: 116; Majidi 2018: 97; Sanchez 2015: 16, 22; Zhang, Sanchez, and Achilli 2018: 8; Zhao 2013: 3), and laws tend to assume they lie at the heart of the phenomenon (Sanchez 2015: 2; Zhang, Sanchez, and Achilli 2018: 8, 13). While some scholars have argued that securitization of borders has caused a convergence of nonnefarious and nefarious actors due to the costs and logistics now necessary (Andreas 2001: 119), others conclude that in most cases they only share limited geographical space instead of integrated operational infrastructure (Kyle and Koslowski 2001: 11; Sanchez and Zhang 2018: 146–149). In other words, distinguishing between individuals with nonnefarious and nefarious intent, despite both acting in a way that is de jure criminal (Human Smuggling and Trafficking Center 2013: 4–5), is a prerequisite for SOF to conduct accurate analysis on true terrorist threats. Though admittedly imperfect, the terms *nonnefarious* and *nefarious* are offered here as an attempt at framing the differences for SOF.

HUMAN SMUGGLING AND THE COUNTERNETWORK PARADIGM

To the US government, human smuggling presents a prima facie terrorist threat corridor, or avenue of approach, since human smugglers by definition demonstrate a willingness to break US laws and find vulnerabilities in border enforcement measures. It is not a tremendous leap in logic to assume that smugglers willing to transport economically motivated migrants, drugs, and gang members might also be willing to transport, wittingly or unwittingly, individuals with nefarious intent against the homeland. This has been the operating assumption of the US government more broadly since at least 2000 (Kyle and Dale 2001: 30–31). Some scholars conclude that US government policy and security approaches have prompted, or actually produced, a merging of human smuggling and criminal syndicates, though it is unclear whether this is an inadvertent policy effect or part of a counternetwork strategy to increase their traceability and signature (Kyle and Dale 2001: 31; Maher 2018: 48–49). Individuals suspected of posing a threat to the homeland are labeled SIAs. Although no SIAs have perpetrated successful terrorist attacks against the US homeland (Bier and Nowrasteh 2018), the absence of evidence is not necessarily evidence of the absence of their intent.

An SIA is defined as "a non-U.S. person who, based on an analysis of travel patterns, potentially poses a national security risk to the United States or its interests. Often such individuals or groups [employ] travel patterns known or evaluated to possibly have a nexus to terrorism" (Department of Homeland Security 2019). SIAs, along with known or suspected terrorists, have become a significant concern for US law enforcement and military personnel since the 1993 bombing of the World Trade Center, the attack on September 11, 2001, and other attacks by Salafi-jihadists in the homeland. Additionally, individuals affiliated with the Iran-backed Lebanese Hezbollah are known to operate in Latin America, and hundreds of individuals from countries in which terrorist organizations operate are routinely arrested at the US border each year (Homeland Security Committee 2019: 6–11). This reality raises the issue of how SIAs might gain entry to the United States with the intent to engage in terrorist attacks.

To bring coherence to the approaches and capabilities the different services bring to military challenges, the Joint Chiefs of Staff in the Department of Defense issue joint publications to provide the force with baseline vocabulary and doctrine. SIAs and human smuggling are predominantly covered by Joint Publication 3-25, *Countering Threat Networks* (Joint Chiefs of Staff 2016), but Joint Publication 3-26, *Counterterrorism* (Joint Chiefs of Staff 2014), also applies due to the known linkages between terrorist organizations and other kinds of threat networks, such as smugglers and money launderers. Both publications are heavily influenced by the counterterrorism operations of the 2000s through which the US military, SOF in particular, successfully adapted to nonhierarchical, network-centric warfare after years of difficulty (McChrystal et al. 2015; Schultz 2016). For decades the US military focused its analysis of the enemy on traditional, hierarchical orders of battle with special attention to the adversary's center of gravity (COG), which, according to military theory, is the opposition's most significant, massed asset and, if identified, can be attacked to cause its decisive defeat (Clausewitz 1984: 595–596; Joint Chiefs of Staff 2017: IV-23–IV-28).

Terrorist operations in Iraq, Somalia, Afghanistan, and other places defied COG analysis and the US military found itself constantly reacting to a perpetually adaptive enemy. Leaders realized they needed new ideas for operating against distributed, cellular organizations (McChrystal et al. 2015: 24–28). By 2006–2007, concepts and tactics, techniques, and procedures on how to combat terrorist networks crystallized, and SOF transformed as an enterprise to provide a dynamic and rapidly adaptive counterterrorism capability that led ultimately to the defeat of Al-Qaeda in Iraq and the restoration of government control in Iraq (Schultz 2016: 66–71).

Importantly, the experience also demonstrated that terrorist organizations rely on a host of witting, unwitting, illicit, and licit organizations that together form networks of enablers. Witting, illicit networks are generically identified as threat networks and typically consist of suppliers, recruiters, transporters, financiers, criminal enterprises, and communication specialists, among others. The commonality is that many of these organizations are part of the fabric of the society in which they operate, so terrorist and threat networks sometimes have direct linkages and utility to the population (Joint Chiefs of Staff 2016: I3–I5). For the joint publications on counterterrorism and counternetwork, the objective is to deny, disrupt, degrade, or destroy the networks in order to take them off the battlefield and enable the government to restore law and order (Joint Chiefs of Staff 2014: IV11–IV13; 2016: IV19–IV21). Nefarious networks are typically framed as security problems to be addressed by police and military forces.

The overt assumption is that the relevant unit of analysis is the network: identify the terrorist or threat network, determine its COG, attack the COG via its vulnerabilities to defeat it, and work with local authorities to fill the void (Joint Chiefs of Staff 2014: IV9, IV11; 2016: III2, III7). While joint doctrine recognizes that networks demonstrate highly adaptive behavior and are therefore difficult to combat (Joint Chiefs of Staff 2016: III2), making the network the unit of analysis obscures the broader social dynamics at play. In other words, the roles of witting, unwitting, illicit, and licit enablers are analyzed through the lens of how the network utilizes them, not why the enablers exist in the first place or how the threat network might establish some degree of utility to the population through which it operates. In military terms, joint doctrine focuses the analysis on the operational to tactical levels, while the strategic level—framed here as the structures of politics, society, and culture—is generally overlooked.

Unfortunately, the social systems in which networks are embedded become obscured because the military thinks it has discussions about the strategic level but, when viewed from the social sciences, effectively does not. The strategic level, from the social systems frame, would consciously explore the world views, mental models, identity constructs, social structures, relationships, and patterns of interaction on which networks draw for generating ideas, social meaning, resources, and personnel. Indeed, for many years, scholars working with US military and security forces on modeling terrorism purposefully avoided researching and modeling the social systems from which networks arise precisely because they are fuzzy and their effects unknowable. They instead reinforced the focus on operational-level networks. Drawing on complexity theory and complex adaptive system modeling techniques, these scholars argued that it would be impossible to gain perfect knowledge about all potential terrorists individually without an oppressive state security apparatus and that strategic-level policy modeling introduces too many unknowns into the equation, with the effect of producing unhelpful "academic speculation" (Vos Fellman 2015: 12). The most fruitful area to model in combatting terrorism or threat networks, they argued, is at the midrange level where organizational behavior and interests can be more readily discerned, mapped, and projected based on past behavior and probabilistic formulas (Mesjasz 2015: 62–63; Vos Fellman 2015: 11–13). As currently understood, eliminating potential terrorist threats to the homeland posed by human smuggling is, therefore, a matter of breaking the networks of smugglers more rapidly than they can reconstitute (Joint Chiefs of Staff 2014: V3–V5; 2016: V12–V13).

The problem for SOF lies with the fact that nowadays so many nonnefarious human smuggling actors have some nexus with nefarious threat networks. In some cases, previously legal activity in other countries came to be viewed as part of the human smuggling chain and was consequently criminalized, often with external political pressure (Brachet 2018: 22). For example, Peter Andreas (2001: 110) and Gabriella Sanchez (2015: 34) note that families on either side of the US-Mexico border would frequently cross without incident early in the twentieth century, but as the borders hardened and flows intensified, border communities with kin-based smuggling networks became essential waypoints in increasingly sophisticated crossing strategies. Similarly, Julien Brachet (2018: 17, 21) notes how Nigerien companies in Agadez legally supported regional labor transportation for years until the European Union identified it as a hub of human smuggling to Europe and successfully pressured the Nigerien authorities to criminalize the industry. While individual violent criminals sometimes become involved in the human smuggling business (Spener 2001: 155–156; von Lampe 2016: 74) and even kin-based networks might turn to criminal syndicates to enforce payment pledges (Zhang 2008: 87), to date scholars tend to conclude that human smuggling networks remain predominantly nonnefarious in terms of threat to the homeland (Brachet 2018: 26; Guevara González 2018: 188; Kook 2018: 122; Sanchez and Zhang 2018: 148–149; Stone-Cadena and Álvarez Velasco 2018: 205; Zhang 2008: 155, 162–164). Unfortunately, every actor now involved in the chain becomes a threat by virtue of the interaction with criminal syndicates, which dilutes SOF's ability to determine where and how to orient their resources and capabilities against truly nefarious networks.

SOF's general approach to counterterrorism and counternetwork shares many similarities with how scholars describe police approaches to human smuggling. Sanchez, who worked with police as a court translator, notes, "I found out the focus of investigations like these was never to develop an understanding of smuggling's dynamics, but simply to arrest as many 'operators' as possible" (Sanchez 2015: 7). David Kyle and Rey Koslowski (2001: 6) note that officials emphasize increasing the number of border agents, eliminating forgery rings, and increasing penalties for involvement in human smuggling. Brachet (2018: 23) even notes that France supported Nigerien security forces with biometric screening equipment and training in Agadez only to realize that towns and villages nearby could not support such capacity due to the lack of electricity. The progressively expanding police and surveillance methods used to combat illegal immigration and human smuggling have resulted in increased costs to migrants, significantly larger border security and enforcement forces, more detention facilities, and a rationale for nefarious actors to become engaged in the activity due to their influence over key territory (Spener 2001: 143–144). Despite this buildup, there remain gaps in enforcement and relatively low probability for migrants and smugglers to be charged with penalties severe enough to deter the activity (147). James Finckenauer observed years ago that human smuggling networks, which tend to be nonhierarchical and susceptible to frequent personnel changes, "are not particularly vulnerable to the strategies and tactics designed to counter genuine organized crime. Use of such techniques as informants, undercover agents, and wiretapping, or (in the United States) of the RICO (Racketeer Influenced and Corrupt Organizations Act) statute, for example, assumes a degree of continuity both over time and over crimes" (2001: 170). These techniques are highly analogous to the ones SOF employ in their counterterrorism and counternetwork activities, but police have yet to discover anything approaching a COG.

A systems-level approach to human smuggling instead explores how a network interjects itself into a preexisting series of relationships and interactions to determine where it brings utility—or not—to specific actors or groups in the overall system of migration. Instead of presuming a priori that actors engaged in human smuggling have nefarious intent, a systems-level approach actually asks the opposite question: To what extent do organizations with nefarious or criminal intent positively or negatively influence the operations of actors engaged in nonnefarious human smuggling? A related question might be, to what extent are migrants who originate from areas with no history of inherent nefarious intent against the US government, infrastructure, or population incentivized or forced to work with criminal organizations as a result of current immigration policy and border security procedures? These questions by nature suggest divergence of experience, a sensitivity to deeper sociocultural dynamics in the country of origin and transit, and an emphasis on analyzing a threat actor's position in the broader system.

The benefit of this perspective is that it enables analysts to start the process of differentiating and categorizing types of actors, their general interests, and their general fears and concerns. While human smugglers are engaged in an activity that results in a violation of US law once individuals cross the border without US government permission, not all actors in the human smuggling system break the law in their own countries, and indeed they find themselves in tension with true threat actors. A systems-level approach to SIAs would seek to leverage these tensions and create alternative incentives at the strategic, policy level to draw the nonnefarious actors away from nefarious ones instead of incentivizing them to work together. But first, it is necessary to determine whether human smuggling fits the military's paradigm of networks with a COG that can be identified, attacked, and defeated. If so, a social systems approach would be unnecessary for SOF.

HUMAN SMUGGLING AS A COMPLEX ADAPTIVE SYSTEM

Academic research on human smuggling suggests, contrary to most government and international organization representations, that human smuggling networks resemble "crime that is organized" instead of organized crime (Finckenauer 2001: 168, 172). The term *organized crime* is associated with criminal structures with hierarchy, chains of command, and generally stable revenue flows that operate in relatively predictable environments. Organized criminal syndicates often involve predatory crimes where individuals are harmed by the activity and are described in this chapter as nefarious actors. *Crime that is organized* is associated with criminal structures with loose connections between actors (i.e., networks), cooperative agreements, and emergent opportunities for financial gain that operate in unpredictable circumstances (von Lampe 2016: 93–97). Criminal networks often become involved in market-based crimes for which the government has deemed a product or service illegal though demand still exists. Human smuggling generally fits this description. Whereas an organized crime syndicate generates the hierarchy to identify a COG, crime that is organized does not. As a result, Klaus von Lampe concludes "that the traditional approach of *reactive policing*, acting upon reported incidents of crime, is less relevant against market-based crime. The policing of market-based crime, instead, depends much more on *proactive policing*. This means that law enforcement agencies have to allocate scarce resources and mobilize community support for actively seeking out illegal market places and illegal market participants (see Abadinsky, 2013, p. 378; Albanese, 2011, p. 255; Chapter 14)" (2016: 75). This distinction is critical for SOF as they develop approaches for dealing with SIAs who attempt to enter the United States through human smuggling networks. The following characteristics of human smuggling elucidate the challenge SOF face.

DECENTRALIZED NETWORKS
Human smuggling as an experience typically consists of numerous small-scale cells performing specialized tasks as migrants move from location to location until they reach their destinations. Included in this network might be legal businesses, corrupt officials, nonmigrant violent criminals, and illegal but nonviolent businesses (Kyle and Dale 2001: 53). Along the chain there might be small organizations that reflect a degree of permanence and hierarchy (Spener 2001: 138), but the overall experience is one of loose affiliation based on emergent circumstances. Scholars involved in ethnographic research on human smuggling describe it as amorphous, community based with strong family and friendship connections, flexible and independent in operations, and small scale with low investment (Achilli 2018: 85; Brachet 2018: 29; Kook 2018: 124; Sanchez 2015: 11, 52–54; Zhang 2008: 108). Victoria Stone-Cadena and Soledad Álvarez Velasco (2018: 205) describe the experience as a "relay race" where migrants are passed on to locally knowledgeable smugglers based on the paths that seem least threatening at a given point in time. Many scholars also report that it is common for nodes in the network to only know the people in the chain immediately before them and after them, with the structure of the overall network remaining a mystery

(Sanchez 2015: 54-55). The decentralized nature of the network results in no appreciable hierarchy or planning logic underlying coherent operations. Instead, the networks cohere based on the desire for future opportunity, norms of behavior and reciprocity, and personal ties (von Lampe 2016: 128).

AD HOC TEAMS
As an industry, human smuggling is ideally suited for ad hoc teams since many of the specialty components of the experience are low skill in nature, which makes for ease of entry and exit as participants see fit. Typical service areas include recruiting, sheltering, financing, chauffeuring, feeding, guiding, and transporting migrants (Brachet 2018: 20-21; Sanchez 2015: 58; Zhang 2008: 113-117). The fluid nature of the networks is in part due to real-time adaptation to changes in border enforcement, individual smuggler and migrant decisions related to risk-reward calculations, weather conditions, ability to finance the trip, and the composition of trusted networks (Kyle and Dale 2001: 32-33; Sanchez 2015: 52; von Lampe 2016: 154-155; Zhang 2008: 124). It is common, for example, for drivers to repay their smuggling fees by completing the assigned role, but invite friends who are recent arrivals to assist to earn extra money. In this way, human smuggling is crime that is organized to the extent that individuals know how they fit as cogs in the machinery of smuggling, but the changing composition of the players prevents a determination of a COG that can break the machine. The combination of decentralized networks with ad hoc teams amplifies the agency and initiative of the migrants who are often motivated by a chance for a better life. With the potential gains of living in freer systems comparing favorably against the risk of capture and the loss of freedom, the allure of smuggling for a short period maintains the industry's viability.

VARIABLE FINANCING
Smuggling exists because an authority deemed trade in a good or service illegal, often a formerly legal activity or trade, which means there is likely to be a penalty associated with getting caught in the act (Andreas 2001: 117; Sanchez 2015: 50; Zhang, Sanchez, and Achilli 2018: 13). The threat of penalty results in a risk premium for those engaged in the activity. This risk premium incentivizes people to engage in the activity to earn profit, ensuring a persistent

pool of people willing to risk the punishment (Sanchez 2015: 51; Stone-Cadena and Álvarez Velasco 2018: 204; Zhang 2008: 33). Risk premiums grow higher the more that authorities seek to eliminate the activity, but despite increasing costs, the smuggling system always seems able to adapt due to variable financing mechanisms.

Financing schemes in human smuggling vary depending on the local circumstances of the sending population and the possibility of payment by friends and family in the receiving country. These financing schemes serve two functions. First, migrants often leave their home countries due to a lack of opportunity and income potential. The various financing techniques reflect local sociocultural norms regarding compensation and credit for helping family and friends achieve a better life (Maher 2018: 37–42; Zhao 2013: 1–2, 22). Second, the financing schemes are often designed to incentivize smugglers to safely deliver the migrant to the agreed-on destination (Andreas 2001: 118; Majidi 2018: 107). Where possible, a migrant or the migrant's family will pay the full cost of the trip in increments, often through the use of intermediaries like *hawala* (money transfer networks popular in Muslim societies) or informal banking arrangements similar to an escrow agreement (Majidi 2018: 107–108; Zhao 2013: 2). When not possible, a mixture of working off the debt and obtaining loans from family is common. Studies of both Mexican and Chinese smuggling operations suggest that the variable financing schemes, especially including family loans and debt bondage, have undermined enforcement-based cost increases because, as a relative matter, the burden compares favorably to their home experiences (Mengiste 2018: 70; Spener 2001: 152; Zhang 2008: 86). Moreover, it is also common for smugglers to offer up to three crossing attempts as a guarantee against potential capture (Kyle and Dale 2001). Once again, the smugglers demonstrate their agency as part of the complex adaptive system by introducing a creative, low-cost, market-based solution to increased border enforcement. They dropped the risk to financing by increasing the odds of successful passage given limited penalties for crossing illegally.

LEGAL ANCHORS

Complicating the identification of nefarious networks is the fact that many illegal immigrants are aided by family, friends, or other communities with long-standing cross-border interactions with the receiving country. Illegal immigration across the US southern border, for example, results both from historical cultural, social, and economic ties between Mexican and US border communities (Sanchez 2015: 34, 40; Spener 2001: 131–132) and from the Bracero Program sponsored by the US federal government from 1942 to 1964, which institutionalized US employer-immigrant labor patterns that persist to this day (Andreas 2001: 109–110). Similarly, Chinese immigration from Canton (Guangdong) and Fujian Provinces in the mid- to late nineteenth century in support of the Western railroad lines was rendered illegal by the end of the century, resulting in illegal immigration pathways through Canada and Mexico (Zhang 2008: 6–8). This characteristic is found outside the US context as well. Female North Korean illegal immigrants to China are often aided by family members who are legal residents in China and who serve as marriage brokers for the women and rural Chinese men (Kook 2018: 120–121, 125). Eritrean migrants are assisted by family members and guides who fled the war for independence with Ethiopia decades ago, but now provide the infrastructure for the sometimes yearslong journey to new destinations (Mengiste 2018: 59–61). Some legal anchors have been subsequently criminalized, such as with the legal migration industry in Niger that contributed heavily to the Agadez economy but that was criminalized under heavy pressure by the European Union (Brachet 2018: 20).

LEGAL BUSINESS AS COVER

As a result of the legal anchors, migrants often have assistance navigating the obstacles to the receiving country. For instance, the Fujianese illegal immigrant community benefits enormously from a thriving business district in New York City with travel agencies, low-skill food and manufacturing infrastructure, and business and social ties across the United States (Zhao 2013: 30–31). In other instances, travel agencies in the sending countries can freely prepare travel arrangements up to the point of the actual crossing without fear of reprisal (Brachet 2018: 21; Kyle and Goldstein 2011). Legal businesses have the ability to gain specialized skills, identify gaps or weaknesses in the migration and importation systems, probe for viability, and exploit for effect. As noted earlier, it is impossible for resource-constrained immigration, customs and border, and police agencies to cover all areas of activity, so legal businesses will be able over time to devise new, viable approaches to human smuggling so long as the demand persists.

More significantly, many scholars note that it is impossible to attack the COG of human smuggling because "most of their members are not engaged in the transportation of migrants on U.S. territory in areas that are heavily patrolled by the immigration authorities" (Spener 2001: 133). Waypoint countries sometimes benefit from temporary migration through their territory by issuing work permits or tourist visas, which provides time and cover for adaptive strategies to emerge (Zhang 2008: 66). Migrant guides sometimes have residency papers for multiple countries through which they might pass, enabling them to avoid immigration control points (Guevara González 2018: 182–183). In other cases, entire communities benefit economically from the migrant business, causing authorities to tread lightly on enforcement (Achilli 2018: 84; Guevara González 2018: 183).

Attacking a COG through either military or police action consequently requires the permission and cooperation of foreign authorities and an alignment of policy aims. In short, it is not practical or possible to attack the COG of a network when the underlying activity is legal in a host country because the law enforcement, military, and financial intervention options are rendered inert. Human smugglers consequently have the freedom of movement to adapt to changes in enforcement, which increases their agency and initiative in the system.

GOVERNMENT CORRUPTION OR DEFERENCE

An unfortunate consequence of increased costs associated with border enforcement is that the risk premium also invites government corruption. Whether in the United States or sending or waypoint countries, human smuggling networks can extract larger bribe funds from migrants, which contributes to the general breakdown of enforcement regimes (Andreas 2001: 121; Kook 2018: 123; Mengiste 2018: 68; Zhang 2008: 67). If interdiction and dismantling require the support of foreign governments, then the complications created by increased incentive for corruption stand to weaken enforcement efforts. At a minimum, the complexity and political challenges associated with negotiating enforcement priorities with foreign countries are problem enough, but adding corruption to the mix diminishes enforcement initiatives even further.

STRONG DEMAND

Whereas Western official government discourse often portrays the decision by migrants to become involved in human smuggling as a choice between certain life at home and possible death abroad, for migrants the decision is often the exact opposite—certain death or persistent misery at home over possible life abroad (Achilli 2018: 89; Kook 2018: 115–120; Mengiste 2018: 62). For this basic reason, the demand for smuggling services remains strong. Though human smuggling was a relatively low-value industry before the 1980s due to lax enforcement, it has since the 1990s become a multibillion-dollar, global one (Kyle and Koslowski 2001: 4; Zhang, Sanchez, and Achilli 2018: 8). Scholars note that smugglers are very often seen by migrants not as criminals but as a means for opportunity beyond what they could otherwise achieve at home. Their utility is in providing a modicum of protection against potential violence and death along perilous, largely unknown roads, a function that would normally be served by states through the issuance of official passports but that is unavailable to migrants who knowingly migrate illegally (Majidi 2018: 98; Mengiste 2018: 59; Sanchez 2015: 22–23; Zhang, Sanchez, and Achilli 2018: 8). Until the costs and penalties for engaging in the practice elevate even further, especially for employers who often have jobs waiting for the migrants, it is unlikely that demand will slow in the near term (Koslowski 2001: 350–351). But with a market that includes loans and family in receiving countries willing to help pay, the question becomes, can authorities ratchet costs up high enough? In addition, increasing the risk premium may perversely incentivize new actors willing to enter the often muddy social norms and legal structures of smuggling actions, especially those overtly helping some escape untenable dangers and persecution in home regions.

FLEXIBLE TIMING

Flexible timing is an essential element for adaptive strategies because it gives smuggling networks the "ability to change routes and destinations in order to overcome obstacles placed in their way by states. In a sense, the smugglers gather and process information about the weak links in terms of transportation systems, border controls, and liberal visa and asylum policies and then provide it to their customers" (Koslowski 2001: 350; Maher 2018: 48; Mengiste 2018: 64, 71). In addition to law enforcement, migrants and their guides must also be wary of threats from violent criminal organizations and armed bandits who see them as targets of opportunity (Guevara González 2018: 189). In other cases, migrants might have to work off debts at waypoints along the path to their ultimate destination (Mengiste 2018: 58). Flexible timing is a crucial aspect of the human smuggling experience nowadays because heightened challenges can only be overcome with informed risk taking, but this raises the overall cost of the journey. Here the agency resides with both the smuggler and the migrant. Each calculates the risk-reward balance of attempting a crossing at particular times and places, and the inherent variability in the determination leads to systemic unpredictability. While patterns of decision-making might emerge, smuggler creativity in devising new paths, different tolerances for personal risk in seeking freedom, and variations in crossing timelines make a COG in the system impossible to discern.

ADAPTIVE STRATEGIES

Despite significant legislative reform in 1986, major crackdowns and international initiatives in the mid-1990s, and increasing penalties in subsequent years (Sanchez 2015: 37), human smuggling and illegal immigration remain vibrant in both the United States and Europe. It is clear from the literature that human smuggling is a highly adaptive enterprise, largely due to the decentralized nature of the system. Where enforcement and government attention are applied, human smuggling can be impeded, but the record shows that smuggling is often displaced, or reconfigured, rather than completely eliminated. For instance, stepped-up enforcement in urban areas of Texas and California redirected illegal immigration to the deserts along the US southern border (Andreas 2001: 115; Sanchez 2015: 40). Similarly, Chinese migrants to the United States utilized oceangoing vessels for years until the *Golden Venture* incident in 1993 revealed the technique, which redirected smuggling networks toward Central America and Eastern Europe (Zhao 2013: 77). Increased European Union pressure on trans-Sahel migration has also pushed migrants into dangerous desert routes (Brachet 2018: 27), and some smugglers have turned to dangerous methods of transportation in the effort to move their customers clandestinely (Maher 2018: 49).

In contrast to the idea of hierarchical, organized crime models of human smuggling, scholars have found that human smuggling networks are highly adaptive precisely because nearly every aspect of the industry is organized for emergent opportunities. Tekalign Ayalew Mengiste describes human smuggling networks as *communities of knowledge*, which "refer to the diverse and dynamic strategies collectively devised and mobilized by migrants, their co-travelers, families and friends settled *en route* and in the diaspora, and friendly strangers and diverse facilitators to reduce risks in clandestine journeys and who allow for successful transits, while not discounting the violence and suffering encountered by migrants and refugees on their paths" (2018: 63). The smuggling networks provide the ground sensing for opportunity in their areas and exploit for effect when windows of opportunity open for their clients. Instead of carefully planned, linear, detailed trips, migrant paths are almost always nonlinear, sensitive to changing weather and policing patterns, and dependent on an infrastructure of ad hoc teams of smugglers (Brachet 2018: 27; Mengiste 2018: 63–67).

Law enforcement, like SOF, functions on the basis of structured, linear planning (Sanchez 2015: 48) and must do so in order to meet statutory obligations for criminal proceedings. Instead of cracking the networks, increased enforcement has driven them underground and into the clandestine world, where it has become harder to comprehend how they function and how they relate to nefarious actors (Andreas 2001: 116; Brachet 2018: 28). The adaptive nature of human smuggling makes identifying a COG an impossible effort since one truly does not exist at the operational level.

CREDIBILITY AND TRUSTWORTHINESS

While there is certainly a range of human smuggling experiences, from kinship- and reputation-based networks to purely profit-oriented criminal enterprises (Kyle and Koslowski 2001: 2, 9; Stone-Cadena and Álvarez Velasco 2018: 206), scholars tend to conclude that the majority of migrants rely on reputation and credibility as key determinants in their choice of network (Zhang, Sanchez, and Achilli 2018: 9–10). Government depictions often create a good/bad distinction, but many migrants view the distinction as the right/wrong smuggler to the extent a choice is even possible with constrained information (Kook 2018: 127; Majidi 2018: 104). The argument holds that human smuggling is, in general, an economic activity in which repeat business only comes in the form of new customers since most stay at their destination. Failure to safely deliver customers, especially those from small communities, could certainly result in the loss of business altogether, but, more importantly, blatant uncaring would violate the moral economy of human smuggling that serves to bind migrant and smuggler in a social compact beyond the financial transaction (Stone-Cadena and Álvarez Velasco 2018: 205; Zhang 2008: 45; Zhao 2013: 74–75). These mutual bonds of trust and credibility are also essential for financing the journeys, since contracts are unenforceable through legal channels, apart from legally collateralized financing schemes (Kyle and Goldstein 2011; Zhang 2008: 47, 144–145; Zhao 2013: 71–72).

ON COMPLEX ADAPTIVE SYSTEMS AND THE COG

Remember for a moment that counterterrorism and counternetwork doctrine orient SOF toward a network's COG, which in theory can be identified, attacked, and defeated. In a network frame, this means identifying key nodes, disrupting their communications, and dismantling their connections faster than they can reconstitute. Yet the characteristics of human smuggling strongly indicate that the networks resemble crime that is organized with a structure especially suited to adapting to systemic stress. While individual nodes and discrete networks might be vulnerable to detection and elimination, the system overall demonstrates extraordinary resilience in the face of pressure due to built-in adaptiveness at nearly every point along the service chain. Human smuggling is a model complex adaptive system for which COG analysis is poorly suited unless truly nefarious actors can be easily distinguished from nonnefarious ones.

Complex adaptive systems present particular challenges because their characteristics defy prediction due to the innumerable relationships available to them at any given moment. Networks exist in open systems, meaning the boundaries of interaction between actors are always in flux, resulting in new opportunities for information transfer and novel behaviors. Complex adaptive systems are particularly interesting because the actors have the capacity to learn and proactively change their preferences and interests (Buckley, Schwandt, and Goldstein 2008: 93–94). Under such conditions, it is impossible to fully model the interactions that constitute the broader system because the underlying variables can always proactively decide to change (Bousquet and Curtis 2011: 47). As Antoine Bousquet and Simon Curtis note, "Self-organization is a key property of open systems. 'Self-organization' refers to the process by which the autonomous interaction of individual entities results in the bottom-up emergence of complex systems. In the absence of centralized authority, the spontaneous appearance of patterned order results from the interaction of the parts of the system as they react to the flow of resources through the system. Self-organization is thus closely related to the concepts of feedback, learning and self-regulation" (47). The key driver of complexity in social systems is emergence, which is the creation of a new social entity as a result of new combinations of actors in the system (47). Emergence tends to happen from the bottom up and on the margins, but it can transform systemic behavior due to the impact of feedback loops (55). What brings these actors and networks into contact to create emergent behavior varies, but certainly policy, technology, and pressure due to securitization are relevant factors. While SOF, and law enforcement more generally, aim to destroy networks, they often just de-structure the relationships for a period of time. But in a complex adaptive system, this simply means that new linkages among the remaining components are likely to reform so long as there is an impetus for the activity to continue (53).

ANTIFRAGILE HUMAN SMUGGLING NETWORKS: A NIGHTMARE OF OUR OWN MAKING?

Scholars have for decades recognized the unintentionally symbiotic relationship between human smuggling and enforcement-based approaches to counter human smuggling (Andreas 2001: 108; Koslowski 2001: 338; Kyle and Dale 2001: 30; Triandafyllidou 2018: 214–215). The inadvertent consequence of the law enforcement approach to human smuggling has been the creation of a self-sustaining industry of clandestine smuggling network–law enforcement gamesmanship that continuously ratchets up the complexity and cost of operations (Brachet 2018: 31). There is a correlation between human smuggling and enforcement, but it is inverse and this should be alarming (Triandafyllidou 2018: 219).

In his book *Antifragile*, Nassim Taleb contends that individuals can position themselves to be fragile, robust, or antifragile. Fragility, in his framework, is based on the individual's need for order, predictability, stability, and only minor disruptions in the system. Fragile individuals and organizations adapt slowly to changing circumstances and can be swept away by pressure exerted on them by the system. Robust individuals and organizations, in contrast, have the ability to weather the unexpected, take shots and lumps, but still survive the turbulence thrown at them by the system. Robustness is certainly better than fragility, according to Taleb, but he says there are certain organizations that take it one step further. Some individuals and organizations have the extraordinary benefit of being antifragile; that is, they actually gain strength by the pressure put on them by the system (Taleb 2014: 31–53)! Taleb invented the term *antifragile* precisely because he could find no better word to describe the phenomenon. Whereas robust individuals and organizations still experience pain and setbacks from systemic stressors, antifragile organizations do not and in fact benefit from the experience.

Human smuggling as an industry benefits from many of the dynamics Taleb associates with antifragility, and noting these characteristics is not to argue that border enforcement and securitization are unwise or inappropriate. They are wholly necessary. The intent in making this observation is simply to clearly elucidate the fact that systemic-level policies can actually make the counterterrorism and counternetwork missions harder for law enforcement and SOF. Indeed, as the previous section illustrated, the complex adaptive system response of the nonnefarious human smuggling networks to increased securitization along the US border has been to generate closer ties to the nefarious criminal organizations with the sophisticated abilities to exploit vulnerabilities in law enforcement and the immigration system (Triandafyllidou 2018: 215). The unintended effect of securitizing the border and incentivizing nonnefarious human smugglers to work with nefarious networks has been to obscure the true SIA threats. As a result, many actors in the human smuggling industry have some connection to threat networks due to being funneled into the same geographic space, and it becomes extremely difficult to determine where to direct limited resources and capabilities against SIAs if so many nodes have only one or two degrees of separation from criminal organizations.

A COMPLEX ADAPTIVE SYSTEMS APPROACH TO SIAS IN HUMAN SMUGGLING

If, as asserted here, human smuggling demonstrates characteristics of antifragility, the question then becomes how to develop a strategy that avoids contributing to the factors enhancing nefarious network strength while intervening at the systemic level to amplify the intrinsic divisions in interest and perspective between nonnefarious human smugglers and truly nefarious actors. Relying solely on existing joint publications on counterterrorism and counternetwork would result only in replicating operational-level concepts of operations to attack the networks to degrade or destroy them. After many years of trying this approach in a multitude of areas, there is growing recognition that new concepts are necessary. Indeed, if this analysis is correct, then the US government might ironically be contributing to the nefarious networks' continued antifragility. So long as the joint publications on counterterrorism and counternetwork focus on the network and the operational level, SOF are likely to replicate each year the challenges they currently face rather than reimagine how systemic-level structural changes might improve their ability to engage the mission.

As noted previously, joint doctrine already accepts complex adaptive systems dynamics at the operational level, but SOF have recently begun exploring ways to address these dynamics at the strategic level. The Joint Special Operations University has developed a concept of applied research inquiries that combines systems thinking, complexity and open systems research, and design thinking environments with diverse groups of SOF personnel, scholars, other US agency personnel, local actors, and others from the private sector. The purpose is to reflexively and constructively critique current approaches to "the problem" to identify structural-level drivers and assumption-laden paradigms underlying policy and strategic thinking (Ellis and Black 2018). In this view, "the problem" is the tip of the iceberg—a symptom of systemic interactions—and cannot be eliminated without persistent and resource-intensive attention. Divergent perspectives and specially designed workshop experiences promote creativity and agency in the bureaucracy and generate the space for new ideas, theories of action, and approaches to complex adaptive systems dynamics to arise. These insights can then be translated into interventions in the system of varying sizes and stripes, such as the publication of a book chapter (as is the case here), US government workshops to change perspectives, realignment of SOF operations or repositioning of SOF personnel, or even potentially changes in policy.

How might a systems-level, complex adaptive systems perspective on SIAs help SOF, and what might a strategic-level intervention look like? First, the complex adaptive systems approach suggests that SOF's existing approaches to counterterrorism and counternetwork will be ineffective in degrading human smuggling networks. While the impulse is to demand more of the existing processes, there is no COG in the human smuggling system to attack and achieve a decisive impact. Second, exploring the history of the human smuggling system is the first step in distinguishing nonnefarious from nefarious networks. Doing so elucidates the differences in motivation, intent, interests, perceptions, and opportunities for engagement between them. For example, economically oriented migrant populations from predominantly nonviolent, Sufi Muslim regions of countries with a multidecade history of smuggling could be easily distinguished from migrants from other regions with a history of Salafi-jihadist violent extremism. Limited SOF resources could then be applied against the most likely threat corridors in concert with US enforcement agencies. Third, it enables a critical evaluation of the changes in the system of immigration and assumptions underlying it—that is, the structural conditions that drive nonnefarious networks to work with nefarious ones. Fourth, with this knowledge it is possible to imagine how different systems and processes—different policies and social structures—might enable the decriminalization of the nonnefarious actors' activities and illuminate nefarious networks. If much of SOF's challenge is distinguishing between nonnefarious and nefarious criminal networks, eliminating the incentives for human smuggling through legislation and administrative process changes might make sense overall. Finally, it enables SOF to recognize how other US government agencies contribute to systemic incentives driving nonnefarious and nefarious networks together in order to identify mechanisms for collaboration or, perhaps, even generate analysis that might change processes or policy.

Admittedly, this chapter explores the human smuggling challenge only from the perspective of SOF as it works to prevent attacks on the homeland from SIAs and known or suspected terrorists. There are likely other considerations and priorities across the US government that might subordinate SOF's challenges as a relative matter. However, the current approach to human smuggling favors the perspective that barriers and enforcement can stem the flow, but the extant literature suggests that, as a complex adaptive system, the illegal flows will find ways around them in time. A more effective, holistic approach might consider policies that can diminish the demand for clandestine human smuggling through the decriminalization of some aspects of the system while incentivizing migrant self-reporting. Such creativity and agency are possible if attachment to existing paradigms is relaxed and updated appreciations of systemic drivers and interactions achieved. Human smuggling as a complex adaptive system is unlikely to change, so devising policies and processes that more productively cycle the flow stands a better chance for revealing to SOF true terrorist threats as SOF continue their essential mission of defending the homeland.

NOTE

The ideas and analysis expressed in this chapter are solely those of the author and do not reflect the views of the Joint Special Operations University, US Special Operations Command, the Department of Defense, or the US government. David C. Ellis serves as a resident senior fellow contractor at the Joint Special Operations University through a subcontract with METIS Solutions.

REFERENCES

Achilli, L., 2018. "The 'Good' Smuggler: The Ethics and Morals of Human Smuggling among Syrians." *ANNALS of the American Academy of Political and Social Science* 676 (March): 77–96.

Andreas, P. 2001. "The Transformation of Migrant Smuggling across the U.S.-Mexican Border." In *Global Human Smuggling: Comparative Perspectives*, edited by David Kyle and Rey Koslowski, 107–125. Baltimore: Johns Hopkins University Press.

Bier, D., and A. Nowrasteh. 2018. "45,000 'Special Interest Aliens' Caught since 2007, but No U.S. Terrorist Attacks from Illegal Border Crossers." *Cato at Liberty* (blog), December 17, 2018. https://www.cato.org/blog/45000-special-interest-aliens-caught-2007-no-us-terrorist-attacks-illegal-border-crossers.

Bousquet, A., and S. Curtis. 2011. "Beyond Models and Metaphors: Complexity Theory, Systems Thinking and International Relations." *Cambridge Review of International Affairs* 24 (1): 43–62.

Brachet, J. 2018. "Manufacturing Smugglers: From Irregular to Clandestine Mobility in the Sahara." *ANNALS of the American Academy of Political and Social Science* 676 (March): 16–35.

Buckley, D., D. Schwandt, and J. A. Goldstein. 2008. "Society as a Complex Adaptive System." *Emergence: Complexity and Organization* 10 (3): 86–112.

Clausewitz, C. v. 1984. *On War*. Edited by M. Howard and P. Paret. Princeton, NJ: Princeton University Press.

Congressional Research Service. 2018. "Defense Primer: Special Operations Forces." December 6, 2018. https://fas.org/sgp/crs/natsec/IF10545.pdf.

Department of Homeland Security. 2019. "MYTH/FACT: Known and Suspected Terrorists/Special Interest Aliens." January 7, 2019. https://www.dhs.gov/news/2019/01/07/mythfact-known-and-suspected-terroristsspecial-interest-aliens.

Ellis, D. C., and C. N. Black. 2018. *Complexity, Organizational Blinders, and the SOCOM Design Way*. Tampa, FL: Joint Special Operations University Press.

Finckenauer, J. O. 2001. "Russian Transnational Organized Crime and Human Trafficking." In *Global Human Smuggling: Comparative Perspectives*, edited by David Kyle and Rey Koslowski, 166–186. Baltimore: Johns Hopkins University Press.

Guevara González, Y. 2018. "Navigating with Coyotes: Pathways of Central American Migrants in Mexico's Southern Borders." *ANNALS of the American Academy of Political and Social Science* 676 (2018): 174–193.

Homeland Security Committee. 2019. *Stopping Terrorist Travel through Illicit Pathways to the Homeland*. House Homeland Security Committee Majority Staff Report, 2018–2019 (January). https://cis.org/sites/default/files/2019-01/396705631-SIA-Report-2018.pdf.

Human Smuggling and Trafficking Center. 2013. *Human Trafficking vs. Human Smuggling*, HSTC2013070001. Human Smuggling and Trafficking Center, US Department of State, July 1, 2013. https://2009-2017.state.gov/documents/organization/226276.pdf.

Joint Chiefs of Staff. 2014. *Joint Publication 3-26: Counterterrorism*. Washington, DC: Joint Chiefs of Staff, US Department of Defense. https://www.jcs.mil/Portals/36/Documents/Doctrine/pubs/jp3_26.pdf.

———. 2016. *Joint Publication 3-25: Countering Threat Networks*. Washington, DC: Joint Chiefs of Staff, US Department of Defense. https://www.jcs.mil/Portals/36/Documents/Doctrine/pubs/jp3_25.pdf.

———. 2017. *Joint Publication 5-0: Joint Planning*. Washington, DC: Joint Chiefs of Staff, US Department of Defense.

Kook, K. 2018. "'I Want to Be Trafficked So I Can Migrate!': Cross-Border Movement of North Koreans into China through Brokerage and Smuggling Networks." *ANNALS of the American Academy of Political and Social Science* 676 (2018): 114–134.

Koslowski, R. 2001. "Economic Globalization, Human Smuggling, and Global Governance," In *Global Human Smuggling: Comparative Perspectives*, edited by David Kyle and Rey Koslowski, 337–358. Baltimore: Johns Hopkins University Press.

Kyle, D., and J. Dale. 2001. "Smuggling the State Back In: Agents of Human Smuggling Reconsidered." In *Global Human Smuggling: Comparative Perspectives*, edited by David Kyle and Rey Koslowski, 29–57. Baltimore: Johns Hopkins University Press.

Kyle, D., and R. Goldstein. 2011. *Migration Industries: A Comparison of the Ecuador-US and Ecuador-Spain Cases*. EU-US Immigration Systems 2011/15. San Domenico di Fiesole, Italy: Robert Schuman Centre for Advanced Studies, European University Institute. https://cadmus.eui.eu/handle/1814/17845.

Kyle, D., and R. Koslowski. 2001. Introduction to *Global Human Smuggling: Comparative Perspectives*, edited by David Kyle and Rey Koslowski, 1–26. Baltimore: Johns Hopkins University Press.

Maher, S. 2018. "Out of West Africa: Human Smuggling as a Social Enterprise." *ANNALS of the American Academy of Political and Social Science* 676 (March): 36–56.

Majidi, N. 2018. "Community Dimensions of Smuggling: The Case of Afghanistan and Somalia." *ANNALS of the American Academy of Political and Social Science* 676 (March): 97–113.

McChrystal, S., T. Collins, D. Silverman, and C. Fussell. 2015. *Team of Teams: New Rules of Engagement for a Complex World*. New York: Portfolio/Penguin.

Mengiste, T. A. 2018. "Refugee Protections from Below: Smuggling in the Eritrea-Ethiopia Context." *ANNALS of the American Academy of Political and Social Science* 676 (March): 57–76.

Mesjasz, C. 2015. "Complex Systems Studies and Terrorism." In *Conflict and Complexity: Countering Terrorism, Insurgency, Ethnic and Regional Violence*, edited by P. Vos Fellman, Y. Bar-Yam, and A. Minai, 35–72. New York: Springer.

Sanchez, G. E. 2015. *Human Smuggling and Border Crossings*. New York: Routledge.

Sanchez, G. E., and S. X. Zhang. 2018. "Rumors, Encounters, Collaborations, and Survival: The Migrant Smuggling-Drug Trafficking Nexus in the U.S. Southwest." *ANNALS of the American Academy of Political and Social Science* 676 (March): 135–151.

Schultz, R. 2016. *Military Innovation in War: It Takes a Learning Organization—a Case Study of Task Force 714 in Iraq*. Tampa, FL: Joint Special Operations University Press.

Spener, D. 2001. "Smuggling Migrants through South Texas: Challenges Posed by Operation Rio Grande." In *Global Human Smuggling: Comparative Perspectives*, edited by David Kyle and Rey Koslowski, 129–165. Baltimore: Johns Hopkins University Press.

Stone-Cadena, V., and S. Álvarez Velasco. 2018. "Historicizing Mobility: Coyoterismo in the Indigenous Ecuadorian Migration Industry." *ANNALS of the American Academy of Political and Social Science* 676 (March): 194–211.

Taleb, N. N. 2014. *Antifragile: Things That Gain from Disorder*. New York: Random House.

Triandafyllidou, A. 2018. "Migrant Smuggling: Novel Insights and Implications for Migration Control Policies." *ANNALS of the American Academy of Political and Social Science* 676 (March): 212–221.

US Immigration and Customs Enforcement. 2017. "Human Smuggling." July 26, 2017. https://www.ice.gov/human-smuggling.

von Lampe, K. 2016. *Organized Crime: Analyzing Illegal Activities, Criminal Structures and Extra-legal Governance*. Los Angeles: Sage.

Vos Fellman, P. 2015. "Modeling Terrorist Networks: The Second Decade." In *Conflict and Complexity: Countering Terrorism, Insurgency, Ethnic and Regional Violence*, edited by P. Vos Fellman, Y. Bar-Yam, and A. Minai, 3–34. New York: Springer.

Zhang, S. 2008. *Chinese Human Smuggling Organizations: Families, Social Networks, and Cultural Imperatives*. Stanford, CA: Stanford University Press.

Zhang, S. X., S. E. Sanchez, and L. Achilli. 2018. "Crime of Solidarity in Mobility: Alternative Views on Migrant Smuggling." *ANNALS of the American Academy of Political and Social Science* 676 (March): 6–15.

Zhao, L. 2013. *Financing Illegal Migration: Chinese Underground Banks and Human Smuggling in New York City*. New York: Palgrave Macmillan.

CHAPTER 6

Migrant Smuggling across the EU-Turkey Border: Structural, Institutional, and Agency-Based Factors

Ahmet İçduygu

THIS CHAPTER AIMS TO DELVE DEEPER into the complexities involved in the diverse dynamics and mechanisms that contribute to the emergence and operation of migrant smuggling. Earlier studies suggest that there are structural and institutional settings, together with the various actors interacting within these settings, that form an environment that is prone to unauthorized border crossings and migrant smuggling activities (İçduygu 2020; Kyle and Koslowski 2011; Triandafyllidou and McAuliffe 2018; Watson 2015; Zhang, Sanchez, and Achilli 2018). Hence this chapter revisits the question of the factors behind migrant smuggling, contextualizing them within the larger picture of an unauthorized mobility system and unpacking its conventionally conceived image, which often reduces smuggling to criminality (Franck 2019) or a threat to state order (Kühnemund 2018).

The debate here will start with key analytical and theoretical issues, presenting an overview of the history of unauthorized migratory movements at the border between the European Union (EU) and Turkey, more specifically between Greece and Turkey. First, this discussion will be advanced by examining the complex structural, institutional, and agency-based factors that have contributed to the dynamics and mechanisms of migrant smuggling as an ingenious activity in the regionally operating mobility system in the southeast corner of Europe. Here, Turkey emerges as a country of transit migration with a corridor from its eastern and southern borders with West Asia and the Middle East to its western ones with Europe. The discussion will then proceed to present a detailed analysis of empirical evidence obtained from Turkey's borders, which have widely been subject to unauthorized migratory movements over the course of the last three decades. After briefly touching on the history of migration smuggling in the region, this chapter will focus on the period of 2015–2020, during which the nature of irregular migration and migrant smuggling has been greatly affected by the actions and discourses of various actors, structures, and institutions involved at the EU-Turkish border. In this context, two central questions are posed: To what extent do three main actors—migrants, smugglers, and state officials—condition migrant smuggling? And how do they interact with the various structural and institutional factors around them? Answering these questions intrinsically engages with the two interrelated conceptual and empirical attributes attached to migrant smuggling activities: the *agency* of the related actors in terms of their ability to affect the smuggling process, and the *creativity* on the part of the actors involved in this phenomenon. In order to better explore the answers to the questions just posed, the argument focuses on the presence and interaction of three distinct elements that condition the larger context of an unauthorized mobility regime: structures (i.e., broader socioeconomic, political, and cultural contexts within which related actors and institutions are embedded), institutions (i.e., formal and informal rules that inform actors' actions), and agencies and actors (i.e., individuals, organizations, and collective entities).

Migration scholars have explored the concept of the migration, or mobility, system by analyzing the complex nature of the elements constituting migration processes—involving origin, transit, and destination points and the trajectories connecting them—elaborating changes over time, and reviewing interactions between individuals' decision-making and structural constraints (Bakewell 2014). In this context, the emphasis in the concept has been on two main dimensions: first, the concept links the different phases of migration that informs the totality of the movement with its causes and consequences; and second, it reveals the exchange between structures and agencies in migration processes. The effects of structural exploratory factors such as macro-level sociopolitical conditions, migration-related macro-level policies, and the larger context of the migratory regime on the types, scale, and duration of the flows between states occupy a prominent place in the system-based explanations developed in migration literature. As a result, the migratory system approach often tends to portray structural factors as a deterministic element influencing migration outcomes. The scholarship on the system approach, particularly in the last decade, also situates the dynamic role of agency in migration processes, but it is difficult to claim that it captures the specifics of the delicate relationship between agents' capabilities and structural constraints. This growing critique of structure-agency perspective needs to be assessed by unpacking its broader complexity and adding the third element—institutions—to the dyad of structure and agency (Bakewell 2014; van Liempt and Doomernik 2006). Therefore, here I carefully examine migrant smuggling from the perspectives of these three distinct elements that condition the larger context of a mobility regime.

Borrowing from scholars using institutional theory in the fields of sociology and public policy (Scharpf 1997; Steinmo 2010), I develop an analytical frame focusing on these three elements that helps to unpack the complex nature of migrant smuggling within unauthorized mobility systems. This analytical framework not only extends beyond the structure and agency dyad formulation but also distinguishes between structures and institutions, highlighting the multiplicity of agencies and dynamic exchanges among structures, institutions, and migrant and smuggler agencies. In an attempt to operationalize these entities in the larger context of unauthorized migration systems, we can boldly refer to the main agents through the examples of migrants, refugees, asylum seekers, smugglers, state actors, and intergovernmental and nongovernmental organizations. On the other hand, institutions can be equated to all formal and informal rules and regulations (policies and administrative practices) in the fields of migration and asylum seeking that inform actions. Finally, structures refer to the broader socioeconomic, political, and cultural contexts within which actors and institutions are embedded.

In recognizing the multiplicity of factors in the operation of smuggling under a migration system, we not only need to see the intricacy of migratory dynamics in an analytical sense but, in doing so, we also need to come to some understanding of the relationship between agency and structure (and institutions). Agency, in this case, is an individual actor's ability to make choices, and structures are those things that are seen to determine actions and behaviors. Indeed, these structures are often seen as determinants that impose obstacles for a creative action. However, as Phillip McIntyre (2012: 57) notes, the limitations on autonomous decision-making could, set by the field and domain, act as both a set of constraints and enabling factors making creative choice possible. In this context, I argue that in the larger setting of the unauthorized migration system, migrant smuggling often systematically exhibits an agentic creativity of related actors in their exchanges with the structures and institutions surrounding them. What is observed, for instance, is that the three main actors—migrants, smugglers, and state officials—seek to develop more creative ways to perform their complementary or contradictory roles in border-crossing activities. In short, these actors in smuggling activities are not the prisoners of the structures and institutions they are involved in; on the contrary, they are active in terms of their own actions that enable the related processes, and they are also enabled by their interactions with these structures and institutions.[1]

LINKING MIGRANT SMUGGLING WITH UNAUTHORIZED MOBILITY SYSTEMS: EVIDENCE FROM THE EU-TURKEY BORDER

Scholarly debates on unauthorized migration date back to the late 1970s. This debate often refers to the political economy of unauthorized migratory systems linking various contexts of the Global South or East and Global North or West. For instance, referring to the inabilities and unwillingness of the US government to manage the country's economic and demographic needs with proper immigration policies, Alejandro Portes (1978: 470) comments about unauthorized Mexican migration to the United States that it is "not a problem, but as a solution to the problem." Later, similar observations were made for the economies of the EU countries, indicating the instrumental and functional importance of unauthorized migratory flows (Flynn 2005; Ghosh 2000). Overall, when the economies in these countries in the Global North or West are structurally in need of labor, unauthorized migratory flows might be inevitable even if the related rhetoric and policies toward these flows are unsympathetic. On the other hand, migratory pressure in several countries of the Global South or East is complementary to the formation of unauthorized migratory flows to the Global North or West. In the absence of legal channels of migration, economically desperate people in the Global South or East tend to find their way to cross borders through clandestine arrangements. Similarly, asylum seekers from politically fragile countries in the Global South or East also choose clandestine arrangements to ensure their border crossings in the absence of legal channels. In short, given established obstacles to crossing borders safely, potential migrants and asylum seekers in need of work and international protection are often compelled to hire smugglers as their only means to flee poverty, deprivation, conflict, and violence. Here, relying on the case study and empirical data from the border between Greece and Turkey, I will substantiate these arguments.

Turkey has been a major transit country for unauthorized migration over the course of the last three decades, mainly because of its geographic position, which makes the country a front line of migratory movements between the Global South or East and the Global North or West (İçduygu and Toktaş 2003; İçduygu and Yükseker 2012). In recent decades, the political history of its neighborhood has exposed Turkey's borders to extensive politically or economically driven unauthorized border crossings and consequently rendered these borders opportunities to human smugglers (İçduygu 2020; İçduygu and Toktaş 2003). In this context, hundreds of thousands of people displaced due to conflict, persecution, or economic depression in various countries in the Middle East, Asia, and Africa find themselves engaging in unauthorized movements, often relying on smuggling networks to move into and out of Turkey, thus creating an unauthorized migratory system in Turkey and its neighboring regions, including Europe. This reflects the historical and structural root causes, or origin, of unauthorized migratory flows and smuggling activities in this particular region.

There are explanatory, and therefore complementary, factors concerning the destination locations. In the last three decades, as the EU's interest in controlling irregular migration and asylum flows has grown, its borders with its neighbors, such as the Greek-Turkish border, have come to be shaped through various forms of border closure policies, essentially becoming "gates" filtering those who are allowed to enter and those who need to be kept out (Düvell 2006, 2011). As the EU borders become subject to different forms of EU externalization policies, a variety of securitization measures are activated that make border crossings more difficult and criminalize them: these gatekeeping activities involve various arrangements such as high-tech investments into the border security apparatus, constructions of walls and fences, and the signing of readmission agreements with the origin or transit countries (Yıldız 2016). However, the efficiency and effectiveness of these policies and practices have always been questionable, as neither unauthorized migration flows nor the smuggling activities that facilitate them have disappeared. It is observed that under the securitization and externalization measures, there were some periods when some declining trends were observed in the unauthorized border crossings, but these declining trends have never been sustainable, indicating that unauthorized migratory flows through smuggling activities have been structurally established in the region over time.

The long history of migratory movements along the Greek-Turkish border in the last three decades reflects the roles and functions of the structural factors and institutional instruments in the unauthorized migration flows and smuggling activities in the region. Regional migratory systems have made Turkey a transit country for thousands of unauthorized migrants from Asia and Africa seeking to enter EU territories (İçduygu and Yükseker 2012). As early as the 1990s, the annual estimated transit migration to the EU via the Greek-Turkish border stood at several thousand migrants, and the issue increasingly became an important agenda item in Turkey's relation with Greece (İçduygu and Aksel 2014). Consequently, as an institutional arrangement, a readmission protocol, aimed at facilitating the return of unauthorized migrants arriving or residing irregularly in Greece to Turkey if they came from Turkey, was signed between these two countries in 2002 to combat unauthorized migration flows (Kirişci 2004). The negotiation and utilization of the readmission agreement has always been very central to the debates around unauthorized migration flows and smuggling activities between the EU and Turkey. In other words, the evolving nature, size, and trends of the unauthorized migration flows and smuggling activities had a critical impact on the bilateral relation between the EU and Turkey before the start of Turkey's accession negotiations in 2005, and even well before the most recent "refugee crisis" of 2015. At the time of the signing of the Greek-Turkish readmission protocol, EU authorities continually stated their concerns about the effective implementation of the protocol, and then considered developing a more structured readmission agreement between the EU and Turkey. These policy-making efforts had shifted toward a more systematic process for harmonization with the EU *acquis*, and in 2005, Turkey adopted the National Action Plan for Asylum and Migration, laying out the necessary tasks and timetable for the development of a migration and asylum management system (İçduygu and Aksel 2014). The plan also directly referred to the initiation and development of various policies and practices, including a readmission agreement with the EU, to deal with unauthorized migration flows and smuggling activities. However, the issue of readmission became an indicator of the deepening mistrust in EU-Turkish relations, reflecting the politicization of migration issues in the region: Turkish authorities worried about Turkey becoming a buffer zone and a dumping ground for unwanted migration to the EU, while the EU begrudged Turkey's unwillingness to make an effort on a highly sensitive issue for many member states (Kirişci 2014).

Despite these setbacks in the 2000s, the migration-related reform attempts once again picked up speed in the early 2010s, resulting in the conclusion of the readmission agreement between the EU and Turkey in 2013. As the readmission agreement's aim was to bring about the expulsion of irregular migrants by establishing obligations and procedures regarding readmission between the contracting parties, it was assumed that the agreement between the EU and Turkey would be an effective tool to combat unauthorized border crossings and its facilitators, such as smugglers. Furthermore, in the context of EU-initiated transformation in Turkey, a new legal arrangement was made: the Law on Foreigners and International Protection was adopted in 2013. The law introduced some landmark improvements, both covering migration, asylum, and mass influx and establishing the Directorate General for Migration Management, which would serve as the main civil coordination authority, with one of its main duties being to develop measures to combat unauthorized migration and smuggling activities and follow up on the implementation of such measures.

Over the course of the past three decades, while the structural and historical conditions continuously matured for the development of unauthorized transit migratory flows through Turkey to Europe, the institutional arrangements for the management of these flows (i.e., new policies and related practices) underwent transformation. However, the institutional arrangements and the changes to them were not reactive enough to effectively deal with unauthorized border crossings and smuggling activities. In the absence of direct measures, the apprehension figures for irregular migrants and smugglers serve as an indicator of the volume of unauthorized border crossings and smuggling activities. It is known that between 1980 and 2010, more than half a million unauthorized migrants were apprehended trying to transit from Turkey—primarily from Middle Eastern, Asian, and African countries—on their way to Europe; alongside these, thousands of smugglers were also detained (İçduygu and Yükseker 2012). Indeed, the most recent case in which Turkey's transit role in Europe's migratory system was intensely debated was during the summer and fall of 2015, when a mass mixed flow of migrants—the majority of whom were Syrian refugees—entered European countries. These migrants were crossing Turkish-Greek sea and land borders, mostly through unauthorized methods including migrant smuggling. The historic unauthorized migratory flow through the transit migration corridor of Turkey in 2015 was not only unique because of the high volume in a short period of time but also fascinating because it highlighted the continuities and ruptures observed in smuggling activities that have occurred for decades in the region.

MIGRANT SMUGGLING AT THE EU-TURKEY BORDER, 2015–2020: ACTS OF MIGRANTS, SMUGGLERS, AND BORDER ENFORCEMENT AGENCIES

The period of 2015–2020, which includes the historic mass unauthorized migratory flows of 2015 to Europe and their aftermath, presents us with a unique study setting in which to unpack the complex nature of migrant smuggling across the EU-Turkey border. It represents an unusual period when the borders between Greece and Turkey became a particularly heated arena of struggle in which not only various high-level governmental and intergovernmental actors negotiated unauthorized border crossing issues but also well-known customary actors in the field—such as migrants, refugees, smugglers, and border law enforcement agents—competed to achieve their goals. In this context, I focus on the emergence of the so-called 2015 migration crisis of Europe, followed by the 2016 EU-Turkey deal and its aftermath, and finally the events of early 2020 when the Turkish government allowed refugees passage to Europe by opening Turkey's border with Greece. These three historical events provide us with a unique setting to revisit the dynamic nature of unauthorized border crossings and smuggling processes. An analysis of this unique setting will reveal the ways various agencies (migrants, smugglers, and border enforcement officials), under the given structural and institutional settings, interact and consequently shape unauthorized migration outcomes, including migrant smuggling.

HISTORICAL LEGACY: BEFORE 2015

When Syria's refugee migration started in 2011, Turkey, as a country of transit migration, was in the midst of developing its immigration and asylum system to meet international—and particularly EU—standards, mainly as part of its long-standing but slow accession process. Although this process resulted in the adoption of a new law and the creation of a new government institution to deal with immigration and asylum policies and practices, Turkey's older migration-related questions, mostly concerning unauthorized border crossings and smuggling, have remained unchanged. Syrian refugees arrived to Turkey as long-standing flows of irregular (transit) migrants and refugees from other countries continued, and migrant smuggling remained a significant element across these flows. Within this historically established migratory picture, Turkey's Iranian border is the main point of entry for the majority of these unauthorized arrivals, and its sea and land borders with Greece are the major departure routes for those who use Turkey as a transit corridor on their journeys to Europe. In short, the main direction of unauthorized migration flows and related smuggling activities in Turkey is from east or south to west or north.

My earlier research findings[2] from these border areas indicate that as migration journeys involve careful decision-making processes, migrants and refugees, as active agents, often exert great effort in planning their journeys even as they deal with various aspects of an uncertain environment. Their journeys are also affected by different external factors and largely conditioned by the broader structural and institutional factors, together with the operation of migrants' own networks through their relatives, friends, and smugglers, as the migrants' relatives and personal social networks often play a prominent role in encouraging, facilitating, and financing a smuggling journey. In this context, the following narrative of a migrant is meaningful:

> I escaped from Afghanistan for its bad economy and politics.... I planned this journey carefully with my relatives, and after moving into Iran, with the help of my friend who lives in Stockholm now.... He went there nine years ago with smugglers.... He said Sweden is a good place, I can work there in good job and establish my life. Neither Afghanistan, nor Iran or Turkey can provide that life to me.... So, I came to Turkey from mountains, with the help of an Afghan smuggler.... He helped me a lot, with a small [amount of] money..., he also gave me some information to find his smuggler friend to take me from Turkey to Greece, and then to Sweden. (Afghan man who came via Iran to Turkey in 2002, interviewed in 2002)

While socioeconomic and political factors appear to push people to migrate, the existence of networks and kinship ties may pull them to destinations. Along with this, the relatively low cost of smugglers and their "friendly" operating networks, an accessible geography, the historical legacy of long-established smuggling traditions, and the conscious ignorance of law enforcement agents who are fully aware of their own limited actions all serve as functional factors facilitating unauthorized border crossings. Interestingly, the trust and informal relations between migrants and local smugglers seem to be a key factor in this process. These interacting factors are illustrated clearly in the narratives of two other main actors of the border crossing process, a smuggler and a border law enforcement agent. The smuggler explained,

> We live close to border, our Iranian relatives take these people to our borders, then we take them into Turkey, and take from Van [close to Iranian border] to Istanbul where they can find another smuggler to go to Europe.... We do not charge them huge amount of money.... We help them.... We are not mafia.... There is a demand for us... and we offer them help.... They are desperate people, they cannot cross borders without us.... We know the behaviour of border guards and migrants... so we can easily deal with them.... Migrants tell us where to go, they trust us and we make plans accordingly. (Local smuggler in Van Province, Turkey, neighboring Iran, interviewed in 2002)

While this quotation refers to the trust relation between migrants and smugglers, and the agency and creative elements in the actions of smugglers, the following quotation reflects the strategic self-positioning of law enforcement agents who are fully aware of the results of their actions and nonactions in the process:

> It isn't so easy to control the border with Iran, very long border and there is no fences, walls, just nature, there are only border stones . . . every one or two kilometres. . . . There are local people who are doing smuggling . . . but they are not big mafia men . . . and many of these poor migrants, they do not want to stay in Turkey, they want to go to Europe, so I often close my eyes . . . if there is no strong order from our top officials. . . . Time to time, government order us to be strong in control, then we try. . . . Otherwise we are quite easy. . . . This is the problem of Europe, they go there. (Gendarme major in Van Province, interviewed in 2002)

SMUGGLING WITHOUT SECRECY AND SELF-MANAGED: MASS FLOWS OF 2015

In 2015, while Turkey was hosting nearly 2.5 million Syrian refugees, the EU countries were overwhelmingly alarmed by the mass arrivals of refugees, most of whom were coming through Turkey. Over the course of the summer and autumn of 2015, the Aegean Sea route and, partly, the land border between Turkey and Greece turned into one of the busiest staging areas for unauthorized border crossings and smuggling activities. Approximately one million refugees and migrants arrived in Europe in 2015, with a significant proportion using Turkey as a transit country. These migratory flows, which were widely referred to as Europe's "refugee crisis" or "migration crisis," called for attention and action from governments, politicians, and European publics who were directed to the issues of unauthorized migration and smuggling activities along Turkey's border with Europe, particularly with Greece. The experience of 2015 showed that within the environment of a mass movement, migrant smuggling gained two main rising attributes: first, becoming overly visible in the sense that different publics have become familiar with it and somehow justified it; and second, increasingly being self-managed as individual migrants initiated and played active roles in organizing and carrying out their journeys. The following narratives demonstrate these two points; in particular, they clearly reflect the active agency role and creativity of main smuggling actors, migrants and smugglers, highlighting the development of self-initiated smuggling journeys.

> These poor refugees and migrants are very desperate, they escape from clashes and poverty. . . . When German government said they are willing to accept refugees in 2015, many migrants in Istanbul found us. . . . We took them to Ayvacık and Behramkale, which are very close to Midillini island of Greece. . . . We provided them with inflatable boats. . . . They took the boat and go there. . . . They themselves arranged their trips. . . . They sail on the sea. . . . It is very easy. . . . Coast guards were not so keen to catch us. . . . I think our government also wanted them to leave the country. (Smuggler who works as an organizer in Istanbul, a hub for transit migrants and refugees, interviewed in 2016)

> We have to escape from war, but here in Turkey we cannot survive. . . . No job, no prospect, no future. . . . Turkey does not give us a refugee status, we are under temporary protection. . . . We want full protection, but Turkey does not give us full and permanent protection. . . . So we have to move to a better place. . . . Particularly for our children. . . . Since we cannot buy a ticket and go to Europe, we go to the hands of smugglers. . . . They provide us with a chance of moving to Europe. In 2015, I arranged a smuggler to take us to İzmir, but police caught us on the way to seaside, . . . but I will try again, and I will manage it. (Syrian refugee in Istanbul, interviewed in 2016)

> They do not cross the borders illegally only with the organization of smugglers, what we see that they, migrants or asylum seekers, increasingly plan their journeys and go alone to the border, and pass to other side themselves. . . . So we cannot do anything, this is publicly known. (Official from the Ministry of Interior, interviewed in 2016)

As these narratives reveal, the events of 2015 indicated that the desperation of migrants and refugees, which was an inevitable outcome of exit pressure from economically and politically fragile states such as Syria and Afghanistan, was pushing many of them to begin their journeys and rely on smugglers to facilitate them. Meanwhile, wider structural and institutional factors affected their journeys, creating an environment of insecurity and uncertainty that simultaneously gave rise to risks and opportunities regarding their journeys. My research in this period highlights that while unbearable living conditions in origin and transit countries were pushing people to migrate to the next possible destination, in the absence of orderly channels of movement, the act of unauthorized border crossing was the only option available, and migrant smuggling was an indispensable element of these journeys. It is necessary to note that many of those who made the journey at that time were refugees who were desperately and urgently seeking protection, and crossing the border by hiring smugglers seemed to legitimize their action under these conditions.

The so-called migration crisis of Europe in 2015 immediately raised questions concerning unauthorized border crossings, smuggling, and issues of "responsibility sharing versus responsibility shifting" to the top of shared EU and Turkish agendas. Following a lengthy and controversial negotiation process, the two parties reached the agreement known as the "EU-Turkey Statement" or "EU-Turkey Deal." This agreement, which signified a new institutional arrangement to combat smuggling, referred to various issues including the return of irregular migrants crossing from Turkey to the Greek islands and the prevention of new routes opening for illegal migration from Turkey to the EU. The agreement was expected to lead to a dramatic decrease in the number of irregular migrants, and such as decrease would be seen as proof of the statement's effectiveness, sending a direct message to migrants that they should not board boats in Turkey and endanger their lives, because they would be returned. The EU-Turkey Deal was also expected to create an environment in which smugglers' business model would be broken (European Commission 2016), thereby further discouraging migrant smuggling. A local smuggler in Küçükkuyu (on the Turkish seaside close to Lesbos, an island of Greece), who was interviewed in 2019, describes the impact of the EU-Turkey Deal on smuggling: "Not only the control of the state agencies has gotten serious, but there is also less demand for us by the migrants or refugees to take them from Turkey to Greece. . . . After 2015, our government became serious with this agreement with the EU. . . . But I cannot say that our business has been closed, but became more complicated . . . and slowed down [a] bit. . . . For instance, we use luxury yachts . . . but only few migrants can pay money for it." In order to better understand the impact of structural and institutional factors on smuggling activities, it is necessary to ask, Did the EU-Turkey Deal bring down the number of unauthorized border crossings and smuggling activities (Spijkerboer 2016)? The narratives that follow also provide an array of observations from various actors in the field. They directly refer to the various exchanges between structural and institutional settings and agency-based factors, which created mixed results, but often also refer to the agentic creativity of related actors.

> We are committed to the application of the EU-Turkey deal, so we are very careful to prevent the passages [of] migrants to Lesbos island. Our coast guards and police forces are very careful to combat against smugglers. . . . Now there is a sharp decline in the number of migrant[s] who manage to cross to Greece; this is the picture on our western borders with Europe. But when we look at our eastern border, particularly with Iran, we have a remarkable increase in the number of arriving irregular migrants in Turkey. . . . It is very naïve thinking that smuggling will disappear, even if you have laws and regulations, and resources, they are not successful to deal with it. . . . This is the movement of people. . . . You cannot control them easily, they are human beings. (Official from the Ministry of Interior, interviewed in 2018)
>
> In my opinion, there are several reasons behind why the number of Syrians in Turkey who tend to go to Europe with smugglers declines. . . . First, many of those who wanted to leave have already left for Europe in 2015, in fact 2015 was a special year, many Syrians acted according to a herd mentality. . . . They mobilized each other. . . . Secondly now Turkey and European countries are very harsh, it is difficult to cross borders . . . but still there are some smugglers available, if you are desperate, they help, and migrants together with smugglers try to develop new strategies to cross the borders. (Syrian man, community leader, interviewed in 2019)

While the EU-Turkey Deal is widely considered an effective measure for border control as it managed to bring down the number of unauthorized crossings from Turkey to Europe, thereby demonstrating a decline in the smuggling endeavors in the region between Turkey and Greece, it is hard to claim that it extensively erased the potential of unauthorized migratory flows and smuggling activities around Turkey, which would likely be targeting Europe. Figures from the field further clarify this picture, as according to the Frontex (European Border and Coast Guard Agency, n.d.) data, the number of unauthorized arrivals from the Eastern Mediterranean corridor to Europe (mainly passing through Turkey) declined from over 885,000 in 2015 to just over 42,000 in 2017, then rose slightly to nearly 57,000 in 2018, and then increased further to over 83,000 in 2019. The corresponding figures from Turkey concerning the number of irregular migrants apprehended imply that unauthorized border crossings and the involvement of smugglers rose and maintain high levels. While the number of apprehended irregular migrants was nearly 146,000 in 2015, it rose to 176,000 in 2017, then to 268,000 in 2018, and finally to 455,000 in 2019. Similarly, there was also an increasing trend in the number of smuggler apprehensions: 4,000 in 2015, 5,000 in 2017, and 9,000 in 2019. From this picture, it is possible to conclude that while the structural factors persisted and institutional settings are developing, the behaviors and attitudes of the major actors in the field are very responsive to these structural and institutional factors, as demonstrated through their purposive actions. While migrants and refugees try their best to cross the borders irregularly, smugglers continue offering their services, and border enforcement agents tend to combat unauthorized border crossings and smuggling activities; all these actors are aware of the extent and limits of their powers, and they act accordingly.

STATE-INITIATED UNAUTHORIZED MIGRATION AND SMUGGLING: EVIDENCE FROM 2020

Interestingly, on the night of February 27–28, 2020, just a few weeks before many countries around the world began to shut their borders completely because of the COVID-19 pandemic, Turkey lifted the strict controls it had enforced on its sea and land borders with Greece since March 2016, prompting thousands of migrants to head to the frontier to cross into Europe. Turkey's decision was a reactionary attempt to draw the attention of European countries to the intensified clashes in northern Syria, which could push nearly one million more Syrians into Turkey. The use of refugees to blackmail states clearly indicates how unauthorized border crossings are being instrumentalized in the EU-Turkey relationship and are part and parcel of Turkey's long-growing disappointment with the 2016 deal as it blames the EU for "responsibility shifting" rather than "responsibility sharing." Following the decision to open the border with Greece, which deliberately encouraged significant numbers of migrants and refugees to head to the Greek border, many migrants and refugees gathered along the land border in the Evros region, and migratory flows through the Aegean Sea from Turkey's mainland to Greek islands also increased. These events on the Greek-Turkish border demonstrate that, as emphasized by Peter Andreas (2011), in the context of the institutionalization of migration and border policies, there are times when states help in the making of smuggling, and smuggling helps to make, or remake, states' policing apparatuses.

Over the days and weeks, violent clashes erupted between the migrants who wanted to cross the border and Greek border authorities who were trying to push them back. This unusual and developing border situation was prone to various types of smuggling activities: while some of the migrants were trying to cross the border on their own, others were relying on the help of smugglers. During the nearly two months that thousands of migrants amassed at the Greek-Turkish border, some managed to cross the border and entered Greece, despite the harsh resistance of Greek border authorities, and others remained on the Turkish side of the border, until the Turkish authorities made a decision, in late March 2020, to evacuate thousands of migrants who had been waiting at the border with Greece hoping to make their way into Europe, as a precaution amid the COVID-19 pandemic. In this highly politicized event, it remains unknown how many migrants and refugees crossed the Greek-Turkish border and entered Greece during the one-month period from late February to late March 2020: while the Greek and EU authorities noted only a couple of thousand, the Turkish officials insisted that tens of thousands crossed. The active involvement of smugglers in the whole process was highly visible. During this period, it was reported that as a growing number of migrants tried to cross from Turkey to Greece, smugglers were working in plain sight to facilitate the unauthorized border crossings. Along the banks of the river near Edirne, which forms part of the border with Greece, and along the Turkish coast off the Aegean Sea, which is close to several Greek islands, many smugglers were openly recruiting migrants who needed someone to take them across the border into Greece. There were cases where smugglers referred to Turkish president Recep Tayyip Erdoğan's comments in televised speeches, mentioning that he allowed the migrants to cross the borders and, indirectly, as smugglers argued, gave smugglers a green light to operate. For instance, one smuggler said,

> You see now that migrants continue to flock here, last two days thousands of people passed through here from Küçükkuyu to Lesbos island.... We help them as we did several years ago, in 2015, you remember... but now we do it openly, as our President Recep Tayyip Erdogan has given instructions on this issue, he has given his approval to their departure from Turkey to Greece.... So I help them... receiving some little money to provide them with boats. I help, and they go. (Local smuggler in Küçükkuyu, on the Turkish seaside close to Lesbos, interviewed in 2020)

The "open-border event of 2020" was a clear manifestation of how states can viciously politicize border-crossing issues, even going beyond their legal commitments, to achieve various domestic and foreign gains. It is necessary to emphasize two major factors here: first, the uneasiness and anxiety in EU states about the influx of refugees, and, second, the enormous impact of irregular migrants on Turkey's responses to the unauthorized border crossings, with a decision to ignore smuggling activities in early 2020. In fact, over the last two or three decades, the Turkish government's approach to migration and refugee issues has been instrumental, frequently using them as an item to bargain with in domestic and foreign politics, but this has become even more perceptible in the last ten years (Cantek and Soykan 2018). The following two quotations clearly reflect this line, as one directly reveals the approach from within the state bureaucracy, and the other echoes it through a migrant's experience:

> Now it isn't the situation that our relation with the European Union is good, we, our government, are, not pro-European now, in the past, we were taking serious to control our borders with the EU, because of EU membership possibility.... So we were serious to prevent illegal flows to Europe.... Now it is not fully the case.... It became an instrument to play with European politicians. (Official from the Ministry of Interior, interviewed in 2020)

They [governments] are playing with us.... Turkish government says, the doors are open you can go to Greece, and Europe, but the other side of the border is not open.... All the states, European Union and others, are playing with us, and smugglers also play with us.... They are not able to take us to Greece.... It is strange that smugglers try to have a deal with us in front of police.... Now I am vulnerable.... But I must be a strong man, I will not be a victim of these governments and smugglers.... I hope my country will get better and I will return there. (Egyptian migrant in Istanbul, interviewed in 2020)

CONCLUDING REMARKS

This chapter aimed to offer responses to the following two questions: How do three main actors in unauthorized border crossings—migrants, smugglers, and state (agents)—affect to varying degrees the conditions of migrant smuggling; and how do these actors experience their activities and position themselves within the migration-related structural and institutional frameworks? This chapter has also examined the agency and creativity that are directly embedded in the multifaceted relationship between the aforementioned actors and those structural and institutional frameworks. In this endeavor, the chapter focused on the case of Turkey's borders, which reveals the experiences of a hotspot where it is possible to observe the various aspects of border politics and migrant smuggling in the southeast corner of the EU, or eastern Mediterranean.

While referring to the structure-agency perspective in migration studies, the chapter argued that it is necessary to assess the nature of migrant smuggling and its connection to unauthorized border crossings by unpacking the complexities of these processes. It also argued that a closer look at the related structures, institutions, and agency-based factors allows for a better understanding of the political and technical realities concerning migrant smuggling and unauthorized border crossings. A historical and structural analysis of the case of Turkey as a transit country and of movements across its border with Greece sheds light on the influence of these factors on the dynamics, processes, and outcomes of migrant smuggling. At a macro-level, it appears that a key structural context for migrant smuggling in the region is both the EU's (and Greece's) and Turkey's attempts to control movements, as well as their interactions concerning this issue, which are mainly institutionalized by the EU, with so-called Europeanization efforts across the region, including Turkey. Border-control and migrant smuggling issues have always been very high agenda items in EU-Turkey relations, with the expectation of Turkey harmonizing its institutional capacity based on EU regulation to combat unauthorized border crossings and smuggling; consequently, this politicized environment has greatly affected the structural and institutional factors surrounding smuggling activities, as well as the acts of the various agents—namely, migrants, smugglers, and state—involved. At a micro-level, as my analysis of the narratives of the three main actors shows, migrant smuggling is a multifaceted process, in terms of both the actors involved and the strategies employed. The findings of this study confirm that the relationship between migrants and smugglers goes beyond the cliché image of predator and victim, taking place in a social context where a variety of interactions occur, including negotiation, assistance, and protection as well as exploitation. Highlighting the social bonds between migrants and smugglers by no means justifies the work of smugglers, but doing so allows us to fully address the complex nature of migrant smuggling and provides us with a better understanding of related migratory contexts and, particularly, the role of agency in these contexts. This study confirms that structures and institutions might occasionally create certain constraints for the smuggling activities, but they also function as enabling factors for agencies of the related actors to provide them with various creative choices in their activities. It also confirms that this symbiotic relationship between migrants and smugglers may also be observed between smugglers and border enforcement actors. As clearly shown by my analysis of the events on the Greek-Turkish borders in early 2020, in the context of the institutionalization of migration and border policies by states, it is possible to conclude that states might also help in the making of smuggling, and smuggling helps to make, or remake, the policing apparatus of the states.

Debates examined in this chapter, mostly in the micro-level analysis, focused on migrants' and refugees' experiences of unauthorized border crossings and smuggling activities, and examined their interactions with multiple actors and structural and institutional settings. Moving beyond binaries used in conventional migration studies, such as migrants and smugglers, or agency and structure, the analysis used in the migratory system approach outlines the multiple paths and agencies emerging in the politics surrounding unauthorized border crossings and smuggling activities. This chapter frames these politics as interactions among the various elements of structures, institutions, and agencies, and of the micropolitical engagements, tensions, and ambivalences that unfold in these interactions. This perspective generates useful empirical questions and provides a critical lens on questions of how to better understand the nature of migrant smuggling.

NOTES

1. Before going into some details concerning our empirical case, a short note must be made on the nature of the data on which the main arguments of this chapter are established. The data used in this chapter were obtained from various research projects conducted since the early 2000s in Turkey, Greece, and various other European countries: "Irregular Migration in Turkey," International Organization for Migration project, 2003; "Irregular Migration and Informal Sectors in Turkey," Istanbul Chamber of Commerce project, 2004; "Transnational Migration in Transition: Transformative Characteristics of Temporary Mobility of People, EURA-NET," EU FP7 project, 2014–2017; and "Evaluation of the Common European Asylum System under Pressure and Recommendations for Further Development, CEASEVAL," EC HORIZON 2020 project, 2017–2019. In particular, narratives from in-depth interviews with migrants, smugglers, and border security officers are used to highlight the interactions of the agencies in smuggling processes, as well as to elaborate their positions within the larger context of the structures and institutions surrounding them.
2. As noted in the introduction of this chapter, the data used in this study were obtained from various research projects conducted since the early 2000s.

REFERENCES

Andreas, P. 2011. "The Transformation of Human Smuggling across the U.S.-Mexican Border." In *Global Human Smuggling: Comparative Perspectives*, 2nd ed., edited by D. Kyle and R. Koslowski, 139–156. Baltimore: John Hopkins University Press.
Bakewell, O. 2014. "Relaunching Migration Systems." *Migration Studies* 2 (3): 300–318.
Cantek, F., and C. Soykan. 2018. *Representation of Refugees in the Media in the AKP Era*. Hâlâ Gazeteciyiz-Media Report-7 (October).
Düvell, F. 2006. "Crossing the Fringes of Europe: Transit Migration in the EU's Neighbourhood." Working paper no. 33. Centre on Migration, Policy and Society.
———. 2011. "Studying Migration from, to and through Turkey: The Context." Turkish Migration Studies Group at Oxford University Paper.

European Border and Coast Guard Agency. n.d. Homepage. Accessed February 16, 2023. https://frontex.europa.eu.

European Commission. 2016. *Communication from the Commission to the European Parliament, the European Council and the Council: Second Report on the Progress Made in the Implementation of the EU-Turkey Statement.* 15.6.2016 COM(2016) 349 Final. Brussels: European Commission. https://eur-lex.europa.eu/resource.html?uri =cellar:78122b4a-339c-11e6-969e-01aa75ed71a1.0002.02/DOC_1&format=PDF.

Flynn, D. 2005. "New Borders, New Management: The Dilemmas of Modern Immigration Policies." *Ethnic and Racial Studies* 28 (3): 463–490. https://doi.org/10.1080 /0141987042000337849.

Franck, A. K. 2019. "Corrupt(ing) Borders: Navigating Urban Immigration Policing in Malaysia." *Geopolitics* 24 (1): 251–269. https://doi.org/10.1080/14650045.2017.1422121.

Ghosh, B. 2000. "Towards a New International Regime for Orderly Movements of People." In *Managing Migration: Time for a New International Regime*, edited by B. Ghosh, 6–26. Oxford: Oxford University Press.

İçduygu, A. 2020. "Decentring Migrant Smuggling: Reflections on the Eastern Mediterranean Route to Europe." *Journal of Ethnic and Migration Studies*, online ahead of print, September 2, 2020. https://doi.org/10.1080/1369183X.2020.1804194.

İçduygu, A., and D. B. Aksel. 2014. "Two-to-Tango in Migration Diplomacy: Negotiating Readmission Agreement between the EU and Turkey." *European Journal of Migration and Law* 16 (3): 337–363.

İçduygu, A., and Ş. Toktaş. 2003. "How Do Smuggling and Trafficking Operate via Irregular Border Crossings in the Middle East? Evidence from Fieldwork in Turkey." *International Migration* 40 (6): 25–54. https://doi.org/10.1111/1468-2435.00222.

İçduygu, A., and D. Yükseker. 2012. "Rethinking Transit Migration in Turkey: Reality and Re-presentation in the Creation of a Migratory Phenomenon." *Population, Space and Place* 18 (4): 441–456. https://doi.org/10.1002/psp.633.

Kirişci, K. 2004. "Reconciling Refugee Protection with Combating Irregular Migration: Turkey and the EU." *Perceptions*, Summer, 5–20.

———. 2014. "Will the Readmission Agreement Bring the EU and Turkey Together or Pull Them Apart?" CEPS Commentary, February 4, 2014. https://www.ceps.eu/wp -content/uploads/2014/02/KK%20EU-Turkey%20readmission%20agreement.pdf.

Kühnemund, J. 2018. *Topographies of "Borderland Schengen": Documental Images of Undocumented Migration in European Borderlands.* Bielefeld, Germany: Transcript Verlag.

Kyle, D., and R. Koslowski, eds. 2011. *Global Human Smuggling: Comparative Perspectives.* 2nd ed. Baltimore: John Hopkins University Press.

McIntyre, P. 2012. "Constraining and Enabling Creativity: The Theoretical Ideas Surrounding Creativity, Agency and Structure." *International Journal of Creativity and Problem Solving* 22 (1): 43–60.

Portes, A. 1978. "Toward a Structural Analysis of Illegal (Undocumented) Immigration." *International Migration Review* 12 (4): 469–484.

Scharpf, F. W. 1997. *Games Real Actors Play: Actor-Centered Institutionalism in Policy Research.* Boulder, CO: Westview.

Spijkerboer, T. 2016. "Minimalist Reflections on Europe, Refugees and Law." *European Papers: A Journal on Law and Integration* 2016 (2): 533–558.

Steinmo, S. 2010. *The Evolution of Modern States: Sweden, Japan, and the United States.* Cambridge: Cambridge University Press.

Triandafyllidou, A., and M. L. McAuliffe, eds. 2018. *Migrant Smuggling Data and Research: A Global Review of the Emerging Evidence Base.* Vol. 2. Geneva: International Organization for Migration.

van Liempt, I. and J. Doomernik. 2006. "Migrant's Agency in the Smuggling Process: The Perspectives of Smuggled Migrants in the Netherlands." *International Migration* 44 (4): 165–190. https://doi.org/10.1111/j.1468-2435.2006.00383.x.

Watson, S. 2015. "The Criminalization of Human and Humanitarian Smuggling." *Migration, Mobility, and Displacement* 1 (1): 39–53. https://doi.org/10.18357/mmd11201513273.

Yıldız, A. G. 2016. "Implications of the External Dimension of European Immigration Policy for Turkey." In *The European Union's Immigration Policy: Managing Migration in Turkey and Morocco*, 97–150. The European Union in International Affairs. London: Palgrave Macmillan.

Zhang, S. X., G. E. Sanchez, and L. Achilli. 2018. "Crimes of Solidarity in Mobility: Alternative Views on Migrant Smuggling." *ANNALS of the American Academy of Political and Social Science* 676 (1): 6–15. https://doi.org/10.1177/0002716217746908.

CHAPTER 7

The Double Duality of Migrant Smugglers

AN ANALYTICAL FRAMEWORK

Jørgen Carling

MIGRANT SMUGGLERS PLAY CENTRAL ROLES in shaping migration. In this chapter, I develop a new framework for understanding migrant smuggling and counter-smuggling measures. Its core is what I call the double duality of migrant smugglers. For states and migrants alike, smugglers embody a typological duality: on the one hand, they are a threat, or a problem, but on the other hand, they are a resource, or a solution. Expressed in these abstract terms, the dualities that migrants and states experience are parallel. Hence the notion of a double duality. This Janus-faced feature is essential to the roles that smugglers have come to play.

A key to new insights lies in reaching across academic grounds. Here I draw connections between the technicalities of migration management, the politics of immigration, and the development of narratives. The last point is anchored in the field of narratology—a rich source of analytical perspectives beyond the widespread but often casual references to "narratives" in migration studies. In the context of this book, narratology offers valuable insights on the creative use of agency to make the most of limited operating space. I show how the dominant narrative on smuggling has changed in response to shifting dynamics of migration and altered geopolitical contexts. The clients of smugglers are increasingly likely to need international protection as refugees, and consequently, migration management and border control have become much more politically fraught than when counter-smuggling measures were a matter of stopping "illegal immigration." When states are cornered by irreconcilable demands, well-crafted narratives can provide a sense of closure and maintain authority. A messy reality of dilemmas and doubt is recast as a compelling plot of victims (migrants), villains (smugglers), and heroes (states). In the process, core realities of the smuggling experience are lost. Most strikingly, the vulnerability of smuggled migrants is often twisted to become a question of the smugglers' character.

The analytical contributions of this chapter are relevant across regional contexts. However, the discussion draws primarily on European experiences with migration across the Mediterranean. Consequently, I focus on smuggling by boat. This form of smuggling not only is numerically important but has also been symbolically and politically prominent and serves as an illuminating focal point for discussions that concern migrant smuggling more broadly.

My analyses can be summarized by the following core argument: disparate aspects of migrant smuggling are all connected, but the connections can be tenderly disentangled. The migrant–smuggler relationship is connected to the state–smuggler relationship; smuggling is connected to other parts of the migration management system, and the management system is connected to the narrative system. In the next section of the chapter, I preface this disentangling of connections with a bird's-eye view of the striking combination of continuities and changes in migrant smuggling across the Mediterranean over the past two decades. Thereafter, I lay out the notion of a double duality in greater detail and proceed to discuss, first, the migrant–smuggler relationship and then the state–smuggler relationship. The penultimate section brings the two together with a focus on the narrative aspect of migration policy. Finally, the conclusion recaps the connections that merit attention in order to understand migrant smuggling and responses to it.

The power of narrative, which I return to, is closely related to terminology. The terms *migrant smuggling*, *human smuggling*, and *people smuggling* coexist as virtual synonyms in the academic and policy literature. I deliberately use *migrant smuggling* because it is smuggling facilitating international migration that is of interest. People are smuggled across borders in other contexts too—for instance, to conduct covert intelligence operations or to escape law enforcement—but those are separate concerns. The case for using *migrant smuggling* is intimately linked to the definition of migrants. International migrants are people who cross borders with the intention of changing their usual place of residence, regardless of their motivations or legal status (IOM 2004). In other words, asylum seekers and refugees are specific categories of migrants. This is particularly important in the context of smuggling since migrants who are smuggled may or may not be fleeing a well-founded fear of persecution and have the right to international protection.

When they are being smuggled, not even the migrants themselves know who will eventually be given refugee status. This ambiguity is a case for using *migrants* in an inclusive manner, encompassing asylum seekers and refugees as well as other people on the move. But this approach is regrettably being thwarted by interagency turf battles in the United Nations (UN) system. The UN Refugee Agency sees this traditional definition of migrants as a threat to the agency's exclusive ownership of refugee issues and has fiercely campaigned against it (Carling 2017c). Its preferred understanding of *migrant* is a person who, by definition, has no right to refugee status. Partly due to the agency's campaign, "migrant smuggling" is often addressed without recognizing the role that smugglers play in bringing refugees to safety.

CONTINUITY AND CHANGE IN MIGRANT SMUGGLING TO EUROPE

Any analytical framework seeks to aid our understanding of a dynamic empirical reality. Thus, a review of both continuity and change since the first edition of this volume was published in 2001 is in order before introducing the conceptual framework. Indeed, European experiences with migrant smuggling have shifted in ways that provide an illustrative window on the mix of continuity and change.

The first obvious continuity is simply that smuggler-assisted irregular migration has been a constant feature at Europe's external borders. Routes have shifted and numbers have fluctuated, but the phenomenon itself—migrants using the services of smugglers to enter Europe in contravention of immigration regulation—has persisted.

Second, anti-smuggling rhetoric has been a consistent part of the government response. By *anti-smuggling rhetoric*, I mean portrayals of smugglers that emphasize negative characteristics in an essentializing, generalized, and often unsubstantiated way. For instance, the Spanish government has since the 1990s referred to migrant smugglers in Morocco as *las mafias*, ignoring the actual variation in organizational forms and the sometimes-blurred line between the smugglers and the smuggled.

The third constant has been that governments have responded to irregular migration with anti-smuggling measures. The exact measures have changed, but that should not distract from the continuity in attempts to curb migrant smuggling. So when the European Union announced the intention to use military action against smuggling vessels in early 2015, the prospect of "bombing the boats" represented newness in terms of its dramatic effect, but it would simply have been another mode of a well-established line of policy: targeting smugglers in order to make unauthorized entry as difficult as possible. In the end, bombing was not part of the plan, but the objective was nevertheless to "identify, capture, and destroy" smugglers' vessels.

A fourth continuity has been that smuggling practices have kept adapting in response to the anti-smuggling measures. As with the other continuities, there is constant change at the superficial level of actual practices. However, there is steadfast stability at the fundamental level of adaptation itself.

But some things have also changed. The first obvious change is the remarkable increase in the number of irregular arrivals in 2014–2015. There have been fluctuations before, but the scale of this increase makes it qualitatively different. Second, the political dimension changed in the sense that irregular migration and migrant smuggling achieved unprecedented prominence on the crowded European policy agenda. Third, there has been a remarkable shift in the composition of the irregular migration flow across Europe's external borders. When such migration first became a concern in the 1990s—and well into the 2000s—only a small proportion of the migrants sought asylum in Europe. This shift has implications for both the management system and the narrative system, to which I return in later sections.

THE DOUBLE DUALITY OF MIGRANT SMUGGLERS

The *double duality of migrant smugglers* refers to their simultaneous roles as (1) a threat, or a problem, and (2) a resource, or a solution, played vis-à-vis both migrants and states. As I will show, the two dualities are also closely intertwined.

TABLE 7.1. The double duality of the migrant smuggler

	Threat or problem	Resource or solution
For migrants	Agents of deception and exploitation	Providers of migration opportunities
For states	Menace to (direct) control of migration	Sources of moral capital for anti-migrant measures

Table 7.1 lays out the basics of the double duality. From the perspective of migrants, smugglers are first and foremost a resource, in the sense that they provide migration opportunities that would otherwise be unavailable. At the same time, smugglers are a threat because of the power they wield in the context of irregular migration, and the concomitant potential for exploitation and abuse. I expand on the relationship between migrants and smugglers in the next section of the chapter.

For states, the obvious role of smugglers, as they tend to view them regardless of their situational motivations, is to undermine state authority and control over migration.[1] "Smugglers," as such, can therefore easily be perceived as an unequivocal menace. Yet they have come to represent a moral resource for states that seek to contain migration. Liberal states are caught in a bind between their international humanitarian commitments and domestic political pressures to minimize immigration. On the one hand, they endorse the institution of asylum, but on the other hand, they want as few asylum seekers as possible given the sharp rise in domestic populist and nationalist movements. These conflicting aims are reconciled by making it as difficult as possible for potential asylum seekers to cross borders and present their claims. Anti-smuggling measures are central to these efforts, even as they result in people who are seeking shelter from persecution, or imminent danger, being prevented from even arriving to claim asylum at the destination. In this context, smugglers become a source of moral capital for states: by referencing the brutality of the smugglers, the very measures that prevent migrants from seeking safety are recast as protective measures for the migrants' own good.

SMUGGLERS AND MIGRANTS

To what extent can smugglers be blamed for the dangers and hardships that smuggled migrants experience? This question is met with disparate answers—some of which reflect the complicated relationship between smugglers and states. But this question also reflects the real duality of the human smuggler as encountered by migrants. On the one hand, the smuggler can fulfill the prospective migrants' wish of arrival; on the other hand, the smuggler embodies potential abuse and exploitation.

The extent of smugglers' blame is an empirical issue, bound to vary across contexts and individuals (see, e.g., Bredeloup 2012; Laacher 2009; Lucht 2011; Schapendonk 2011; van Liempt 2004; van Liempt and Sersli 2013). However, it is striking that in-depth ethnographic accounts repeatedly describe a more complex and ambiguous relationship than government portrayals of smugglers. A good example of government rhetoric was offered by the Norwegian government on the occasion of proposing new legislation in response to the European Union's Directive 2002/90/EC. "Migrant Smuggling Is Cynical Exploitation of People in Distress" was the heading of the press release, a quotation attributed to the minister in charge, who later became prime minister (Norwegian Ministry of Local Government and Regional Development 2004). Many smugglers are cynical and exploitative, but presenting these characteristics as inherent to migrant smuggling is obviously misleading. If we reject this sweeping characterization, how can we make sense of the variable relationship between migrants and smugglers, and the associated risks of being smuggled?

FOUNDATIONS OF VULNERABILITY

A first analytical approach lies in examining what exactly exposes migrants to danger when they are being smuggled. When smuggling involves transportation, as opposed to provision of documents that enable migrants to travel independently, the following foundations of vulnerability are common:

- Physical isolation: Smuggling typically takes place in isolated areas, be it the sea, deserts, forests, or mountains. Whatever emergency arises, assistance is often unavailable.
- Concealment: The need to travel undiscovered often comes at the cost of safety. This concerns not only the choice of route but also modes of travel, such as being hidden in trucks or containers.

- Strategic exposure: Smuggling at sea has sometimes adopted a modus operandi that depends on being rescued; consequently, unseaworthy vessels and other conditions that underpin the need for rescue have at times had strategic purpose.
- Overcrowding: Boats and trucks are often filled with a number of migrants that jeopardizes safety. There is an obvious economic incentive for smugglers to do this, since costs only increase slightly with the number of passengers while income increases proportionally.
- Absence of legal protection: The clandestine nature of smuggling means that migrants who are smuggled have little or no recourse to protection by law enforcement officials.
- Operational failures: Smuggling can be quite a challenging operation that is vulnerable to equipment failure and navigation problems. Many of the deaths in deserts and seas can be attributed to such issues.
- Psychological duress: The dangers of being smuggled can be exacerbated through vicious circles in which stress, fear, and other psychological reactions play a role.

On the whole, none of these sources of vulnerability result directly from smugglers' ill will. But their impact on migrants is mediated by smugglers' actions and priorities. Smugglers can take steps to minimize the risks—for instance, by not overcrowding vehicles and by safeguarding against equipment failure. At the same time, the vulnerability inherent in the smuggling context creates opportunities for exploitation that smugglers can abuse. The choices smugglers make are partly a matter of conscience but can also be interpreted with respect to the incentive structures that smugglers navigate.

INCENTIVE STRUCTURES

Across different settings, migrant smugglers are influenced by two overarching incentives: (1) to not get caught and prosecuted and (2) to secure, or maximize, their profits. Empirical research has shown how smugglers operate with other motivations too—including altruism (Achilli 2018; Mohammadi, Nimkar, and Savage 2019)—but these two incentives stand out as reasonable elements of a general analytical framework. The question is how they are likely to affect the safety of migrants.

Avoiding arrest and prosecution has become a growing concern for smugglers in different parts of the world as states have increased penalties and devoted greater operational resources to counter-smuggling measures. Luigi Achilli (2018: 91) recounts the assessment of a young Syrian smuggler's assistant in Turkey: "Look, it's a dangerous job, if the Turkish or Greek police catch you, you can spend up to 10–15 years in prison." One consequence of such risks is that smugglers avoid accompanying migrants farther than necessary. In the early 2000s, smugglers in the Mediterranean typically brought migrants near the coast, ordered them overboard and told them to swim ashore, and then returned with the boat (Carling 2007a). In recent years, migrants have more often made the entire journey by boat on their own (Mandić and Simpson 2017). Along the US-Mexico border, too, migrants are often endangered by abandonment when smugglers sense a risk of being intercepted and flee (Slack and Martínez 2018). As Danilo Mandić and Charles Simpson (2017) point out, counter-smuggling measures create risks that are shifted onto migrants as smugglers seek to minimize their own exposure.

The second overarching incentive—profit—translates into strategies for maximizing income and minimizing costs. Smugglers often push the number of paying clients on a single journey to the limits, with dire consequences for migrants' safety. An obvious example is the overcrowding of boats, which has contributed to large numbers of migrant deaths in the Mediterranean (Last and Spijkerboer 2014). Similarly, smugglers can cut costs by minimizing precautionary spending on reserve fuel, water, and life-saving equipment, for instance. Within this logic of short-term income maximization, the profits that smugglers make increase with the risks that migrants endure.

But smugglers also take a longer-term perspective on their own business and the reputation that they build (Bilger, Hofmann, and Jandl 2006; Biner 2018). A smuggler in northern Ethiopia summarized this business aspect of protecting migrants en route: "You think about their wellbeing because you need a good reputation. It affects the business if we don't treat them well" (Breines et al. 2015: 28). Indeed, most migrants who are smuggled across the Mediterranean or the US-Mexico border found their smuggler through referrals (Crawley et al. 2016; Slack and Martínez 2018). Moreover, smugglers commonly receive the full payment only after the migrant has reached the destination, in a deliberate arrangement to change incentives.

These observations show that, while migrants are in an unequal power relationship with smugglers, they potentially enjoy some protection from their consumer power. However, such protection requires a well-functioning market in which migrants can choose between smugglers based on other migrants' past experiences. Counter-smuggling measures can result in fragmented journeys and smuggler monopolies that erode migrants' opportunities for making informed choices.

FACILITATION AND EXPLOITATION

So far, I have referred to the straightforward notion of "the smugglers" that dominates discussions about migrant smuggling. However, this image has been undermined by field research and evolving empirical developments, in two ways. First, the distinction between smugglers and their clients is often blurred. Migrants work in smuggling on their way, they take on smuggling responsibilities (such as piloting a boat) against a discount, and they engage in self-smuggling. Second, migrants engage with a range of people on their way, and it is not always clear who is a smuggler and who is not. Taking a step back from the empirical specifics of different routes and experiences, it is useful to distinguish between two forms of interaction with migrants: facilitation and exploitation.

Facilitation occurs when migrants are helped to proceed on their journey, assisted across bureaucratic or geographic obstacles. Exploitation takes place when migrants are deprived of their resources or physical integrity for someone else's gain, be it through violence, coercion, or deceit. Facilitation and exploitation are both questions of degree, and they can occur in combination. Figure 7.1 illustrates this relationship and identifies different roles that people who interact with migrants can play.

By definition, smuggling entails facilitation. Smugglers therefore always occupy the upper part of the figure. But the smuggling may or may not also be exploitative. Point X represents a smuggler who simply provides a service for a price, in a reasonable transaction: facilitation without exploitation. Point Y, by contrast, represent a smuggler who facilitates mobility but also exploits or abuses his or her clients. The area between X and Y invites dis-

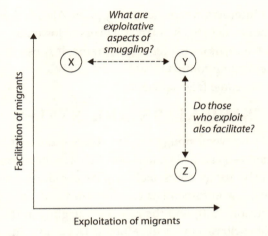

FIGURE 7.1. The relationship between facilitation and exploitation in interactions with smuggled migrants

cussions about the exploitative elements of smuggling. For instance, what is reasonable compensation for the smugglers' risk and expenses and what is exploitative overcharging? And when does undercommunication of the dangers amount to exploitation?

When migrants are clearly exploited, the exploiters are not necessarily smugglers. Long and fragmented journeys expose migrants to risks of exploitation and abuse from a range of individuals including officials, criminals, militias, and other migrants. Point Z represents actors who take advantage of the smuggling context to exploit migrants, without facilitating their journey. An example of growing concern is the kidnapping of migrants for ransom. Eritreans being smuggled through Egypt and Latin Americans transiting through Mexico have been victims of such crimes on a substantial scale (Breines et al. 2015; Leutert and Yates 2019). In some cases, the smugglers are involved, directly or indirectly; in other cases, the exploiters are completely detached from the smuggling activity. Often, the role of smugglers remains unknown and contested (Slack and Martínez 2018). This diversity of roles also challenges the notion of "the smuggler" as an unequivocal figure. Figure 7.1 thus invites an alternative perspective focused on the actions rather than the categorical identities of the people who interact with migrants who are being smuggled.

The type of interaction represented by point Z is a serious threat to migrants, but in policy debates it is usually overshadowed by concerns about smuggling. With a focus on protecting migrants, it is essential to acknowledge that the smuggling context creates vulnerabilities, but that the dangers do not necessarily come from smugglers.

SMUGGLERS AND STATES

The relationship between smugglers and states—like that between smugglers and migrants—is an ambivalent one. Scholars have examined this relationship through various lenses, including the paradoxical interdependence of smugglers and law enforcement for their own existence (Andreas 2012; Keen and Andersson 2018) and the role of smuggling in the securitization of migration (Ghezelbash et al. 2018; Moreno-Lax 2018). This chapter makes two original contributions to the field. First, it connects the smuggler–state relationship to the smuggler–migrant relationship through the notion of a double duality. The analytical value of doing so will become clear in the sections that follow. Second, the chapter shows how the smuggler–state relationship can be understood through the interaction of two systems: the management system and the narrative system. As will become clear, both are "systems" in the sense that they are made up of parts that are interconnected but may change through ripple effects. The analyses help specify what kind of problem smugglers represent to states, and also how they represent solutions.

THE MANAGEMENT SYSTEM

Migrant smuggling is part of a wider system of pathways and obstacles to migration. Since this is the system that migrants encounter, I have referred to it elsewhere as "the immigration interface" (Carling 2002, 2007a). From the state's perspective, it constitutes a management system—a totality of physical, organizational, and legal elements through which the state exercises migration management (Geiger and Pécoud 2010). The nature and significance of migrant smuggling—and hence the relationship between smugglers and states—depends on its shifting role within this system.

The European experience since the late 1990s contained a series of such shifts, illustrated in Figure 7.2. Initially, migrant smuggling was a direct pathway to illegal residence and work in the large unregulated sectors of southern European labor markets (King, Lazardis, and Tsardanidis 2000). Many more migrants entered illegality through overstaying legal permits, so smuggling was of limited significance. But the role that smuggling played was nevertheless clear (see Figure 7.2, phase I).

Throughout the different phases, destination states have fought smuggling directly, through criminal prosecution. But the strategic policy priorities vis-à-vis migrant smuggling have shifted. Initially, when smuggling offered access to illegal residence and work, an obvious priority was to intercept and apprehend migrants as they arrived. Spain, in particular, invested heavily in surveillance infrastructure. The so-called integrated system of external vigilance incorporated systems for detecting vessels well before they approached shore and dispatching patrols to intercept the passengers (Carling 2007b).

In theory, migrants who were intercepted could be detained and returned to their countries of origin, ultimately erasing the demand for smuggling. But obstacles to readmission meant that thousands of boat migrants were simply issued with expulsion orders and released when the maximum duration of detention was reached (Carling 2007b). The growing policy concern was the pathway smuggling–interception–detention–release–illegality (see Figure 7.2, phase II). As a result, policy efforts shifted to cooperation with countries of origin and transit in order to facilitate returns. The maximum detention periods were also extended.

More recent shifts in the composition of boat migration across the Mediterranean has added further complexity to the system (see Figure 7.2, phase III). A large proportion of migrants now seek asylum upon arrival and thereby enter the asylum-processing system. When applications are rejected, governments are tasked with ensuring return. This challenge is, to a certain extent, a continuation of past experience and depends on cooperation with countries of origin and transit. But in a larger proportion of cases, compared with previously, smuggled migrants seek asylum, have their applications approved, and are allowed to remain.

I would argue that, especially since the crisis of 2015, states' greatest anxiety is the pathway smuggling–interception–asylum claim–processing–approval, which does not include situations of illegality. Rejected asylum claims may represent logistical challenges, financial costs, and substantial risks of illegality, but granted asylum applications represent something

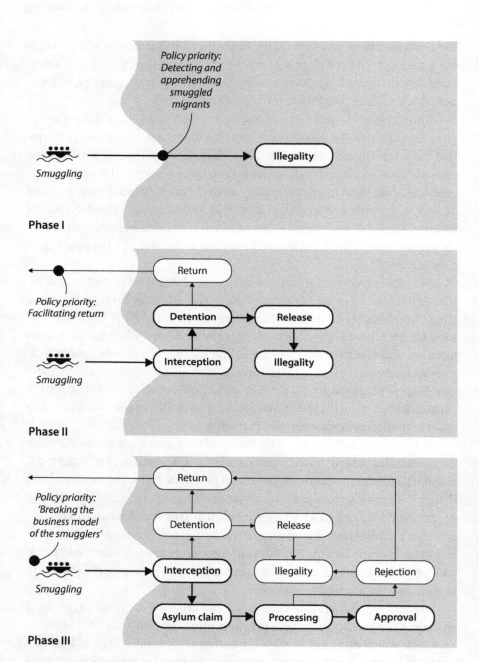

FIGURE 7.2. The shifting role of smuggling in the European migration management system

potentially worse: submission to unpopular and unwanted immigration (Carling 2011; Joppke 1998).

The most salient policy priority is to curb smuggling at the outset. The catchphrase is "breaking the business model of the smugglers," which has been applied quite loosely to diverse measures. Some measures, such as cutting the supply of vessels, do not alter the management system. Others, such as classifying transit states as safe third countries and returning all asylum applicants, effectively undercut the business model providing access to the asylum system by means of smuggling (European Commission 2016).

The contextual changes have altered the significance of smuggling for states. Interception is no longer the critical issue it once was, since migrants who intend to seek asylum have no incentive to enter undetected. But the challenge of containing unauthorized migration is also radically different when the migrants are, for the most part, seeking protection and can be labeled refugees. "Illegal immigration" may be a legitimate target for assertive political action, but "refugee flows" are not. The repercussions of this dilemma play out through the narrative system.

THE NARRATIVE SYSTEM

The narrative system of migration is the sense-making structure through which a complex reality is interpreted and represented. The term *narrative* is often used quite loosely and suggestively in migration research, including in work on smuggling. By contrast, it has particular meanings in research that incorporates narratological theory (Altman 2008; Bal 2009; Borins 2011; Franzosi 1998). In my approach to narratives of smuggling, I do not take specific texts as the starting point but instead address the underlying levels through which smuggling is interpreted and represented by states.

The analysis of narratives connects with this volume's crosscutting themes of creativity and agency. Narratology has developed primarily from the study of creative work, such as literature and film, and provided tools that also contribute to social science. The agency expressed in shaping narratives about smuggling also has a creative component. It can be illuminating to recognize this dimension, but the value of doing so hinges on our understanding of creativity. Seeing creative accounts simply as contrasts to "truth" is an analytical dead end. Rather, creativity is required to construct sense-making stories about overly complex realities. Some accounts portray the realities of smuggling in more meaningful ways than others, but they are necessarily selective.

Narratological approaches vary in terminology, yet all distinguish between two or three analytical levels of narrative. One influential model denotes them text–story–fabula, with the last denoting the series of logically and chronologically related events that are caused or experienced by actors (Bal 2009). Within this approach, the term *actants* is used to describe classes of actors who have an identical relation to the principle of the fabula.[2] In the story world of migration management and migrant smuggling, we might identify the key actants as (1) destination states that seek to control migration, (2) migrants, who seek to enter the destination state, and (3) smugglers, who enable migrants to enter. We can add (4) origin and transit states, which play important roles but have less clearly defined aspirations. Each of these four is a collection of different actors, but they are singular actants by virtue of their place in the fabula.

The analytical value of this perspective lies in examining how the same bare-facts fabula gives rise to divergent stories about migrant smuggling, which in turn are represented in specific texts, including policy documents, speeches, media coverage, and academic works. I leave the last step—textual representations—aside in this chapter and instead address how the divergent stories are premised on assigning particular character roles to the actants. These roles are simultaneously shaped by the characteristics of each actant and by their relations to each other—hence my reference to a narrative "system."

Figure 7.3 displays these four actants and the connecting relationships of greatest interest. The changes that have occurred in the migration management system since the 1990s are reflected in the nature of relations between actants, and in the character roles they are given by the dominant storyteller: destination states. In phase I, when smuggling was primarily a pathway to illegal residence, European destination states portrayed their role primarily in terms of protecting the integrity and security of European societies. Transit states were accused of turning a blind eye to smugglers, or colluding with them, and the trans-Mediterranean relationship was a largely antagonistic one. The relationship with smuggled migrants, too, was fundamentally hostile, in the sense that the phenomenon they represented—illegal immigration—was a legitimate target in mainstream politics.

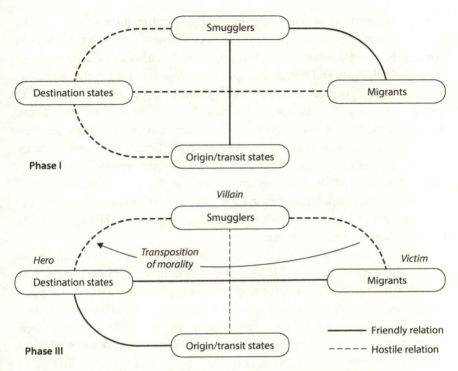

FIGURE 7.3. Actants in the narrative system of migration management

Two subsequent shifts in the migration management system have incited a new narrative. Figure 7.3 displays the resulting narrative system, labeled phase III because it overlaps with the third phase of the migration management system illustrated in Figure 7.2. The early years of the new millennium saw the adoption of Europe's Global Approach to Migration and Mobility, widespread externalization of European migration control, and the rise of "migration management" as the favored designation of the policy field (Collyer 2012; Geiger and Pécoud 2010). Cooperation with origin and transit states was needed to manage migration—not least to facilitate returns (see Figure 7.2). In the migration narrative system, origin and transit states were consequently given a new character role as "partners," symbolically and formally reinforced through "migration partnerships."

This policy-driven shift was followed by a shift in external events, with further repercussions for the narrative system. As mentioned earlier, a growing proportion of boat migrants in the Mediterranean were seeking asylum in Europe. When Syrians became the largest nationality in 2013, it not only boosted this trend in numerical terms but also shaped the image of smuggled migrants and hence their possible character role in the narrative. The salient refugeeness of Syrians strengthened the perceived legitimacy of boat migration, and the simultaneous surge in the number of migrant deaths demonstrated the vulnerability of smuggled migrants (Kallio, Häkli, and Pascucci 2019). In combination, these changes complicated destination states' relationship with smuggled migrants, who no longer represented unequivocally undesirable "illegal immigration." This shift in the character role of migrants in the mainstream destination-state narrative is vital, even as populist anti-migration narratives have simultaneously flourished and gained a foothold, also in national governments.

When destination states' relationships with migrants and with transit states are softened, political leaders are also deprived of potential targets for assertive action. The relationship with smugglers thus gains importance partly because of its residual position. In other words, when destination-country leaders are under mounting pressure to "do something" in a forceful manner, they have nowhere else to turn. Such pressure grew with the number of arrivals and fatalities, and so did the need for a good enemy.

A systemic analysis reveals how the triangular relationship between destination states, migrants, and smugglers evolved in this situation (see Figure 7.3). Smugglers and migrants are to a lesser extent portrayed as teaming up to undermine the integrity of destination states. Rather, the relation between them is portrayed in villain–victim terms. When the relationship is imbued with this moral dimension—virtuous refugees being exploited by cynical criminals—and destination states assertively target smugglers, states assume a heroic character role. So while the sympathy for migrants directly challenges states' scope for containment, it indirectly bolsters the legitimacy and virtuousness of counter-smuggling action. In other words, the good–evil representation of the migrant–smuggler relationship generates moral capital that is appropriated by destination states—even as they successfully seek to limit or deny the ability to even claim asylum.

Going back to the question of the facilitation and exploitation of migrants (see Figure 7.1), it is striking that the destination-state narrative only accommodates agents who both facilitate migration and exploit migrants (point Y in the figure). In other words, smugglers are seen as inherently exploitative, and the exploitation of migrants is attributed to smugglers. There is no room for smugglers who simply deliver a service as agreed (point X), and there is little attention to other agents of exploitation and abuse (point Z) (Carling 2017a, 2017b). This fixation on exploitative smugglers is rhetorically reinforced by the recurrent conflation of smuggling and trafficking.

The appropriation of moral capital has proved particularly powerful because of how smuggling is covered in the media (cf. Sanchez 2013). The good–evil representation of the migrant–smuggler relationship has immediate journalistic appeal, easily overshadowing the complexity of the relationship. Even the International Organization for Migration's head of media and communications has called the use of migrant smugglers "foolhardy" because migrants "walk into the hands of smugglers who have nothing but cynicism in their hearts" (Nebehay 2014). The more ruthless the smugglers, the more noble the cause of fighting them—even as it prevents migrants from accessing the asylum system. This humanitarian narrative of protection has become increasingly central, paradoxically, to the migration management mode of addressing migration smuggling.

CLOSURE AND CONTESTATION

The idea that smugglers represent both a resource and a problem for migrants and states alike—the idea of a double duality—points to the fundamental paradoxes and diverging interests in migration management and refugee protection (Andreas, this volume, chap. 2; FitzGerald 2019). Migration remains a demanding policy field with daunting challenges that, for a range of operational, ethical, and political reasons, cannot be "solved." This makes the narrative realm even more important. Narratives can provide a sense of closure when policy outcomes cannot. With the rising urgency and higher stakes of migration management in Europe since around 2013, we have perhaps witnessed not only an evolution of narratives but also a strengthened narrativity of policy making. In the context of narratives about migrant smuggling, closure does not require a resolution of the conflict between the actants, as much as a resolution of the ethical and operational dilemmas of policy making.

The simple scheme of narrative phases does not do proper justice to the coexistence of different narratives over time, especially the longer history of the protection narrative and the persistent importance of the integrity and security narratives (Boswell, Geddes, and Scholten 2011; Carling and Hernández-Carretero 2011). But the simplification makes salient the connection between the operational and narrative spheres, the internal logic of each narrative, and the specific nature of contention. Table 7.2 provides a schematic overview of the earlier and later destination-state narratives and contrasts them with the dominant counternarrative.

The destination-state narratives of integrity and protection both provide closure: each populates the story world in a way that gives destination states a virtuous character role with a clear sense of purpose. They are also broadly compatible. The contrasts between their portrayals of actants, evident in Table 7.2, can be resolved. Migrants are increasingly described as "migrants and refugees" with an understanding that migrants, by definition, do not have a well-founded fear of persecution (Carling 2017c). And states of

TABLE 7.2. Portrayal of key actants in contrasting narratives about migrant smuggling

Actants	Destination-state narrative of integrity	Destination-state narrative of protection	Counternarrative of containment
Destination states	Guardians of law and order who act to ensure territorial and administrative integrity	Champions of refugees who act to undermine smugglers' business model	Hypocritical states that seek to minimize protection responsibilities
Origin and transit states	Corrupt and irresponsible bystanders or accomplices	Partners in the fight against smuggling	Opportunistic states that use migration politics to their advantage
Migrants	Illegal entrants who are motivated by material aspirations	Naïve and vulnerable victims of exploitation	Rational actors with a legitimate need for protection
Smugglers	Organized criminals who run a low-risk, high-reward business	Cynical profiteers who prey on migrants	Service providers of varying quality who provide access to the asylum system

origin and transit are, in practice, regarded both as partners and with suspicion, even if the partnership aspect dominates the public discourse.

The problem with the destination-state narratives, of course, is that they can be challenged by facts. A growing body of research on migrant smuggling presents a counternarrative that emphasizes what is left out of destination-state narratives. In particular, it is evident that smugglers are, in most cases, a necessity for accessing the asylum system, and that destination states use counter-smuggling measures to minimize their protection obligations. This counternarrative is, in other words, a story about the containment of unwanted migration. The actants and their basic functions are the same, but their characteristics and motivations differ, with moral implications. Taken to the extreme, the character roles are even reversed, with smugglers as heroes who ensure protection for migrants, while destination-state villains seek to contain migrant victims in places of danger and hardship (Achilli 2018; Aloyo and Cusumano 2018; Mohammadi, Nimkar, and Savage 2019). The emergence of a state-led narrative and a counternarrative illustrates not only the importance of narratology but also the multiple layers of agency—playing out not only along borders, on smuggling routes, and in detention centers on the ground but also in organizing on-the-ground agency into sense-making stories.

CONCLUSION

This chapter set out by presenting the double duality of smugglers—the notion that they represent a resource and a threat for states and migrants. I conclude by recasting the argument as a call for making four types of connections.

The first is between the two dualities—that is, between the smuggler–state relation on the one hand and the smuggler–migrant relation on the other. These are not just parallel in their ambivalence, but functionally connected: the resource that smugglers represent to migrants is a threat for destination states, and the threat that they represent for migrants is a resource for destination states. The danger that smugglers represent vis-à-vis migrants is useful to states not only because danger can deter migration but also because it serves as a source of moral justification for counter-smuggling measures.

Second, we must be attentive to the connection between migrant smuggling and the other parts of the migration management system, through which the meaning and significance of smuggling are defined. This connection has determined the shifting policy priorities in Europe. Two decades ago, the greatest concern was the undetected arrival of migrants seeking work on the black market; today it is the arrival of asylum seekers with legitimate needs for protection.

The third connection is between the management system and the narrative system. The deepening paradoxes of the management system have been mollified by a sense of closure in the protection narrative. This narrative, centered on states protecting migrant-victims against smuggler-villains, manages to mobilize moral capital from the vulnerability of migrants to lessen the vulnerability of states.

Finally, there are the connections between the actants of the narrative system. Stories about migration management are defined by the character roles given to destination states, migrants, smugglers, and origin and transit states, and these roles are essentially relational. In this system, the role of smugglers is increasingly shaped by the lack of other targets for liberal states' assertive action in the field of immigration policy. Smugglers are the only remaining good enemy.

NOTES

1. Table 7.1 and my arguments so far simply refer to "states." By this I mean destination-country governments at the national and supranational levels, such as the European Union. Clearly, disagreements and power games *between* and *within* these states also play key roles in migration management and in efforts to contain smuggling. Others have examined these dimensions, and I leave them aside for now to let the chapter concentrate on the relationship between destination states and other actors.
2. The notion of actants, defined in relation to a fabula, as mutually constitutive diverges from the social-scientific notion of "agency," as it is used in this volume and elsewhere. It is this tension between the stylized actants in narrative representations and the bewildering actors in real life that opens analytical perspectives.

REFERENCES

Achilli, L. 2018. "The 'Good' Smuggler: The Ethics and Morals of Human Smuggling among Syrians." ANNALS *of the American Academy of Political and Social Science* 676 (1): 77–96.

Aloyo, E., and E. Cusumano. 2018. "Morally Evaluating Human Smuggling: The Case of Migration to Europe." *Critical Review of International Social and Political Philosophy*, online ahead of print, September 28, 2018. https://doi.org/10.1080/13698230.2018.1525118.

Altman, R. 2008. *A Theory of Narrative*. New York: Columbia University Press.

Andreas, P. 2012. *Border Games: Policing the US-Mexico Divide*. Ithaca, NY: Cornell University Press.

Bal, M. 2009. *Narratology: Introduction to the Theory of Narrative*. Toronto: University of Toronto Press.

Bilger, V., M. Hofmann, and M. Jandl. 2006. "Human Smuggling as a Transnational Service Industry: Evidence from Austria." *International Migration* 44 (4): 59–93.

Biner, Ö. 2018. "Crossing the Mountain and Negotiating the Border: Human Smuggling in Eastern Turkey." *New Perspectives on Turkey* 59:89–108.

Borins, S. F. 2011. "Making Narrative Count: A Narratological Approach to Public Management Innovation." *Journal of Public Administration Research and Theory* 22 (1): 165–189.

Boswell, C., A. Geddes, and P. Scholten. 2011. "The Role of Narratives in Migration Policy-Making: A Research Framework." *British Journal of Politics and International Relations* 13 (1): 1–11.

Bredeloup, S. 2012. "Sahara Transit: Times, Spaces, People." *Population, Space and Place* 18 (4): 457–467.

Breines, M., M. Collyer, D. Lutterbeck, C. Mainwaring, D. Mainwaring, and P. Monzini. 2015. *A Study on the Smuggling of Migrants: Case Study 2: Ethiopia–Libya–Malta/Italy*. Brussels: European Commission, Directorate-General for Migration and Home Affairs.

Carling, J. 2002. "Migration in the Age of Involuntary Immobility: Theoretical Reflections and Cape Verdean Experiences." *Journal of Ethnic and Migration Studies* 28 (1): 5–42.

———. 2007a. "Migration Control and Migrant Fatalities at the Spanish-African Borders." *International Migration Review* 41 (2): 316–343.

———. 2007b. "Unauthorized Migration from Africa to Spain." *International Migration* 45 (4): 3–37.

———. 2011. "The European Paradox of Unwanted Immigration." In *A Threat against Europe? Security, Migration and Integration*, edited by J. P. Burgess and S. Gutwirth, 33–46. Brussels: Brussels University Press.

———. 2017a. "Batman in Vienna: Choosing How to Confront Migrant Smuggling." Blog post, September 5, 2017. https://jorgencarling.org/2017/09/05/batman-in-vienna-choosing-how-to-confronting-migrant-smuggling/.

———. 2017b. Expert Panellist Statement on the Smuggling of Migrants. New York: Office of the President of the General Assembly, United Nations.

———. 2017c. "Refugee Advocacy and the Meaning of 'Migrants.'" PRIO Policy Brief, Peace Research Institute Oslo.

Carling, J., and M. Hernández-Carretero. 2011. "Protecting Europe and Protecting Migrants? Strategies for Managing Unauthorized Migration from Africa." *British Journal of Politics and International Relations* 13 (1): 42–58.

Collyer, M. 2012. "Migrants as Strategic Actors in the European Union's Global Approach to Migration and Mobility." *Global Networks* 12 (4): 505–524.

Crawley, H., F. Düvell, K. Jones, S. McMahon, and N. Sigona. 2016. *Destination Europe? Understanding the Dynamics and Drivers of Mediterranean Migration in 2015.* MEDMIG Final Report. Coventry: Coventry University.

European Commission. 2016. "Six Principles for Further Developing EU-Turkey Cooperation in Tackling the Migration Crisis." Press release, March 16, 2016, Brussels.

FitzGerald, D. 2019. *Refuge beyond Reach: How Rich Democracies Repel Asylum Seekers.* New York: Oxford University Press.

Franzosi, R. 1998. "Narrative Analysis—or Why (and How) Sociologists Should Be Interested in Narrative." *Annual Review of Sociology* 24 (1): 517–554.

Geiger, M., and A. Pécoud. 2010. "The Politics of International Migration Management." In *The Politics of International Migration Management*, edited by M. Geiger and A. Pécoud, 1–20. New York: Palgrave Macmillan.

Ghezelbash, D., V. Moreno-Lax, N. Klein, and B. Opeskin. 2018. "Securitization of Search and Rescue at Sea: The Response to Boat Migration in the Mediterranean and Offshore Australia." *International and Comparative Law Quarterly* 67 (2): 315–351.

IOM (International Organization for Migration). 2004. *Glossary on Migration*. Geneva: IOM.

Joppke, C. 1998. "Why Liberal States Accept Unwanted Immigration." *World Politics* 50 (2): 266–293.

Kallio, K. P., J. Häkli, and E. Pascucci. 2019. "Refugeeness as Political Subjectivity: Experiencing the Humanitarian Border." *Environment and Planning C: Politics and Space* 37 (7): 1258–1276. https://doi.org/10.1177/2399654418820915.

Keen, D., and R. Andersson. 2018. "Double Games: Success, Failure and the Relocation of Risk in Fighting Terror, Drugs and Migration." *Political Geography* 67:100–110.

King, R., G. Lazardis, and C. Tsardanidis, eds. 2000. *Eldorado or Fortress? Migration in Southern Europe.* London: Macmillan.

Laacher, S. 2009. "Passeurs, passagers et points de passage." In *L'enjeu mondial: Les migrations*, edited by C. Jaffrelot and C. Lequesne, 147–153. Paris: Presses de Sciences Po.

Last, T., and T. Spijkerboer. 2014. "Tracking Deaths in the Mediterranean." In *Fatal Journeys: Tracking Lives Lost during Migration*, edited by T. Brian and F. Laczko, 85–106. Geneva: International Organization for Migration.

Leutert, S., and C. Yates. 2019. "Migrant Smuggling along Mexico's Highway System." In *Critical Insights on Irregular Migration Facilitation: Global Perspectives*, edited by G. Sanchez and L. Achilli, 16–18. Florence: European University Institute.

Lucht, H. 2011. *Darkness before Daybreak: African Migrants Living on the Margins in Southern Italy Today.* Berkeley: University of California Press.

Mandić, D., and C. M. Simpson. 2017. "Refugees and Shifted Risk: An International Study of Syrian Forced Migration and Smuggling." *International Migration* 55 (6): 73–89.

Mohammadi, A., R. Nimkar, and E. Savage. 2019. *"We Are the Ones They Come to When Nobody Can Help": Afghan Smugglers' Perceptions of Themselves and Their Communities.* Migration Research Series, 56. Geneva: International Organization for Migration.

Moreno-Lax, V. 2018. "The EU Humanitarian Border and the Securitization of Human Rights: The 'Rescue-through-Interdiction/Rescue-without-Protection' Paradigm." *JCMS: Journal of Common Market Studies* 56 (1): 119–140.

Nebehay, S. 2014. "Record Number of Migrant Deaths at Sea, in Deserts This Year—IOM." *Reuters* (Geneva), September 30, 2014.

Norwegian Ministry of Local Government and Regional Development. 2004. "Menneskesmugling er kynisk utnyttelse av mennesker i nød." Press release, 170/204. Oslo.

Sanchez, G. 2013. "Four Corners: Human Smuggling and the Spectacle of Suffering." *Conversation*, November 19, 2013.

Schapendonk, J. 2011. "Turbulent Trajectories. Sub-Saharan African Migrants Heading North." PhD thesis, Department of Human Geography, Radboud University, Nijmegen.

Slack, J., and D. E. Martínez. 2018. "What Makes a Good Human Smuggler? The Differences between Satisfaction with and Recommendation of Coyotes on the U.S.-Mexico Border." *ANNALS of the American Academy of Political and Social Science* 676 (1): 152–173.

van Liempt, I. 2004. "De sociale organisatie van mensensmokkel." *Amsterdams Sociologisch Tijdschrift* 31 (1): 1–24.

van Liempt, I., and S. Sersli. 2013. "State Responses and Migrant Experiences with Human Smuggling: A Reality Check." *Antipode* 45 (4): 1029–1046.

CHAPTER 8

Financial Elements of Clandestine Journeys
HOW YOU PAY YOUR SMUGGLER MATTERS

Kim Wilson

THE ROLE OF INFORMAL FINANCE in the world at large has been explored by economic historians, journalists, policy analysts, and scholars and practitioners in international security. But less is written about how the mechanics of informal payment and financing systems undergird the smuggling of human cargo. In this chapter, I set out to explain a few of the financial and payment mechanisms used to source journey funds and finance transcontinental, largely clandestine journeys, highlighting how different modes of sourcing, financing, and payment affect the risks of a journey as experienced by smugglers, financial middlemen, and clandestine travelers.

My key messages are simple: First, the methods of financing used in human smuggling are varied, often customized, and depend on the traveler's country of origin. Such factors include the distance traveled, the number and nature of borders crossed, the traveler's budget, the smuggler's preferences and intermediaries, and the negotiating skills of the traveler. Second, while licit institutions like banks may play a part in human smuggling, where they do not, duplicate versions in the informal economy emerge to take their place. In many cases, a highly sophisticated system of financing evolves to include a web of informal money agents, banks, and family actors, a web whose beginnings extend back to ancient times. Born of necessity, the institutions in use and the financial mechanisms they deploy are creatively improvised and ever changing. Third, the financing and payment methods chosen (not just the agreed-on pricing) affect the safety and success of a journey.

RESEARCH METHODS

Between 2016 and 2020, a team of Tufts University researchers conducted studies on the financial journey of refugees. In all, we interviewed more than 438 migrant and refugee respondents, which we referred to as "travelers," across twelve countries and research sites. We also interviewed local smugglers and dozens of key informants. During the course of our interviews, various specifics on the financial elements of smuggling emerged.

Our research approach rested primarily on face-to-face, one-on-one, open-ended interviews. Critical to our methodology was using interviewers who were native speakers of the language of the travelers (Welch and Piekkari 2006). For example, our research in Costa Rica involved a team of twelve graduate students who hailed from India, Bangladesh, Nepal, Algeria, Morocco, Lebanon, and Costa Rica. These students spoke native-level Hindi, Urdu, Nepali, Bangla, French, Arabic, and Spanish and could interview Africans and South Asians directly in their natal languages (or in the case of West Africans, at least in their national language of French or English). In our Mediterranean studies, researchers came from countries including Afghanistan, Syria, and Tunisia and thus spoke Dari, Farsi, and various dialects of Arabic. In the United States and Mexico, researchers included native-level Spanish and Haitian Creole speakers. In all cases, we followed a constructed grounded theory approach, whereby we allowed findings to emerge unrestricted by the assumptions of a particular hypothesis (Charmaz 2014).

THE COSTS OF A JOURNEY

Before delving into the creative financial and payment instruments characteristic of clandestine finance, it is worth taking a look at the costs associated with travel. Smuggling services represented the single largest reported expense for transcontinental journeys. For travelers who used smuggling services (considering that many did not), their costs represented 75 to 85 percent of overall journey expenses. For those travelers who had purchased all-inclusive door-to-door smuggling packages where the smuggling ring handled all journey activities, smuggling costs represented nearly 100 percent of their journey expenses.

Smuggling prices varied considerably. To give one example, Nepalis who were under the care of their smuggling networks for the entire length of their journeys reported that their costs to get to the United States ranged between US$16,000 and $41,000, including smuggler fees. These high prices were independently confirmed (Adhikari 2020) and even surpassed, with one journalist reporting a price of $68,000 (Sapkota 2019). We saw similar variations for Afghans and sub-Saharan Africans trying to reach Europe. And while smuggling prices for Syrians attempting to reach Germany or Denmark were lower than for Afghans or sub-Saharan Africans aspiring to the same destinations, there were similar pricing variations.

What accounted for the wide variance? According to our respondents, first and foremost was the smuggling package on offer. While some packages were the door-to-door type just discussed—where smugglers manage all finances, including pocket change—others offered a bare minimum of service across short passages (Koser 2008; UNODC 2018).

A second factor that influenced pricing was the number of legs of the journey that required smuggling services. Journeys often incorporated segments that were not clandestine but involved legal travel with visas or transit passes easily obtained, which could cost less than completely clandestine journeys (Brigden 2018). A third factor was the degree of difficulty in obtaining ID documents, forged or purchased (Kyle and Koslowski 2011). A fourth was the mode of travel—overland versus air. A fifth was one's gender and family status. As told by many of our male and female respondents, smugglers did not like smuggling women. Women needed more protected shelter than men; they were perceived to move more slowly during the trekking, mule- and horse-riding, or river-fording segments; and most of all, women tending to children were seen to delay passages that required people to move in large groups. For instance, passage through the Darién wilderness that divides Colombia and Panama often had smugglers assembling travelers into groups as large as eighty members. The passers—that is, the local smugglers—were not inclined to look after women and children, whom they told travelers slowed their trek, unless compensated with a greater fee (Wilson 2009b).

Finally, a traveler's ability to negotiate was crucial to the final price of the smuggling deal. In places where smugglers were ubiquitous, competition abounded and prices were more transparent and varied little. However, in places where smugglers were fewer, or less conspicuous, a good price depended on an individual's ability to negotiate. As one Afghan researcher noted, individual negotiating skills were critical to getting a good deal: *jor amad*, meaning the way in which parties come to terms with one another, was key. Each pricing arrangement was tailor-made.

SMUGGLING SERVICES WORTH PAYING FOR

Depending on the smuggling package, smugglers offered logistical services in the same way that legitimate travel agents would. They would secure lodging and transportation by plane, train, bus, boat, or horse. Some hoteliers in Colombia and Costa Rica, working in tandem with larger smuggling operations, offered remittance services for those travelers who followed a pay-as-you-go plan (discussed later in this chapter). Hoteliers would instruct the lodgers to have their remittances sent in the name of the hotelier. The hotelier would then visit the remittance kiosk, use his or her own ID to receive the remittance, and deduct the cost of lodging from the remittance.

Regarding bribes, door-to-door smuggling packages covered them—both the petty kind designated for specific border officials or police and the grander bribes involving higher-level officials (Busse and Vásquez Luque 2016).

Forged, stolen, purchased, or rented documents—particularly passports with fake visas—were also standard offerings of smugglers. For travelers who purchased door-to-door packages, smugglers provided all documents. Smugglers adopted different strategies to procure documents (Kyle and Koslowski 2011). A first strategy was to obtain a quality forged document—a passport or a visa or both. Forgeries ranged markedly in quality with many we spoke to, underscoring the notion of "you get what you pay for." A second strategy had members of the smuggling network purchasing or renting look-alike passports from legitimate passport holders in the destination country and making arrangements to ship the documents to the traveler. For door-to-door smuggling services, the cost of procuring the documents was bundled into the overall package. Others paid à la carte.

One service widely reported by our travelers but not as often discussed in the literature was allowances that smugglers dispensed to travelers. Smugglers would dole out money along various stages of the journey, a service that travelers appreciated and that naturally was part of what they purchased in a door-to-door package. Cash allowances were not just used as pocket money but could also serve as a payment for those journey legs where a local passer could not accompany the traveler (Wilson 2019b). An Indian venturing north from Chile described how he used the $1,000 allowance handed to him by smugglers:

- $200 for a bribe to the border police in Chile.
- $20 for the hotel in Peru.
- $550 paid to the smuggler's local handler in Lima.
- $20 to the man posing as a handler at the border of Ecuador, who vanished with the funds. (Their landlord rescued them and helped them board the bus.) After spending money on bus and food, he was left with only $30.
- They had yet to bribe the border "cops" between Peru and Ecuador. An Ethiopian, being handled by their same smuggler, paid $180 on their behalf.
- From there, his trip and funds were coordinated by a ring of handlers and he had no more out-of-pocket expenses.

Travelers appreciated the cash allowances, even with specific instructions attached. They were grateful that they did not need to incur the risk of carrying cash nor the hassle of trying to convert their money in and out of local currencies.

MUSTERING FUNDS TO PAY FOR SMUGGLING SERVICES

Travelers gathered funds in varied ways. For those who escaped with nothing but the clothes on their back, there was no time to secure smuggling services. For those who had time to plan, there was an ability to assemble a financial portfolio that would afford them the hope of a safe passage. As one might imagine, borrowing, liquidating assets into cash, and receiving gifts were the main ways of mustering travel money.

The size, cost, and terms of loans varied by region. Few Africans reported borrowing large sums from friends and family to finance their travel to the United States. This was because so few—none that we spoke to—needed to fund transcontinental smuggling services. They only began to pay for services once in South America.

But for South and Central Asians traveling to Europe or the United States, borrowing was critical. Those interviewed in Greece, Turkey, and Jordan reported borrowing heavily from friends and family to fund their travel. Taking on debt from third parties (nonfamily lenders) was a more salient strategy for South Asians traveling through South America to the United States. Their portfolios contained both moneylender debt and debts to friends and family. Family debt was often not in the regular size and shape of a specific loan but leaned more toward a tacit promise to send money home.

Details came from travelers whose journeys originated in Nepal. Those who had made it as far as New York City reported that portions of their journeys were funded by Nepalese moneylenders at the per annum rate of 18 to 36 percent. Interestingly, they could garner those loans only if they were bound for the United States. At one point, destinations in Europe and Australia were equally attractive investments, but as of December 2019 when we completed interviews in New York City, this was no longer the case. One cab driver in the hilly, touristed areas of Nepal exclaimed, "If you want to buy land for a hotel here, you cannot find the money. If you want to invest in a taxi service, you cannot find the money. If you want to migrate to the US, the moneylenders will line up behind you."

A second way travelers gathered sums for smuggling was by tapping their own savings. Afghan travelers described in careful detail how they had accumulated savings over the years with the intent of financing a long-distance journey. They had stored money in their places of business, in their homes, and in banks. Some had put their savings with money guards—trusted neighbors and shopkeepers (Collins et al. 2009). The source of their savings was typically earnings, but occasionally a colorful story would emerge. For instance, a young Afghan couple hoping to leave for Turkey had amassed close to $5,000 to pay for a smuggler, an amount that was topped up by an additional $5,000 win from the Afghan version of the quiz show *Who Wants to Be a Millionaire?* (Amiry 2020).

A researcher from our team in Nepal reported that many journeys were financed by the Nepali travelers themselves, with money sourced from their own wages and savings. They had earned comparatively good incomes by working in places like Dubai and Qatar. The work, though, was so grueling that they did not wish to return to the Gulf. Their brokers based in the Gulf would take their passports and make them "work long days in unbearable heat." When they returned to Nepal with cash to spare, they decided the best investment would be to get to the United States.

A third method to collect funds was to sell assets for cash. Travelers relayed how they liquidated land, homes, or livestock. "We sold everything: refrigerators, a washing machine, everything," an Iranian woman said in Greece. "We sold the house, closed the bank account, liquidated anything to get here." She went on to describe how she sold off, fire-sale style, equipment from her business—she was a beautician with her own shop—as well as the electronics and furnishings from her home. It took her about a month to liquidate everything.

Imminent danger compressed the time allotted for selling assets. This was the case for many fleeing Syria, all of whom needed to be smuggled through various internal checkpoints or, if crossing to Turkey, then at the Turkish border. The selling of assets took place over a matter of days, generating funds that were a pittance of what they would be during a peacetime liquidation.

A fourth way to muster funds was to receive gifts from family, friends, and the local temple, church, or mosque. Mustering funds for smuggling services was less of a task for West and Central Africans than for Asians, as the segments of their journeys that required smuggling services were not transcontinental but confined to South and Central America. To pay for these services, they amassed funds from local family and religious networks. And those with relatives in the United States or Europe pressed family relationships into service, asking relatives to send remittances.

A fifth way was a variation on the method just described, one to which we assigned the appellation "crowdfunding from the diaspora with a pay-it-forward twist." Many diasporas span continents, their reach allowing people trapped behind political boundaries to secure the help of smugglers. One example from Eritrea is particularly instructive. When a person tries to leave the country, he or she signals relatives who press into use a network of kin. Their method of mustering funds blended an ethical contract with the tactic of crowdsourcing. In this scheme, the traveler benefiting from the smuggling service incurred no debt per se but did incur an obligation of providing support to other travelers in the future. Instead of taking out a personal loan to be paid back with interest, the traveler became part of a human network where savings from family and friends were collected into a mobile phone of one member of the network, then transferred via a digital money-transfer service to the smuggler as soon as the traveler reached his or her destination. For example, Zain was one money-transfer service that travelers mentioned repeatedly. Rose, an Eritrean woman, discussed her experience:

> I spoke to my parents and told them I wanted to leave. I called my Eritrean friends in Sudan. One of them arranged everything for me. She looked for a smuggler.... I didn't have to sell anything: my husband's family, my family, all our friends in other Arab countries sent money to my friend [in Sudan]... My friend told me I had to meet a driver at 3pm a week later, in Asmara. I stayed home for a week and waited. I had about $200 with me. I didn't take clothes with me—only something to eat. I knew nothing about what would happen. In the car, there were four other women. The driver was nice. He didn't speak or anything. He brought us to Khartoum—the driver knew everything about the border and he went through a secret way. Maybe he paid police. I don't know. When I got to Khartoum, I called my friend and told her I had arrived. She paid the $5,000 (which she had collected from Eritreans around the world) to the smuggler and I went to her house. I spent three months in Sudan, not working. I was very afraid of the Eritrean security in Sudan. I knew people who had been sent back from Sudan, so I was hiding.

But Rose realized she could not continue in hiding forever, and her sister repeated the crowdfunding exercise until Rose reached Greece. Other Eritreans echoed that this blended crowdfunded "pay-it-forward" model was crucial to their own journeys.

A male Eritrean confirmed the norms surrounding these arrangements. Asked whether travelers were expected to repay the people who helped them, he responded, "No, no, no, not at all. But if my Eritrean friend asks for my help, I must give it. I will give back this way. It's a collective system. All Eritreans understand each other on this."

PAYING FOR SMUGGLING SERVICES

Modes of payment can be critical to a journey's success. While the price of a journey mattered to smugglers, middlemen, and travelers, so did the form of payment. As reported by our respondents, negotiating payment methods and payment timing meant balancing two competing risks: one dominating the *smugglers'* concerns, and the other dominating the *travelers'* concerns (Koser 2011; Mandić and Simpson 2017; Williams and Baláž 2012).

Travelers were concerned with *performance risk*—the risk that the smuggler would not safely transport them to their final destinations or predetermined waypoints. Smugglers were concerned with *payment risk*—the risk that travelers would not be able to make full payment for smuggling services. Table 8.1 illustrates the range of payment methods to reduce these two risk categories.

The table also illustrates something else: the range of informal options, meaning the range of options that are not regulated by legitimate government institutions, are mirror images of formal and legitimate options. For instance, on routes that lead to the Mediterranean, if the smuggler and traveler agree that the smuggler will be paid leg by leg (pay-as-you-go), then one option is for a money agent—a local agent who assists traveler customers with paying their smugglers—to hold the travelers' money and release funds to the kingpin at each waypoint (Wilson 2020; Wilson and Krystalli 2017). This is an informal reflection of well-established formal services known as "placing funds in trust" or "in escrow" (Kim 2007).

Financial relationships and the transactions they spawned were never confined solely to a formal (regulated) space or an informal (unregulated) space. What was clear was that in the absence of formal services, informal actors would create mirror-image services. Products like informal insurance, guarantees, and escrow were as much a part of the informal economy as were more formal options like Western Union, MoneyGram, and mobile money—for example, M-Pesa, Tigo, MTN, and the like.

The variations on informal services revealed what appeared to be an almost infinite number of ways in which a service could be customized. We saw major patterns emerge from a dense tangle of financial detail. Next, I highlight a few of the variations described by our respondents, categorizing them by when smugglers were paid.

TABLE 8.1. Modes of paying a smuggler

Mode of payment	Payment timing		Financial enhancements (for demand side—travelers)	Financial enhancements (for supply side—smugglers)
	Prepay (Traveler or family pays in full for entire journey before departure)	Postpay (Traveler pays in full after destination is reached)		
Pay directly to smuggler or his or her agent	Pay leg by leg, pay-as-you-go (Traveler pays on reaching predetermined waypoints)		Insurance and refunds offered by "financial supplier" (money agent, smuggler, or other third party) for acceptance of partial payments	Physical collateral (Required by smuggler)
	Yes, evidence of this; common in Syria	Yes, usually for shorter legs, as in Syria (e.g., one border crossing)	Yes, but based on initially negotiated terms	In many instances in the Mediterranean and also South America where the traveler himself became the collateral
	Yes, evidence in Nepal and Bangladesh, where funds may be deposited directly into the smuggler's bank account or into another bank account as instructed by the smuggler	Used when smuggler wants to see proof that traveler has the cash	Some "third-party insurance" available Some partial payment accepted based on where on the route the journey ended, if not at the final destination	Smugglers do not release the traveler until the family makes the payment
Via money-agent system	Yes, the traveler pays money agent, and money agent pays smuggler upon reaching final destination	Yes, money agent releases funds to smuggler at predetermined waypoints	Yes, some instances where the refugee can get money back if the journey failed In many cases, no refunds; in some instances, partial payment would be accepted based on where the traveler ended up	Yes; in instances where the smuggler chooses or recommends the money agent, the smuggler knows that if he or she applies certain pressures, the money agent will pay the smuggler
	Yes, in this case the money agent is just a money-transfer agent (*hawala*) Very common for travelers hailing from Afghanistan and Iran			

(continued)

TABLE 8.1. (continued)

Mode of payment	Payment timing		Financial enhancements (for demand side—travelers)	Financial enhancements (for supply side—smugglers)
Via family member or trusted person (kinship finance)	Yes, trusted neighbor or family member pays smuggler entire amount before travel	Yes, trusted neighbor or family member releases funds to smuggler when traveler reaches predetermined waypoints	Yes, money is sent through money agent or bank according to family member instructions	Yes, in many instances in the Mediterranean and also South America where the traveler himself or herself becomes the collateral
		Yes, money can be returned to the traveler or family by the smuggler or his or her agent if the traveler does not reach destination	Traveler may be detained or beaten while waiting for smuggler to get paid	Smugglers do not release the traveler until the family makes the payment
Via a bank	Yes, where available	Yes, where available; in Nepal and Bangladesh refugee's family deposits money into the smuggler's bank account	None reported	None reported

POSTPAYING A SMUGGLER FOR EACH SUCCESSFUL LEG

Traveling through the Americas, Nepalis and Bangladeshis paid their smugglers in installments, using a bank or local agent back in their country of origin. Payment was linked to the traveler's safe arrival at a specific place—for example, Quito, Ecuador, or Izmir, Turkey. To pay smugglers in the Mediterranean, travelers worked not through banks but through kin or informal money agents. The *sarafi* system, which I will refer to more broadly as a "money-agent system," served a double purpose.[1] Money-agent systems not only made payment to smugglers convenient, bypassing the need for travelers to carry large sums of cash, but they also served as a form of guarantee. If the smuggling network did not deliver the traveler to the specified waypoint, presumably the money agent would not release funds to the kingpin.

A third-party money agent offered a buffer between the *nonperformance risk* potentially experienced by the traveler and the *nonpayment risk* potentially experienced by the smuggler—as well as reducing the risk of carrying cash along the way. Releasing payment upon completing a successful journey seemed to at least partially insure the traveler. An Afghan man described traveling with his family from Turkey to Greece: "Once we reached Greek territory the Greek police saw us. They came to our rescue and transferred everyone from our boat to a ship. I had put money with the *saraf* and he released it once we reached each of our destinations. The smuggler had people in each location who transferred us along our assigned routes. The smuggler doesn't get paid if anyone was deported—only if the destination is reached." Because of this system in which the smuggling network was compensated only when the traveler reached specific waypoints, smugglers had financial incentive to move travelers to those waypoints, even if they were sick, exhausted, or injured. This could spell disaster for travelers. An egregious example involved one of our respondents from Nepal. His smuggling ring was shepherding him through Nicaragua—a country hostile to travelers—when they were apprehended. The traveler was shot and landed in a hospital and then prison. He was finally dumped at the Costa Rica border two months after being apprehended. Though severely injured and wanting to return to Nepal, he knew the smuggler would not receive his fee until he had deposited the traveler in Mexico, the agreed-on waypoint for a final payment. The traveler had to escape the smuggler's clutches, literally, and sought the help of the International Organization for Migration (the UN's migration agency) for a voluntary return.

PREPAYING THE SMUGGLER DIRECTLY OR THROUGH KIN

In this method, the traveler, before departure, pays to the smuggler either the full price of the entire journey or the price for parts of the journey. We found this was often the case when crossing the Aegean by boat from Turkey to Greece. It was also common within Syria and when crossing the Syrian border to Turkey. Often friends and family would make payments on behalf of the traveler, either because the traveler lacked sufficient funds or because a family member had more access to the smuggler.

For example, a male Syrian traveler found a smuggler through his hotel in Istanbul. The smuggler was in contact with his cousin, who paid the smuggler just over $18,000. The cousin gave the money "to someone in Syria," who gave the money to someone in Turkey, who then gave the money to the smuggler. He said, "When I met the smuggler, he had already been paid."

This method of prepayment clearly places the traveler at risk. He or she has little recourse if the smuggler balks. When asked about such fears, a male Syrian in Greece responded, "It is the fact that you don't have a choice but to trust a smuggler who is a criminal, and you always have to fear that he will rob you or not honor the deal and not get you to your destination."

POSTPAYING THE SMUGGLER DIRECTLY OR THROUGH KIN FOR ENTIRE JOURNEY

On the opposite end of the payment spectrum were various forms of postpayment—paying for the journey in whole or in part after the journey had been completed. While this option may reduce performance risk for travelers, travelers also run the risk of becoming "human collateral" as the smuggler seeks to ensure payment.

We heard of the many harms endured by travelers who were unable to make their payments expeditiously. One Afghan man in Greece reported that from Zahedan, Iran, he traveled with five other men. They were passed from smuggler to smuggler like a baton "in an unbroken chain from one border to the next." Once he arrived in any predetermined destination, he would call his parents and have them wire funds to the smuggler's bank account.

When asked what would happen if someone failed to pay, he continued, "That happened to others, but not to me. I saw boys get their ears cut off for lack of payment of their smugglers' fees."

"PAY-AS-YOU-GO" FOR SMUGGLING SERVICES

Many families and individuals paid for smuggling services at various points in their journey. This was especially common for Syrian travelers. One Syrian woman we met in Greece told us that her trip cost $12,000, or $3,000 per family member. It took her ten days to cross Syria via multiple internal checkpoints. Seven smugglers were involved, each requiring a payment.

Nowhere was the pay-as-you-go system more prevalent than in the Americas. Africans traveling from South to North America hired smugglers piecemeal. They could haggle at the Darién Gap, the passage through or around Nicaragua, and at the border crossing between Ecuador and Colombia.

In the Darién Gap, travelers would often group themselves together to retain one *donker* (a migrant term for a local smuggler, adopted by South Asians who had crossed the Darién). Typically, the *donker* would require a twenty-dollar payment each morning before that day's jungle march began. Quickly, travelers realized that the *donker* had no incentive to make the jungle trek a swift one. Many reported walking in circles for days as the *donker* would stretch the journey and thus his earnings over the course of weeks.

Finessing the final price of a leg took frequent exchanges. One Cameroonian woman described her experience after she had been forcibly returned from Nicaragua back to Cameroon:

> I let my smuggler know that we had been returned. He seemed to have this information already and promised that without paying more, I could try again. He told everyone who had paid $330 that they would have to pay another $80. He asked me to pay another $150 (for a total of $300), but I said no. I would only pay $50 more. When we met up to make the crossing attempt, he said that I would have to wait because he had customers who were willing to pay more. He was very nice and said, "Don't worry, I will take you, just not tonight." That was last night, and I will try again tonight.

The good bargaining skills deployed by this shrewd traveler could be a cause for alarm for others. The research team heard grumblings about her specific negotiations. Some questioned whether she was inflating the price in order to pocket the difference, or if she had lied about the timing of their anticipated departure so as to secure her own spot. While these questions resolved themselves when this traveler reached Honduras, her strategies had the potential to backfire.

WRITTEN CONTRACTS AND GUARANTEES

Financial guarantees worked to reduce uncertainty in clandestine travel. An informant in Athens described a system he called "three tries," popular among travelers as well as smugglers. Such a system may or may not include a financial middleman. In this scheme, a smuggler agrees to procure plane tickets and documents—forged or stolen—for three trips. He only procures the tickets and documents for the second trip if the first fails, and for the third if the second fails. He (overwhelmingly "he," as discussed) has calculated the costs so that he makes a large profit if the traveler successfully journeys from Athens onward to Europe on the first try. He still makes a profit if the second try is successful. But on the third try, if the traveler does not make it, the smuggler loses or makes very little money.

We learned of various forms of insurance whereby, for a small fee (typically fifty dollars), a smuggler would guarantee a successful journey, and should the journey fail, the smuggler would issue a refund.

A range of guarantees existed that would protect either the service providers (the smuggler or the money agent) from *nonpayment risk* or the traveler from *nonperformance risk*, or both. Most arrangements between travelers and money agents were verbal, but not in all cases. Our informant in Kabul described the story of a traveler, Amjal, and the representative of a smuggler, Shuja:

> Shuja, someone whom Ajmal knew, knew the smuggler. Amjal was helping his brother to cross from Afghanistan to Europe. Shuja, a representative, speaking on behalf of the smuggler had asked Ajmal to find someone that he trusts to "freeze" the money with them. Shuja had also recommended one *saraf* [money agent] in a Kabul neighborhood. When Ajmal showed up at the *saraf* with Shuja, the money agent wrote, signed and stamped a letter acknowledging the receipt of the money as an "amanat" (a kind of guarantee in this case where

the money is held in trust) good for three months. Ajmal, who has worked in administration and finance for the past ten years, insisted on putting some concrete terms in this letter: for example, what is the money for, the name of the person traveling, destination, conditions for release of installments, etc. For the *saraf*, it was either *amanat* (a less formal guarantee) or no deal. *Amanat* means when you trust something with someone. In this case, putting the money in the *saraf*'s trust.

The letter served less as a contract and more as an acknowledgment for receipt of deposit.

Money agents and smuggler insurance agents ran risks beyond nonpayment risk: they ran both reputation and legal risks. Their reputations as trustworthy businesspeople were valuable and worth protecting. Many money agents were involved in other businesses, such as trading in cloth and foodstuffs, that were attached to, but separate from, financial services. In this sense, their venerable family histories held a valuable form of social and economic capital, not to be eroded.

Risks associated with breaking laws also weighed on certain money agents in ways that surpassed the risks that smugglers faced. While smugglers were the ones who transported human travelers, money agents were the ones who transported the money that travelers needed to finance their journeys. Smugglers whose locations, physical cell phones, phone numbers, and SIM cards are in constant flux are difficult to trace. By contrast, money agents, who often operate from fixed market stalls, are easily traced. According to an informant, a sign in the Sarai Shazada neighborhood of Kabul chock-a-block with money agent counters warns that involvement with *qachaq-e-insan* (smuggling) is illegal. So while money agents may be duped by families failing to reach their agreed-on destinations, they have no available legal remedy. They must choose between disappointing traveler families and disappointing smugglers. In either case, the "trust is broken."

COMPLETING THE FINANCIAL CIRCUIT

Financing and paying for smuggling services did not stop once a traveler reached their destination. Our research in Queens, New York, illustrated how Nepalis continued to repay their debts, helped newcomers repay their debts, and proceeded to finance the journeys of Nepalis interested in migrating to the United States.

The system that helped the Nepalis is known as the *dhikuti*, a traditional means of rotating savings. Dhikutis are found all across Queens, each operating a little differently based on customs from their specific geographic, ethnic, and caste communities. I can offer this rough general description: Each month, Nepali contributors pay a predetermined amount into the dhikuti, and each month, one member takes home the lump sum. A typical contribution is $1,000. If there are twenty members in the dhikuti (twenty was the most commonly mentioned number), then one person would receive the $20,000 payout. This process would continue until each member of the dhikuti had received his or her $20,000 payout. Then, the dhikuti would start afresh. "In this way," our key informant explained, "the Nepali immigrant can pay off his debt or accumulate funds to invest in the smuggling of another Nepali." Those who could work eventually paid off their smuggling debts and many of them became the financiers of inbound Nepali migrants, adding in an extra charge of an annual 36 percent interest (or 3 percent per month).

These types of systems can be found in many communities across the United States—known as *tandas* for Mexicans, *tontines* for Congolese, and *ekubs* for Ethiopians—and all can help amass funds for smuggling services. To the degree that they use funds to pay for smuggling services, we do not know, but future research might help us find out.

LOOKING TO THE PAST TO HELP US UNDERSTAND THE PRESENT: HISTORICAL MECHANISMS OF FINANCING

The financial instruments of contemporary migration described in this chapter did not surface in a vacuum to abet smugglers and travelers along their migration routes. They had been steeping for millennia, evolving through the experiences of groups ranging from the Sumerians in 2000 BCE to the Knights Templar in 1150 CE, and then being refined over the following centuries (Graeber 2012: 291).

At the convergence of the Tigris and Euphrates Rivers, the Sumerians developed a financial system that would help them to better distribute food and other necessities locally while enabling them to secure goods from afar.

In the center of this system stood a contract that could extend through time: a promissory note, which over the years and through other ancient cultures was made tangible in the form of clay tokens, cylindrical seals, and later, coin and paper (Goetzmann 2016: 22–27). Debt started to take on a fantastical dimension with the *fei qian* (flying money) of the Chinese during the T'ang dynasty, considered a precursor to the *hawala* and *hundi* systems of South and Central Asia and the Middle East (Goetzmann 2016: 180). In these instances, a party would make deposits in one locale and take the slip or token—proof of their deposit—to retrieve it in another.

Similarly, in the twelfth century, the Knights Templar, a Catholic military order, discerned a way to get money from the beginning of a pilgrim's journey to a financial waypoint or destination without his actually having to carry cash. For example, pilgrims would deposit cash at a bank in London and then retrieve it in Jerusalem. Historians speculate that a system of letters of credit and various codes, tallies, and ciphers connected the traveler to his money (Goetzmann 2016: 209). In all these instances, debt had graduated from being intertemporal to being both intertemporal and interspatial and thus useful for trade.

As these financial systems evolved, community trust in financial institutions evolved in tandem. Often, systems of credit were established between communities with common ethnicities, languages, currencies, and practices. The dhikuti method described earlier provides a good example. Such rotating systems of credit can be traced back to thirteenth-century Japan, and other examples of mutual aid extend back over time to ancient Egypt and the Roman Empire (Archambault 2010; Dekle and Hamada 2000). As technologies of credit evolved (e.g., from a clay promissory note to a bill of exchange), communities of trust could expand beyond locals to include distant kin and even strangers who could prove their "credit" (which, in the Latin sense of the word *credere*, means "to believe in" or "to trust"). Thus, these systems became sticky, enduring across great expanses of time, and importantly, lengthening themselves geographically.

In our contemporary research, an informant in Greece explained that as his fellow Syrians had settled in Germany, they began to yearn for Syrian spices and Syrian clothing. In response, Syrian shops sprang up and, in turn, trade with Syria expanded to keep those shops in stock. With commerce in place, a money-agent system could materialize. Our informant in 2017 was able to receive funds from family in Germany via a Germany-based money agent. He could then retrieve the money at a Greece-based money agent, a financial action that had not been possible a year earlier.

The origins of payment and lending schemes within the money-agent system in contexts across the world become clear through such examples. These schemes enable a person in one country to send money to another person in another country without sending actual cash. While in earlier times the sender would carry a bill of exchange or cash, with digital technology, physical cash or cash substitutes are no longer required. A system of debits and credits between money agents, facilitated by digital payment systems, enables settlements to happen nearly instantaneously. In our research, we saw evidence of the same systems operating in Costa Rica, connecting smugglers and their cargo to remitters in the United States. Locals referred to it as "the Colombian system" for reasons they did not explain. Another researcher, referencing the same system, mentions that the *hawala* transfer system is equivalent to the Black Market Peso Exchange and links it to drug money in Latin America (Peters 2010: 187). In these cases, transactions operate under the regulatory radar of the state.

Along with the deepening ruts of money movement came deepening routines—routines passed down through families, over generations, governed by parables (such as hadiths) and proverbs ("The best among you are those who are best in paying off debt", Muslim) and burnished by practice (Obaidullah 2008: 14). Recent studies in human behavior show that the costs of switching to a new system or a new practice are perceived to be high, whether or not in actuality they are (Polites and Karahanna 2012). This means that if using a system of chits—as in the *hawala* or *hundi*—is familiar, it may be preferred, even if a more efficient, more effective system were available. This reliance on the familiar was echoed again and again by our respondents. As a Syrian remarked, "I never did it the official way, through Western Union or anything. I transferred to my brother and sister the same way I do now. Which is through friends who want to move money to Turkey" (Wilson 2019a: 32).

CONCLUSION

The means of financing clandestine segments of a journey are as varied as the payment systems that accompany them. These systems patch together a welter of institutions in the formal sector, such as money transfer and banking services, and institutions in the informal sector, such as money agents. Together they mingle like coins in a change purse, out of which pours variation upon variation of financing and payment schemes.

If, according to the anthropologist James C. Scott, the business of the state is to organize its subjects into universal, standardized systems that are legible, rigid, bureaucratic, and hierarchical, then it should be no surprise that state-regulated financial services construct their *own* standardized and bureaucratic financial systems (Scott 2012: 35). And, in fact, they do. Formal financial institutions—banks, mobile money operators, money transfer operators, financial technologies (fintechs), and others—must comply with a maze of rules and restrictions. Nor should we be surprised that the characteristics of underground finance that support the smuggling enterprise run counter to those of the state: they do not follow universal principles, but draw on local practices that are familiar and acceptable to both smuggler and traveler; they are inherently illegible, flexible, free of bureaucracy, and without hierarchy.

While formal banking and money transfers may offer traceable digital footprints, the services of informal money agents are difficult, if not impossible, to track (Tinti and Reitano 2016: 71). Most transactions are recorded off the books, leaving no paper trail. Invisible to regulators and financial global standard-setting bodies, their transactions, systems of accounting, and reconciliation are well understood in the underground economy. Centuries of use and refinement make these systems familiar to agents and travelers, and in many instances more trusted than formal options. Operating under the radar, informal systems do not carry the tremendous cost burden of compliance faced by banks.

Unshackled by the expense and hassle of regulatory obedience, clandestine financing can adjust itself exclusively to meeting the needs of the traveler and the smuggler with zero regard for the state, its jurisdictions, its financial intelligence units, its global standard-setting bodies, or its hegemonic financial power vested in entities like the US Treasury (Tinti and Reitano 2016). Nor does such financing need to concern itself with the policies of customer due diligence that precede it. Without the constraints of bureaucratic compliance, financial services for smuggling purposes can mold themselves to the particular needs of the various parties. Collectively, they can offer up a suite of services, infinitely adjustable for matching the needs of smugglers, financial middlemen, and travelers.

One might infer from history and habit that informal financing is not going to vanish or be tamped down anytime soon. As long as there is a market for these services—seen not only in the financial footprints of migration but also in long-distance trade—they will continue to flourish and be available to smugglers and their human cargo for years to come.

NOTE

1. Study subjects also referred to the *sarafi* system or the *hawala* system—which I call the "money-agent system"—as the "*sarafi-hawala* system" or the "guarantee scheme." For more on the *hawala*, see Maimbo (2003).

REFERENCES

Adhikari, Deepak. 2020. "From the Hills of Nepal to the Colombian Jungle: A Migrant's Story." Organized Crime and Corruption Reporting Project, July 9, 2020. https://www.occrp.org/en/cruel-road-north/from-the-hills-of-nepal-to-the-colombian-jungle-a-migrants-story.

Archambault, Edith. 2010. "Mutual Organizations/Mutual Societies." In *International Encyclopedia of Civil Society*, edited by Helmut K. Anheier and Stefan Toepler, 1–9. New York: Springer.

Amiry, Qiamuddin. 2020. *Searching for Smugglers in Kabul: A Recollection*. Medford, MA: Henry J. Leir Institute for Human Security at the Fletcher School of Law and Diplomacy, Tufts University. https://sites.tufts.edu/journeysproject/files/2020/09/SearchingSmugglers_Papers_PB_v2.pdf.

Brigden, Noelle Kateri. 2018. *The Migrant Passage: Clandestine Journeys from Central America*. Ithaca, NY: Cornell University Press.

Busse, Erika, and Tania Vásquez Luque. 2016. "The Legal-Illegal Nexus: Haitians in Transit Migration Deploying Migrant Capital." *International Journal of Sociology* 46 (3): 205–222.

Charmaz, Kathy. 2014. *Constructing Grounded Theory: A Practical Guide through Qualitative Analysis*. London: Sage.

Collins, Daryl, Jonathan Morduch, Stuart Rutherford, and Orlanda Ruthven. 2009. *Portfolios of the Poor: How the World's Poor Live on $2 a Day*. Princeton, NJ: Princeton University Press.

Dekle, Robert, and Koichi Hamada. 2000. "On the Development of Rotating Credit Associations in Japan." *Economic Development and Cultural Change* 49 (1): 77–90.

Goetzmann, William N. 2016. *Money Changes Everything: How Finance Made Civilization Possible*. Princeton, NJ: Princeton University Press.

Graeber, David. 2012. *Debt: The First 5,000 Years*. Brooklyn, NY: Melville House.

Kim, Tae H. 2007. "Borderline Disaster: The Case for Escrow in Reducing Human Vulnerability." *Geopolitics* 12 (2): 320–329.

Koser, Khalid. 2008. "Why Migrant Smuggling Pays." *International Migration* 46 (2): 3–26.
——. 2011. "The Smuggling of Refugees." In *Global Human Smuggling: Comparative Perspectives*, 2nd ed., edited by David Kyle and Rey Koslowski, 256–272. Baltimore: John Hopkins University Press.
Kyle, David, and Rey Koslowski, eds. 2011. *Global Human Smuggling: Comparative Perspectives*. 2nd ed. Baltimore: Johns Hopkins University Press.
Maimbo, Samuel Munzele. 2003. "The Money Exchange Dealers of Kabul." World Bank Working Papers.
Mandić, Danilo, and Charles M. Simpson. 2017. "Refugees and Shifted Risk: An International Study of Syrian Forced Migration and Smuggling." *International Migration* 55 (6): 73–89.
Obaidullah, Mohammed. 2008. *Introduction to Islamic Microfinance*. India: International Institute of Islamic Business and Finance.
Peters, Gretchen. 2010. *Seeds of Terror: How Drugs, Thugs and Crime Are Reshaping the Afghan War*. New York: Picador.
Polites, Greta L., and Elena Karahanna. 2012. "Shackled to the Status Quo: The Inhibiting Effects of Incumbent System Habit, Switching Costs, and Inertia on New System Acceptance." *MIS Quarterly* 36 (1): 21–42.
Sapkota, Janakraj. 2019. "A Nepali Man's Odyssey from Dang to San Diego." *Kathmandu Post*, June 29, 2019. https://kathmandupost.com/national/2019/06/29/a-nepali-mans-odyssey-from-dang-to-san-diego.
Scott, James C. 2012. *Two Cheers for Anarchism: Six Easy Pieces on Autonomy, Dignity, and Meaningful Work and Play*. Princeton, NJ: Princeton University Press.
Tinti, Peter, and Tuesday Reitano. 2016. *Migrant, Refugee, Smuggler, Saviour*. London: Hurst.
UNODC (United Nations Office on Drugs and Crime). 2018. *Global Study on Smuggling of Migrants 2018*. Vienna: UNODC. https://www.unodc.org/documents/data-and-analysis/glosom/GLOSOM_2018_web_small.pdf.
Welch, Catherine, and Rebecca Piekkari. 2006. "Crossing Language Boundaries: Qualitative Interviewing in International Business." *Management International Review* 46 (4): 417–437.
Williams, Alan, and Vladimír Baláž. 2012. "Migration, Risk, and Uncertainty: Theoretical Perspectives." *Population, Space and Place* 18 (2): 167–180.
Wilson, Kim. 2019a. *Financial Biographies of Long Distance Journeyers*. Medford, MA: Henry J. Leir Institute for Human Security at the Fletcher School of Law and Diplomacy, Tufts University. https://sites.tufts.edu/journeysproject/files/2019/06/FinancialJourneys_Papers_PB_vFIN.pdf.
——. 2019b. *The Other Migration: The Financial Journeys of Asians and Africans Traveling through South and Central America Bound for the United States and Canada*. Medford, MA: Henry J. Leir Institute for Human Security at the Fletcher School of Law and Diplomacy, Tufts University. https://sites.tufts.edu/journeysproject/files/2019/05/FinalReport_Papers_PB_vFIN.pd.
Wilson, Kim, and Roxanne Krystalli. 2017. *The Financial Journeys of Refugees*. Medford, MA: Henry J. Leir Institute for Human Security at the Fletcher School of Law and Diplomacy, Tufts University. https://sites.tufts.edu/ihs/files/2018/02/Final-Journeys_Briefing-Paper-1.pdf.

CHAPTER 9

The Burners

SMUGGLING NETWORKS AND MAGHREBI MIGRANTS

Matt Herbert

SINCE 2020, THE NUMBER OF IRREGULAR migrants from the three Maghreb states (Tunisia, Algeria, and Morocco) embarking for Europe has surged. The rise has been led by Tunisians, with over forty-eight thousand migrants apprehended at European borders between January 2020 and December 2022, with Tunisian forces intercepting another thirty-six thousand (FRONTEX 2023).[1] Movement by irregular migrants from Morocco and Algeria also remained high, with more than eighty-four thousand migrants from the two countries caught by European authorities during the same time period as above. This surge in mobility placed North Africans as the top nationalities arriving from Africa, accounting for about 40 percent of all irregular migrant interceptions (FRONTEX 2023).

Organized migrant smuggling networks have played an important role in many of these departures. The networks offer a range of services: from cheap, basic options for transport in overloaded and often unseaworthy boats to high-end services involving European-owned yachts and comprehensive assistance to the migrants in moving through Europe. Crucially, the networks involved in transporting nationals from the Maghreb are largely distinct from those aiding foreign migrants moving through the region. For Maghrebi migrants, the smuggling networks are viewed as service providers, offering options and agency to those challenged by structural impediments to economic and social advancement at home. The complex interplay between migrants and smugglers is just one aspect of a dynamic, highly fluid system predicated on the creative subversion of European and Maghrebi states' efforts to limit irregular migration.

A significant amount of academic and policy research has been conducted on the smuggling networks in the Maghreb, but most look into those that move non-Maghrebi migrants through the region and to Europe. This literature details key factors such as methods employed by smugglers, pricing, the complex relationships between migrants and smugglers, and the impact of enforcement efforts by Maghrebi and European states on smuggler operations (see, e.g., Carling 2007; Coluccello and Massey 2007: 80; Freedman 2012; Monzini 2007; Pastore, Monzini, and Sciortino 2006: 16–17; Reitano 2015; Tinti and Reitano 2016; Triandafyllidou and Maroukis 2012). Due to high levels of irregular migration from Libya since 2011, most recent literature has focused on that country (see, e.g., Kuschminder and Triandafyllidou 2020; Lahlou 2018; Micallef 2017; Micallef, Horsely, and Bish 2019; Reitano and Tinti 2015; Schapendonk 2018).

Research on migrant smuggling networks catering to Maghrebis is more limited, often heavily focused on Morocco and largely dated (see, e.g., Arango and Martin 2005; Berriane, de Haas, and Natter 2015; Boubakri 2013a; Chadia 2007; Hendow 2013; Monzini 2007; Przybyl and Ben Tayeb 2013; Souiah 2012, 2016). The latter issue is particularly problematic due to the fluidity and speed of change in the regional migrant smuggling ecosystem. For example, between 2016 and 2023 new techniques of smuggling, new networks and new routes arose in each of the Maghreb states. One new practice, self-smuggling, in which collectives of migrants source vessels and transit autonomously, evolved during the period from a niche activity to one that is popular and common.

This chapter aims to address this gap by describing and analyzing the forms of smuggling utilized by Maghrebi irregular migrants. It begins by describing the evolution of Maghrebi migration and migrant smuggling. Next, it details the nature of smuggling networks, including types of services offered and the structure of the organizations. The life cycle of a migrant smuggling attempt is then traced. The chapter concludes with a look at the complicated interactions between migrants, smuggling networks, and state agents.

The chapter draws on over 200 interviews conducted between 2014 and 2023 in Tunisia, Algeria, and Morocco with migrants, smugglers, local activists, and government officials. These interviews were supplemented with Arabic- and French-language communiqués by regional governments, media reports, and academic literature.

Significant data collection challenges exist in researching migrant smuggling networks. Participants in illicit activities can be difficult to identify and interview, government officials can be reticent to candidly discuss dynamics, and information can quickly become outdated. The author has endeavored to address these challenges; however, the chapter should be read as an illustrative snapshot of Maghrebi migrant smuggling in the Maghreb in the late 2010s and early 2020s, rather than a definitive analysis of the subject.

THE DEVELOPMENT OF CROSS-MEDITERRANEAN MIGRATION AND MIGRANT SMUGGLING

Tunisia, Algeria, and Morocco have witnessed waves of their citizens head north to Europe since their independence from France was gained in the middle of the twentieth century. Migration was particularly intense between the 1960s and 1980s, leading to the establishment of large diaspora communities throughout Europe (Gatrell 2019: 124–143).

At first, Maghrebi migrants went to Europe in search of jobs, and they were largely welcomed by postwar countries in need of laborers to help rebuild and to replace native workers who had emigrated abroad (Seccombe and Lawless 1985: 125). Despite consistent economic growth in the Maghreb between the 1960s and 1980s, the economic opportunities available in Europe were better paid and offered a more accessible path toward a career, especially for migrants from marginalized regions or ethnic groups.

Unlike those who came later, nearly all migrants arriving during this era moved via legal channels, arriving on tourist visas or as part of guest-worker programs, before later crossing into informality. Access was straightforward enough that circular migration became the norm for some Maghrebis, who would informally work for a season or two in Europe before returning home, only to undertake the process again the following year (Natter 2015). The ease of licit ways to travel to Europe led to a limited demand for migrant smuggling. However, cross-Mediterranean maritime smuggling of other goods, such as cannabis, existed, foreshadowing the later emergence of the migrant smuggling industry (Herbert and Gallien 2020: 12).

The era of easy legal transit ended in the late 1980s and early 1990s, when European states began to impose visa requirements on Maghrebi nationals due to rising concerns over the level of migration from the region to Europe and as part of the Schengen Agreement's visa harmonization articles (see, e.g., Ferrer-Gallardo 2008; Natter 2014). For many Maghrebis, especially those from the middle and lower classes who formed the bulk of migrants to Europe, the cost and bureaucratic hurdles involved in accessing these documents placed them largely out of reach. "I remember [in 1991] people began queuing at two or three in the morning near the French consulate to hand in their visa files; the queues were 40 meters long," recounted one Algerian worker (Herbert 2019: 4).

European imposition of visa requirements did little to halt migration. Demand for low-skilled labor in Europe remained plentiful, in stark contrast to the dearth of economic opportunities for unskilled and educated workers in Tunisia, Algeria, and Morocco (Arango and Martin 2005: 262; Berriane, de Haas, and Natter 2015: 506). Rather, the primary impact of visa tightening was to change how migrants traveled to Europe.

Facing barriers to travel, Maghrebis adopted a variety of methods to get to Europe. Those able to afford and receive tourist visas continued to head north on buses and planes. Others stowed away on cargo ships. One Algerian port worker remembered that in the early 1990s, in Oran and Arzew, "people began to enter the ships secretly at night, often with the complicity of [port officials]." These stowaways constituted "the birth of the *harga* [irregular migration]" in Algeria (interview, former trade unionist, Oran, December 2018).

Europe's visa tightening also spurred the emergence of migrant smuggling networks. The first generation of these networks, which emerged in the 1990s, were small, often ad hoc enterprises with limited geographic reach. They typically comprised fishermen or sailors who transported migrants north while also continuing their other formal professions (Herbert 2016: 3). Some established maritime contraband networks, also diversified into migrant smuggling, though their numbers were relatively low.

First-generation smuggling networks were clustered in Morocco and Tunisia, and provided services primarily to citizens of those countries. From northern Morocco, migrants were transported across the Strait of Gibraltar or the Alboran Sea into southern Spain, or across the land border into Spain's enclaves of Ceuta and Melilla. In Tunisia, smugglers shuttled migrants from the country's north to Sicily, and from the center and southern coast to the Pelagic islands (Simon 2006: 55).

Cross-Mediterranean migrant smuggling was not a significant domestic concern for Maghreb states. Rather than a problem, migration was viewed as a solution to chronic unemployment and underemployment, a means of lessening politically dangerous social tensions (interview, Tunisian security expert, Tunis, September 2014). A Tunisian migration expert recounted that under former president Zine al-Abidine Ben Ali, in power from 1987 to 2011, "the main instruction for anyone intending to migrate clandestinely was that, if caught, the person should deny as much as possible that they were Tunisian, throw away their identification, and change their dialect" (interview, Tunis, July 2016).

The laissez-faire approach by Maghreb states toward migration changed in the early 2000s, largely at the behest of the European Union (EU) and member states. Wielding diplomatic pressure and aid inducements, European states enlisted Morocco and Tunisia to counter irregular migration through the passage of new laws, heightened enforcement, and the agreement to readmit irregular migrants caught in Europe (Badalič 2019: 85; European Commission 2005: 16–17, 28–31; United Nations Office on Drugs and Crime 2010: 11). Bilateral law enforcement coordination between Morocco and Spain, as well as Tunisia and Italy, became increasingly robust, including intelligence sharing and joint maritime patrols (International Organization for Migration 2005: 79). Apprehended migrants, including those deported from Europe, nominally risked fines and imprisonment, with more severe sanctions meted out on those suspected of being smugglers (Badalič 2019: 92; Hendow 2013: 203–204).

Migrant smugglers responded to increased enforcement by changing their operations. Many Tunisian smuggling networks shifted their operations into Libya, which was under international embargo and hence not a participant in Europe's countermigration programming (Boubakri 2013b: 6; United Nations Office on Drugs and Crime 2010: 32). While Tunisian migrants were the early users of this route, Moroccans soon came to dominate it, with most flying from Casablanca to Tripoli before heading to embarkation zones (United Nations Office on Drugs and Crime 2010: 9). Some flew to Libya on their own and then contacted smugglers, while others contracted with Morocco-based smugglers who arranged the entire journey, partnering with Tunisian and Libyan smuggling networks. By 2006, Italy intercepted more Moroccan migrants than Spain (Coluccello and Massey 2007: 80; Fondation Européenne pour la Formation et Association Marocaine d'Études et de Recherches sur les Migration 2013: 16).

As irregular migration from Libya grew, Tunisian smuggling networks were slowly taken over by Libyans, who were better placed to negotiate permission to operate with local police and intelligence officials. The Libyan networks were less ad hoc and were more focused on migrant smuggling as a full-time business. The average number of migrants per boat increased, and smugglers began to actively offer their services to migrants from outside North Africa (Herbert 2016).

In 2011 uprisings in Tunisia and Libya, and social unrest in Morocco and Algeria, affected migration and migrant smuggling networks in the region. After the Tunisian uprising, chaos in the security forces allowed close to thirty thousand youths to sail for Italy. One former migrant recounted that "the coastal areas were almost deserted [of security forces]. It was the opportunity of a lifetime" (interview, former irregular migrant, Tunis, January 2019). Few established smuggling networks were involved in the 2011 exodus: rather, migrants transited north either by paying local fishermen or by acquiring boats and steering northeast. It underscored the latent potential for widespread migration despite nearly a decade of countermigration efforts by Tunisia and European states.

The 2011 pulse was, however, the exception to the norm. Between 2010 and 2017, most Maghrebi irregular migrants flew to second countries before crossing toward Europe. Many went via the Eastern Mediterranean / Balkan route, a dynamic that preceded the broader irregular migrant surge through the region in 2015 (FRONTEX 2013a: 21; 2013b: 13). However, the number of Maghrebi migrants also increased sharply during the surge, with 8,839, primarily Moroccans and Algerians, apprehended (International Organization for Migration 2016; interview, journalist, Algiers, May 2016).

To reach the Eastern Mediterranean / Balkan route, Maghrebis flew to Turkey, entering with licit tourist visas or falsified work contracts (FRONTEX 2010: 11; interview, migration researcher, Rabat, May 2016). Upon arrival, migrants contracted with local migrant smugglers to cross into Greece or Bulgaria. Finding smugglers was reportedly straightforward, with information on specific locations to go to or individuals to speak with shared via word of mouth or social media (interview, freelance journalist, Beirut, July 2016; interview, Moroccan irregular migrant, remote, March 2019).

Following the 2016 agreement between the EU and Turkey, Maghrebi migration was displaced from the eastern to the central Mediterranean. Western Libya reemerged as the dominant departure point, as local migrant smuggling networks exploited the anarchic postrevolutionary situation (interview, international migration official, Nouakchott, June 2016). To get to western Libyan embarkation points, Maghrebis—primarily Moroccans and Tunisians—moved overland, typically with the assistance of smuggling networks. Once they were in Libya, separate maritime smuggling networks offered passage to Europe (mainly to Italy's Pelagie Islands).

In the wake of Libya's revolution, the smugglers there had become infamous for employing overloaded and barely seaworthy vessels, leading to a high number of fatalities among sub-Saharan African and South Asian migrants. However, the same networks offered better and safer passage to Tunisians, Algerians, and Moroccans, nominally on the grounds of regional solidarity (interview, journalist, Tunis, March 2015). As an Algerian journalist explained, "For Maghrebis who can afford 2,000 euros for the crossing, there are old networks which are safe" (interview, Algiers, May 2016).

By 2018, Maghrebi irregular migration changed yet again. The Libyan route became increasingly unpopular for migrants, particularly Moroccans. European agreements with formal and informal security actors in Libya to halt migration drove some of this (see Herbert 2019). However, Libya also fell out of favor after several high-profile instances of mass detention or violence against Moroccan migrants (Kadiri 2017). This drove a reversion to earlier smuggling routes to Europe. In 2018 nearly all Maghrebi irregular migrants embarked directly from their home countries toward Europe. While this alteration in routes was driven by factors largely outside the Maghreb, it was enabled by the existence of numerous migrant smuggling networks in the region that were able to expand their activities to meet increased demand.

The advent of the COVID-19 pandemic in the late winter of 2020 initially drove a sharp decline in the number of migrant embarkations from Tunisia, Algeria, and Morocco, largely due to internal mobility constraints imposed by the states to counter the spread of the disease. This pause in mobility proved fleeting, however, with rising number of embarkations recorded from mid-June onward (Micallef et al 2021). In some locations, the rise in mobility seems linked to the lifting of mobility constraints. However, in others smuggling networks actively sought out routes which evaded heightened controls. This was most noticeable in Morocco, where smuggling networks based in the north of the country forged partnerships with small networks in the disputed Western Sahara region, further fueling movement to Spain's Canary Islands (Global Initiative against Transnational Organized Crime 2022).

The most intense and sustained surge in movement, however, occurred from Tunisia. There, worsening economic, social, and political dynamics drove a sharp rise in embarkations by Tunisian irregular migrants beginning in the mid-Summer of 2020 and continuing to rise up to the time of writing (Herbert 2022a; Herbert 2022b). Notably, the surge involved not only young men, the traditional demographic for most Maghrebi migration, but also heightened numbers of unaccompanied minors, women, and entire families (Herbert 2022a).

The overwhelming majority of Tunisian irregular migrants since 2020 embarked in boats from Tunisia's coastline. While some groups of migrants engaged in self-smuggling—sourcing boats, engines, and GPS units and departing autonomously—most employed the services of smuggling networks in order to reach Europe (Herbert 2022a). The Tunisian surge also led to a reinvigoration of the Balkans route, as thousands of irregular migrants flew to Serbia, often via Turkey, and contracted with smuggling groups along the Serbian-Hungarian border to cross into Europe.

The history of migration and migrant smuggling in the Maghreb is one defined by creativity and flexibility. Efforts by European and regional states to constrain migration had limited impact in reducing demand for migration. Rather, they enabled the growth of a migrant smuggling industry—one that proved capable of adapting to circumvent or subvert state actions.

THE SOCIAL COMPOSITION, STRUCTURE, AND SERVICES OF MIGRANT SMUGGLING NETWORKS

Migrant smugglers play an important role in the current process of Maghrebi irregular migration. While some migrants reach Europe unaided by smugglers, most interact with one or more smuggling networks along the way.

There is broad homogeneity among migrant smuggling networks across the Maghreb. The smuggling industry emerged at roughly the same time in

Tunisia, Algeria, and Morocco, and it has developed similar organizational structures and offered generally similar services. While some national and subnational variation exists, the similarities shared by networks catering to Maghrebi migrants—and how they engage with and subvert state actions—make possible cross-regional analysis of the social composition, structure, and services offered.

THE SOCIAL COMPOSITION OF MAGHREBI SMUGGLING NETWORKS

Migrant smuggling in the Maghreb involves a large number of networks, each operating within a relatively narrow geographic area. "In every small town in my governorate,' explained a Tunisian smuggler, 'there is at least one main network and other smaller networks." (Herbert 2022b: 10). Nearly all networks in the region are rooted in the communities that dot the Mediterranean shoreline. In these communities there is a dearth of economic options, with fishing an important but economically tenuous activity (Colloca, Scarcella, and Libralato 2017: 1). Fishermen formed the first generation of Maghrebi smugglers and continue to play an important role. Participation in the smuggling trade has expanded, with smuggling networks frequently drawing in other individuals with and without direct maritime experience.

There is significant variation in how smugglers are referred to, even within a single country. In western Algeria, for example, the term *harraba* is common, while in Annaba, in the east of the country, the term *tlayna* is frequently used as code for smugglers offering transit to Italy (personal communication, Algerian researcher, remote, June 2020).

For present-day smugglers, the activity is a relatively full-time vocation, with networks operating year-round (though crossings by Maghrebis are limited in the winter due to poor weather). Because smuggling is often far more lucrative than other available economic options, those involved often operate for lengthy periods, undeterred even by official sanctions. Some smugglers in Tunisia, for example, have been caught and imprisoned several times, only to return to smuggling upon their release (interview, Tunisian security expert, Tunis, February 2018; Herbert 2022a).

Some of the more institutionalized networks for smuggling migrants also transport other contraband commodities. Most poly-smuggling networks are concentrated in northern Morocco and are linked to the cannabis industry (Guardia Civil 2017; Herbert 2016: 18; interview, Ministry of Interior official, Rabat, January 2019; interview, nongovernmental organization [NGO] official, Rabat, January 2019). At least one such network has been uncovered in Tunisia, involving black-market cigarettes (Pantaleone 2017).

In addition to professional smugglers, a variety of other actors continue to participate in smuggling on a part-time or as-needed basis. It is often an attempt at income substitution when their main livelihood has been disrupted. For example, a sharp decline in fisheries in Tunisia's Gulf of Gabes in 2017 and 2018 led a number of fishermen to become involved in smuggling to make up for the shortfall in their income (Herbert 2019: 17). Such cyclical, ad hoc smuggling represents a minority of active networks. Because their operations can commence and cease rapidly, such part-time smugglers are particularly difficult for government agents to detect, apprehend, and deter.

Both professional and ad hoc smuggling networks are rooted in existent social networks, with members drawn from family or trusted friend connections (Herbert 2016: 16). Reliance on existent social bonds is an effective means of subverting states' efforts to investigate and eliminate the smuggling networks, but it has also placed limits on how big the networks grow and where they operate. Consequently, most are small and localized, operating in areas close to the members' communities of origin. "[Smugglers] work more effectively in their hometowns," explained a Tunisian security officer. "There they are more connected to the communities and able to reach out to potential migrants" (interview, Sousse, February 2019). A local focus also enables the networks to better manage relations with government officials, often by leveraging family or friendship connections.

Less frequently, a smuggling network may operate across a greater geographic swath, either autonomously or in partnership with other networks. Mostly this involves south-north connections, with a network or a partnership of networks offering services on both sides of the Mediterranean. For example, one network in northern Morocco maintained operations in Morocco, geared toward recruiting migrants and transporting them to Spain, and a Spanish component tasked with collecting and transporting them inland (Guardia Civil 2018a). In central Algeria, networks targeting Spain's Balearic Islands partner with Spanish networks that move migrants from the islands to the mainland (Guardia Civil 2019). Some lateral connections also exist, with Moroccan smugglers occasionally partnering with Tunisian networks in order to move Moroccan migrants from Tunisia to Italy.

Maghrebi smuggling is often highly gendered. Networks are composed primarily of young and middle-aged men, while women are only infrequently involved, often in specific support roles, such as recruiting. While some instances of women involved in piloting vessels have been documented, it is rare. The gender disparity in smuggling networks is likely a result of social norms regarding female participation in extralegal activity and the wider gap in female participation in linked licit activities, such as fishing. It also reflects the gender imbalance in Maghrebi migration, which has historically skewed toward young males.

THE STRUCTURE OF SMUGGLING NETWORKS

Maghrebi smuggling networks are small, usually comprising a half dozen members or fewer. Most offer a single type of smuggling service—such as transit via fishing boat, semirigid craft, or speedboat. There is little indication that powerful, poly-trafficking organizations have become involved in the trade or sought to tax it, a dynamic that has arisen in other global migration corridors such as on the US-Mexico border.

Two basic types of networks exist in the Maghreb: hierarchic and cooperative. In hierarchic networks, the smuggling activity is organized around a single leader. Often an experienced smuggler or businessman, the leader supplies the capital to purchase boats and engines, and hires other network personnel. Because of the layers within the network, migrants rarely meet the leader until the moment of departure when the payment is collected. Most networks in the Maghreb—especially in Morocco and Tunisia—follow this organization.

In cooperative networks, the structure is much flatter. Groups of smugglers pool their money in order to buy boats, engines, and GPS units (interview, journalist, Annaba, June 2016). The smugglers also cooperate on other smuggling activities, including negotiating with potential migrants, sourcing supplies, operating the boats, and handling the sensitive relationships with government officials. Within cooperative networks, the profits earned from migrants are split among the members of the cooperative. Such networks form the minority of those operating in the Maghreb and are seen most frequently in eastern Algeria.

In both hierarchic and cooperative networks, a number of different roles and activities are required for a smuggling effort to succeed (United Nations Office on Drugs and Crime 2010: 27–28). The networks are led by experienced smugglers (in Tunisia known as a *harrak*) who draw on personal networks and knowledge to coordinate the different actors and steps in the smuggling process. "They are always fishermen who know the sea, know how to get to Italy, and know the movements of the Coast Guard," explained one Tunisian smuggler (Herbert 2022a: 22).

The most delicate role is that of the recruiter (known as *wassit* or a *samsar* in Tunisia), who is tasked with making contact with potential migrants. Recruiters are the most visible and identifiable members of a smuggling network. While this is necessary if migrants are to find them, or vice versa, it leaves them the most exposed to arrest by the security forces. For this reason, recruiters are often circumspect in their activity, requiring that a prospective migrant be vouched for by a trusted intermediary or otherwise vetted. Efforts to avoid security attention have also led to the use of women in this role, due to smuggler beliefs that the recruiters' gender will better enable them to evade arrest (Herbert 2019: 19). The recruiter also is tasked with vetting migrants and managing the financial arrangements, including handling negotiations and sometimes collecting an initial payment, as well as supplying information close to the date of departure on specifics of the trip (Benyakoub 2018; interview, returned migrant #3, Tunis, January 2019; interview, irregular migrant, Sousse, February 2019; interview, journalist, Annaba, June 2016). In some instances, the recruiter operates in a freelance capacity, supporting several smuggling networks, and earning a percentage from each paying migrant recruited (Herbert 2022a).

Logisticians (also known as a *wassit* in Tunisia) source the necessary boats and engines for the trip, which is facilitated by the ubiquity of such goods in littoral towns and villages across the Maghreb. Engines, GPS units, and petrol are readily available from local businessmen, while boats are procured secondhand, bought from businesses, or crafted by local artisans. In instances in which safe houses are used, such as on Tunisia's Kerkennah Islands or in southern Spain, logistical personnel are tasked with housing and feeding migrants (Guardia Civil 2018a; Herbert 2019: 19).

Interactions with and payments to authorities are usually managed by a single individual. In hierarchic networks this can be the group leader, but responsibility can devolve to a subordinate who has existing links—due to family ties, former employment, or charisma—with the officials (interview, Tunisian security expert, Tunis, February 2018).

The final role within the smuggling networks is the boat pilot. When the trip involves a return of the boat to the embarkation area, the pilot is nearly always a network member, often with experience in maritime navigation. Most are men, though in at least one high-end network in western Algeria women are involved as pilots. Smuggling networks that use and then abandon boats on reaching Europe often delegate navigation and piloting of the vessel to one of the migrants, sometimes one with maritime experience but often not. In exchange for piloting, networks typically offer reduced or free passage to the migrant.

The actual composition and size of the various networks throughout the Maghreb can vary substantially. One Tunisian smuggler underscored this:

> In big networks there is the main fisherman, the owner of the boat, the captain that drives the boat, and a [recruiter] who recruits people for the crossing. In a big network, there could be more than one [recruiter], and in some cases up to 10 people in all in the network. In smaller networks there is the captain, [who] usually is the owner of a small boat or has a boat that he stole. In these cases, it is usually just him alone or with one [recruiter]. (Herbert 2022b: 10)

Finally, profiteering off smuggling extends beyond the network members themselves, with other categories of workers benefiting through the assistance they provide to the networks. These include fishermen, boatbuilders, maritime supply vendors, and petrol distributors. Migrant smuggling in Tunisia, Algeria, and Morocco has not had nearly the economic impact it has had in postrevolutionary Libya, but the benefits are significant for communities with limited economic opportunities.

TYPES OF SERVICES OFFERED BY MIGRANT SMUGGLING NETWORKS

There are a variety of different services offered by the various migrant smuggling networks operating in the Maghreb. These range from basic and inexpensive options to higher-end packages that provide transit north and assistance for migrants in gaining papers in Europe. "When we pay the high price, smugglers assure us we will arrive safe and sound. If we pay a lower price, then we are told . . . there is a chance that the crossing could fail," explained one Algerian migrant (Hagani 2019).

Networks offering basic options to migrants form the bulk of those active in the Maghreb. One Algerian observer estimated that 90 percent of the smugglers in his area of Oran provided crossing via basic options, including older fishing boats sold secondhand, artisanally produced craft, and semi-rigid boats purchased in local stores (interview, former trade unionist, Oran, 2019). On average, one to two dozen migrants were packed into these boats for seven-to-fourteen-hour trips.

Depending on the network, the departure location, and the country, basic smuggling options cost migrants the equivalent of 400 to 2,500 euros, with higher prices sometimes charged for women and children (Herbert 2022a; Global Initiative against Transnational Organized Crime 2022). While some smuggling networks shuttle back and forth between Europe and their point of departure in North Africa, for many networks the trip is one-way, with the boat abandoned upon arrival in Italy or Spain.

Networks specializing in high-end smuggling efforts are less common. However, such networks do operate in each of the three Maghrebi countries. In Morocco, networks operate jet skis that traverse the Strait of Gibraltar in about thirty minutes and speedboats across the Alboran Sea (Europol 2018). In Algeria, a network near Oran operates speedboats that traverse to Europe in about three hours. In northern Tunisia, speedboats travel from the country's northern coast to Sicily in about four hours (Pantaleone 2017, 2019). Some networks in Tunisia offer a far more leisurely transit for up to six migrants aboard private yachts owned by Europeans and piloted to disembarkation points in Italy and France (Herbert 2022a). Such higher-end options generally cost between 1,000 and 4,000 euros, though more can be charged if the smuggling network supplies falsified residency papers or aids the migrants in transiting through Europe to their final destination (Guardia Civil 2018a, 2018b, 2019; interview, NGO coordinator, Tangier, January 2019).

As detailed in this section, migrant smuggling networks catering to Maghrebis are small and often hyperlocalized, drawing their members from among the littoral communities across the Maghreb. The networks offer their members, their clients, and the broader communities from which they come livelihood opportunities in otherwise economically difficult locales. In situations in which the average citizen has little economic agency, with structural inequalities often limiting livelihood options, smugglers create options—for themselves and for the migrants. Because of this, few network members are perceived to engage in deviant criminality. Rather, they are service providers who—as long as they do not gain a reputation for callous disregard for migrant lives—are generally viewed positively within their communities as actors able to help effect an improvement in migrants' situations. This matches a dynamic observed in a variety of other locations, from the Eastern Mediterranean to Mesoamerica, in which the smuggler-migrant relationship is defined as trust based and cooperative, often rooted in "deep, socially cemented ties" (Sanchez 2015: 17; also see Achilli 2018; Slack and Martinez 2018).

The entrenched perception that local smugglers are offering a service and prioritize locals' safety is also likely grounded in practical realities. Because human smugglers in the Maghreb—especially in Tunisia and Algeria—source many clients from their own local communities, they have to live in proximity to the families and friends of local migrants whom they transport. A reputation for recklessness or abuse incurs business costs, as migrants avoid them, and social costs.

This effectively limits the diffusion of innately unsafe smuggling approaches within the region. Smuggling models employed in Libya, involving vessels overloaded with large numbers of migrants, which often sink or capsize, were briefly attempted in Tunisia in 2017. The sinking of two vessels and death of over a hundred Tunisian migrants, however, led to significant protests and social unrest in the victims' home communities. This social pressure, and the political and law enforcement pressure it catalyzed, led smugglers to revert to transporting smaller numbers of migrants in better-maintained vessels (Herbert 2019: 18). This underscores that while networks engaged with foreign migrants can seek to maximize profits, those whose primary clientele are their conationals are constrained in how they approach the process of smuggling, balancing profit and social tolerance for their activities.

THE PROCESS OF MIGRANT SMUGGLING IN THE MAGHREB

Migrants experience the process of migrant smuggling in different ways. For some—especially those with little means—the process is full of risk, defined by overfilled or unseaworthy boats and minimally experienced pilots. For those able to pay more, transit is rapid and fairly safe, involving well-maintained boats captained by experienced sailors and smuggling networks that continue to aid migrants in reaching their ultimate destination even after the maritime journey has ended.

However, for migrants of all economic means, the process of embarking involves a number of similar steps. This section will illustrate each of those, including how contact is made between migrants and smugglers, migrants' transit to embarkation points, the process of embarkation, and the maritime trip. The section will underscore the similarity in how these steps occur in the three Maghrebi countries, as well as the dynamic complexity of the activities of migrant smuggling networks.

CONTACT BETWEEN MIGRANTS AND SMUGGLERS

For migrants the process of choosing to depart is often one that is long and highly subjective. However, once a decision has been arrived at, the first step toward carrying it out is remarkably similar for irregular migrants, involving an effort to find a network capable of getting the individual to their desired destination.

The first contact that Maghrebi irregular migrants have with smuggling networks is often the recruiter. The process of finding a recruiter differs depending on how far from home a migrant needs or plans to travel before embarking for Europe. If the prospective migrant hails from a coastal area, there is a good chance that he or she is already aware of who in their neighborhood is a recruiter, as well as the identities of local smugglers. One Algerian youth explained that "it is easy to get in touch with ... traffickers or smugglers. Everyone in our neighborhood, for example, knows the name of one guy who organizes embarkations west of Oran" (interview, Oran, December 2018).

Due to the arrest risks, some recruiters require that even locals be introduced by a trusted mutual acquaintance or contact (interview, journalist,

Annaba, June 2016). "I met my middleman through a friend," explained a Tunisian migrant. "He was a very good guy. He gave us advice and allowed us to bargain with him on the price of the passage" (Herbert 2019: 19). Such flexibility in pricing is the norm, with recruiters often negotiating rates with each migrant individually. The rate paid can differ based on whether a migrant has personal connections to and the trust of a recruiter (interview, NGO official, Tangier, January 2019; interview, Ministry of Interior official, Rabat, January 2019).

Recruiters are not always passive actors, with some actively seeking prospective clients. "In poor districts, in the cities and on the coast, people know people, and it is easy for smugglers to target those who might be interested," noted one observer (interview, economic journalist, Algiers, May 2016). In other places, recruiters may overtly advertise their services. "Over the last 24 months, smugglers have become much more visible in the markets, offering a range of services," bemoaned one Moroccan community leader (interview, Khouribga, January 2019). The degree to which recruiters are overt is in part connected to the level of security force pressure against smugglers, but it is also a manifestation of the complex interplay between migrants and smugglers in times of heightened migration. Smugglers may be emboldened to be overt in their advertisement of services when they know a significant number of individuals want to migrate, the risk of exposure thus being outweighed by the likelihood of pecuniary gain.

For those not from coastal areas, the process of finding a recruiter is more challenging. Some migrants travel first to towns and areas known as migrant embarkation zones—such as Tangier in Morocco, El Kala in Algeria, and Sfax in Tunisia. There they seek out recruiters. The approach can be successful, especially in areas in which recruiters actively seek clients. However, there is also the risk of failure, due to either an inability to contact a recruiter or the price of smuggling standing in excess of the finances the migrant has available with them (interview, returned irregular migrant, Azrou, December 2018).

Because of these risks, most irregular migrants attempt to contact a recruiter before leaving home. Much of the information is shared via personal or neighborhood contacts. As one Algerian mother explained, "A friend of [my sons] came from Annaba and spent about a month with them at Meissonnier. As far as I know, he introduced them to someone who organises *harga* [irregular migration attempts] from El Kala" (author translation of quote from Benyakoub 2018). Information on smugglers also comes from family members and friends who have already successfully migrated irregularly to Europe (interview, returned irregular migrant, Morocco, February 2019; interview, NGO official, Rabat, January 2019). This dynamic can create a self-reinforcing trend, with extended families and communities utilizing the same migrant smugglers and same routes over extended periods of time.

The process of acquiring information on and contact information for recruiters has been upended since 2015 by social media. This has enabled the emergence of a dynamic, largely borderless Maghrebi social media ecosystem on migration issues, comprising videos posted to YouTube; posts and livestreams on WhatsApp, FaceTime, Instagram Live, and Facebook; and dedicated Facebook pages and WhatsApp groups (Herbert and Ghoulidi 2019). Content is mainly created by recently arrived irregular migrants in Europe and is focused on practical advice for prospective migrants (interview, Ministry of Interior official, Rabat, January 2019; interview, NGO official, Rabat, January 2019; interview, lawyer, Annaba, December 2018). This includes different routes, prices, and levels of security enforcement in different areas.

While the videos may mention smuggling trends, they rarely detail specific smugglers. However, in the comments, viewers can find information on recruiters, including names and phone numbers, and on groups of migrants planning to depart collectively. Conversations that begin on open social media pages can continue into more secure mediums—such as WhatsApp or Facebook Messenger—allowing for more specific information to be shared or communication to be established with smuggling networks. In a small number of instances, migrants leverage these channels in order to negotiate passage with recruiters and agree on the location and general date of the departure (interview, international migration official, Cairo, July 2016).

The rise of mobile social media has changed how far information on smugglers and recruiters can diffuse. Previously, reliance on personal contacts meant that information on smuggling networks was narrowly siloed within specific communities or regions. However, diffusion of information on smuggling via social media allows for a far broader reach. The mutual intelligibility of Moroccan, Algerian, and Tunisian Arabic dialects allows for information—either in the videos or in the comments sections—to reach across borders. Due to this, smuggling networks that once catered only to a local market can now appeal to a far larger potential market. This allows for greater resilience and adaptability of the migrant smuggling market as a whole, with national-level action to curtail smuggling networks merely redirecting prospective migrants to other smugglers or other departure points in the region, rather than stymying their options for transiting north.

The social media ecosystem also enables a dynamism in route and smuggler selection for migrants once in transit. Information is routinely communicated on security force pressure, smuggler availability and cost, and new strategies for arriving in Europe. Responding to this information, Maghrebi migrants can shift their plans to account for emergent challenges and opportunities, leading to a systematic fluidity and complexity that significantly hinder governments' efforts to halt the activity.

TRANSIT TO MARITIME EMBARKATION ZONES

For most migrants, the step after contacting a recruiter for a migrant smuggling network involves transiting to the embarkation area. This is not usually a challenge for migrants embarking directly from their home countries. While there is a risk of security force attention, especially if migrants are traveling in groups, for most the process is a straightforward, legal trip. However, migrants intending to embark for Europe from a country other than their own face a more difficult journey that can require contracting with land-based migrant smuggling networks to cross the borders between Maghrebi states.

The number of smuggling networks an individual migrant contracts with depends on the distance and number of borders transited. "There were two different groups in the smuggling network that took me [to Libya]," explained one Tunisian migrant. "The first group was made of Tunisians who gathered the [migrants] in Tunis and took us to the southern border. There we met the second group, who took us from the borders to the harbor we left from" (interview, returned irregular migrant, Tunis, January 2019).

For Moroccans embarking from Libya, the number of networks involved is even larger. Journeys can include Moroccan groups to cross the Algerian border, Algerian networks to transit that country's interior, and Libyan smugglers to travel to the coast and to Europe (interview, journalist, Tlemcen, June 2016; interview, journalist, Algiers, May 2016).

AT THE EMBARKATION POINTS
Even after migrants' arrival close to the embarkation point, Maghrebi smugglers rarely provide specific, advance information on embarkation dates and times. Rather, information is given at the "the last possible moment" to limit the risk of the security forces uncovering the plan (interview, economic journalist, Algiers, May 2016; interview, female Tunisian irregular migrant, Paris, February 2019).

When an embarkation involves mainly local migrants, notice is usually given by the recruiter to migrants to gather payment and personal items, depart home, and meet at a specific gathering point (interview, journalist, Algiers, May 2016). A young Tunisian woman recounted, "[After arranging passage] I got news to wait for the climate and sea to be calmer. I waited for ten or eleven days at my house, and then got a call two days prior to prepare. I was told only to take necessary things and one backpack" (interview, irregular migrant, Paris, February 2019).

If migrants come from farther away, networks sometimes rent or acquire houses close to the embarkation point for the migrants to wait in or to be collected from (known as a *gouna* or hiding place in Tunisia). A network member typically watches over the house, providing food and other supplies to migrants, which is included in the overall cost of passage.

In the hours before a departure, smugglers will collect payment from the migrants, usually in cash. Typically, migrants must show they have the funds to pay for their journey before being allowed into a hiding place; however, in some cases smuggling networks will shuttle them to ATMs, post offices, or banks if funds need to be collected (interview, Tunisian security expert, Tunis, February 2018; Herbert 2022a: 22). There are three main structures for payments. First, some smugglers demand all funds be paid prior to departure. Second, half of the payment is made prior to departure, with the remainder disbursed while the migrant is at sea. Third, half of the payment is made before leaving, with the remainder sent when the migrant successfully reaches Europe (Herbert 2022a: 23). Typically payment is in local currencies, though more expensive smuggling networks require payment in euros (interview, irregular migrant, Tangier, January 2019).

EMBARKATION AND THE TRANSIT

Embarkation often takes place at night, to limit the risk of apprehension. It is often the only time migrants meet the network leader, who typically collects outstanding payments (interview, female Tunisian irregular migrant, Paris, February 2019).

Most departures involve individual boats. However, some networks in Algeria and Tunisia coordinate their activities so that several craft depart simultaneously, in order to lessen the risk of interdiction (Herbert 2016; Herbert 2022a). The number of migrants per boat differs based on the vessel size and the cost paid. In most basic options, the boats are significantly overloaded. For example, in 2017 ninety-four Tunisian migrants were found packed on a craft designed for thirty (Republic of Tunisia, Ministry of Interior, 2017). Crowding is rarely so extreme, with departures from Maghrebi states averaging a dozen to two dozen passengers.

For migrants who pay a premium, the voyage to Europe can last from thirty minutes to four hours. Boats are often new, in relatively good shape, and a pilot is supplied by the smuggling network (and expected to come back after dropping off the migrants). Less well-heeled Maghrebi migrants, however, face a different experience. Vessels are often in poor shape and engines at risk of breaking down. Most vessels are abandoned once the migrants reach Europe. Because of this, as previously mentioned, networks rarely supply pilots or GPS, with a migrant acting as the pilot, in return for a reduced or free trip (interview, security official, Sousse, February 2019). While some such ad hoc pilots hail from littoral areas and have some maritime experience, others are inexperienced and ill-equipped for the task.

The female Tunisian migrant mentioned earlier explained that her pilot was one of the migrants:

> One of the guys had a traditional compass made from sand and a thread, and so that's how we steered. We had to stop a lot and ended up throwing most of the provisions overboard because the boat was so small and heavy. The engine's safety belt ripped, so we stopped and tried to fix it with our coats. We thought we were going to die, and so we had to stay still so that the boat kept stable. Finally, an hour later, the engine began working again. (Interview, irregular migrant, Paris, February 2019)

In part due to such an ad hoc approach to navigation, as well as poorly maintained boats and general risks of maritime transits, disappearances and deaths on the route are common. In 2019, their frequency became a political issue in the Maghreb, featuring prominently in Algeria's 2019 protests (Herbert and Naceur 2019).

However, some smugglers have a better reputation for safety. Mostly they are part of high-end smuggling networks. However, in some cases, smuggling networks exist that seem to focus on ensuring that migrants reach Europe relatively safely. For example, in Tunisia and Morocco, smugglers utilize mother ships to move migrants close to Italian and Spanish borders before transferring their passengers to smaller boats for the remainder of the journey (FRONTEX 2018: 20).

STATE AGENTS AND SMUGGLING NETWORKS

State agents are key actors shaping migrant smuggling in the Maghreb. Smuggling networks exist even in the absence of state agents—as demonstrated by Libya's postrevolutionary governance vacuum—but the activity of Maghrebi state agents has affected the form and activities of smuggling networks.

Laws criminalizing migration and migrant smuggling exist in Tunisia, Algeria, and Morocco, and each country routinely arrests migrants and smugglers. This affects the practice of migrant smuggling and the routes used. Most significantly, it has increased the need for clandestine approaches to mobility and heightened the need for an organized network to ensure a crossing was successful.

State actions also affected the visibility of smuggling, especially around departures. "[When we departed] we needed to get on the boat, which [was] already in the sea. There was no one by the beach except for us. The [smuggler] gave us a sign that it was all clear by flashing his lights four times. Then we waded out to it," explained a Tunisian migrant (interview, female Tunisian irregular migrant, Paris, February 2019). This underscores that the process of smuggling is largely hidden from public view, even if the act of smuggling is widely discussed in Maghrebi societies and in the media.

However, across the region, enforcement is uneven and prone to shifts in government prioritization of the phenomenon, leading to sharp though often brief crackdowns on smuggling and migrant embarkations, followed by long periods involving seemingly limited activity. One reason for sometimes sharp shifts in approach is that for Maghrebi governments, emigrants—and by default the smuggling networks that aid them—offer tangible benefits to the state. Irregular migration reduces social pressures in Maghrebi states by providing youths who have limited domestic livelihood options with a means to find options abroad. Significantly increasing migration enforcement risks exacerbating such social tensions for little tangible domestic reward.

When smuggler activities challenge societal stability, however, states can act decisively. This was demonstrated in Tunisia in 2017, when after two vessels sank, killing over a hundred, social unrest in the victims' communities prompted government action. Smugglers were arrested, policing was increased in embarkation areas, and travel to embarkation points was strictly controlled. This curtailed migration from these areas and, more importantly for the Tunisian government, deflated social tensions.

One downside of Maghrebi states' tacit toleration of migration and migrant smuggling is the impact it has on their relations with the EU and member states. Since the late 1990s, the bloc has sought to entice Morocco and Tunisia, and to a lesser degree Algeria, to support European border security priorities. When large numbers of migrants are caught by European states in the central and western Mediterranean, it leads to diplomatic repercussions, often followed by offers of aid or political inducements to entice Maghrebi states to halt departures and target smuggling networks. These crackdowns have limited long-term impact on migrant smuggling due to the domestic political imperatives of allowing smuggling to continue.

Uneven enforcement also reflects capacity gaps in Maghrebi states. The sheer number of Maghrebi migrants departing per year risks overwhelming judicial and penal systems should zero-tolerance policies be implemented. "Our penitentiary institutions do not have the capacity to accommodate hundreds of thousands of [migrants and smugglers]," an Algerian lawyer explained (interview, Annaba, December 2018). An even more acute challenge exists in Tunisia, leading to the fairly rapid release of those detained at sea (Herbert 2022a). Court cases for smuggling and migration are fairly low across the region, with prosecution typically reserved for smugglers whose activities are particularly substantial, seen as reckless or which resulted in injury or death (Herbert 2022a). Rather than acting as a deterrent, official approaches have influenced the nature of smuggling, with smugglers self-limiting the number of migrants they carry and avoiding bad weather in order to lessen risk (Herbert 2022a).

Corruption also enables smuggling networks to operate with limited apprehension risk. Mostly, this involves relatively low-ranking officers, primarily those who occupy field roles that offer engagement with and discretionary power over smugglers and migrants.

Uneven enforcement—due to politics, capacity, or corruption—should not be confused with no enforcement. Maghrebi states routinely arrest smugglers and migrants, and can act aggressively to curtail smuggling in specific areas or by specific smuggling networks, often when the networks become too large, risky, or deadly, and so impact broader state stability interests. In so doing, regional countries have shaped a migrant smuggling ecosystem that subverts state enforcement while otherwise being constrained in power and scope, posing little challenge to core state stability or security concerns. "The smuggling networks in Algeria are highly surveilled by the security services," explained one Algerian terrorism expert. "If the security services find out that one has been used by a terrorist or someone trying to reach the [Islamic State], the entire network will be taken down" (interview, Algiers, May 2016).

In this way, even as smuggling networks act extralegally, they also de facto reinforce state power and control. This underscores the central difficulty European states face in limiting migrant smuggling networks and embarkations from the Maghreb.

CONCLUSION

Irregular migration and migrant smuggling networks have a long history in Tunisia, Algeria, and Morocco. Since the 1990s, irregular migrants embarking from the Maghreb have relied on a vibrant smuggling ecosystem. In contrast to Libya, where migrant smugglers have gained a reputation for callous disregard for their clients' lives, smuggling networks catering to Maghrebis focus more on ensuring safe and successful arrivals. Boats still sink and deaths result, but Maghrebi migrants' mortality rates are far lower than those of foreign migrants transiting the region.

This chapter has illustrated how migrant smuggling networks developed, their composition and structure, the process of smuggling, and the complicated interactions between state agents and smugglers. A theme throughout the chapter has been the agency that smuggling networks provide among their own members and the agency they offer to migrants. Facing limited economic opportunity in their home areas, smugglers leverage their maritime knowledge and connections to create livelihood options and offer migrants the opportunity to access livelihoods in Europe.

In countries in which state control is ubiquitous, and politically subversive activities are dealt with harshly, smuggling networks have carved out a degree of latitude to transgress and subvert laws as long as they do not threaten core state control or interests. For states, migration and migrant smuggling networks offer a means of buttressing stability and deflating social tensions. Selective and uneven enforcement allows regional governments to demonstrate action against the migration phenomenon to the EU and member states without significantly affecting the migrant smuggling industry as a whole.

The utility of migrant smuggling for the state, smugglers' creativity, and the deep demand of the migrants themselves for opportunities unavailable at home suggest that Maghrebi migrant smuggling from Morocco, Algeria, and Tunisia is unlikely to abate. Ultimately, regional youths will continue to dream of migrating, legally or irregularly, and the smuggling networks dotted along the Maghreb's littoral will continue to reap the profits of that demand.

NOTE

1. Tunisian apprehensions calculated based on compilation and analysis of media releases issued by the Tunisian Ministry of Interior and Ministry of Defense.

REFERENCES

Achilli, Luigi. 2018. "The 'Good' Smuggler: The Ethics and Morals of Human Smuggling among Syrians." *ANNALS of the American Academy of Political and Social Science* 676 (March): 77–96.

Arango, Joaquin, and Philip Martin. 2005. "Best Practices to Manage Migration: Morocco-Spain." *International Migration Review* 39 (1): 258–269.

Badalič, Vasja. 2019. "Tunisia's Role in the EU External Migration Policy: Crimmigration Law, Illegal Practices, and Their Impact on Human Rights." *Journal of International Migration and Integration* 20 (1): 85–100.

Benyakoub, R. M. 2018. "Je n'ai pas pu dire adieu à mon fils." *El Watan*, December 21, 2018.
Berriane, Mohamed, Hein de Haas, and Katharina Natter. 2015. "Introduction: Revisiting Moroccan Migrations." *Journal of North African Studies* 20 (4): 503–521.
Boubakri, Hassan. 2013a. "Les migrations en Tunisie après la revolution." *Confluences Méditerranée*, no. 87, 31–46.
———. 2013b. *Revolution and International Migration in Tunisia*. Migration Policy Center Research Report 2013/04. San Domenico di Fiesole, Italy: Robert Schuman Centre for Advanced Studies, European University Institute.
Carling, Jørgen. 2007. "Migration Control and Migrant Fatalities at the Spanish-African Borders." *International Migration Review* 41 (2): 316–343.
Chadia, Arab. 2007. "Le 'hrague' ou comment les Marocains brûlent les frontiers." *Hommes et Migrations*, no. 1266, 82–94.
Colloca, Francesco, Giuseppe Scarcella, and Simone Libralato. 2017. "Recent Trends and Impacts of Fisheries Exploitation on Mediterranean Stocks and Ecosystems." *Frontiers in Marine Science* 4 (August): article 244.
Coluccello, Salvatore, and Simon Massey. 2007. "Out of Africa: The Human Trade between Libya and Lampedusa." *Trends in Organized Crime* 10 (4): 77–90.
Dipartimento della Pubblica sicurezza. n.d. "Cruscotto statistico giornaliero." http://www.libertaciviliimmigrazione.dlci.interno.gov.it/it/documentazione/statistica/cruscotto-statistico-giornaliero.
European Commission. 2005. *Annexes to the Communication from the Commission to the Council on the Monitoring and Evaluation Mechanism of Third Countries in the Field of the Fight against Illegal Immigration*. Brussels: European Commission.
Europol. 2018. "From Morocco to Spain in 30 Minutes: How a Crime Group Smuggled Migrants and Cannabis on Jet Skis." April 26, 2018. https://www.europol.europa.eu/newsroom/news/morocco-to-spain-in-30-minutes-how-crime-group-smuggled-migrants-and-cannabis-jet-skis.
Ferrer-Gallardo, Xavier. 2008. "The Spanish-Moroccan Border Complex: Processes of Geopolitical, Functional and Symbolic Rebordering." *Political Geography* 27:301–321.
Fondation Européenne pour la Formation et Association Marocaine d'Études et de Recherches sur les Migration. 2013. *Migration et compétences au Maroc: Résultats de l'enquête 2011–12, sur la migration et le lien entre compétences, migration et développement*. Turin: Fondation Européenne pour la Formation.
Freedman, Jane. 2012. "Analysing the Gendered Insecurities of Migration." *International Feminist Journal of Politics* 14 (1): 36–55.
FRONTEX (European Agency for the Management of Operational Cooperation at the External Borders of the Member States of the European Union). 2010. *FRAN Quarterly: Issue 4, October–December 2010*. Warsaw: FRONTEX.
———. 2013a. *Annual Risk Analysis 2013*. Warsaw: FRONTEX.
———. 2013b. *Western Balkans Annual Risk Analysis 2013*. Warsaw: FRONTEX.
———. 2018. *FRAN Quarterly: Quarter 3 2017*. Warsaw: FRONTEX.
———. 2023. *Detections of Illegal Border-crossings Statistics (FRAN and JORA Data as of March 2023)*. Warsaw: FRONTEX.

Gatrell, Peter. 2019. *The Unsettling of Europe: How Migration Reshaped a Continent.* New York: Basic Books.

Global Initiative against Transnational Organized Crime. 2022. *Morocco: Organized Crime, Geopolitics and Economic Woes Drive New Trends in 2021.* Global Initiative against Transnational Organized Crime. Human Smuggling and Trafficking Ecosystems—North Africa and The Sahel, 2022 Series. Geneva: Global Initiative against Transnational Organized Crime, July. https://globalinitiative.net/wp-content/uploads/2022/06/Human-smuggling-and-trafficking-ecosystems-MOROCCO.pdf.

Guardia Civil. 2017. "La Guardia Civil desarticula una organización criminal que favorecía la inmigración irregular." March 22, 2017. https://www.guardiacivil.es/es/prensa/historico_prensa/6145.html.

———. 2018a. "La Guardia Civil desarticula una organización criminal dedicada a favorecer la inmigración irregular." May 11, 2018. http://www.guardiacivil.es/es/prensa/noticias/6596.html.

———. 2018b. "La Guardia Civil desarticula una organización criminal dedicada al tráfico de personas desde Marruecos a España." July 16, 2018. http://www.guardiacivil.es/es/prensa/noticias/6676_0.html.

———. 2019. "La Guardia Civil detiene a siete personas por organización criminal para el tráfico de personas entre el Norte de África y Baleares." February 23, 2019. http://www.guardiacivil.es/es/prensa/noticias/6913.html.

Hagani, Lakhdar. 2019. "Partir à tout prix! Oran-Mostaganem, plaque tournante de la harga." *El Watan,* January 2, 2019.

Hendow, Maegan. 2013. "Tunisian Migrant Journeys: Human Rights Concerns for Tunisians Arriving by Sea." *Laws* 2:187–209.

Herbert, Matthew. 2016. "At the Edge: Trends and Routes of North African Clandestine Migrants." ISS Paper 298, Institute for Security Studies and the Global Initiative against Transnational Organized Crime, November.

———. 2019. *Less than the Sum of Its Parts: Europe's Fixation with Libyan Border Security.* Policy Brief 126, Institute for Security Studies, April.

———. 2022a. *Losing Hope: Why Tunisians Are Leading the Surge in Irregular Migration to Europe.* Geneva: Global Initiative against Transnational Organized Crime, January.

———. 2022b. *Tunisia: Growing Irregular Migration Flows Amid Worsening Political Fragility.* Geneva: Global Initiative against Transnational Organized Crime, July.

Herbert, Matt, and Max Gallien. 2020. *A Rising Tide: Trends in Production, Trafficking, and Consumption of Drugs in North Africa.* Geneva: Global Initiative against Transnational Organized Crime, May.

Herbert, Matt, and Amine Ghoulidi. 2019. "Social Media Bridges North Africa's Divides to Facilitate Migration." *ISS Today,* March 25, 2019. https://issafrica.org/iss-today/social-media-bridges-north-africas-divides-to-facilitate-migration.

Herbert, Matt, and Sofian Philip Naceur. 2019. "Algeria's Protests and Migration: The Fearmongers Have It Wrong." *ISS Today,* March 15, 2019. https://issafrica.org/iss-today/algerias-protests-and-migration-the-fearmongers-have-it-wrong.

International Organization for Migration. 2005. *World Migration 2005: Costs and Benefits of International Migration.* Geneva: International Organization for Migration.

———. 2016. *Mixed Migration Flows in the Mediterranean and Beyond: Compilation of Available Data and Information Statistical Data for Reporting Period 2015*. Geneva: International Organization for Migration.

Kadiri, Ghalia. 2017. "Des ressortissants marocains pris au piège des prisons libyennes." *Le Monde*, November 23, 2017. https://www.lemonde.fr/afrique/article/2017/11/23/le-maroc-decouvre-avec-effroi-que-ses-ressortissants-sont-aussi-vendus-en-libye_5219461_3212.html.

Kuschminder, Katie, and Anna Triandafyllidou. 2020. "Smuggling, Trafficking, and Extortion: New Conceptual and Policy Challenges on the Libyan Route to Europe." *Antipode* 52 (1): 206–226.

Lahlou, Mehdi. 2018. "Migration Dynamics in Play in Morocco: Trafficking and Political Relationships and Their Implications at the Regional Level." Middle East and North Africa Regional Architecture: Mapping Geopolitical Shifts, Regional Order and Domestic Transformations, Working Paper No. 26, November.

Micallef, Mark. 2017. *The Human Conveyor Belt: Trends in Human Trafficking and Smuggling in Post-revolutionary Libya*. Geneva: Global Initiative against Transnational Organized Crime, March.

Micallef, Mark, Rupert Horsely, and Alexander Bish. 2019. *The Human Conveyor Belt Broken: Assessing the Collapse of the Human Smuggling Industry in Libya and the Central Sahel*. Geneva: Global Initiative against Transnational Organized Crime, March.

Micallef, Mark, Matthew Herbert, Rupert Horsley, Alex Bish, Alice Fereday, and Peter Tinti. 2021. *Conflict, Coping and Covid: Changing Human Smuggling and Trafficking Dynamics in North Africa and the Sahel in 2019 and 2020*. Geneva: Global Initiative Against Transnational Organized Crime, April.

Monzini, Paola. 2007. "Sea-Border Crossings: The Organization of Irregular Migration to Italy." *Mediterranean Politics* 12 (2): 163–184.

Natter, Katharina. 2014. "The Formation of Morocco's Policy towards Irregular Migration (2000–2007): Political Rationale and Policy Processes." *International Migration* 52 (5): 15–28.

———. 2015. "Revolution and Political Transition in Tunisia: A Migration Game Changer." *Migration Information Source*, May 28, 2015. http://www.migrationpolicy.org/article/revolution-and-political-transition-tunisia-migration-game-changer.

Pantaleone, Wladimir. 2017. "Italy Busts Ring Smuggling Migrants from Tunisia in Speedboat." Reuters, June 6, 2017. https://www.reuters.com/article/us-europe-migrants-italy-smugglers/italy-busts-ring-smuggling-migrants-from-tunisia-in-speedboat-idUSKBN18X26J.

———. 2019. "Italy Breaks Up Smuggling Ring Run by Islamic State Sympathizer." Reuters, January 9, 2019. https://www.reuters.com/article/us-italy-security-smuggling-idUSKCN1P316G.

Pastore, Ferruccio, Paola Monzini, and Giuseppe Sciortino. 2006. "Schengen's Soft Underbelly? Irregular Migration and Human Smuggling across Land and Sea Borders to Italy." *International Migration* 44 (4): 95–119.

Przybyl, Sarah, and Youssef Ben Tayeb. 2013. "Tanger et les harraga: Les mutations d'un espace frontalier." *Hommes et Migrations*, no. 1304, 41–48.

Reitano, Tuesday. 2015. "A Perilous but Profitable Crossing: The Changing Nature of Migrant Smuggling through Sub-Saharan Africa to Europe and EU Migration Policy (2012–2015)." *European Review of Organised Crime* 2 (1): 1–23.

Reitano, Tuesday, and Peter Tinti. 2015. "Survive and Advance: The Economics of Smuggling Refugees and Migrants into Europe." ISS Paper 289, Institute for Security Studies and Global Initiative against Transnational Organized Crime, November.

Republic of Tunisia, Ministry of Interior. 2017. بلاغ. November 2017. http://www.interieur.gov.tn/actualite/2837/بلاغ.

R.S. 2019. "Ils activaient à travers la wilaya de Mostaganem: Trois réseaux d'organisation de voyages clandestins démantelés." *El Watan*, January 19, 2019.

Sanchez, Gabriella. 2015. *Human Smuggling and Border Crossings*. London: Routledge.

Schapendonk, Joris. 2018. "Navigating the Migration Industry: Migrants Moving through an African-European Web of Facilitation/Control." *Journal of Ethnic and Migration Studies* 44 (4): 663–679.

Seccombe, I. J., and R. J. Lawless. 1985. "Some New Trends in Mediterranean Labour Migration: The Middle East Connection." *International Migration* 23 (1): 123–148.

Simon, Julien. 2006. "Irregular Transit Migration in the Mediterranean: Facts, Figures and Insights." In *Mediterranean Transit Migration*, edited by Ninna Nyberg Sørensen, 25–66. Copenhagen: Danish Institute for International Studies.

Slack, Jeremy, and Daniel E. Martinez. 2018. "What Makes a Good Human Smuggler? The Differences between Satisfaction with and Recommendation of Coyotes on the U.S.-Mexico Border." *ANNALS of the American Academy of Political and Social Science* 676 (March): 152–172.

Souiah, Farida. 2016. "La pénalisation des 'brûleurs' de frontières en Algérie." *Après-demain* 3 (39): 19–21.

———. 2012. "Les harraga algériens." *Migrations Société*, no. 143, 105–120.

Tinti, Peter, and Tuesday Reitano. 2016. *Migrant, Refugee, Smuggler, Saviour*. London: Hurst.

Triandafyllidou, Anna, and Thanos Maroukis. 2012. *Migrant Smuggling: Irregular Migration from Asia and Africa to Europe*. London: Palgrave Macmillan.

United Nations High Commissioner for Refugees. n.d. "Operational Data Portal." Accessed February 21, 2023. https://data2.unhcr.org/en/situations.

United Nations Office on Drugs and Crime. 2010. *Smuggling of Migrants into, through and from North Africa: A Thematic Review and Annotated Bibliography of Recent Publications*. New York: United Nations.

CHAPTER 10

Smuggling Migrants from Africa to Europe

THREAT, RESOURCE, OR BARGAINING CHIP?

Luca Raineri

MIGRANT SMUGGLING DYNAMICS are the result of the complex interplay between the demand of cross-border mobility, its regulatory framework, and the smuggling practices bridging the gap between the two. Aiming to contribute to the understanding of these phenomena, this chapter explores the European Union (EU) response to the unprecedented rise of irregular migration from Africa since 2014 and discusses the impact of the fight against migrant smuggling in African countries of transit, including Libya, Niger, and Sudan. Undoubtedly, EU policing measures have had a profound impact on the volume and dynamics of the smuggling of migrants. In many cases, though, these diverged considerably from the expectations of the EU planners. Explaining these outcomes requires one to move past the determinism which is often implicit in EU strategizing and to focus instead on the perceptions and agency of smuggling providers and customers—that is, on their capacity to evade, adjust, and deform in creative ways the policing and policy constraints imposed on them at the structural level. Accounting for multidirectional causality and social rules paves the way to more nuanced interpretations of how smuggling unfolds in a complex field of political struggles.

Migrant smuggling between Africa and Europe is not a new phenomenon. Beginning in the late 1990s, the hardening of EU external borders and common migration policies pushed part of the EU-bound migration from

Africa outside the regulatory framework of both transit and receiving countries, prompting the rise of large-scale irregular migration schemes.[1] In response, since the early 2000s migrants and asylum seekers have tried to reach Europe with the help of smugglers, crossing by boat from the shores of Senegal and Mauritania heading toward the Canary Islands, or from northern African countries to southern Europe. Border cooperation treaties such as those signed between Spain and Morocco (2004), Spain and Mauritania (2007), and Italy and Libya (2008) contributed to significantly curtailing these flows to a few thousand detected irregular crossings per year (UNODC 2011). However, the political changes brought about by the so-called Arab Spring[2] destabilized this framework, with violent conflicts in Syria and Libya resulting in massive population displacement and increased border porosity in the southern European neighborhood. With migratory flows booming across southeast Europe at the same time, European media and policymakers were quick to label the situation a "EU migration crisis."[3]

In this context, migratory flows from Africa to Europe reached an unprecedented scale between 2014 and the first half of 2017, when more than half a million people crossed the Mediterranean Sea along the so-called Central Mediterranean route (CMR) from Libya to Italy. While the embarkation points to cross the Mediterranean were confined to a handful of localities in western Libya, the root of the CMR stretched deep into the African continent. Among the migrants who landed in Italy irregularly between 2014 and 2017, the largest majority came from sub-Saharan African countries, including more than 100,000 Eritreans, 85,000 Nigerians, and 30,000 Gambians. According to the International Organization for Migration (IOM), more than half of the total number of migrants and asylum seekers having reached Lampedusa at the peak of the migration "crisis" passed through the Nigerien town of Agadez (Tinti and Westcott 2016), where flows increased markedly from an estimated 40,000 to 60,000 crossings in the early 2010s (UNODC 2011) to 330,000 in 2016. At the same time, Sudan became the hub of the migration route from East Africa toward Libya and Europe; although the lack of reliable data makes the flows difficult to quantify, estimates suggest that migrants' and asylum seekers' crossings to Libya for Europe surpassed 50,000 per year (Tubiana and Gramizzi 2017). In this context, Libya and Italy became countries of transit or destination for migration from Africa. And in both cases, the restriction of legal migration avenues has resulted in the widespread resort to smuggling schemes in order to cross international and regional borders.

Scholars have put forward several factors to explain this sudden surge: the relapse of Libya in a civil war in 2014, leading to the collapse of law enforcement and the rise of extralegal economies (Shaw and Mangan 2015); the massive inflow in Libya of asylum seekers escaping the Syrian conflict, whose relative wealth paved the way to the creation of a smuggling economy of scale across the continent (Reitano and Tinti 2015); and the economic crises affecting several African countries in those years, incentivizing massive migratory flows (Benattia, Armitano, and Robinson 2015). While all these hypotheses have explanatory value, they remarkably all share the same framing: migrant smuggling is seen as an economic activity, akin to and interacting with market dynamics. Smugglers and their clients are understood as rational agents driven by utility maximization, while their aggregate behavior is considered sensitive to (and deducible from) the market incentives and variations of supply and demand. Implicit in this perspective is that positivist economic thinking is best suited to describing the main features and to explaining the main variations of migrant smuggling.

Such a framing of the smuggling of migrants from Africa to Europe has gained some traction not only in policy analysis but also and most importantly in policy making. Stirred by sensationalistic media reports and growing political concern in the EU, the policy response crafted by European authorities to an ill-defined "migration crisis" appeared to build on the assumption that the behavior of smuggling actors—including both smugglers and smuggled individuals—is akin to that of social atoms driven by a utility-maximization function. From this perspective, the trajectory and volume of actual migratory flows are presumed to be deducible from the availability and affordability of smuggling opportunities that bridge the gap between social universes characterized by large income differentials. In the same vein, the drivers of migration and migrant smuggling are seen not only as predictable through a cost-benefit calculation but also as highly sensitive to the supply of constraints and incentives at the structural level. In EU migration jargon, the widespread resort to framing metaphors taken from the hydraulic lexicon such as *push factors* and *pull factors* provides a clear illustration of this.

The abstract determinism implicit in this view, though, systematically downplays the agency and creativity of the actors involved in the smuggling world—that is, their capacity to deform and transform power structures by reacting to external stimuli in ways that economic variables alone are unable to predict. The observation of the migrant smuggling dynamics along the CMR suggests that EU incentives have often failed to mechanically bring about the expected outcomes. Aiming to investigate this discrepancy, this contribution explores the hypothesis that the failure to consider the political and social entrenchment of migrant smuggling contributes to explaining the unexpected outcomes of EU anti-smuggling policies along the CMR.

To this end, the chapter first outlines the policies and measures devised by the EU to tackle irregular migration along the CMR, trying to unearth the positivist economic thinking underlying them. Subsequently, two sections explore how smuggling and anti-smuggling efforts along the CMR have become entangled in a complex struggle for legitimacy and resources that a focus on local actors' agency is better suited to grasping.

The chapter is based on ethnographic primary data collected by the author through interviews with migrants, smugglers, law enforcement, and humanitarian actors. This provides not only a basis to overcome the oft-noticed challenge of illuminating inherently opaque extralegal economies but also the fine-grained qualitative evidence capable of calling into question the assumptions of positivistic approaches to studying and governing migrant smuggling. In particular, the chapter builds on extensive fieldwork carried out in and out of Mali, Niger, and Tunisia since 2013. This includes most notably semidirective interviews with stakeholders of migration governance in countries of transit, such as officials in national ministries of interiors and of foreign affairs; law enforcement officers (police, gendarmerie, customs); officials for EU Common Security and Defence Policy (CSDP) missions along the CMR (EU Capacity Building Mission [EUCAP] Sahel Mali, EUCAP Sahel Niger, EU Border Assistance Mission Libya, EU Naval Force–Mediterranean Operation Sophia); and humanitarian actors (IOM, UN High Commissioner for Refugees, international and local nongovernmental organizations [NGOs]). Additional interviews took place with EU, Italian, and UN officers in Brussels and Rome, as well as with migrants, former migrants, deported migrants, smugglers, and former smugglers met in Agadez (Niger) and Bamako (Mali). Traveling by public transport on the same West African routes hit by migrants has also provided a valuable opportunity to triangulate interview information with direct observation.[4]

FIGHTING SMUGGLERS TO TACKLE IRREGULAR MIGRATION

In April 2015, eight hundred migrants and asylum seekers died in a major shipwreck in front of Lampedusa on the CMR. This event shocked the European public and prompted an urgent reaction by European authorities. In the subsequent weeks, the EU issued some key policy documents that provided an overarching strategic framework to address the challenges of irregular migration: a ten-point action plan (Mogherini Plan) on migration, issued jointly by the Foreign and Home Affairs Councils on April 20, 2015 (European Commission 2015b), whose key ideas were reiterated in a special meeting of the EU Council on April 23 (Council of the European Union 2015); and a EU-wide Agenda on Migration (European Commission 2015a), issued on May 13, updating and replacing the 2005 EU Global Agenda on Migration and Mobility in light of the emerging challenges.

While these documents put forward a variety of measures and tools to address the challenges of irregular migration, all emphasized the "fight against migrant smuggling and trafficking" (often conflated without further specification) through police and security means. The Mogherini Plan, for instance, underscores the goal of undertaking "systematic effort to capture and destroy vessels used by the smugglers" and to leverage Europol's expertise so as "to gather information on smugglers' modus operandi" (European Commission 2015b). Noting that "instability in Libya creates an ideal environment for the criminal activities of traffickers," the conclusion of the EU Council special meeting further elaborated on the need to "disrupt trafficking networks, bring the perpetrators to justice and seize their assets, through swift action by Member State authorities in co-operation with EUROPOL," and to "reinforce our political cooperation with African partners at all levels in order to tackle the cause of illegal migration and combat the smuggling and trafficking of human beings" (Council of the European Union 2015).

The EU Agenda on Migration articulated this strategy even more explicitly. It called for streamlining the fight against migrant smuggling networks in CSDP operations, including both existing ones in the Sahel and new ones to be launched in the Mediterranean. A few weeks later, the council launched the CSDP mission EU Naval Force–Mediterranean Operation Sophia with the mandate "to disrupt the business model of human smuggling and trafficking networks in the Southern Central Mediterranean" (EEAS 2017). At the same time, the annual report of the Sahel Regional Action Plan, meant to monitor the implementation of the EU Security and Development Strategy in the Sahel, noted that "the three CSDP missions in the Sahel [EU Training Mission, EUCAP Sahel Niger, and EUCAP Sahel Mali] have been adapted to the political priorities of the EU, notably following the EU mobilization against irregular migration and related trafficking" (EEAS 2016).

On paper, EU migration strategies entail a variety of measures that go beyond the fight against smugglers, including enhanced humanitarian action to save lives at sea, development efforts to tackle the root causes of migration, and the review of EU asylum policies to help frontline member states address the high volume of arrivals during the migration "crisis." However, subsequent reports noted that these measures have been implemented only poorly, if at all (Cusumano 2017; Oxfam 2017). By contrast, the fight against migrant smuggling not only was streamlined but has also come to subsume and reconfigure the overall EU approach to migration and broader engagement in North Africa and the Sahel. The negotiation of the EU Migration Partnership Frameworks with countries of origin and transit of migratory flows highlighted the EU's determination to make development aid conditional to the beneficiaries' genuine commitment to clamp down on smuggling, measured in terms of reduction of flows and increase of arrests. From this perspective, the growing emphasis on the enhancement of borders, security-sector capacity-building, and criminalization of smugglers clearly highlights the underlying priorities of the EU and its member states.

The EU Agenda on Migration makes the rationale of this choice explicit: "Action to fight criminal networks of smugglers and traffickers . . . would act as a disincentive to irregular migration. The goal must be to transform smuggling networks from 'low risk, high return' operations for criminals into 'high risk, low return' ones" (European Commission 2015a: 7). An EU officer interviewed in Niamey further elaborated on this point: "We need to increase the costs of migration, by adding obstacles, shrinking legal corridors, and empowering local police forces" (interview, EU officer, Niamey, Niger, September 2015). The economic mentality underpinning EU policy making surfaces clearly: on the one hand, the criminalization of smuggling is expected to drive many operators out of the market, with the reduction of crossing options' supply leading to higher prices; on the other hand, the criminal professionalization that remaining smuggling cartels are likely to experience—if only to evade detection and live up to the raising entry barrier in the newly illegal(ized) market—would entail greater costs and personal risks for both smugglers and smuggled. And in this context, a rational-choice calculation of the costs and benefits of migration is likely to rule out the option of smuggling to Europe as too expensive and too dangerous for a larger share of smuggling providers and customers.

The desired outcome of curtailing irregular migration to Europe is thus achieved by leveraging the (supposed) structural determinants of migration through the administration of incentives and disincentives. As for the balls on a billiard table, the trajectories of African migrants to Europe are considered predictable from, and modifiable through, a set of given stimulants, underscoring the positivist bent of EU migration governance. This framework, however, pays inadequate attention to diverse sources of migrants' agency that fall beyond a supposedly rational cost-benefit calculation, including cultural norms, embedded practices, and social expectations.

At the same time, the almost exclusive focus on the (reduction of) the supply side of smuggling is reminiscent of the measures adopted to curtail other forms of smuggling, including most notably that of illicit drugs (Horwood 2019). However, the fundamental differences between the two sectors, and the spectacular failure of the war on drugs, should have suggested a more cautious approach to the issue of irregular migration, rather than a mere transposition of one-size-fits-all measures.

THE SOCIOPOLITICAL ENTRENCHMENT OF MIGRANT SMUGGLING

The stereotypical image of migrant smuggling networks—in which EU policies indulge—is that of a tightly organized criminal cartel, whose tentacles would stretch from remote African villages to North Libya's embarkation points, and farther into Europe, with the purpose of luring vulnerable individuals into a perilous journey through deception and fraud. Such a framing tends to take two key characteristics of the smuggling of migrants for granted: its criminality and its exploitative nature. While neither aspect is entirely inaccurate, this framing lays an exaggerated emphasis on the victimization and passivity of the smuggled migrants, implicitly equating migrant smuggling to a social evil that migrants have no other choice but to succumb to.

Beyond sensationalistic media reports, though, ethnographic studies suggest that local perceptions significantly diverge from these assumptions. In the Saharan borderlands along the CMR, smuggling is largely viewed as a normal, socially legitimate activity (Scheele 2012; Tidjani-Alou 2012). The smuggling of migrants makes no exception, with the oft-noticed moral ambiguity of human smuggling depending less on the illegal nature of the practice than on the specific conduct of the individual smugglers involved (Achilli 2015). And in fragile countries, where jobs are in short supply but corruption abounds, smugglers often enjoy a significant degree of legitimacy and trust, while it is the discontinuation of the smuggling flows that is perceived as criminal. This is especially the case in the Saharan space, where human mobility predates the legal framework criminalizing it by decades. Local sources contend that "smuggling is a noble activity, while being with the state means to be enslaved. The international community has attempted to reduce all traffics, but it cannot turn them off completely, for all the wealth of the community depends on that" (interview, young Tuareg activist from the Ifoghas tribe of Kidal, Mali, November 2014).[5] Rather than being seen as exploitative, then, smugglers are often seen as allies, if not saviors (Tinti and Reitano 2016), who help people escape social insecurity and stifling constraints.

As observed elsewhere (Sanchez 2017), smugglers in this region typically share the same cultural, social, and national background of their customers. This contributes to explaining that smugglers are often recommended by migrants' acquaintances at home or abroad. Many studies have found that the infrastructure of migratory flows from Africa (and especially West Africa) to Europe depends less on hierarchically integrated, professionally organized clandestine networks than on small-scale, "homespun" smuggling initiatives, loosely coordinated (al-Arabi 2018; Benattia, Armitano, and Robinson 2015; Raineri 2018). This has to do with the fact that, as is increasingly the case for transnational criminal activities in general, migrant smuggling is not separate from but deeply woven into the texture of ordinary social life, where criminal contacts intermesh with habitual social patterns (Hudson 2014).

Looking at the determinants of departure, smugglers do not appear to have a significant role in triggering migration (with the possible exception of migrants from Nigeria; see Molenaar and Ezzedinne 2018). Available data suggest that, rather than stimulating the demand for migration, smugglers are more often seen as service providers who meet an exogenously given social demand of mobility. One's determination to migrate is more influenced by peer pressure, social expectations, and the construction of gender roles than by mere economic considerations or incentives offered by the smugglers.[6] These observations suggest not only that the assumption about migrants' passivity is inaccurate but also that the demand of mobility stems from a variety of factors much broader than economic considerations of cost-benefit alone.

An inadequate consideration of the crucial influence of collective perceptions and local political agendas may help explain the initial failure of EU policies to curb irregular migration and migrant smuggling along the CMR. In Niger, for example, the adoption of a stringent law criminalizing migrant smuggling (in May 2015) and the reconfiguration of EU security-sector support to fight migrant smuggling (in July 2015) failed to produce any tangible impact for several months. In the remote borderlands of North Niger, in fact, migration is considered a social security valve contributing to the economic resilience of both migrants and smugglers (Reitano and Shaw 2014). According to a survey, the economy of human mobility contributed to the incomes of approximately half of Agadez households in 2016 (Molenaar et al. 2017). As a result, human smuggling enjoys a considerable social legitimacy. Even more importantly, the high degree of forbearance demonstrated by local authorities has led to the normalization and widespread impunity of human smuggling in Niger (IOM 2014), which a *political* economy analysis helps illuminate. Among the main actors contributing in different capacities to the facilitation of migrants' mobility across Niger, in fact, one could find local businessmen, who were also well-known sponsors of the incumbent government in Niamey (Raineri 2018), as well as former Tuareg and Tebu rebels, who agreed to lay down weapons in exchange for a relative toleration of their involvement in the economy of smuggling (Tubiana, Warin, and Saeneen 2018). Local authorities, including within the administration and the security sector, were also known to benefit from the revenues of migrant smuggling through the enforcement of informal taxation and protection rackets (Molenaar 2017; Tinti and Westcott 2016).

The discrepancy between (inter)national legality and local norm(ality) contributes to explaining why, in spite of the EU's urging the government of Niger to criminalize migrant smuggling, flows have continued to soar and prices to decline for several months (Raineri 2018). Local smugglers used to provide quite a telling illustration of this: "They [state authorities] do not bother us, because the whole city lives out of smuggling [*trafic*].[7] It is an evidence, there is no other job opportunity in Agadez. Sometimes we undergo a few formalities, we register the passengers' names, we pay a local 'tax,' and they let us go" (phone interview, Nigerien smuggler, May 2016).[8] Arguably, local networks of patronage politics—deeply entrenched in the human smuggling economy—have filtered and dispersed EU incentives, thereby undermining the planned curtailment of irregular migration.

Niger is not an isolated case. With Sudan emerging as the hub of mixed migration flows from East Africa, the EU engaged Sudanese authorities to prevent and fight migrant smuggling and trafficking. Authorities in Khartoum, however, managed to attract EU aid with the aim to bolster the formal security and police sector, but at the same time outsourced anti-smuggling functions to a paramilitary force largely composed of former counterinsurgency militiamen. With the backing of the government, these fought existing migrant smuggling networks, but only to replace them in the management of the lucrative smuggling business. Reportedly, this did not lead, at least initially, to any significant change in the volume of irregular migration from Sudan, nor to a rise of the price extorted to migrants smuggled to Libya (Tubiana, Warin, and Saeneen 2018). Again, the complexities of Africa's hybrid political orders trumped the expectations of EU anti-smuggling policies, demonstrating the resilience of smuggling to changing structural inputs and its creative adaptation to unstable political equilibria.

Libya is another case in point. Here, too, the security-centered approach promoted by the EU initially failed to bring about the desired outcome of curtailing irregular migration. On the one hand, the EU stepped up its cooperation by supporting the strengthening of a Libyan coastguard and the creation of a Libyan maritime rescue coordination center, in order to increase Libya's capacity to intercept and return migrants at sea. However, the EU's reliance on local security partners proved misguided, as—just like in Niger and Sudan—it failed to consider the capacity of local patronage networks to capture and divert the incentives theoretically aimed at curtailing irregular migration. The UN Panel of Experts on Libya found out that the Libyan coastguard's leaders, including some of the beneficiaries of EU aid, were protecting rather than fighting the smuggling of migrants (UNSC 2017), and the contribution of the Libyan coastguard to the fight against human smuggling and the reduction of irregular migration remained marginal (Micallef, Horsley, and Bish 2019).

On the other hand, Operation Sophia proved relatively successful in intercepting the vessels used by migrant smugglers across the Mediterranean, with approximately eight hundred boats seized in the first two years of the mission (declaration of Admiral Enrico Credendino, Operation Sophia Commander, during the Shade Med event in Rome, November 2017).[9] However, this did not lead to a "disruption of the smugglers' business model," as per the mandate of Operation Sophia, but only to its reconfiguration. Facing the deployment of Operation Sophia's sophisticated assets for interception and surveillance, in fact, smugglers were swift to replace medium-sized wooden boats with much cheaper inflatable rubber boats (dinghies). Purchased online for $300–$500, they could be filled with approximately one hundred passengers per journey, thus making the assets easily disposable with a negligible impact on the final profitability (Stocker 2017). At the same time, the massive use of unseaworthy rubber boats crammed with passengers resulted in a dramatic surge of the rate of shipwrecks and migrants' deaths at sea. Both Operation Sophia and humanitarian NGOs thus engaged in systematic search-and-rescue operations in front of Libya's territorial waters.

Critics argue that this may have paradoxically eased the smuggling of migrants (Micallef, Horsley, and Bish 2019). In the subsequent months, in fact, the price of a (irregular) sea crossing from Libya to Italy, or at least to international waters, declined markedly, while the volume of mixed migration flows from Libya continued to increase. This prompted media and political entrepreneurs to voice concern that search-and-rescue activities in the Mediterranean were providing a "pull factor" of migrant smuggling, thereby implicitly reproducing the same positivist assumptions of EU anti-smuggling policies. Subsequent studies, however, called into question the validity of such a correlation (Cusumano and Villa 2019). Although it may well be that smugglers do react to incentives and constraints, then, a mechanistic interpretation fails to explain the resilience of cross-Mediterranean migrant smuggling. It is rather the smugglers' agency that foiled EU anti-smuggling policies. Illustrations of this include, on the one hand, the creativity of the smugglers and their capacity to turn adverse circumstances to their own advantage and, on the other hand, the criminal capture of law enforcement in Libya, strategically pursued to ensure the social and political entrenchment of extralegal economies, including migrant smuggling (Lacher and al-Idrissi 2018; Shaw and Mangan 2015).

FROM SMUGGLING TO ANTI-SMUGGLING: A STRUGGLE FOR LEGITIMACY

The neglect of the social and political entrenchment of migrant smuggling contributes to explaining the initial failure of the EU strategy to bring about a reduction of migrant smuggling from Africa. Similarly, the changes of local politics and legitimization processes help us understand why prominent actors with stakes in migrant smuggling eventually turned to fight smugglers. While EU incentives are certainly one of the factors prompting this shift, assuming that they are the only factor mechanically bringing about a predetermined outcome would be misleading.

In Niger, it was only in late 2016 that the first symbolic measures against smugglers were adopted, with the arrest of several Agadez-based drivers and ghetto operators, and the confiscation of numerous pickup trucks (Molenaar et al. 2017). One may speculate that the timing of these measures points to the decisive influence of the EU incentives, including most notably the EU Partnership Framework on Migration, negotiated with Niamey since the summer of 2016. At the same time, one should not underestimate the significance of Niger's domestic electoral deadlines: given the widespread legitimacy of migrant smuggling, its criminalization could not take place in the run-up to the presidential election. An international observer commented that "before the election, it was hard to implement the law [criminalizing smugglers]. After the election, the implementation of the law allows local authorities to raise their international legitimacy" (interview, EU officer, Niamey, November 2018). That took place only in mid-2016—that is, one year after the passing of the law criminalizing migrant smuggling, which until then had remained "the most unpopular in the country" (interview, officer of EUCAP Sahel Niger, Niamey, May 2016). And while the shift of the Nigerien government's attitude certainly pleased European donors, there are indications that the criminalization of migrant smuggling was implemented only halfheartedly by Niamey: of the alleged smugglers arrested, few were actually judged, even fewer convicted, and only with light penalties. Similarly, some well-known smuggling kingpins rumored to have political protections were forced to discontinue (or at least reduce) their business, but without formal charges (interviews with civil society actors, law enforcement, and former smugglers, Niamey and Agadez, November 2018). Even more controversially, the criminalization of migrant smuggling seemed to be focused solely on the region of Agadez, while there is very limited evidence of anti-smuggling measures being implemented elsewhere in the country (interviews with EU officer, Nigerien human rights activist, and regional authorities, Niamey, Agadez, and Tillabéry, November and December 2018). As a result, while the reduction of mixed migration from Niger to Libya was undoubted, anecdotal evidence suggests that new routes were developed to avoid detection (Micallef, Horsley, and Bish 2019). Mixed migration across Niger thus remained sustained well into 2017 (Raineri 2018).[10]

In this context, EU insistence on the priority to fight migrant smuggling prompted entrepreneurial Nigerien actors to boast and advertise anti-smuggling credentials in an attempt to win the support of influential foreign partners in the framework of a domestic power struggle. For instance, Niger's minister of interior, who was rumored to maintain links with smuggling networks in Niger, proclaimed his determination to clamp down on irregular migration. The support of the EU and its member states that ensued gave him access to large material and symbolic resources that he successfully mobilized to build his patronage networks, climb the echelons of the ruling party, and be designated as the president's successor (interviews with journalists and local politicians, Niamey, November 2018). At the same time, prominent Nigerien businessmen with stakes in the smuggling economy were compensated for the losses resulting from the reduction of migratory flows by receiving tax cuts and trading licenses with the sponsorship of the government. Even more importantly, some of them managed to benefit from the shift to anti-smuggling policies and related economies by capturing lucrative international contracts as partners in the construction of military bases along the CMR, or in the return of migrants repatriated by EU measures and deported from Algeria (interviews with journalists and local politicians, Niamey, November 2018). And in the north of the country, Tebu tribesmen formerly involved in smuggling formed a local militia in the (short-lived) attempt to posture as reliable partners in the control of the border with Libya and the fight against all forms of smuggling. In this case, too, the shift to anti-smuggling should be interpreted in the framework of a competition over resources and legitimacy against rival armed factions, ethnic groups, and patronage networks (Tubiana, Warin, and Saeneen 2018).

In Libya, too, the interactions between foreign agendas, local political struggles, and changing legitimization dynamics are crucial to understand the shift from smuggling to anti-smuggling. It is not a coincidence that such shifts hardly occurred in the southern regions of the country. Here, as local communities suffered from acute political marginalization and the deterioration of livelihoods, the smuggling of all sorts of goods, including migrants, kept on representing a lifeline enjoying a widespread legitimacy (Tubiana and Gramizzi 2017). At the same time, this gave an opportunity to the unrecognized militia leader Khalifa Haftar to set a foothold in the unruly south and make military advances vis-à-vis its Tripoli-based rivals, posing as the only credible interlocutor of the international community capable of enforcing border protection and fighting migrant smuggling in southern Libya (Micallef, Horsley, and Bish 2019). It soon turned out, however, that Haftar's acceptance by southern tribes was premised on a tacit agreement that, in spite of much rhetoric, he would not disrupt the informal economy vital to local communities, including migrant smuggling. Local smuggling organizations simply integrated Haftar's patronage network so as to ensure the relative protection of their business, both in the southeast (UNSC 2018) and in the southwest (interview with Nigerien military deployed at the border with Libya, September 2019).

In the north of the country, in the vicinity of the smuggling hubs used to cross the Mediterranean, the situation was very different. Here, the criminal drift of large-scale smuggling resulted in soaring abuses vis-à-vis both migrants and local communities. As a result of the rapid erosion of the legitimacy of migrant smuggling, popular revolts successfully managed to kick the smugglers out of the towns of Zuwara and Garabulli, which used to be embarkation points of large-scale migratory flows to Europe. In the meantime, local militias emerged to enforce a strict anti–migrant smuggling policy in an attempt to consolidate their political legitimacy and institutional grip (Micallef, Horsley, and Bish 2019; Stocker 2017).

In the highly fragmented landscape of Libya's politics, other towns followed different trajectories, yet most converged toward a shift from smuggling to anti-smuggling. As extralegal economies thrived in postrevolutionary Libya, militias formed during the civil war initially competed to enforce a protection racket over all sorts of economic activities, including migrant smuggling (Shaw and Mangan 2015). Progressively, though, the antagonism and turf wars among militias precipitated a situation of political anarchy, economic crisis, and widespread corruption in Libya (Lacher and al-Idrissi 2018). This, in turn, prompted a rising demand for rule of law, domestically, and for stability, internationally. In this context, local security providers who succeeded in being perceived as committed to the pursuit of law and order—no matter how strictly conceived and how harshly implemented—quickly increased their domestic legitimacy and international standing (ICG 2019). With the unfolding of the complex political negotiations to establish a unified government in Libya, the capacity of Libyan militias to attract symbolic and material support by foreign sponsors—such as Egypt, the United Arab Emirates, Saudi Arabia, Italy, France, and the EU—became even more important than (or perhaps instrumental to) the control over national resources. The alignment with international priorities, including the fight against migrant smuggling, thus became a crucial asset in local power struggles, while the collusions with smugglers were increasingly perceived as a toxic liability in the pursuit of legitimacy (Micallef, Horsley, and Bish 2019).

It is noteworthy that the shift from the protection racket of migrant smuggling to the (if only outward posture of) anti-smuggling law enforcement by Libyan armed groups was not harmless, with charges of "corruption" fueling intermilitia clashes in several northern Libyan towns. The case of Sabratha is illustrative of these dynamics. Until mid-2017, Sabratha was the main embarkation point of migrant smuggling flows to Europe, as well as a demonstration of the Libyan coastguard's failure to tackle migrant smuggling (UNSC 2017). The situation radically changed in July 2017 when, almost overnight, a prominent local smugglers' network discontinued its operations and turned from fostering smuggling to joining anti-smuggling efforts. This surprising shift prompted allegations that former smugglers had traded their "conversion" in exchange for economic compensations and political co-optation, perhaps with the financial and political support of foreign actors (a rumor further corroborated by one of the accused themselves, as reported by Wintour 2017). The discontinuation of Sabratha's lucrative smuggling economy stirred the violent reaction of the rival smuggling networks and the militias protecting them. Yet when the latter managed to remove the former smugglers turned cops, they did not resume migrant smuggling but rather joined the anti-smuggling security apparatus (Micallef, Horsley, and Bish 2019). That the aim of the struggle was not so much to challenge the anti-smuggling apparatus but to secure a place within it is an indication of the shifting *political* economy of migrant smuggling in Libya.

Additional examples indicate that the case of Sabratha was not an oddity but an instance of a broader trend of general value: from the northeast of Libya to the Fezzan, from Sudan to Niger, state, nonstate, and parastate armed actors were sucked into a competition to demonstrate their reliability as local partners in the EU-sponsored fight against migrant smuggling. At the same time, these dynamics appear to have prompted a transition in how irregular migration along the CMR unfolds: from migrant exporting schemes to slave importing operations (Kyle and Dale 2001). According to David Kyle and John Dale, migrant exporting schemes are poorly criminalized, highly opportunistic enterprises to ship migrants out of a sending country or region; slave importing operations, instead, are performed by highly organized networks, often involving large-scale corruption, whose core business is centered in the country of destination, where exploitation takes place. And "in most of the cases, victims of these operations are duped into believing that it is a migrant exporting scheme in which they are about to embark" (Kyle and Dale 2001: 33), which is a precondition for exploitation. Illustrations of this trend along the CMR include the rise of debt-bound travel schemes in Sudan and Chad (Tubiana, Warin, and Saeneen 2018); banditry, extortions, and kidnapping for ransom of smuggled migrants in Niger and Mali (Molenaar et al. 2017); the systematic exploitation of the labor of migrants trapped in connection houses and detention centers in Libya, including most notably in Sebha and Bani Walid (al-Arabi 2018); the scale-up of the market for prostitution of trafficked Nigerian women inside Libya (Micallef, Horsley, and Bish 2019); and the overall blurring of the lines between migrant smuggling and trafficking along the CMR.

This outcome is unsurprising: the compression of migrants' actual agency—which the shift from migrant exporting schemes to slave importing operations entails—may be seen as one of the unintended consequences of the disregard for migrants' and smugglers' agency that permeates EU anti-smuggling policies' structural determinism.

CONCLUSION: SMUGGLING (RESEARCH)— HIGH RISK AND LOW RETURNS?

At the time of writing (2020), irregular migration along the CMR has radically shrunk in comparison with the peak of the migration "crisis" in 2014–2017. However, as this chapter has argued, this is less the direct outcome of EU measures to fight migrant smuggling than it is the result of a complex realignment of actors, interests, and practices at local and international levels that was catalyzed around mid-2017.

It is questionable whether the conversion from smuggling to anti-smuggling, outlined in this chapter, represents a "disruption of the smugglers' business model." Rather, it has the potential to further cement the political clout of patronage networks devoted to extralegal economic activities. There are indications that many smugglers have simply shifted to the smuggling of other commodities, just as (if not more) profitable, but less politically sensitive, and therefore subject to less international scrutiny. This is exemplified by the rise of drug, gold, and fuel smuggling across Niger, Sudan, and Libya and the alleged involvement of former migrant smugglers in it (Micallef, Horsley, and Bish 2019; Tubiana, Warin, and Saeneen 2018). These developments are transforming the structural constraints in which migrant smuggling takes place, although it is not clear whether they are contributing to curbing the demand of clandestine migration.

This ambiguity paves the way to a concluding remark. Critical migration scholarship has argued that the tightening of border controls and the criminalization of irregular migration in fact fuels the demand for smuggling services, thereby generating, somewhat paradoxically, incentives for the perpetuation and entrenchment of the very phenomenon these measures are supposed to fight—that is, migrant smuggling. There is indeed no lack of evidence to corroborate this claim. This argument reproduces and adapts to the field of migration studies a long-established trope in critical criminology literature, whereby criminalization often leads to criminogenic, or "iatrogenic," effects. However, one may argue that this way of reasoning, too, indulges in an understanding of social phenomena that is fundamentally deterministic, and probably too rigid to be entirely accurate. Critical scholars would then run the risk of reproducing, reiterating, and possibly legitimizing the same epistemological standpoint that contributes to generating the policies they condemn.

Understanding the agency of both smuggling providers and customers becomes then even more necessary, in order to move past the overemphasis on structural determinants and rational choice. Migrant smuggling is a complex phenomenon that economic variables alone are unable to grasp. The case of the CMR highlights the need for a *political* economy analysis that factors the social and political embeddedness of migrant smuggling in, against the background of specific sociohistorical contextualization. Acknowledging this should prompt scholars to complement the study of migrant smuggling and anti-smuggling with a greater reliance on qualitative methodologies and ethnographic methods.

However, the ongoing overbureaucratization of fieldwork research, in combination with the securitization of migrant smuggling, runs the risk of foreclosing to ethnographers access to smuggling practices. In other words, the criminalization of migrant smuggling runs the risk of making of ethnographic migration scholarship a high-risk, low-return enterprise, in the same way it is supposed to do with irregular migration itself. Nevertheless, in the face of the limits of existing anti-smuggling policies, discourses, and theories—to which the deaths of thousands of migrants along the CMR are not alien—the alternative of "business as usual" seems no longer viable.

NOTES

1. UNODC (2018) acknowledges that "there is no clear or universally accepted definition of irregular migration, but it is generally understood as movements that take place outside the regulatory norms of sending, transit, or receiving countries." (20)
2. The nickname denotes the upheavals against authoritarian regimes that ignited political transitions in the Middle East and North Africa in 2011.
3. The qualification of migration "crisis" appears poorly fitting if one considers that many countries less resourced than the EU have been targeted in the same years by much larger flows of migrants and asylum seekers. It would be more appropriate to speak of a *political* crisis prompted by large-scale migratory flows.
4. Journeys were undertaken in particular in 2016, most notably from Freetown (Sierra Leone) to Bamako (Mali) via Conakry (Guinea), and from Niamey toward Agadez (Niger).
5. The quote refers to smuggling in general, which includes migrant smuggling but also the smuggling of licit and illicit goods. The social contexts prevailing in Mali in

the aftermath of the Tuareg insurrection of 2012 may have influenced the audacity of the statement. This remains, however, indicative of widespread social perceptions in the region, which fail to disqualify—let alone criminalize—smuggling.
6. The data on the determinants of migration elaborated on in this paragraph are taken from the surveys conducted by the Mixed Migration Monitoring Mechanism in Sahel and Libya. See Mixed Migration Centre (n.d.).
7. While the interviewee explicitly used the word *trafic* (smuggling), ethnographers have found that iterations of the notion of "fraud" such as *al-frud* (Scheele 2012) and *afrod* (Kohl 2013) are locally widespread and often employed as equivalent of trade in general.
8. The interviewee added—without being asked—that he was in charge of a "Bureau des Trafiquants" (smugglers office) tasked with representing the "legitimate interests" of the smugglers vis-à-vis local authorities.
9. However, subsequent informal comments made in the same circumstances suggested that the majority of such seizures concerned inflatable rubber boats.
10. As an illustration of this, the analysis of IOM data on mobility in Niger reveals some important gaps that require a cautious interpretation: in 2017, for instance, only 2,700 migrants and asylum seekers from Nigeria were observed in transit through Niger to Libya, yet 18,000 Nigerians reached Italy the same year. See IOM 2014.

REFERENCES

Achilli, Luigi. 2015. *The Smuggler: Hero or Felon?* Policy Brief 2015/10. Florence: Robert Schuman Centre for Advanced Studies.
al-Arabi, Abdulrahman. 2018. *Local Specificities of Migration in Libya: Challenges and Solutions.* Policy Brief 2018/04. Florence: Robert Schuman Centre for Advanced Studies.
Benattia, Tahar, Florence Armitano, and Holly Robinson. 2015. *Irregular Migration between West Africa, North Africa and the Mediterranean.* Paris: Altai Consulting.
Council of the European Union. 2015. "Special Meeting of the European Council—Statement." Foreign Affairs and Home Affairs Council meeting, Brussels, April 23, 2015.
Cusumano, Eugenio. 2017. "Straightjacketing Migrant Rescuers? The Code of Conduct on Maritime NGOs." *Mediterranean Politics*, online ahead of print, September 27, 2017. https://doi.org/10.1080/13629395.2017.1381400.
Cusumano, Eugenio, and Matteo Villa. 2019. *Sea Rescue NGOs: A Pull Factor of Irregular Migration?* Policy Brief 2019/22. Florence: Robert Schuman Centre for Advanced Studies.
EEAS (European External Action Service). 2016. *Annual Report on the Sahel Regional Action Plan.* Brussels: European Commission, December 23.
———. 2017. *Strategic Review on EUBAM Libya, EUNAVFOR MED Op Sophia & EU Liaison and Planning Cell.* Brussels, May 15.
European Commission. 2015a. "A European Agenda on Migration." Communication to the European Parliament, the Council, the European Economic and Social Committee and the Committee of Regions, Brussels, May 13, 2015.

———. 2015b. "Ten-Point Action Plan on Migration." Joint Foreign and Home Affairs Council, Luxembourg, April 20, 2015.

Horwood, Cristopher. 2019. *The New "Public Enemy Number One": Comparing and Contrasting the War on Drugs and the Emerging War on Migrant Smugglers*. Geneva: Mixed Migration Centre.

Hudson, Ray. 2014. "Thinking through the Relationships between Legal and Illegal Activities and Economies: Spaces, Flows and Pathways." *Journal of Economic Geography* 14 (4): 775–795.

ICG (International Crisis Group). 2019. *Addressing the Rise of Libya's Madkhali-Salafis*. Middle East and North Africa Report No. 200. Brussels: ICG, April.

IOM (International Organization for Migration). 2014. *Fatal Journey: Tracking Lives Lost during Migration*. Geneva: IOM, October.

———. 2017. *Population Flow Monitoring—Niger Overview Report*. Geneva: IOM, December.

Kohl, Ines. 2013. "Afrod, le business touareg avec la frontière: Nouvelles conditions et nouveaux défis." *Politique Africaine* 4 (132): 139–159.

Kyle, David, and John Dale. 2001. "Smuggling the State Back In: Agents of Human Smuggling Reconsidered." In *Global Human Smuggling: Comparative Perspectives*, edited by David Kyle and Rey Koslowski, 33–59. Baltimore: Johns Hopkins University Press.

Lacher, Wolfram, and Alaa al-Idrissi. 2018. *Capital of Militias: Tripoli's Armed Groups Capture the Libyan State*. Geneva: Small Arms Survey.

Micallef, Mark, Rupert Horsley, and Alexandre Bish. 2019. *The Human Conveyor Belt Broken: Assessing the Collapse of the Human-Smuggling Industry in Libya and the Central Sahel*. Geneva: Global Initiative against Transnational Organized Crime.

Mixed Migration Centre. n.d. "A Summary of the Mixed Migration Monitoring Mechanism Initiative (4Mi) Methodology and Approach." Accessed February 22, 2023. http://www.mixedmigration.org/wp-content/uploads/2018/08/4mi_summary_methodology.pdf.

Molenaar, Fransje. 2017. *Irregular Migration and Human Smuggling Networks in Niger*. CRU report. The Hague: Netherlands Institute of International Relations "Clingendael."

Molenaar, Fransje, and Nancy Ezzedinne. 2018. *Southbound Mixed Movement to Niger: An Analysis of Changing Dynamics and Policy Responses*. CRU report. The Hague: Netherlands Institute of International Relations "Clingendael."

Molenaar, Fransje, Elena-Anca Ursu, Bachirou Tinni, Annette Hoffmann, and Jos Meester. 2017. *A Line in the Sand: Roadmap for Sustainable Migration Management in Agadez*. CRU report. The Hague: Netherlands Institute of International Relations "Clingendael."

Oxfam. 2017. *An Emergency for Whom? The EU Emergency Trust Fund for Africa: Migratory Routes and Development Aid in Africa*. Oxfam Briefing Note. Brussels: Oxfam.

Raineri, Luca. 2018. "Human Smuggling across Niger: State-Sponsored Protection Rackets and Contradictory Security Imperatives." *Journal of Modern African Studies* 56 (1): 63–86.

Reitano, Tuesday, and Mark Shaw. 2014. "People's Perspectives of Organised Crime in West Africa and the Sahel." ISS Paper 254, Institute for Security Studies, Dakar, April.

Reitano, Tuesday, and Peter Tinti. 2015. "Survive and Advance: The Economics of Smuggling Refugees and Migrants into Europe." ISS Paper 289, Institute for Security Studies, Dakar, November.

Sanchez, Gabriella. 2017. "Critical Perspectives on Clandestine Migration Facilitation: An Overview of Migrant Smuggling Research." *Journal on Migration and Human Security* 5 (1): 9–27.

Scheele, Judith. 2012. *Smugglers and Saints of the Sahara: Regional Connectivity in the Twentieth Century*. Cambridge: Cambridge University Press.

Shaw, Mark, and Fiona Mangan. 2015. "Enforcing 'Our Law' When the State Breaks Down: The Case of Protection Economies in Libya and Their Political Consequences." *Hague Journal on the Rule of Law* 7 (1): 99–110.

Stocker, Valerie. 2017. *Leaving Libya: Rapid Assessment of Municipalities of Departures of Migrants in Libya*. Tunis: Altai Consulting.

Tidjani-Alou, Mahamadou. 2012. "Monitoring the Neopatrimonial State on a Day-by-Day Basis: Politicians, Customs Officials and Traders in Niger." In *Neopatrimonialism in Africa and Beyond*, edited by Daniel Bach and Mamadou Gazibo, 142–154. New York: Routledge.

Tinti, Peter, and Tuesday Reitano. 2016. *Migrant, Refugee, Smuggler, Saviour*. New York: Hurst.

Tinti, Peter, and Tom Westcott. 2016. "The Niger-Libya Corridor: Smugglers' Perspectives." ISS Paper 299, Institute for Security Studies, Dakar, November.

Tubiana, Jérôme, and Claudio Gramizzi. 2017. *Tubu Trouble: State and Statelessness in the Chad–Sudan–Libya Triangle*. Geneva: Small Arms Survey and Conflict Armament Research.

Tubiana, Jérôme, Clotilde Warin, and Gaffar Saeneen. 2018. *Multilateral Damage: The Impact of EU Migration Policies on Central Saharan Routes*. CRU report. The Hague: Netherlands Institute of International Relations "Clingendael."

UNODC (United Nations Office on Drugs and Crime). 2011. *The Role of Organized Crime in the Smuggling of Migrants from West Africa to the European Union*. Vienna: UNODC, January.

———. 2018. *Global Study on Smuggling of Migrants*. Vienna: UNODC, June.

UNSC (United Nations Security Council). 2017. *Final Report of the Panel of Experts on Libya Established Pursuant to Resolution 1973 (2011)*. S/2017/466. New York, June.

———. 2018. *Final Report of the Panel of Experts on Libya Established Pursuant to Resolution 1973 (2011)*. S/2018/812. New York, September.

Wintour, Patrick. 2017. "Italy's Deal to Stem Flow of People from Libya in Danger of Collapse." *Guardian*, October 3, 2017.

CHAPTER 11

Irregular Migration and Human Smuggling Networks
THE CASE OF NORTH KOREA

Kyunghee Kook

MORE THAN THIRTY THOUSAND North Koreans have left their home country and reached South Korea through a perilous journey via China, Russia, Mongolia, and Southeast Asian countries with the assistance of networks of facilitators (South Korean Ministry of Unification 2022). Their journeys are guided by smuggling groups, churches, or nonprofit networks operated by religious and nongovernmental organizations (NGOs). Scholarly literature and humanitarian reports generally assume that there is a rigid dichotomy between smugglers and the other groups (e.g., Human Rights Watch 2002, 2013; International Crisis Group 2006; Kim 2011; Lankov 2004). On one side of this narrative, there are smugglers organized in often hierarchical groups, who are depicted as reckless criminals whose interest in facilitating people's mobility purely and simply derives from greed and who lure innocent North Korean migrants into exploitative situations. On the other side, there are missionaries and NGOs with various mandates, whose networks are described in a substantially more positive light and who are perceived as operating for altruistic purposes deriving from a genuine interest to "rescue" and "save" those seeking to escape the North Korean regime.

Drawing from ethnographic evidence, this chapter engages with conventional wisdom by focusing on the facilitation of irregular migration and the main routes used to smuggle North Koreans out of their country. In doing so, it argues that the very broad and divergent range of interests that involve human smuggling among North Koreans cannot be encompassed by clear-cut distinctions between altruistic missionaries and humanitarian actors, on one hand, and profit-oriented smuggling networks, on the other. On the contrary, North Koreans' migratory journeys have mostly been facilitated by decentralized networks of people and groups in partnership with one another. These networks comprise a variety of actors, including smugglers, NGOs, pastors, missionaries (or small churches), family members, and relatives, who cover a plurality of roles as organizers, smugglers, intermediaries, guides, drivers, and external collaborators. Different interests are in play, and these are not deterministically bound to specific typologies of actors. As this chapter demonstrates, many smugglers in fact operate for altruistic or political reasons, whereas some pastors have provided smuggling services in pursuit of financial gain.

METHODS

This chapter builds on empirical research largely consisting of interviews with and participant observations of North Korean migrants and those who facilitate their journeys, which was conducted in Seoul, South Korea, from 2014 to 2016. Interviews were conducted with forty-five North Korean men and women, half of whom were smuggled to South Korea via China, Mongolia, and Southeast Asian countries such as Laos, Cambodia, and Thailand. The other half of the North Korean interviewees were professional smugglers or other actors who previously worked—often interchangeably—as organizers or intermediaries in smuggling networks in North Korea, China, or South Korea. I also conducted twenty interviews with Korean Chinese and Chinese smugglers, South Korean NGO activists, American pastors, Korean Chinese pastors and missionaries, and Chinese missionaries who facilitated North Koreans' irregular migration at various stages.

Although in-depth and semistructured interviews were the predominant and primary data-collection modes used for this research, I also engaged in participant observation of North Korean migrants and those who assisted their movements. Intensive exposure to the community of facilitators and migrants led to several informal conversations and field observations. To recruit participants, I relied on social contacts obtained through my involvement in NGOs and churches. I previously worked part time with an NGO founded by North Korean migrants that helps those stranded in China to reach South Korea and organizes public events and conferences to raise awareness of human rights abuses in North Korea. A large part of data collection entailed interviews and informal conversations with men and women attending three churches based in South Korea, North America, and North Korea, all of which operate networks of safe houses in China that support North Korean asylum seekers who wish to escape their country and reach South Korea.[1]

In the America-based church, where I volunteered as an interpreter between American pastors or missionaries and North Korean migrants, I had many opportunities to engage in conversations with both parties. In the South Korea–based church, I made frequent visits to temporary shelters set up for North Korean migrants and built a solid relationship with the community by assisting them with daily living, bureaucratic issues with council offices, and banking or school administrations in South Korea. I became familiar with the North Korea–based church through the NGO where I worked, which enabled me to share their daily life and routine without needing to spend a great deal of time building rapport, and they spoke openly about how underground churches, shelters, and smuggling were operated in China.

JOURNEYS TO SOUTH KOREA VIA SMUGGLING ROUTES

Amid the country's economic breakdown in the 1990s, hundreds of thousands of North Koreans crossed the border to China in search of food, shelter, jobs, and better lives. Although their exact numbers are unknown due to their illegal status, estimates of North Korean migrants living in China range between one hundred thousand and three hundred thousand (Song 2013: 165). Recognized by the Chinese government as illegal immigrants, North Korean migrants are subject to violence and forcible repatriation. International humanitarian groups have depicted these escapees as veritable "modern slaves" (Muico 2005: 3), as they are bound into various forms of enslavement, including forced marriage, forced labor, trafficking, and similar practices (Charny 2005; Human Rights Watch 2002). For these reasons, many seek refuge in South Korea, where their asylum claims are granted and protected. This journey is extremely dangerous and expensive; only a small minority can afford it, and even fewer actually make it to South Korea.

At the time of my fieldwork between 2014 and 2016, North Korean escapees had two legal options to reach South Korea: border passes and working permits. Extremely difficult to obtain, border passes are only accessible to a very small minority of people—usually highly ranked officers in the North Korean establishment or prominent businesspeople. Alternatively, prospective migrants can be employed as guest workers in other countries. The North Korean government claimed that in 2016, approximately sixty thousand North Korean workers were sent to twenty or so countries, the most common destinations being Russia, Kuwait, Mongolia, China, and the United Arab Emirates (Do et al. 2017). However, only very few of these guest workers managed to move to Seoul (Do et al. 2017); most are dissuaded by strict surveillance at work by the North Korean government and the threat of retaliation against families left behind.

With few notable exceptions, North Koreans have most frequently used illegal channels to leave their country, crossing the border to China either alone or with the aid of smugglers and then moving on to South Korea through a third country. Before Kim Jong-un's regime, quite a few people escaped by familiarizing themselves with the geography around the border or paying bribes to border guards. However, since Kim Jong-un's rise to power in 2011, the installation of electric fences and introduction of harsher punishments for illegal border crossings have substantially increased migrants' reliance on third parties as facilitators to reach China.

Increasingly restrictive and abusive measures have changed the nature of the smuggling business. Smugglers are recognized as political criminals who incite ordinary North Koreans to betray their Great Leader by supporting their journeys away from the regime, and penalties for smugglers arrested in China or North Korea are much more severe than those for the smuggled North Koreans found with them. Smugglers' sentences at reeducation prison camps (*kyowhaso*) are typically much longer than those given to their clients, and they also may be sent to political prison camps (*kwalliso*), where release is unlikely, or sentenced to public execution in extreme cases (Kook 2019: 14). The prospect of harsh punishment has led a number of smugglers to quit their jobs in North Korea, and those who have continued to work have raised their commission fees. As Kyung-chul, who had worked as a smuggler for the past five years, explained, "Once smugglers are caught, they will be sent to prison camps, including political prison camps from which they may never be released. Besides, they could even be executed. How much money would you require for that? It's the price of your life. We need to call for a high price so that, in case we get caught, we might at least get an opportunity to bribe the border guards to save our life." The drastic increase in smuggling fees has resulted in a substantial decrease in irregular border crossings. The number of North Korean migrants moving to South Korea has declined to 1,000–1,200 per year, which is less than half the rate of escapees documented during mid- to late 2000s (South Korean Ministry of Unification 2022).

Irrespective of whether their crossing was legal or illegal, once North Koreans enter China, they heavily rely on smuggling networks to move on to South Korea, as there are no legal routes for that stage of the journey. According to interviewees, there are three main routes for North Koreans to move from China to South Korea. The first route is to use a fake passport to board an airplane or a ship, which is the most expensive option but also the safest and fastest, as it only takes them three to seven days to arrive in Seoul. Since the introduction of e-passports in South Korea in 2008, costs have considerably increased from $10,000 in the early 2000s to $25,000 or more (Williamson 2011). The very few who choose this option generally have family members in South Korea who can financially support their journey. My informants described this route as also being a favorite among smugglers. Not only is it safer, as they merely need to get migrants to the airport rather than crossing the border with them, it is also physically less demanding.

The second path is the northern route, whereby migrants cross the border from China to Mongolia and then enter South Korea, and the third route is via Southeast Asian countries; migrants travel from southern China to Laos or Myanmar and then cross the Mekong River to Thailand before entering South Korea. Whereas the northern route takes between three days and a week, the southern route is considerably more time consuming, requiring a week or even a month. However, the northern route is more physically demanding, as weather conditions in Mongolia can be particularly harsh. Moreover, beginning in the mid- to late 2000s, China increased the level of surveillance at the Mongolian border. Thus, over the last decade, the weight has largely shifted to the southern route. At the time of my fieldwork in 2016, the price for the journey was between $3,000 and $5,000, and the duration was dependent on the weather and smugglers' level of preparation. Moving from China to Thailand does not take much time; however, North Korean migrants can end up staying in a refugee shelter for three months to a year while awaiting the South Korean government's approval for them to enter the country.

My research indicated that the choice of route and smuggling group carried a set of social and moral signifiers. Those who reached South Korea with fake passports were generally proud of this choice, as the ability to access this route reflected more prestigious social ranks and backgrounds. Other researchers have shed light on the intersection of social status with smuggling and irregular mobility (Zhang, Sanchez, and Achilli 2018). However, among my informants, social and moral values were deeply intertwined with economic motives.

The more widely the smuggling networks and routes are known, the more likely migrants and facilitators are to be caught by Chinese authorities or North Korean security police. Unsurprisingly, information concerning smuggling networks is a source of power among North Korean migrants, who can sell their knowledge for high prices in the Chinese, North Korean, and South Korean black markets.[2] Participants usually only spoke in detail about their journeys and fake passports after a certain level of rapport had been built. Many participants spoke of smugglers as acquaintances or helpers who needed to be protected.

SEON: THE STRUCTURE AND COORDINATION OF SMUGGLING NETWORKS

North Koreans' journeys have mainly been facilitated by decentralized networks known as *seon*. The term—which translates literally and interchangeably into the English equivalent of "networks"—refers to the coordinated action of professional smugglers, pastors, missionaries (or small churches), NGOs, and family members. All of the interviewees had been involved with seon in one way or another. Those who had journeyed to South Korea through China and other countries did so as clients of seon. After arriving in China or South Korea, some migrants worked as seon organizers or intermediaries, whereas others founded NGOs, worked as activists for NGOs, or became pastors or missionaries in churches in China. Along with professional smugglers, NGO workers, pastors, and missionaries play varying key roles in facilitating the irregular journeys of North Korean escapees at different stages. Although seon were not depicted as hierarchically structured organizations, they operate based on a complex division of labor.

According to study participants, seon can be schematically classified into three groups depending on the focal organizers around whom smaller sub-networks operate: North Korean facilitators who have settled in South Korea, NGOs, and Christian networks. The first group is the largest due to their connections with or former status as North Korean smugglers, border guards, and military men. They play a crucial role in the organization of journeys due to their awareness of the political circumstances in North Korea as well as internal border security situations. Moreover, North Korean escapees who have stayed in China or have relatives in the country have better access to groups of facilitators who can help escapees cross the border to China and then to a third country. Most importantly, North Korean escapees who have completed the journey themselves have firsthand knowledge of what it entails. Shin-young, who had escaped from North Korea and had been working in South Korea as a seon organizer for three years, described the mechanisms of the networks as follows:

> If someone wants to come to South Korea from North Korea, I get notified. I first contact the Korean-Chinese intermediaries who in turn get in touch with North Korean smugglers. When the price is agreed, the smugglers take the migrants to the intermediaries. From there, Chinese smugglers help them cross the border to Laos where a Laos boatman would be in charge of delivering them to Thailand. In Thailand, they contact the South Korean embassy to enter Seoul. When they arrive in South Korea, I receive the money some of which would be sent to the intermediaries who would also send some to the smugglers in turn. In a sense, I act as the manager of the whole journey.

The second group comprises NGOs established to protect and promote the human rights of North Koreans, which are predominantly South Korea-based but also present in the United States and Canada. At the peak of North Korea's food crisis in the 1990s, a large number of refugees went to China to escape starvation. NGOs began helping them by providing them with food and safe houses in China. They also facilitate the journey from North Korea or China to South Korea.

However, due to the covert nature of all of the aforementioned activities, it is often difficult to identify which NGOs are involved in seon, although there are a handful of NGOs that explicitly promote their involvement in "rescues." Among NGOs in South Korea, those established by North Korean migrants tend to be more active in rescue efforts, and those established by non–North Koreans recruit and rely on such migrants and their networks for their knowledge of North Korea, China, and the border area between the two countries.

The third group constitutes networks of evangelical Christians—namely, South Koreans, Americans, Chinese, and Korean Chinese who share a common religious faith. Such networks consist of pastors and missionaries as well as ordinary believers who have volunteered for missionary work to preach the gospel (Han 2013). During my fieldwork, I met with American pastors, Chinese missionaries, and South Korean pastors who had their own churches and were involved in organizing the journey for North Koreans. The Christian networks operated safe houses in China, Laos, Myanmar, and Cambodia. These safe houses are shared among Christian communities as well as North Korean professional smugglers and NGOs because although each of the three types of groups possess their own organizers, they share the Chinese intermediaries, which implies that they have the same modus operandi. For example, Hyun-joong's son contacted a North Korean migrant organizer who lived in Seoul to arrange his journey and moved from North Korea to China with the aid of a professional North Korean smuggler. When he arrived in China, Korean Chinese intermediaries took him to a church, and a Chinese missionary guided him to the Laotian border.

Chinese seon serve as intermediaries between the organizers of seon involving North Korean migrants working in South Korea, NGOs, and Christian networks, on the one hand, and North Korean clients who wish to move to South Korea, on the other. They receive North Koreans near the Chinese–North Korean border and then travel with them through China and cross the border to Laos, Cambodia, Myanmar, or Thailand. They also hire local drivers as agents when crossing borders defined by rivers.

The intermediaries in China are generally of lower- or lower-middle-class status. Most are Korean Chinese men, although some are Chinese men whose backgrounds as former members of police or military give them an advantage during the physically demanding journeys with the migrants. Their main responsibility is to take North Koreans to China or a third country so that they can eventually reach South Korea or another destination. Intermediaries tend to have networks in both North and South Korea; as they live in the border area, they are familiar with the geography of the region and may also have connections with security guards in both North Korea and China. According to interviewees who worked as organizers, the aid of these intermediaries—in particular the Korean Chinese—is highly sought after by various organizers in South Korea, as it is illegal in China to help North Korean escapees and it is safer for the organizers to delegate traveling with the migrants to Chinese intermediaries who are familiar with the language and the regions. Due to their rarity and the illegality of rescue activities, they and their networks are usually shared among a number of groups and organizers.

One common characteristic of the Chinese intermediaries is that they tend to form decentralized underground networks to evade surveillance. These groups are run by independent individuals operating their parts in the journey rather than a hierarchical organization, and the selection of smugglers for different tasks tends to be flexible. Their roles are generally classified as smugglers, guides, drives, agents, and so on; however, they tend to take on different parts in rotations, as occupying a fixed position increases the chance that they will be exposed to authorities. In this regard, the concept of seon relates to decentralized and flexible networks capable of adapting to the changing scenarios of border-control systems.

THE MOTIVES AND AGENCY OF SEON

North Korean migrants are often represented in South Korean media as being impoverished, traitors to their country, or unwanted guests who increase welfare budgets (Choi 2018; Chung 2008). In the historical, political, and social context of South Korea, the reputation of North Korean migrant smugglers is constructed as that of criminals largely motivated by profit, whereas pastors, missionaries, and nongovernmental agents are represented as risking their own safety to rescue people for humanitarian purposes.

However, my research shows that professional smuggling networks help other North Koreans escape for several reasons: family affection and emotional ties (i.e., they want to help their family members or friends to escape); ideological and political reasons (namely, opposition toward the North Korean regime); a sense of brotherhood toward their people; a desire to participate in a struggle for freedom; the lack of job opportunities for migrants in South Korea.

Just as NGOs are typically motivated by altruism to rescue North Koreans, so are many North Korean smuggling networks. Participants described North Korean–operated migrant smuggling networks as being informally organized to help families and friends rather than composed of a well-structured group of professionals. For example, Man-su, who had been organizing North Korean journeys to South Korea for five years, first became involved with the seon while engineering his own younger brother's escape. After unsuccessfully seeking the help of professional smugglers, Man-su had no option but to bring his brother to South Korea on his own, after which he brought his mother and other relatives. As his experiences accumulated, Man-su became a professional smuggler and an established organizer. Another organizer among my interviewees explained, "I came to South Korea without smugglers and had to face a few life-threatening moments. I decided to become an organizer in smuggling networks myself to provide aid so that others do not have to go through the same."

However, smuggling is also a means of earning money. Indeed some North Korean organizers among the interviewees acknowledged that they had become involved in smuggling due to difficulties finding employment in South Korea. For example, Ki-han, who had worked as an organizer for three years, explained that he had worked several jobs since arriving in South Korea but ended up organizing North Korean journeys in order to increase his income:

> There are few jobs available for North Korean migrants in South Korea because of discrimination and racism against them; for example, working at construction sites or factories, which are unwanted jobs in the society. I worked there for years with a very low salary, too. I felt so angry and desperate. Did I risk my life to come all this way to live miserably? I thought it was unfair, and to do something that I could get compensation for my efforts, I looked for what I could do for earning a lot of money and ended up doing it. I have

worked as an organizer for three years. It does not bring a very high income. But compared to the minimum wage, I normally earn three or four times more a month.

Some North Korean smugglers and organizers work for political purposes. For example, Chul-soo, who previously worked as a professional smuggler in North Korea and had worked as an organizer in South Korea for five years, stated that he began to help North Korean escapees as a means of taking down the regime:

> Do you really think North Korea will collapse? It is hard to grasp any ideas from outside. I do not think it will, even if millions starve to death. That is the scary part of the established system and regime. I believe that the only way it could collapse or be influenced is if a significant number of people leave the country. I have been told that there are about 30,000 North Korean migrants in South Korea. If the number reaches ten times that [i.e., 300,000], North Korea will begin to shake.

Thus, Chul-soo aimed to help more North Koreans leave the country as a means to trigger the gradual collapse of the regime. In a sense, this purpose can be characterized as ideological and political rather than deriving from a more personal altruism.

In contrast, Min-su attempted to escape North Korea with his parents; however, they were caught near the Laotian border and sent to a prison camp. Following his release, he escaped to South Korea by himself with the assistance of smugglers. Min-su then became involved in organizing North Koreans' journeys. Although one of his purposes was to retaliate against Kim Jong-un, his motivation was more personal than that of Chul-soo:

> My parents and brother were sent to prison and died there. Kim Jong-un is the enemy who is responsible for it. Smuggling more people is the only way to pay him back. Do you know what he is most afraid of? It is that his people know the reality of North Korea. We need to inform other North Koreans that Kim Jong-un lied to his people and we were all deceived by his propaganda. We need to realize that Kim Jong-un made his people starve to death, that North Korea is very poor while South Korea is a rich country. If people find

out about it, no one would give loyalty to him anymore. In order for this to happen, more North Koreans need to come out of the country and see the reality with their own eyes. People in the border area who get to hear this earlier than other parts of the country have changed a lot already, and it needs to spread out to the whole country.

Min-su expressed the belief that as more North Korean people escape from the country or interact with people outside its borders, thereby fostering the accumulation of social remittances, North Korea is likely to change, and long-held ideologies such as freedom and peace will emerge. Thus, although rooted in personal retaliation, Min-su's motivation for smuggling extends to a desire to participate in fostering social and political change. Similarly, Jin-su, an organizer in South Korea, had previously worked as a smuggler in North Korea as an act of resistance to the regime and argued that smuggling was a means to bring democracy to North Korea. Jin-su stated that although smuggling is illegal and the related surveillance and penalties have increased and intensified in recent years, he was willing to accept the risk due to a firm belief that it was the only "good" that he could perform. As such, smuggling activities can be perceived as a form of patriotism and a means for North Koreans to help their people.

My research indicates that the Christian networks also seek to perform good works by delivering the gospel of God to North Korea through the routes used for smuggling escapees. Their mission is twofold: to help illegal North Korean migrants living in China and support their journey to South Korea, and to smuggle church-related objects such as the Bible and the cross into North Korea. The religious freedom promised in the Constitution does not apply to North Koreans in reality, and operating a church could lead to the death penalty or imprisonment in political prison camps. For example, Gye-sook, who escaped from North Korea through a Christian network, had been an underground church pastor who was caught secretly leading a church and in possession of the Bible and other religious paraphernalia obtained through human smuggling networks. As she was in her eighth month of pregnancy when convicted, she was sentenced to fifteen years in prison rather than receiving the death penalty. Following her escape to South Korea, Gye-sook was willing to sacrifice herself to preach the gospel, bring the Bible and the cross to North Korean people, and obtain goods for them. Such deep faith was not uncommon among participants involved in Christian networks. Emma, an American missionary engaged in fundraising in South Korea in order to rescue North Koreans from the regime, explained that her activities were a way for her to preach the gospel and perceived her work as a mission from God.

Many NGOs help to facilitate North Koreans' journeys as a means of protecting their human rights. According to this perspective, smuggling North Koreans to South Korea is a moral act because it provides migrants with the opportunity to live as humans. For example, Byung-Jin, an NGO activist who has brought more than one hundred North Koreans to South Korea over the past decade, cited the desire to protect human rights and dignity along with a political purpose for her work: "I wish to enter North Korea and end Kim Jong Un's dictatorship, and help the people out. But it is not easy. The best we can do to make them live a life as humans, with the basic needs fulfilled, is to help them escape from North Korea."

As elucidated earlier, many migrant smugglers are not only motivated by greed but rather are driven by other factors. In particular, a number of smugglers and organizers perceive a moral good in their activities. As such, the perspectives I have presented can be seen to align with Lawrence Cohen's (2011) and Luigi Achilli's (2018) arguments that smuggling is often perceived as constituting an ethical act. Similarly, Gabriella Sanchez's (2015: 77–78) empirical research found that human smugglers along the US-Mexico border made migrants feel safe and facilitated border crossings to improve others' lives, and Wendy Vogt's (2018) research revealed the spiritual and political motivations for smuggling operations.

The groups that smuggle North Koreans share ethical and moral motivations in common. However, there are also some important distinctions among the three groups: NGOs stress humanitarian reasons, whereas Christians put more weight on religious faith and values and North Korean migrants are focused on brotherhood and family ties. Such variations in motivations among the three groups dismantle the stereotype of human smugglers being exclusively profit driven.

A consideration of the concept of agency as referring to an individual's ability to improve circumstances within structural limitations can help foster a more nuanced understanding of the motivations for participating in seon. My findings indicate that many smugglers recognize their activities as a form of ideological agency. Such a framework encompasses different types of agency: economic agency used to accomplish financial accumulation and upward mobility (for the "greedy" ones); political agency in the case of those who perceived smuggling North Koreans as a way of undermining the regime; and religious or faith-based agency exercised among those who saw smuggling as a sort of spiritual path to become better Christians and bring the gospel to others. However, as Ruth Lister (2004: 126) asserted, "agency does not operate in a vacuum; rather it is located in a dialectic relationship with social structures and is embedded in the context of social, economic and political relations." Thus, smugglers and organizers exercise their agency through their struggles and negotiations with structural forces, and different types of agency are not always exercised discretely—one may engage in smuggling for a combination of reasons: as a path to wealth, to become a better person, to disrupt the North Korean regime, as an expression of faith, and so on.

SMUGGLERS AND REFUGEES: RISK, BETRAYAL, AND REPAYMENT

As described earlier, North Korean migrants cross irregularly to China and then travel to South Korea via Mongolia or Laos, Cambodia, or other Southeast Asian countries. The Chinese government recognizes them as not refugees but illegal migrants, and those who are caught are forcibly repatriated. Once returned to North Korea, they are sent either to a labor training camp (*rodong danryundae*) or a reeducation camp (*kyowhaso*) for a period ranging from one to several years. Reports indicate that prisoners experience severe human rights abuses, including forced labor, beatings, torture, starvation, unsanitary conditions, and sexual violation (Davis 2006: 134–135).

Because North Koreans are recognized as illegal migrants in China, helping them is also considered a criminal act, and Chinese intermediates who are caught by the authorities are normally given prison sentences exceeding three years. Thus, not being caught by Chinese police is their top priority. Typically, migrants travel in groups of ten to twelve people when moving through China, and in order to avoid raising suspicions, they closely adhere to the instructions given by guides or intermediaries.

However, there are occasions when migrants are caught regardless of how cautious and resourceful they are. This often happens when spies disguise themselves as migrants and travel with a group to the southern border with Laos or Myanmar. As they approach the border, these spies contact Chinese border guards or police and denounce their fellow travelers. For example, Sook-jung, who had traveled with a group that was infiltrated by one of these spies and was caught and repatriated, recalled her experience: "When I arrived at the border by bus, the police suddenly stopped the bus and spoke to each of us in Chinese so all North Koreans were identified.... The spies are trained by the North Korean Security Department and sent to China on purpose to find the escapees. They join the migrant groups and travel together until they get caught—they are also sent back to North Korea, but to the Security Department rather than prisons." Spies wait until the migrants reach the border because it is more difficult to catch smugglers while they travel inland. Moreover, if caught while traveling inland, the escapees would be only charged for illegally crossing the border between China and North Korea. However, those apprehended near the border of another country are punished for treason, which is a far heavier offense. Thus, guides and intermediaries emphasize the need to be alert about spies. Jung-chul, who had worked as a guide in China for several years, explained that due to the difficulty of identifying a spy in a group of eight to twelve people, he confiscated migrants' mobile phones while traveling in case of espionage.

In other cases, migrants report smugglers and intermediaries to Chinese police after arriving in South Korea. According to the interviewees, they might be reported as a form of retaliation for personal grievances that migrants have accumulated through the journey; however, one of the main reasons for such reports is for the migrant simply to avoid paying the smuggling fee. Since the currency reform in 2009, North Korean money is worthless outside the country, and unless migrants have family members in South Korea who can pay for their journey upfront, payment is usually deferred until their arrival in Seoul. The organizer pays for housing accommodations, transportation, meals, and guidance in advance. Once they arrive in South Korea, migrants receive housing benefits and a settlement bursary of approximately $6,400. Taking this into account as a kind of collateral, smugglers, guides, or intermediaries issue promissory bills, which are usually kept by the organizer in South Korea. As soon as the migrants receive their settlement funds, they pay the fee to the organizer, who subsequently distributes it among all parties involved in the process.

Chul-jin, a North Korean escapee who worked as an organizer in South Korea, described his experience of being reported by migrants: "I need to be paid so that I can send some [money] to the intermediaries in China. I repeatedly asked the migrants for the fee, but they did not want to pay and instead reported the two guides who traveled with them through China to the Chinese authorities." The two guides were arrested by the Chinese authorities and sentenced to three years in prison.

Jin-hyung, who worked as an organizer in South Korea, was blackmailed by a migrant who threatened to report him and his accomplices to Chinese authorities if he did not cancel their debt. Another organizer, Hyuk-min, was also threatened but nevertheless insisted on collecting his payment. Rather than paying the travel fee, the migrants reported him, and his fellow facilitators were eventually reported to the Chinese authorities, which led to the arrest of one of them. Hyuk-min was forced to quit his work as an organizer, as his name and identity had been exposed to the authorities, and he and the Chinese intermediaries felt frustrated and betrayed: "I could not understand why they reported us, as we helped them move to South Korea. So later I asked them about it, and they said that they thought the debt would disappear if I got arrested. I felt bitter and betrayed. We only helped them and yet they reported us. . . . I could not trust the escapees any more so could not continue to work." Other participants recounted similar experiences. For example, Soon-chang, who had worked as a guide in China, stated, "I did it more as a voluntary work so did not get paid, so why did they have to report me to the Chinese authorities?" According to him, as in the case of Hyuk-min, the escapees claimed that they had reported him to avoid paying their debt, and his experience had discouraged him from continuing his work.

Chul-soo, who was forced quit his guide job in China soon after being reported by a migrant, argued that anyone who took on the job solely for financial gain would not be able to do it for long. Rather, one would desperately need some other motivation such as brotherhood (i.e., a sense of fellowship among compatriots) or family ties to continue such work. Chul-jin similarly highlighted the possibility of not being paid and described smuggling as a form of voluntary work. Although they smuggle North Korean people at least partly for economic gain, because payment is not ensured, many organizers—in particular those who are also North Korean migrants—

often work as part-time taxi drivers, construction workers, deliverymen, and other positions to sustain their livelihoods.

The literature on human smuggling tends to highlight the ways that smugglers exploit migrants (Salt 2000; Salt and Stein 1997). Migrants' travel expenses are often prepaid, and smugglers may exploit them for additional funds. However, in the case of North Korean migrants, postpayments are understandably conventional; thus, smugglers risk not being repaid as well as facing the risks of the journey itself. The possibility of being reported and imprisoned is a very dangerous dimension of the process, which some migrants use to their advantage in a reversal of the logic that assumes migrants are victims at the mercy of the smugglers. Many North Korean smugglers are motivated by the moral imperative of saving their own people from what they perceive as an abusive regime, whereas some migrants will not hesitate to denounce their own saviors to the authorities in order to avoid paying what they owe.

Of course, there are also cases that align more closely to what is typically described in the literature. However, notably, even these cases disrupt worn-out categories of exploitative smugglers, vulnerable migrants, and humanitarian saviors. Some of my interviewees were brought to South Korea through Christian networks in what they were told was a voluntary service, only for the pastor or missionary to demand a travel fee upon their arrival in Seoul. As Young-Chul, a pastor who had retrospectively requested travel payments, explained, "We do not talk about the travel expenses to North Korean migrants. If we speak about the money, they are reluctant to leave the country. They believe that churches do not require money, but in reality, we also need money to run our services. So, when they arrive in Seoul and receive the settlement fund from the government, we ask them to pay for the travel fee." Young-Chul added that there was little he could do if a North Korean migrant refused to pay the fee; however, he tried to be repaid in other ways. One migrant who did not pay his travel fee worked unpaid as a cleaner at Young-Chul's church for a year. In another case, Young-Chul helped a migrant who had not made her payment obtain employment and collected her salary while telling her that he was depositing it into her bank account, which was possible due to her ignorance of South Korean society. Such actions vastly diverge from the aim of spreading the gospel or salvation that is widely associated with churches involved in the seon, which is often contrasted with the profit-driven motivation of individuals.

CONCLUSION

This chapter has described how North Korean refugees' journeys are accomplished through decentralized smuggling networks called seon, which are largely composed of North Korean professional smuggling networks, NGOs, and Christian groups. Although these groups may seem to operate separate networks, they share intermediaries in China. In other words, rather than being hierarchically structured, a seon is a decentralized organization based on a complex division of labor. While these three groups share a common interest in rescuing North Koreans from China and North Korea, their actions are motivated by different agendas. Whereas evangelical Christians emphasize spreading the gospel, NGOs assert humanitarian purpose, and North Korean migrants become involved due to a combination of factors ranging from financial gain to political goals, whereby smuggling is perceived as a way of ultimately destroying the regime and bringing democracy to North Korea.

International law condemns smuggling as a heinous crime that violates the human rights of migrants as well as state sovereignty. In the current legal framework, smuggling is illegal and thus smugglers are criminals. However, many North Korean facilitators perceive their work as part of the struggle to free their people from the dictatorship of the Kim family. Thus, the unusual political situation of North Korea reveals a paradox in international law. Ironically, North Koreans must violate international laws prohibiting smuggling in order to claim the very human dignity and freedom that these laws were created to protect.

Although acutely aware of the illegality of their activities, North Korean smugglers believe that smuggling is a worthy cause that is morally correct because it saves people. In this sense, the political motivation to oppose the North Korean regime can be seen to outweigh that of financial gain in importance. This perspective helps us to understand their willingness to continue providing what they regard as a "voluntary service" despite receiving their payment postmigration and taking the risk of being reported. That smuggling may be regarded as a good and altruistic act refutes the conventional dynamics of human smuggling in dominant migration discourses. The participants' perspectives and experiences challenge the conventional image of smugglers as greedy, immoral, ruthless, and profit-driven individuals and depictions of smuggling networks as transnational criminal organizations engaged in systematic deception and exploitation that violate migrants' human rights and dignity for financial gain.

NOTES

1. All necessary procedures, including anonymization and omission of sensitive information, have been followed to protect my informants' privacy.
2. The journey of North Korean migrants is often compared to that of enslaved African Americans along the Underground Railroad on their passage to freedom (see Demick 2010; Kirkpatrick 2014). However, whereas African American escapees often widely shared details concerning their routes, North Korean migrants often conceal such information so that they can bring their families to join them.

REFERENCES

Achilli, L. 2018. "The 'Good' Smuggler: The Ethics and Morals of Human Smuggling among Syrians." *ANNALS of the American Academy of Political and Social Science* 676:77–95.

Charny, J. R. 2005. *Acts of Betrayal: The Challenge of Protecting North Koreans in China*. Washington, DC: Refugees International.

Choi, G. 2018. "North Korean Refugees in South Korea: Change and Challenge in Settlement Support Policy." *Korean Journal of International Studies* 16 (1): 77–98.

Chung, B. H. 2008. "Between Defector and Migrant: Identities and Strategies of North Koreans in South Korea." *Korean Studies* 32:1–27.

Cohen, L. 2011. "Ethical Publicity: On Transplant Victims, Wounded Communities, and the Moral Demands of Dreaming." In *Ethical Life in South Asia*, edited by A. Pandian and A. Daud, 253–274. Bloomington: Indiana University Press.

Davis, K., 2006. "Brides, Bruises and the Border: The trafficking of North Korean Women into China." *SAIS Review* 26(1): 131–141.

Demick, B. 2010. *Nothing to Envy: Ordinary Lives in North Korea*. London: Granta.

Do, K., S. Kim, D. Han, K. Lee, and M. Hong. 2017. *White Paper on Human Rights in North Korea 2017*. Seoul: Korean Institute for National Unification.

Han, J. H. J. 2013. "Beyond Safe Haven: A Critique of Christian Custody of North Korean Migrants in China." *Critical Asian Studies* 45 (4): 533–560.

Human Rights Watch. 2002. *The Invisible Exodus: North Koreans in the People's Republic of China*. New York: Human Rights Watch.

———. 2013. "The World Report 2013: North Korea." http://www.hrw.org/world-report/2013/country-chapters/north-korea.

International Crisis Group. 2006. *Perilous Journeys: The Plight of North Koreans in China and Beyond*. Asia Report No. 122. https://www.crisisgroup.org/asia/north-east-asia/korean-peninsula/perilous-journeys-plight-north-koreans-china-and-beyond.

Kim, J. 2011. "Trafficked: Domestic Violence, Exploitation in Marriage, and the Foreign-Bride Industry." *Virginia Journal of International Law* 51 (2): 443–497.

Kirkpatrick, M. 2014. *Escape from North Korea: The Untold Story of Asia's Underground Railroad*. New York: Encounter Books.

Kook, K. H. 2019. "Refugee Smuggling from North Korea to China." In *Critical Insights on Irregular Migration Facilitation: Global Perspectives*, edited by G. Sanchez and A. Luigi, 13–15. Florence: European University Institute.

Lankov, A. 2004. "North Korean Refugees in Northeast China." *Asian Survey* 44 (6): 856–873.

Lister, R. 2004. *Poverty*. Cambridge, UK: Blackwell/Polity.

Muico, N. K. 2005. *An Absence of Choice: The Sexual Exploitation of North Korean Women in China*. London: Anti-Slavery International. https://www.antislavery.org/wp-content/uploads/2017/01/full_korea_report_2005.pdf.

Salt, J. 2000. "Trafficking and Human Smuggling: A European Perspective." *International Migration* 38:31–56.

Salt, J., and J. Stein. 1997. "Migration as a Business: The Case of Trafficking." *International Migration* 35 (4): 467–494.

Sanchez, G. E. 2015. *Human Smuggling and Border Crossings*. Abingdon, UK: Routledge.

Song, J. Y. 2013. "'Smuggled Refugees': The Social Construction of North Korean Migration." *International Migration* 51 (4): 158–173.

South Korean Ministry of Unification. 2022. "Status of North Korean Migrants Entering South Korea with Statistics (in Korean)." https://www.unikorea.go.kr/unikorea/business/NKDefectorsPolicy/status/lately/

Vogt, W. 2018. *Lives in Transit: Violence and Intimacy on the Migrant Journey*. Oakland: University of California Press.

Williamson, L. 2011. "Shadowy World of Korea's People Smugglers." BBC, July 7, 2011. http://www.bbc.com/news/world-asia-pacific-14044794.

Zhang, S. X., G. E. Sanchez, and L Achilli. 2018. "Crimes of Solidarity in Mobility: Alternative Views on Migrant Smuggling." *Annals of the American Academy of Political and Social Science* 676:6–15.

CHAPTER 12

People Smuggling in Southeast Asia

ROHINGYA AND CHIN STORIES OF AGENCY, FREEDOM, AND POWER IN CROSS-BORDER MOVEMENT

Gerhard Hoffstaedter

THIS BOOK AND ITS PREVIOUS EDITIONS (Kyle and Koslowski 2001, 2011) have sought to disentangle the complexities inherent in making sense of human smuggling, trafficking, and irregular migration globally. There was great optimism in the late 1980s about globalization and regional political formations, such as the European Union, opening borders and making way for freer movement and exchange, but the hope was quickly shattered by the 1990s, which saw a reconstruction of borders as sites of national sovereignty (Wonders 2007). Thus, international migration continues to be managed and regularized through national bordering regimes that see regular migration as the orderly and legal movement across their borders. These regimes rely on techniques that police, surveil, and administratively capture individuals in order to subject them to state control (Hoffstaedter 2019). Irregular migration, on the other hand, is characterized by the mass movement of people across borders without documentation in pursuit of protection, employment, and other life opportunities. People smuggling—also referred to as human or migrant smuggling—has emerged as one of the key facilitators of irregular migration. As such, it has attracted increasing attention from both governments and international organizations as they seek to respond to the political, economic, and social costs of the arrival of significant numbers of unauthorized migrants. Human trafficking is another key type of irregular migration, although it often merges with people smuggling (Gallagher and

McAuliffe 2016). There are clear legal and conceptual differences between the two. The reality, however, is that the lines between people smuggling and human trafficking are often blurred, and consensual arrangements can become exploitative (see also Stanslas 2010; Wahab 2018). Within this fraught policy and legal environment, it is vital to "recognize the extreme diversity of smuggling operations and activities both among and within sending regions and how they are integrated into wider regional social structures" (Kyle and Dale 2001: 29). In this volume we shine a light on this diversity and how the key concepts of creativity, agency, and freedom are articulated in these structures. This chapter aims to provide more ethnographic data to argue that in Southeast Asia people smuggling is a necessary response to regional inequalities, conflict, displacement, and hitherto freer movement.

This chapter is informed by long-term ethnographic fieldwork in Malaysia and Southeast Asia, working primarily with refugees to document their everyday lives. I have tried to document refugee movement not just in terms of displacement and eventual emplacement somewhere else but also in terms of the enveloping social, political, and personal drivers for movement, immobility, and the role that religion, culture, and ethnic or kin networks play in facilitating such movement or prohibiting it. Over the last decade I have spent over twenty months in the field, with most of the data for this chapter based on a prolonged one-year fieldwork stay in peninsular Malaysia in 2015–2016. I conducted fieldtrips to Penang and other regional centers but was primarily based in Kuala Lumpur and conducted extensive fieldwork across the Klang valley, stretching from Kuala Lumpur to the port of Klang. Most refugees in West Malaysia live in this urban conglomeration to be near established refugee communities, find work in the large informal sector, and apply for registration with the United Nations High Commissioner for Refugees (UNHCR) office, situated in the middle of Kuala Lumpur. The largest refugee groups are Rohingya and Chin, both from Myanmar, where they have fled persecution, violence, and poverty.

I conducted fieldwork with the help of several research assistants, most drawn from the refugee communities themselves. Together with my partner, an oral historian, we trained and conducted in-depth semistructured interviews with over eighty research participants and attended many public, community, and personal events for participant observation. In discussions about their journeys to Malaysia, many refugees talked about the people who had facilitated their journeys in muted tones, not wanting to relive traumatic events or still frightened about people they owed money to. Others were forthright about their role in hiring people to facilitate cross-border movement. This chapter attempts to draw out a range of narratives about the availability of smugglers, the agency people have in contracting and influencing the journey and cost, and the definitional issues between smuggling and trafficking.

PEOPLE SMUGGLING IN SOUTHEAST ASIA

Irregular migration is widespread in Southeast Asia, and most movement is motivated by the search for employment (Coyne and Nyst 2017). There are also strong historical roots to such movement across the region, as people were trafficked for sex work and labor as well as through the slave trade until the nineteenth century, as well as people engaging in unforced irregular migration for work opportunities (Tagliacozzo 2002). Irregular labor migration relies heavily on the use of smugglers, which results in much overlap between regular and irregular migration, migrant smuggling, and human trafficking in the region (UNODC 2012: 8). There are also significant movements of displaced peoples, who traverse national borders in search of protection and a better future. They also avail themselves of people smugglers to facilitate cross-border movement.

Major flows of people occur from countries in the Mekong region, especially Myanmar, to Thailand and Malaysia, two major global people smuggling hubs and regional transit points as well as two key destination countries for smuggled migrants and refugees in Asia (Coyne and Nyst 2017; Missbach and Hoffstaedter 2020; UNODC 2018: 118). Both countries have strong economies compared with their neighbors and offer relative ease of access due to their vast coastal borderlands, which remain poorly policed (Tagliacozzo 2002: 210–211). In addition, Thailand's extensive land borders facilitate undetected entry, while Malaysia issues visas on arrival for many visitors from the Middle East and the Association of Southeast Asian Nations (Coyne and Nyst 2017). The specific methods of smuggling depend on a range of variables relating to the specific route: these include geography, border control, transport, knowledge, and the skill of the smugglers themselves, as well as the available funds of the smuggled (UNODC 2018: 117).

As a result, there has been a regional focus on curtailing people smuggling activities by criminalizing cross-border movement and thereby tying people smuggling to trafficking and international crime. This has made it harder for refugees fleeing persecution to cross borders in search of protection. Refugee protection remains extremely weak in Southeast Asia, with only East Timor, the Philippines, and Cambodia signed up to the UN refugee convention. Refugees find it increasingly difficult to seek protection in neighboring countries of conflict areas such as Myanmar. Thus, most refugees travel vast distances to more prosperous countries, such as Malaysia, that do not recognize refugees legally but can offer them a modicum of protection through the UNHCR and the opportunity to earn money in the vast informal economy. Regionally, the Bali Process on People Smuggling, Trafficking in Persons and Related Transnational Crime approaches refugees solely as a security issue. Indeed, regional bordering practices and state policies produce the very structural conditions that create a need for people smuggling. Migrants and refugees must use their agency or capacity, resources, and capital (social, cultural, and financial) to overcome these structures that limit their choices for cross-border movement. Some politicians are aware of this, and one former Malaysian opposition member of parliament recounted in an interview,

> The government must realize when you don't recognize them [refugees], that feeds trafficking [and smuggling]. They have to find ways to come into the country because they're not recognized.... You see, the whole issue of trafficking is, the people who are being trafficked are voluntary in this position because they're escaping something, which is even worse. They are prepared to take the risk of being trafficked, of being bullied by the traffickers because staying back in the original situation, say Rohingya for example, is even more dangerous. So, for them, the traffickers..., the illegal smugglers, are actually serving a purpose. But they are there because the legal routes to arrive in Malaysia are closed. The borders are too strong, impermeable and we don't let them in. They must smuggle them in because of us. It's our policy that creates trafficking. If we have a clear policy, people running away can come and they assess, they don't have to go to Thailand to sneak their way in. (Fieldwork interview, 2017)

While the politician in the interview merged smuggling and trafficking, it is striking that he noted the direct relationship between Malaysia's inaction in recognizing refugees and its actions along the border as producing the necessary environment for people smuggling to flourish. In early 2015, for example, a mass grave of people trafficked across the Thai-Malaysian border was discovered. The then deputy home minister for Malaysia told a press conference near the site of the mass grave that the Malaysian government is considering building a wall along the entire border with Thailand (Bernama 2015). Grandiose projects such as this had been considered before but were deemed too costly and unfeasible due to the rugged mountainous terrain. However, the government's relentless pursuit of formally closing the borders, coupled with a lack of recognition of refugees, internally drives the need for agents or people smugglers to provide passage across borders.

This leaves refugees at the mercy of often unscrupulous smugglers and traffickers, the definitional difference of which most of our interlocutors did not subscribe to. Many refugees are aware of the illegality of crossing borders without documentation and therefore see their actions as illegal, albeit necessary. The people facilitating this journey were often described either as friends, "good people," and helpers in the case of Chin or as agents, traffickers, and criminals by Rohingya. These descriptions are based on the differences in the smuggling experiences of these groups, as will be described in detail later. *Smuggling* and *smugglers* were rarely used in the vernaculars, as they were seen as foreign and legalistic terms that did not adequately describe or capture people's experiences and relationships to the people facilitating their journey The following, sadly common, story of Rohingya fleeing Rakhine State highlights the transitional nature of such legalistic terminology and its concomitant meaning.

A Rohingya couple we interviewed in 2016 described their experience of arranging what they believed to be a safe journey with a smuggler to take them from Rakhine State in the east of Myanmar to Thailand and then on to Malaysia, where the husband already had a network of friends and family. They had paid a people smuggler a considerable amount of money, some of it borrowed from family, friends, and village neighbors. They arrived in Malaysia via the "back road," the clandestine routes that cut through jungles across international borders and allow undetected travel from one country to another. They had heard they would be safe from persecution in Malaysia, which they believe to be an Islamic country. Their journey toward freedom was arduous and, as is the case for many people who begin journeys as part of a smuggling operation, it turned into one of human trafficking. Once they reached Thailand they were separated, shackled, and imprisoned in rudimentary bamboo jails in a human trafficking camp in the jungle. Aisyah's husband was forced to call one of his uncles to secure more money for her and their child's freedom. Her husband remained in the human trafficking camp, badly beaten, and scared for his life as he could not organize enough extra money from his relatives in Malaysia to secure all of their releases. It took more negotiations and ransom monies to achieve his eventual release. Many Rohingya face this extortionate smuggling-trafficking business model, because they often do not know the smugglers or have enough money to pay up front for the journey. Without adequate resources to facilitate their irregular migration or the agency to decide on a suitable time, the route or mode of transportation is severely curtailed. The fewer resources refugees have at their disposal, the more dependent they become on any possible path toward safety and freedom.

People smugglers and traffickers facilitate this irregular movement across international borders through the provision of transport, accommodations, and sometimes falsified travel documents. These services are part of a larger migration industry, partially legal, partially not, that has developed to provide opportunities for movement in increasingly complex migration regimes (Betts 2012). The impetus is commercial in nature; however, not all smugglers are "migration merchants" with an economic motive (Kyle 2000). I have documented a number of cases of hospitality, mutual aid, and support networks often based on coreligiosity or ethnic and kin networks that could be mobilized for help to cross borders among Chin refugees especially.[1] People smuggling can take many forms, ranging from large-scale international smuggling networks, to small groups of organized smugglers, to those best described as amateur smugglers. In Southeast Asia, there is no single business model, nor are there any monopolies or structured hierarchical organizations (Barker 2013; UNODC 2018). Instead, people smuggling networks in this region consist of small, diffuse networks characterized by flexibility and resilience that allow adaptation to the ever-changing context (Barker 2013; Coyne and Nyst 2017).

The profile of smugglers varies, and although in Southeast Asia most are men, some women have been involved, and some may have been smuggled themselves. For those engaging smugglers to cross national borders, trust and reputation are central. Thus, some smugglers work hard to establish their credibility. Other times reputation is secondary to the availability of smugglers. Following eruptions of violence in Rakhine State, Myanmar, in 2012, many Rohingya and other Muslims fled the area onto smuggler boats without knowing either the smuggler's reputation or the price of the journey. This sort of spontaneity was evidenced by a Rohingya refugee interlocutor, who had initially fled to Cox's Bazar, where a friend told him that he was going to Malaysia the following day: "My friend told me: 'you can go also, you can find a good job, you can make a good future.' And then I come to Malaysia by boat." Without any knowledge about the price, journey, or, in some cases, destination, desperate people are willing to risk their lives in the pursuit of freedom and for the opportunity at a better life. For this twenty-five-year-old Rohingya man, the journey ended in Penang after his uncle had to pay an inflated ransom for his release. Nonetheless, he was happy to have come to Malaysia, as it did afford him the opportunity his friend had promised: a job and a regular income to secure his future.

SMUGGLING OF ROHINGYA AND CHIN TO MALAYSIA

People smuggling is considered inevitable due to the high demand of many ethnic and religious minorities fleeing violence and persecution in Myanmar. These push factors drive people to creatively imagine ways to flee to safety and, hopefully, prosperity. They all seek freedom from fear, want, and indignities—in short, to live a life worth living. Refugees experience different levels of agency in displacement and flight, based on the financial, social, and cultural resources or capital they have. They all engage smuggling and even forms of trafficking as a necessary step in realizing their route to freedom and a better life. I will demonstrate how their agency, freedom, exploitation, and dependence interconnect and complex contradictions abound in how these people ultimately reach their goal of flight from persecution and poverty to a new life in Malaysia.

Recent figures from the UNHCR show that Malaysia hosts the second-highest number of refugees and asylum seekers from Myanmar globally:

178,140, although the actual figure is likely to be much higher (UNHCR, n.d.). This section details two stories from the largest refugee groups in Malaysia: Rohingya and Chin. The most numerous refugees in Malaysia are the Rohingya, a minority Muslim group from Rakhine State, who have sought asylum in Malaysia to escape widespread persecution and a "slow-burning genocide" (Khairi and Wahab 2018: 79; Zarni and Cowley 2014). Although reliable data are unavailable, estimates suggest that many tens of thousands of Rohingya refugees have used smuggling networks to travel to Malaysia. The following story is not the most common, but one that exemplifies the many complex turns journeys to safety can take, especially when they begin straightforward and easy.

AHMAD'S STORY: COMPLEXITY AND CREATIVITY FOR FREEDOM

Ahmad had fled Myanmar to Bangladesh in the 1990s with his parents, as his father was politically active fighting for Rohingya rights. In Bangladesh, they were not confined to the refugee camps and Ahmad was able to gain some education by claiming he was Bangladeshi. After school he worked in a variety of jobs, ending up in a garment factory. The work was hard, and he recounted that his life was getting harder due to rising living costs when friends told him about getting a boat to Malaysia, where life was easier. He was interested but had heard of the danger posed by the often unseaworthy boats used to ferry Rohingya and Bangladeshis across the Andaman Sea. Many boats have gone missing and their passengers are presumed drowned. Ahmad sought out a safer journey by air. This already marks out his creative use of the resources at his disposal: money and time. He was not in need of immediate safety; he could wait and find a better solution that he felt comfortable with. So instead of joining his friends on the boat, he tried to get a Bangladeshi passport illegally, but his first attempt failed to get past the police verification report. Thereafter, he met a friend who told him about a *dalal* (broker or agent) who could arrange everything to transport him to Malaysia safely via airplane. Ahmad was taken by this proposition of safe and direct passage and agreed on a price with the agent. He said,

> They gave me a ticket, everything they gave me. "You have to go there," they would say, "when you go to Thailand, there is a procedure,"

some procedure they say. So, our first airplane was Singapore Airlines. They said this plane will land in Singapore. Then, from Singapore you have to take another terminal, then you will go to Thailand. So, we just follow the instruction. Dhaka to Singapore first. And from there we need to change terminal; we change terminal, it was all in the tickets as well.

So, anyways after Singapore, next to it was to Chiang Mai, Thailand. I don't have any idea whatsoever, then I got to Chiang Mai. There was a person, a trafficker, they had a number, they gave me a sim card. With that sim card he used to communicate with me. They asked "Ahmad, did you arrive here? Ok. Then one person will come to pick up." Two ladies came with a car and they . . . took me into a car. Then they took me to a hotel to live there. (Fieldwork interview, 2017)

Ahmad's supposedly direct journey to Malaysia had already taken him halfway across Southeast Asia, but not much closer to Malaysia, as he entered northern Thailand. This was the end of his air travel and the beginning of his overland trek south toward Malaysia.

Over many more days that turned into weeks, his odyssey led him to the Thai-Malaysian border. There, smugglers and traffickers gather people in transit camps before attempting the last leg across the border. At this camp Ahmad met many other refugees and migrants from Myanmar and Bangladesh, and his experience growing up in Bangladesh meant he was often mistaken for a Bangladeshi migrant. People discussed their journeys that had brought them together in the middle of a jungle, so close to their destination, yet so far away from the future lives they envisaged. Ahmad recounted the poor condition of the camp, which was full of cockroaches and other insects feasting on the detritus of wave after wave of smuggled people. The insects also began feasting on Ahmad: "We found insects on our body. Then I suddenly realized one thing. It's better to just feel comfortable with the situation. It's better just to calm down . . . with my body. That's how it was. They were biting me. After one hour or two hours, it became normal" (fieldwork interview, 2017). More encounters with new species he had never seen or felt before lay ahead once his group started the trek through the dense jungle across the border: leeches. They soon occupied his body and sucked the blood from him, and all the while he just kept going, knowing that he had no alternatives.

It had grown dark and he used his mobile phone's flashlight to light the way so he would not stumble in the thicket. The smugglers started to shout at him to turn off the flashlight, presumably as any light source could give away their position.

> In the middle of walking, one person came and he wanted to take away my phone from my hand. Then I wanted to fight with him because it's the only cell phone that I had. If I lost it, I might lose myself. If something happened, this is my only chance that I have, to do something. And there are many contacts in my handphone. Almost 3–5 minutes we fight each other. Then he hit me and suddenly I was the loser. Then I give him my phone and he take away the phone from there. Then, we start walking again for another two hours. (Fieldwork interview, 2017)

Having lost the fight and the phone, he had no choice but to carry on walking. Once they reached the Malaysian border, the smugglers warned him, "Now you have to be careful. Everybody is responsible for [them]self. It's very risky right now. Everything can happen here." Ahmad was afraid. At twenty-three years of age, he was the youngest in the group and had no one to look out for him; he felt alone. His journey, so far, had been arduous, complex, and dangerous. Many times, he was reliant on his creativity, resilience, and hope for what lay beyond the journey to carry him through. Nonetheless, arriving in Malaysia was not the end of the journey, as the traffickers still needed to get paid, and the last part of the journey was among the most harrowing he described. He explained how two young women who were traveling in his group were repeatedly raped by multiple traffickers and how he, as the youngest member, was powerless. He was disturbed by the rape, but also by the inaction of the others in the group, who, he remarked, were older and "knew about this thing," but "they were all thinking about themselves" (fieldwork interview, 2017).

It had taken Ahmad seven to eight days just to cross the border to Malaysia; the whole trip had taken several weeks, but he could not remember how long exactly, as days became weeks and had rolled into each other along the way. The last leg through Malaysia to its capital, Kuala Lumpur, was again marked by violence. They were transported by van and had to keep a low profile. Every now and then curiosity got the better of Ahmad and he would stick his head out to catch a glimpse of the surroundings, as they passed through towns or drove along the highway. The traffickers did not want anyone to see their human cargo, so they hit Ahmad and anyone else who stuck their head up. Everyone had to lie flat in the back. Ahmad described how they stopped intermittently and how the two young women in their group were assaulted and raped again by the traffickers, once in front of the rest of the group. When they finally arrived in Kuala Lumpur, the traffickers took everyone to an apartment to "freshen up" and then call their family and friends for the ransom demands. In Ahmad's case it was very costly and he had to find US$4,500 from family and friends to buy his freedom in Malaysia.

In interviews with dozens of Rohingya interlocutors, I found that they often recounted stories about their journeys to Malaysia from Bangladesh or Myanmar that began as a conscious decision to escape persecution, violence, and lack of hope. They sought freedom from fear and want, and Malaysia often featured as a (Muslim) land of hope that would shelter them (Hoffstaedter 2017). For many the easiest way is to follow their friends, family, and acquaintances onto boats, where this hope for a safe passage quickly transforms into a complex story of human trafficking as the price for passage increases and a price becomes a ransom. In Ahmad's case, he demonstrated creativity to seek out a safer way by researching, collecting information about boats and alternative means of travel to make his way to Malaysia. As for his friends on the boat, his agency, often limited to begin with, was quickly diminished. Nonetheless, people embarking on these journeys cannot easily turn back. They often carry with them the hope of entire families and communities who often do not have the means to travel themselves but contribute money to buy someone's safety and life. Many Rohingya incur great debts to unscrupulous money lenders with hugely inflated interest that they must pay back for years as a result. Yet this very poor outcome is still considered an improvement to the situation in internally displaced camps in Rakhine State or refugee camps in Bangladesh. Therefore, Rohingya continue to pursue the dangerous route to Malaysia with the help of people smugglers and traffickers, always in the hope that they will make it.

RUTH AND VAN: FAMILY AND FRIENDS FOR FREEDOM

Remittances sent to Myanmar also play a crucial part in the story of many Chin coming to Malaysia. The Chin are an ethnic minority from the mountainous northwest of Myanmar. They were missionized by American preachers in the late nineteenth century, who converted formerly animist tribes to a range of Christian faiths, predominantly of an evangelical nature. Since then Christianity has formed the basis of a modern, unified Chin identity (Sakhong 2003). Chin have been fleeing religious persecution and the "Burmanisation" of religious minorities in Myanmar for decades (Mang 2011). Many fled to India initially but were attracted to Malaysia by stories from the Chin diaspora there about the work opportunities and access to the UNHCR resettlement scheme to third countries like the United States and Australia that now house a significant Chin diaspora. Thus, many Chin were able to make a more informed decision about where to go to seek freedom from fear and from want. Many knew from fellow Chin refugees in India about the hardship there and the relative ease of finding work and resettlement places in Malaysia (Bartolomei 2015).

In Chin State in Myanmar, some agents set up shop to provide passage to Malaysia for largely economic reasons. However, many refugees in the past fled at a moment's notice and did not have access to agents to help them guide their journey. A couple I interviewed in 2013 recounted a common narrative among Chin refugees who had fled some form of violence or persecution initially and found themselves relying on a series of friends, family, and agents to guide them across the borders to Thailand and, eventually, Malaysia. Van and Ruth were from a small hamlet not far from Hakha, the Chin State capital. In the early 2000s fighting between the Chin National Army and the Myanmar Army caught many ordinary farmers and villagers in the crossfire. Many Chin men were conscripted into portering duties (the carrying of heavy materials across mountainous terrain) for the Myanmar Army, which maintained an extensive presence in the Chin hills.[2] Their bases often occupy mountain ridges, and they went on extensive patrols for which they commandeered locals to carry their gear and supplies. When some men Van and Ruth knew were conscripted in a nearby village, they decided to leave Chin State. They packed only essentials and headed from their village to Mandalay and then Yangon. There, a contact from a childhood friend set them up with an agent. The agent was eager to get them to leave immediately because he had a group waiting, but they disliked the agent enough to pass on the opportunity and await another. After two weeks they met a new agent who had been recommended by family members who had made the trip to Malaysia successfully. They had praised his fair price and the safety provided along the journey. Among Chin, family and village networks are essential, and connections through these networks allow them to identify people within their extended and neighboring kin group (Hoffstaedter 2014: 876). This agent was related to a member of Van's extended kin network and therefore trustworthy to them.

They made their way through southeastern Myanmar by small van until they reached the Myanmar-Thai border. They could not remember which border town they crossed at, only that they had to disembark before reaching the town and then walk through the hilly forest and jungle. Ruth mentioned a long walk through dense jungle that was arduous. Their group consisted of about twenty people guided by two smugglers, one leading the group, the other following behind. They walked up and down several hills before they were picked up on the Thai side by another van for the journey to the Thai-Malaysian border. They already knew about the trek through the hilly jungles of the Thai-Malaysian border crossing from one of Van's uncles, who had been helped by a fellow villager across the border. Therefore, they were prepared for the second large trek and supplied with enough water to make the crossing safely. Once they arrived in Malaysia, they were transported by car to Kuala Lumpur, where they quickly connected to the large Chin community network made up of members of their village or language group and Chin church-based organizations that help new arrivals settle in Malaysia. They found a small room to rent in a shared apartment and both were soon employed in jobs they received via the Chin refugee community organization they had joined. But their journey to freedom was not over yet, as they now face considerable challenges in Malaysia and hope for fast resettlement to the United States or Australia (Hoffstaedter 2014).

While the first parts of their journey to a new life were dependent on smugglers, family, and friends, the last part is up to the UNHCR and its resettlement program. However, here too, community creativity is paramount and has been most beneficial to the most organized refugee communities, such as the Chin. The Chin diasporas in the United States and Australia have been very effective in lobbying politicians to support further Chin resettlement. The United States ran a special program favoring Chin for resettlement in US cities with existing Chin communities. In Australia, Chin have also benefited from an upsurge in resettlement from Malaysia in the past ten years (Hoffstaedter and Lamb 2019). For many Chin, a happy confluence of factors has provided them with a relatively safe pathway to freedom and prosperity through people smugglers. Most have agency in choosing a suitable smuggler who will provide safe passage. Due to creative thinking and strategic forethought from community leaders in Malaysia and key resettlement countries, many Chin have access to strong support networks and a clear pathway toward freedom, legal status (citizenship in a resettlement country), and prosperity.

CONCLUSION

Each of the stories in this chapter is about achieving freedom—freedom from fear, freedom from want, and freedom from indignities. All share the crucial push factor of having experienced forms of persecution, crimes committed against people based on their religion or ethnicity, and even genocide. They also share pull factors to Malaysia that focus on some appreciation of limited protection and the greater opportunity to provide for themselves and their families through paid work in Malaysia's informal sector. In order to achieve this, these refugees are willing to risk their lives; indeed, many have paid with their lives for the mere opportunity to flee. The inability to traverse borders safely and legally means they have to engage smugglers to facilitate their journey. Refugees use their agency and their connections through kin and friendship networks to find the best way to reach Malaysia. People smugglers provide this crucial service, and sometimes they can be a last resort for protection facilitation in conflict areas, such as Myanmar. Javier Hidalgo (2016) argues that in such cases people smuggling can be morally justified because it directly assists people fleeing persecution or threats to their rights. However, people smugglers also act as facilitators for a perceived improvement in life chances and opportunities—that is, refugees engage them for economic reasons. For some, this has largely worked out well, as is the case for thousands of Chin refugees who smuggled themselves or were smuggled to Malaysia and were ultimately resettled to third countries like the United States and Australia. They are often held up as the lucky ones who have made it. There are countless others at the other end of the spectrum, many of them Rohingya, who have perished at sea or at the hands of human traffickers in Thailand and Malaysia. Thus, in the search for freedom, agency in determining one's mobility is often a matter of resources, connections, and money. Those with more resources are able to be more creative in how and how often they move across borders and, of course, which borders to cross. This is also reflected in the agency people have and are able to deploy. The more resources one has access to, the more power over individual journeys they have.

This is especially crucial to the smuggling and trafficking nexus in irregular cross-border movement. The area beyond the legal definitional divide remains a particularly gray area due to the nature of the push factors that continue to drive desperate people to flee conflict, discrimination, and poverty. Using one's creativity to escape and find refuge in Malaysia in this complex mixed migration environment comes in many guises: for some it is in the agency of being able to choose their agent or smuggler and find the most trusted and trustworthy; for others it is in surviving the extremely difficult and life-threatening migration experiences to muddle through and find a way to safety at all. Ahmad had only limited agency in his decision-making to leave Myanmar and how his cross-border journey unfolded. Ruth and Van had more agency in the way they made decisions about whom to engage to smuggle them across the border and choosing to wait for a better and more trustworthy agent, for example. Malaysia has joined the chorus of regional states, led by Australia, calling to improve border protection and find extreme and more creative ways to stop people smuggling to their shores (Missbach and Palmer, this volume, chap. 16). In the case of Malaysia, the chorus remains largely one of rhetoric, allowing people smuggling to continue along alternative routes but with the same outcomes. As long as persecution, human rights abuses, and structural violence persist in places like Myanmar, people will be forced to flee in search of freedom, a better life, and a better future for their children—whether or not that path is complicated, expensive, or even dangerous.

ACKNOWLEDGMENTS

I was the recipient of an Australian Research Council Discovery Early Career Award (DE140100052) to document the lives of refugees in Malaysia. I thank the many refugees who have participated in this research project, gave their time, and shared their stories with us. I thank Nicole Lamb for her unwavering support and Sue Scull and Aslam Abd Jalil for their research assistance.

NOTES

1. This corresponds with much recent ethnographic data from around the world that challenges the view of smugglers as purely profit-driven criminals and presents evidence of smugglers as protectors and caretakers; see Vogt (2018). Sometimes family members seek to support kin; see Kook (2018). On working based on solidarity and reciprocity, see Achilli (2018).
2. A 2011 report used a cluster survey technique to determine that 92 percent of households in Chin State had been subjected to forced labor, including portering, road building, and growing cash crops for the Myanmar military; see Physicians for Human Rights (2011).

REFERENCES

Achilli, Luigi. 2018. "The 'Good' Smuggler: The Ethics and Morals of Human Smuggling among Syrians." *ANNALS of the American Academy of Political and Social Science* 676 (1): 77–96.

Barker, Cat. 2013. "The People Smugglers' Business Model." Research Paper No. 2, 2012–13, Department of Parliamentary Services, Parliament of Australia, Canberra.

Bartolomei, Linda. 2015. "Surviving the City: Refugees from Burma in New Delhi." In *Urban Refugees: Challenges in Protection, Service and Policy*, edited by Gerhard Hoffstaedter and Koichi Koizumi, 139–163. New York: Routledge.

Bernama. 2015. "Wan Junaidi: Government Plans to Wall Parts of Malaysia-Thailand Border." *Star* (Malaysia), March 1, 2015.

Betts, Alexander. 2012. "The Migration Industry in Global Migration Governance." In *The Migration Industry and the Commercialization of International Migration*, edited by Ninna Nyberg Sorensen and Thomas Gammeltoft-Hansen, 45–63. London: Taylor and Francis.

Coyne, John, and Madeleine Nyst. 2017. "People Smuggling in Southeast Asia." In *People Smugglers Globally, 2017*, edited by John Coyne and Madeleine Nyst, 12–17. Barton, Australian Capital Territory: Australian Strategic Policy Institute.

Gallagher, Anne, and Marie L. McAuliffe. 2016. "South-East Asia and Australia." In *Migrant Smuggling Data and Research: A Global Review of the Emerging Evidence Base*, edited by Marie L. McAuliffe and Frank Laczko, 211–241. Geneva: International Organization for Migration.

Hidalgo, Javier. 2016. "The Ethics of People Smuggling." *Journal of Global Ethics* 12 (3): 311–326.

Hoffstaedter, Gerhard. 2014. "Place-Making: Chin Refugees, Citizenship and the State in Malaysia." *Citizenship Studies* 18 (8): 871–884.

———. 2017. "Refugees, Islam and the State: The Role of Religion in Providing Sanctuary in Malaysia." *Journal of Immigrant and Refugee Studies* 15 (3): 287–304.

———. 2019. "Arrested Refugee Mobilities: Optics as Bordering Techniques in Malaysia." *Sojourn: Journal of Social Issues in Southeast Asia* 34 (3): 521–546.

Hoffstaedter, Gerhard, and Nicole Lamb. 2019. "'It's God's Plan to Be Here': Displacement, Transit and Resettlement of Chin and Karenni Refugees to Australia." *Australian Journal of Politics and History* 65 (4): 584–599.

Khairi, Aizat, and Andika Abdul Wahab. 2018. "The Smuggling Activity and Irregular Migration to Malaysia: A Case Study of the Muslim Rohingya from Myanmar." *Global Journal Al-Thaqafah* 8 (1): 73–81.

Kook, Kyunghee. 2018. "'I Want to Be Trafficked So I Can Migrate!': Cross-Border Movement of North Koreans into China through Brokerage and Smuggling Networks." *ANNALS of the American Academy of Political and Social Science* 676 (1): 114–134.

Kyle, David. 2000. *Transnational Peasants: Migrations, Networks, and Ethnicity in Andean Ecuador*. Baltimore: Johns Hopkins University Press.

Kyle, David, and John Dale. 2001. "Smuggling the State Back In: Agents of Human Smuggling Reconsidered." In *Global Human Smuggling: Comparative Perspectives*, edited by David Kyle and Rey Koslowski, 29–57. Baltimore: Johns Hopkins University Press.

Kyle, David, and Rey Koslowski, eds. 2001. *Global Human Smuggling: Comparative Perspectives*. Baltimore: Johns Hopkins University Press.

———, eds. 2011. *Global Human Smuggling: Comparative Perspectives*. 2nd ed. Baltimore: Johns Hopkins University Press.

Mang, Pum Za. 2011. "Separation of Church and State: A Case Study of Myanmar (Burma)." *Asia Journal of Theology* 25 (1): 42–58.

Missbach, Antje, and Gerhard Hoffstaedter. 2020. "When Transit States Pursue Their Own Agenda: Malaysian and Indonesian Responses to Australia's Migration and Border Policies." *Migration and Society* 3 (1): 64–79.

Physicians for Human Rights. 2011. *Life under the Junta: Evidence of Crimes against Humanity in Burma's Chin State*. Cambridge, MA: Physicians for Human Rights.

Sakhong, Lian H. 2003. *In Search of Chin Identity: A Study in Religion, Politics and Ethnic Identity in Burma*. Copenhagen: Nordic Institute of Asian Studies Press.

Stanslas, Pooja Theresa. 2010. "Transborder Human Trafficking in Malaysian Waters: Addressing the Root Causes." *Journal of Maritime Law and Commerce* 41 (4): 595–606.

Tagliacozzo, Eric. 2002. "Smuggling in Southeast Asia: History and Its Contemporary Vectors in an Unbounded Region." *Critical Asian Studies* 34 (2): 193–220.

UNHCR (United Nations High Commissioner for Refugees). n.d. "Figures at a Glance in Malaysia." Accessed February 23, 2023. https://www.unhcr.org/en-my/figures-at-a-glance-in-malaysia.html.

UNODC (United Nations Office on Drugs and Crime). 2012. *Migrant Smuggling in Asia: A Thematic Review of the Literature*. Bangkok: UNODC.

———. 2018. *Migrant Smuggling in Asia and the Pacific: Current Trends and Challenges*. Vol. 2. Bangkok: UNODC.

Vogt, Wendy A. 2018. *Lives in Transit: Violence and Intimacy on the Migrant Journey*. California Series in Public Anthropology. Oakland: University of California Press.

Wahab, Andika A. 2018. "The Colours of Exploitation: Smuggling of Rohingyas from Myanmar to Malaysia." *Akademika* 88, no. 1 (2018): 5–16.

Wonders, Nancy A. 2007. "Globalization, Border Reconstruction Projects, and Transnational Crime." *Social Justice* 34, no. 2 (108): 33–46.

Zarni, Maung, and Alice Cowley. 2014. "The Slow-Burning Genocide of Myanmar's Rohingya." *Pacific Rim Law and Policy Journal* 23 (3): 681–752.

CHAPTER 13

What the Experiences of Women Tell Us about the Facilitation of Irregular Migration

Gabriella E. Sanchez

MIGRANT SMUGGLING IS OFTEN REPRESENTED in the global migration discourse as a complex and sophisticated crime. Simultaneously, its facilitators are depicted as inhumane, reckless criminals capable of adapting their modus operandi in ways that law enforcement activities and migration policy and control can hardly keep up with, mobilizing an almost preternatural capacity to avoid detection through their savvy use of advanced technology. These allegedly intrepid, risk-prone, high-tech mercenaries who engage in audacious, dangerous journeys across vast oceans and deserts are also gendered as male and racialized as people of color, dominated both by an inherent, uncontrollable sex drive that leads them to prey on the naïveté of young and innocent migrant women, and by boundless greed driving them to exploit the vulnerable and the desperate who are seeking to reach the promised lands of Europe or North America (Sanchez 2018).

In migration discourse, the emphasis on the smuggler as male and on smuggling as inherently evil is problematic. Among other reasons, it provides a monolithic understanding of the practice, while rendering invisible its many actors, which include not only adult men but also children and women. Like men, women coordinate logistics, collect fees, and recruit clients and other smuggling facilitators. They house and feed migrants in transit or care for those who are injured or sick. They are also known for driving people across checkpoints or serving as decoys, or even engaging in violent behavior when under attack.

Despite their roles, women and their experiences as facilitators have hardly been the subject of migrant smuggling research. Every once in a while, they emerge in some journalistic report or academic article, depicted as odd if dangerous figures, or as "taking over" the hypermasculine world of smuggling, often with devastating consequences (see Kilgannon and Singer, 2014). These kinds of reporting are invariably accompanied by testimonies by law enforcement officials or organized crime experts who argue that women are becoming more visible, more daring, more creative, presenting skills and talents not seen even among men (CLIP 2021).

And yet, men are not being forced out of smuggling by women, nor have women suddenly found a way to disrupt sexism through their involvement in the facilitation of irregular migration. Believing so implies falling for the same simplistic claim that labels women's presence in smuggling as "unprecedented" or "never before seen." The dominant discourse of migrant smuggling only seems to acknowledge the presence of women in smuggling as legitimate or worthy of commentary when they appear as victims, or when their deviant actions are seen as echoing those believed to be performed only by men. This reveals what has long been a problematic reluctance to incorporate gender perspectives into the analysis not only of smuggling but of organized crime in general (UNODC 2019).

Gender is performed in smuggling in a wide range of ways and is an important element in the creation of critical forms of inequality that exist within the practice itself. In other words, the fact that scholars have privileged the persona of the smuggler as male is not the ultimate problem: it is the way in which, by rendering smuggling as male, the vast context in which it takes place, and its many other actors, is made invisible.

In what follows, I situate the facilitation of irregular migration for profit—known legally as migrant smuggling—as a collective, community-based enterprise that, while criminalized, is relied on in communities on the migration trail as one of the few remaining mechanisms available for physical and social mobility amid increasing migration restrictions worldwide. With that purpose in mind, I examine the experiences of women charged with migrant smuggling on the US-Mexico border. I purposely avoid situating women's actions as unparalleled or unprecedented, or equating them to those of men. I do so by showing not only that they participate in smuggling but that this in fact constitutes a series of collective efforts performed by multiple individuals and households seeking their survival and those of their communities amid stepped-up migration enforcement worldwide. Granted, said participation imposes on actors often problematic gendered demands made invisible by the focus on the violent male smuggler, which, as I will argue, may be behind the significant increase in the number of women prosecuted for migrant smuggling in the United States, a number that has almost doubled since the 1990s (USSC 2021).

MIGRANT SMUGGLING IN THE UNITED STATES

The UNODC Protocol against the Smuggling of Migrants by Land, Sea and Air defines migrant smuggling as "the procurement, in order to obtain, directly or indirectly, a financial or other material benefit, of the illegal entry of a person into a State Party of which the person is not a national or a permanent resident" (UNODC 2000). A signatory of the protocol, the United States simultaneously relies on the term *alien smuggling* to designate the "conceal[ment], harbor[ing], or shield[ing] from detection, or attempts to conceal, harbor, or shield from detection, [of] an alien in any place, including any building or any means of transportation" (8 U.S.C. § 1324).

In the United States, smuggling is prosecuted at both the federal and state levels. However, data concerning smuggling convictions is hard to come by. The US Sentencing Commission has maintained statistics concerning federal smuggling cases since the late 1990s, when the alien smuggling designation was first introduced into US law. These statistics show that the number of federal convictions for migrant smuggling in the United States grew more than 50 percent between 2012 and 2021, going from 2,231 cases to 3,551 (USSC 2021). The vast majority of smuggling cases heard in federal court in 2021 (that is, 3,346) involved convictions in five district courts along the US-Mexico border, which are, coincidentally, in communities with some of the highest poverty rates in the United States (Guilamo-Ramos and Thimm-Kaiser 2018; Texas Health and Human Services, n.d.) and, ironically, critical locations for the smuggling of migrants due to their location (Guerra 2015; Sanchez 2016). While men constitute the majority of those convicted—76 percent in 2021

(USSC 2021)—the number for women has gone from about 13 percent in the late 1990s to 24 percent in 2021. In 2020, 889 women were convicted for migrant smuggling—until then, the largest number on record (USSC 2020).

How to explain the growth? I argue that, among other factors, it is the consequence of increased levels of precarity in the US-Mexico borderlands, which has led growing numbers of border residents to engage in the facilitation of clandestine border crossings, alongside the aggressive growth of immigration enforcement and its racialized enforcement practices in the region. Historically, the southern US border has not only been ground zero for the efforts to contain irregular migration into the United States; the region's residents—the vast majority of which are of migrant origin—have for generations been denied their basic rights on the grounds of their speech, attire, and even musical tastes, which have made them the target of systematic discrimination and abuse, many times in violation of their human and civil rights (Romero 2006). Multiple scholars have also denounced the excessive levels of militarization, patrolling, and surveillance to which border communities are subjected to, and which have increasingly relied not only on technology (see Maass 2023) but also on the employment of men and women from the same communities as border control officers (Cortez 2021; Vega 2017).

For many of these officers, joining a law enforcement agency implies adopting the code that labels long-standing community-based practices like the facilitation of border crossings as a threat to US national security (Vega 2017)—doing otherwise puts them at risk of being ostracized, or even pushed out of enforcement institutions (Cantu 2018). As much sought-after candidates for their very knowledge of the landscape where they operate, border officers adopt, and in some cases fully embrace, the discourse that redefines local community practices and their actors as inherently illicit if not criminal. And so while smuggling is defined as a sophisticated, complex, and transnational criminal network–like operation during trainings and induction programs, the ability of agents to counter it often relies not on intelligence gathering alone, but on their intimate understandings of their own communities, on their personal awareness of the spaces where the practice takes place, and, quite often, on their familiarity with the very people who carry it out. In other words, efforts to counter smuggling on the US-Mexico border rely on border agents' intimate knowledge of their communities, and the rendering of selected members as criminal.

In sum, the increase in the number of smuggling convictions in the United States can be traced at least in part to the violent escalation of migration control and border enforcement along the US-Mexico border via the deployment of insiders who—not unlike smuggling facilitators—rely on their personal and intimate knowledge of the land to enforce US counter-smuggling strategy. But most importantly, while said strategy relies on the claims that smuggling takes place in wild, exotic locales under the control of ethnic gangs, counter-smuggling involves the criminalization of communities with long-standing histories of impoverishment and marginalization (Guevara González 2018; Sanchez 2016; Stone-Cadena and Álvarez Velasco 2018), spaces where gender inequality thrives.

THE WOMEN IN MIGRANT SMUGGLING

I didn't get into this to *hacerme rica* [get rich], you know? I was making more selling my burritos in my food truck. We used to get up really early and go to the construction sites and sell there, you know. [Smuggling] was just for those times when we needed things that were really urgent—like a part or repairs for the food truck. Or money for rent. One time I did it because my kid was graduating from junior high school and I wanted to throw him a little party. It is not like we were *traficantes* [smugglers] or anything. It was just to cover those things we really didn't have enough money for.

Since 2004 I have conducted research among men, women, and children either charged with migrant smuggling or involved in the facilitation of irregular border crossings into the United States. Granted, and as reflected by the available numbers, the vast majority of those who participate in and are convicted of smuggling are men (see USSC 2021). Men's roles, as shown in other contexts (see Achilli 2018; Zhang 2008), tend to be quite specific, if not narrow—most of them perform transportation-related activities as drivers, scouts, and guides.

Women, on the other hand, perform a wider range of tasks—among those I have interviewed are a fourteen-year-old mother of one who worked as a decoy and a sixty-four-year-old grandmother who housed migrants overnight in her living room. Many women also pick up smuggling fees wired to Western Union or MoneyGram stores. They also care for migrants, provide them with food and board, set up safe houses (the locations where migrants stay while waiting to be transported), and help provide or secure services for those who arrive (they may help them receive medical attention, obtain legal assistance, or even connect with potential employers).

Most smuggling facilitators I have interviewed live in towns and medium-size cities along the US-Mexico border with limited employment or income-generating alternatives. But as Marina's testimony at the beginning of this section shows, hardly anyone turns to smuggling as a way to "get rich." It is in fact not hard to uncover that despite the claims from international organizations concerning the vast profits enjoyed by the participants in the smuggling market (Europol and INTERPOL 2016; IOM 2012; UNODC 2018), facilitating border crossings is neither an easy job nor a fast income generator. Not once have I come across a smuggling facilitator who was not employed in one or, in fact, many other jobs at the same time they were involved in smuggling (see Sanchez 2016). Smuggling, due to its unpredictability—many facilitators in fact offer up to three crossing attempts per fee paid—does not guarantee an income, and most facilitators are prompt to emphasize that their participation only provides supplemental earnings (Sanchez 2016; Sanchez and Thibos 2022; Zhang 2008).

Furthermore—and this is where a gender perspective becomes necessary—not everyone profits from their labor the same way. Men, by virtue of performing tasks considered to involve higher risks—for example, driving vehicles transporting migrants to other states in the United States, or guiding groups through the desert—tend to command higher earnings. Despite the importance of their roles, and their visibility during counter-smuggling raids and undercover operations, most women report only being paid symbolic amounts, receiving in-kind compensation, or, at times, being offered no payment at all, as their tasks are often seen or rationalized as part of their regular household obligations (Sanchez 2016). In other words, supporting smuggling tasks is often explained as part of women's social obligations, despite the potential exposure to criminalization. Mariana, a woman charged with human smuggling for delivering food to a safe house, explained,

> My husband had a job, but we could not afford rent, so his aunt and uncle took us and my children in. They were already working for a

pollero,[1] bringing food for the people at the safe house. I didn't have papers so I couldn't work. But what was I supposed to do, just sit there? No, we owed it to them, you know. I had an obligation because they had taken us in. So whenever they had to bring food I helped them load the car, get the water ready because those packages are heavy and they couldn't carry them on their own, they were elderly people. That was what I did.

Gendered demands for care—ensuring the well-being of their children or elderly parents, for example—also translate into women often having to limit their involvement in smuggling to locations they can travel to and from easily. Unlike men, women are not expected to be absent for prolonged amounts of time or to participate in long-distance travel.

While many of these roles are convenient to women in the sense that they may allow them to balance gendered demands with work, they may ultimately reinforce their perceptions as caregivers and nurturers who must remain in close proximity to their children, which may also explain their limited profits. Ramon's testimony exemplifies some of the logic behind these arrangements:

I knew a woman who worked at the same hotel I did who had a baby boy with a disability. The baby needed special care, and my coworker was working the night shift so that she could spend the day with him. But then suddenly her [work] hours got cut, and she had to get another job during the daytime. I felt sorry for her because she could not take care of the baby, and I told her I could connect her with someone who could pay her a bit of money if she housed a few people at her apartment every once in a while. That way she didn't have to go out to work. She was most grateful.

Researchers have also noted that many of those who participate in smuggling or are prosecuted for smuggling are migrants in transit themselves (Achilli 2018; Campbell and D'Agostino 2022; Frank-Vitale 2020). While data on the specific experiences of migrant women as facilitators of other migrants' journeys are limited, the literature includes testimonies of those who, having hired the services of a facilitator, sought or received discounts or special pricing in exchange for the performance of smuggling-related tasks (Guevara González 2018; Sanchez 2022; Vogt 2018; Yates and Leutert 2020).

While most migration literature (see Stoebenau et al. 2016) tends to define the interactions between smuggling facilitators and migrants along the lines of transactional sex, or focuses on cases in which sexual intimidation or assault has in fact occurred, the experiences of women with facilitators are not limited to sexual encounters. In my research, I have documented cases of women who were offered significant reductions of their smuggling fees in return for performing cleaning, cooking, or babysitting tasks, while others have also reported having traveled for free or for reduced amounts by accepting to pose as drivers' girlfriends, wives, or daughters (Sanchez 2016; Sanchez and Thibos 2022). These agreements are highly valued by migrants, for they can reduce smuggling debt significantly, while allowing them to reach their destinations.

Granted, migrants often hold the short stick of these deals, and it is common to hear about smuggling facilitators delaying or even backing out of their promises—not to mention that the likelihood of being charged with smuggling as a migrant is real. Juliana, a migrant woman who was apprehended in Texas for her alleged involvement in smuggling, explained,

> [The coyotes] said I had to pay more once we got to Reynosa, that I had to pay them more. And I told them, well if that is the case then you better send me back because I do not have any more money—you know, my husband and I had spent everything we had. Everything. And so one of the coyotes said, no, no: stay here, help us cook and clean. We need help with that. So I stayed there. The only problem was that that went on for many days and they would not let me go. Like those cases, you know, that people say they are kidnapped. I felt kidnapped. They kept saying they were just waiting to fill up a car of people going the same direction I was, and that once that happened I could go. And that was the case. They finally got the people they needed to complete the trip. I got in the car, and they still asked me if I wanted to stay. They even said they would pay me [a salary]. But I just wanted to go be with my husband, so I got in the car and left. That was when the police [intercepted] us and everyone got arrested.

While it is common to come across male-centric stories of women entering the market as a result of falling in love with male facilitators—who are portrayed almost invariably as heads or leaders of organized criminal groups (Christiansen 2016; Ovalle and Giacomello 2006)—entry and participation in smuggling by women is significantly more complex, and it is fueled by economic, familial, and social dimensions, rather than by romantic prospects alone. During an interview, Susana, a woman convicted for smuggling, resented being asked whether her former partner had a role in her involvement:

> He didn't know anything when he came to me. He had been working as a cook at a restaurant but wanted to do something else. I was the one who taught him; I had been doing this for a long time with my brothers, and so he asked that I showed him how it was done—he had just moved to the state. So I sent him with my friend's husband, and they went to the border and he got to meet everybody who was doing something—the drivers, the guides, the debt collectors, the recruiters. He just went around and asked questions, a lot of questions. A few years later we started fighting a lot because he was [seeing] other women and so I left him, and so now he is not that nice to me anymore, so I do not always like working with him.

Some women also report having experienced domestic violence, so the prospect of being involved with a partner who may engage in abusive behavior often translates into their decision to avoid any kind of romantic relationship. They remain single, focused on their jobs and their children, and securing additional income through smuggling side jobs. Cynthia, a small business owner, explained,

> I divorced [my ex-husband] because he used to beat me. But we had been doing this [smuggling] thing for a long time. I had always worked [as a hairdresser] and I had my own money. But whenever somebody needs a favor, like picking up money or driving a group of people I call [my ex-husband] and I tell him and he does it. I only do it because of [my] kids, they are his too so he has to [find ways to financially support] them.

As this section has shown, women are critical actors in the facilitation of irregular migration. Smuggling often provides them with the flexibility they need to simultaneously care for their families and children. Granted, the importance of their roles is often minimized, even by the women themselves, and simply rationalized as a way to perform favors or fulfill reciprocity demands, their profits frequently being significantly lower than those of men. The fact that many of these activities take place in domestic settings renders them even more invisible, leading to their perception as unimportant or inconsequential, not only by fellow facilitators but by scholars and commentators alike.

THE UNSEEN SIDE OF MIGRANT SMUGGLING

The tasks women tend to perform in smuggling are essential for the successful completion of clandestine journeys. But alongside them, the provision of physical and emotional protection, companionship, and care by both male and female smugglers constitutes a fundamental component of the journey and ultimately plays a role in a clandestine journey's success (Hagan 2008; Maher 2018; Van Ramshorst 2019).

Care *can* foster solidarity and collaboration among migrants and smuggling facilitators alike. While underexamined, there is evidence of migrants and smugglers protecting each other, developing strategies to prevent being the target of violence or criminalization in the course of their journeys. Migrants may assist facilitators by helping other men, women, and children complete particularly difficult segments of the journey. Migrants often refuse to reveal the identity of the guide or facilitator to authorities if found. Granted, many of these partnerships or forms of cooperation may be temporary and short lived, and may also be motivated by fear, by expectations of material profit, or by the hope of securing additional crossing attempts. Yet accounts referring to moments of happiness and hope derived from interactions that take place on the migration pathway are frequent in the testimonies of migrants and smuggling facilitators alike. Uber—a male, teenage guide—remembered,

> I got to cross this older guy, but we had a difficult crossing; we climbed the fence and then had to walk for a while without shoes and our feet were all covered with thorns. And he then began to cry, and I felt bad, poor old man, I thought, and he looked at me and said, encourage me my son, tell me something that will make me keep

going because I am ready to give up. And I told him, hey mister, don't get sad, can't you see how close we are? Come on, let's keep walking, we are almost there. And I encouraged him and he got happy again and we got to the safe house and his family was already there waiting for him. Everyone cried. Man, I felt so happy, I thought I was going to cry too, because I knew how hard it had been for him and I was able to give him hope. It was nice.

While romance is not commonly mentioned in smuggling accounts, lifelong friendships often emerge between those who share the migration trail. As Vogt (2018), Maher (2018), and Guevara González (2018) argue, the opposite would in fact be strange among people who share incredibly precarious experiences, spending significant amounts of time together traveling across vast distances. Many people do in fact remain in touch with those who facilitate their journeys, with the help of social media and apps. Josh, a male teenage driver, remembered,

We would get in the car and we would be all quiet, but then I will try to put [the girls] at ease by telling them jokes, and when they asked me how old I was and I told them "I am thirteen, I am fourteen" they would laugh because they couldn't believe I was that young, and that would break the ice. I wanted them to feel safe, that they could trust me. I used to think of my mom and my sisters, and how they would feel if they were in the same situation. Sometimes we would exchange [cell phone] numbers and people would text me when they arrived at their destination. It felt nice to be part of what they went through, to feel that I had been of help.

What these testimonies demonstrate is how the apparently unremarkable moments in the interactions of migrants and those who facilitate their journeys are in fact critical components of the experience of traveling irregularly, and that smuggling's narrow conceptualization as a crime alone dangerously obscures the importance and value of moments like these on the migration trail. The constant talk of smuggling abiding by specific business models controlled by particularly heinous and hypersexual men driven by greed and relying on advanced technology is good at generating public support for counter-smuggling activities. Privileged by most academics, law enforcement, and policymakers, the narrative of the facilitation of irregular migration and its actors as inherently criminal systematically and selectively oversimplifies the dynamics present on the migrant trail and allows for the reproduction of enforcement measures that ultimately victimize the most vulnerable.

CONCLUSIONS

Media depictions of counter-smuggling activities along the US-Mexico border portray self-confident border guards chasing fearless male smugglers and frightened migrants in the vastness of the desert and river lands, supported by all-terrain vehicles, night-vision goggles, and powerful helicopter lights.

This contribution instead shows how a significant part of the activities that allow migrants and smuggling facilitators to complete their irregular journeys into the United States take place under far less impressive circumstances and involve the actions of men and women from the margins who—relying on their friends and families, the scant resources available to them, and their geopolitical knowledge—help migrants reach their destinations. I decided to focus on the experiences of women not to ignore those of men but to show how the tendency to conceptualize smuggling along sensationalistic, organized-crime, and male-centric lines makes invisible the not less critical, extraordinary moments that arise in the interactions between migrants and those who facilitate their journeys. Surprisingly—and then perhaps not—many of these moments involve the work of women and young people, who are largely absent in the smuggling literature discourse unless described as victims.

The growth in the number of women prosecuted for smuggling in the United States is proof of the targeting by law enforcement of the weakest actors in the migration facilitation process: those who pose the least risk, involved in activities performed away from the spotlight, in community settings and extended households, where the risk of encountering violence and resistance is slim. Federal data on smuggling convictions in the United States show that these actors are concentrated in borderland communities where extraordinary displays of policing and surveillance collide with historical marginalization and impoverishment (Maass 2023; Núñez and Heyman 2007). This would suggest that despite the tendency to portray smuggling as occurring "in the wild," convictions are the result of the hyperpolicing of community, private, even intimate settings, where women, for a series of gendered reasons that often constrain them to specific locations and spaces, also live.

Masked as part of the fight against irregular migration along the US-Mexico border, counter-smuggling raids and apprehensions attract scant attention from migration activists and civil society (especially given the tropes surrounding the persona of the smuggling facilitator), furthering the invisibilization of the criminalization of border communities.

As dignified employment opportunities become less and less available in border communities, side jobs in underground, illicit, and criminalized markets will continue to provide legitimized if risky alternatives to reduce household precarity. In this sense, the increase in the number of women prosecuted for migrant smuggling also stands as a sign of the impact of border and migration enforcement and control practices on the precarization of women's lives. The growth of convictions involving women has gone hand in hand with the intensification of US immigration policing and enforcement on the border and with the arrival of vast groups of people seeking to reach the United States. The story along the border is not only that of children being forcefully separated from their families or caged in detention facilities, or of vast groups of migrants turning themselves in to the US immigration system, but of the rampant criminalization that people from the border itself face.

Why have the experiences of women remained largely invisible in the way we talk about the facilitation of migrants' journeys? The answer may be connected to the dominant narratives put forth by counter-smuggling efforts worldwide—and the stories we tell ourselves. Smuggling tends to be monolithically described as an illicit industry in which men from the Global South who are organized in vast criminal networks extract financial profits from a seemingly unstoppable number of desperate people. Within this framework, references to women are limited to the kind that portrays them as victims of smugglers' sexual impulses, as their conniving partners, or as heads of dark smuggling gangs. Yet, beyond the headlines, it is fundamental to contextualize the experiences and lives of the people who participate in smuggling as manifestations of the precarity present in their communities. It is also important to keep in mind, beyond the feminization of poverty, the feminization of responsibility (see Chant 2008), as women become increasingly responsible for the survival of their households, given the criminalization to which growing numbers of migrants and people of color are subjected nationwide.

The forms of violence that migrants face in the course of their journeys must not be ignored. Sexual and gender-based violence does exist and has profound implications in the lives of migrants. Yet to attribute it solely to "smugglers" or organized crime overshadows the vast range of actors, including the state, who play a role in the emergence of such violence. Furthermore, the focus on violence (and more specifically on sexual violence) often leads to the fetishization of the bodies of migrant people of color, rather than showcasing the structural conditions that create sexual and gender-based violence to start with (Sanchez 2022), while simultaneously obscuring the very strategies people deploy for their protection and that of those who travel with them, and neglecting the relationships that they forge along the way for survival, companionship, and care (Guevara González 2018; Vogt 2018). Additionally, conceiving the facilitation of irregular migration solely as under the control of an organized criminal element hides the emotional and intimate labors behind the facilitation of mobility (the kind deployed by friends, family members, ordinary people, and facilitators too).

In sum, an examination of women's experiences as smuggling facilitators does not seek to "give them a voice" or "make them visible." It reveals the complex, gendered, and certainly often unequal interactions present in the smuggling market, which, ironically, depends on the deployment of forms of care. It would not succeed otherwise.

NOTE

1. *Pollero* and *coyote* are colloquial terms used throughout the Americas to designate smuggling facilitators.

REFERENCES

Achilli, L. 2018. "The 'Good' Smuggler: The Ethics and Morals of Human Smuggling among Syrians." *ANNALS of the American Academy of Political and Social Science* 676 (1): 77–96.

Campbell, Z., and L. D'Agostino. 2022. "Rebel Boat: Hacked Phones, Undercover Cops, and Conspiracy Theories: Inside Italy's Crackdown on Humanitarian Rescue."

Intercept, December 21, 2022. https://theintercept.com/2022/12/21/italy-iuventa-humanitarian-rescue/.

Cantu, F. 2018. *The Line Becomes a River: Dispatches from the Border.* New York: Riverhead Books.

Chant, S. 2008. "The 'Feminisation of Poverty' and the 'Feminisation' of Anti-poverty Programmes: Room for Revision?" *Journal of Development Studies* 44 (2): 165–197.

Christiansen, M. L. 2016. "'La insoportable levedad del discurso': Timos epistemológicos en la construcción mediática de la narcoviolencia." *Mitologías hoy* 14:25–40.

CLIP (Centro Latinoamericano de Investigación Periodística). 2021. *Migrantes de otro mundo.* New York: Penguin Random House and Editorial Aguilar.

Cortez, D. 2021. "Latinxs in La Migra: Why They Join and Why It Matters." *Political Research Quarterly* 74 (3): 688–702.

Europol and INTERPOL. 2016. *Migrant Smuggling Networks: Joint Europol-INTERPOL Report, Executive Summary, May 2016.* The Hague: Europol. https://www.europol.europa.eu/sites/default/files/documents/ep-ip_report_executive_summary.pdf.

Frank-Vitale, A. 2020. "Stuck in Motion: Inhabiting the Space of Transit in Central American Migration." *Journal of Latin American and Caribbean Anthropology* 25 (1): 67–83.

Guerra, S. I. 2015. "La Chota y los Mafiosos: Mexican American Casualties of the Border Drug War." *Latino Studies* 13 (2): 227–244.

Guevara González, Y. 2018. "Navigating with Coyotes: Pathways of Central American Migrants in Mexico's Southern Borders." *ANNALS of the American Academy of Political and Social Science* 676 (1): 174–193.

Guilamo-Ramos, V., and M. Thimm-Kaiser. 2018. "Youth Living in Settlements at US Border Suffer Poverty and Lack of Health Care." Conversation, October 10, 2018. https://theconversation.com/youth-living-in-settlements-at-us-border-suffer-poverty-and-lack-of-health-care-103416.

Hagan, J. 2008. *Migration Miracle: Faith, Hope and Meaning in the Migration Journey.* Cambridge, MA: Harvard University Press.

IOM (International Organization for Migration). 2012. "IOM Document Examination Centre in Bangkok Aims to Help Combat Trafficking." IOM News Global, June 7, 2012. https://www.iom.int/news/iom-document-examination-centre-bangkok-aims-help-combat-trafficking.

Kilgannon, C., and J. Singer. 2014. "A Smuggler of Immigrants Dies in Prison, but Is Praised in Chinatown." *New York Times*, April 27, 2014. https://www.nytimes.com/2014/04/28/nyregion/cheng-chui-ping-a-smuggler-of-immigrants-dies-in-prison-but-is-praised-in-chinatown.html.

Maass, D. 2023. "CBP Is Expanding Its Surveillance Tower Program at the US Mexico Border—and We Are Mapping It." Electronic Frontier Foundation, March 20, 2023. https://www.eff.org/deeplinks/2023/03/cbp-expanding-its-surveillance-tower-program-us-mexico-border-and-were-mapping-it.

Maher, S. 2018. "Out of West Africa: Human Smuggling as a Social Enterprise." *ANNALS of the American Academy of Political and Social Science* 676 (1): 36–56.

Núñez, G., and J. Heyman. 2007. "Entrapment Processes and Immigrant Communities in a Time of Heightened Border Vigilance." *Human Organization* 66 (4): 354–365.

Offenses Related to Aliens. 8 U.S.C. § 1324(a) (1907). https://www.justice.gov/archives/jm/criminal-resource-manual-1907-title-8-usc-1324a-offenses#:~:text=Subsection%201324(a)(1,any%20of%20the%20preceding%20acts.

Ovalle, P., and C. Giacomello. 2006. "La mujer en el 'narcomundo.' Construcciones tradicionales y alternativas del sujeto femenino." *La Ventana* 24: 297–318.

Romero, M. 2006. "Racial Profiling and Immigration Enforcement: Rounding Up the Usual Suspects in the Latino Community." *Critical Sociology* 32 (2–3): 447–473.

Sanchez, G. 2016. *Border Crossings and Migrant Smuggling*. London: Routledge.

———. 2018. "Portrait of a Human Smuggler: Race, Class and Gender among Facilitators of Irregular Migration on the US-Mexico Border." In *Race, Criminal Justice and Migration Control: Enforcing the Boundaries of Belonging*, edited by M. Bosworth, A. Parmar, and Y. Vazquez, 29–42. Oxford: Oxford University Press.

———. 2022. "The Danger of a Single Story: The Migrant Smuggling Narrative." In *EMM5: Euromesco Euromed Survey*, 74–81. Barcelona: EuroMeSCo.

Sanchez, G., and C. Thibos, eds. 2022. *The Violent, Hopeful World of Children Who Smuggle People*. London: Beyond Trafficking and Slavery/OpenDemocracy.

Stoebenau, K., L. Heise, J. Wamoyi, and N. Bobrova. 2016. "Revisiting the Understanding of 'Transactional Sex' in Sub-Saharan Africa: A Review and Synthesis of the Literature." *Social Science and Medicine* 168:186–197.

Stone-Cadena, V., and S. Álvarez Velasco. 2018. "Historicizing Mobility: Coyoterismo in the Indigenous Ecuadorian Migration Industry." *ANNALS of the American Academy of Political and Social Science* 676 (1): 194–211.

Texas Health and Human Services. n.d. "Border Report Section 3: Population and Demographics of the Texas-Mexico Border Region." Accessed February 24, 2023. https://www.dshs.state.tx.us/hivstd/reports/border/sec3.shtm.

UNODC (United Nations Office on Drugs and Crime). 2000. Protocol against the Smuggling of Migrants by Land, Sea and Air. Vienna: UNODC. https://www.unodc.org/documents/middleeastandnorthafrica/smuggling-migrants/SoM_Protocol_English.pdf.

———. 2018. *Global Study on the Smuggling of Migrants*. Vienna: UNODC. https://www.unodc.org/documents/data-and-analysis/glosom/GLOSOM_2018_web_small.pdf.

———. 2019. "Module 15: Gender and Organized Crime." E4J University Module Series on Organized Crime. https://www.unodc.org/e4j/en/organized-crime/module-15/key-issues/gender-and-organized-crime.html.

USSC (US Sentencing Commission). 2020. *Quick Facts: Alien Smuggling, Fiscal Year 2020*. Washington, DC: USSC. https://www.ussc.gov/sites/default/files/pdf/research-and-publications/quick-facts/Alien_Smuggling_FY20.pdf.

———. 2021. *Quick Facts: Alien Smuggling, Fiscal Year 2021*. Washington, DC: USSC. https://www.ussc.gov/sites/default/files/pdf/research-and-publications/quick-facts/Alien_Smuggling_FY21.pdf.

Van Ramshorst, J. P. 2019. "Laughing about It: Emotional and Affective Spaces of Humour in the Geopolitics of Migration." *Geopolitics* 24 (4): 896–915.

Vega, I. 2017. "Empathy, Morality and Criminality: The Legitimation Narratives of US Border Patrol Agents." *Journal of Ethnic and Migration Studies* 44 (15): 2544–2561.

Vogt, W. A. 2018. *Lives in Transit: Violence and Intimacy on the Migrant Journey*. Berkeley: University of California Press.

Yates, C., and S. Leutert. 2020. "A Gender Perspective of Migrant Kidnapping in Mexico." *Victims and Offenders* 15 (3): 295–312.

Zhang, S. 2008. *Chinese Human Smuggling Organizations: Families, Social Networks and Cultural Imperatives*. Palo Alto, CA: Stanford University Press.

CHAPTER 14

Enter the Boogeyman
REPRESENTATIONS OF HUMAN SMUGGLING IN MAINSTREAM NARRATIVES OF MIGRATION

Luigi Achilli and Alice Massari

THE FIGURE OF THE HUMAN SMUGGLER has been the subject of greatly increased coverage by media since the early 2000s and especially since the beginning of the European migrant "crisis" in 2015.[1] In this chapter, we observe and analyze the gap between a linguistic emphasis on "the smuggler" and their visual absence in media representations and journalistic reporting on the subject. This narrative regime, we argue, provided a language that placed the "refugee crisis" on the shoulders of the smugglers at the same time that it afforded the European Union (EU) with a means of distancing itself from the clear responsibility of this drama.

These facilitators of irregular mobility, from that of economic migrants to that of refugees, have gained infamy as some of the most widely recognized and despised global predators of our time. Smugglers are commonly referred to as the sole orchestrators of senseless human tragedies along migration corridors, the masterminds behind sexual exploitation rings, and greedy amassers of untold riches made at the expense of asylum seekers, migrants, and their families. Their clients, in turn, have often been narrowly portrayed as passive victims lacking agency and freedom (e.g., Miklaucic and Brewer 2013; Naim 2010; Shelley 2014). In general, the relationship between migrants and human smugglers tends to be subsumed under the category of "modern slavery." A defining feature of slavery is that it involves people depriving other human beings of their capacity to act and be free (Bales 2007). In this framework, relationships are characterized primarily by their nonconsensual nature as presumed victims lose any form of control over their own lives (Howard 2017). Their condition "in effect amounts to becoming an object of ownership" or a "thing" (O'Connell Davidson 2016: 233).

Taking advantage of this position of absolute domination, smugglers are said to prey on migration crises, creating in the process global syndicates of organized crime that are swiftly bypassing, evading, corrupting, and subverting state controls and authority (Europol 2016). The sense of pure evil, communicated through mainstream academic and policy writing in this field, has had considerable influence on public and political discourse, serving as a key legal, moral, and political justification for consolidating more intrusive and authoritarian forms of border security and migration policies (Arrouche, Fallone, and Vosyliūtė 2021; Pallister-Wilkins 2015).

This narrative regime is supported and amplified by the power of images, which—as the adage goes—are worth a thousand words. Since the beginning of the so-called European migration crisis, there has been a pronounced tendency to try to identify migrants and smugglers on extralegal grounds, and one of the key terrains where this takes place is in the visual cultural space. A broad and transnational traffic in images and visual signs of irregular migration has increasingly populated our visual landscape. The pictorial representation of irregular migration occurs in many arenas: in the media, in the publications of international and nongovernmental organizations, in humanitarian advertisement for fundraising, and so on. A growing body of literature observes how these representations dehumanize migrants (Bleiker et al. 2013), turn them into embodiments of an "emergency imaginary" (Musarò 2013), and relegate them to simplistic categories of "threat" and "victim" (Chouliaraki and Georgiou 2017; Friese 2017; Horsti 2016).

Yet despite the current hypervisibility of smugglers in media narratives, their visual representation has been surprisingly overlooked by the relevant literature. Our contribution intends to fill this gap through an investigation of the visuality of the smuggler. In this chapter, we examine the images that accompany, and visually narrate, the media discourse on smuggling in two main Italian newspapers—*Il Corriere della Sera* and *La Repubblica*—between January and December 2015. As Lilie Chouliaraki and colleagues have pointed out, "Media represent a key domain for Europe to encounter refugees and new migrants" (Chouliaraki et al. 2017: 1). Our goal is to shed light on how aesthetic patterns reproduced by powerful media affect our understanding of the issue. In order to do so, we have decided to focus on the case of Italy, a central node of the migratory route, circumscribing the time period to 2015, at the peak of the European "refugee crisis" (News European Parliament 2017).

FRAMING THE FIELD

The analysis is based on the theoretical assumption that photos, far from being objective mirrors of reality, constitute that reality (Barthes 1981; Burgin 1982; Sontag [1973] 2005). Beginning in the mid-1990s, visuality started to get much more attention in social research, not only because of the wide presence of images in our wall-to-wall visual landscapes but also because of the pivotal role of visuality in the production and exchange of meaning, especially in Western societies (Rose 2001). Particularly, media images play a key role in framing the perception of an issue and the political debate around it (Bleiker et al. 2013).

Through archival research of all the articles published during 2015 by the two most-read newspapers in Italy (Watson 2022), we systematically collected all images appearing in the news accompanied by the Italian words for "smugglers" and "smuggling"—namely, *scafista, scafisti, trafficante, trafficanti, traffico di uomini,* and *passeur*.[2] The analysis has been carried out through the combination of two visual methodologies: visual social semiotics, for its attention to semiotic resources within situated cultural and social contexts; and iconography, for its potential to identify visual trends and patterns in a large body of images. Through the latter, images have been classified on NVivo according to the subjects and the iconographic elements present in the pictures. Visual social semiotics, with its attention to three layers of meaning—representational, interactive, and compositional (Kress and Van Leeuwen 1996)—has guided the qualitative analysis of a smaller group of photos. Of the 401 pictures collected, 10 represented smugglers and 255 represented migrants (43 images of single individuals, 115 of groups, and 4 of corpses). In 63 photos, the subjects were politicians, while law enforcement people were present in 35 and humanitarian personnel in 32. When looking at nonhuman subjects, the only consistently recurrent visual element is that of a boat (present in 80 pictures).

Visual social semiotics is extremely helpful in making sense of the different meanings present in an image and showing how visual representations of reality are inevitability an interpretation of that reality. Yet this methodology presents some limitations. The strong interpretative component of the analysis can undermine the strength of its heuristic potentiality precisely for the impossibility to affirm that there is a *unique* or *right* way to look at a visual artifact. However, when we analyze an image in its entirety, the various layers of meaning and semiotic resources considered together can help point toward one specific reading. The interpretation of an image is based on the complex agglomeration of the multiple semiotic resources at play and the interplay of the different layers of meaning—representational (what is shown in the image), interactive (the kind of relationship with the viewer the image is suggesting), and compositional (how representational and interactive meanings are integrated within the visual output). In each picture, the potentially infinite combination of semiotic resources can reinforce or, on the contrary, weaken a particular reading (Barthes 1977)—a reading that is situated in a geographically and historically specific cultural milieu. The analysis is based on a specific situatedness that is linked with our positionality as part of the Western contemporary audience, which is exactly the one to which the images in this study are directed. Since any reading is situated in a particular cultural milieu, as Roland Barthes (1977) has noticed, cultural and social expectations are brought to the image. Being part of the same cultural milieu as the primary audience of the image is therefore crucial to unpack the various meanings that are possible in that specific culturally, geographically, and historically situated public.

As we have argued, the study of images is integral to exposing the meanings conveyed by visual narratives about human smuggling. However, in order to be able to fully grasp the implications of their representation, it is also important to first understand the actual dynamics of the phenomenon as experienced by the main actors at the center of the events: smugglers and migrants. For this reason, we combined visual methodologies with ethnographic research based on interviews with, and participant observation among, migrants and irregular migrant facilitators in Europe (Italy and Greece), Turkey, the Arab region (Lebanon and Jordan), and the United States (California) between 2011 and 2018. A large part of data collection involved interviews and informal conversations with men and women formerly smuggled across the Eastern Mediterranean route—mostly from Syria—who either reached their destination or were in transit. It is difficult to quantify the number of interviews that we carried out, since a large part of the empirical data came from informal conversations and interactions with research participants; however, we talked with approximately ninety migrants and over forty people involved in the facilitation of irregular migration. We conducted several face-to-face, phone, and web-based interviews with refugees, facilitators, and activists. It is not always easy to disentangle these three categories since in many cases smugglers, migrants, and even activists were the same people. We augmented the interviews with many hours of informal conversations during day-to-day interactions with most research participants. We also had long-term interactions via Skype, email, and phone conversations with some of them. Follow-up interviews were semistructured or unstructured and, in several cases, entailed multiple meetings over the course of months and even years. All interviews and informal talks were either transcribed during the meetings or, if possible, recorded with prior authorization from the involved people and subsequently transcribed and analyzed. These interviews were conducted in a plurality of settings: private homes, migrant shelters, public squares, and other public spaces where our informants felt most comfortable to be interviewed.

CONVERGING NARRATIVES ABOUT HUMAN SMUGGLING

For the United Nations' 2000 Convention against Transnational Organized Crime and its accompanying Protocol against the Smuggling of Migrants, the smuggler is a person who transports people illicitly into a third country or state (United Nations 2000: 54–55). However, *human smuggler* does not mean, for most people, what the official definition claims it means. This is because media and political discourses have placed more emphasis on the moral dimension of these actors than on their logistical skills. These facilitators of irregular migration have earned notoriety, especially in Western Europe and North America, as evil criminals.

A profusion of photos of migrants crammed into wretched boats circulates in the media; several accounts report the recklessness of smugglers who do not hesitate to toss human beings into the sea or sabotage their own vessels to force authorities to carry out rescues (Europol 2016). The rhetoric that characterizes human smugglers as greedy and immoral depicts migrants as helpless victims and calls for smashing smuggling rings and tightening borders, which—advocates believe—would ensure the safety of migrants and their freedom from the alleged perpetrators (Liempt and Sersli 2013).

A growing, yet still small, body of scholarship has questioned oversimplified depictions of the relationships among the smuggling facilitator, the travelers, and their communities. As early as 2001, David Kyle and John Dale (2001) summarized the complex relationship between smugglers and migrants as a spectrum that ranges from the altruistic assistance provided by family members or friends to dynamics of exploitation based on the intent of hardened criminals. Since their work, empirical research has shown that trust and cooperation seem to be more the rule than the exception in the interaction between smugglers and migrants (Bilger, Hofmann, and Jandl 2006; Koser 1997; Kyle 2000; Kyle and Koslowski 2011; Spener 2004). Sheldon Zhang (2007: 89), for example, points out that Chinese migrants coming to the United States often perceive smugglers as philanthropists, and a number of studies have revealed a strong bond of trust that ties smugglers and migrants together (Ayalew Mengiste 2018; Baird 2016; Brachet 2018; İçduygu and Koser Akcapar 2016). More than just exploitation and lack of agency, the migrant-smuggler relationship is a complex bond that can entail also the development of friendships (Sanchez 2014) and love affairs (Vogt 2018), the mobilization of political activities and ideology (Achilli and Abu Samra 2019; Kook 2023), and even the strengthening of spiritual and religious credos (Achilli 2018; Hagan 2008).

Along with these studies, our field research also unearthed a much more complex picture. The time spent with our interlocutors showed us how human smuggling held strong social and moral significance for both migrants and smugglers. Despite public perceptions of deceit and deception, trust and cooperation seemed to be common in the interactions between migrants and those behind their journeys. Most smugglers operated by helping members of their immediate circles to reach destinations that would have otherwise been blocked to them through legal channels. Remarkably, not only did smugglers depict themselves as service providers who privileged ethical choices over mere profit, but even migrants often described them as decent and respectable people.

And yet, most if not all of our interlocutors, including the smugglers themselves, spoke of smuggling in abstract terms as a very abusive and evil practice. Crucial elements in a mechanism of protection from below, smugglers were widely perceived by migrants and even themselves as abusive exploiters who prey on the need for safety of their victims, the migrants. This inconsistency was puzzling. When interacting with smugglers, migrants never called them by their vernacular equivalents, all words with a negative connotation that evokes exploitation, predation, and violence. The perception of irregular migration as fundamentally predatory and dangerous in nature is evident in the terminology used for indicating human smugglers and their clients across the world (Papadopoulos and Tsianos 2008)—respectively. A smuggler could not be good by definition. For example, among Arabic-speaking communities, migrants referred to their own facilitators by using their personal names or honorific appellatives such as *hajj* or *ammi* (lit. paternal uncle).[3] However, our interlocutors, including the smugglers themselves, used the word *muharrib* to refer to smugglers at large. And when they were asked to comment on the characteristics and moral dispositions of these facilitators of irregular migration, their narratives did not diverge from mainstream narratives of migration. Smugglers were bad.

In sum, quite like the "vox populi" in Europe, even for our research companions the smuggler was a constant source of social anxiety. Certainly, differences emerged in the way the figure of the smuggler was sketched out in their accounts, and how the different actors positioned themselves in relation to this character. However, the degree of consensus was surprising: smugglers were fundamentally evil. The real wonder was that smugglers and migrants shared with mainstream narratives of migration the same understanding of what a smuggler ultimately is: a reckless criminal who preys on migrants' vulnerability. But does this come as a surprise?

It is worth remembering that a plethora of studies on enforcement have demonstrated how the tightening of border controls and the implementation of restrictive immigration policies reduces safe migration mechanisms and encourages the emergence of increasingly dangerous routes where relationships between migrants and their facilitators tend to be more exploitative (Achilli 2018). Furthermore, narratives of smugglers as violent, especially if circulated by powerful media, have the tendency to be resilient and highly contagious.

This does not mean the migrants play a passive role; rather, they interact in complex ways with this system of representations by challenging, accommodating, or even reenacting its authoritative messages (Achilli 2019).[4]

However, as the militarization of the Mediterranean increased the risks faced by irregular migrants, migration flows along the Eastern Mediterranean route in 2015 reinforced in the European public opinion the feeling of being under siege. In mainstream media, the smuggler was blamed for the countless deaths of migrants and the alleged invasion of Europe. Small wonder that facilitators of irregular migration and migrants so anxiously dissociated themselves from the criminal label stuck onto them by iterating dominant narratives in expressing outrage and condemning the "smuggler mafia." "Nobody takes pride in being called *muharrib*," Ashraf told us. A formerly smuggled migrant from Syria who spent over a year with Syrian smugglers in Greece, he knew that his friends "might be proud of smuggling, might even enjoy what they do, but they would never be happy to be called smugglers." His words echoed what a smuggler said a few months earlier in a coastal town in western Turkey when he was asked to reflect on his involvement in what is commonly perceived as an unsavory business. In truth, he said, he did not even think of himself as a smuggler. "If I were [like these smugglers], . . . I would not have so many friends around Europe, so many people praying for me!" "I've never sent anyone to death," the man insisted. "I never overload my boats with men, women and children. I do not send them adrift waiting for the coastguard to rescue them."

The more the field research progressed, the more it became clear that the discourses around smuggling and smugglers were more about moral judgments than the real life of people involved in everyday practices of irregular migration. As we shall see in what follows, the point is not investigating whether a smuggler—a person intrinsically bad in the eyes of our interlocutors—could be good. It is rather to unearth the mechanics and the consequences of this process of manufacturing that sees the transformation of facilitators of irregular migration into the bogeymen of the modern age.

THE (IN)VISIBILITY OF THE SMUGGLER

Two interesting observations emerge from our investigation of media images: the almost invisibility of the smuggler and his elusive nature. Against the significant presence of the figure of the smuggler in the media discourse on the "European migrants crisis," the number of pictures representing smugglers in the two main Italian newspapers is extremely limited. Among the 401 images collected from articles mentioning the Italian equivalent of the words *smuggler(s)* and *trafficker(s)*, only 10 represented them visually, constituting around 2.5 percent of the total. The almost invisibility of the smugglers is coupled with the absence of a clear visual referent. Considered together, images with "smugglers" display a quite heterogeneous visual pattern: individuals behind bars or in a mugshot; close-up shots of people standing among (presumably) migrants; standard passport-type pictures of the alleged smugglers; or a man whipping another man outside a house in an urban environment. In other pictures of smugglers, the confusion only grows—as in the case of a series of snapshots that show men initially identified as victims of smugglers but subsequently accused of being smugglers and eventually acquitted of these accusations. There is even a picture of a white female smuggler: the half-length picture portrays the honorary French consul in Bodrum, who has been accused of smuggling people. Ultimately what all the pictures share is a lack of distinguishing markers that would identify the subjects as belonging to the same category.

A picture captures particularly well this visual vagueness. The photo was published on April 21, 2015, in the Italian newspaper *La Repubblica* to accompany the article "Malek, lo scafista si nascondeva tra i sopravvissuti a bordo della Gregoretti" (Malek, the smuggler was hiding among the survivors on the Gregoretti ship). The image is a medium-close frontal shot of two men. Although the forefront is dark and out of focus, the shape on the bottom left is quite clearly the half body of a man wearing a white disposable suit and plastic protective glasses leaning over, seemingly intent on an action that is out of the picture's frame. The bottom right forefront is also dark, but the viewer can see parts of two men who are walking away from the scene of the picture. The subject of the image is in the in-focus and lit background. We see two men standing near a white wall and iron stairs on the right side. From the article's title, we can deduct that the men are on a boat, while the disposable suits (the uniform of humanitarian rescue personnel) suggest that the image has been taken during a rescue operation. One of the two subjects of the image is wearing the same type of disposable white suit as the out-of-focus person in the forefront. The other person in the focal point of the image wears a blue jacket with the hood raised up. The man in the white suit is facing the man in blue; we cannot see the former's face, although we might assume that he is speaking with the other one. The man in the blue jacket seems to be listening while he stares directly into the camera with what appears as a spiteful snigger. The medium-close shot and the frontal angle, which in social semiotic language imply a certain degree of social closeness and involvement of the viewer in the action, are counterbalanced by the back view we have of the most salient character, who excludes us from the scene. In semiotic terms, the elements at play in this photo suggest that, although the viewers are personally extraneous to the world represented in the image (that of migrants, smugglers, and boats), the malicious smile of the man in the dark hood bridges the social distance: if smugglers are a threat for migrants, it is a threat that somehow also involves "us," the viewers. And yet, this sense of looming threat is coupled with the absence of a clearly distinguishable referent. The iconographic and symbolic signs of the image leave us completely confused about who the smuggler is. Not only are the two men dressed differently, but we even learn in the text accompanying the image that the man in white—dressed exactly like the humanitarian rescue officers—is the chief smuggler, while the other has been identified by some migrants as a minor associate.

The picture is representative of a well-defined visual pattern. These facilitators of irregular migration are represented in only 10 out of 401 pictures accompanying articles that use the word *smuggler*. When we look at the totality of pictures depicting smugglers, we find an evanescent character, so diluted into the heterogeneity of visual patterns as to almost disappear. The only shared element—if we exclude the French consul—is a racialized and gendered image of human smugglers as young men from the Global South (see also Sanchez, this volume, chap. 13). Apart from that, it is hard to visually disentangle smugglers from other actors populating the world of irregular migration, such as humanitarian actors and migrants.[5] The archetypical figures of victim, hero, and villain are conflated in these pictures. It should not come as surprising that, among the ten collected images, there is one identifying as a smuggler the father of Alan Kurdi, the child whose corpse was photographed lying lifeless on western Turkey's shores after the boat he was traveling in with his family and other migrants wrecked. The exact same picture is used in other newspapers' articles to illustrate the grieving father mourning in his dead son's room in Syria. The confusion about who the smuggler is only grows when we look at the picture of a smiling blond middle-aged woman, the French consul accused of smuggling. In a context in which the fight against irregular migration has been camouflaged with the moral imperative of fighting human smuggling, this quasi-invisibility has visible reverberations.

Susan Sontag has defined photography as a "grammar and, even more importantly, an ethics of seeing" ([1973] 2005: 1). However, if Sontag is right when she affirms that photography makes things represented worth being seen, we should seriously engage what is left out from our vision. Roland Bleiker and colleagues (2013) have argued that, by shaping what can be seen (and what cannot), images indirectly shape what can be thought (and what cannot). In this sense, representation is as much about presence as about absence (Manzo 2008), and visual studies has by now recognized the importance of the unseen (Foster 1988) and the need to conceptualize the absence (Rogoff 2000).[6] In this perspective, the absence of visual representation becomes as important to consider as what is represented. This observation is crucial if we want to appreciate the role of invisibility in contemporary discourses about migration. Only if we give enough credit to what cannot be seen, can we understand how specific aesthetic regimes reproduce a discourse of securitization. Put simply, if visibility works powerfully in the construction of securitized utterances (Campbell and Shapiro 2007), so does invisibility.

How, in practice, does invisibility contribute to the securitization of the discourse on migration? The visual absence of the smuggler in mainstream media representations covering the "European refugee crisis" appears particularly relevant when inscribed into the wider discourse on the fight against irregular migration. The quasi-invisibility of the smuggler and the evanescence of his image confirm the idea that in mainstream discourses on migration, the smuggler is clearly the evil. However, when it is necessary to identify who the smuggler is, everything becomes foggy (on this point, see also Achilli 2019). Invisibility and evanescence unite in reproducing the idea of the smuggler as a threat that is both looming on us and difficult to identify and therefore very hard to fight. The smuggler's invisibility, or at least to see clearly (evanescence), feeds into the fear of the unknown and the "moral panic of our multi-mediated society" (McRobbie and Thornton 1995). Invisibility and evanescence contribute to reinforce a rhetoric of the emergency that has dominated the media account of migration over the last few years. And this sense of crisis and impending catastrophe constitutes a large part of mainstream media's securitized discourse. The lack of a visual iconography of the smuggler and the confusion about his identification, produced by pictures like the one portraying the father of Alan Kurdi or the one of the French consul, combine to raise the level of uncertainty about whom to fear and whom not to fear.

THE VISIBILITY OF MIGRANTS

If the smuggler is blurred (if not altogether invisible), what do pictures represent in his stead? Migrants. These are the subjects of two-thirds of the images collected for this study (253 pictures). Photos that accompany articles discussing smugglers predominantly represent migrants, and they do so through three main visual patterns: masses, stranded people, and boats. All of them, although through different processes, contribute to reinforce a securitized account of migration in general and of smugglers more particularly. All of them justify the necessity of an external intervention and legitimize severely restrictive migration policies. On the one hand, images of masses and boats—through the visual trope of the threat—evoke the necessity of intervention to contrast the invasion of which human smugglers appear as the facilitators. On the other hand, pictures of stranded people—through the visual trope of the victim—strongly emphasize the need to fight smuggling to protect the migrants.

The picture that accompanied the article "Colpire i traffici di uomini con ogni mezzo" (Hit human smuggling at any cost), published in the newspaper *Il Corriere della Sera* on May 11, 2015, is a paradigmatic example of journalistic representation of migrants as simultaneously victims and threat. The photo is a close shot from a slightly elevated perspective that shows a group of people sitting close together on the ground and seemingly waiting for something. All the people in the image are men, adults, and black skinned. Each one of them is looking in a different direction, and most show a puzzled air. They seem waiting for something and the caption, at the bottom right corner, confirms: "Stopped. Tens of migrants from Sub-Saharan Africa brought the day before yesterday to the identification center of Misurata in Libya." To begin with, the image reinforces the portrayal of migrants as potential threats. Also, in this case, what we do not see is as important as what we see. Although we can easily recognize individual traits and facial expressions, the frame selection suggests that these men are just part of a bigger group that is too large to fit into the picture. We can just guess that they are many. In this sense, the picture seems to suggest that the story of the article is not only about those we can see—with whom we could also feel emotionally involved, given the relative closeness of the shot (a semiotic technique connected with social intimacy). The frame indicates that the story is also about the larger and potentially dangerous multitude left outside the visual frame—the horde that is crowding at Europe's security doors.

Quite contradictorily, the picture also represents migrants as passive and helpless victims. The high angle of the shot establishes a relationship in which the viewer has power over the represented participants, whose subaltern position is also reinforced by the larger context: a crowd of people who sit and wait passively, without any apparent form of interaction. The lack of activity occurring and the absence of a focal point to which the subjects' attention is directed reveal the conceptual structure of an image that represents "participants in terms of their more generalized and more or less stable and timeless essence, in terms of class, or structure or meaning" (Kress and Van Leeuwen 1996: 79). More specifically, the mass of refugees is represented in its suggestive symbolic process. Details are overlooked in favor of an "atmosphere" (106), underlined by the represented participants' homogeneous ages, genders, and skin colors. The dilution of distinguishing characteristics and colors accentuates the symbolic value of the carrier: a crowd of passive and inactive people, portrayed in their generic essence.

As in the case of the picture accompanying *La Repubblica*'s article on the smuggler, the photo included in *Il Corriere della Sera*'s article on migrants is representative of a broader visual pattern. Along with images of boats, the visual elements of masses and stranded people constitute the most recurrent aesthetic patterns present in the pictures that depict migrants collected for this study. First, one-fourth of the photos collected represent people on the move as masses. Indeed, in a great number of cases, migrants are depicted in very large groups (115 pictures out of the 251 represent groups of more than ten people). Faces and individual traits are basically indistinguishable. Such visual framings "suppress or overlook the types of factors that make people human" (Bleiker et al. 2013: 411), as the distance of the shot—an index of social distance in visual social semiotics—prevents the establishment of a personal emotional connection with the viewer. Images of masses of people therefore tend to evoke a sense of fear and threat, reinforcing narratives of crisis, emergency, and invasion (see also Falk 2010;

Friese 2017; Musarò 2017). These kinds of pictures are likely to arouse various degrees of discomfort, apprehension, and anxiety (Bleiker et al. 2013), thus reinforcing a politics of fear in which people on the move are considered a threat to sovereignty and security.

Second, images of masses of indistinguishable people are also very often combined with another recurrent visual pattern: overcrowded boats, typically portrayed adrift at high sea (present in eighty images, almost 20 percent of the total number of images). The iconography of the boat crammed with migrants has become, over the last decades, a symbol of large migration flows and a visual element quite familiar to the Western audience. Vessels full of people inspire feelings of threat and fear (Bleiker et al. 2013; Falk 2010; Friese 2017; Musarò 2017; Pugh 2004). The blurred blend of bodies, the indistinctiveness of the represented participants, the frame size, the perspective, and the point of view all work together to create a representation of boat people that nourishes inquietude and fear, reproducing and reinforcing a securitizing discourse that depicts migrants in terms of threat. Furthermore, the idea of the ship resonates with discourses of penetration and invasion. The texture of water, with its fluid power of infiltration, is present in several liquid metaphors for migration that commonly describe it in terms of relentless floods, waves, and flows (see, among others, Pugh 2004).

Finally, a third form emerges among images of helpless migrants hidden in trucks' engine compartments, groups of people passively sitting and waiting for something to happen, and people covered in blankets in inclement weather: the stranded pattern. At the visual level, this pattern conveys victimhood in several ways—such as through shots of people on the move from a high angle, captured during a moment of inactivity, and with expressions of suffering, as well as through the overrepresentation of children. Clearly, media images aim to show what is happening and provide sympathetic testimony of their suffering. By doing so, however, they fuel a stereotypical and overly simplified narrative of the migrant as an object of compassion (Ticktin 2011), as helpless and passive (Calain 2012; Fassin 2007; Kleinman and Kleinman 1996; Rajaram 2002) and at the mercy of reckless smugglers. This sense of misery has had considerable influence on public and political discourse, serving as a key legal, moral, and political justification for consolidating more authoritarian migration policies (Campos-Delgado 2020; Pallister-Wilkins 2015).

CONCLUSION

This study has highlighted how the almost total absence of smugglers from visual representations stands in striking contrast with the abundance of narrative accounts about them at the media and policy levels. On the contrary, the visual narrative is dominated by an aesthetic rhetoric based on the overrepresentation of migrants. All this has important consequences.

First, this discrepancy turns *smuggler* into a morally laden term that, in fact, fails to identify any actual person in the field (Achilli 2019). More than anything else, the figure of the smuggler speaks of a generalized condition of moral panic over immigration that media have contributed to generating. The simultaneous ubiquity and salience of the smuggler is largely explained by the absence of a clear referent. Blame is located firmly on the smuggler; yet it is less clear who the smuggler is. What the struggle to pin down the smuggler ultimately tells us is that the term has lost its capacity to describe local contexts of human movement. As Wendy Vogt aptly puts it, smugglers "are the boogeymen of the migration industry, an omnipresent danger, but disembodied and difficult to see" (2018: 134). Against this background, if the smuggler becomes the ideal enemy—a threat easy to evoke but hard to locate—migrants rise to the role of perfect victims. The almost invisibility of the smuggler is combined with the hypervisibility of migrants. The latter are simultaneously represented both as passive victims with no agency who are at the mercy of evil criminals and as threatening masses of people who attempt to reach Europe's borders by boat and on foot.

Second, the visual representation of the so-called migration crisis is not merely descriptive: it is agentive. It is in every instance a clear political project, if we want to give credit to French philosopher Jacques Rancière, for whom reframing the real is an intrinsic political action. Narratives of smugglers as violent, especially if circulated by powerful media, have the tendency to be resilient and highly contagious. As the militarization of the Mediterranean increased the risks faced by irregular migrants, migration flows along the Eastern Mediterranean route in 2015 reinforced in the European public opinion the feeling of being under siege. In mainstream media, the smuggler was blamed for the countless deaths of migrants and the alleged invasion of Europe. As we have shown in this chapter, the interplay of visible and invisible becomes a grammar for political enunciation. The effect of these representations is clear: the threat of the smuggler, which increases in size with its elusiveness, compels Europe to intervene. Press coverage of crime and violence provided a language that placed the "refugee crisis" on the shoulders of an invisible and ubiquitous enemy at the same time that it afforded the EU the moral authority to act on the behalf of those who suffer a chronic lack of agency: the migrants.

NOTES

1. On this point, it is important to clarify that we use the term *crisis* critically. We agree here with those who have argued that the "crisis" narrative is part and parcel of a European discourse on "migration" or "refugees" that fails to reflect the empirics and ultimately depoliticizes the context in which migration occurs (see, among others, De Genova and Tazzioli 2016). At the same time, it is undeniable that the specter of the "refugee crisis" has come to define a specific historical phenomenon that entails important political implications in the way refugees are represented, perceived, and ultimately managed.
2. It is important to note that although there are substantial differences in the meanings of these terms in the Italian language, media articles often used them as synonyms.
3. The word is used to refer to someone who has successfully completed the pilgrimage to Mecca. In the Middle East it is also often used as an honorific title for an older and respected person.
4. Hacking's idea of a "looping effect" is particularly relevant to our analysis for it highlights the role of people in interacting with and manufacturing their own categorization. As the Canadian philosopher puts it, "People . . . can become aware that they are classified as such. They can make tacit or even explicit choices, adapt or adopt ways of living so as to fit or get away from the very classification that may be applied to them." However, they inevitably change the original categorization: "What was known about people of a kind may become false because people of that kind have changed in virtue of what they believe about themselves. . . . This phenomenon [is] the looping effect of humankinds" (1999: 34).
5. In sum, smugglers are almost invisible, and when they appear, their contours remain quite blurred. This confirms the empirical findings of a critical body of literature that has shown how the smuggler is a rather complex and fluid figure, not easily distinguishable on the ground from the migrants, humanitarian actors, and other actors (e.g., Zhang, Sanchez, and Achilli 2018).
6. Rancière (2014) has pointed out how systems of meaning function at the visual level, limiting or encouraging thought. Paying attention to Rancière's "systems of visibility"—aesthetic regimes that decide what should be and should not be visible—allows us to reach a better understanding of smugglers' representation and the relevance of what is left out of the picture.

REFERENCES

Achilli, Luigi. 2018. "The 'Good' Smuggler: The Ethics and Morals of Human Smuggling among Syrians." *ANNALS of the American Academy of Political and Social Science* 676 (1): 77–96.

———. 2019. "Waiting for the Smuggler: Tales across the Border." *Public Anthropologist* 1 (2): 194–207.

Achilli, Luigi, and Mjriam Abu Samra. 2019. "Beyond Legality and Illegality: Palestinian Informal Networks and the Ethno-political Facilitation of Irregular Migration from Syria." *Journal of Ethnic and Migration Studies*, online ahead of print, September 30, 2019. https://doi.org/10.1080/1369183X.2019.1671181.

Arrouche, Kheira, Andrew Fallone, and Lina Vosyliūtė. 2021. *Between Politics and Inconvenient Evidence: Assessing the Renewed EU Action Plan against Migrant Smuggling.* CEPS Policy Brief No. 2021-01. Brussels: Center for European Policy Studies.

Ayalew Mengiste, Tekalign. 2018. "Refugee Protections from Below: Smuggling in the Eritrea-Ethiopia Context." *ANNALS of the American Academy of Political and Social Science* 676 (1): 57–76.

Baird, Theodore. 2016. *Human Smuggling in the Eastern Mediterranean.* Vol. 8. London: Taylor and Francis.

Bales, Kevin. 2007. "Defining and Measuring Modern Slavery." Free the Slaves. https://freetheslaves.net/wp-content/uploads/2015/01/DefiningMeasuringModernSlavery.pdf.

Barthes, Roland. 1977. *Image, Music, Text.* London: Fontana.

———. 1981. *Camera Lucida: Reflections on Photography.* New York: Hill and Wang.

Bilger, Veronika, Martin Hofmann, and Michael Jandl. 2006. "Human Smuggling as a Transnational Service Industry: Evidence from Austria." *International Migration* 44 (4): 59–93.

Bleiker, Roland, David Campbell, Emma Hutchison, and Xzarina Nicholson. 2013. "The Visual Dehumanisation of Refugees." *Australian Journal of Political Science* 48 (4): 398–416.

Brachet, Julien. 2018. "Manufacturing Smugglers: From Irregular to Clandestine Mobility in the Sahara." *ANNALS of the American Academy of Political and Social Science* 676 (1): 16–35.

Burgin, Victor. 1982. "Looking at Photographs." In *Thinking Photography*, edited by Victor Burgin, 142–153. London: Palgrave.

Calain, Philippe. 2012. "Ethics and Images of Suffering Bodies in Humanitarian Medicine." *Social Science and Medicine* 98:278–285.

Campbell, David, and Michael J. Shapiro. 2007. "Guest Editors' Introduction." In "Special Issue on Securitization, Militarization and Visual Culture in the Worlds of Post-9/11." *Security Dialogue* 38 (2): 131–137.

Campos-Delgado, Amalia. 2020. "Abnormal Bordering: Control, Punishment and Deterrence in Mexico's Migrant Detention Centres." *British Journal of Criminology* 61 (2), online ahead of print, November 5, 2020. https://doi.org/10.1093/bjc/azaa071.

Chouliaraki, Lilie, and Myria Georgiou. 2017. "Hospitality: The Communicative Architecture of Humanitarian Securitization at Europe's Borders." *Journal of Communication* 67 (2): 159–180.

Chouliaraki, Lilie, Myria Georgiou, Rafal Zaborowski, and W. A. Oomen. 2017. *The European "Migration Crisis" and the Media: A Cross-European Press Content Analysis*. London: London School of Economics and Political Science.

De Genova, Nicholas, Martina Tazzioli, and Soledad Álvarez-Velasco. 2016. "Europe/Crisis: New Keywords of 'the Crisis' in and of 'Europe.'" *Near Futures Online* 1:1–16.

Europol. 2016. *Migrant Smuggling in the EU*. European Police Office. https://www.europol.europa.eu/cms/sites/default/files/documents/migrant_smuggling_europol_report_2016.pdf.

Falk, Francesca. 2010. "Invasion, Infection, Invisibility: An Iconology of Illegalized Immigration." In *Images of Illegalized Immigration: Towards a Critical Iconology of Politics*, edited by Christine Bischoff, Francesca Falk, and Sylvia Kafehsy, 83–100. Bielefeld, Germany: Transcript.

Fassin, Didier. 2007. "Humanitarianism as a Politics of Life." *Public Culture* 19 (3): 499–520.

Foster, Hal. 1988. *Vision and Visuality: Discussions in Contemporary Culture*. Seattle: Dia Art Foundation and Bay Press.

Friese, Heidrun. 2017. "Representations of Gendered Mobility and the Tragic Border Regime in the Mediterranean." *Journal of Balkan and Near Eastern Studies* 19 (5): 541–556.

Hacking, Ian. 1999. *The Social Construction of What?* Cambridge, MA: Harvard University Press.

Hagan, Jacqueline Maria. 2008. *Migration Miracle*. Cambridge, MA: Harvard University Press.

Horsti, Karina. 2016. "Visibility without Voice: Media Witnessing Irregular Migrants in BBC Online News Journalism." *African Journalism Studies* 37 (1): 1–20.

Howard, Neil. 2017. *Child Trafficking, Youth Labour Mobility and the Politics of Protection*. London: Palgrave Macmillan.

İçduygu, Ahmet, and Sebnem Koser Akcapar. 2016. "Turkey." In *Migrant Smuggling Data and Research: A Global Review of the Emerging Evidence Base*, 137–160. Geneva: International Organization for Migration.

Il Corriere della Sera. 2015. "Colpire i traffici di uomini con ogni mezzo." May 11, 2015. https://archivio.corriere.it/Archivio/interface/slider.html#!Colpire-i-traffici-di-uomini-con-ogni-mezzo/NobwRAdghgtgpmAXGA1nAngdwPYCcAmYANGAC5wAepSYAwtgDYAOAlrnAAQsem5QBm-FgGNu+bgFdsMFhG7DsEDtgDmcjvABem7GAC+AXSA.

Kleinman, Arthur, and Joan Kleinman. 1996. "The Appeal of Experience; the Dismay of Images: Cultural Appropriations of Suffering in Our Times." *Daedalus* 125 (1): 1–23.

Koser, Khalid. 1997. "Social Networks and the Asylum Cycle: The Case of Iranians in the Netherlands." *International Migration Review* 31 (3): 591–611.

Kress, Gunther R., and Theo Van Leeuwen. 1996. *Reading Images: The Grammar of Visual Design*. London: Routledge.

Kyle, David. 2000. *Transnational Peasants: Migrations, Networks, and Ethnicity in Andean Ecuador*. Baltimore: Johns Hopkins University Press.

Kyle, David, and John Dale. 2001. "Smuggling the State Back In: Agents of Human Smuggling Reconsidered." In *Global Human Smuggling: Comparative Perspectives*, edited by David Kyle and Rey Koslowski, 29–45. Baltimore: Johns Hopkins University Press.

Kyle, David, and Rey Koslowski, eds. 2011. *Global Human Smuggling: Comparative Perspectives*. 2nd ed. Baltimore: Johns Hopkins University Press.
La Repubblica. 2015. "Malek, lo scafista si nascondeva tra i sopravvissuti a bordo della Gregoretti." April 21, 2015. https://www.repubblica.it/cronaca/2015/04/21/foto/gregoretti-112496373/1/.
Liempt, Ilse, and Stephanie Sersli. 2013. "State Responses and Migrant Experiences with Human Smuggling: A Reality Check." *Antipode* 45 (4): 1029–1046.
Manzo, Kate. 2008. "Imaging Humanitarianism: NGO Identity and the Iconography of Childhood." *Antipode* 40 (4): 632–657.
McRobbie, Angela, and Sarah L. Thornton. 1995. "Rethinking 'Moral Panic' for Multi-mediated Social Worlds." *British Journal of Sociology* 46 (4): 559–574.
Miklaucic, Michael, and Jacqueline Brewer, eds. 2013. *Convergence: Illicit Networks and National Security in the Age of Globalization*. Washington, DC: National Defense University Press.
Musarò, Pierluigi. 2013. "'Africans' vs. 'Europeans': Humanitarian Narratives and the Moral Geography of the World." *Sociologia della Comunicazione* 45:37–59.
———. 2017. "Mare Nostrum: The Visual Politics of a Military-Humanitarian Operation in the Mediterranean Sea." *Media, Culture and Society* 39 (1): 11–28.
Naim, Moises. 2010. *Illicit: How Smugglers, Traffickers and Copycats Are Hijacking the Global Economy*. New York: Random House.
News European Parliament. 2017. Europe's Migration Crisis. https://www.europarl.europa.eu/news/en/headlines/society/20170629STO78630/asylum-and-migration-in-the-eu-facts-and-figures.
O'Connell Davidson, Julia. 2016. "'Things' Are Not What They Seem: On Persons, Things, Slaves, and the New Abolitionist Movement." *Current Legal Problems* 69 (1): 227–257.
Pallister-Wilkins, Polly. 2015. "The Humanitarian Politics of European Border Policing: Frontex and Border Police in Evros." *International Political Sociology* 9 (1): 53–69.
Papadopoulos, Dimitris, and Vassilis Tsianos. 2008. "The Autonomy of Migration: The Animals of Undocumented Mobility." In *Deleuzian Encounters: Studies in Contemporary Social Issues*, edited by Anna Hickey-Moody and Peta Malins, 223–235. London: Palgrave Macmillan.
Pugh, Michael. 2004. "Drowning Not Waving: Boat People and Humanitarianism at Sea." *Journal of Refugee Studies* 17 (1): 50–69.
Rajaram, Prem Kumar. 2002. "Humanitarianism and Representations of the Refugee." *Journal of Refugee Studies* 15 (3): 247–264. https://doi.org/10.1093/jrs/15.3.247.
Rancière, Jacques. 2014. *The Emancipated Spectator*. London: Verso Books.
Rogoff, Irit. 2000. *Terra Infirma: Geography's Visual Culture*. London: Routledge.
Rose, Gillian. 2001. *Visual Methodologies: An Introduction to Researching with Visual Materials*. London: Sage.
Sanchez, Gabriella. 2014. *Human Smuggling and Border Crossings*. London: Routledge.
Shelley, Louise I. 2014. *Dirty Entanglements: Corruption, Crime, and Terrorism*. Cambridge: Cambridge University Press.

Sontag, Susan. (1973) 2005. *On Photography*. Electronic ed. New York: RosettaBooks.
Spener, David. 2004. "Mexican Migrant-Smuggling: A Cross-Border Cottage Industry." *Journal of International Migration and Integration/Revue de l'integration et de la migration internationale* 5 (3): 295–320.
Ticktin, Miriam I. 2011. *Casualties of Care: Immigration and the Politics of Humanitarianism in France*. Berkeley: University of California Press.
United Nations. 2000. United Nations Convention against Transnational Organized Crime and the Protocols Thereto. https://www.unodc.org/documents/treaties/UNTOC/Publications/TOC%20Convention/TOCebook-e.pdf.
Vogt, Wendy A. 2018. *Lives in Transit: Violence and Intimacy on the Migrant Journey*. Oakland: University of California Press.
Watson, Amy. 2022. "Leading Daily Newspapers in Italy as of December 2021, by Number of Copies Sold." Statista, April 22, 2022. https://www.statista.com/statistics/729663/top-daily-newspapers-italy/.
Zhang, Sheldon. 2007. *Smuggling and Trafficking in Human Beings: All Roads Lead to America*. Westport, CT: Praeger.
Zhang, Sheldon, Gabriella Sanchez, and Luigi Achilli. 2018. "Crimes of Solidarity in Mobility: Alternative Views on Migrant Smuggling." *ANNALS of the American Academy of Political and Social Science* 676 (1): 6–15.

CHAPTER 15

Ecuadorean Migrant Smuggling
CONTEMPORARY PATTERNS AND DYNAMICS

Soledad Álvarez Velasco

COYOTERISMO, AS MIGRANT SMUGGLING is known in Ecuador, is an enduring dimension of undocumented migration taking place from that South American country to diverse destinations worldwide. For the past five decades, Ecuadoreans have steadily immigrated to the United States with the aid of coyotes. Similarly, over the past four decades, and greatly increasing since 2008, regional migrants (mainly from the Caribbean region) and extracontinental migrants (from African, Asian, and Middle Eastern countries) have reached Ecuador with the intention of transiting from there to elsewhere, principally to the United States, also guided by coyotes. Amid the current so-called Venezuelan migrant crisis, Venezuelans have resorted to local coyotes, either to cross Ecuadorean borders or to transit from there to other South American destinations, or even to the United States. All this provides evidence of two separate, overarching modes of migrant smuggling taking place in Ecuador: a *domestic mode*, through which traditional local smuggling networks facilitate irregularized[1] movements of Ecuadoreans abroad, and an *international mode*, through which international migrant[2] smuggling networks make use of Ecuador as a transit country for the movement of regional or extracontinental migrants, asylum seekers, and refugees to reach the United States or other destinations with the aid of coyotes. This chapter delves into those two modes of migrant smuggling. The analysis focuses on three interconnected aspects: (1) the structural causes that explain their endurance in relation to Ecuadorean migratory history, (2) their new patterns, and (3) the role that technology has played in reshaping both modes of migrant smuggling.

The argument that runs through the chapter is that coyoterismo is a historical process that must be examined in order to comprehend the role that Ecuador has played as an "articulating node" (Heyman 2004) within the neoliberal world economy. In addition to providing raw materials for world exports, from the late 1960s to the present, Ecuador has provided labor power, embodied in Ecuadorean and international undocumented migrants. Coyotes have been enablers of those irregularized journeys traditionally to the United States and more recently to other destinations in the Americas. They have empowered not only migrants' mobilities amid reinforced border regimes but also the configuration and operation of a profitable business within the Ecuadorean illegalized economy, which benefits a multiplicity of actors on the local, national, and transnational scales. As the chapter proves, coyoterismo is intimately related to social, economic, cultural, and religious dynamics in present-day Ecuador; therefore, the production of interdisciplinary research based on empirical data must dismantle the hegemonic approach that aims to analyze a historical process as complex as migrant smuggling simplistically based on criminal tags.

The empirical data I present arise from a larger research project on why and how Ecuador became a global space of transit toward the United States.[3] I combined a historical analysis (the 1960s–2016) with a multisited ethnography and an ethnography of migrants' digital space. My research was conducted between 2015 and 2016 and allowed the reconstruction of twenty trajectories of transit migrants from Cuba, the Dominican Republic, Haiti, Syria, Iraq, Zimbabwe, Sudan, and Nigeria and of Ecuadorean deportees. These findings were complemented by some recent empirical and journalistic information gathered between January and September 2019. During those months, I conducted fieldwork in various rural towns of the province of Azuay, one of the historical migrant-sending hubs to the United States. All this material has been the basis for historicizing Ecuador's transit condition and for understanding its contemporary complexities. The time frame of this analysis covers the history of coyoterismo in Ecuador between the mid-1960s and the present, analyzing dynamics right up until 2019, the end of the second decade of the twenty-first century.

COYOTES: HISTORICAL ENABLERS OF IRREGULARIZED TRANSITS

Since the mid-twentieth century, South American countries have primarily been migrant-sending countries (IOM 2019). Ecuador has been no exception. With an estimated stock of around two to three million emigrants, for the past decade, Ecuadoreans have ranked sixth among the ten principal Latin American sending countries (World Bank 2011). Though during the first years of the twenty-first century Spain and Italy arose as important migratory destinations, the United States has remained the principal destination (Herrera, Moncayo, and Escobar 2012).

The endurance of coyoterismo has to be understood as a consequence of two structural conditions, which together have prompted undocumented migrations of Ecuadoreans: recurrent national socioeconomic crises and the reinforcement of the global border regime. Ecuador, as a periphery dependent country, has been and still is disproportionately oriented toward supplying commodities or raw materials (e.g., textiles, bananas, cacao, and oil) to external markets (Velasco 1972), and since the mid-twentieth century it has provided labor power through massive migrations mainly to the United States.

This movement of people may be explained as a response to continuous socioeconomic crisis. In the mid-1960s, the crisis in the production of toquilla straw and in the exports of toquilla hats from the southern highland provinces of Azuay and Cañar resulted in pioneering movements to the United States. The 1986 and 1990 international oil crises, which coincided with the turn to neoliberalism, also induced massive departures. The Ecuadorean new millennium crisis in 1999, which resulted in the dollarization of Ecuador's economy, drove massive urban migration toward the United States, Spain, and Italy. Furthermore, in the face of the 2008 global financial crisis, the answer was migration, only this time return migration to Ecuador (Herrera, Moncayo, and Escobar 2012). This accumulation of historical crises and migrants' autonomous responses make it evident that Ecuadorean migrants have been coming and going from Ecuador to elsewhere for the past five decades, deploying a diversity of patterns and strategies.

Against this constant and massive migratory movement, the United States and other countries in the region that function as preliminary US borders have imposed visa restrictions on Ecuadoreans. Such has been the case for Mexico, Guatemala, El Salvador, and Costa Rica (Velázquez and Schiavon 2006). Ecuadoreans have resorted to coyotes as a way to slip through enforced borders to accomplish their migratory projects. This explains why the number of Ecuadoreans residing in the United States has had sustained growth, becoming the tenth-largest Latino group (Noe-Bustamante, Flores, and Shah 2019).

Ecuadorean coyoterismo was shaped amid the first migratory wave, or during the first massive exit of Ecuadoreans, which took place at the end of the 1960s. In response to the crisis of the production of toquilla straw, pioneer male Indigenous peasants followed the straw-hat trade route to reach the United States via Mexico. Initially, they learned from Mexican coyotes their strategies to traverse borders; later they themselves guided other Ecuadorean migrants (Kyle 2000). This first movement influenced the historical outline of a social process that has facilitated the transnational clandestine mobility of undocumented Ecuadoreans along the Ecuador–Mexico–US route.

From the late 1960s to the present, coyoterismo has been a profitable activity involving multiple local actors engaged around irregularized transits to the United States. Over the years, the cost of immigrating to the United States with the aid of coyotes has risen, from around US$5,000 in the 1980s to no less than $10,000 to $20,000 at present, an amount of money that has benefited actors involved in the irregularized transits of Ecuadoreans. For this reason, David Kyle (2000: 66–67), in his study of the Ecuadorean coyoterismo, asserts that a "migrant export model" operates in Ecuador, where "migration merchants" have played a key role in configuring social networks based on trust and usurious financing to enable clandestine transits. In this sense, coyotes and other local actors (including moneylenders, lawyers, document forgers, intermediaries, travel agents, airline staff, and even representatives of international consulates or local government offices) have taken part in an expansive, profitable social network (Ruiz and Álvarez Velasco 2019).

Coyoterismo is also a key element of local culture. Although there are plenty of harrowing stories, thousands of successful experiences equally proliferate. This explains why in the southern province of Azuay, coyotes are seen as facilitators, benefactors, protectors, or even *padrinos* (godfathers)

(Stone-Cadena and Álvarez Velasco 2018). While conducting fieldwork, I confirmed the religiosity that has developed around Ecuadorean undocumented migration and coyoterismo. In some migrant-sending communities in Azuay, there are temples with patron saints of migrants, where families and migrants themselves pray for the travelers, and where offerings are solemnly made. That is the case, for example, for the Church of Nuestra Señora de La Merced of the Missionary Oblates, where a weekly mass for the travelers is offered. There, migrants and their relatives usually leave to Father Julio Maria Matovelle, patron saint of the travelers, their passport-size photos with their names written on the back as a sort of offering, so that they can be protected along the route (see Figure 15.1).

In the rural town of Guapachala, on the other hand, there is a temple devoted to the Lord of Andacocha, another patron saint of migrants. Each September 14, a local festivity is held in his honor, which includes a massive mass and a popular celebration with music, food, and dancing. Families of migrants and returned and deported migrants pilgrimage on foot toward the temple. They leave their votive offerings to express their gratitude for having arrived safely in the United States or for having a good job there. They also request that the Lord of Andacocha give them protection when traversing the Mexican-US border (see Figures 15.2 and 15.3).

These public expressions of religiosity confirm that coyoterismo is embedded in Ecuadorean migratory culture. Since the mid-1980s, the priest of the parish of the rural town of Guachapala has been directly working with migrants. He is an expert on Ecuadorean migration and its intimate nexus with coyoterismo. While explaining to me the dynamics of the festivities to honor the Lord of Andacocha, he mentioned,

> Migration to the U.S. cannot be understood without the figure of coyotes. The Lord of Andacocha, he is *"¡el coyote mayor!"* [the major coyote]. I tell you this because in the imaginary of people, he is the one who allows them to reach the U.S. when they go *por la chacra*.[4] Because of this, they pray as a form of gratitude. The complex figure of a coyote needs to be understood within the cultural and religious practices of local people.

As the priest asserted, "the complex figure of a coyote" cannot be analyzed outside the cultural, religious, and historical dynamics of Ecuadorean

FIGURE 15.1. Families and communities in Cuenca, Ecuador, participating in La Misa para los Viajeros (The Mass for Travelers), devoted to their family members who left Ecuador for the United States. Congregants ask for protection, blessings, and the well-being of loved ones as they traverse multiple countries to the Mexico–US border, make that particularly risky crossing, and, following the journey, settle and find work in the United States. The mass takes place every Wednesday at the Iglesia de La Merced Catholic Church. Photos by author

FIGURE 15.1. (continued)

FIGURE 15.2. Gratitude altarpiece for the Lord of Andacocha. The temple of the Lord of Andacocha is located in Guachapala, Azuay, Ecuador. Photo by author

> Thankfulness to the Lord of Andacocha. I thank you for protecting
> and helping me during the journey I started and for getting
> me with happiness and health to the EE.UU.
> Your loyal devout
> Elmer Salvay
> EE.UU. 9th June 2016

emigration. Undocumented migration from Ecuador to the United States has meant making a dreadful journey and bearing the latent threat of perhaps being incarcerated, deported, abused, kidnapped, or even killed. Against open unprotection, faith and religiosity have come to be sources of hope, reassurance, and protection for the migrant passage (Hagan 2008). That is why prayers to coyotes requesting their care or thanking them for arriving alive to the United States are remarkably common. To the extent that stories of successful crossings have been accumulated in Ecuadorean migrant memory, coyotes have turned into protectors. This confirms what the priest

FIGURE 15.3. Gratitude altarpieces for the Lord of Andacocha. The temple of the Lord of Andacocha is located in Guachapala, Azuay, Ecuador. Photo by author

*Thankfulness to the Lord of the miracles of Andacocha
for my journey to the EE.UU.
Your devotees,
Family Tacuro Morocho*

of Andacocha said: beyond being merely a problematic figure associated with an illegal act, coyotes need to be understood as guides, enablers, and protectors of migrants.

During Ecuador's so-called second migratory wave (1996–2006), the domestic mode of migrant smuggling changed. The new millennium's socioeconomic and political crisis triggered a second massive migration to the United States and European destinations, mainly Spain and Italy, where Ecuadoreans were not required to have a Schengen visa (Acosta, López, and Villamar 2006). Because of this, coyotes were not as important figures as *chulqueros* (usurious money lenders). As Kyle and Rachel Goldstein (2011: 5) describe, during this migratory wave—under a scheme that required a high level of trust and loyalty among those involved—a local *tramitador* (middleman) would connect the migrant with a chulquero, who provided travel funds (between US$6,000 and $10,000)[5] under usurious interest rates, while the migrant's land, animals, and possessions were held as guarantee. This scheme remained popular until 2003 when the European Union imposed tourist visa requirements for Ecuadoreans, deaccelerating this migratory flow (Herrera, Moncayo, and Escobar 2012).

Just as Ecuadoreans have historically resorted to smuggling networks to reach the United States, the same is true for international migrants using Ecuador as a transit country. During fieldwork, oral accounts from local actors made it clear to me that the historical configuration of the international mode of migrant smuggling goes back over four decades. The testimony of Norberto, a sixty-three-year-old man I met in Tulcán (a town at the Ecuadorean-Colombian border), provides a clear example: "I have been working as a taxi driver for more than 30 years. I know this border. I have seen people from China, Africa, and the Middle East during these years. They do not stay; they move on. I have also known Ecuadoreans that have left. Some in their third or fourth attempt. All of them, foreigners and nationals, heading to the US."

Norberto's perceptions were consistent with journalistic investigations that suggested that extracontinental migrants (overall from the Middle East and Africa) have reached the United States via clandestine pathways through Ecuador, facilitated by smugglers since at least the 1970s (Santos 2004). Ecuador's geographic position on the South American continent, the existence of local smuggling networks, and scarce control explain its historical role as a strategic crossing point on transcontinental routes. While conducting press review, I identified an illustrative case of an Iranian smuggling network that, during the 1990s, smuggled migrants from Jordan, Iraq, Palestine, and Egypt to the United States via Ecuador. In 2003, the leader of that network was apprehended and went to trial in the United States. During that legal procedure, the US Citizenship and Immigration Services gave evidence that at least from the late 1970s, Ecuador had been a "mecca of illegal migration" where smuggling networks operated virtually without any control (Arrillaga and Rodríguez 2005; Santos 2004). When reviewing declassified archives of national security information from the US Central Intelligence Agency from the 1970s and approved for release in 2013, I also confirmed that Ecuador has long been considered a "source of illegal migration" directed to the United States (CIA 2013). All this evidence confirms that international migrants have historically transited through Ecuador to the United States assisted by smuggling networks.

NEW DEVELOPMENTS IN THE TWO MODES OF MIGRANT SMUGGLING IN ECUADOR

Since the 2000s, structural violence produced by wars, political and religious conflicts, and the deepening of poverty and inequality across the globe have encouraged the movement of people searching for safe places to recommence their life projects (Castles, De Haas, and Miller 2014). Yet insofar as people coming from poor or conflict-affected countries have set themselves into motion, barriers to enter the United States and the European Union (EU)—the most highly desired migratory destinations worldwide—have greatly increased. These global conditionalities have reshaped global migratory patterns to the point that South American countries have acquired multiple migratory conditions: as sending, receiving, and transit countries (IOM 2019).

As an example of this phenomenon, Ecuador continues to be a migrant-sending country while being a receiver of worldwide migrants, refugees, and asylum seekers. The country also receives voluntarily returned Ecuadorean migrants, as well as Ecuadorean deportees, and in the past years, it has become increasingly recognized as a space of transit used both by Ecuadorean deportees who restart their journeys northward and by international migrants to reach other destinations (IOM 2019).

A confluence of global and national conditions explains these changes. On the one hand, systemic inequality, wartime conflicts, ecological devastation, and fortressed U.S. and Europe converge to explain the diversions of extracontinental and Caribbean migrations, mainly from Cuba, Haiti, and the Dominican Republic to South America (De Haas, Miller, and Castles 2021). On the other, at a national level, Ecuador's dollarized economy and its progressive open-border constitution attracted regional and extracontinental migratory flows. Consistent with its migratory history but then buoyed by a "post-neoliberal" leftist new regime in 2008 (Acosta 2010), Ecuador embraced one of the most progressive constitutions concerning migratory matters, which includes the principles of "universal citizenship," "free mobility," "equality between foreigners and nationals," and its commitment to safeguarding "the right to seek asylum" (Articles 40, 41, and 416). Likewise, in that same year, a free-visa regime was adopted that granted a tourist visa of up to ninety days to citizens worldwide. It is undeniable that the adoption of this migratory legal frame played a key role in stimulating the arrival of continental and extracontinental flows of migrants who reach the country either to try their luck there or to transit from there to elsewhere (Álvarez Velasco 2020). Amid the new Ecuadorean migratory pattern, the two traditional modes of migrant smuggling have therefore experienced modifications and new routes and dynamics have emerged (see Figure 15.4).

THE DOMESTIC MODE OF MIGRANT SMUGGLING: ECUADOR AS A COUNTRY OF ORIGIN OF MIGRANT SMUGGLING NETWORKS

At present, 71 percent of people dwelling in rural areas are poor (INEC 2019). Because of this, emigration, mainly from impoverished rural zones, has persisted, mostly directed to the United States via coyotes. That explains why between 2007 and 2016, the number of Ecuadoreans residing in that country increased from ~533,000 to ~738,000 (Noe-Bustamante, Flores, and Shah

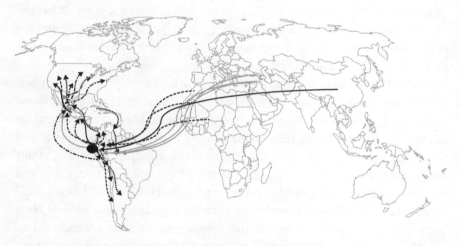

FIGURE 15.4. Ecuadorean and international migrant smuggling routes from and through Ecuador. Ruiz and Álvarez Velasco 2019

2019). In the past two decades, Ecuadorean coyoterismo has undergone three major changes: (1) in who resorts to coyotes to reach the United States, (2) in the migratory strategies, and (3) in the costs and risks associated with these new strategies. Three tiers reflect diversity in terms of the social profile of those who resort to coyotes. From the early 2000s to the present, mostly young parents and their children have been the clients of coyoterismo (Ruiz and Álvarez Velasco 2019). According to Ecuador's latest census, 37 percent of those Ecuadoreans who immigrated to the United States left their children with close relatives. Data from the Observatory on the Rights of Children and Adolescents demonstrate that 2 percent (~200,000) of Ecuadorean children and adolescents have one or two of their parents living abroad (ODNA 2012). Up to now, in the United States, no legislation allows for family reunification schemes when migrant parents are undocumented. Hence, the only possible mechanism to bring about reunifications of Ecuadorean undocumented migrant parents with their children is via coyoterismo (Álvarez Velasco and Guillot 2012). This implies paying coyotes considerable sums of money: between US$15,000 and $25,000 to transport Ecuadorean minors to the United States, a journey on which they are likely to encounter various degrees of violence, as explain later.

Ecuadorean deportees are among those who at present also resort to coyotes. In the past decade, deportation has come to be a form of "post-entry social control" that mainly targets Latin American and Caribbean undocumented male migrants (Kanstroom 2012). Ecuadoreans have been part of that target: between 2012 and 2016, approximately 1,500 Ecuadoreans were deported from the United States per year, positioning Ecuador among the ten principal countries of origin of deportees (ICE 2016). Yet "deportation is not the final word" (De Genova 2017: 253) o: in many cases, deportees restart their irregularized mobilities to the United States. Felix (thirty-eight years old) and Andrés (twenty-nine years old) both were deported from the United States to Ecuador and were among my interlocutors during fieldwork. The former lived in Ecuador for two decades, the second for one decade. Felix said, "When the judge gave the sentence, it was the beginning of a horrible moment. I had never felt before the weight of being shackled. It is tremendous. Returning to the US will be the only way to forget all this.... Almost 20 years ago I got there *con guía* [with *coyote*]. This time, I will do the same." Andrés said, "The menace of deportation was always present.

Experiencing it was true shock: I felt as if I were a thug. But, from the moment I was detained, I said to myself: I have to recover my life and return to the U.S. . . . Maybe I will pay or maybe I will leave without anyone's guidance, except mine. I guess I am able to guide myself." In their reflections, their desire to go back to the United States stands out. Like Felix and Andrés, other deportees who were part of my investigation confirmed that enforced returns lead to a restarting of irregularized journeys from Ecuador to the United States either by resorting to coyotes recommended by family or friends or guided by themselves using migratory knowledge shared within the migrant community or obtained in the digital space (mainly Facebook, Google, or WhatsApp) on the road ahead.

In addition to the changes in who resorts to coyotes, new strategies have been developed. Today a "relay race" strategy has emerged for defying reinforced border control. Ecuadorean coyotes have been incorporated into broader transnational smuggling networks operated via digital communications. They have turned into local brokers of those networks responsible for Ecuadorean migrants only along one stretch of the route: from Ecuador to Peru, Ecuador to Colombia, Ecuador to Bolivia, or even Ecuador to Mexico. From there on, responsibility shifts to Mexican or Central American coyotes. Via mobile phones, Ecuadorean coyotes are connected with those foreigner coyotes along the route. They exchange information and coordinate payments via Western Union or MoneyGram (Stone-Cadena and Álvarez Velasco 2018). According to local testimonies, with this new modality Ecuadorean coyotes lose control of what happens in the later stretches of the route, and Ecuadorean migrants and their families do not know who the international coyotes are. For them, coyotes have turned anonymous or become "coyotes without a face," as local people told to me. This means that Ecuadorean coyotes' traditional roles as guiders and caregivers along the whole route are being called into question: When Ecuadorean migrants face violence, disappear, or die, who can be held responsible?

Regarding the costs and risks along the clandestine Ecuador–Central America–Mexico–US route, it is likewise possible to identify certain modifications. Since the mid-2000s, Ecuadoreans have flown to Central American countries that do not require visas and continued their irregularized crossings by land to Mexico and then to the United States. Depending on the contingencies of the route, it can take approximately one to three months to reach the United States. Coyotes allow for three attempts to get to the United States, and the total cost of the journey includes transport services, food, accommodations, fake documents, and bribes for local authorities in the countries to be crossed (Calderón 2007).[6]

Confronting complex forms of violence is now a constant in the irregularized journeys from Ecuador to the United States. In the same way that Central American migrants face violence along the Mexico–US corridor, Ecuadorean migrants, adults and children, are likely to encounter some type of violence along the route, which can range from assault, kidnapping, accident, rape, and disappearance to the death of migrants. These forms of violence can be perpetrated with varying levels of intensity and in diverse ways by corrupt border agents, thieves, members of drug cartels, gangs, ordinary people, or even the same coyotes. Yet usually no responsibility is assigned, nor any legal process carried out against the perpetrators (Álvarez Velasco 2016).

While I was concluding my fieldwork in 2018, a major change regarding the mechanisms to control mobility took place that immediately affected Ecuadorean coyoterismo. On November 29, 2018, Mexico's secretary of foreign affairs withdrew the requirement to obtain a ninety-day tourist visa for Ecuadorean citizens before their arrival to Mexico (Mexican Secretary of Foreign Affairs 2018). One of the main historical barriers to reaching the Mexico–US corridor was eliminated; Ecuadoreans with a valid passport can now fly directly to Mexico. Since Mexico withdrew the tourist visa requirement for Ecuadoreans, empirical findings confirm that Ecuadoreans have been departing to Mexico, including adults, children, and Ecuadorean deportees. According to recent journalistic reports (*El Telégrafo* 2019), as well as empirical data gathered from the Austral region, the withdrawal of Mexico's visa requirement modified migrant smuggling strategies. On the one hand, the Ecuador–Mexico land route was substituted by a direct air flight to Mexico. This means that Ecuadoreans did not need to hire coyotes to traverse the land route to reach Mexico. Ecuadorean coyotes' role as brokers within transnational smuggling networks was accentuated, and they charged for guaranteeing the connection between Ecuadorean migrants and Mexican coyotes who serve as guides to traverse the Mexican-US border. On the other hand, the traditional role of chulqueros as money providers become more prominent. Local actors suggested that these changes led to complex forms of extortion and arbitrary taxations of interest for the borrowing and lending of cash, which might provoke scams and the exacerbation of power conflicts between chulqueros and migrants or their families.

The withdrawal of visa requirements to enter Mexico also meant that Ecuadoreans, children and adults, are at less risk of violence. As Zoila, a fifty-five-year-old Ecuadorean and former intermediary who used to work within a local smuggling network, mentioned, "The news has been very well received because the risk of crossing goes completely down. The same is true for our fears and our anxiety about moving from here to Mexico. But, the major problem is still there: migrants have to cross the Mexican border to enter the US, and that is tough, let me tell you it is not a joke. That is why coyotes are still needed."

The withdrawal of the Mexican visa accelerated the exit of Ecuadoreans, which reached a peak during the pandemic years. Ecuador, like the rest of Latin America, was deeply impacted by the pandemic. Faced with the convergence of health and economic crises and the collapse of the Andean country's social protection system, the departure of thousands of Ecuadorian families to the United States via Mexico multiplied. Between January and August 2021, out of the ~112,000 Ecuadoreans who traveled to Mexico, ~70,000 did not return to the country (El Comercio, 2021). In other words, as confirmed by Mexican authorities, between 2020 and 2021, only one out of every three Ecuadoreans who flew to Mexico did so for tourism purposes, the rest continued to the United States (España and Varela 2021). To curb the massive arrival of Ecuadoreans to the United States, and as an effect of the reinforcement of the externalization of the US border on the continent, on August 24, 2021, Mexico reimposed visas for Ecuador (El Comercio, 2021). Thus, the period between 2018 and 2021, when Mexico withdrew the visa requirement, was a time when the dynamics of coyoterismo changed and at the same time many Ecuadoreans and entire families emigrated to the United States. Since 2021, new migratory routes have been opened, such as the crossing through the Darien jungle, between Panama and Colombia (Oquendo, 2023), while maintaining the traditional exit by land or via Central American countries, always with the guidance of coyotes.

ECUADOR AS A TRANSIT COUNTRY OF SMUGGLING NETWORKS USED BY INTERNATIONAL MIGRANTS

The international mode of migrant smuggling, which involves the departure of continental and extracontinental migrants from Ecuador to northern and southern continental destinations with the aid of coyotes, has to be understood in the light of recent changes in Ecuadorean migratory policies. As mentioned before, Ecuador's constitutional principles of "free mobility," "right to refuge," "universal citizenship," and an "open border policy" provoked a powerful "calling effect" among worldwide migrants and refugees. Some of them arrive with the aim of staying in Ecuador, others with the intention of transiting to other continental destinations, mostly the United States, and guided by coyotes.

Fieldwork findings revealed that international migrants departing from Ecuador to elsewhere resort to coyotes under three different schemes. In the first, Ecuador is a stepping-stone within larger transnational routes. Taking advantage of Ecuador's progressive migratory policies, international migrants enter the country by air routes and regularized paths. On arrival, they obtain a ninety-day tourist visa, and once in Ecuador they depart almost immediately by either land or air, sometimes with the use of forged documents. International coyotes residing in Ecuador are usually in control of these movements. Migrants are charged a minimum of US$20,000. This scheme is common among Chinese, Indian, Nepalese, Cameroonian, and Senegalese migrants en route to the United States (Mena Erazo 2010; Wells 2013). In an example of how this first scheme operates, police investigations confirmed the operation of an international migrant smuggling network coordinated by a Pakistani coyote residing in Ecuador. This was its modus operandi: Pakistani and Indian migrants traveled from their home countries to Ecuador by plane via Brazil. On arrival, a coyote waited for them at Quito's airport and took them to a waiting house near the airport. After a couple of weeks, migrants departed by land to Colombia to continue their journey up north. In 2017, this network was disarticulated (*El Telégrafo* 2017).

In the second scheme, international migrants enter Ecuador via regularized paths (with a ninety-day tourist visa) but, unlike in the previous scheme, they stay for a while in Ecuador. It is during their stay that they contact coyotes who can facilitate their journeys via clandestine paths mostly to the United States, but also to South American destinations. This is the case of Haitians en route to the Mexico–US corridor with the guidance of coyotes or who use the Ecuador–Peru–Chile route; of Dominicans using the Ecuador–Peru–Chile route; or of African migrants en route from Ecuador to the United States or to Argentina, as in the case of Nigerians or Senegalese. Depending on the destination, migrants pay from US$500 to $5,000 (Bernal 2014; Correa 2014). This second scheme can also be applied for cases where migrants reached Ecuador with the intention of residing there but, while their migratory experience unfolded, they opted to depart to other destinations due to inconsistencies between their migratory expectations and everyday life in Ecuador. The experience of Mustafa, a thirty-five-year-old Sudanese migrant who departed from Ecuador to the United States, is a clear case in point:

> I was persecuted in Sudan. I was able to enter Ecuador without problems. But I could not regularize myself. I did not meet the conditions. Not having papers has been very hard. I work in a poultry shop, peeling chickens. I earn less than 100 USD a month. It's not enough for me. My cousin, who lives in the U.S., has lent me money and I am going to Peru, from there I will pay to go up [migrate to the United States]. I do not have a choice anymore; I cannot stay here [Ecuador].

Like Mustafa, many other international migrants have chosen to leave the country because the Ecuadorean migratory dream in one way or another ended up tricking them. Inconsistencies between Ecuador's progressive constitution and permanent setbacks in migration policies, together with unbearable precariousness within the Ecuadorean dollarized economy, constant racism, and xenophobia, have ended up speeding international migrants' decisions to migrate again, mostly to the United States with the aid of coyotes, as in Mustafa's case, or to other destinations on the South American continent such as Peru, Chile, or Brazil (Álvarez Velasco 2020).

In the third scheme, international migrants enter undocumented, via irregularized paths, to the Andean country to reach other destinations. While dwelling irregularly in Ecuador, they contact local coyotes to continue their clandestine journeys. This modality applies for several cases, such as Cubans, who, after the 2015 reimposition of visa requirements, have entered Ecuador following the clandestine route Cuba–Guyana–Brazil–Peru–Ecuador, and from there they have hired coyotes to continue their route to the United States. It is also the case of African migrants who arrive to Ecuador via irregularized paths, usually after entering the continent via Brazil. Once they get to Ecuador, they hire local coyotes to reach Peru or Colombia with the intention of moving from there to other continental destinations, such as Chile, Argentina, or the United States. More recently, the Venezuelan case also illustrates the third scheme.

Since 2015, due to the Venezuelan political and economic crisis, some seven million Venezuelans have fled from their country to several destinations on the American continent and abroad (R4V, 2023). Between 2015 and 2019, Ecuador received around 350,000 Venezuelans. Data from the Ministry of Interior (2019) assert that around 3,000 Venezuelans traverse Ecuadorean borders on a daily basis. Against this massive and continual arrival of Venezuelans, Ecuador adopted strict control measures: in August 2018, the government implemented the requirement of a valid passport for Venezuelan citizens who want to enter Ecuador (Ministry of Interior 2019). At present, meeting this requirement is impossible for Venezuelans, particularly for impoverished migrants. According to Ecuadorean authorities, this measure was adopted to regulate the entrance of Venezuelans and also supposedly diminish the risk that Venezuelans would be trapped by migrant smuggling networks (*El Comercio* 2018). This measure has, paradoxically, increased the use of coyotes to traverse Ecuador's northern border. As Rigoberto, a twenty-eight-year-old Venezuelan undocumented migrant, explained to me, "There are no passports in my country. We are in a state of war, and we do not have any means to get a passport. Simply we cannot have a passport. If we want to save ourselves, we have to move out of the country, even if we have to enter Colombia or Ecuador *por trocha* (via irregularized paths)."

According to fieldwork findings, Venezuelans pay between US$20 and $50 to coyotes to traverse Ecuador's northern border. Those coyotes are usually Venezuelan migrants who have already crossed the border or who put them in contact with local coyotes. Once in Ecuador, it is known that Venezuelans also embark on irregularized movements to reach Peru or Chile, or even pay US$2,000 to $4,000 to local coyotes to reach Belize, as part of a larger mobility project to later reach the United States.

Just as Ecuadorean deportees resort to digital information to autonomously emigrate from Ecuador to the United States, international migrants also resort to digital social networks to gather information. Fieldwork findings confirmed that in many cases international migrants increasingly depart guided by their own migratory knowledge gathered from other migrants or sourced from the internet. These new irregularized transits from and through Ecuador are highlighted globally as a creative combination of autonomous movements and the contracting of coyotes' services. No matter whether they resort to coyotes or not, international migrants also confront violence en route (Vogt, 2017). The forms of social and state violence that occur on the Ecuador–Mexico–US route, previously described, also impact international migrants who cross borders. Hence, violence is another common feature between both modes of migrant smuggling that take place in contemporary Ecuador.

CONCLUSIONS

I have analyzed how both the domestic and international modes of migrant smuggling are evolving social processes embedded in Ecuadorean social formation, reflecting its long migratory history. Irregularized transits of both Ecuadoreans and international migrants toward the United States are not a recent development within Ecuador's migratory pattern. Due to the dependent structural character of Ecuador's economy, since colonial times, diverse "connecting factors" have articulated Ecuador with the world system, and since at least the end of the 1960s, one of these factors has been undocumented labor power, embodied in undocumented migration. It thus makes sense to conceive of Ecuador as an articulating "node in the world system" (Heyman 2004), whereby Ecuadoreans and international migrants have been coming and going to the United States, while profitable smuggling networks have established a long-standing social process of cultural, social, and economic relationships to facilitate and augment irregularized transit.

For this, as I have argued, coyotes have been and still are key enablers, or play a key agentic role within transnational mobilities. Were it not for coyoterismo, the spatial shaping of Ecuador as a global space of transit would have hardly taken place. This is because coyoterismo is a nodal element of Ecuador's migratory history and culture. It is a historical, ever-changing, socioeconomic, and cultural process that derives from systemic inequality while being at the same time a direct outcome of deficient national policies and the reinforced global border regime. Coyoterismo is not alien to uneven geographical development, nor to the current neoliberal border regime, and even less to Ecuadorean national dynamics. Coyoterismo is a direct outcome of these processes.

The convergence of global dynamics and local contexts affects the contemporary modifications of both modes of migrant smuggling. The violence of poverty, wars, and religious and political conflicts, together with the fortress Europe policy and the battle against undocumented migrants via the US deportation regime, has had reverberations across both modes of migrant smuggling and in the new migratory patterns currently found in Ecuador. Ecuador has a five-decade history of undocumented migration to the United States, a process that has often entailed detention, deportation, and the restarting of migratory journeys northward.

This analysis has also allowed me to explain how the externalization of the US border regime southward has not halted mobility but rather provoked other forms of irregularized transit via smuggling networks (Kyle and Koslowski 2011). Understanding the historicity of Ecuador as a global space of transit also critically underscores how, during recent decades, the United States has subtly externalized remote control practices southward, a mechanism that has directly affected Ecuadorean migration, confining it to irregularized mobilities.

Scrutinizing the historicity of Ecuador's transit condition is crucial, for it adds analytical elements necessary to understand its present condition within the new geography of transit migration and transit states. The production of undocumented migrants in Ecuador and the expulsion of their nationals via irregularized transit feed a systemic attempt to control mobility configured between the intimate relation between irregularized transits, deportation, and migrant smuggling. Both modes of human smuggling are integral to the Ecuadorean formation of migratory patterns over four decades. Undocumented migration and the various strategies it creates and deploys, such as resorting to coyotes, are in permanent transformation. Their contiguous character, as this chapter confirms, is incessant. Hence, future research should not rule out an in-depth analysis of possible interlinkages between the domestic mode and the international mode of migrant smuggling taking place in Ecuador, particularly in a global context that is increasingly hostile to migration. A clear example of how both modes are constantly transforming derives from the undeniable impact of technology. Currently both Ecuadorean migrants (including deportees) and international migrants increasingly resort to the digital to undertake irregularized journeys, either guided by coyotes or with the migrants themselves serving as their own guides or guides for other migrants.

Because of all this, it can be stated that coyoterismo, as I have shown, has changed throughout the past several decades. The production of interdisciplinary research information on both modes of migrant smuggling taking place from and through Ecuador can improve understandings that extend beyond a simplistic criminalist approach. Producing original studies based on a migrant-centric perspective could well contribute to the assumption that both Ecuadorean and international migrants are active decision-making subjects and not simply passive victims, and to expand the social, historical, cultural, and political comprehension of both modes of migrant smuggling. This means inquiring about migrant subjectivity, including that of children and adolescents, but also understanding who is a coyote or chulquero, beyond the criminal tags, and their social, economic, and political roles in local communities. The complex figure of the coyote obliges us to adopt a historical and critical gaze to comprehend its intimate nexus with migration. It is time to discard and surpass the hegemonic approach that mainly and simplistically conceives coyoterismo as a criminal practice within a binary yet inexistent world of "criminals" and "good" people.

NOTES

I gratefully acknowledge the work of Oswaldo Suin as a research assistant during fieldwork conducted between January and September 2019.

1. Drawing on critical migration scholars who appeal for an understanding of the social and political processes that render certain types of mobility "irregularized," I use the term *irregularized* and not *irregular*. To these scholars, the term *illegalised* or *irregularised* accurately brings attention to the social, political, and juridical conditionalities that have produced migrants as "illegalized" or "irregularized" subjects (see De Genova 2002).
2. I use the term *international migrants* to refer to regional and extracontinental migrants who have reached Ecuador and who depart from there to elsewhere with the aid of smuggling networks. Using this term also allows me to distinguish them

from Ecuadorean migrants who also resort to those networks, though they do it with their own specificities and own dynamics, as I describe later.
3. This project was my doctoral research (Álvarez Velasco 2019).
4. "Ir por la chacra," "por el camino," and "por la pampa" are common expressions colloquially used to name the irregularized route from Ecuador to the United States.
5. The money provided by a *chulquero* is locally known as *bolsa de viaje*.
6. Between the mid-1990s and early 2000s, coyotes offered a sea journey from Ecuador to Guatemala by boat, and afterward by land. However, it turned tremendously dangerous, causing countless deaths at sea, and was mostly supplanted by the air route (Calderón 2007).

REFERENCES

Acosta, A., S. M. L. O. López, and D. Villamar. 2006. *La migración en el Ecuador: Oportunidades y amenazas*. Quito: Centro Andino de Estudios Internacionales, Universidad Andina Simón Bolívar.

Acosta, A. 2010. *El Buen Vivir en el camino del post-desarrollo: Una lectura desde la Constitución de Montecristi*. Vol. 9. Quito: Friedrich-Ebert-Stiftung-ILDIS.

Álvarez Velasco, S. 2016. *Frontera Sur Chiapaneca: El Muro Humano de la violencia*. México: CIESAS-UIA.

———. 2019. "Trespassing the Visible: The Production of Ecuador as a Global Space of Transit for Irregularized Migrants Moving towards the Mexico-U.S. Corridor." PhD diss., King's College London, June.

———. 2020. "From Ecuador to Elsewhere: The (Re)configuration of a Transit Country." *Migration and Society* 3 (1): 34–49.

Álvarez Velasco, S., and S. Guillot. 2012. *Entre la violencia y la invisibilidad: Un análisis de la situación de los niños, niñas y adolescentes ecuatorianos no acompañados en el proceso de migración hacia Estados Unidos*. Quito: Gobierno Nacional de la República del Ecuador, Secretaría Nacional del Migrante.

Arrillaga, P., and O. R. Rodríguez. 2005. "The Terror Immigration Connection." NBC News, March 7, 2005. http://www.nbcnews.com/id/8408009/ns/us_news-security/t/terror-immigration-connection/#.W_gLMi2ZP2X.

Bernal, G. 2014. "La migración haitiana hacia Brasil: Ecuador, país de tránsito." In *La migración haitiana hacia Brasil: Características, oportunidades y desafíos*, Cuaderno Migratorios No. 6, 33–51. Buenos Aires: Organización Internacional para las Migraciones.

Calderón, J. C. 2007. *Naufragio: Migración y muerte en el Pacífico*. Quito: Paradiso Editores.

Castles, S., H. De Haas, and M. J. Miller. 2014. *The Age of Migration: International Population Movements in the Modern World*. 5th ed. New York: Guilford.

CIA (Central Intelligence Agency). 2013. National Security Information. Unauthorized Disclosure Subject to Criminal Sanctions. Approved for release April 29, 2013. https://www.cia.gov/readingroom/docs/CIA-RDP79T00912A001900010018-0.pdf.

Correa, A. 2014. *Del Caribe a la mitad del mundo: Migración cubana en Ecuador*. Quito: Abya-Yala.

De Genova, N. 2002. "Migrant 'Illegality' and Deportability in Everyday Life." *Annual Review of Anthropology* 31:419–447.

———. 2017. "The Incorrigible Subject: Mobilizing a Critical Geography of (Latin) America through the Autonomy of Migration." *Journal of Latin American Geography* 16 (1): 17–42.

De Haas, Hein, Mark Miller, and Stephen Castles. 2020. *The Age of Migration: International Population Movements in the Modern World*. New York: Guildford Press.

El Comercio. 2018. "Redes criminales atacan a venezolanos." March 11. https://www.elcomercio.com/actualidad/redes-criminales-atacan-venezolanos.html.

El Telégrafo. 2017. "Policía desarticuló red que traficaba con migrantes de Pakistán e India." March 25. https://www.eltelegrafo.com.ec/noticias/judicial/1/policia-desarticulo-red-que-traficaba-con-migrantes-de-pakistan-e-india.

———. 2019. "Los viajes hacia México crecieron en diciembre." https://www.eltelegrafo.com.ec/noticias/economia/4/viajes-ecuador-mexico-incremento-diciembre.

España, S. and M. Varela. 2021. "México reinstaura la visa de entrada para ecuatorianos ante una nueva oleada Migratoria." *Diario El PAIS*. August 24. https://elpais.com/internacional/2021-08-24/mexico-reinstaura-la-visa-de-entrada-para-ecuatorianos-ante-una-nueva-oleada-migratoria.html.

González, J. 2021. "El 76% de los ecuatorianos que viajó a México en 2021 salió desde Quito." September 21. *Diario El Comercio*. https://www.elcomercio.com/actualidad/politica/ecuatorianos-vuelos-mexico-migracion-quito.html.

Hagan, J. M. 2008. *Migration Miracle: Faith, Hope, and Meaning on the Undocumented Journey*. Cambridge, MA: Harvard University Press.

Herrera, G., and G. Cabezas. 2019. "Ecuador: De la recepción a la disuasión: Políticas frente a la población venezolana y experiencia migratoria 2015–2018." In *Crisis y migración de población venezolana: Entre la desprotección y la seguridad jurídica en Latinoamérica*, edited by L. Gandini, F. Lozano Ascencio, and V. Prieto, 125–157. Mexico City: Universidad Nacional Autónoma de México.

Herrera, G., M. I. Moncayo, and A. Escobar. 2012. *Perfil migratorio del Ecuador 2011*. Quito: Organización Internacional para las Migraciones.

Heyman, J. M. 2004. "Ports of Entry as Nodes in the World System." *Identities: Global Studies in Culture and Power* 11:303–327.

ICE (Immigration and Customs Enforcement). 2016. *Fiscal Year 2016 ICE Enforcement and Removal Operations Report*. https://www.ice.gov/sites/default/files/documents/Report/2016/removal-stats-2016.pdf.

INEC (Instituto Nacional de Estadísticas y Censos). 2019. "Ecuador en Cifras." https://www.ecuadorencifras.gob.ec/documentos/web-inec/POBREZA/2019/Diciembre-2019/Boletin%20tecnico%20de%20pobreza%20diciembre%202019_d.pdf.

IOM (International Organization for Migration). 2019. *World Migration Report 2020*. Geneva: IOM. https://publications.iom.int/system/files/pdf/wmr_2020.pdf.

Kanstroom, D. 2012. *Aftermath: Deportation Law and the New American Diaspora*. Oxford: Oxford University Press.

Kyle, D. 2000. *Transnational Peasants: Migrations, Networks, and Ethnicity in Andean Ecuador*. Baltimore: Johns Hopkins University Press.

Kyle, D. J., and R. Goldstein. 2011. *Migration Industries: A Comparison of the Ecuador-US and Ecuador-Spain Cases*. Florence: Robert Schuman Centre for Advanced Studies, European University Institute.

Kyle, D., and R. Koslowski, eds. 2011. *Global Human Smuggling: Comparative Perspectives*. 2nd ed. Baltimore: Johns Hopkins University Press.

Mena Erazo, P. 2010. "Ecuador pedirá visa a ciudadanos de nueve países de Asia y África." BBC Mundo, September 10, 2010. http://www.bbc.com/mundo/america_latina/2010/09/100907_ecuador_inmigrantes_africa_asia_visa_rg.shtml.

Mexican Secretary of Foreign Affairs. 2018. "Avisos Embajada de Mexico en Ecuador." https://embamex.sre.gob.mx/ecuador/index.php/avisos/402-1-mexico-suprime-el-requisito-de-visa-en-pasaportes-ordinarios-a-los-nacionales-de-ecuador.

Ministry of Interior. 2019. "Ministerio del Interior aclara situación sobre ingreso de extranjeros al Ecuador." https://www.ministeriodegobierno.gob.ec/comunicado-3/.

Noe-Bustamante, L., A. Flores, and S. Shah. 2019. "Facts on Hispanics of Ecuadorian Origin in the United States, 2017." Pew Research Center, September 16, 2019. https://www.pewresearch.org/hispanic/fact-sheet/u-s-hispanics-facts-on-ecuadorian-origin-latinos/.

ODNA (Observatorio de la Niñez y Adolescencia de Ecuador). 2012. *Los niños y niñas del Ecuador a inicios del siglo XXI: Una aproximación a partir de la primera encuesta nacional de la niñez y adolescencia de la sociedad civil*. Quito: ODNA.

Oquendo, C. 2023. "El alarmante incremento de migrantes ecuatorianos cruzando por el Darién." *El País*, January 13. https://elpais.com/america-colombia/2023-01-13/el-alarmante-incremento-de-migrantes-ecuatorianos-cruzando-por-el-darien.html.

Peutz, N., and N. De Genova. 2010. Introduction to *The Deportation Regime: Sovereignty, Space, and the Freedom of Movement*, edited by N. De Genova and N. Peutz, 1-33. Durham, NC: Duke University Press.

R4V Regional Interagency Coordination Platform for Refugees and Migrants of Venezuela. 2023. "Refugees and Migrants from Venezuela." https://www.r4v.info/en/refugeeandmigrants.

Ruiz, M. C., and S. Álvarez Velasco. 2019. "Excluir para proteger: La 'guerra' contra la trata y el tráfico de migrantes y las nuevas lógicas de control migratorio en Ecuador." *Revista Estudios Sociológicos* 37 (111). http://dx.doi.org/10.24201/es.2019v37n111.1686.

Santos, T. 2004. "Ecuador, base de red internacional de coyotaje." *El Universo*, February 15, 2004.

Stone-Cadena, V., and S. Álvarez Velasco. 2018. "Historicizing Mobility: *Coyoterismo* in the Indigenous Ecuadorian Migration Industry." *ANNALS of the American Academy of Political and Social Science* 676 (1): 194–211. http://journals.sagepub.com/doi/abs/10.1177/0002716217752333.

Velasco, F. 1972. *Ecuador, subdesarrollo y dependencia*. Quito, Editorial El Conejo.

Velázquez Flores, R., and J. A. Schiavon. 2006. "El 11 de septiembre y la relación México Estados Unidos: ¿Hacia la securitización de la agenda?" *Revista Enfoques: Ciencia Política y Administración Pública* 6 (8): 61–85.

Wells, M. 2013. "Ecuador Breaks Up Nepalese Human Smuggling Ring." InSight Crime, October 11, 2013. http://www.insightcrime.org/news-briefs/ecuador-busts-nepalese-human-smuggling-network.

World Bank. 2011. *Migration and Remittances Factbook 2011*. Washington, DC: Migration and Remittances Unit, World Bank. http://go.worldbank.org/QGUCPJTOR0.

Vogt, W. 2017. "The Arterial Border: Negotiating Economies of Risk and Violence in Mexico's Security Regime." *International Journal of Migration and Border Studies* 3 (2-3): 192–207.

CHAPTER 16

Combatting People Smuggling with the Same Crime?

AUSTRALIA'S "CREATIVE" ANTI-SMUGGLING EFFORTS IN INDONESIA

Antje Missbach and Wayne Palmer

It is not yet unlawful to move or to migrate, or to seek asylum, even if the criminalisation of "irregular emigration" by sending states seems to be desired by the developed world. (Goodwin-Gill 2011)

In the first two decades of this century, Australia has sought to deter any potential maritime asylum seekers long before they reach the Australian border (Missbach and Hoffstaedter 2020; Watkins 2017). In the mid-1970s, when Vietnamese asylum seekers sailed into Darwin Harbor, Australia was a desirable and, to a certain extent, even welcoming destination for refugees arriving by sea (Stevens 2012). The number of asylum seekers arriving in Australia has fluctuated significantly over the last two decades, and their countries of origin have varied migration policies to shield the country from unwanted migrants (Grewcock 2013a). We concentrate our analysis on the disruption and prevention of people-smuggling activities in Indonesia, not only because Indonesia is one of the most important transit countries for maritime asylum seekers en route to Australia but also because Australia has instigated and financed the bulk of anti-people-smuggling activities in

Indonesia (Hirsch 2017). While the majority of Australia's anti-people-smuggling efforts are legally sound, there are policies that border on illegality, as our case study here illustrates. By this we mean that such efforts may not violate an explicit law (Klein 2014), but they may violate the spirit of the law, which refers to the actual intentions of the lawmakers, who, at the time of drafting the law, did not intend to discriminate against asylum seekers on boats.[1]

Whereas much of the literature regarding people smuggling focuses on the role of the state as an inhibitor of irregular migration and mobility (e.g., Kyle and Koslowski 2001; Weber and Bowling 2004), the possibility of states as smugglers is rarely discussed (Grewcock 2013b). This omission is noteworthy, given that the state has been studied from rather critical perspectives in the social sciences. For example, there are many well-documented examples that show how states have intentionally resorted to illegal trade or imports in order to advance their interests and achieve certain political gains (Andreas 2013; Cribb 1991; Jenss 2018). Many law- and policymakers tend to define people smuggling as a crime against the state, because the primary victim is deemed to be the state whose immigration laws are violated (Kyle and Dale 2001; Kyle and Siracusa 2005). This narrow understanding overlooks the possibility of states facilitating illegal border crossings into other states in order to get rid of unwanted migrants. By embedding our analysis in the debate about the state-illegality nexus, we demonstrate that states can also act as smugglers.

This chapter also uses the concept of creativity to further analyze one such case that was both unprecedented and unconventional. Creativity is usually assumed to produce something that is not only new but also of value. While creativity is a highly sought-after talent in people, it would be dangerously naïve to ignore the dark sides of human creativity and inventiveness (Gino and Ariely 2012). We use this starting point to examine an instance in which Australian authorities tested a new border-control practice as part of their broader deterrence objectives. We describe in detail how they returned sixty-five asylum seekers to Indonesia by providing financial, material, and practical support to the Indonesian transporters who had smuggled them out of Indonesia.

The Australian government refuses to provide information that it deems "operationally sensitive," as it might be useful to smugglers (Operation

Sovereign Borders Joint Agency Task Force 2015). Consequently, it is impossible to produce a fully corroborated version of events described in this chapter. For our analysis we have triangulated a range of relevant sources to produce the most accurate narrative of the Australian government's turnback of asylum seekers. An Amnesty International (2015) report provided a detailed nongovernment perspective, which was complemented by the report of an inquiry by the Australian Senate's Legal and Constitutional Affairs References Committee (2016) and documents from the Indonesian courts that eventually convicted the Indonesian boat crew for people smuggling but none of the Australian members of the "anti-people-smuggling" taskforce that returned the asylum seekers to Indonesia. Several interviews with an Indonesian boat captain, during his imprisonment and after his release, provided extra detail about the organizational roles that the Australian authorities played in the interception and turnback.

This chapter is in four parts. First, we provide some insights into Australia's role in combatting people smuggling within the Indo-Pacific region, which reveal the underlying deterrence impetus. Next, we offer a detailed case study of one of Australia's more controversial border management practices, which clearly demonstrates that it is prepared to use potentially unlawful means to deter unwanted asylum seekers. Then, we discuss the legality of those practices, according to Australian and international law, before considering the possible consequences of other countries following suit. In conclusion, we argue that such "creative" approaches to combatting and preventing people smuggling pose a threat to regional cooperation, as they could erode trust in bilateral and multilateral relationships among participating nations.

AUSTRALIA'S ROLE IN COMBATTING PEOPLE SMUGGLING IN THE INDO-PACIFIC

When it comes to anti-people-smuggling activities in Australia and its neighboring countries, in which Australia is known to be involved in externalized border control (Missbach 2015; Watkins 2017), the Australian government shrouds those activities in secrecy (Bevitt 2017). Occasionally, strong allegations of illegal and semilegal direct interference have been made by asylum seekers who have been intercepted by Australian naval and customs officers, but by and large, the general public is left in the dark. Kevin (2012:

61) mentions that the Australian Federal Police and the Indonesian National Police cooperated in disruption campaigns from 1999 to 2001 and again from 2009 to 2011 in order to prevent the departure of asylum seekers' boats from Indonesia by physically sabotaging the vessels. It was not until 2012, when the Indonesian anti-people-smuggling taskforce—primarily financed by the Australian government—started operating, that the Australian Federal Police switched from disruption operations to providing investigative support and intelligence on the people-smuggling networks (Connery, Sambhi, and McKenzie 2014).

Before Tony Abbott won the Australian federal election in 2013, he announced plans he intended to implement during his prime ministership, which were criticized by both Australian and Indonesian observers who doubted the promises' merit, benefit, and effectiveness. For example, Abbott pledged funds to buy old Indonesian fishing boats to reduce the number available for smugglers to transport their clients. Another plan he announced involved Australian intelligence agencies buying information on upcoming unauthorized maritime departures of asylum seekers from Indonesian informants in coastal areas where people smugglers operated. A third proposal was for intercepted boats to be towed back to Indonesia (Missbach 2015: 191–192). Although Indonesian politicians and representatives of government have a genuine interest in securing borders and curtailing irregular migration, they did not welcome Abbott's proposed interventions, which they saw as demeaning and disrespectful of Indonesian sovereignty. While the first two plans were completely abandoned for having unrealistic prospects, the interception of asylum seekers' boats and their forced return became Australia's signature strategy for dealing with maritime asylum seekers.[2] A joint agency taskforce, named Operation Sovereign Borders, was formed in September 2013; it is a military-led interagency border-security initiative that incorporates activities to disrupt and deter people smuggling, including the interception of asylum seekers' boats (Chia, McAdam, and Purcell 2014).

In most cases of forced returns, the Australian navy would escort asylum seekers' boats back to the edges of Indonesian waters with instructions to return to shore.[3] However, in less than three months of the operation, the Australian government had on at least six occasions entered Indonesia's territorial sea, which extends only twelve nautical miles from the coast, thus violating Indonesian sovereignty under international law. In one case, Australian Border Force boats were only three miles from the Indonesian coast (Taylor 2014). Indonesia's minister for foreign affairs, Marty Natalagawa, warned that Australia was on a "slippery slope" in resorting to such unilateral actions, which had already strained relations with Indonesia. Despite strong protests from Jakarta, Australia continued to turn back boats, which not only continued to anger the Indonesian government but could also, as we will argue in this chapter, be seen as tantamount to people smuggling (Saul 2015).

It is generally assumed that only criminal individuals and networks commit transnational organized crimes, such as people smuggling. To show how states employ innovative means in their attempts to secure their borders by using methods that resemble people smuggling, we use the example of the Australian government's turnback of asylum seekers, in which officials bribed Indonesian boat crews to return to Indonesia. In other words, Australia paradoxically attempts to fight people smuggling from Indonesia by paying smugglers to take asylum seekers back to Indonesia. The geographic direction of people smuggling is reversed, as the boat crew and asylum seekers now cross maritime borders to enter Indonesian, instead of Australian, territory. But in this chapter, we argue that the turnback also meets conditions that define people smuggling in legal terms—facilitating the crossing of an international border without the authorization of the state being entered.

FROM INTERCEPTION TO PEOPLE SMUGGLING

On May 5, 2015, an asylum seekers' boat, the *Andika*, set sail from Indonesia's Pelabuhan Ratu on Java's southwest coast (Figure 16.1). On board were sixty-five asylum seekers and six Indonesian transporters, destined for distant New Zealand, over 7,700 kilometers away. Normally, the final destination of asylum seekers' boats is Australia or one of its remote islands, such as Christmas Island, just 350 kilometers from Java but 1,560 kilometers from the Australian mainland. This time, however, the asylum seekers' boat intended to risk the longer and more dangerous journey, largely because the Australian government had restricted access to the shorter and less perilous routes in the eighteen months of Operation Sovereign Borders.

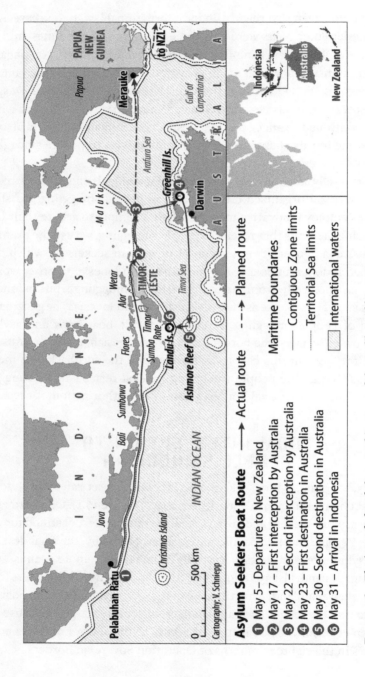

FIGURE 16.1. The intended and the actual journey of the *Andika* and her passengers

On May 17, after the *Andika* had been at sea for almost two weeks, two Australian Border Force vessels intercepted the boat in international waters near Indonesia and Timor Leste's territorial waters.[4] At first, the Indonesian boat crew on board the *Andika* objected to being stopped in international waters so far from Australia, claiming it was an Indonesian-flagged vessel over which the Indonesian government had exclusive jurisdiction as the flag state. If Australian Border Force officers were certain that the *Andika* was an Indonesian boat, the legal way to board would have been for them to request permission from the Indonesian government (United Nations 2000: Article 8(2)). The Australians could have boarded the vessel without permission if the Indonesian government did not "respond expeditiously" (Article 8(4)). Alternatively, the Australian Border Force could have boarded the *Andika* without notifying Indonesia at all if they held a "reasonable suspicion that the vessel has engaged in crime" (Klein 2014: 8). Either way, once they had boarded, six Australian Border Force personnel inspected the *Andika*, took photographs, and, before disembarking, left pamphlets in multiple languages warning the Indonesian crew and asylum seekers that they could not enter Australian territory without a valid visa or complete set of travel documents. The *Andika* then continued on its way to Merauke in Papua, its last scheduled stop in Indonesia, but not alone, as the Australian Border Force followed it for the next five days.

On May 22 an Australian naval ship, HMAS *Wollongong*, stopped the *Andika*. The Australian government reports that the boat was in international waters, so the Australian Border Force could use the same justification for boarding the ship as for the earlier interception. The *Andika*'s captain disputes the claim, however, alleging that the boat was in Indonesian waters at the time (interview with the captain, Yohanis Humiang, February 1, 2019). He used a global positioning system (GPS) to navigate the area that was based on an Indonesian map. On this occasion, the Australian Border Force confiscated the GPS and the maps. Further complicating independent efforts to verify the allegation, the Australian government has not released coordinates, even though there is no other publicly available evidence to support or disprove the claim. However, it is useful to keep in mind previous territorial transgressions "inadvertently" committed by the Australian navy.[5] The Australian Border Force later justified the interception by claiming that it did so out of concern for the safety of the Indonesian crew and asylum seekers. According to the Australian Border Force, adverse weather conditions had been forecast for the area and they doubted that the *Andika* could withstand them—a claim the captain also disputed in later interviews.

On this second interception, the *Andika*'s captain had to accompany the Australians who had boarded his boat onto HMAS *Wollongong* to discuss options for aborting the operation. Through an interpreter, the Australian officers asked the captain to turn the boat around and return to Indonesia (interview with the captain, Yohanis Humiang, August 2, 2016). In response, he explained that it would be very difficult to convince the other crew members to do so. The asylum seekers had paid thousands of dollars for the passage, and the fact that they outnumbered the Indonesian crew made the captain fear for the crew's physical safety. Furthermore, the crew had not yet received any payment and wanted to continue working; they had agreed to a total payment of Rp 100 million (US$6,500) but would receive it in two installments—the first 50 percent after reaching Merauke and the second after reaching New Zealand, the final destination. Merauke was only a short distance away, so the crew wanted to at least complete that leg of the journey to receive the first payment of Rp 50 million (US$3,250). Before returning to the *Andika* with eight Australian personnel, the captain agreed to sail the boat to Australia, hoping that he could leave the asylum seekers there and be deported with his crew back to Indonesia, thereby escaping going to court and subsequently to jail in Australia.

Most of that evening, the *Andika* remained at the interception site. The five women and children were permitted to sleep in the cabin, but the other fifty-eight asylum seekers and six transporters stayed outside on the deck with eight armed Australian personnel. The Australian Border Force reported that weather conditions had steadily worsened, but Amnesty International (2015: 3) claims that the Australians provided "no protection from the elements." At a public hearing nearly nine months later, on February 5, 2016, the commander of Operation Sovereign Borders revealed that the decision to keep most people outside was a risk management strategy; if the *Andika* started to sink, it would be easier to rescue people from the deck rather than from inside the cabin (Australian Senate, Legal and Constitutional Affairs References Committee, 2016: 16). The people on board the *Andika* were provided with life jackets, and later that evening, the Australian Border Force began escorting the asylum seekers' boat to Australia.

Late in the evening of the next day, May 23, the boats reached Greenhill Island, near Darwin in Australia. Soon after arriving, Australian officials boarded the *Andika* to interview and photograph the asylum seekers (Amnesty International 2015: 17). The officials did not explain the purpose of the interviews, but it is clear that they were not for the assessment of their claims for asylum. Few other authorities even knew about the boat's arrival. The Australian Border Force attempted to separate the transporters and passengers by promising the asylum seekers the option of showering and sleeping in a bed on board another vessel, an offer that fifty asylum seekers accepted, but they later reported that they were then detained in two small rooms for around a week. It is also alleged that the Australian Border Force treated them poorly. One asylum seeker recalls that the Australian officials denied a request for medicine, recommending instead that the asylum seekers "just relax . . . and drink water" (Amnesty International 2015: 19). Of the fifteen asylum seekers who remained on board the *Andika*, eight men were later transferred to other Australian Border Force vessels, where conditions were also poor.

While on Greenhill Island, Australian officials allegedly made payments to the Indonesian crew so that they would return to Indonesia. Reports of the payments vary, with Amnesty International (2015) claiming that it was US$32,000. Media reports range between US$30,000 and US$32,000 (Stewart 2015), and the Australian Senate inquiry and testimonies by the Indonesian boat crew in court report that a total of US$31,000 was paid (US$6,000 to the captain and US$5,000 to each of the other five Indonesian crew members) (Australian Senate, Legal and Constitutional Affairs References Committee, 2016). On board the HMAS *Wollongong*, the captain had asked for US$10,000 (interview with the captain, Yohanis Humiang, August 2, 2016), presumably as financial compensation for each of the Indonesian crew, because he had almost reached Merauke before being intercepted by the Australian Border Force. The actual amount they received was between 40 and 50 percent less and, according to an asylum seeker who had remained on board the *Andika*, was allegedly handed over to the captain by the Australian officials in the boat's kitchen. Allegedly, the asylum seeker also witnessed the captain accept a "thick white envelope" and noticed that the other members of the crew were "very happy" as they began "joking with the Australian officers, whereas beforehand they had seemed frightened and nervous" (Amnesty International 2015: 17).

After this, the *Andika* remained at Greenhill Island for about a day before Australian Border Force officers instructed those on board to get ready for the return trip. The promised destination is disputed, as the Indonesian boat crew understood that the Australian Border Force would escort them to the edge of Indonesian waters near Cidaun on the southwest coast of Java. After some time at sea, the Indonesian boat crew became suspicious when they saw the white sand that is characteristic of Indonesian islands near Rote Island in southeast Indonesia (interview with the captain, Yohanis Humiang, August 2, 2016). As the Indonesian boat crew no longer had either a GPS or a map, they could not confirm their location independently. Late in the evening of May 30, the Australian Border Force officers finally informed the captain and his crew that they would transport all sixty-five asylum seekers from Australia's Ashmore Reef to Indonesia's Rote Island. The Indonesian boat crew were disappointed, but they were in a weak position to resist the change in plan, both because the Australian Border Force was in control of their vessel and because they had accepted payment to return to Indonesia.

Early the next morning, May 31, the Australian Border Force officers divided the Indonesian boat crew and asylum seekers more or less equally between two new boats, the *Jasmine* and the *Kanak*. Ten Australian vessels then escorted the boats to the edge of Indonesian waters, not far from Rote Island, and left the boats there. Before reaching the destination, the *Jasmine* ran out of fuel, so everyone crowded onto the *Kanak* for the final stretch. A few hours later, at around five o'clock in the afternoon, the *Kanak* struck a reef off the southeast coast of Rote Island, and asylum seekers who could swim abandoned the shipwreck and made their way to the closest beach. The others, including women and children, relied on locals to rescue them from the stricken vessel. Once on shore, and fearing arrest for people smuggling, the Indonesian crew fled, leaving behind the confused, frightened, and angry asylum seekers, who then gathered in the local village head's house. Four hours later, the police arrested the crew, who were later convicted for their failed attempt to smuggle asylum seekers to New Zealand.

On January 14, 2016, the boat captain and five crew were convicted of people smuggling in the Rote Ndao District Court. The prosecution had pursued charges for the offense of attempted smuggling, largely because the transporters did not reach their intended destination, New Zealand. The judges, however, decided that the transporters did successfully smuggle migrants across international borders. They reasoned that evidence proved the transporters' criminal liability for the three components of the offense that criminalize people smuggling. The defendants had (1) transported migrants; (2) done so without valid immigration permission to leave and then reenter Indonesia; and (3) done so for profit.

BREACHES OF INTERNATIONAL AND DOMESTIC LAW

While the Indonesian court decided to ignore the involvement of the Australian agencies, others have argued that the Australian officials indeed appear to have organized or directed the Indonesian crew to commit a people-smuggling offense and thus to have breached the international smuggling protocol. International law defines people smuggling as "the procurement, in order to obtain, directly or indirectly, a financial or other material benefit, of the illegal entry of a person into a State Party of which the person is not a national or a permanent resident" (United Nations 2000: Article 3a). The available evidence suggests that the Indonesian crew may have acted under duress when they followed the instructions of Australian officials. According to Amnesty International (2015: 6), it was under Australian officials' instruction and with their material assistance (including two boats, fuel, maps, and GPS) that the offense of smuggling people into Indonesia took place. The mode of entry to Indonesia that, according to the crew, the Australian officials directed them to follow—landing at identified points on Rote Island rather than presenting themselves to Indonesian border officials and complying with procedures for entry by boat to Indonesia—amount to illegal entry within the terms of the smuggling protocol. The US$32,000 constitutes a financial benefit to the crew to procure the illegal entry. The Australian officials who paid the smugglers and instructed them to land on Rote Island in May 2015 may also have participated as accomplices in the transnational crime of people smuggling.

While Australia still disputes the illegality of this act, we argue that the bribery can indeed be understood as a creative means of state-sponsored people smuggling. Its very creativity lies in the fact that the act of bribing Indonesian transporters is an innovative, unconventional way of avoiding processing asylum seekers' claims by removing them from a geographic jurisdiction where they otherwise would be entitled to have their legal claims for asylum heard by a court, with support from legal aid groups or lawyers. As far as we know, this approach, in which Australia tests legal and diplomatic boundaries, has not been used elsewhere, thus highlighting its highly creative nature.

Leading legal scholars in Australia have argued that, besides committing breaches of the international smuggling protocol, Australian officials may also have breached people-smuggling provisions in the Australian Criminal Code (as documented in submissions to the Senate inquiry; Australian Senate, Legal and Constitutional Affairs References Committee, 2016). The Australian Senate's Legal and Constitutional Affairs References Committee published an interim report on the incident in May 2016, and it seems unlikely that any further investigations will take place in Australia. There is a lack of interest in seeking the truth about what happened during the return of the *Andika*'s asylum seekers and whether it equated to state-sponsored people smuggling, together with a lack of political will on the part of the Australian government, which has shielded its Operation Sovereign Borders from any public scrutiny. Under the people-smuggling provisions of the Australian Criminal Code, the attorney general's written consent is required to begin proceedings for the offense of people smuggling, and it is safe to assume that no current or future attorney general will voluntarily initiate such proceedings, unless driven to it by a royal commission. Moreover, it needs to be noted that certain categories of public officials, such as Australian Secret Intelligence Service officials, may enjoy immunity from liability under Australian law. Such exemptions from liability are inconsistent with the United Nations Convention against Transnational Organized Crime, as signatory states are required to prevent transnational organized crime and to promote the development of standards and procedures to safeguard the integrity of public entities. Unless special exemptions for intelligence officers are abolished, Australian agencies have no fear of criminal prosecution in this affair.

Under questioning by the Australian Senate's Legal and Constitutional Affairs References Committee in February 2016, Operation Sovereign Borders commander Andrew Bottrell and Immigration Department secretary Michael Pezzullo refused to confirm or deny the bribery allegations but maintained that officials had acted within Australian and international law. However, in the submission the Operation Sovereign Borders Joint Agency Task Force had made earlier to that committee, the government claimed that the interception of the *Andika* was intended to save lives following a distress call. This claim was denied both by the asylum seekers and by the boat crew, who were interviewed separately by Amnesty International (2015). In fact, the post-interception conduct of Australian officials, as described by passengers and crew, did not fit the definition of a rescue operation. To the contrary, as we have detailed in this chapter, the available evidence shows that the return actually put the lives of people at risk. Because of such conflicting statements, together with the overall secrecy surrounding the Australian government's actions against asylum seekers at sea, the Australian public is left in the dark and prevented from mounting any substantial public protest that could lead to effective change within Australia's untransparent border policies. In order to correct previous wrongs, the Australian government should not only allow for more transparency and accountability for its previous actions, for which there is strong evidence that they have prioritized deterrence policies over human rights, but also allow for impartial supervision of Operation Sovereign Borders' current maneuvers.

While then prime minister Tony Abbott neither confirmed nor denied the initial allegation, he stated publicly that his government was committed to stop the boats "by hook or by crook" (Conifer 2015). This statement suggests that the Australian government was prepared to test legal boundaries and diplomatic relations with Indonesia in its attempts to "stop the boats," arousing even more the interest of scholars studying people smuggling and related issues, such as migration and mobility, border studies, and refugee studies. Australia and Indonesia have not always had such disparate stances on how to best deal with irregular migrants, as the two states acted in concert at times (Missbach 2022), with both dedicating significant resources and commitment to "enhancing regional cooperation and capacity building in addressing irregular migration, including people smuggling," in the multilateral regional consultation that they co-chair (Co-chairs of the

Bali Process 2013). Interestingly, one year after the bribery scandal, officials engaged in the Bali Process once again embraced their well-worn diplomatic formulas and urged "members [of the Bali Process] to effectively criminalise people smuggling and trafficking in persons, in accordance with relevant international law, and regional instruments" (Co-chairs of the Bali Process 2016).

STATE, ILLEGALITY, AND A NEW GENERATION OF BORDERING PRACTICES

Putting aside the *Andika* case and taking a wider look at the advancement of global bordering practices employed by states, it becomes apparent that bordering practices to combat people smuggling are diversifying and are not always legal. Littoral states, for example, are known to "intercept" people traveling without the required documentation, whether in the country of departure, in a transit country, within territorial waters, or even on the high seas before they reach their territory. Interceptions are often used to prevent unauthorized arrivals of vessels and their passengers but are only permissible in certain situations as outlined in international law. While some bordering practices used to control migratory movements are legal under international and domestic law, many others are not. When called to account by the public, governments in destination countries are known to "quarantine national law and policy from [their] international legal obligations"—for example, by attempting to prevent the application of international law when assessing the legality of their interception activities (Chia, McAdam, and Purcell 2014: 64). They also selectively choose articles in international laws to justify their interception activities, while ignoring obligations in others.

While there is a growing body of literature dealing with various forms of illegal interceptions (Ghezelbash 2018; Klein 2011; Morris 2003), we wish to advance this scholarship by, first, pointing out that state personnel can and do break laws in their official capacity to achieve policy objectives, including reducing the number of unauthorized maritime arrivals. Second, the new generation of unilateral and "creative" anti-people-smuggling activities might further erode any meaningful bilateral or multilateral collaboration when it comes to enforcing anti-people-smuggling laws in the region. Destroying trust in regional collaboration that had been built in the past will therefore thwart attempts to find regional solutions for dealing with increasing numbers of irregular migratory movements in the mid- to long term. Although the number of boats reaching Australia has decreased substantially since the start of Operation Sovereign Borders, the direct and indirect costs of interceptions and returns of asylum seekers' boats and of the detention of asylum seekers in offshore camps (on Manus Island and Nauru) are extremely high, both in financial and in human terms, and are therefore deemed unsustainable. Unilateral action might bring quick results in preventing people smuggling, but it cannot guarantee long-term success. The nature of the Australia-Indonesia relationship in seeking to combat and prevent people smuggling makes this risk very clear.

Not only do we argue that state-sponsored people smuggling is a particularly perfidious form of creativity employed to generate human suffering, but we also suggest that our case study serves as a stern warning of how this creative approach to combat and prevent people smuggling could undermine a growing commitment to international cooperation and any existing regional collaboration in regard to the protection of migrants and asylum seekers. Ignoring binding international law in regard to deterring asylum seekers threatens to start a "race to the bottom," in which states continue to prioritize border protection over the competing responsibility to protect the human rights of migrants and refugees. If other countries in the Indo-Pacific were to follow Australia's example and pay the transporters of asylum seekers to take them away from areas where they could access protection, international arrangements and regional cooperation might start to collapse.

The most imminent danger of the erosion of regional trust is that other countries might follow suit when it comes to breaching international law that was established to protect asylum seekers and refugees. As Australia has not been scrutinized internationally regarding its turnbacks of asylum seekers at sea, Malaysia, Thailand, and Indonesia did not have to fear international criticism when pushing back Rohingya asylum seekers fleeing Myanmar in 2015 (Human Rights Watch 2015). Although it is hard to prove that the pushbacks by the Malaysian, Indonesian, and Thai governments were a direct consequence of Australia's actions, there is a real danger that the Australian turnbacks will further undermine international and domestic legal obligations put in place to rescue people in distress at sea, regardless of their migration status. For example, according to the newly implemented standard operational procedures of the Indonesian Search and Rescue Agency, foreign asylum seekers will not always be brought to the nearest port, where they could then apply for international protection. Unless their boats are damaged beyond repair, Indonesian authorities will fix their boats, refuel their tanks, and provide additional food and water, so that the asylum seekers can sail to another but more distant destination (Komaeny 2019).

Australia's turnback actions, as detailed in our account of the bribery case, have shown that destination countries can actively facilitate people smuggling to other countries as part of their own anti-people-smuggling policies. Despite the ever-present rhetoric of multilateral collaboration within wider border protection, unilateral policies such as those pursued by the Australian government under its Operation Sovereign Borders threaten to undermine the fragile regional collaborative frameworks established to find joint solutions to combat and prevent people smuggling in the Indo-Pacific region. Pursuing its own interests at a neighbor's expense will not only weaken Australia's diplomatic relations but also severely undermine international trust in Australia's adherence to the rule of law. In this regard, Australia is considered to be playing with fire by setting dangerous precedents that might then be copied by other states beyond the region.

NOTES

1. The case study we present here draws on an earlier publication on the matter (Missbach and Palmer 2020).
2. Thirty-six boats carrying 852 people were turned back under Operation Sovereign Borders between September 2013 and July 2019 (Asylum Insight 2019).
3. If the landing site was a densely populated area, Indonesian authorities would often arrest the passengers on the beach. In other places, the arrivals would disappear into the Indonesian hinterland, which is largely unknown to the Indonesian government.
4. Unreferenced statements in this case study refer to facts corroborated in the following sources: Amnesty International (2015); Australian Senate, Legal and Constitutional Affairs References Committee (2016); Legal Decision No. 37/Pid.Sus/2015/PN.Rno (2015); Legal Decision No. 38/Pid.Sus/2015/PN.Rno (2015); Legal Decision No. 40/Pid.Sus/2015/PN.Rno (2016).
5. The Australian Defence Force and the Australian Customs and Border Protection Service completed in February 2014 a joint review of the six occasions on which Australian vessels entered Indonesian waters between December 2013 and January 2014.

REFERENCES

Amnesty International. 2015. *By Hook or by Crook: Australia's Abuse of Asylum-Seekers at Sea*. London: Amnesty International.

Andreas, Peter. 2013. *Smuggler Nation: How Illicit Trade Made America*. Oxford: Oxford University Press.

Asylum Insight. 2019. "Statistics." Accessed February 13, 2020. https://www.asyluminsight.com/statistics/#.XAjXI2gzbIV.

Australian Senate, Legal and Constitutional Affairs References Committee. 2016. *Payment of Cash or Other Inducements by the Commonwealth of Australia in Exchange for the Turn Back of Asylum Seeker Boats: Interim Report*. Canberra.

Bevitt, Nicola. 2017. "The Australian Border Force Act 2015 (Cth) Secrecy Provisions—Borderline Unconstitutional." *Sydney Law Review* 39 (2): 257–275.

Chia, Joyce, Jane McAdam, and Kate Purcell. 2014. "Asylum in Australia: Operation Sovereign Borders and International Law." *Australian Yearbook of International Law* 34:33–64.

Co-chairs of the Bali Process. 2013. Bali Process Senior Officials Meeting, Bali, Indonesia, April 1, 2013, Co-Chairs' Statement. https://www.baliprocess.net/UserFiles/baliprocess/File/SOM%20Co-Chairs%20Statement%20-%20FINAL(2).pdf.

———. 2016. Bali Declaration on People Smuggling, Trafficking in Persons and Related Transnational Crime. Sixth Ministerial Conference of the Bali Process on People Smuggling, Trafficking in Persons and Related Transnational Crime, Bali, March 23, 2016. https://www.baliprocess.net/UserFiles/baliprocess/File/BPMC%20Co-chairs%20Ministerial%20Statement_with%20Bali%20Declaration%20attached%20-%2023%20March%202016_docx.pdf.

Conifer, Dan. 2015. "Asylum Seekers: Tony Abbott Refuses to Deny Australia Paid Thousands to People Smugglers." ABC News, June 12, 2015. https://www.abc.net.au/news/2015-06-12/abbott-refuses-to-deny-people-smugglers-paid-to-turn-back/6540866.

Connery, David, Natalie Sambhi, and Michael McKenzie. 2014. *A Return on Investment: The Future of Police Cooperation between Australia and Indonesia*. Special report. Barton, Australian Capital Territory: Australian Strategic Policy Institute.

Cribb, Robert. 1991. *Gangsters and Revolutionaries: The Jakarta People's Militia and the Indonesian Revolution, 1945–1949*. Honolulu: University of Hawaii Press.

Ghezelbash, Daniel. 2018. *Refuge Lost: Asylum Law in an Interdependent World*. Cambridge: Cambridge University Press.

Gino, Francesca, and Dan Ariely. 2012. "The Dark Side of Creativity: Original Thinkers Can Be More Dishonest." *Journal of Personality and Social Psychology* 102 (3): 445–459.

Goodwin-Gill, Guy S. 2011. "The Right to Seek Asylum: Interception at Sea and the Principle of Non-Refoulement." Inaugural lecture given at the Palais des Académies, Brussels, February 16, 2011.

Grewcock, Michael. 2013a. "Australia's Ongoing Border Wars." *Race and Class* 54 (3): 10–32.

———. 2013b. "People Smuggling and State Crime." In *Crime, Justice and Social Democracy*, edited by Kerry Carrington, Matthew Ball, Erin O'Brien, and Juan Marcellus Tauri, 327–343. London: Palgrave Macmillan.

Hirsch, Asher Lazarus. 2017. "The Borders beyond the Border: Australia's Extraterritorial Migration Controls." *Refugee Survey Quarterly* 36 (3): 48–80.

Human Rights Watch. 2015. "Southeast Asia: End Rohingya Boat Pushbacks: Thailand, Malaysia, Indonesia Should Act Urgently to Save Lives." May 14, 2015. https://www.hrw.org/news/2015/05/14/southeast-asia-end-rohingya-boat-pushbacks.

Jenss, Alke. 2018. "A Criminal Commodity Consensus: The Coloniality of State Power, State Crime and the Transformation of Property Relations in Mexico." *State Crime Journal* 7 (2): 306–328.

Kevin, Anthony C. 2012. *Reluctant Rescuers: An Exploration of the Australian Border Protection System's Safety Record in Detecting and Intercepting Asylum-Seeker Boats, 1998–2011*. Manuka, ACT: self-published.

Klein, Natalie. 2011. *Maritime Security and the Law of the Sea*. Oxford Monographs in International Law. Oxford: Oxford University Press.

———. 2014. "Assessing Australia's Push Back the Boats Policy under International Law: Legality and Accountability for Maritime Interceptions of Irregular Migrants." *Melbourne Journal of International Law* 15 (2): 1–30.

Komaeny, Abdullah. 2019. "The Handling of Refugees in Distress in Indonesian Territorial Waters according to the Presidential Decree 125/2016." Presentation, Depok, March 20, 2019.

Kyle, David, and John Dale. 2001. "Smuggling the State Back In: Agents of Human Smuggling Reconsidered." In *Global Human Smuggling: Comparative Perspectives*, edited by David Kyle and Rey Koslowski, 29–57. Baltimore: Johns Hopkins University Press.

Kyle, David, and Rey Koslowski, eds. 2001. *Global Human Smuggling: Comparative Perspectives*, Baltimore: Johns Hopkins University Press.

Kyle, David, and Christina A. Siracusa. 2005. "Seeing the State like a Migrant: Why So Many Non-criminals Break Immigration Laws." In *Illicit Flows and Criminal Things: States, Borders, and the Other Side of Globalization*, edited by Willem van Schendel and Itty Abraham, 153–176. Bloomington: Indiana University Press.

Legal Decision No. 37/Pid.Sus/2015/PN.Rno with defendant Yohanis Humiang. Decided December 22, 2015.

Legal Decision No. 38/Pid.Sus/2015/PN.Rno with defendants Marthen Karaeng, Medi Ampow, Yapi Aponno, Indra Reza Rumambi and Stevan Ivan Janny Worotitjan. Decided December 22, 2015.

Legal Decision No. 40/Pid.Sus/2015/PN.Rno with defendant Vishvanathan Thineshkumar alias Thines alias Kugan. Decided January 16, 2016.

Missbach, Antje. 2015. *Troubled Transit: Asylum Seekers Stuck in Indonesia*. Singapore: ISEAS.

———. 2022. *The Criminalisation of People Smuggling in Indonesia: Asylum out of Reach*. London: Routledge.

Missbach, Antje, and Gerhard Hoffstaedter. 2020. "When Transit States Pursue Their Own Agenda: Malaysian and Indonesian Responses to Australia's Migration and Border Policies." *Migration and Society* 3 (1): 64–79.

Missbach, Antje, and Wayne Palmer. 2020. "People Smuggling by a Different Name: Australia's 'Turnbacks' of Asylum Seekers to Indonesia." *Australian Journal of International Affairs* 74 (2): 185–206.

Morris, Jessica. 2003. "The Spaces in Between: American and Australian Interdiction Policies and Their Implications for the Refugee Protection Regime." *Refuge: Canada's Journal on Refugees* 21 (4): 51–62.

Operation Sovereign Borders Joint Agency Task Force. 2015. "Submission No 9: Payment of Cash or Other Inducements by the Commonwealth of Australia in Exchange for the Turn Back of Asylum Seeker Boats." Senate Legal and Constitutional Affairs Reference Committee.

Saul, Ben. 2015. "Submission No 1: Payment of Cash or Other Inducements by the Commonwealth of Australia in Exchange for the Turn Back of Asylum Seeker Boats." Senate Legal and Constitutional Affairs Reference Committee.

Stevens, Rachel. 2012. "Political Debates on Asylum Seekers during the Fraser Government, 1977–1982." *Australian Journal of Politics and History* 58 (4): 526–541.

Stewart, Cameron. 2015. "Sinking Fears Sparked Emergency Rescue of Asylum 'Bribes' Boat." *Australian*, June 17, 2015.

Taylor, Lenore. 2014. "Australia's Naval Incursion Will Worsen Relations, Indonesia Warns." *Guardian*, January 17, 2014.

United Nations. 2000. Protocol against the Smuggling of Migrants by Land, Sea and Air, Supplementing the United Nations Convention against Transnational Organized Crime.

Watkins, Josh. 2017. "Bordering Borderscapes: Australia's Use of Humanitarian Aid and Border Security Support to Immobilise Asylum Seekers." *Geopolitics* 22 (4): 958–983.

Weber, Leanne, and Benjamin Bowling. 2004. "Policing Migration: A Framework for Investigating the Regulation of Global Mobility." *Policing and Society* 14 (3): 195–212.

CHAPTER 17

The Rise of "Border Security"

CHAOS, CLUTTER, AND COMPLEXITY IN A TECHNOLOGICAL ARMS RACE

Victor Manjarrez Jr.

THE UNDERSTANDING OF BORDER security has ebbed and flowed since the birth of the United States, depending on numerous variables, typically designed to welcome some people or to keep others out. The past thirty-five years have generally seen governmental movements to strengthen border security policies that have drastically increased resources and funding dedicated to border enforcement. Although significant border security enforcement improvements were made at border locations such as those in San Diego, California; Nogales, Arizona; El Paso, Texas; and McAllen, Texas, before September 11, 2001, the issue was viewed as one of immigration versus security. In reality, before the terrorist attacks of September 11, 2001, illegal immigration was generally considered, by most of America, a southwest border problem (Andreas 2003).

The notion of securing our nation's borders has been important but not essential. It would be inaccurate to believe that no effort was made to control the southwest border of the United States before the September 11, 2001 attacks. Efforts by the US Border Patrol such as Operation Gatekeeper and Operation Hold the Line (Andreas 2000) were conducted to control illegal immigration in San Diego and El Paso in the early 1990s. These operations were a result of local residents and local politicians raising the issue to such a level that it caused local policymakers to take action. The efforts were not nationally coordinated and lacked the national incentive of policymakers to sustain the enforcement efforts. However, they were seen as successful by local residents. More importantly, these operations introduced a new concept of border security that was based on "prevention through deterrence" (Alden 2012). The new strategy was anchored to the idea of confronting illegal immigration entering the United States as close as possible to the border itself.

The paradigm shift in enforcement tactics involved the concept of moving border patrol agents from the interior of border cities to the immediate border in an attempt to discourage the illegal entry of humans and contraband. The advancement of this new tactic proved to be the basis for future border security strategies. These included clearly delineating the international border, in many areas for the first time, and placing border patrol agents in highly visible locations to discourage the entry of illegal entrants (Andreas 2000). The intent of this concept was to remove the advantage that human and narcotic smugglers (often referred by border security agencies as the "criminal element") had in urban areas adjacent to the border, as well as to shift the flow of illegal activity to locations where border enforcement entities would have an advantage. Not only did the change in border enforcement tactics clearly delineate change for border security entities, it also denoted a change in other actors who aimed to exploit massive illegal migration. I argue that as the US government places greater emphasis on border security through the use of greater personnel resources, infrastructure, and technology, so will illicit actors who aim to smuggle humans into the country. The last thirty-five years have taught us that the process of security and smuggling is a cyclical race between the state and smugglers and to defeat each other.

This chapter does not attempt to make sense of border security policy in the United States but rather examines the evolution of technology by both border security personnel and smugglers of humans and contraband. First, I begin by describing the southwest border of the United States in geographical terms and the volume of legitimate and illegitimate activity. Second, I outline the actors and their roles regarding border security efforts. Third, I discuss the chaos and clutter that is created by the combination of the geography, border activity, and border security actors, which form a complex border ecosystem. Finally, I discuss the evolution of technology from the perspectives of the various border actors.

DIMENSIONS OF THE SOUTHWEST BORDER OF THE UNITED STATES

GEOGRAPHY

The US border with Mexico is 1,954 miles long, excluding the maritime boundaries of 18 miles in the Pacific Ocean and 12 miles in the Gulf of Mexico (GAO 2008). The western point is Border Field State Park in California, and the easternmost point is Brownsville, Texas (Beaver 2006). The international border from California to New Mexico is approximately 700 miles in length and is categorized as low and mid-highland desert. Small and large US and Mexican municipalities segment the desert areas. This portion of the land border contains twenty-four border crossings that commercial, vehicular, and pedestrian traffic utilize to enter or depart the United States (USCBP, n.d.). The Rio Grande River constitutes over 1,200 miles of the international border between the United States and Mexico (Beaver 2006) and the entire border between Texas and Mexico. The river winds itself from New Mexico and enters Texas at the city of El Paso, flows toward Brownsville, and eventually empties into the Gulf of Mexico. Small and large US and Mexican municipalities encompassing twenty-eight international bridges allow commercial, vehicular, and pedestrian traffic to flow across the river border (USCBP, n.d.). The number of designated ports of entry in Texas has contributed to Mexico's status as Texas's number one trading partner.

VOLUME OF ACTIVITY AT AND BETWEEN PORTS OF ENTRY

The volume of commercial goods through the ports of entry along the southwest border of the United States greatly increased after the implementation of the North American Free Trade Agreement (NAFTA) on January 1, 1994 (Alden 2012). As a result of NAFTA, the United States realized an increase of exports of goods and services to Mexico of 485 percent from 1993 pre-NAFTA (Office of the United States Trade Representative, n.d.). In addition, there has been a 687 percent increase in goods and services imported into the United States from Mexico when compared with 1993 pre-NAFTA. The volume of trade and travel with Mexico not only increased significantly, but it also amplified the complexity of border security efforts at ports of entry. The large volume of legitimate trade and travel easily masks criminal activity occurring at ports of entry.

In 2017 US goods and services traded with Mexico totaled approximately $615.9 billion (Office of the United States Trade Representative, n.d.) across the fifty-two land and bridge ports of entry. The dollar volume in trade makes Mexico the United States' third-largest trading partner after Canada and China. The volume of trade with Mexico can readily be inferred from the 2017 daily average of 514,974 individuals who were inspected on trains, buses, and other vehicles and as pedestrians as they entered the country (US Bureau of Transportation Statistics, n.d.). On average, nearly 20,000 commercial truck and rail containers and 212,085 trains and buses are inspected daily across the fifty-two ports of entry along US-Mexico border. The volume of trade is important to both economies and the livelihood of residents of the two countries (Office of the United States Trade Representative, n.d.). The complexity of processing legitimate trade and travel at ports of entry is further exacerbated by the 216,370 inadmissible aliens (an individual who is present in the United States without being lawfully admitted or paroled into the country) processed, over $65 million in US currency seized, and 479,585 pounds of cocaine, heroin, marijuana, methamphetamines, and fentanyl seized (USCBP 2019).

The increase of legal cross-border commercial traffic, due to NAFTA, created the political drive to portray a sense of order on the border (Longmire 2014). Not only does the agreement require the relatively unrestricted movement of people, goods, and services across the border, it also inevitably provides the opportunity for transnational criminal organizations to exploit the high level of legitimate activity (Cottam and Marenin 2005). As a result, government officials and criminal organizations recognized that enforcement efforts were not effective or coordinated. It also became clear that the annual multibillion-dollar industry of illegal drug smuggling was not going to cease any time soon. An acceptance of this dynamic and the creation of NAFTA were the premises for the rapid escalation of border enforcement in the early 1990s. The escalation of border enforcement operations beginning in 1993 in El Paso and San Diego captured national and international attention (Andreas 2000). The link between a chaotic (high levels of legitimate activity) and uncontrolled (high levels of illegal narcotics and immigration) border was not yet identified or viewed as a border security issue within the United States. During this time, illegal immigration was not considered a criminal act by most Americans and was simply viewed as a "victimless crime" (Alden 2012).

ACTORS AND THEIR ROLES

The southwest border of the United States has been the home of a plethora of federal law enforcement agencies for the last thirty-five years. In addition, the last twenty years have also been marked by significant citizen activism around the issue of immigration and border security, in large part because many feel current immigration or border security policy is not working, whether they critique it from the left or from the right. For example, for most of the 1990s, the epicenter for overwhelming illegal immigration and nongovernmental organizations' activity could be found along the international border in San Diego. The high levels of illegal immigration in Southern California caused a backlash by the public that culminated in a referendum known as Proposition 187. The proposition, among other things, would have established a state-run screening system to prohibit illegal aliens from using public health care and other social services. This referendum was described by its supporters as a giant step to ultimately end the significant flow of illegal immigration into Southern California that became the stimulus for other "grassroots" activities (Foley 2003). While both pro- and anti-immigrant groups have lengthy histories with prior waves of immigrants, this could arguably be considered the relative peak for such activity. In this section, I discuss law enforcement entities and border security threats that shape the notion of border security along the US-Mexico border.

LAW ENFORCEMENT ENTITIES

The Department of Homeland Security was formed as a result of the Homeland Security Act of 2002 (Phelps, Dailey, and Koenigsberg 2014), and over twenty agencies were merged into the new department. A key agency created within the department is US Customs and Border Protection (USCBP), in which the US Border Patrol, enforcement functions of the Department of Agriculture, and the US Customs Service were grouped together to form an agency with border enforcement responsibilities. While USCBP is responsible for overall border enforcement, a distinction is made within the agency concerning border security at and between ports of entry into the United States. The US Border Patrol was founded on May 28, 1924, to be the nation's primary law enforcement entity responsible for border security between ports of entry. The creation of the Department of Homeland Security on March 1, 2003, added to the traditional immigration and drug interdiction duties of the US Border Patrol. The agency was now tasked, as its primary mission, with detecting and preventing the entry of terrorists and weapons of mass destruction between ports of entry. The agency patrols nearly nine thousand miles of international borders with Mexico and Canada and the coastal waters around the Gulf of Mexico, Florida, and Puerto Rico.

The US Customs Service was established on July 31, 1789, primarily to collect import tariffs and conduct selected border security duties. The agency had two significant law enforcement functions: US Customs special agents investigated smuggling and other violations of customs, narcotics, and revenue laws; and US Customs inspectors served as uniformed officers at airports, seaports, and land border ports of entry who inspected people and vehicles entering the United States for contraband and dutiable merchandise. The creation of the Department of Homeland Security transferred the jurisdiction of the US Customs Service from the Department of the Treasury to the new department (Phelps, Dailey, and Koenigsberg 2014). As a result, US Customs inspectors combined with inspectors of the Immigration and Naturalization Service and the Plant Protection and Quarantine division of the US Department of Agriculture to form the Office of Field Operations (OFO). The agency is responsible for border security and the processing of legitimate trade and travel into the United States through ports of entry. Most importantly, OFO has the complex mission of screening all foreign visitors, returning American citizens, and imported cargo entering the United States at more than 320 land, air, and seaports (GAO 2011). Along the US-Mexico border, the work conducted by OFO is at 52 land and river ports of entry and multiple international airports and seaports. The investigative arms of the US Customs Service and the Immigration and Naturalization Service combined to form US Immigration and Customs Enforcement.

The Homeland Security Act of 2002 not only created the US Immigration and Customs Enforcement agency, it also provided a unique combination of civil and criminal authorities to better protect the United States. The new agency's primary mission is to promote homeland security and public safety through the criminal and civil enforcement of federal laws governing border security, customs, trade, and immigration (GAO 2008). In addition, the agency is tasked with investigating criminal and terrorist activity of foreign nationals residing in the United States. Immigration and Customs Enforcement has two primary operational components: Homeland Security Investigations and Enforcement and Removal Operations. Homeland Security Investigations probes a wide range of issues that threaten the national security of the United States, such as human trafficking, human smuggling, drug trafficking, and arms trafficking (GAO 2008). The Enforcement and Removal Operations branch of Immigration and Customs Enforcement is responsible for enforcing the nation's immigration laws and ensuring the departure of removable immigrants from the country. Although both entities conduct immigration, customs, and counterterrorism duties, their primary location of operation is not between or at designated ports of entry; they operate in the interior of the United States to include cities identified as border cities.

The Department of Justice has a significant presence along the US-Mexico border through agencies such as the FBI and Drug Enforcement Agency (US Department of Justice 2017). The FBI enforces laws and conducts investigations related to combatting transnational and national criminal organizations. The Drug Enforcement Agency is tasked with combatting drug smuggling and distribution within the United States. The fact that the agency may conduct drug investigations along the international border with Mexico makes it prominent along the border region. In both cases, the agencies' operational footprints are small when compared with USCBP.

The United States has within the four border states of California, Arizona, New Mexico, and Texas twenty-four state counties that have at least one border extending to the US-Mexico international border (GAO 2013). The border counties all have sheriff departments ranging in organizational size and geographic patrol areas. In addition, the counties all have municipal police departments and state law enforcement entities such as the Highway Patrol or Department of Public Safety. A key component to these agencies is that they contend with border crime issues and typically coordinate efforts with their law enforcement partners from the Department of Homeland Security and Department of Justice.

THREATS

This section reviews two types of threats that are the most prominent in the US-Mexico international border region. *Threat* in this context is defined as an individual or a group that has an implicit or explicit objective to violate US criminal law. In addition, these same individuals have demonstrated the organizational capability and possess the means to carry out the illegal activity. The term *threat* denotes an activity that law enforcement must either address or respond to in the immediate region of the US-Mexico border.

First, the human smuggler who either assists another individual to make an entry into the country or helps further the entry once inside the United States is one of the more distinct actors on the border. Interestingly, human smugglers outside the United States are often viewed by those people who contract their services as individuals who help their fellow countrymen. In many cases, human smugglers are independent contractors who are loosely organized and assist others for a fee in their travels to the United States. This type of human smuggler is often viewed as a necessary evil by the individuals who employ them. Others are part of a larger and more complex organization that smuggles individuals into the United States. The latter category of human smuggler typically operates within the immediate border region both north and south of the international border. This type of human smuggler is viewed by law enforcement as a callous individual who does not have a high regard for human life and is simply executing a business transaction. Interestingly, the person who is paying a fee for the smuggling service and is actually being smuggled tends to be vulnerable to abuse and exploitation by the very same smugglers (United Nations Office on Drugs and Crime, n.d.). As reported by the United Nations Office on Drugs and Crime, the safety of the individuals being smuggled is often put at risk, yet individuals seek human smugglers to assist them in their journey to enter the United States surreptitiously.

The illegal narcotic smuggler is the second category of threat discussed. Narcotic smugglers in this context are generally not high-level members of a drug cartel organization but rather the conveyance drivers and mules who transport the illegal narcotic, supported by guides or scouts. The guides serve as the listening and lookout extensions of the narcotic organization, and their responsibility is to avoid detection and apprehension. This group is the primary focus for law enforcement entities along the international border.

The individuals generally operate in teams of multiple members coordinating the movement of the illicit contraband. The concept is the same as at a port of entry; the goal of the narcotic organization is to avoid detection of the contraband and subsequent seizure. The guides are invariably involved in nearly every type of criminal activity between designated ports of entry and at a port of entry.

UNDERSTANDING THE COMPLEXITY

Securing the nation's borders is an emotional topic for the American people and lawmakers. Due to the issue's complexity, viewpoints usually emerge that are not only significantly disparate but unrealistic and irrational. While illegal immigration and border security are two different and divergent issues facing the United States, both issues undoubtedly have significant bearing and influence on each other. Understanding the complexity of the issue hinges on understanding the correlation between illegal immigration and border security. The basic premise is that opportunistic criminal elements will exploit border regions experiencing overwhelming legitimate trade and travel as well as illegitimate immigration. The overwhelming trade, travel, and migration flows provide illicit actors the opportunity to be less visible in plain sight by blending in with legitimate activity to evade detection and subsequent arrest. This is because the environment is disorderly (i.e., there are high levels of activity and creativity by criminal actors) and border security agencies simply have a difficult time managing the high levels of activity. As the environment becomes busier, criminal actors, who have embedded themselves in the very fabric of an open society (Ackleson 2005), find favorable opportunities to flourish in this chaotic and cluttered milieu. Criminal organizations, realizing border enforcement entities such as the US Border Patrol can be overcome by a large volume of illegal activity, exploit the chaos by simply masking their illicit activities. The clutter of this type of environment makes it difficult for law enforcement entities to identify threats to national and public safety.

High illegitimate immigration and a high volume of legitimate trade and travel produces an area that is vulnerable to exploitation. Transnational criminal organizations conducting narcotic smuggling, human smuggling, illegal trade, illicit financing schemes, and other illegal activities rely on the dynamic to conceal their illicit activities in plain sight of an open society.

The high activity and lack of clarity generated by both legitimate and illegitimate activity become the real threat of an uncontrolled border. The "prevention through deterrence" strategy becomes even more significant in locations where the threat and risk are high because the aim is to reduce the clutter along the border by preventing illegal entry (USCBP 2004). The reduction in activity provides additional situational awareness (clarity) to what is occurring, so the greater threats (criminal organizations and terrorists) cannot exploit the environment. Reducing the chaos and clutter becomes key when the aim of border security is to have a high probability of detection coupled with a high probability of interdiction. The aim is to have threats and vulnerabilities identified, prioritized, and targeted in order to reduce the criminal element's critical requirements and capabilities to operate.

The constant challenge of the cat-and-mouse game played out on the border is the foundation for the criminal element's ingenuity in attempting to defeat law enforcement efforts. Thus, the goal of law enforcement is to quickly learn about the criminal element's adaptation. The dynamic is played out along the southern border on a daily basis, and nothing has been more riveting than the evolution of technology used by both law enforcement and transnational criminal organizations that deal with an array of illicit activities. The creativity, speed, and complexity with which transnational criminal organizations adapt is akin to that of *Fortune* 500 companies with robust research and development capabilities (Basu 2013). The technological complexity of the adaptation can range from low to high. It is the use of technology in highly active and cluttered environments that makes border enforcement operations unique and dynamic.

BORDER SECURITY TECHNOLOGY BEFORE SEPTEMBER 11, 2001

LAW ENFORCEMENT ORGANIZATIONS

The very term *border security* did not enter the American lexicon until after the terrorist attacks of September 11, 2001. Generally, the Immigration and Naturalization Service and the US Customs Service were the only agencies operating consistently within the border region. The Drug Enforcement Agency also operated along the US-Mexico border, but its efforts were not border-centric. The antiquated tools and outdated technology of the time reflected the level of importance US policymakers placed on border control.

The equipment carried by border patrol agents typically consisted of only their firearm, a flashlight, and binoculars. The agents relied on traditional and in some cases decades-old techniques learned on the job (e.g., following footprints) rather than on equipment or technology to perform their daily duties. Personal night-vision goggles were available on a very limited and shift-by-shift basis, and they were very outdated. In some locations, the transnational criminal organizations attempting to smuggle narcotics or people equipped their guides and smugglers with better equipment.

The bulk of border security technology usually consisted of long-range thermal surveillance equipment with Vietnam-era technology that had far exceeded the manufacturers' recommended use. By the 1990s a limited number of locations—such as Nogales and Douglas, Arizona; and El Paso—had received, as part of the American Shield Initiative, remote video surveillance systems (RVSSs) (Ordonez 2008). These RVSSs offered the US Border Patrol the latest in night-vision capabilities as well as daytime surveillance resources. The RVSS provided short-, medium-, and long-range persistent surveillance from towers or structures. Before the advent of RVSS, the US Border Patrol utilized mobile vehicle surveillance systems that contained short- and medium-range surveillance cameras mounted on telescoping masts, which were, in turn, mounted in vehicles. In addition, seismic, passive infrared, acoustic, or magnetic unattended ground sensors provided short-range persistent surveillance to support detection. Border patrol agents were provided with air support that consisted of fixed-wing (small airplanes) and rotary-wing (helicopters) platforms. The helicopters were Vietnam War–era OH-5 light observation aircraft and Bell UH-1s (better known as Hueys). It was common to see both styles of helicopters with multiple bullet holes from their time in combat zones in Vietnam.

Although surveillance technology has been a critical aspect of border security operations, the implementation of the Automated Biometric Identification System (IDENT) in 1994 was the largest technological leap for the US Border Patrol (Office of Border Patrol 2005). Before the implementation of the system, there was no reliable method to determine how many times an individual was apprehended illegally entering the United States, nor the identity of the individual. The system allows the agency to identify and track individuals who are repeatedly apprehended. All individuals apprehended, except those ages thirteen and under, have their fingerprints entered into the system for comparison against previously entered prints. In addition, IDENT is linked to biographical data within the Enforcement Case Tracking System and the FBI's Integrated Automated Fingerprint Identification System. The latter system contains the Criminal Master Files of individuals who have been arrested for criterion offenses. These systems allow greater latitude in categorizing those who have attempted to enter the United States illegally. IDENT has allowed the agency to conduct analysis of recidivism, the origin of recidivists, demographic characteristics of recidivists, and recidivism totals by specific identifiers (nationality, gender, age, etc.).

Before the terrorist attacks of September 11, 2001, personnel operating at ports of entry did so under the US Customs Service. The agency, operating at ports of entry, focused on trade and illegal narcotics entering the United States. The agency relied principally on three pieces of technology to conduct inspection of trucks, cargo, and personally owned vehicles. First, the Vehicle and Cargo Inspection System (VACIS) is a nonintrusive inspection system that uses gamma-ray technology to produce images of tankers, commercial trucks, and sea air containers to search for drugs, weapons, currency, and humans hiding (US Department of Justice 2017). The images produced by the VACIS are used by law enforcement personnel to determine whether the containers require further physical inspection. The system was first developed as a joint project between the Department of Homeland Security, the Office of National Drug Control Policy, and the Department of Defense. The VACIS system can verify the contents of a package or container without breaking the package seal. This examination is conducted at a port of entry where cargo vehicles are inspected. Second, density meters, utilizing low-intensity gamma radiation, are used to scan vehicles to measure the density of certain parts. The meter does not detect contraband but provides inspectors with the knowledge that something is awry with the composition of the vehicle compartment (Ordonez 2008). In essence, the density meter is a queuing system for further inspection. Lastly, fiberscopes are used to conduct direct visual inspections of closed compartments of vehicles to alert an officer of the possibility of contraband. Typically, the fiberscopes are used to look inside fuel tanks, via a small video camera, to determine whether contraband is being concealed. Officers disassemble the compartment if contraband is detected.

THREATS

Generally, technology used by human and narcotic smugglers before September 11, 2001, was considered low tech and consisted mainly of countersurveillance activities. Human smugglers and guides were observed utilizing binoculars and, in some cases, commercial-brand night-vision goggles. In the more remote areas of the US-Mexico border, narcotic and human smugglers not only used commercial-brand night-vision but also encrypted "push-to-talk" radios. The more sophisticated criminal organizations developed radio repeater systems in the remote areas of the border. The objective was to provide additional communication capabilities in order to smuggle illicit goods and perform countersurveillance activities against law enforcement entities. The most significant technological breakthrough for criminal organizations was the extensive use of tunnels. In 1990, the first US–Mexico tunnel was discovered in Douglas, Arizona (Ordonez 2008). Although the tunnel was only approximately one hundred yards in length, it represented a significant technological leap for criminal organizations. The hydraulic, electrical, and ventilation systems employed in the tunnel demonstrated significant engineering accomplishments and became a model for the most complex criminal organizations.

BORDER SECURITY TECHNOLOGY AFTER SEPTEMBER 11, 2001

Successful border security efforts are often gauged by the manner in which transnational criminal organizations change their modus operandi as a result of them (Alden 2012; Bach 2005). As the "prevention through deterrence" enforcement concept was applied in El Paso and San Diego, the US Border Patrol noticed guides and smugglers initially resorting to violence (Office of Border Patrol 2006). As border patrol agents were positioned very close to the border in highly visible positions, they began to be assaulted by rocks thrown by individuals just inside Mexico. The intent of these assaults was not to actually assault the border patrol agents but to get the agents to move away from their positions. Once the agents left their positions, the individuals on the Mexican side of the border would exploit the gap in enforcement coverage by making an illegal entry (Office of Border Patrol 2006).

In addition to changing tactics, the US Border Patrol received technological advances in the era immediately following September 11, 2001. The agency acquired improvements to its surveillance technology with the procurement of mobile surveillance capability systems, expansion of the RVSS, and the development of surveillance systems such as Project 28 and the Integrated Fixed Tower system. The mobile surveillance capability systems are vehicle-mounted radar and camera sensors that provide long-range mobile surveillance, automatic detection, and tracking of items of interest while providing the operator with data and video of the observed activity. The vehicles can be deployed in any area in which a truck can be driven and moved in response to tactical decisions by field supervisors. The existing RVSS received technological upgrades and was expanded to other urban locations along the border. The Integrated Fixed Tower system aims to develop a web of sensor towers with radar, day/night cameras, and command-and-control software, which correlates sensor information to provide a single operating picture. Information from all the towers is networked into a border patrol station command-and-control center, which increases situational awareness for border patrol agents. Coupled with the new enforcement tactics, which included additional resources, the "prevention through deterrence" strategy resulted in some unintended consequences. One such unintended consequence was transnational criminal organizations' increased pressure on enforcement entities at ports of entry.

The increased smuggling through ports of entry was realized at points along the southwest border as a result of the application of significant levels of personnel, technology, and border infrastructure between ports of entry. OFO within USCBP reported it had encountered a growing trend of individuals using authentic and valid immigration documents, not issued to them, to lawfully enter the United States (Phelps, Dailey, and Koenigsberg 2014). These individuals have been termed "imposters" by USCBP. The tactic had been amplified in southern Arizona, where the Tucson Sector Border Patrol was focusing its border security enforcement efforts and resources. The Nogales Port of Entry (the largest and most active port of entry in Arizona) encountered a strategy in which multiple vehicles operating together were driven by and contained individuals presenting legitimate immigration documents belonging to someone else. This was being done because the perception was that border security was more effective between the ports of entry. The belief resulted in criminal organizations attempting alternative methods of gaining unlawful entry into the United States.

OFO has embarked on a multiyear effort to improve illicit cargo detection by upgrading legacy scanning systems such as the VACIS by linking them to new analysis and information sharing tools. Scanning capabilities at the border have also been enhanced with new equipment such as the Z Portal, which is designed as a drive-through nonintrusive passenger vehicle inspection system. Like the VACIS, it utilizes gamma-ray technology to perform a rapid scan of passenger vehicles in order to detect the presence of hidden merchandise, narcotics, and humans. One significant benefit the Z Portal provides is clearer images of objects and humans hidden in vehicles.

The rapidly advancing technologies of biometrics have found a niche in the mission of OFO. For example, facial recognition software is being implemented at various ports of entry along the southwest border of the United States. The aim of the biometric system is to detect imposters attempting to enter the country. Although the system is in place in only sixteen locations (Phelps, Dailey, and Koenigsberg 2014), the technology is proving to be useful in facilitating the movement of people through ports of entry. A key component to OFO's efforts is the ability to improve the performance of nonintrusive inspection systems. The aim is to increase the agency's ability to interdict illicit actors without slowing commerce through advanced data analytics, advanced imaging systems, and standardized nonintrusive inspection system metrics.

As a result of a political environment in the United States that focused on border security, cross-border smuggling organizations turned to utilizing alternative and more sophisticated methods to enter the United States, over land, by air, and by sea, to successfully move their illicit contraband. It is clear that technology is readily available to smuggling organizations and is being deployed creatively. The following sections highlight three creative ways contraband is being smuggled across the US-Mexico border (LaSusa 2016).

TUNNELS
One of the unintended consequences of the advent of border security infrastructure between the ports of entry was the utilization of tunnels by criminal organizations. The Department of Homeland Security categorizes tunnels in three groups (USCBP 2017). The first group is called the sophisticated group, which are elaborately constructed tunnels that have electricity, water,

and ventilation and are significantly long and deep (up to one mile long). The second group of tunnels is the rudimentary group, which are crudely constructed, shallow, and not very long (up to seventy-five feet long). The last group of tunnels is the interconnecting group and is the most common type of tunnel found along the international border. These types of tunnels exploit and connect to municipal infrastructure such as storm and sewer drains. This type of tunnel usually works in conjunction with either a sophisticated or rudimentary tunnel in order to be effective. The Department of Homeland Security (USCBP 2017) reported that over two hundred tunnels have been discovered along the US-Mexico border since 1990, and over 80 percent of the discoveries occurred after 2008. Nearly 75 percent of all tunnels have been discovered in the state of Arizona.

The first tunnel was discovered in 1990 and was located in downtown Douglas, Arizona (Ordonez 2008). The tunnel was 273 feet long and spanned from a home in Agua Prieta, Mexico, to a warehouse in Arizona. The tunnel was complex and sophisticated, as it was fully equipped with lighting, drainage, and a trolley system to move contraband. The tunnel entrance on the Mexican side included a hidden switch inside the luxury home that, when activated, raised a pool table and the concrete slab below to provide access to a narrow entrance to the tunnel (LaSusa 2016). Since 1990 more than sixty sophisticated tunnels have been discovered in San Diego. One of the largest tunnels discovered was one mile long from Tijuana, Mexico, to San Diego. The exit points for this tunnel and for most tunnels rely on the ability to blend in with daily legitimate trade activity. Although tunnels have traditionally been considered an endeavor of those smuggling narcotics, USCBP has reported the growing use of tunnels to facilitate human smuggling (O'Neill 2017).

ULTRALIGHT AIRCRAFT
In 2005 the US Border Patrol became aware of the use of ultralight aircraft to smuggle illicit contraband into the United States. The aircraft are constructed with fabric wings that are attached to aluminum tubing frames. The aircraft are powered by small two-stroke gas engines that sound very much like a lawn mower and power a rear propeller. The pilot sits in a sling seat that gives the aircraft the appearance of a winged tricycle. Although the aircraft are rigged with all-terrain tires for landing, the pilots rarely land. They

generally prefer to drop their illicit cargo, weighing up to five hundred pounds, from an elevation of about 1,500 feet at a predetermined location. The cargo is later picked up by an accomplice. Ultralights have been spotted up to two hundred miles into the United States after making their illegal incursion. The use of ultralight aircraft allows criminal organizations to use the cover of darkness at night, and the small frames go undetected by radar. Significantly, unlike other manners of transporting illicit contraband, this method can transport a human being. Although the Department of Homeland Security has previously suggested this manner of smuggling has been used primarily for illegal contraband, the department has recently reported a growing use of ultralights for the smuggling of high-paying foreign nationals who seek entry into the United States (Hong 2018). This may be the result of transnational criminal organizations understanding the Department of Homeland Security has a difficult time detecting, tracking, and interdicting this manner of smuggling (GAO 2008). It continues to remain a significant challenge to the Department of Homeland Security, and in large part it remains unresolved. In 2009, the department was so concerned about its inability to detect and interdict the ultralights, it spent $100 million on new sensor technology to detect the aircraft (Mendoza and Bunker 2009).

DRONES
In October 2018 both the Department of Homeland Security and the FBI identified unmanned aerial systems or drones as one of the greatest security risks to the United States (Giaritelli 2018). Drones have become popular in the personal and commercial markets as "techie toys," but the capabilities were soon recognized by drug cartels. Typically, the drones range from a few ounces to a few pounds in weight and travel up to fifty miles per hour while flying up to one thousand feet in the air. In 2015, the first known cross-border drug smuggling incident via drone occurred. Now, the use of drones is a daily occurrence in many places along the US-Mexico border, but arrests of the people operating the drones or the actual seizure of the device is rare. In 2018, the Department of Homeland Security reported (Giaritelli 2018) that drug and human smugglers had begun using the drones to spy on USCBP officers at ports of entry. The agency described how drones can hover above a port of entry and watch officers screen passenger vehicles and commercial trucks attempting to enter the United States. The risk is that the

practice will expose critical capabilities of the agency to conduct screenings and will expose vulnerabilities of these same processes to be exploited at a later date, but the agency is powerless to stop the activity because of existing federal laws.

Criminal organizations have used technology not only to smuggle illicit contraband but also for communications and defense operations (GAO 2011). Large smuggling operations have become complex, requiring reliable communications systems. Transnational criminal organizations in the Mexican states of Sonora, Chihuahua, and Tamaulipas have created encrypted cellular phone networks to help them conduct their business operations. These newly created networks are clandestine, with antennas and repeaters connected to their own sources of power. In addition, the organizations have created "push-to-talk" systems along the US-Mexico border. Not only has this new technology improved the manner in which drug and human smuggling organizations transport illicit contraband and communicate their movements, the same technology has become a defensive mechanism for the organizations. The technology has allowed for a system of alarms and layers of protection for transnational criminal organizations against rivals and law enforcement interdiction.

CONCLUSION

As we have seen from the last thirty-five years, the complexity of border enforcement and the role of technology are not always well understood. Before the enhanced border security measures, there was really no need for illicit actors in human smuggling to use extreme measures such as tunnels, ultralight aircraft, or unmanned drones. The increased technological security measures put in place by the US government, particularly after the terrorist attacks of September 11, 2001, have been met by an equally capable foe who has demonstrated a penchant for sophistication based on the notions of persistence and audacity (Tory 2018). The cyclical nature of the competition between smugglers and the state has in essence created a technological race to defeat each other.

While there have been significant improvements in border enforcement in the last thirty-five years, the challenge is that our policy approach to border security has not changed. When deciding future border security strategies, we should look to our past for insight into the next evolution of border enforcement. Globalization of our economies with the use of trade agreements such as NAFTA has been embraced by almost every sector of our society, yet we continue to view our borders in the same static manner. Borders exist, in one sense, as lines on a map, a delineation of authority and control, yet they do more than just mark spaces; they influence the creation of new spaces both near and far. By understanding the complexities of the border environment, we can look at how it can be possible not only to propose new policy on border security but how technology should play a role in the future. It is clear that criminal organizations fluidly adapt to policy and law enforcement approaches to border security. Revisiting border security paradigms may provide insight into the cyclical nature of the cat-and-mouse game that border security entities and human smugglers play along the US-Mexico border.

REFERENCES

Ackleson, Jason. 2005. "Border Security in Risk Society." *Journal of Borderlands Studies* 20 (1): 1–22.

Alden, Edward. 2012. "Immigration and Border Control." *Cato Journal* 32 (1): 107–124.

Andreas, Peter. 2000. *Border Games: Policing the U.S.-Mexico Divide*. Ithaca, NY: Cornell University Press.

———. 2003. "A Tale of Two Borders: The U.S.-Mexico and U.S. and Canada Lines after 9/11." Working Paper 77, Center for Comparative Immigration Studies.

Bach, Robert. 2005. "Transforming Border Security: Prevention First." *Homeland Security Affairs* 1 (1): 1–14.

Basu, Gautem. 2013. "The Role of Transnational Smuggling Operations in Illicit Supply Chains." *Journal of Transportation Security* 6 (4): 315–328.

Beaver, Janice Cheryl. 2006. *U.S. International Border: Brief Facts*. Report Number RS21729. Washington, DC: Congressional Research Service.

Cottam, Martha L., and Otwin Marenin. 2005. "The Management of Border Security in NAFTA: Imagery, Nationalism, and the War on Drugs." *International Criminal Justice Review* 15 (1): 5–37.

Foley, Neil. 2003. Review of *Operation Gatekeeper: The Rise of the "Illegal Alien" and the Making of the U.S.-Mexico Boundary*, by Joseph Nevins. *Journal of American History* 90 (3): 1108–1109.

GAO (US Government Accountability Office). 2008. *Homeland Security: DHS Has Taken Actions to Strengthen Border Security Programs and Operations, but Challenges Remain*. Report Number 08-542T. Washington, DC: GAO, March 6.

———. 2011. *Border Security: Preliminary Observations on Border Control Measures for the Southwest Border*. Report Number 11-374T. Washington, DC: GAO, February 26.

———. 2013. *Southwest Border Security: Data Are Limited and Concerns Vary about Spillover Crime along the Southwest Border.* Report Number 13-175. Washington, DC: GAO, February 26.

Giaritelli, Anna. 2018. "Drones Swamp U.S.-Mexico Border but Federal Agents Powerless to Stop Them." *Washington Examiner,* October 12, 2018.

Hong, Joseph. 2018. "Ultralight Aircraft, Second in Three Days, Crosses into U.S. in Suspected Human Trafficking Operation." *Palm Springs Desert Sun,* December 18, 2018.

LaSusa, Mike. 2016. "5 Clever Ways Mexican Cartels Move Drugs across U.S Border." InSight Crime, October 4, 2016. https://www.insightcrime.org/news/analysis/5-clever-ways-mexico-cartels-move-drugs-over-us-border/.

Longmire, Sylvia. 2014. *Border Insecurity: Why Big Money, Fences, and Drones Aren't Making Us Safer.* New York: Palgrave Macmillan.

Mendoza, Marissa, and Robert J. Bunker. 2009. "Mexican Cartel Tactical Note #32: Ultralight Aircraft and Border Drug Smuggling." *Small Wars Journal,* March 11, 2009.

Office of Border Patrol. 2005. *Analysis of IDENT Capabilities.* Washington, DC: Office of Border Patrol.

———. 2006. *National Border Patrol Strategy Briefing—BP101.* Washington, DC: Office of Border Patrol.

Office of the United States Trade Representative. n.d. "U.S.-Mexico Trade Facts." Accessed March 10, 2023. https://ustr.gov/countries-regions/americas/mexico.

O'Neill, Natalie. 2017. "Human-Smuggling Tunnel Discovered Near Mexican Border." *New York Post,* August 28, 2017.

Ordonez, Karina. 2008. "Securing the United States-Mexico Border: An On-going Dilemma." *Homeland Security Affairs* 2:1–10.

Phelps, James R., Jeffrey Dailey, and Monica Koenigsberg. 2014. *Border Security.* Durham, NC: Carolina Academic Press.

Tory, Sarah. 2018. "As the Border Wall Grows, Smuggling Tunnels Proliferate." *High Country News,* November 8, 2018.

United Nations Office on Drugs and Crime. n.d. "Smuggling of Migrants: The Harsh Search for a Better Life." Transnational Organized Crime. Accessed March 10, 2023. https://www.unodc.org/toc/en/crimes/migrant-smuggling.html.

US Bureau of Transportation Statistics. n.d. "Border Crossing and Entry Data." Accessed March 10, 2023. https://www.bts.gov/content/border-crossingentry-data.

USCBP (US Customs and Border Protection). 2004. *National Border Patrol Strategy.* Washington, DC: Office of Border Patrol.

———. 2017. *Cross Border Tunnels and Border Tunnel Prevention: Fiscal Year 2017 Report to Congress.* Washington, DC: USCBP.

———. 2019. "On a Typical Day in Fiscal Year 2018." Customs and Border Protection. https://www.cbp.gov/newsroom/stats/typical-day-fy2018.

———. n.d. "Border Wait Times." Customs and Border Protection. Accessed March 10, 2023. https://bwt.cbp.gov/.

US Department of Justice. 2017. *2016 National Drug Assessment Summary.* US Drug Enforcement Agency, Department of Justice.

CHAPTER 18

Transnational Struggles and the "State"

BIOPOWER AND BIOPOLITICS IN THE CASE OF A NIGERIAN HUMAN TRAFFICKING RING

Gregory Feldman

BY NOW THE STORIES ARE COMMONPLACE: people undergoing arduous journeys across land and sea in the hope of securing a better living for themselves and their families. They flee poverty, persecution, warfare, lack of opportunity, or all of the above. They are pushed by circumstances and pulled by hope, much like anyone else. Mainstream media outlets have reported in detail on their stories for years. Academic scholarship has published reams of research on the phenomenon ranging from fine-grained ethnographic studies to large-scale statistical research. These tales of people smuggled or trafficked no longer surprise but they continue to unsettle. Why? They make mincemeat of the foundational, and doggedly persistent, myth of global order: that each person is a citizen, identical to fellow citizens, all of whom embody a territorial nation protected by a bureaucratic apparatus called a state, which interfaces with other nation-states through the protocols of diplomacy. What Liisa Malkki (1995; see also Löfgren 1989) long ago critiqued as the "national order of things"—a static view of the world as divided into clearly bordered states, each representing a homogeneous nation—still premises our understanding of global security as a matter of professional expertise and of unreflective daily life.

This chapter offers an alternative perspective of global security, with respect to human trafficking, so that our policy and banal viewpoints more closely correspond to empirical reality. To do so, it relies on Michael Hardt and Antonio Negri's (2000) distinction between "biopower" and "biopolitics," where the former signifies state capital's exploitation of labor and the latter signifies the horizontal networks that labor utilizes to resist for the sake of attaining a "livable life" (Butler 2015: 25), if not democratic political spaces.[1] The chapter thus demonstrates, first, how transnational flows help to instantiate nation-states as an effect of the biopower-biopolitics struggle; and second, how people caught up in global migration circuits constitute particular locations as distinct places (Trouillot 2001). This approach avoids the fallacy of "methodological nationalism" (Wimmer and Glick Schiller 2002) in which the nation-state is regarded as a basic and irreducible unit of analysis in the study of global migration. Instead we must treat references to a pregiven nation-state as "representations of space"—that is, conceived spaces, such as the territorial nation-state, that have the effect of imposing order when deployed by such actors as planners, scientists, technocrats, businesspeople, and border officials (Lefebvre [1974] 1991: 38–39).[2] This move allows us to understand how the nation-state as a concept (rather than a pregiven thing) creates state-like effects when state agents strive to impose order on the unruliness of global migration, for example.

Therefore, the key question is not, How does the *state* engage global migration? Instead, the question is twofold: (1) How is the nation-state—as a symbolic trapping of situated power—invoked by those authorized as its agents? And (2) how do so many other people moving around the world constitute their lives, and so the specific places where they are living, in a shared relational field with those agents? This definition opens a vista on global order that is dynamic rather than *static* (or *state*-like; both cognates imply immobility and lack of change). More fully, it paints a clearer picture of how a range of actors—for example, border officials, policymakers, migrants, smugglers, and traffickers—constitute, and reconstitute, nation-states and particular places through their struggles in a relational field. Yet, given the legal issues involved, many of these struggles must occur in secret. In keeping with the larger edited volume, this chapter is an exploration of human agency, which necessarily implies human creativity, but not as something sensational or out of the ordinary. Rather, agency and creativity are daily phenomena perhaps deployed more frequently by those on the margins of global power where the state's reach might be less concentrated (Das and Poole 2004).

This chapter's case study relies on extensive ethnographic fieldwork undertaken in various intervals from 2013 to 2017 with an undercover police investigation team in a southern European Union (EU) member state. It focuses on a case involving a Nigerian trafficking ring that operated through their country and its capital city.[3] As one part of a large ethnographic project (Feldman 2019), I participated in several of the surveillance runs described here; conducted extensive interviews with the team and the Nigerian woman, Sadie, whose situation I describe; and studied the legal issues surrounding the case. This trafficking ring included a loose affiliation of actors stretching from West Africa to southern Europe to Germany. The country in which this team works remains confidential as a condition of ethnographic access. I obtained permission to conduct this fieldwork, and publish research from it, first from the team members themselves, then their immediate superior officer, and finally the national director of the team's home bureaucracy. All people in this chapter are identified through English pseudonyms.

SURVEILLANCE ON THE NIGERIAN CASE: THE STATE EFFECT IN THE BIOPOWER-BIOPOLITICAL STRUGGLE

A Nigerian ring that operated in the country frustrated the investigative team because it worked slowly and its members were loosely associated with one another, unlike the Romania- or Georgia-based criminal networks that they previously faced. The members of the Nigerian network hardly thought of themselves as a "ring," but rather as acquaintances who would do mutual favors for each other because they might be from the same place in Nigeria or know other people in common. Otherwise, they went about their own daily affairs (Feldman 2019: 158–159). Nevertheless, they pushed security officials among different states to collaborate in their efforts to control what law identifies as illicit migratory flows. These efforts occur not only within state spaces but across open ill-defined spaces like deserts and seas, which cannot be properly "secured" from a statist perspective.

On a drizzly May afternoon just after lunch, Brian, David, and Max (three of seven members of the street-level investigative team) received a phone call from a desk investigator. She had just received a call from an official in the national immigration service center where noncitizens apply for and pick up travel documents. The desk investigator had placed an alert on the file of a young woman whom her staff determined had entered the country two years earlier on a false Ghanaian passport. That passport falsely indicated her age at seventeen years. They suspected that she was actually eighteen to twenty years old but was taking advantage of juvenile status in her asylum application. That status allowed her to stay at an open hostel from which she soon disappeared. She reappeared in Germany during a sting operation in which she and some of her handlers were arrested. Due to her age and circumstances, the arrest resulted in her receiving temporary residence for humanitarian reasons (which is not asylum) in Germany. In March 2014, she then returned to the first country to apply for a document allowing her to travel while her asylum decision remained outstanding. At that point the lead investigator placed the alert on her file, as she would have to reappear in the country to pick up the document when it was ready. Two months later when she returned, an official notified the desk investigator by phone. Without missing a beat, the desk investigator phoned the street investigative team requesting that they follow the young woman. She did not ask the team to arrest the woman for traveling on a false Ghanaian passport but rather to collect possible evidence of a criminal ring that might be facilitating her movement and perhaps that of others as well (Feldman 2019: 160).

The young Nigerian woman arrived at the immigration office at four o'clock on a May afternoon. David, Brian, and I sat across the street at an outdoor café to watch for her exit. Frank and John remained in a car parked nearby. The woman exited forty minutes later and walked toward a bus stop before getting into a taxi. She arrived at a travel agency in the main bus station where Brian had earlier recruited a travel agent as an informant. They would soon enough learn where the woman intended to travel (Feldman 2019: 161–162). Brian had expedited the immigration paperwork of the travel agent's brother, which had gotten bogged down in red tape. His cultivation of this informant had entered dubious legal territory, as a judicial warrant might be needed both to get involved in the brother's paperwork and to obtain the information from her. Nevertheless, he explained, "this way, we have a friend for life" (111). As the team suspected, but still needed to confirm, the woman had bought a bus ticket for the journey back to Germany. She was to depart the station at seven forty-five the next morning.

David explained as we kept up with the taxi why he suspected, but was not yet sure, that the woman worked as a prostitute (a fact that was not confirmed until the arrest took place in Germany, as described earlier). He reasoned, "She has a nice slim body, she is Nigerian, and the shoes she is wearing are those like prostitutes would wear. They are just sandals with only two leather straps attached to a thin ankle brace. Do you see how they are studded with shiny metal squares?" He also noted that even though she wore jeans, uncommon for street prostitutes, these sandals were probably used on the job. It was suspicious, he thought, that she was wearing them on a day of heavy rain. "She must not have any other shoes to wear," David concluded. She left the next morning by bus for Germany (Feldman 2019: 162).

The team quickly gained reason to suspect that, before she left for Germany, a transnational ring handled this woman. This inference led to a fuller investigation, conducted with counterparts in Germany and other countries, focusing on four main suspects in their own country: three Nigerian men along with a lawyer. The young woman's handlers in this country hired the lawyer to take legal responsibility for her asylum application with the purpose of slowing the case down.[4] Juvenile asylum seekers are transferred to open-door hostels and provided with a living stipend if their cases take longer than sixty days to process. The lawyer can slow the adjudication process down with queries to reach that limit. The asylum seeker can then come and go at will at the hostel. They eventually leave the hostel for good once someone from the ring contacts them. Many of the young Nigerian women who end up in prostitution in Europe enter this way. The trafficker's first goal is to simply get the woman into the Schengen Area (the territory comprised of EU member states that opened borders between them). From there she can be easily moved to the most lucrative location within it (Feldman 2019: 159–160). Frank explained further:

> The center let us know that the girl from the airport has left and they haven't seen her. We had taken pictures. We got contact numbers they had sewn into the seam of their pants. She later arrived in Germany. The Germans found her and two other missing girls from our center when they busted a Nigerian ring there. So, we confirmed that Ghana was using our airport as a platform. After that, we analyzed asylum requests back to 2012 to see the pattern of what the Nigerians do. We ask Europol to consult member states for names

of girls who vanished from our centers. There were dozens of them, and a lawyer from our country was involved with many of these cases. (Feldman 2019: 164–165)

Some young Nigerian women from whom they took testimonies claimed they met a Nigerian man under suspicion in the country known as Raul. The team confirmed through phone taps that Raul would contact two other Nigerians and the lawyer to let him know that the women were coming and what names they would be using. The Nigerian men would collect the women from the bus station when they returned from Germany to pick up their asylum documents and then return them to the station the next day for them to travel back to Germany. The lawyer would provide the women with any necessary legal assistance. The team identified everyone from Nigeria who was tied to the asylum requests since 2012 and they learned that the same men always escorted the young women (Feldman 2019: 164–165). Frank noted, "We did 60 surveillances in this case. We had two meetings in person with the Germany. There was bilateral cooperation with them and also cooperation with Europol. The information from Germany that was valuable was that we learned that we were a platform for Germany and other places. We needed help from other countries too. We also needed judiciary cooperation to get information about the girls that were held in Spain in protective custody" (165). The team also searched twelve houses and offices,[5] tapped phones, and gathered numerous testimonies. Their overall investigation revealed their own country was not a final destination but only a way station to other EU countries and to Russia in a few cases. Ultimately, the team arrested the lawyer and the three Nigerian men on orders from the state prosecutor responsible for the case. While proving the existence of a ring is difficult, the team had gathered enough evidence for the prosecutors to gain at least convictions for human trafficking: the three Nigerian men were sentenced to ten years in prison, while the lawyer was disbarred for two years (165–166).[6]

Two features of the investigation stand out. First, there was a large amount of subterfuge by both the investigators and the smugglers. The smugglers made false statements about age, fled unsupervised hostels, and relied on intermediaries who could plausibly deny guilt. The investigators made use of undercover surveillance and informants whose support remained confidential. The ingenuity from both sides required that they function at the margins of the law, if not outside it. Second, the smugglers and investigators (and state officials more generally) competed with each other in an open-ended space through which smuggling channels get carved. These channels force investigators to cooperate with security officials in a host of other states. These facts compel us to broaden the analytic scope for the sake of accuracy. Specifically, we need not ask how the "state" as an entity based on territorial law should respond to global human smuggling and trafficking. That question assumes its pregiven existence. Rather, we need to ask how situated struggles over freedom of movement have the effect, on the one hand, of generating nation-states in certain manifestations relative to the migrants encountering that effect and, on the other, of both conditioning and enabling certain modalities of global migration. The state is not a *thing* but rather a lived phenomenal experience.

Even if the "state" lacks territorial fixity, there are certainly places where people coexist in one way or another. So what happens when people arrive at a place where they are not from? The simple answer is that they play a part in constituting it as a distinct place, thus revealing that particular places emerge as the effect of how people put their mark on them through daily practice.

SADIE AND THE HISTORIC SQUARE: STRUGGLES, DESIRES, AND GLOBAL NETWORKS

Sadie is a Nigerian woman in her late twenties living and working in the country as a street prostitute. The global networks through which she, along with many others, has moved help to concretize particular places, thus testifying to their agency. In Sadie's situation, that place appears in the form of a small square with a neglected historical statue sitting next to an auto repair shop. She shares it with two or three other Nigerian prostitutes. Sadie hails from Benin City in the Nigerian state of Edo, a common source of women working in prostitution in Europe (UNODC 2011: 17). She earns at least fifteen euros per customer, while in Edo, at best, she could earn ten euros per month as a cleaner. She might have had better prospects back home if she held a diploma, but the cost was likely too high, and her education was not prioritized ahead of her male siblings'. As she explains it, she contacted a man in Edo who knew about employment first in Morocco, then in Spain, with a Nigerian woman who needed help caring for her baby and herself as she moved to Europe. The woman advanced Sadie the cost of transportation to Morocco (Feldman 2019: 155).

Sadie had to seal her agreement to repay the advance by participating in a voodoo ritual. Its purpose was to bind the woman in a pact with her handlers in Nigeria. Through a covenant with a deity symbolized in anthropomorphic form, she agreed to pay back the sum advanced to her to travel to Europe. The doll symbolizing the deity was crafted to induce fear. "You would be afraid of it," Sadie insisted. "They make the doll with eyes and nose and mouth. Then, they talk, talk, talk, and drink whiskey. When you see it, you are afraid, so I ask God to help me. They did it with me. It's for them to know that you will do what you are supposed to. If you don't pay, then there is a problem. Life is difficult" (Feldman 2019: 155). The voodoo ritual is an instructive example of how agreements between people are based on a social bond that locks in the involved parties by means of fear of violating it. That bond is then rendered sacred by appeal to an abstract third entity. Thus, a voodoo ritual appealing to a frightful doll that symbolizes supernatural power is only exotic from a *statist* standpoint. From a different standpoint, one could just as easily conclude that smearing ink in the shape of one's name on paper and then depositing it in something called a "court" vested with "state" authority is no less exotic and irrational. The same explanation would apply in both ethnographic cases: the sacred aspect of the agreement (the doll's supernatural power or the court's authority derived from a mythical state) increases the fear of violating it, because the parties reasonably believe that the consequences would be grave.

Sadie traveled first to Togo by bus with six other young women. The *gidma* (a young man who works for the woman in Nigeria, who herself is colloquially known as a "momma") told her which bus to take and where to stay. After a few days, the gidma instructed them to board a different bus bound for Abidjan, Ivory Coast. He likewise gave them instructions about where to stay in that city so one of the gidma's contacts could keep watch on them. They remained in Abidjan for three months in order to avoid the police. Sadie remarked that "girls are not supposed to go on the street. We couldn't come out. No phone calls. We leave when the man tells us it is time." When the time came, they boarded a smaller bus and drove from Abidjan to

Morocco, across the western Sahara via Mali and Algeria, in two weeks. The gidma arranged for the food along the way, which usually came in the form of bread and bananas. They slept on the bus during rest stops. They traveled with dozens of young men and women and the gidma himself, who negotiated with police at the various borders and checkpoints along the way (Feldman 2019: 156). The state (formally understood) had a less uniform presence here in West Africa insofar as a clear, abstract border policy was not implemented along the way. Border crossing amounted to ad hoc arrangements based on the demands of local police and the ability of the gidma to negotiate a reasonable price.[7]

Sadie lived for two years in Morocco working for the momma. However, she was never to be employed as a caretaker. (In fact, the momma had told the same story to the six other women who traveled with Sadie out of Nigeria.) The momma explained that she had no money to pay Sadie, so she could not work off her debt through caretaking. Instead, she would have to become a prostitute. After two years, Sadie paid the momma 2,000 euros, at which point the momma left. Through contacts Sadie had cultivated in Morocco, she managed to find transport to Spain by arranging a similar deal with a momma based in Germany. She boarded a boat for a voyage that would take eight days, despite the short distance compared with her Saharan journey. "Everybody was afraid," she recalled. Upon her arrival in Spain, the police collected the entire group and took them to a camp. Sadie asked for asylum but did not get it. Most likely, the authorities concluded that she was an economic migrant, not someone who had endured persecution, though she explained, "Nigeria is difficult. I need to help my friends and I have a son." Due to delays in concluding her asylum request, she managed to leave Spain without any papers and travel by bus to the country discussed in this chapter. Another gidma put her in touch with people with whom she could live. Her work as a prostitute began again in the decrepit historic square, which is situated only two bus stops away from the apartment that she shares with a man from Sierra Leone and a woman and baby from the Ivory Coast (Feldman 2019: 156).

The intersection where Sadie solicits clients is formed by a side street and a main avenue linking the downtown to the residential districts on the city's outskirts. Sitting closer to downtown, the intersection is also close to small businesses, municipal offices, and residential apartments. The apartments contain a mix of elderly nationals who never moved out of the neighborhood because of favorable rent control laws and immigrants from a range of African, South Asian, and East European countries. Foot traffic through the intersection is busy with locals plus tourists, students, and visitors from everywhere in the world. Many of these people stay in the hostels and pensions that dot the urban landscape. The foot traffic is good for Sadie's business (Feldman 2019: 157).[8]

Sadie takes her clients past the monument, around a bend in the road, and up to a tucked-away pension called the Petit Palace. That pension, like the global networks to which it is tied, serves both the licit and the illicit dimensions of global circulations (see Nordstrom 2007). I went with Sadie to the pension to conduct interviews away from the busy intersection. A dark interior staircase leads to a locked glass door where one must ring a bell to have the proprietor unlock the door leading to the lobby. Sadie knows the proprietor. They exchanged greetings and a joke. When Sadie brings a client, the proprietor gives her a key, and the client pays him the room charge of five euros per hour. During my visit, I saw one open closet in the corner that contained stacks of neatly folded towels tended by a cleaning woman. The woman proceeded down one corridor and was passed by a man with a small suitcase. He appeared to be staying at the hostel as a conventional guest. Sadie takes her clients down a different corridor and into a small room with an old double bed. She explained that she does not take Nigerian men in case she knows their wives or they know her, and under no circumstances does she allow videotaping. Some clients are Chinese who own small businesses in the area but live in the suburbs. Casual observation of the intersection also shows many nationals, both young professionals and pensioners, who purchase her services and those of the other Nigerian women who wait there. Their attitudes toward her vary widely. Some ask her questions to learn more about her situation and offer sympathy. Some, she explains, "are crazy." They range from men as old as her father to young boys. She has not told her family in Nigeria about the nature of the work she performs here because of the shame, but the money she sends to them pays for school fees and food. As we exited the pension's lobby, Sadie nervously pointed to a doll shaped like a witch on top of a tall cabinet, saying, "It is like that," as she sped down the staircase, referring to the doll in the voodoo ritual.

This disheveled historic square was not always subject to what we myopically call globalization. More specifically, the EU accession and the 1995 implementation of the Schengen Area drew in ever more people from the union and abroad. Similarly, the rise of global tourism since the 1980s, South-North migration, international students coming from elsewhere, and entrepreneurs from around the world all now make a distinctive mark in a part of town that would have been known for national homogeneity decades earlier. (Of course, in previous decades, domestic migrations mainly composed this square as a particular place.) People are drawn to and through this square, or most any place, by their variously expressed struggles to better their lot in life. Simultaneously, agents authorized to act in the state's name try to condition and control those travelers' actions for the sake docility and productivity. The result of these tensions and struggles is the composition of the historic square in any given moment.

CONCLUSION: SECRECY, STRUGGLES, AND THE STATE

Both the Nigerian trafficking ring and Sadie's historic square open up the analytical question, What is the state? This is no mere philosophical exercise because the answer pushes us directly to the question of how human agency manifests itself to constitute the state (and the wider system of states) against the initiatives that people will inevitably take to improve their lives. The use of the term *state* betrays an intellectual laziness that leaves this fundamental issue, a rigorously empirical one, obscured. Analysis must begin with the struggles, desires, and needs of people themselves, out of which emerge sophisticated global networks to profit from it all. "States" do not merely attempt to deter or regulate these networks. Instead, agents authorized to act in the state's name constitute (and reconstitute) state-like entities in the very measures they deploy in reaction to how they are provoked by the global circulation of labor (and most migrants are labor migrants whether working with valid documentation or not).

To that end, we should recognize that transnational engagements between networks of state officials and networks of migrants and smugglers coconstitute a global order out of which "states" and particular places precipitate. Such relationality transpires in the biopower-biopolitical struggle, with both sides often acting clandestinely: the Nigerian ring and the investigative team with their colleagues in Germany, Europol, and Eurojust. Neither side wants to be recognized for what it is, so it either hides from view or presents itself publicly as something it is not. The Nigerians' phone calls from Ghana to the country were made on open lines, but the terms they used would not suggest criminality. They openly moved the young women through airports, but with fraudulent passports (which appeared to be authentic). The women work the streets with the intent of being seen by potential clients but in ways that do not reveal their handlers (in most EU countries, prostitution is not a crime, but profiting from someone's work as a prostitute is). Similarly, Sadie has to maintain discretion, and often tell lies, within the local Nigerian community, with her relations back home in Edo, and with the investigative team to protect herself and her son.

Similarly, the investigators either engaged in actions entirely undercover, with their presence undetected, or presented themselves publicly as normal bystanders. Phone taps are conducted so that suspects will speak freely, unaware the authorities are listening in. Surveillance operations are carried out in order to convince the suspect and bystanders that the investigators are simply ordinary people. (It worked so well in one such operation that Raul asked Brian and me if we knew how to purchase subway tickets from the automatic dispenser. Brian helped him without raising his suspicion.) The team does not make themselves known during an arrest when they and the suspects come face-to-face, because they wear ski masks. Their faces are only revealed when they are called in to testify in court in front of the suspects when they are on trial.

Hardt and Negri's biopower-biopolitics distinction provides an alternative perspective to make sense of the messiness involved in human trafficking and investigations of it. That perspective implies that nation-states and particular places are constituted out of the concrete struggles that make up the daily lives of migrants, state agents, and countless others. Importantly, they point out that in the biopower-biopolitics relationship, labor has the initiative as it makes new demands (better conditions, shorter hours, more benefits). Similarly, those marginalized in the capitalist system (propped up by the system of nation-states), such as migrants and refugees, push that system to somehow find safety and prosperity for themselves. That system constitutes itself in reaction to migrants' initiatives, and it transforms accordingly into something new and different each time. In this arrangement, the state, far from being identified as a coherent, institutionalized apparatus governing a territorial state, functions as a "representation of space." Such representations condition, but do not determine, lived experience by how their image of spatial order appears in policy, the law, and other technocratic initiatives. If we regard states as merely status quos, then we more accurately see the sheer globality and dynamism of how any place is constituted and then reconstituted. This nonstatist frame opens up a view of how the agency and creativity of migrants themselves both challenge and constitute global order through their efforts to secure their own lives from their particular position in the global hierarchy. Surely, this should be the starting point for our studies of "state" power.

NOTES

1. While Hardt and Negri see this conflict primarily in terms of labor and capital (backed up by the power of the state), we can expand their perspective to include the state's task of preserving the integrity of the nation-states understood in cultural terms, and, in any case, recognize that undocumented migration is largely composed of people seeking work abroad. Nation-states, especially European Union member states, work together on the political front because the integrity of any given nation-state is best preserved by guaranteeing the integrity of the system of nation-states (Feldman 2005). The cooperation of multiple states gives biopower its transnational quality as it seeks to halt the biopolitics of human smuggling and trafficking.
2. "Representations of space" are only one type of space that Lefebvre identifies as constituting place. For a fuller application of Lefebvre's ideas, see Feldman (2008) and Merrifield (1993, 1995).
3. *Trafficking* and *smuggling* can be difficult to distinguish as a legal matter. The former refers to moving people illegally across borders either against their will or under false pretenses, while the latter involves illegally moving people who knowingly and willfully consent to it. Of course, knowledge and willful consent can be difficult to establish.
4. The lawyer's presence signals the limits of Hardt and Negri's biopower-biopolitics distinction. The two sides of this struggle are not entirely distinct insofar as the lawyer straddles both: a legal expert who can advance the cause of each. Recent ethnographic work on police focuses on their interface, mainly in domestic contexts (Garriott 2011, 2013; Karpiak and Garriott 2018). Also see Jauregui (2016) and Martin (2019) for extensive ethnographic analyses of the blending of state authority with local social networks to establish very different types of political order. In a different argument, Sausdal (2018) points out how Danish investigators actually refrain from conducting their surveillance duties, thus ceasing to perform their duties of biopower.

5. The searches reveal such clues as plane tickets, bus tickets, unusually large amounts of case, and evidence found on phones and computers, which usually show peoples' contacts.
6. The legal term is not *ring* but rather *criminal association*. The relevant law is divided into three areas (see Feldman 2019: 165–166). The first area involves the action, or what the suspects actually did to facilitate human movement. Generically, these actions include extending bogus job offers, conducting recruitment efforts, giving shelter during transportation, and others. Specifically, the team had evidence of the suspects arranging transport from the phone taps and the women's own testimony that the first went to the lawyer's office in Ghana before meeting the suspects based in this country. The second area pertains to the means of their action. How did they manage to move these women either against their will or under false pretenses? The team obtained two pieces of crucial evidence: the use of voodoo to ensure their compliance in repaying their transportation costs, and phone taps confirming the detention, abuse, and rape of one of the women. The third area is the objective of their actions, which in this case would be prostitution. Frank shared all of this information with Eurojust so as to make it available to the team's German counterparts. Eurojust ensures that evidence obtained in one EU member state meets the legal standards in the courts of another. It also helps member states agree on legal standards when they participate in a joint investigation.
7. Much research is available on the situated character of border policy and state-making in West Africa with respect to global migration (Andersson 2014; Cold-Ravnkilde and Nissen 2020; Gaibazzi 2018; Richter 2019).
8. She did not make it clear to me whether she is working for a momma anymore. If not, then her profit margin is much greater than in Morocco because she is no longer paying off the debt incurred for her transportation from Morocco to Spain.

REFERENCES

Andersson, Ruben. 2014. *Illegality, Inc.: Clandestine Migration and the Business of Bordering Europe*. Berkeley: University of California Press.

Butler, Judith. 2015. *Notes toward a Performative Theory of Assembly*. Cambridge, MA: Harvard University Press.

Cold-Ravenkilde, Signe Marie, and Christine Nissen. 2020. "Schizophrenic Agendas in the EU's External Actions in Mali." *International Affairs* 96 (4): 935–953.

Das, Veena, and Deborah Poole, eds. 2004. *Anthropology in the Margins of the State*. Santa Fe: School of American Research Press.

Feldman, Gregory. 2005. "Estranged States: Diplomacy and the Containment of National Minorities in Europe." *Anthropological Theory* 5 (3): 219–245.

———. 2008. "The Trap of Abstract Space: Recomposing Russian-Speaking Immigrants in Post-Soviet Estonia." *Anthropological Quarterly* 81 (2): 311–342.

———. 2019. *The Gray Zone: Sovereignty, Human Smuggling, and Undercover Police Investigation in Europe*. Stanford, CA: Stanford University Press.

Gaibazzi, Paolo. 2018. "West African Strangers and the Politics of Inhumanity in Angola." *American Ethnologist* 45 (4): 470–481.

Garriott, William. 2011. *Policing Methamphetamine: Narcopolitics in Rural America*. New York: New York University Press.

———. 2013. "Introduction: Police in Practice: Policing and the Project of Contemporary Governance." In *Policing and Contemporary Governance: The Anthropology of Police in Practice*, edited by William Garriott, 1–28. New York: Palgrave Macmillan.

Hardt, Michael, and Antonio Negri. 2000. *Empire*. Cambridge, MA: Harvard University Press.

Jauregui, Beatrice. 2016. *Provisional Authority: Police, Order, and Security in India*. Chicago: University of Chicago Press.

Karpiak, Kevin G., and William Garriott, eds. 2018. *Anthropology of Police*. London: Routledge.

Lefebvre, Henri. (1974) 1991. *The Production of Space*. Oxford: Blackwell.

Löfgren, Orvar. 1989. "The Nationalization of Culture." *Ethnologia Europaea* 19:5–23.

Malkki, Liisa. 1995. "Refugees and Exile: From 'Refugee Studies' to the National Order of Things." *Annual Review of Anthropology* 24:495–523.

Martin, Jeffrey. 2019. *Sentiment, Reason, and Law: Policing in the Republic of China on Taiwan*. Ithaca, NY: Cornell University Press.

Merrifield, Andrew. 1993. "Place and Space: A Lefebvrian Reconciliation." *Transactions of the Institute of British Geographers* 18 (4): 516–531.

———. 1995. "Lefebvre, Anti-logos and Nietzsche: An Alternative Reading of the *Production of Space*." *Antipode* 27 (3): 294–303.

Nordstrom, Carolyn. 2007. *Global Outlaws: Crime, Money, and Power in the Contemporary World*. Berkeley: University of California Press.

Richter, Line. 2019. "Doing *Bizness*: Migrant Smuggling and Everyday Life in the Maghreb." *Focaal: Journal of Global and Historical Anthropology* 85:29–36.

Sausdal, David. 2018. "Everyday Deficiencies of Police Surveillance: A Quotidian Approach to Surveillance Studies." *Policing and Society*, online ahead of print, December 13, 2019. https://doi.org/10.1080/10439463.2018.1557659.

Trouillot, Michel-Rolph. 2001. "The Anthropology of the State in the Age of Globalization: Close Encounters of the Deceptive Kind." *Current Anthropology* 42 (1): 125–138.

UNODC (United Nations Office on Drugs and Crime). 2011. *The Role of Organized Crime in the Smuggling of Migrants from West Africa to the European Union*. Vienna: UNODC.

Wimmer, Andreas, and Nina Glick Schiller. 2002. "Methodological Nationalism and Beyond: Nation-State Building, Migration, and the Social Sciences." *Global Networks: A Journal of Transnational Affairs* 2 (4): 301–334.

CHAPTER 19

The Transformation of Mexican Migrant Smuggling Networks during the Twenty-First Century

Simón Pedro Izcara Palacios

THERE IS A GENERAL UNDERSTANDING that before the 1990s buildup of policing along the southwest US border, the business of migrant smuggling was dominated by small-scale freelance smugglers. In one of the earliest studies on migrant smuggling along the US-Mexico border, Gustavo López Castro (1997) depicted the figures of local and border migrant smugglers who came from the same hometown or region as their clientele and gained their knowledge of entering the United States illegally from their own experiences as migrants. However, as the physical and financial costs of migrant smuggling escalated, freelance smugglers, left at a competitive disadvantage, were driven out of business (Andreas 2009: 97).

The official discourse, disseminated by mainstream media and shared by US and Mexican authorities, as well as nongovernmental human rights organizations (Spener 2004: 301), usually overemphasizes the connection between migrant smuggling and organized crime to legitimize measures against smugglers. Likewise, the dominant discourse among academics points out that as a result of the criminalization of unauthorized migration and the militarization of the border, clandestine crossings became a business operated largely by transnational gang networks involved in the smuggling of people and trafficking of drugs (Alonso Meneses 2013: 104, 115; Andreas 2009; Slack and Whiteford 2011: 14). Although academics tend to be critical of US border policies, they are usually uncritical about government institutions' released data on human smuggling. Mainstream media reports on human smuggling, which almost never question official claims (Sanford, Martínez, and Weitzer 2016: 153), are frequently quoted uncritically in scholars' papers.

In the academic literature, there is a romanticized nostalgia about past border-crossing practices carried out by freelance smugglers embedded in the migrant-sending communities in Mexico. These guides were believed to be friends of the migrants, to belong to the same community as their clientele, and to fulfill an important social function, as they reduced the risks associated with crossing the border. With these smugglers, who were members of migrants' social networks, the crossing process was forged from a social obligation to ensure the safety of the border crossers (Alonso Meneses 2013: 117; Mora Martínez 2018: 18; O'Leary 2009: 34). These mythical figures are contrasted with today's dangerous migrant smugglers, who belong to criminal organizations, follow a mafia-capitalist logic, see migrants as a commodity, and take advantage of them through the use of coercion (Martínez 2010: 141). Migrant smuggling is frequently depicted as an activity in which scrupulous people no longer work as smugglers. Smugglers' abuses include charging exorbitant fees, abandoning those who are not able to keep up with the group, committing sexual abuse, or even causing migrant deaths. However, if we analyze the literature on migrant smuggling, smugglers' representations in the past did not differ much from today's views. According to Albert N. Thompson (1956: 78), the illegal entry of Mexicans into the United States was instigated by unscrupulous smugglers or coyotes who frequently used fear with considerable force and effectiveness, terrorized migrants with tales of what would happen if this illegal entry were discovered, and stripped them of all their funds. Likewise, Julia María Schiavone Camacho (2012) points out that in the early 1930s coyotes were depicted both as good men and as brutal villains.

In contrast, some academics argue that the business of migrant smuggling did not change as a result of increased enforcement, and call into question the alleged transformation of the migrant smuggling business into one dominated by large criminal syndicates (Spener 2004: 308; 2009: 160; Zhang, Sanchez, and Achilli 2018: 11). David Spener (2009: 104; 2011: 162) describes as dubious the assertion that transnational organized crime groups are engaged in migrant smuggling and compares this discourse with the claims about the national security threat posed by migrant smugglers linked to foreign communists in the 1920s, 1950s, and early 1980s.

My argument builds principally on the second body of scholarship, but it intends to contribute to the critical literature by shedding light on the actual changes that have affected migrant smuggling along the US-Mexico border. On the eastern side of the US-Mexico border, migrant smuggling is not dominated by large criminal syndicates; and yet migrant smuggling networks are more complex than two decades ago and freelance smugglers operating on their own have declined. This chapter centers on the hypothesis that, during the twenty-first century, migrant smuggling across the US-Mexico border became a more complex and expensive practice as a result of three factors: (1) the Mexican war on drugs, (2) the tightening of border controls in the United States, and (3) the decline of Mexicans' willingness to cross the border surreptitiously.

In this chapter, I argue that in order to cope with a changing scenario on the US-Mexico border, Mexican migrant smuggling networks have been refashioned in five ways during the last two decades. First, former migrant smugglers are being recruited by drug cartels in greater numbers for activities ranging from kidnappings to drug trafficking. Second, simple networks, composed of one cell and one line, have evolved into more complex networks, composed of several cells per line and several lines. Third, migrant smugglers have evolved from autonomous entrepreneurs into salaried workers. Fourth, US employers' role in migrant smuggling has been strengthened and corruption has become more widespread as border-control buildup has made the border more difficult to cross. Finally, smugglers have turned their eye to Central Americans because of Mexicans' reluctance to cross the border.

This chapter, based on interviews with 185 Mexican migrant smugglers, studies how and why Mexican migrant smuggling networks have been adapted to a riskier and less profitable environment. On the one hand, I examine the creativity of migrant smugglers, who, in order to cope with a changing scenario, have built large-scale organizations from small-scale ones and have started recruiting an increasing number of migrants from Central America. On the other hand, I analyze the reasons for the reduction of migrants' space for maneuver in negotiations with smugglers, as well as the reasons why migrant smugglers have lost autonomy and have traded freedom for security.

METHODOLOGY AND SAMPLE DESCRIPTION

Due to the nature of this study, a qualitative methodology was used. The technique used to collect discursive data was the in-depth interview; all interviews were recorded and transcribed. Contact with interviewees was made via social networks and snowballing in a number of different Mexican states: Tamaulipas, Nuevo León, San Luis Potosí, Veracruz, Mexico City, the State of Mexico, and Chiapas. Tamaulipas was selected because it is a border state with the United States where the number of smugglers is very high, as it is in Chiapas, the main entry point into Mexico of Central Americans seeking migrant smugglers to help them reach the United States. Mexico City and the State of Mexico were selected because they are the main nodal points from which smugglers' networks spread across the country. Finally, the three main transit points of migrant smuggling networks that operate along the eastern sector of the US-Mexico border were selected: Nuevo León, San Luis Potosí, and Veracruz. More than half (52.4 percent) of migrant smugglers interviewed were born in Tamaulipas; 8.6 percent in Veracruz; 7.6 percent in Nuevo León; 7.0 percent in Mexico City and San Luis Potosí; 5.4 percent in Chiapas; 2.2 percent in Puebla; 1.6 percent in Coahuila and Tabasco; 1.1 percent in the State of Mexico, Guanajuato, Oaxaca, and Sonora; 0.5 percent in Chihuahua and Guerrero; and 1.1 percent in the United States (Table 19.1).

I am aware that this study is biased in different ways. The sample is not random. In addition, more than half of the interviewees came from Tamaulipas, and most of them transported migrants to Texas. This has an impact on the information reported about the evolution of smuggling groups' structure and modus operandi, because violence against migrants in this area is higher than on the western part of the border. Also, drug cartels in Tamaulipas are more dependent on the fees paid by smugglers. Therefore, I want to emphasize that this is not a study of human smuggling in Mexico at large.

TABLE 19.1. Place of origin of migrant smugglers interviewed

	n	%		n	%
Tamaulipas	97	52.4	Tabasco	3	1.6
Veracruz	16	8.6	State of Mexico	2	1.1
Nuevo León	14	7.6	Guanajuato	2	1.1
Mexico City	13	7.0	Oaxaca	2	1.1
San Luis Potosí	13	7.0	Sonora	2	1.1
Chiapas	10	5.4	Chihuahua	1	0.5
Puebla	4	2.2	Guerrero	1	0.5
Coahuila	3	1.6	United States	2	1.1

Source: Compiled by the author from data recorded in the interviews.
Note: N = 185.

The findings of this chapter principally describe the eastern side of the border.

Between April 2008 and June 2018, I interviewed 185 migrant smugglers. Informants were people who led a cell that transported migrants and were supported by a small number of assistants. All but two of them were men. All had considerable experience in the business of migrant smuggling, as they had spent between one and thirty-one years in migrant smuggling. The respondents had on average six years of schooling, and their low level of education was the result of needing to work from childhood to sustain the family financially. The age when they started working fluctuated from five to twenty-three. They started working as migrant smugglers between the ages of sixteen and forty-one, and on average they dedicated 9.5 years to this activity (Table 19.2).

The cases discussed represent principally the southeast of the United States. Texas, Florida, and North Carolina were the states where most Mexican smugglers operated (Table 19.3).

THE RECRUITMENT OF FORMER MIGRANT SMUGGLERS BY DRUG CARTELS

Since the launch of military operations against drug cartels in 2006, violence in Mexico has reached unprecedented levels. As Guadalupe Correa Cabrera (2018: 1) explains, drug trafficking organizations "have diversified their operations and are now involved in new lucrative businesses" ranging from

TABLE 19.2. Selected characteristics of Mexican migrant smugglers interviewed

	Average	Minimum	Maximum
Age	36.8	21	49
Number of years involved in migrant smuggling	9.5	1	31
Years of schooling	6.0	0	16
Age when started working	10.1	5	23
Age when started working as migrant smuggler	26.9	16	41

Source: Compiled by the author from data recorded in the interviews.
Note: N = 185.

TABLE 19.3. States in the United States where interviewees operated

	n	%		n	%
Texas	112	60.5	Mississippi	3	1.6
Florida	21	11.4	Tennessee	3	1.6
North Carolina	15	8.1	Alabama	2	1.1
California	15	8.1	Arkansas	2	1.1
Virginia	12	6.5	Georgia	2	1.1
Louisiana	11	5.9	Kansas	2	1.1
Oklahoma	6	3.2	Minnesota	2	1.1
South Carolina	6	3.2	Idaho	1	0.5
Arizona	4	2.2	Iowa	1	0.5
Missouri	4	2.2	Michigan	1	0.5
New Mexico	4	2.2	Montana	1	0.5
Oregon	4	2.2	Nevada	1	0.5
Colorado	3	1.6	New Orleans	1	0.5
Illinois	3	1.6	New York	1	0.5

Source: Compiled by the author from data recorded in the interviews.
Note: The sum of N is higher than 185 because some of the interviewees brought migrants to different states in the United States.

kidnapping for ransom to the smuggling of hydrocarbons and their derivatives. As drug cartels' operations have diversified, criminal organizations have recruited new members with new areas of expertise. Consequently, in recent years an increasing number of former migrant smugglers have been recruited by drug cartels. Two-thirds of those interviewed who addressed this issue indicated that they knew of former migrant smugglers who had gone to work with drug cartels. Only one-fifth (22 percent) of the interviewees did not know whether former migrant smugglers were involved with drug cartels. Near half of respondents interviewed in 2011 and 2012 did not know whether former migrant smugglers were involved with drug cartels. By contrast, in 2013 most interviewees (94.4 percent) knew about former smugglers involved with drug cartels, and all those interviewed in 2014, 2015, and 2018 knew about some former migrant smugglers who worked for drug cartels (Table 19.4). These data give us some indication that the number of former Mexican migrant smugglers involved with drug cartels has increased in recent years.

One-quarter of the interviewees did not know about the activities carried out by former migrant smugglers involved with drug cartels, because they had lost all contact with them. When migrant smugglers go on to work for drug cartels, these groups usually force them to cut ties with the social world outside these organizations.[1] They no longer frequent the locations they used to, and they enter a new social world where old colleagues do not

TABLE 19.4. Interviewees' knowledge about the involvement of former migrant smugglers with drug cartels

Year	Knows former smugglers who work for drug cartels n	%	Does not know whether former smugglers are involved with drug cartels n	%	Total n	%
2011	4	50.0	4	50.0	8	6.8
2012	23	57.5	17	42.5	40	33.9
2013	34	94.4	2	5.6	36	30.5
2014	14	100.0	0	0.0	14	11.9
2015	9	100.0	0	0.0	9	7.6
2016	2	50.0	2	50.0	4	3.4
2017	3	75.0	1	25.0	4	3.4
2018	3	100.0	0	0.0	3	2.5
2011–2018	92	78.0	26	22.0	118	100.0

Source: Compiled by the author from data recorded in the interviews.

belong.[2] However, some smugglers involved with drug cartels have sporadic encounters with their former colleagues. Three-fourths of respondents had some knowledge about the activities carried out by former migrant smugglers involved with drug cartels. As can be seen from Table 19.5, drug trafficking was the most important activity carried out by migrant smugglers during the first years, especially in 2011; however, after 2013 the kidnapping of migrants for ransom became the most important activity carried out by them, and from 2014 they became involved in increasingly dangerous activities, such as serving as hit men. This was a result of the war on drugs. As hit men were the first and main casualties of the war on drugs, drug cartels gradually replaced fallen professional hit men with newcomers.

CHANGE IN THE STRUCTURE OF MIGRANT SMUGGLING NETWORKS: FROM AUTONOMOUS ENTREPRENEURS TO SALARIED WORKERS

Sociological and anthropological research based on interviews with smugglers depicts human smuggling as an activity generally carried out by small-scale organizations (López Castro 1997; Spener 2009). In contrast, the criminological perspective based on criminal court proceedings or police files focuses on forms of migrant smuggling that resemble highly organized, mafia-like criminal activities (Napoleoni 2016; Perrin 2013). In small-scale organizations it is assumed that smugglers and migrants share common interests and that the former take good care of the latter and often act out of humanitarian motives (Sanchez 2015; Zhang, Chin, and Miller 2007: 712). By contrast, in large-scale mafia-like businesses, it is supposed that smugglers are merciless criminals who only act to make huge profits (Napoleoni 2016). The data collected from interviewees indicate that on the eastern side of the US-Mexico border, the number of amateurs and small-scale smugglers has decreased rapidly while the number of large-scale smugglers has climbed. However, large-scale organizations do not resemble mafia-like businesses. Small-scale organizations gradually have been swallowed by large-scale organizations because the latter are able to negotiate better arrangements with drug cartels and have more resources to bribe border agents. However, the nature of the business has not changed much because smugglers in large-scale organizations are not merciless criminals; many of them are the same people who ran small-scale organizations a decade ago.

TABLE 19.5. Interviewees' knowledge about the activities performed by former migrant smugglers involved with drug cartels (percentages of *n*)

Activity	2011	2012	2013	2014	2015	2016	2017	2018	Total
Drug trafficking	25.0	4.3	8.8	7.1	11.1	0.0	0.0	0.0	7.6
Trafficking of drugs and weapons	25.0	13.0	8.8	0.0	0.0	0.0	0.0	0.0	7.6
Trafficking of drugs, weapons, and kidnapping of migrants	0.0	0.0	5.9	0.0	0.0	0.0	0.0	0.0	2.2
Trafficking of drugs and kidnapping of migrants	0.0	0.0	2.9	0.0	0.0	0.0	0.0	33.3	3.3
Drug trafficking, robbery, kidnapping of migrants and *sicariato* (hit men)	0.0	0.0	2.9	11.1	11.1	50.0	0.0	0.0	4.3
Kidnapping of migrants	0.0	13.0	38.2	11.1	11.1	50.0	0.0	0.0	20.6
Extortion of migrant smugglers	0.0	13.0	0.0	0.0	0.0	0.0	0.0	0.0	3.3
Giving information	0.0	0.0	2.9	0.0	0.0	0.0	0.0	33.3	5.4
Serving as *sicariato*	0.0	0.0	0.0	11.1	11.1	0.0	0.0	0.0	3.3
Engaging in illicit activities in general	25.0	21.7	14.7	22.2	22.2	0.0	33.3	0.0	17.4
Do not know what they do	25.0	34.8	14.7	33.3	33.3	0.0	66.7	33.3	25.0
n	4	23	34	14	9	2	3	3	92

Source: Compiled by the author from data recorded in the interviews.

They usually take good care of their clients, because this business depends on migrants' recommendations.

Large-scale migrant smuggling organizations in Mexico share some peripheral features of mafia-like structures: there is an internal hierarchy, smugglers receive a salary (Campana 2011: 222), they specialize in illegal economic activities, and they corrupt civil servants. However, migrant smuggling organizations do not share any of the core elements of mafia-like structures. First, they are not involved in the sale of protection (Gambetta 1993: 1). On the contrary, smugglers themselves pay protection fees (Izcara Palacios 2012). They provide genuinely desired services and do not exact a price for unwanted services. The so-called false *coyotaje* (Spener 2009: 155) is not a feature of large-scale migrant smuggling organizations.

Second, these organizations are not entrenched in a territory (on the contrary, they require territorial flexibility) and do not monopolize the markets in which they operate. Smugglers compete in attracting clients, but disputes are unusual. The way they compete is by gaining fame for delivering a good service. As a migrant smuggler from Tamaulipas who was involved in a complex network pointed out when interviewed in 2015, "Every *pollero* [smuggler] looks and fights for their people, but people go with those who are good and know better." Interviewees used to repeat the phrase, "The sun rises for everyone," meaning that there were customers for all of them.

Finally, smuggling organizations do not resort to violence. Mexican smugglers do not carry guns, and men of violence[3] are of little use in migrant smuggling. Only five of the interviewees could be described as men of violence. One was involved in drug trafficking before becoming a migrant smuggler. Four left the Mexican army because it was very hard to stay away from their families for such long periods. One of these four put their skills to profitable use trafficking weapons and finally became a migrant smuggler. The other three tried to find legitimate jobs but finally decided to become migrant smugglers because, during their time in the army, they got in touch with the bosses of large smuggling organizations.[4] In contrast, the other 180 interviewees did not have violent pasts.

Mexican migrant smuggling networks[5] can be divided by their degree of complexity. Those networks composed of one cell led by a migrant smuggler can be defined as simple, while those consisting of one or more lines, with two or more cells per line, can be defined as complex (Izcara Palacios

2015). A cell is a structure led by a migrant smuggler supported by a small number of assistants who transport migrants. A line is a group of actors involved in the transportation of a group of migrants from the country of origin to the country of destination. In simple networks, a single cell transports migrants from the point of origin to the point of destination. In complex networks, a line is usually composed of several cells. As it was explained by a migrant smuggler from Veracruz interviewed in 2012, "A *pollero* brings migrants from Chiapas to Mexico City, and from there they go to San Luis, and from here I take them to the border, and there I bring them to other *pollero* working in the same line.... A line is a team of *polleros* working for the same boss. There are several lines, and every line has its *polleros*."

Simple networks are composed of one cell led by a migrant smuggler, with the support of a small number of assistants. Migrant smugglers involved in simple networks are autonomous entrepreneurs who lead the network. Some of them satisfy the labor demand of US employers and receive economic compensation from them; others tend to work primarily for migrant social networks. In complex networks, each cell appears to be led by a migrant smuggler who has the support of several assistants. Migrant smugglers involved in complex networks are salaried workers. They lead the cell but not the network they are involved in. The one who leads the network is a person the smugglers call *patrón* (boss). Smugglers receive orders from the patron who manages the network and receive a salary that is paid by their patron.

As can be seen from Table 19.6, before 2012 the majority of migrant smugglers interviewed were autonomous entrepreneurs involved in simple networks. However, from 2013 most interviewees were salaried workers involved in complex networks. Therefore, the data from Table 19.6 give some indication that during the last decade, the number of autonomous smugglers involved in simple networks has declined while the number of salaried smugglers involved in complex networks has increased.

As a result of the Mexican war on drugs, the tightening of border controls along the US-Mexico border, and the change in migrant composition, the organigram of smuggling networks has changed as groups have moved from small-scale to large-scale businesses; consequently, the roles and the very agency of smugglers inside the group have also undergone drastic transformations. In a small-scale business, the smuggler has the freedom to

TABLE 19.6. Interviewees' knowledge about the degree of complexity of migrant smuggling networks

Year	Simple networks n	Simple networks %	Complex networks n	Complex networks %	Total n	Total %
2008	17	89.5	2	10.5	19	10.3
2009	14	77.8	4	22.2	18	9.7
2010	3	100.0	0	0.0	3	1.6
2011	24	82.8	5	17.2	29	15.7
2012	36	78.3	10	21.7	46	24.9
2013	8	22.2	28	77.8	36	19.5
2014	7	50.0	7	50.0	14	7.6
2015	4	44.4	5	56.6	9	4.9
2016	3	75.0	1	25.0	4	2.2
2017	0	0.0	4	100.0	4	2.2
2018	0	0.0	3	100.0	3	1.6
2008–2018	116	62.7	69	37.3	185	100.0

Source: Compiled by the author from data recorded in the interviews.

decide where and when to travel and how much to charge for their services. By contrast, in a large-scale organization, the smuggler is a salaried worker who has to obey to their patron. Smugglers have a minor role in the decision-making process. At the top of the pyramid is the patron. Under the patron are the bosses of every line, and smugglers receive orders from their immediate bosses. The patron is in charge of paying bribes, although smugglers pay from their salary to the recruiters and other people helping them.[6] In a riskier environment, small-scale smugglers have joined forces to form large-scale organizations. It makes sense for migrant smugglers to renounce their freedom in exchange for higher security.

TIGHTENING UP BORDER CONTROL: US EMPLOYERS' ROLE IN MIGRANT SMUGGLING AND BORDER CORRUPTION

Beginning in the twenty-first century, Mexican illegal migration to the United States dropped as a result of border enforcement, and the supply of migrant labor was outpaced by the demand. According to interviewees, two decades ago migrants came on their own to the United States in search of employment, and US employers had plenty of labor. Migrants selected the destination and smugglers acted as the facilitators. Therefore, smuggled migrants had an important role in the decision-making process of selecting their destination. However, as a result of higher border enforcement, illegal immigration decreased and some US employers started building alliances with migrant smugglers in order to obtain migrant labor on a regular basis (Izcara Palacios 2019). As a result, migrants' space for maneuver in negotiations with smugglers decreased. In recent times, smugglers have decided where migrants ended up.

Near two-thirds (118, or 63.8 percent) of the interviewees transported migrants to a concrete destination to work for one or several US employers.[7] By contrast, more than a third (67, or 36.2 percent) of the interviewees worked for migrants' social networks. Eighteen interviewees worked exclusively for migrants' networks, while 49 interviewees worked for migrants and employers. Migrants are aware of the destination, the job, and the salaries before getting smuggled. However, many do not know how many hours they should work to get the promised salaries. For example, a smuggler from Tamaulipas, interviewed in 2016, immigrated in 1999 to Texas to work in agriculture. In 2007, he told his employer that he was returning to Mexico and not coming back. At that time, the smuggler working for this employer had quit smuggling migrants. Therefore, the US employer convinced the interviewee to smuggle migrants to his ranch. The agribusinessman had an agreement with some immigration agents to allow the interviewee to smuggle migrants to the ranch. Consequently, he was never apprehended. He decided to become a smuggler because, as he said, this agribusinessman "is friend with the *migras* [US immigration officers], not with all, but with some, and I cross the border the day they are working." He crossed the border with fifteen migrants twice a year, in January and June. He had some people helping him in Mexico and three more people helped him in the United States, one who was in a safe house and two more who gave him information about the roads, the checkpoints, and a safe route to follow. He charged migrants US$4,000 but also received economic compensation from the US agribusinessman. He was not free to take anyone with him. His job was to select people with a strong work ethic. As he said, migrants "should be people who like the heavy work." Payment of the fee was not the only condition to be smuggled. As the interviewee said, "They have to work where they are brought, only there they have to be working." Migrants acquired an obligation to work for the employer that had the agreement with immigration authorities. As the interviewee said, "They should work for a few years when they are given the job. If they are brought, they are compelled to work." Being a hard worker was the requirement for being smuggled, because hardworking people with no money could be patronized. When the smuggler's fee was paid by the Texan agribusinessman, migrants received a reduced salary until the debt was paid. However, having the debt paid did not mean that migrants were free to leave the job.

The space for negotiations between smugglers and migrants has been severely reduced. Smugglers working for US businessmen bring migrants to the place where their labor is needed (Izcara Palacios and Yamamoto 2017). However, migrants cannot be described as victims without agency; they have room to maneuver. Migrants decide whether they want to migrate, although they cannot negotiate where to go or where to work. In 63.8 percent of the cases, smugglers brought migrants to an employer, a group of employers, an association of employers, or a pseudo-agency of employment. Smugglers offered migrants a place to go and a job to do, not a general location to go. If a migrant does not agree to do the job, he is not smuggled. Migrants decide whether they want to go, but smugglers determine whether migrants comply with the requisites set by US employers: age, physical strength, labor experience, work ethic, behavior, and so on. By contrast, in 36.2 percent of the cases studied, the requisite to be smuggled was payment of a fee.

Respondents pointed out that the smuggling business had changed in the last two decades in response to a growing demand for cheap labor. Interviewees used the words *before*, when there were plenty of migrants, and *now*, when migrant labor had become a scarce commodity. According to interviewees, rather than Mexican drug cartels, it was US businessmen who took over the business of migrant smuggling in order to import cheap labor. Interviewees pointed out that some US employers, in order to have access to cheap labor, have not only built alliances with migrant smugglers but also bribed US immigration agents (Izcara Palacios 2019). Some respondents indicated that during the last two decades, US employers participated directly in the recruitment of migrants, lessening the financial and legal obstacles of the journey. As can be seen from Table 19.7, before 2011 just a few respondents spoke about arrangements between US employers and US immigration agents to allow undocumented migrants to cross the border or to employ them; however, after 2012 more than half of interviewees spoke about these kinds of agreements.

Therefore, as a result of border enforcement and employers' involvement in migrant smuggling, migrants' role in the decision-making within the smuggling process has been weakened. Smuggled migrants have lost autonomy in deciding where to travel.

TABLE 19.7. Interviewees' knowledge about the arrangements made between US employers and US immigration agents

Year	Interviewees said that US employers, foremen, or employers' associations had some kind of monetary arrangements with immigration authorities to allow undocumented migrants to cross the border or to employ them *n*	%	Interviewees said that US employers had arrangements with immigration agents, but they did not specify the nature of these arrangements *n*	%	Total *n*	%
2008	1	5.3	1	5.3	2	10.6
2009	0	0.0	3	16.7	3	16.7
2010	0	0.0	0	0.0	0	0.0
2011	7	24.1	2	6.9	9	31.0
2012	23	50.0	5	10.9	28	60.9
2013	12	33.3	1	2.8	13	36.1
2014	9	64.3	0	0.0	9	64.3
2015	6	66.7	0	0.0	6	66.7
2016	2	50.0	0	0.0	2	50.0
2017	1	25.0	2	50.0	3	75.0
2018	2	66.7	0	0.0	2	66.7
2008–2018	63	34.1	14	7.6	77	41.6

Source: Compiled by the author from data recorded in the interviews.

THE RECRUITMENT OF MIGRANTS FROM CENTRAL AMERICA

Mexican migration to the United States has declined rapidly during the last two decades. From 2009 to 2014, 1 million Mexicans left the United States for Mexico, while only 0.87 million Mexicans left Mexico to come to the United States (Gonzalez-Barrera 2015: 5). As can be seen from Table 19.8, in the early 2000s more than 90 percent of foreign nationals apprehended by the border patrol or arrested by US Immigration and Customs Enforcement for violating the Immigration and Nationality Act were Mexicans (US Department of Homeland Security 2012, 2015, 2017). In contrast, less than 5 percent of foreign nationals apprehended were born in the Northern Triangle of Central America. After the 2008 US economic crisis, the number of Mexicans apprehended declined gradually, and by 2016 only half of those apprehended were Mexican nationals. By contrast, the number of foreign nationals apprehended from the Northern Triangle of Central America rapidly soared, and by 2016 near 42.7 percent of those apprehended came from this region.

J. Edward Taylor, Diane Charlton, and Antonio Yúnez-Naude (2012: 593) documented a decreasing supply of Mexican labor to the United States beginning in 2008 as a result of long-term structural changes rather than a temporary response to US recession. Accordingly, the figure of Mexican nationals apprehended by the border patrol or arrested by US Immigration and Customs Enforcement fell every single year from 2008 and did not recover when the US economy expanded (US Department of Homeland Security 2012, 2015, 2017). Increasing costs of migration, a decline in birth rates, and improvement of local conditions in Mexico have been mentioned as the causes of the decline in international migration (Jones 2014: 754). In contrast, the number of nationals from Central America's Northern Triangle who were apprehended fell slightly during the recession years (from 2008 to 2011) but soared when the US economy recovered (Table 19.8). Beginning in 2012 not only did the US economy grow rapidly, but the purchasing power of US wages in Mexico climbed as the Mexican peso tumbled against the US dollar. Therefore, over the last decade, the persistence of relatively high wages in the United States did not create pressure for illegal immigration from Mexico (Hanson and Spilimbergo 1999).

TABLE 19.8. Aliens apprehended by country of nationality

Year	Mexico n	Mexico %	Central America Northern Triangle El Salvador	Guatemala	Honduras	Nicaragua	n	%	Total n
2002	994,724	93.6	9,209	8,344	11,295	823	29,671	2.8	1,062,270
2003	956,963	91.5	11,757	10,355	16,632	1,055	39,799	3.8	1,046,422
2004	1,142,807	90.4	19,180	14,288	26,555	1,664	61,687	4.9	1,264,232
2005	1,093,340	84.7	42,885	25,909	55,756	4,272	128,822	10.0	1,291,065
2006	1,057,206	87.6	46,315	25,135	33,383	3,228	108,061	9.0	1,206,417
2007	854,275	88.9	19,699	23,907	28,265	2,119	73,990	7.7	960,772
2008	884,082	84.7	27,152	33,697	33,779	2,802	97,430	9.3	1,043,863
2009	715,914	82.3	26,778	33,882	31,822	2,674	95,156	10.9	869,857
2010	598,004	79.5	27,539	36,230	29,942	2,417	96,128	12.8	752,329
2011	489,547	76.3	25,594	39,153	29,122	2,150	96,019	15.0	641,633
2012	468,766	69.8	38,976	57,486	50,771	2,532	149,765	22.3	671,327
2013	424,978	64.1	51,226	73,208	64,157	2,712	191,303	28.9	662,483
2014	350,177	51.5	79,321	97,151	106,928	2,912	286,312	42.1	679,996
2015	267,885	57.9	51,200	66,982	42,433	1,577	162,192	35.1	462,388
2016	265,747	50.1	78,983	84,649	61,222	1,756	226,610	42.7	530,250

Sources: US Department of Homeland Security (2012, 2015, 2017).

Note: Total *n* is the sum of all aliens apprehended by the border patrol. While nearly 95% of aliens come from Mexico and the Central America Northern Triangle, 5% come from other countries (Venezuela, Colombia, Haiti, etc.).

TABLE 19.9. Origin of migrants recruited by interviewees

	Mexico		Central America		Total	
Year	n	%	n	%	n	%
2008	19	100.0	1	5.3	19	10.3
2009	18	100.0	5	27.8	18	9.8
2010	3	100.0	0	0.0	3	1.6
2011	29	100.0	8	27.6	29	15.7
2012	41	89.1	13	28.3	46	24.9
2013	19	52.8	31	86.1	36	19.5
2014	7	50.0	9	64.3	14	7.6
2015	7	77.8	8	88.9	9	4.9
2016	4	100.0	4	100.0	4	2.2
2017	4	100.0	4	100.0	4	2.2
2018	2	66.7	3	100.0	3	1.6
2008–2018	153	82.7	86	46.5	185	100.0

Source: Compiled by the author from data recorded in the interviews.

The decline in the flow of Mexican immigrants has been attributed to two factors: the slow recovery of the US economy and the stricter enforcement of US immigration laws (Gonzalez-Barrera 2015: 6). By contrast, according to interviewees, the contraction of Mexican illegal migration to the United States was a result of border enforcement and drug-related violence along the border. Respondents said that Mexicans had fear about migrating. As a consequence, migrant smuggling networks replaced Mexican migrants with Central Americans, who, according to interviewees, are more inclined to take risks than Mexicans. As can be seen from Table 19.9, nearly half (46.5 percent) of the migrant smugglers that were interviewed recruited migrants from Central America. Less than one-third of the smugglers interviewed from 2008 to 2011 recruited Central Americans. By contrast, beginning in 2013, the percentage of migrant smugglers who recruited Central Americans grew rapidly.

CONCLUSION

As a consequence of the Mexican war on drugs, harsher border controls in the United States, and the decline in Mexican migration, migrant smuggling has become more hazardous and costly than two decades ago, and smugglers' clientele has decreased significantly. Mexican smugglers have adapted to a new environment using several strategies. Many smugglers who in the past were autonomous entrepreneurs involved in simple networks are now salaried workers in complex networks. To work as a salaried worker in a complex network is less profitable that working on one's own in a simple network, but it is safer in the more dangerous environment that has resulted from tougher border controls and rising drug cartels' violence. Moreover, smugglers have combatted the growing costs and decreasing revenues of engaging in this business by recruiting an increasing number of Central American migrants, who pay larger fees than hesitant Mexicans.

On the other hand, according to interviewees, as the supply of undocumented migrants became insufficient to fill the demand by US employers because fewer people were migrating from the south, some US employers not only started building alliances with smugglers in order to obtain migrant labor, they also commenced paying bribes to US immigration officials to allow migrant smugglers to cross the border.

Finally, Mexican drug cartels are recruiting former migrant smugglers in greater numbers. The latter are involved in activities such as drug trafficking and kidnapping of migrants. In some cases, former migrant smugglers became involved voluntarily with drug cartels, whereas others were forced. Criminal groups not only recruit former migrant smugglers, they also monopolize a great portion of the revenues generated by migrant smuggling, as migrant smugglers are paying dues to cross the territories dominated by drug cartels. Migrant smugglers and drug trafficking organizations have built close ties during the last decade; however, Mexican drug cartels do not transport migrants to the United States. Migrant smuggling and drug trafficking are different businesses. Migrant smugglers and criminals are involved in a kind of symbiotic relationship, where the latter benefits at the cost of the former. According to interviewees, drug cartels are parasites benefiting from migrant smugglers' work, while the latter only experience harm from the former. Therefore, migrant smuggling is not an activity conducted by Mexican drug cartels, but it is a business from which criminals profit.

For decades, the US government has argued that Mexican drug cartels have taken over human smuggling. According to interviewees' narratives, it is US businessmen and not criminal organizations who have taken over migrant smuggling. The numbers of visas issued and administered by the Department of Homeland Security and the Department of Labor for bringing in foreign workers are not enough to fill the jobs rejected by US workers that do not require much formal education. Therefore, as US employers cannot import migrant labor in a legal fashion, they are resorting to migrant smugglers.

NOTES

1. A smuggler from Veracruz interviewed in 2015 said that his best friend decided to work for a drug cartel because he was offered a better salary. The interviewee did not know what his friend was doing, because as soon as he entered the cartel, he did not speak to him anymore. As he said, "I had a *cuate muy mi cuate* [a very close friend] that told me: 'I was invited to work, I leave.' He is not a *pollero* [smuggler] anymore. He is doing another job. He left because there [with drug cartels] he does better. I do not know what he really does because since he left, he stopped being my friend, we no longer talk each other or anything." By contrast, a smuggler from Oaxaca interviewed the same year said that he had some friends who were kidnapped to work for a drug cartel. From the time they were recruited under duress, he had not received any news about them. As he said, "Since you stop knowing about them, you don't know anything, I had some friends who were taken [by drug cartels] and nothing is known."
2. Smugglers used to frequent the same locations. The recruitment of migrants consumes most of the time of many smugglers. Smugglers sometimes take a proactive role and search for the migrants, but on other occasions they take a reactive position and just wait for the migrants to come to them. The first approach can be challenging because on many occasions the smuggler spends a large amount of time trying to convince a person and comes back with empty hands. For example, in November 2018 many smugglers from Tamaulipas traveled more than two thousand kilometers to recruit Central American migrants from the caravans, but they had very little success. According to smugglers, most migrants from the caravans did not have money, had vices, and had a weak work ethic. In contrast, the reactive role can be more rewarding, because when a migrant approaches a smuggler, he or she has money and is eager to migrate. Therefore, in some cases smugglers wait for the migrants to come to them. The locations of smugglers are very well known, and any migrant looking for them can find them. As one smuggler pointed out, "We are well known, so popular, in certain places anyone knows us, because we move from one place to another. It's like a seamstress or a *curandera* [healer] of the *colonia* [district], anyone knows where to find her, because they know her, it's the same in this work of *pollero* [smuggler]." Also, at certain times of the year, such as Easter, migrant smugglers gather in specific places. They travel hundreds or thousands of kilometers to meet in a certain place on a certain day. In contrast, when a migrant smuggler is

recruited by a drug cartel, he no longer frequent these locations; it is as if he has disappeared. He does not meet his colleagues anymore. They see one another only on rare occasions. In some cases they become enemies, because smugglers recruited by cartels sometimes participate in kidnappings of migrants and smugglers.
3. Men of violence are armed men accustomed to dispensing violence (Gambetta 1993: 252).
4. They received bribes to protect smugglers' safe houses and so on. As a former soldier from Mexico City interviewed in 2012 pointed out, "I knew him [the boss of a migrant smuggling network] because he was the one who gave us the *cuotas* [bribes] to let him work. So, when I retired, I looked for him to ask him for a job."
5. Many studies carried out in the area have demonstrated the need to be conscious about terms and notions that might reiterate mainstream and noxious narratives about criminal convergence and highly hierarchical groups, such as the notion of networks (Sanchez and Natividad 2017). By using the word *network*, I do not want to insinuate that migrant smuggling is an activity carried out by criminals, or that migrant smuggling is a transnational organized crime.
6. This interviewee's statement marks clearly the distance between a smuggler and their patron: "He orders me, or he talks to me, but I don't know him. I know he is the *patrón* [boss], the one in charge, but I haven't seen him personally. Those *patrónes* at the top do not mix with the ones below. He wants the job done well and commands, that is what he does" (migrant smuggler from Veracruz, interviewed in 2014). Under the patron is the leader of a line. In some cases smugglers are not allowed to speak with the patron, only with the leader of their line. As it was pointed out by a smuggler from the city of Mexico interviewed in 2018, "With that patron I haven't spoken. My patron doesn't allow me to talk to him. I have been present when they talk, but I don't talk to the *mero, mero patrón* [very, very boss]. Few know him because he makes a deal with my boss and my boss with me [leader of the cell]."
7. This figure must be taken with some caution because smugglers were not selected randomly. I have principally studied smugglers working for US employers.

REFERENCES

Alonso Meneses, G. 2013. *El desierto de los sueños rotos: Detenciones y muertes de migrantes en la frontera México-Estados Unidos 1993-2013*. Tijuana: El Colegio de la Frontera Norte.

Andreas, P. 2009. *Border Games: Policing the US-Mexico Divide*. 2nd ed. Ithaca, NY: Cornell University Press.

Campana, P. 2011. "Eavesdropping on the Mob: The Functional Diversification of Mafia Activities across Territories." *European Journal of Criminology* 8 (3): 213–228.

Correa Cabrera, G. 2018. *Los Zetas Inc.: La corporación delictiva que funciona como empresa trasnacional*. Ciudad de México: Editorial Planeta Mexicana.

Gambetta, D. 1993. *The Sicilian Mafia: The Business of Private Protection.* Cambridge, MA: Harvard University Press.

González Barrera, A. 2015. *More Mexicans Leaving than Coming to the U.S.* Washington, DC: Pew Research Center. https://www.pewresearch.org/hispanic/wp-content/uploads/sites/5/2015/11/2015-11-19_mexican-immigration__FINAL.pdf

Hanson, G. H., and A. Spilimbergo. 1999. "Illegal Immigration, Border Enforcement, and Relative Wages: Evidence from Apprehensions at the US-Mexico Border." *American Economic Review* 89 (5): 1337–1357.

Izcara Palacios, S. P. 2012. "Coyotaje y grupos delictivos en Tamaulipas." *Latin American Research Review* 47 (3): 41–61.

———. 2015. "Coyotaje and Drugs: Two Different Businesses." *Bulletin of Latin American Research* 34 (3): 324–339.

———. 2019. "Corruption at the Border: Intersections between US Labour Demands, Border Control, and Human Smuggling Economies." *Antipode* 51 (4): 1210–1230.

Izcara Palacios, S. P., and Y. Yamamoto. 2017. "Trafficking in US Agriculture." *Antipode* 49 (5): 1306–1328.

Jones, R. C. 2014. "The Decline of International Migration as an Economic Force in Rural Areas: A Mexican Case Study." *International Migration Review* 48 (3): 728–761.

López Castro, G. 1997. "Coyotes and Alien Smuggling." In *Migration between Mexico and the United States: Binational Study,* 965–974. Research Reports and Background Materials, vol. 3. Mexico City: Mexican Ministry of Foreign Affairs; Washington, DC: US Commission on Immigration Reform.

Martínez, O. 2010. *Los migrantes que no importan.* Barcelona: Icaria Editorial.

Mora Martínez, L. 2018. "De la sierra a la costa: Migración otomí transnacional: Los hñähñü de la Huasteca Poblana." *Migraciones internacionales* 9 (3): 9–36.

Napoleoni, L. 2016. *Traficantes de personas: El negocio de los secuestros y la crisis de los refugiados.* Barcelona: Paidós.

O'Leary, A. O. 2009. "The ABCs of Migration Costs: Assembling, Bajadores, and Coyotes." *Migration Letters* 6 (1): 27–35.

Perrin, B. 2013. "Migrant Smuggling: Canada's Response to a Global Criminal Enterprise." *International Journal of Social Science Studies* 1 (2): 139–153.

Sanchez, G. E. 2015. "Human Smuggling Facilitators in the US Southwest." In *The Routledge Handbook on Crime and International Migration,* edited by S. Pickering and J. Ham, 275–286. New York: Routledge.

Sanchez, Gabriella, and Nicholas Natividad. 2017. "Reframing Migrant Smuggling as a Form of Knowledge: A View from the U.S.-Mexico Border." In *Border Politics: Defining Spaces of Governance and Forms of Transgressions,* edited by Günay Cengiz and Witjes Nina, 67–83. Cham: Springer International Publishing AG.

Sanford, R., D. E. Martínez, and R. Weitzer. 2016. "Framing Human Trafficking: A Context Analysis of Recent U.S. Newspaper Articles." *Journal of Human Trafficking* 2 (2): 139–155.

Schiavone Camacho, J. M. 2012. *Chinese Mexicans. Transpacific Migration and the Search for a Homeland, 1910–1960.* Chapel Hill: University of North Carolina Press.

Slack, J., and S. Whiteford. 2011. "Violence and Migration on the Arizona-Sonora Border." *Human Organization* 70 (1): 11–21.
Spener, D. 2004. "Mexican Migrant-Smuggling: A Cross-Border Cottage Industry." *Journal of International Migration and Integration* 5 (3): 295–320.
———. 2009. *Clandestine Crossings: Migrants and Coyotes on the Texas-Mexico Border*. Ithaca, NY: Cornell University Press.
———. 2011. "Global Apartheid, Coyotaje, and the Discourse of Clandestine Migration: Distinctions between Personal, Structural, and Cultural Violence." In *Global Human Smuggling: Comparative Perspectives*, 2nd ed., edited by David Kyle and Rey Koslowski, 157–185. Baltimore: Johns Hopkins University Press.
Taylor, J. E., D. Charlton, and A. Yúnez-Naude. 2012. "The End of Farm Labor Abundance." *Applied Economic Perspectives and Policy* 34 (4): 587–598.
Thompson, A. N. 1956. "The Mexican Immigrant Worker in Southwestern Agriculture." *American Journal of Economics and Sociology* 16 (1): 73–81.
US Department of Homeland Security. 2012. *2011 Yearbook of Immigration Statistics*. Washington, DC: Office of Immigration Statistics. https://www.dhs.gov/sites/default/files/publications/Yearbook_Immigration_Statistics_2011.pdf.
———. 2015. *2014 Yearbook of Immigration Statistics*. Washington, DC: Office of Immigration Statistics. https://www.dhs.gov/sites/default/files/publications/DHS%202014%20Yearbook.pdf.
———. 2017. *2016 Yearbook of Immigration Statistics*. Washington, DC: Office of Immigration Statistics. https://www.dhs.gov/sites/default/files/publications/2016%20Yearbook%20of%20Immigration%20Statistics.pdf.
Zhang, S. X., K. L. Chin, and J. Miller. 2007. "Women's Participation in Chinese Transnational Human Smuggling: A Gendered Market Perspective." *Criminology* 5 (3): 699–733.
Zhang S. X., G. E. Sanchez, and L. Achilli. 2018. "Crimes of Solidarity in Mobility: Alternative Views on Migrant Smuggling." *ANNALS of the American Academy of Political and Social Science* 676 (1): 6–15.

CHAPTER 20

In Search of Protection
IRREGULAR MOBILITY AMONG PALESTINIAN YOUTH IN GAZA

Caitlin Procter

MOUSA, A TWENTY-ONE-YEAR-OLD YOUNG MAN from the north of Gaza, died while attempting to swim across a fast-running river in Bosnia in the late summer of 2019. The first his family knew of his death was through a series of screenshots of Facebook stories and live videos. Friends Mousa had made in Turkey before traveling on along the Balkan route had photographed his corpse, tagging other friends from Gaza they had met along the way in the hope that through a long process of sharing and tagging, they might find someone who could reach his family with the news. A long back-and-forth of comments between Mousa's brother and the men who had been with him when he died ensued, in the public space of Mousa's Facebook wall, trying to work out whether there was a way to return his body to Gaza. I had met Mousa in the spring of 2019 as he was preparing to leave in an effort to get to Europe. "It really doesn't matter where I end up, I'll go anywhere. But I can't stay here in Gaza, waiting to die. I'd rather die trying to make something of my life than waiting here for a missile to hit my house," he explained. The tragedy that ended Mousa's life is a painfully familiar story among Palestinians from Gaza who risk their lives to journey to Europe in search of protection.

I began conducting ethnographic field research for this project with the intention of understanding how young people in Gaza who had lived through over a decade of Israeli-Egyptian blockade and three large-scale military attacks on Gaza conceptualized their futures. What I quickly found was that the overwhelming majority of young people I met in Gaza were trying to find ways to escape their besieged land. The Arabic word for migration, *hijra*, has religious connotations drawn from the Prophet Muhammad's emigration (*hijra*) from Mecca to Medina, and the term implies a process of mobility with the intention of settling permanently. The term *muhajirin* (permanent migrants) is used to refer to the individuals undertaking this process, as opposed to other terms that could be used in a discussion of mobility, such as *mughtaribin* (living away from home) or *musafirin* (traveling). In Gaza, youth only spoke of their intention to leave as their intention to become *muhajirin*. In the context of Palestine, this is significant. Efforts among Palestinian youth to leave Gaza are new, and they exemplify the impact of the continuing expansion of Israeli settler colonial control in the occupied Palestinian territories—to the extent that Palestinians in Gaza now feel that their only option for a secure future is to migrate. Although grounded in this political context, this chapter explicitly focuses on the processes of irregular mobility required to leave Gaza, and on the ways young people in a context of protracted political and economic crisis come to view these new forms of mobility as fundamental to their own protection.

Describing any form of mobility as "irregular" might conjure up a number of images: large sums of money paid to greedy individuals who seek to exploit vulnerable individuals; hidden processes that are illicit, if not illegal; actions that need to be concealed from authority. In Gaza, mobility is not completely licit, in that it is not managed through a formal or governmental authority. In spite of the draconian security and movement restrictions imposed on Palestinians in Gaza by Israel, young people continue to elaborate new ways to leave. The pursuit of irregular processes is therefore undertaken in Gaza as the only way to attempt to secure protection and safety. This chapter argues that, among Palestinian youth, individuals who enable this process (be they smugglers or other kinds of migration facilitators) are not seen as exploitative individuals. On the contrary, they are perceived as resourceful service providers who can conjure up mobility in a distinctly immobile place. The mundane, routine interactions between these facilitators of irregular migration and the young Palestinians are formed on the basis of community links and shared solidarities where the financial cost of leaving Gaza is seen as the required compensation for a valuable service intended to bypass the movement restrictions imposed by Israel.

This chapter draws from fieldwork conducted in the Gaza Strip between November 2018 and August 2019, involving interviews and informal conversations and discussions with over two hundred young people aged between twenty-one and thirty-five who were either in the process of leaving Gaza through irregular means or seriously considering engaging in the process. Research participants were recruited initially through civil society organizations and later through the friends and connections of other interlocutors. Semistructured interviews and informal conversations and discussions were my principal research methods, although a significant amount of time was also spent doing participant observation among groups of young people and their families, as well as with the families of young people who had died in the process of trying to leave Gaza. I was also able to spend limited periods of time doing participant observation among youth waiting to leave at the southern Rafah border crossing out of Gaza. This was complemented by twenty-two interviews and numerous informal conversations with Palestinian academics and policy experts, Palestinian and international humanitarian aid workers, and leaders of civil society organizations. I subsequently conducted follow-up fieldwork with fifteen young people once they reached various destinations in Europe, primarily via phone, WhatsApp, and Instagram.

MOVEMENT RESTRICTIONS UNDER BLOCKADE IN GAZA

Drinking fresh juice on the beach in Gaza as the sun sets is one of the small pleasures of living there. Year round, children run in and out of the sea to play, body-boarders catch small waves, and boys do parkour jumps from crumbling wooden structures, once home to restaurants, that stick out from the beach over the water. Music blasts out of mobile phones, and carts selling roasted sweet corn and sweet potato make their way up and down the beach. Looking out at the sea, one could almost be anywhere on the Mediterranean. But as the sun sets, a stream of beaming bright lights appears on the horizon: Israeli military ships, demarcating the six-nautical-mile radius of the sea blockade on the Gaza Strip. It is immensely claustrophobic. Under an Israeli-Egyptian blockade of land, air, and sea since 2007, the vast majority of Palestinians in Gaza have not left the strip of land stretching just forty-one kilometers in length since the Hamas take-over in the same year.

In order to make sense of the arguments that follow, it is vital to understand the broader political context of Gaza and, within that frame, the movement restrictions placed on Palestinians in Gaza that control much of everyday life and opportunities. The Oslo Accords have failed to realize "peace" in Palestine and Israel, and yet "the peace process" remains the principal discursive framework in which the relationship between Palestine and Israel is discussed by the overwhelming majority of political partnerships on both sides, as well as the global media. The majority of the young people who are the central focus of this study were born in the aftermath of the Oslo peace process and have grown up under the structural conditions ushered in by the accords.

In the aftermath of the first intifada (uprising), the Oslo peace process was initiated in 1991. Bringing hope among Palestinians and Israelis that some kind of resolution could be achieved, the Oslo agreements proposed a two-state solution, in which a Palestinian state on the West Bank and Gaza would exist alongside an Israeli state. What emerged instead was a "peace process" that, by design, fundamentally changed the landscape of Palestine politically, economically, and physically (Al Husseini and Bocco 2009; Roy 2007). The conditions imposed on Palestinians by the Oslo process were intrinsically shaped by Israel's closure policy,[1] established early in 1991. This policy sealed off the occupied territories from each other (Gaza, the West Bank, and East Jerusalem), from Israel, and from external markets, removing any prospect for the development of the Palestinian economy in doing so (Roy 2007). It severely restricted Palestinian access to natural resources, movement of people, and movement of goods, leading to rising unemployment and limitations on any prospects for sustained economic development. Negotiations under the Oslo process wore on throughout the 1990s, during which time Israel steadily reshaped the reality of occupation in both the Gaza Strip and the West Bank.

The Gaza Strip has been under blockade since 2007, when Israel declared the enclave to be a "hostile territory" following a Hamas coup.[2] Under this blockade of air, land, and sea, life in Gaza has become increasingly stifling. While movement within the enclave is heavily surveilled and regulated through checkpoints operated primarily by Hamas and Islamic Jihad, freedom of movement beyond Gaza is almost exclusively prevented by the siege. Particularly relevant in this sense is the Coordination of Government Activities in the Territories—an administrative unit within the Israeli Ministry of Defense with a specific mandate to "implement the government's civilian policy within the territories of Judea and Samaria and toward the Gaza

Strip" (Government of Israel, n.d.). The tasks of the Coordination of Government Activities in the Territories include the policing of not only the movement of people in and out of Gaza but also the entry and exit of all food and goods. With a chilling degree of accuracy, this includes a calculation of the required number of calories needed to avert a situation of mass starvation in Gaza (Hass 2012).

Within this complex political landscape, a generation of Palestinians in Gaza have grown up through three Israeli military attacks, in 2008, 2012, and 2014. The latest of these attacks was the most devastating: during the attack, which lasted fifty-one days between July 8 and August 26, 2014, 2,251 Palestinians were killed; a further 11,231 were injured (10 percent of whom now suffer a permanent disability); 18,000 homes were severely damaged or destroyed; at the height of the onslaught, 500,000 Gazans became internally displaced persons and 100,000 Gazans were left displaced by the end of the war (OHCHR 2015). Demolished buildings and streets are found across Gaza, and Israeli drones overhead buzz day and night, conducting surveillance. Spilling beyond the already densely populated refugee camps, many families live under makeshift structures on the beach and on small patches of agricultural land. Gaza sits on the brink of a major public health crisis, as only 3 percent of the freshwater along this stretch of the Mediterranean meets World Health Organisation standards (RAND 2018). Households receive a maximum of eight nonconsistent hours of electricity a day, with many families receiving only three to four hours and relying on generators when they can afford to do so (OCHA 2018). After twelve years of Israeli-Egyptian blockade, unemployment in Gaza is among the highest in the world (OCHA 2022); almost exclusively, the young people I interviewed during this research were unemployed.

Under blockade, leaving and returning to the Gaza Strip has become almost impossible, but movement restrictions in Gaza in fact long predate the Hamas takeover in 2007. Since the start of Israel's occupation of the West Bank and Gaza in 1967, Israeli policies have consistently limited the possibility of domestic economic development, as part of a bid to preclude the possibility of a Palestinian state (Roy 2016), within which movement restrictions have played a key role. Later, in June 1989, Israel introduced a card system to restrict the movement of Palestinians in Gaza, limiting the number of individuals who could leave the Gaza Strip. After the signing of the

Oslo Accords in 1994, Israel built a barrier around Gaza. Although it was still possible to get in and out, this access was conditional on permits and the crossings would regularly close without warning, leaving Palestinians trapped on either side. The bombing of the airport and seaport in Gaza in 2001 intensified the need for access to goods and materials, which was made possible by a tunnel network managed by different political factions between Gaza and Egypt that had existed infrastructurally since the early 1980s (Pelham 2012). After the Hamas takeover of the Gaza Strip in 2007, Hamas set about formalizing the tunnel economy through the Tunnel Affairs Commission, regulating the movement of goods and people through tunnels. Although Israel made concerted efforts to disrupt the tunnel network in Operation Cast Lead (2008–2009), it was not until Operation Protective Edge in 2014 that the tunnel network was substantially destroyed and largely stopped being used for the movement of people.

Before turning to the ways that youth navigate these movement restrictions, it is worth examining the political event that has dominated much of the political discussion about Gaza for the last two years, the Great March of Return, which has implications for the discussion of political agency in migration facilitation that follows. From March 2018 to the winter of 2019, tens of thousands of Palestinians in Gaza took part in weekly demonstrations in what was called the Great March of Return. While demonstrators took part for varying reasons, which were significantly shaped by gender and class, the overarching drive for participation was the desperate need to change the status quo in Gaza, and to pressure Israel to lift the blockade. A number of interlocutors described the march as having been the last hope for change that could have persuaded them to stay. In reality, the protest achieved few substantive gains and left more than thirty-six thousand Palestinians injured and hundreds killed. What started as an effort to revive a collective political mobilization among Palestinians in Gaza ended with many feeling that every option for change had been tried—now there was nothing left but to attempt to leave Gaza.

COMPLICATING MIGRANT-SMUGGLER RELATIONSHIPS

There is a devastating regularity to reports in both mainstream and social media that document individuals crossing the Mediterranean by perilous means. Images of inflatable boats packed with people, of individuals scrambling over walls or under fences, of makeshift refugee camps, of people drowning, and of people driving in trucks across deserts have all become somewhat usual. Individuals like Mousa who migrate to Europe by irregular means are pitied for their desperation in even considering such forms of mobility, while blame is levied at profit-oriented individuals, typically men, who facilitate these journeys (UNODC 2015).

The response of European governments has been predominantly focused on implementing a security-based policy aimed to curb irregular migration and criminalize the practice of migrant smuggling—an approach pioneered through the 2000 United Nations Protocol against the Smuggling of Migrants. These efforts at criminalization not only have been proved incapable of either explaining or reducing irregular migration (Sanchez 2017) but have concurrently delegitimized the work of nongovernmental organizations in migrant search-and-rescue missions in the Mediterranean (Cusumano 2017). Indeed, the consequences observed as a result of European Union anti-smuggling policies have radically called into question the extent to which such policies can ever have the well-being and best interests of migrants at heart (Aloyo and Cusumano 2018; Carrera et al. 2019). In Hamas-administered Gaza, the populist narratives I encountered among the international and diplomatic community often compounded this imagery with alarmist assumptions of the culpability of smugglers in Gaza who facilitate the migration of Salafi-jihadists to Europe.

A growing critical literature explaining the multiplicity of relationships between individuals facilitating migration and migrants has done important work in challenging these assumptions, focusing on the roles and relationships between individual migrants, their families, and the kinds of networks with which they engage in order to move, as well as the interaction between structural forces that dictate the possibility of mobility and individual desires and aspirations. The question of migrant agency underlies public and policy discourse in which migrants are characterized as holding little to no agency, as well as the way academics theorize different forms of migration. Indeed, operationalizing the notion of "migrant agency" in processes of irregular migration is about showing how migrants in tightly restrained and vulnerable situations still look for ways to regain control of their circumstances (Squire 2017). We know, for instance, of solidarities that exist between smugglers and migrants who engage their services (Achilli 2018); that often smugglers are asylum seekers or migrants themselves and are relying on their own past migratory experiences to provide a service to others (Stone-Cadena 2016); that many share the same nationality or place of origin as those they work for (Zhang 2007); that migrants can have a certain autonomy and choice in decisions made during journeys (van Liempt and Doomerik 2006); and that, as individuals, smugglers can be ordinary citizens, self-defining as entrepreneurial in their attempts to help others to be mobile (Achilli 2015). Finally, we know that, to a certain extent, irregular migration facilitation achieves its aim of enabling the movement of those who might otherwise be immobile. The reliance of individuals and families on these mechanisms and methods is evidence of how increased state control and policing of borders has led to a deeper reliance on smuggling activities (Andreas 2009; Sanchez 2017). Receiving help to escape violence is considered by many to be invaluable, and a service worth paying for if necessary (Koser 2013). Indeed, in some contexts it can be considered immoral not to ask for money in exchange for the provision of a service, since not doing so can be seen as evidence of concealing a secret agenda (Osella 2015: 370). Taken together, these studies have built a constructive counter to the notion that, once in the hands of smugglers, migrants are left helpless to whatever fate has in store. Instead, this scholarship points to the myriad ways in which both individuals and communities navigate processes of irregular migration.

Attention to agency in irregular migration establishes a more nuanced picture of closed borders, and in this context blockade, as contested spaces. However severely constrained the circumstances of the Gaza Strip, I argue in this chapter that Palestinians who navigate the tightly controlled siege on the Gaza Strip are critical agents of change. A failure to recognize this reifies the power of the state to control a population under siege and, following Ċetta Mainwaring (2016: 291), "conceals the contested politics of mobility security evident in negotiations between migrants [and other actors]." This chapter builds on this growing body of critical scholarship, focusing on a different migratory population and drawing from the concept of navigation to add to existing constructions of migrant agency. Writing about the efforts of individuals and communities to live in uncertain and unstable circumstances, Henrik Vigh (2009) advocates for the usefulness of the concept of "navigation" of a "social terrain." In his analysis, he uses navigation as a tool to bridge the gap between "agency" and "social forces." This, he argues, denotes the extent to which acts are inseparable from their environments. Navigation can help us to understand how actors behave in environments that are constantly changing. Drawing on Vigh, rather than trying to fix notions of subject and object or agency and resistance to the lives of the young people I worked with, I explain the actions as navigations in the face of protracted insecurity attempts in order to provide a fuller description of their social and political worlds, under extreme pressure from different sources. Reading actions as navigations can lead us to a better understanding of the constant efforts of youth in Gaza to find new ways of surviving under the imposed conditions of blockade in which they live. I suggest that by navigating irregular processes and procedures of mobility, these young people engage in a mechanism that allows them to assert some control over their own lives. The process of coordination, which enables Palestinians to leave Gaza in order to be smuggled elsewhere, is not seen here as an exploitative process, but rather becomes a vehicle through which personal lives and broader political struggles can continue.

THE ROLE OF COORDINATION IN IRREGULAR MOBILITY

Today, there are two operational crossings for people to move in and out of Gaza: the Erez crossing from the north of Gaza into Israel (and the only subsequent way to travel into the West Bank), and the Rafah crossing from the south of Gaza into Egypt. The Erez crossing is controlled by Israel and is a highly securitized passage limited to trade permit holders, medical patients, travel facilitated by diplomatic missions, and sometimes students taking up scholarship or training opportunities abroad. Indeed, a number of young people I met in Gaza were applying for permits to leave through Erez on such grounds, after which they would be escorted directly to the Jordanian border, without stopping in historic Palestine on the way. Once in Jordan, they would be permitted to fly from Amman to their destination. However, even the limited number of Palestinians granted permits often have them denied at the last minute or at the crossing itself, typically on account of a "security block" that suggests (with no requirement of evidence) that the Palestinian in question would pose a security threat to the Israeli state.

The focus here, however, is on the southernmost crossing out of Gaza, located in Rafah, which borders Sinai. This crossing has been predominantly closed since the blockade of Gaza began.[3] To use the Rafah crossing, Palestinians are required to meet Egyptian travel criteria, subject to preregistration with the Hamas authorities in Gaza. Palestinians are required to prove foreign residency or present a foreign passport; possess a medical referral for treatment in Egypt; or hold a visa for work, study, or tourism in another country. Indeed, many who cross Rafah do so because although they possess the required visas and invitations, they are denied the possibility of crossing Erez for so-called security reasons. The list of Palestinians in Gaza registered to leave through Rafah is hundreds of thousands of names long—and thus, a process of *tansiq* emerged to "coordinate" the option for individuals to leave sooner in exchange for a fee.

Tansiq was seen as the first rung of the ladder to climb in the long process of reaching Europe by irregular means. In practical terms, tansiq meant paying a fee to an individual to move names up the list and increase the likelihood of crossing Rafah sooner. Individuals who could facilitate tansiq were sometimes referred to as "travel agents" and other times as individuals in a community (in both instances, in Gaza these individuals were always men). The fee fluctuated depending on how regularly the Rafah crossing was open. In early 2017, for instance, the fee for coordination was reportedly as much as US$5,000; but by late 2019, this had reduced to around US$1,200–$1,500. Although the process of tansiq had nothing to do with Hamas, the government also did not actively police the practice. There were rumors within the communities in which I worked that Hamas wanted to control the price of tansiq in order to ensure they could take a cut, but the price continued to fluctuate dramatically during the period of my research.

This process of tansiq was differentiated by youth from the process of *muharrib* (smuggling), even though the goal of both was to enable individuals to move across a border, and both processes involved financial exchange. Neither process was seen as more licit than the other; rather, they were described as concretely separate processes that were part of a migration journey to reach Europe. Finding a *muharribiin* (smuggler) with whom to journey to Europe was widely discussed among youth as being the next stage in the journey after they succeeded in leaving Gaza. Once through the Rafah crossing, the next stage would ideally be to fly to a country where it was easy for Palestinians to obtain a visa. In practice, this meant flying to Turkey and then continuing with a smuggler on the Balkan route, or flying to Mauritania to go with a smuggler across the West Mediterranean route. The prospect of going directly with a smuggler overland from Egypt and through the Central Mediterranean route was largely considered too dangerous, because of the ongoing instability in Libya.

As migration became an increasingly popular subject of conversation in Gaza, the Hamas government remained publicly quiet on topic. Some young people commented that they were in fact doing Hamas a favor by leaving: "It's less work for them to govern a smaller population! Maybe they'll do a better job when we are gone," said Nur. Over the course of 2019, more and more people told stories of relatives or friends who had left or were leaving, with no clear destination or reason for travel in mind: "We're not living anymore here in Gaza, we are simply not alive. It's like watching dead people walk the streets," said Jamal, a twenty-four-year-old who was still living in Khan Younis, waiting for his name to be called to leave through Rafah, when we met. Several of Jamal's close friends had already left, and among his wider social circle, the possibility of leaving Gaza and migrating elsewhere was a constant subject of discussion. "What is there to be afraid of? The worst that can happen is that I die. I live every day of my life thinking I might die, so does everyone in Gaza. I know people say going with a smuggler can be bad, but it's better to try it and see than to just stay here and wait to be killed by an airstrike."

The process of finding out about the travel agents or individuals who could facilitate tansiq in Gaza was described by many research participants in straightforward terms: "It's not a big deal," Nur explained. At twenty-four years old, she had recently got married and was planning to leave Gaza with her husband for an unknown destination imminently. "There are a lot of these travel agents in Gaza to choose from, thirty or forty or something. You can shop around, find the best deal!" Once they reached Egypt, Nur and her husband planned to fly to Turkey and then contact the smuggler who had facilitated the journey of friends of theirs several months earlier. Their friends had gone from Gaza to Turkey and had, according to Nur, ended up in Belgium. In spite of the European Union–Turkey agreements, which were poorly understood among interlocutors, a significant number of young people planned to fly from Cairo to Istanbul and then attempt to reach

Greece with the help of smugglers they assumed they would be connected to once they arrived, typically by other friends already in Turkey. Nur spoke of the process calmly and confidently. "It's easy to get information, the guy our friends went with was good. . . . They didn't have to pay all the money up front, just a deposit at first and the rest when they arrive."

Although she and her husband did not have the full amount of money that they believed they would need to travel, this was not prohibitive to their journey. On the contrary, Nur explained that staying in Gaza was prohibitive to her ability to fulfill expectations that she perceived as essential to being fully recognized as an adult woman. As a newlywed couple, Nur explained the pressure on her and her husband to have a child as soon as possible, but she was determined to do this outside Gaza: "Never ever would I consider having a child here in Gaza, I want my child to have access to another life than this one—there is no hope for us, let alone another generation here in Gaza. I only want to get pregnant after we have left." There is a global and long-standing literature on the pursuit of adulthood (or escape of "waithood") that migration can enable among young men (Monsutti 2007; Wojnicka and Pustułka 2019). This literature suggests that migration requires material resources that men can more easily mobilize at the household and community levels, as well as personal attributes most often associated with masculinity. Nur explains how in the context of Gaza, migration was also undertaken in the pursuit of social processes and culturally desired trajectories toward female adulthood (see Alpes 2017 for a similar discussion in the context of migration of women from West Africa). Contrary to the idea that leaving Gaza necessitated engagement in illicit processes that would carry risks for her and her husband's safety, Nur described the process as ʻadi (literally translated as "ordinary"), used in this context to describe the process as something banal and mundane. This disrupts the idea that once in the hands of a smuggler, individuals who were traveling lost any sense of agency or choice. On the contrary, they were using irregular migration in this context as a mechanism to fulfill broader aspirations connected to adulthood.

Nur and her husband planned to stay in Egypt with friends before traveling to Turkey, where they would stay with family until they assessed the situation, found a smuggler they were able to trust, and were ready to travel onward. Deciding whom to trust was largely dependent on individual social networks, and in the experience of my interlocutors the routes they took to reach Europe were based on the advice they received from friends who had already traveled. Adham was an example of an individual whose journey inspired many of his friends. He had successfully reached Belgium some four months after leaving Gaza, where he was seeking asylum, and was highly regarded for his success in doing so among his group of friends in the middle area of the Gaza Strip. I met this group of friends before I spoke to Adham himself, and they each recounted varying elaborations of his journey—one that they all planned to emulate. At twenty-two years old, Adham had spent months gathering money from different relatives, neighbors, and friends to enable him to leave Gaza. Rather than actively seeking out a travel agent in Gaza, he had gotten into a conversation with someone in the camp by chance who suggested the possibility of tansiq to enable him to leave quickly. At the time he left, the Rafah crossing was open regularly, and the price of tansiq had dropped to US$1,500. The man he met was a friend of his family and was known in the community for working in various odd jobs in community organizations. According to Adham, there was nothing underhanded about their interactions—he was just trying to help. He promised to secure Adham a visa to Turkey within a week, and once Adham reached Cairo, he would put him in touch with "friends of his," implying migration facilitators, who could help him out along the way. According to Adham's friends, the journey to Europe had been *'aadi* (straightforward), each *muharrib* had passed him on to the next one seamlessly, and he had not been asked to pay more than a small deposit until he got to Belgium.

The story that Adham told of his own journey was somewhat different, and he admitted that he had spared his friends and family most of the details of the conditions he had endured during the journey. "But, compared to some of the stories you hear, mine wasn't so bad.... If one of my friends wants to do the same journey, I'll try to help him come the same way," Adham explained. "To be honest, what my friends live with by staying in Gaza is more dangerous than anything I faced in this journey." Adham, like many young people across Gaza, had taken part in the Great March of Return, in the hope that this might be a way to finally change the status quo of blockade and occupation: "We had so much hope at the start of the march, that it was finally a way to change our circumstances—it was really something different, something new. But it ended just like everything else, the only thing the march achieved was ruining the futures of so many young people in Gaza. When the march turned bad, I felt there was no choice, I had to leave if I wanted to make anything of my life." Although his journey had been full of precarity and uncertainty, Adham felt more in control of his life during this process than he ever did while living in Gaza. "We're used to this life, to living each day at a time, to believing that death is waiting for you down the street. When you're moving from place to place, even though you don't know where you are going, you are going somewhere."

While Adham's journey had been successful, many young people in Gaza also knew of Palestinians whose journeys to Europe had, like Mousa's, ended in death. A young woman from a refugee camp close to Gaza City was killed in a fire in an overcrowded building where she had been made to wait in Turkey before boarding a boat to Greece. And a young man from a refugee camp in Jabalia had jumped from a building in an effort to escape police in Greece and had died. Many individuals had disappeared in Cairo. One man from Beit Lahia in the north of Gaza had reportedly been sent to Syria from Turkey, since he had no papers to prove that he was from Gaza. Other journeys "failed" as a result of structural constraints. Mohammed, for example, had attempted to leave Gaza two years earlier, in 2016. He had paid for a tourist visa to visit Turkey, using a loan from an international funded association in Gaza that loaned money for start-up projects. Having paid for his visa, Mohammed then had to wait for the Rafah crossing to open. At that time, in 2016, Rafah was only open sporadically, usually for several days a month that were unannounced. In order to stand a chance of crossing on one of only four buses that would leave each day, he explained, he had to first register on a public list to leave, and then pay a travel agent US$3,500 to increase his chances of leaving sooner. He kept a packed suitcase in his room for seven weeks, waiting for a day when the border would be open and his name would be called to board a bus at the crossing that would take him to Cairo. His visa to Turkey expired before Rafah opened again, and he lost all his money because the travel agent had already used it to try to secure his crossing. This adds another perspective to the growing literature on "waiting" in irregular migration processes (Zharkevich 2020). While substantial attention has been paid to the potential for individuals to be cheated and exploited, made to wait long periods of time for smugglers to facilitate a crossing or journey, in the case of Mohammed the journey failed because of structural factors—namely, the siege. The emphasis in his explanation was not on the travel agent who had taken his money but on the broader political environment. Although his father was still paying off his debt, which added an enormous financial burden to the family, Mohammed was still focused on trying to leave and was talking to multiple travel agents in Gaza to try to secure a deal whereby he could pay for his journey only after he arrived in Europe.

CONCLUSION

The ways that young people in Gaza talk about and prepare for the processes of smuggling between Gaza and Europe, of which tansiq is a critical part, are important to developing our understanding of how they conceptualize this process, and how and why they might make certain decisions along the way. In the public discourse, which is preoccupied by the arrival of migrants in Europe, little attention has been paid to the state machinery that leaves individuals with no choice but to find forms of irregular mobility in order to protect their own lives. This discourse has similarly failed to account for the myriad processes that go into what is broadly described as "being smuggled." Nor does it account for the social and political agency of individuals in planning and undertaking these journeys. While narratives that victimize migrants as vulnerable and passive subjects of abusive smugglers are common, young people on the move from Gaza did not attribute significant importance to the dangers or difficulties faced along the way. Leaving Gaza remains extraordinarily challenging. There are no official data available on the numbers who have left with no plans to return in the past eighteen months since the Rafah border began to be more regularly open, but border monitoring suggests that over forty thousand Palestinians have left Gaza during that period. Out of a population of just over two million, this figure is significant, and likely to be a conservative estimate. The blockade of the Gaza Strip means that those who want to leave have no choice but to engage the help of travel agents and smugglers in doing so. Often, money to pay for leaving Gaza is not demanded as an up-front payment, but individuals can pay fees for their coordination once they reach Europe.

For young people in Gaza, the processes necessary to migrate to Europe (raising enough money to leave, coordinating the Rafah crossing, finding a smuggler, choosing which route to attempt) were seen as somewhat secondary to their overall life projects of attempting to secure their own protection. The legality of this process was entirely inconsequential to their plans, and however dangerous the journey might be, it was seen to be the only path toward a longer-term goal. Further, when the uncertainties posed by a journey are no more than the uncertainties that already exist in daily life, there is little to deter people from forms of irregular mobility. On the contrary, in spite of the uncertainties of the journey, these unplanned routes present individuals with a far greater series of choices and opportunities to exercise agency than remaining in Gaza.

By attending to the ways young people attempt to defy the siege and leave Gaza, this chapter has shown how the facilitation of irregular migration is, for young Palestinians from Gaza, a means to different social and political goals. The overemphasis on the criminal dimension of human smuggling overshadows the structural and political regimes that have forced such choices in the first place. In the case of Gaza, migration with no intention to return represents an unprecedented shift away from the practice of nationalist struggle in a resistance movement that has defined Middle Eastern politics for almost a century. That young Palestinians in Gaza see no alternative for their futures but to undertake journeys that they know might fail is indicative of the extent people will go to in the pursuit of protection, and ultimately of freedom.

NOTES

This project has received funding from the European Union's Horizon 2020 research and innovation programme under the Marie Skłodowska-Curie grant agreement No 101032492.

1. Detailed analyses of the closure policy can be found in Roy (1999, 2007) and Turner and Shweiki (2014).
2. For a history of Hamas's thirty-year transition from fringe military resistance to governance, see Baconi (2018).
3. In recent years, the Rafah crossing has rarely been open: in 2015, it was only open for thirty-two days throughout the year; in 2016 for forty-four days; and in 2017 for thirty-six days (figures taken from border monitoring conducted by OCHA [2017]).

REFERENCES

Achilli, L. 2015. *The Smuggler: Hero or Felon?* Policy Brief 2015/10. Florence: Robert Schuman Centre for Advanced Studies.

———. 2018. "The 'Good' Smuggler: The Ethics and Morals of Human Smuggling among Syrians." *ANNALS of the American Academy of Political and Social Science* 676:77–96.

Al Husseini, J., and R. Bocco. 2009. "The Status of Palestinian Refugees in the Near East: The Right of Return and UNRWA in Perspective." *Refugee Studies Quarterly* 28 (2-3): 260–285.

Alpes, M. J. 2017. *Brokering High-Risk Migration and Illegality in West Africa: Abroad at Any Cost*. New York: Routledge.

Aloyo, E., and E. Cusumano. 2018. "Morally Evaluating Human Smuggling: The Case of Migration to Europe." *Critical Review of International Social and Political Philosophy* 24 (2): 1–24.

Andreas, P. 2009. *Border Games: Policing the US-Mexico Divide*. Ithaca, NY: Cornell University Press.

Baconi, T. 2018. *Hamas Contained: The Rise and Pacification of Palestinian Resistance*. Stanford, CA: Stanford University Press.

Carerra, S. et al. 2019. "When Mobility Is Not a Choice: Problematizing Asylum Seekers' Secondary Movements and Their Criminalization in the EU." *CEPS Paper in Liberty and Security in Europe*. https://www.ceps.eu/wp-content/uploads/2019/12/LSE2019-11-RESOMA-Policing-secondary-movements-in-the-EU.pdf.

Cusumano, E. 2017. "Straightjacketing Migrant Rescuers? The Code of Conduct on Maritime NGOs." *Mediterranean Politics*, online ahead of print, September 27, 2017. https://doi.org/10.1080/13629395.2017.1381400.

Government of Israel. n.d. "Coordination of Government Activities in the Territories." Last updated May 25, 2020. https://www.gov.il/en/departments/about/aboutcogat.

Hass, A. 2012. "2,279 Calories per Person: How Israel Made Sure Gaza Didn't Starve." *Haarez*, October 17, 2012.

Koser, K. 2013. "The Smuggling of Refugees." In *Global Human Smuggling: Comparative Perspectives*, edited by D. Kyle and R. Koslowski, 2nd ed., 256–272. Baltimore: John Hopkins University Press.

Mainwaring, C. 2016. "Migrant Agency: Negotiating Borders and Migration Controls." *Migration Studies* 4 (3): 289–308.

Monsutti, A. 2007. "Migration as a Rite of Passage: Young Afghans Building Masculinity and Adulthood in Iran." *Iranian Studies* 40 (2): 167–185.

OCHA (United Nations Office for the Coordination of Humanitarian Affairs). 2017. "Overview of Access of Palestinians from Gaza in 2016." February 10, 2017. https://www.ochaopt.org/content/overview-access-palestinians-gaza-2016.

———. 2018. "Electricity Crisis Brings Gaza to the Brink of Disaster." February 6, 2018. https://www.ochaopt.org/content/un-electricity-crisis-brings-gaza-verge-disaster.

———. 2022. "Gaza Strip: The Humanitarian Impact of Fifteen Years of Blockade." June 29, 2022. https://www.ochaopt.org/content/gaza-strip-humanitarian-impact-15-years-blockade-june-2022.

OHCHR (United Nations Office of the High Commissioner for Human Rights). 2015. *Report of the Detailed Findings of the Commission of Inquiry on the 2014 Gaza Conflict* (A/HRC/29/CRP.4).

Osella, F. 2015. "The (Im)morality of Mediation and Patronage in South India and the Gulf." In *Patronage as Politics in South Asia*, edited by A. Piliavsky, 367–395. Cambridge, MA: Cambridge University Press.

Pelham, N. 2012. "Gaza's Tunnel Phenomenon: The Unintended Dynamics of Israel's Siege." *Journal of Palestine Studies* 41 (4): 6–31.

RAND. 2018. *The Public Health Impact of Gaza's Water Crisis*. Santa Monica, CA: RAND.

Roy, S. 1999. "De-development Revisited: Palestinian Economy and Society since Oslo." *Journal of Palestinian Studies* 28 (3): 64–82.

———. 2007. *Failing Peace: Gaza and the Palestinian Israeli Conflict*. London: Pluto.

———. 2016. *The Gaza Strip: A Political Economy of De-development*. Washington, DC: Institute for Palestine Studies.

Sanchez, G. 2017. "Critical Perspectives on Clandestine Migration Facilitation: An Overview of Migrant Smuggling Research." *Journal on Migration and Human Security* 5 (1): 9–27.

Squire, V. 2017. "Unauthorised Migration beyond Structure/Agency? Acts, Interventions, Effects." *Politics* 37 (3): 254–272.

Stone-Cadena, V. 2016. "Indigenous Ecuadorian Mobility Strategies in the Clandestine Migration Journey." *Geopolitics* 21 (2): 345–65.

Turner, M., and O. Shweiki. 2014. "Decolonizing the Study of the Political Economy of the Palestinian People." In *Decolonizing Palestinian Political Economy: De-development and Beyond*, 1–12. London: Palgrave Macmillan.

United Nations. 2000. Protocol against the Smuggling of Migrants by Land, Sea and Air, Supplementing the United Nations Convention against Transnational Organized Crime.

UNODC (United Nations Office on Drugs and Crime). 2015. *Migrant Smuggling*. Vienna: UNODC.

Van Liempt, I., and J. Doomernik. 2006. "Migrant's Agency in the Smuggling Process: The Perspectives of Smuggled Migrants in the Netherlands." *International Migration* 44 (4): 165–190

Vigh, H. 2009. "Motion Squared: A Second Look at the Concept of Social Navigation." *Anthropological Theory* 9 (4): 419–438.

Wojnicka, K., and P. Pustułka. 2019. "Research on Men, Masculinities and Migration: Past, Present and Future." *International Journal for Masculinity Studies* 14 (2): 91–95.

Zhang, S. X. 2007. *Smuggling and Human Trafficking in Human Beings: All Roads Lead to America*. Santa Barbara, CA: Praeger.

Zharkevich, I. 2020. "'We Are in the Process': The Exploitation of Hope and the Political Economy of Waiting among the Aspiring Irregular Migrants in Nepal." *Environment and Planning D: Society and Space*, online ahead of print, September 9, 2020. https://doi.org/10.1177/0263775820954877.

Contributors

LUIGI ACHILLI is senior researcher at the European University Institute in Florence, Italy, and at the Christian Michelsen Institute in Bergen, Norway. He holds an MA and a PhD in social anthropology from the School of Oriental and African Studies in London. His research and writing focus on irregular migration, transnational crime, refugee studies, political engagement and nationalism, and the Palestinian issue. Ethnographic in approach, his work is based on extensive field research in the Middle East, southern Europe, and Mexico. He has taught at Cambridge, the School of Oriental and African Studies, and various universities in the Middle East. On this and related topics, Achilli has published several articles and other influential works.

PETER ANDREAS is the John Hay Professor of International Studies at Brown University, where he holds a joint appointment between the Department of Political Science and the Watson Institute for International and Public Affairs.

JØRGEN CARLING is research professor of migration and transnationalism studies at the Peace Research Institute Oslo and codirector of the PRIO Migration Centre. His research covers diverse aspects of global migration and transnationalism, often with an emphasis on theoretical innovation.

Among his most influential work is the analysis of aspiration and ability in international migration, the phenomenon of involuntary immobility, and the scripting of remittance transactions. His empirical work has focused on Africa, using a combination of ethnographic and quantitative methods. He has authored more than fifty scientific publications and been a visiting fellow at the University of Oxford, the National University of Singapore, and the University of Maastricht and United Nations University–Maastricht Economic and Social Research Institute on Innovation and Technology.

JOHN DALE is associate professor, Department of Sociology and Anthropology, and director of Movement Engaged, Center for Social Science Research, at George Mason University. He serves on the steering committee of the American Association for the Advancement of Science's Science and Human Rights Coalition and on the Scientific Council and Advisory Board of the European Research Council—Consolidator Project Transnational Advocacy Networks and Corporate Accountability for Major International Crimes (2021–2026). Prof. Dale is author of *Free Burma: Transnational Legal Action and Corporate Accountability* (2011) and coauthor of *Political Sociology: Power and Participation in the Modern World* (2009).

DAVID C. ELLIS is president of Ellis Analytics, Inc., a firm dedicated to helping organizations navigate complexity and diverse sociocultural landscapes. He served as a resident senior fellow at the Joint Special Operations University from 2016 to 2022. He holds a doctorate in international relations and comparative politics from the University of Florida and a master's degree in international development from the George Washington University. Previously, he served as an intelligence analyst in the United States Special Operations Command Directorate for Intelligence, deployed to Afghanistan in support of Special Operations Forces, and worked closely with interagency personnel. His current research focuses on the intersection of complexity, organizational learning within the special operations enterprise, and integrated campaigning and statecraft.

GREGORY FELDMAN is a political anthropologist teaching at the University of Windsor, Canada. His work focuses on migrant political action; borders, policing, and human smuggling and trafficking; and migration policy with emphasis on migration circuits tying North and Central Africa to the European Union and Canada. He is the author of four books: *The Subject of Sovereignty: Relationality and the Pivot Past Liberalism* (2023); *The Gray Zone: Sovereignty, Human Smuggling, and Undercover Police Investigation in Europe* (2019); *We Are All Migrants: Political Action and the Ubiquitous Condition of Migrant-hood* (2015); and *The Migration Apparatus: Security, Labor, and Policymaking in the European Union* (2012).

MATT HERBERT is a senior expert at the Global Initiative against Transnational Organized Crime's North Africa and Sahel Observatory. He specializes in the study of irregular migration, human smuggling, transnational organized crime, and state fragility and stabilization. He also researches and advises on policy responses to these issues. He began his career as a policy aide to the governor of New Mexico, before working on organized crime issues on the US-Mexican border. Dr. Herbert holds a PhD in international relations and a MA in law and diplomacy from the Fletcher School of Law and Diplomacy, Tufts University. He has authored numerous articles, reports, and book chapters on irregular migration, illicit markets, and stability and resilience issues.

GERHARD HOFFSTAEDTER is associate professor in anthropology in the School of Social Science at the University of Queensland. He conducts research with refugees in Southeast Asia, on refugee and immigration policy, and on religion and the state. His first book, titled *Modern Muslim Identities: Negotiating Religion and Ethnicity in Malaysia*, was published in 2011. He coedited a volume titled *Urban Refugees: Challenges in Protection, Services and Policy* that was published in 2015. He is course director for the social anthropology massive open online course World101x: The Anthropology of Current World Issues, which has taught tens of thousands of students how to think more anthropologically.

AHMET İÇDUYGU currently holds a dual appointment as a full professor at Koç University, one in the Department of International Relations and the other in the Department of Sociology. He is also the director of the Migration Research Center at Koç (MiReKoc). He holds a PhD in demography from the Australian National University. He is an elected member of the Science Academy in Turkey. He is the editor-in-chief of the well-established scholarly journal *International Migration*. He teaches on migration studies, theories and practices of citizenship, international organizations, civil society, nationalism and ethnicity, and research methods. He has authored numerous articles and books, including *Critical Reflections in Migration Research: Views from the South and the East*, coedited with Ayşem Biriz Karaçay (2014).

KYUNGHEE KOOK is currently an independent researcher. She holds an MA in migration studies from Oxford University and a PhD in sociology from Bristol University. Her research and writings focus on gender, trafficking, refugee studies, irregular migration, and smuggling networks. Ethnographic in approach, her work is based on field research in East Asia focusing on China and North Korea. Her previous research on North Koreans' irregular migration culminated with the publication "'I Want to Be Trafficked So I Can Migrate!': Cross-Border Movement of North Koreans into China through Brokerage and Smuggling Networks" (2018). Kook is now carrying out field research on migrant North Koreans living in the Korean community in London.

DAVID KYLE holds a faculty appointment at the University of California at Davis and a PhD in sociology from Johns Hopkins University. Pioneering work on transnational communities and entrepreneurship in 1991, building on his previous research in Belize concerning transnational politics, he also initiated the noncriminological comparative approach to our understanding of migrant smuggling in 1995. More recently, Kyle's concept of cognitive migration, which he developed with Finnish researcher Saara Koikkalainen and first presented in 2011, based on our ability to pre-live possible futures using the prospective social imagination, has influenced researchers in diverse cognitive social sciences globally, in both research and applied settings. His current project examines the narrative stories and ideologies of creativity, talentism, and meritocracy around the theme of buried talent at work.

SARAH P. LOCKHART is associate professor of political science and director of International Studies at Fordham University. She is a graduate of Mount Holyoke College and the University of California, Davis. Her research focuses on when and how states work together to address migration policy challenges, and the role of international organizations. She is particularly interested in the links between immigration enforcement, refugee and asylum policy, smuggling, and trafficking. She is the coauthor of *Migration Crises and the Structure of International Cooperation* (2018) and the coeditor of *Introduction to International Migration: Population Movements in the 21st Century* (2021).

VICTOR MANJARREZ is the director of the Center for Law and Human Behavior at the University of Texas at El Paso. The center is partially supported by the Department of Homeland Security. The center is recognized internationally for its applied research in support of the homeland security enterprise. Chief Manjarrez served for more than twenty years in the US Border Patrol and filled key operational roles both in the field and at headquarters over the course of his extensive homeland security career. He was consistently recognized as one of the Department of Homeland Security's most dynamic and innovative operational leaders.

ALICE MASSARI is a Marie Curie Global Fellow at the Canada Excellence Research Chair in Migration and Integration at the Toronto Metropolitan University and the University of Copenhagen. She obtained a PhD in political science, European politics, and international relations and an MA in international relations. Since 2007, Dr. Massari has worked on migration and humanitarian aid in various capacities, including as a researcher, aid worker, and consultant. Her experience includes leading an international nongovernmental organization during the Syrian emergency, working as a European Union expert on migration, and serving as a humanitarian analyst for the UK Foreign Commonwealth and Development Office. Dr. Massari's research and writing have focused on migration, visuality, humanitarianism, and governance. She is the author of the book *Visual Securitization: Humanitarian Representations and Migration Governance*.

ANTJE MISSBACH is professor of sociology at Bielefeld University, Germany, specializing in global and transnational migration and mobility. She is the author of *Separatist Conflict in Indonesia: The Long-Distance Politics of the Acehnese Diaspora* (2012) and *Troubled Transit: Asylum Seekers Stuck in Indonesia* (2015) and coauthor of *Indonesia: State and Society in Transition* (2019). Her latest book, *The Criminalisation of People Smuggling in Indonesia* *and Australia: Asylum out of Reach*, was published in 2022. Her latest research interests include maritime mass movements in the Andaman Sea and state rejections of maritime asylum seekers.

MORGANE NICOT joined the United Nations Office on Drugs and Crime in 2009 to take on the portfolio relating to the implementation of the Smuggling of Migrants Protocol supplementing the UN Convention against Transnational Organized Crime. After leading the knowledge development team on migrant smuggling and human trafficking, she now coordinates the program for the review of the implementation of the convention and its protocols. She holds an LLM in international criminal justice and armed conflict from the University of Nottingham and a postgraduate degree in international administration from the University of Paris Pantheon-Sorbonne.

SIMÓN PEDRO IZCARA PALACIOS is a professor of sociology at the Department of Sociology (UAMCEH), Tamaulipas University, Mexico, and is a member of the National System of Researchers of Mexico. He specializes in immigration studies, migrant smuggling, and sex trafficking. Recent publications include "Smuggling Women for Sex Work in North America: The Smugglers' Perspective" (2022), "'Males Are Undeserving; Females Are Ideal Victims': Gender Bias Hides Demand in Human-Smuggling Networks" (2022), and "The Lucrative Networks Smuggling Women from Mexico and Central America for the Sex Commerce in the United States" (2022, in Spanish).

WAYNE PALMER is a research fellow at Bielefeld University, where he teaches courses on migration and integration, mobility, global migration governance, and labor exploitation in the global fisheries. His publications include studies of the intersections between labor migration, human trafficking, and people smuggling through Indonesia. Palmer's main research project focuses on institutional responses to the violation of migrants' work rights involving three groups of migrants in Indonesia: foreign professionals, foreign spouses, and foreign fishers. He also is a chief investigator on the research project Employment Relations in Indonesia's Commercial Fishing Industry (with Michele Ford and Dede S. Adhuri).

CAITLIN PROCTER is a Marie Curie Research Fellow at the Centre on Conflict, Development and Peacebuilding at the Graduate Institute, Geneva. She received her doctorate in international development at the University of Oxford and previously held a Max Weber Fellowship at the European University Institute. Her research focuses on youth, forced and irregular migration, and postconflict reintegration. She has conducted extensive ethnographic fieldwork in Palestine and has also conducted research on Jordan, Lebanon, Syria, and Tunisia. Alongside her academic work, Procter works regularly as a consultant and adviser to the United Nations Relief and Works Agency for Palestine Refugees in the Near East, UNICEF, and the UN High Commissioner for Refugees.

LUCA RAINERI is a researcher in security studies at the Sant'Anna School of Advanced Studies in Pisa, Italy. His work investigates transnational phenomena of security relevance (organized crime, migration, terrorism, climate change) with reference to the European Union extended Mediterranean neighborhood and Africa at large. Dr. Raineri holds a master's degree in political theory from the Ecole des Hautes Etudes en Sciences Sociales in Paris and a PhD in global politics and human rights from the Sant'Anna School of Advanced Studies. His research has been published in scientific journals, edited volumes, and the monograph *La crisi libica e l'ordine internazionale* (2022). Dr. Raineri has also worked as a consultant for research centers and international organizations dealing with security, development, and migration.

GABRIELLA SANCHEZ is a sociocultural anthropologist with a background in law enforcement, and her work examines irregular migration facilitation and crimes related to migration. She has a special interest in the recruitment and involvement of men, women, and children as smuggling and trafficking facilitators. Her work (carried out on the US-Mexican border and in the Americas, North Africa, the Middle East, and Europe) relies on a community-centered and participatory approach.

EILEEN P. SCULLY is on the faculty of Bennington College, where she teaches history, international law, and public action courses. Scully's publications explore extraterritoriality in treaty port China, human trafficking, international law, and nineteenth-century international history. Her most recent publications include "The United States and International Law: From the Transcontinental Treaty to the League of Nations Covenant, 1819–1919," in *The Cambridge History of America and the World* (2022). Her current research projects focus on pre–World War II diplomatic conflicts over the repatriation of indigent foreign nationals.

SOLEDAD ÁLVAREZ VELASCO is an assistant professor in the Latin American and Latino Studies Program and the Department of Anthropology at the University of Illinois Chicago. She investigates the intersection between irregularized Global South–North and Global South–South transit migration, border regimes, the formation of migratory corridors across the Americas, and the migrant struggle across these transnational spaces, including that of migrant children. She is the author of the book *Frontera sur chiapaneca: El muro humano de la violencia* (2016) and coeditor with Ulla D. Berg and Iréri Ceja of the book *Migraciones*, Colección Palabras Clave (2021). She founded and co-coordinated the transnational digital project (Im)mobility in the Americas and COVID-19.

KIM WILSON is a senior research fellow at the Leir Institute for Migration and Human Security at the Fletcher School, Tufts University, where she also teaches courses in international business and development. Since 2016, Wilson has focused her research on the financial aspects of long-distance migration. As part of her work, she has launched and maintains a web portal called the Journeys Project (https://sites.tufts.edu/journeysproject/). On the portal, a signature set of publications, named Financial Biographies, highlights how refugees and migrants finance their journeys and manage their resources as they adapt to new surroundings.

Index

Page references followed by an "f" indicate a figure; followed by a "t" indicate a table.

A21, 117
Abbott, Tony, 374, 383
Achilli, Luigi, 25, 181, 282
Advisory Committee on Social Questions, 98
Advisory Committee on the Trafficking of Women and Children (CTW), 95–98
Afghanistan and Afghan refugees, 161, 163, 200–201, 203, 209–10, 212
African migration: EU cooperation, 253, 255; increase in, 159, 220, 249; indentured labor and, 88; local networks, 27; motivation, 251; payment systems for, 202, 211; sub-Saharan countries and, 200, 226, 250
Aldeen, Salam, 19
Algeria: embarkation, 238; EU relationship, 242, 261; harga (irregular migration), 223, 237; harraba or tlayna (smugglers), 228; increases or declines, 29, 222, 225–26, 241; networks of, 229–30, 232, 234–35, 243–44; smuggling fees, 233; smuggling from, 220; transit from, 238, 240, 418

Álvarez Velasco, Soledad, 29, 136, 381
American National Vigilance Committee, 91
American Purity Alliance, 91
Amnesty International, 373, 378–79, 383
Andika, 375, 376f, 377–80, 382–84
Andreas, Peter, 18, 38, 133, 167
Antifragile (Taleb), 145–46
Antislavery and Aborigines Protection Society, 100
Anti-Slavery International, 116
Arab Spring, 250, 266n2
Association of Southeast Asian Nations (ASEAN), 51, 292
asylum and asylum seekers: agency and, 9; Australia and, 18, 371, 374; claim requirements, 120–21, 176; EU destination, 22, 189; nonnefarious, 129; policies for, 38, 118, 178; rejected claims, 185; smugglers and, 193, 455. *See also Andika*; Operation Sovereign Borders

INDEX

Australia, 371–75, 377, 381–83, 385–86. *See also* Operation Sovereign Borders
Australian Border Force, 375, 377–80
Australian Criminal Code, 382
Australian Federal Police, 374
Azuay, Ecuador, 42–45, 47–48, 55–56, 346–49, 352f, 353f

Bales, Kevin, 60
Bali Process on People Smuggling, Trafficking in Persons and Related Transnational Crime, 293, 384
Bangladesh, 209, 297–98, 300
Barthes, Roland, 328
Binational Study on Migration, 77
biopower-biopolitics, 411, 420–21, 422n1, 422n4
Bleiker, Roland, 335
border control: Australian strategy, 372–73; corporations and, 82, 427; criminality of, 17; EU-Turkey and, 165, 170; government power, 69, 71, 74–75, 81; Mexican border and, 76, 78; officers, 265; state tightening, 18, 22, 28, 38, 78, 265, 311, 427, 435, 442–43; strategies, 358; technology of, 68, 399; United Nations and, xiii, 111
Bottrell, Andrew, 383
Bousquet, Antoine, 144
Bracero Program, 70–71, 139
Brachet, Julien, 133–34
Braun, Marcus, 67
Butler, Josephine, 90
Byung-Jin (NGO activist), 282

California, 67–68, 73, 75, 82, 142, 392, 394, 396
Campana, Paolo, 16, 22
Cañar, Ecuador, 43–45, 347
Carling, Jørgen, 22, 120–21
Central Americans: coyotes, 358; dangerous journeys of, 83; massacre of, 62; networks of, 4, 27, 47; smugglers and, 427; smugglers target, 427–28, 442–43, 444n2; through transit, 72, 119, 360; violence encountered, 359
Central Mediterranean Route (CMR), 250, 252–53, 256–57, 261, 264–66
Charlton, Diane, 440
children, 5, 7, 13, 31, 43–44, 55
Chinese Exclusion Act (1882), 67
Chinese immigration, 31, 66–67, 139, 142
Chinese seon (networks), 277–78, 283–84, 286
Chouliaraki, Lilie, 326
Chul-jin (seon organizer), 285
Chul-soo (professional smuggler), 280, 285
climate change, 2–3, 30
Clinton, Bill, 74, 109
Coalition Against Trafficking in Persons, 113
Cohen, Lawrence, 282
colonialism, 43, 89, 100–101, 364
Commission of Enquiry into Traffic in Women and Children in the East, 96
Contagious Diseases Acts (1864–1869), 89–90
control, complexity, and *creativity*, 10–12, 31
Correa Cabrera, Guadalupe, 429
Corriere della Sera, Il (newspaper), 326, 336–37
corruption, xiii, 3, 6, 41, 47, 55–56, 61
Countering Threat Networks (Joint Chiefs of Staff), 131
Counterterrorism (Joint Chiefs of Staff), 131
Counterterrorism and *Countering Threat Networks*, 128, 131
COVID-19, 3, 30, 83, 166–67, 226, 360
coyotes, 20, 29, 47–48, 62, 66, 129, 321n1, 426
creativity: African migrants and, 251–52; agency and, 174, 187; Australia and, 372–73, 382; complications, 165; financing smuggling, 199; global meritocracy, 24; Maghreb smuggling

and, 29, 227; migrants and, 26–27; Nigerian trafficking investigation, 416; resettlement programs and, 302–3; Rohingya and Chin and, 304; smugglers and, 26; smuggling and, 153, 155, 162–63, 169, 259–60, 297, 299–300; smuggling-migrant activity, 12, 24–25; social dimension of, 27–28, 32; state-sponsored people smuggling, 384–85

crime, organized: causal stories of, 37, 61; drug smuggling, 110, 427, 432; encrypted cellular phone networks, 407; global networks, 4; mass undocumented migration and, 56; migrants narratives and, xv; smuggling networks, 9, 135, 144, 432, 436, 445n6

crime, state-organized, 56

crime, transnational organized: drones, 406; fluid adaptation of, 408; infrastructure of, 79–80; Myanmar and Thailand and, 49; not involved, 55; ports of entry and, 403; smuggling and, 15, 66, 119, 427; tunnels, 402, 404; tunnels and, 405; ultralight aircraft, 405–6; US-Mexico border and, 393, 398–99

criminal association, 423n6

Crowdy, Rachel, 95

Cuenca, Ecuador, 43–45, 48, 350–51f

Curtis, Simon, 144

Dale, John, 18, 264, 330

debt, 42, 52–53, 60

debt peonage, 43, 52–53

deportation, 118–19, 357, 365

destination states, 108–10, 118–19, 185, 188, 190–94, 194n1

de Witt-Schlumberger, Marguerite, 96

documents, 73, 80–81, 200–201

Dominguez, Miguel E., 44

Doomernik, Jeroen, 20

Draft Convention for the Suppression of the Exploitation of the Prostitution of Others (1937), 98

drug cartels, 359, 397, 406, 427–31, 430t, 431t, 432, 438, 443, 444n1

drugs, 16–17, 28, 130, 255, 401, 426–27, 435, 442

economy: criminal markets and, 21; dollarization of, 62; effect on immigration, 107–8, 228; formal, 26–27; global, 3, 9, 25, 43–44; regional, 56; rural, 45; skilled migrants and, 12; smuggling and, 140; Soviet Union collapse, 108

Ecuador: *chulquero* (smuggler/moneylender), 46–48, 353–54, 360, 366, 367n5; coyoterismo, 345–49, 357–60, 364–66; document forging, 47; dollarization of, 347; domestic smuggling, 345, 353, 356; *encomienda* system, 43; government corruption and, 47; Guapachala, 349; international migrants, 361–63; international smuggling, 345, 354, 361; Iranian smuggling network, 354; labor from, 364; migrant families, 357; migrants and violence, 359; migrants to United States, 365; moneylending in, 46–47; narratives, 354, 362; out-migration to Spain, 62; progressive migratory policies, 355–56, 361; raw material exporting, 347; religiosity of, 349, 350–51f, 352f; sending state, 347, 355, 360; smuggling from, 348; smuggling history, 29, 38; smuggling routes, 356f; social media and, 366; socioeconomic crises, 347; straw (Panama) hat industry, 43–44, 348; *tramitador* (middleman), 354; transit migration, 345, 355, 365; travel routes, 358–59, 367n6; Venezuelan migrants and, 363. See also Azuay, Ecuador; Cañar, Ecuador; Cuenca, Ecuador

Ellis, David C., 16

El Paso, 67–68, 75–76, 390, 393, 400, 402

El Paso *Herald-Post*, 67

employers, 45, 49, 56, 59–61

Entry and Residence of Foreign Nationals and the Right to Asylum (France), xvin5
Erdoğan, Recep Tayyip, 168
Eritrean migrants, 139, 183, 204–5, 250
EU Agenda on Migration, 253–54
EU Common Security and Defence Policy (CSDP), 252–54
EU Migration Partnership Frameworks, 254–55, 260
Eurojust, 421, 423n6
European Migrant Smuggling Centre, 5
European Union (EU), 187; anti-immigration sentiment, 5; boat migration and seizures, 177, 185, 189, 253, 259; border control and, 156–57, 170, 355; border cooperation treaties, 250; criminalization of smuggling, xi, xii, 118; destination priorities, 185; Facilitation Directive, xi, xii; Global Approach to Migration and Mobility, 189; immigration policies, 22, 155, 160, 177; Lampedusa shipwreck, 253; Maghreb states and, 224; Mexican back door to US, 68–69; migration crisis (2015), 159, 162, 164, 185, 250–51, 266n3, 325–27, 332, 339, 340n1; migration management, 186f, 189, 194, 252; migration strategies, 253–55, 260; Mogherini Plan, 253; Nigerian trafficking investigation, 412–16, 421, 423n5; redirection to desert routes, 142; sending countries and, 185, 255; smuggling history, 152–53, 162, 249–50. *See also* Turkey
European Union–Turkey agreements, 458
Europol, 4–5, 253, 414–15, 421
"EU-Turkey Statement" (or Deal), 159, 164–65

families: border crossing and, 133; criminals' treatment of, 20; daughters' exploitation, 52; elite, 56; kin-based networks, 129, 133; kinship and migrants, 47, 133, 161, 204, 209, 234; kinship networks, 291, 295, 302–3; mestizo, 45; money sent home, 58; North Koreans to China, 139; smuggling and, 22, 41, 45–46, 55, 129, 139, 229; smuggling payments, 210; taxes and slave labor, 58; unification, 13
Federal Bureau of Investigation (FBI), 80, 92, 396, 401, 406
fees, 2, 38, 41, 48, 77, 134, 458
Feldman, Gregory, 23
financial systems, 214–16
Finckenauer, James O., 55, 134
Free the Slaves, 117
Friman, H. Richard, 49
Frontex, 166

Gadsden Purchase (1853), 66
Gallagher, Anne, xiii
Gaza Strip: Coordination of Government Activities in the Territories, 451; crossing locations and restrictions, 456–57; Great March of Return, 453, 460–61; Hamas and, 451, 453, 458; irregular migration from, 29, 454, 457–62; Israeli-Egyptian military blockade, 450–52, 456; movement restrictions, 452–53; *muharrib* (smuggling), 457, 460; social and political situation, 449–50, 452–53, 462–63; *tansiq* (fee to enter Egypt), 457, 460; Tunnel Affairs Commission, 453. *See also* Palestinians
Global Alliance Against Trafficking in Women, 113
global border practices, 18, 293, 304, 383–86
Global Compact on Migration, xiv, xv
globalization: border control and, 290; currency crisis and, 49; global tourism, 420; slavery and, 60; smuggling and, 14, 39; smuggling and smugglers, 2; social and cultural practices, 10; technology and, 25; transportation and, 108–9

Golden Venture incident, 39, 142
Goldstein, Kyle and Rachel, 353
Gonzalez, Elián, 39–40
government corruption, 41–42, 47, 57–58, 140
Greek-Turkish border, 19; boat migration and seizures, 210, 461; crowdfunding and, 205; EU-Turkey deal, 164, 166–67; financial system, 216; Global South and, 156; irregular migration, 152, 157, 169, 170n1; mass migration period, 159–60; smugglers and, 209; through transit, 161–62, 225, 459
Greek-Turkish readmission protocol, 157–58
Guevara González, Yaatsil, 282, 318
Gye-sook (Church pastor), 281

Haftar, Khalifa, 262
Hardt, Michael, 410, 421, 422n1, 422n4
Harris, Sidney, 99
Herbert, Matt, 29
Herzog, Silva, 57
Hidalgo, Javier, 303
HMAS *Wollongong*, 377–79
Hoffstaedter, Gerhard, 22
Homeland Security Act (2002), 394–95
human rights: abuses, 3, 50; international agreements and organizations, 93, 97–98, 100–102, 106–7, 111–12, 121; international laws, xi; migrants and refugees, xii; sex-work industry, 50, 102, 113; smuggling and, 62, 112–13
Human Rights Caucus, 113
Human Rights Council on Extrajudicial, Summary or Arbitrary Executions, xiii
human smuggling, 19, 30–31, 32n1
human trafficking: Advisory Committee on the Trafficking of Women and Children (CTW), 95–98; anti-smuggling conventions, 107; anti-trafficking conventions, 106–7; anti-trafficking efforts, 14, 87–88, 96–98, 101; anti-trafficking organizations, 116–17; Asian women, 96; children and, 110–11; Commission of Enquiry into Traffic in Women and Children in the East, 96; distinction with smuggling, 37, 422n3; Draft Convention for the Suppression of the Exploitation of the Prostitution of Others (1937), 98; human cargo trope, 4; International Congress on the White Slave Trade, 89; International Convention for the Suppression of the Traffic in Women of Full Age (1933), 91–95, 97; international instruments against, 108; International Union for the Suppression of the White Slave Trade, 91; London Congress on the White Slave Trade (1899), 87; organized crime and, 119–20; prostitutes and, 95; regional elites and, 56; responses to, 87; Rohingya extortion, 294–95; state organized crime, 56; transnational organized crime and, 55, 61; treaties prohibiting, 87; victimized trafficked migrants, 113–14, 117, 291; White Russian women and, 96. *See also* League of Nations; United States; Vienna Process
Hyuk-min (seon organizer), 285
Hyun-joong (migrant's father), 277

İçduygu, Ahmet, 15
iconography, 237, 336, 338
IDENT, electronic identification system, 74, 400–401
Illegal Immigration Reform and Immigration Responsibility Act (1996), 75
Immigration Act (1907), 92
Immigration Act (1910), 92
immigration agencies, 139–40, 143
Immigration and Nationality Act, 440
Immigration Law (1924), 69
Immigration Reform and Control Act (IRCA) (1986), 72–73

Indonesia, 17–18, 371–72, 374, 377, 381, 386n3. *See also* Operation Sovereign Borders
Indonesian National Police, 374
International Abolitionist Federation, 90
International Agreement for the Suppression of the White Slave Trade (1904), 87, 91, 92–94, 98, 122n3
International Alliance of Women for Suffrage and Equal Citizenship, 95
International Association for the Promotion of Child Welfare, 95, 97
International Bureau (IB), 91, 93, 95–96
International Bureau for the Unification of Penal Law, 98
International Congress on the White Slave Trade, 89
International Convention for the Suppression of the Traffic in Women and Children (1921), 94–95
International Convention for the Suppression of the Traffic in Women of Full Age (1933), 97
International Convention for the Suppression of the White Slave Traffic (1910), 91–93
International Convention on the Protection of the Rights of All Migrant Workers and Members of Their Families, 110, 115
International Court of Justice, 115
International Crime Control Strategy, 78
International Criminal Police Commission (Interpol), 98
International Human Rights Law Group, 113
International Labor Organization, 97
international migrants, 29, 176, 345, 354–55, 361–62, 364, 366n2
International Monetary Fund, 49, 52
International Organization for Migration, 110, 191, 210
International Union for the Suppression of the White Slave Trade, 91
Interpol, 98
irregular migration: criminalization of, xi, 17, 107–8, 110, 118, 130, 265–66, 332, 454; definition of, 266n1, 290, 345, 366n1, 449; goals of, 454; official narratives of, 5; processes of, 454; treatment en route, 6–7
Israel, 448–53, 456. *See also* Oslo Accords
Italy, 25–26, 120, 224–25, 228, 230–31, 250, 259, 267n10
Izcara Palacios, Simón Pedro, 28

Japan and Japanese, 49, 68, 215
Jasmine (asylum boat), 380
Jin-su (seon organizer), 281
Juárez, Mexico, 67, 69

Kanak (asylum boat), 380
Keefe, Daniel, 92
Keller v. United States (1909), 92
Kellogg, Frank, 97
Kellogg-Briand Pact (1927), 97
Ki-han (seon organizer), 279
Kim Jong-un, 273, 280, 282
Kmett, Guy Henry, 80–81
Kook, Kyunghee, 23
Koslowski, Rey, 134
Kurdi, Alan, 121, 334, 336
Kyle, David, 9, 18, 20, 134, 264, 330, 348
Kyung-chul (smuggler), 273

labor: agribusiness, 70, 437–38; biopower-biopolitics, 411; coerced, 58; Ecuadorean migrants and, 346; exploitation of, 45; irregular migration and, 292; shortages, 50, 155–56; skilled or unskilled, 24–25; slavery and, 100; smuggling and, 66, 437–38; undocumented, 40, 59, 62; unskilled and farm, 8, 60, 69, 74; US employers and, 437–38, 439t, 443; vulnerable women, 41–42. *See also* talents and talentism

La Patria, 69
League Health Organization, 97
League of Nations: Advisory Committee on the Trafficking of Women and Children (CTW), 95–97; Committee of Equal Status for Women, 97; human trafficking conference, 93–94; International Alliance of Women for Suffrage and Equal Citizenship, 95; International Association for the Promotion of Child Welfare, 95; Social Hygiene Bureau, 95. *See also* human trafficking
League of United Latin American Citizens, 57
Legal and Constitutional Affairs References Committee (Australia), 373, 382–83
Libya: anti-smuggling agenda, 3; dangerous journey through, 120; embarkation, 238, 250; EU cooperation, 258; EU migration, 250; EU relationship, 264; focus on, 221; governance, 241; Maghreb states and, 224–25; motivation for migration, 251; Sabratha anti-smuggling agenda, 263–64; transit migration, 250; unseaworthy vessels, 120, 226
Lister, Ruth, 283
Lockhart, Sarah P., 13–14
Lockheed Martin, 82
London Congress on the White Slave Trade (1899), 87
López Castro, Gustavo, 425

Maghreb states: boat pilot, 232, 240; corruption and enforcement, 243; criminalization of smuggling, 241–42; economic motivation, 229, 232, 234; embarkation, 238–40; EU relationship, 242; gender-based, 229; logisticians, 231; migrant history, 221–26; non-Maghrebi migrants and, 221, 226; payment systems for, 239; recruiters, 231, 235–37; Schengen Agreement, 223; smuggling history, 243; smuggling networks, 29, 228–31; smuggling services, 232–33; social ties with smugglers, 234; travel methods, 224–27, 234; Turkey and, 225; vessel dangers, 240–41. *See also* Algeria; Morocco; Tunisia
Maher, Stephanie, 282, 318
Mainwaring, Ćetta, 455
Malaysia, 292–96, 298–300, 303
Malkki, Liisa, 410
Mandić, Danilo, 181
Manjarrez, Victor, 28
Mann Act (1910). *See* White Slave Traffic Act
Man-su (seon organizer), 279
Marx, Gary, 65
Massari, Alice, 25
Massey, Douglas, 73
Matovelle, Julio Maria, 349
McIntyre, Phillip, 155
media: developed countries lifestyle, 42; gendered and racialized images, 334; migrant portrayal, 8, 329, 336–38; migration crisis coverage, 332; Myanmar and, 58; photography, 335; smuggler portrayal, 5–6, 19, 25; smugglers' portrayal and invisibility, 329, 333–35, 339, 340n5; smuggling and, 3, 14–15, 19, 37, 325; smuggling coverage, 15, 191, 327; systems of visibility, 335, 340n6
Mediterranean sea: asylum seekers, 185, 190; dangerous and deadly journey, 116, 120, 181, 454; dangerous journeys of, 5; EU and partners, 26, 188, 253; Israeli blockade, 450; Maghreb states and, 224, 242; militarization of, 332; Operation Sophia, 259; smuggling across, 175; smuggling goods, 222; smuggling networks, 228–29, 262; smuggling payment, 206, 209. *See also* Central Mediterranean Route

Meissner, Doris, 77–78
Mengiste, Tekalign Ayalew, 143
Mexico: backdoor to the United States, 108; Bracero Program, 70–71, 139; drugs and criminal syndicates, 62, 429–32; employment destinations, 428, 437; false *coyotaje*, 434; farm workers, 69–70; freedom of exit, 72; migrant recruitment, 444n2; migrants' dangers, 83; migrant smuggling networks, 29, 427–28, 434–36, 436t, 442, 445n4, 445n5; migration from, 440, 443; money sent home, 57–58; polleros, 314, 321n1, 434–35, 444nn1–2; smuggler recruitment, 429–31, 430t, 431t; smuggling history, 66, 139; tourist visas and, 359–60
migrant exporting schemes: chulquero (smuggler/ moneylender), 46–48, 353–54, 360, 366, 367n5; coyotes, 29, 47–48; criminal syndicates and, 41; money laundering comparison, 41; overland route to US, 47; residente (green-card holder), 47–48; sending states, 40–41; tramitadores (facilitators), 45–48, 354
migrants and refugees: agency of, 9, 160–61, 256–57, 454–56, 459, 462; definition of, 176; displaced persons, 292; economically desperate people, 156, 164; empathy and concern for, 121–22; exploitation of, 285–86; facilitation and exploitation, 182–83, 183f, 190–91; facilitators relationship, 7, 177, 317–18; kidnapping of, 183; media portrayal, 325–26, 338, 340n4; migrant protection, 293; moral ambiguity of smuggling, 256; numbers from Myanmar, 296–97; numbers of Africans, 250; numbers of Ecuadoreans, 356, 360; numbers of Mexicans and Central Americans, 440, 441t, 442t; numbers through Eastern Mediterranean, 166; refugee status, 163, 176; smugglers and, 9, 182; symbiotic relationship with smugglers, 65, 170, 443; travel methods, 223; vulnerability of, 175, 179–80, 235
migrant–smuggler relationship, 175, 190–91, 193, 330
migrant smuggling: criminal enterprises and, 38–39; definition of, 175–76; globalization and, 39; mass transnational migration, 56–57; state action, 38
migration process, 153–55, 163, 169, 184–85, 251–52
military, center of gravity analysis (COG), 131–32, 134–37, 140, 142–44, 148; Myanmar and, 50–53, 58–59; technology and, 31, 74–75. *See also* Operation Sovereign Borders; US–Mexico border, security agencies
Min-su (seon organizer), 280–81
Missbach, Antje, 17–18
Morocco, 220–21, 224, 227–28, 238
Morona Santiago, Ecuador, 45
Myanmar: Burmese virgin market, 49, 52–53; destination states, 292; enslavement of villagers, 51; foreign investment and, 51; military government of, 58–59; minority persecution, 296; money sent home, 58–59; Muslims and, 296–97; political history, 50–51; religious persecution, 301; Shan state, 49–50, 52–53; smugglers to Malaysia, 301; state organized crime, 56; Thailand and Malaysia, 292; transnational trafficking of girls and boys, 38, 48–50, 52

narratives: actants, 188, 189f, 192t, 194, 194n2; analysis of, 174, 187; management system and, 194; media, 19; migrant accounts, 19, 30, 160–61, 163, 170; official, 5, 10, 15; policy making and, 191–92; smuggler as criminal, 20, 25
narrative system, 175, 177, 184, 187, 189, 194
Natalagawa, Marty, 375
National League for Democracy (Myanmar), 50–51

National Vigilance Association (NVA), 89–91, 93
nation-state, 411, 416, 420–21, 422n1
Negri, Antonio, 411, 421, 422n1, 422n4
Nepal, 200, 203–4, 209, 213–14
New York Declaration, xiv
New York Times, 99
New Zealand, 375, 378, 380–81
Niger, 133–34, 139, 249–50, 257–58, 260–62, 267n7, 267n8, 267n10
Nigeria, 23, 256, 412–15, 417–18, 420–21, 423n8
nongovernmental organizations: arrest and prosecution of, xii; humanitarian assistance, 51, 91, 252, 270, 326, 394; rescue vessels, xvin5; treaty reporting, 95, 99, 102; United Nations and, 111
North American Free Trade Agreement (NAFTA), 392–93, 408
North Korean migrants: China and, 139, 272, 274; Chinese authorities and, 283–85; financing smuggling, 284–86; legal immigration and, 273; Mongolia and, 274; political situation, 287; smugglers or NGOs, 23, 270; smuggling penalties, 273–74; Southeast Asian countries and, 274–75
North Korean seon (networks): Christian networks, 276–77, 281–82, 286–87; motivation of, 278–83; NGOs, 276–77, 282, 287; North Korean facilitators, 275; professional smugglers, 287; smugglers or NGOs, 275; Underground Railroad comparison, 288n2
Northrop Grumman, 82
Norway, 179
Not For Sale, 117

Observatory on the Rights of Children and Adolescents, 357
Operation Gatekeeper, 76, 390–91
Operation Hold the Line, 76, 390–91
Operation Mare Nostrum, 120
Operation Sophia, 252–53, 259, 267n9
Operation Sovereign Borders, 374–75, 378, 382–83, 385–86, 386n2, 386n5
Oslo Accords, 451, 453
overland journeys, 47, 200, 226, 298–99, 458

Palermo Protocols (2000), 13, 102, 106–7, 110, 112, 114–16, 119–22
Palestinians, 448–49, 451–52
Palmer, Wayne, 17–18
Passport Act (1918), 68
passports, 46–47, 96, 201, 274–75, 297, 363–64, 412
patronage networks, 258, 261–62, 265
Peraltas smuggling organization, 81
Pezzullo, Michael, 383
Polaris Project, 117
politics and migration: Afghanistan, 163; Africa and, 260; biopower-biopolitics, 17, 411, 420–21, 422n1, 422n4; corruption and, 3; Gaza Strip and, 449–50, 452–53, 462–63; human trafficking and, 88; Myanmar, 50–51; North Korea and, 287; Syria, 163; Turkey and, 168–69, 171; US-Mexico border, 38
Portes, Alejandro, 155
Procter, Caitlin, 29
prostitution, 53–54, 89, 96; abolitionism, 90, 94, 97–99, 101; brothels, 52; colonial empires and, 89; consensual or coercive, 91, 93, 101–2, 113; criminalization or regulationism, 90–91, 93–94; frontier boomtowns and, 89; indentured labor and, 88; necessary evil debate, 101; Nigerian street prostitute, 416–19, 421; Nigerian trafficking ring and, 413–15; Schengen Area, 414, 419–20; slave importing operations, 42; social evil, 89; state sanctioned, 95, 99; trafficking history, 14; victim targeting, 96; virgins, 56; voluntary, 113. *See also* white slave trade

484 INDEX

Protocol against the Illicit Manufacturing and Trafficking in Firearms, 122n1

Rackete, Carola, xvin5
Racketeer Influenced and Corrupt Organizations Act (RICO), 134
Raineri, Luca, 28
Rancière, Jacques, 339, 340n6
Raytheon, 82
receiving states, 38, 57, 59, 106, 109, 111–12, 115, 119
refugees: asylum, 9; camps, 5, 51–52; climate crisis and, 3, 31; dangerous journeys of, 5, 21, 178, 461–62; exploitation of, 15; financing, 21; humanitarian assistance, xii; killing of, xiii; law, xi; sea rescues, 19; smuggling and, 22; translation skills, 52; vessel dangers, 175, 181, 185, 240–42; youth, 29
remittances, 41, 57–59
Repubblica, La (newspaper), 326, 333
research methods: Ecuador as a transit space, 346; EU undercover case, 412; Gaza Strip, 449–50; interviews, 199, 222, 271–72, 312, 328–29; Mexican interviews, 428–29, 445n7; Mexican smugglers, 427–28; Mexican smugglers place of origin, 429t; migrant routes, 252, 266n4, 291–92; migrants and smugglers, 199; newspaper images, 327–28
Reuter, Peter, 71
Rockefeller Foundation, 95, 98
Rockwell, Stephen, 79
Rohingya and Chin, 22, 291, 293–304, 305n1, 305n2
Ronfeldt, David, 71
Roosevelt, Theodore, 91–92

Sanchez, Gabriella E., 23, 133–34, 282
San Diego, California, 74, 76–77, 80, 390, 393–94, 402, 405
San Ysidro, 80

Schiavone Camacho, Julia María, 426
Schwab, Klaus, 7, 25
Scott, James C., 217
Scully, Eileen P., 14
Secure Fence Act (2006), 82
sending states: benefit to, 57; economic incentives to, 119–20; human rights and, 110–12; Maghreb states, 224, 242; obligations to migrants, 115; politics and migration, 38, 41, 109; surplus labor and, 114
Shin-young (seon organizer), 276
Simpson, Charles, 181
Skerry, Peter, 79
slave importing operations, 40–42, 264
slavery, 1, 325
Slavery Convention (1926), 96, 100
smuggling and smugglers: from Africa, 116; anti-smuggling conventions, x, 106; anti-smuggling efforts, 14, 119–20, 134, 177–78, 185; anti-smuggling rhetoric, 176–77; asylum and, 193; business of, 181–82; characterization of, 19, 330; commercial trucks, 79; complexity of, 20–21; definition by states, 117, 178; definition of, 2, 19, 66, 310; distinction with trafficking, 422n3; double duality of, 174, 177, 178t, 191, 193; EU migration, 176; financing schemes, 21–22, 137–38, 300; flexibility and adaptation, 141–43, 177; fragility and antifragility, 145–47; gendered and racialized, 308–9; humanitarian motives, xiii, 2, 13–14, 21, 278, 282, 287, 432; incentives for, 114, 141, 180–81; law enforcement and, 145, 162, 181; local view of, 256, 266n5; media portrayal, 325–26; moral ambiguity of smuggling, 19; motives for, 1, 295; negative portrayals, 426; pejorative terms, 129; policing and, 136; policy paradox, 14, 106, 121; professional smugglers, 38, 41, 66, 71–72, 77–80, 229, 271, 275, 277, 279–80;

redirection to remote locations, 68, 80, 82, 142; responsibility for danger, 17–18, 178–79; root causes for, xiv; self-organization, 144–45, 162, 221, 230; self-smuggling, 66, 182; seon (networks) from North Korea, 275; state relationship, 22–23, 184, 193; state-sponsored, 382, 385; technology and, 402; travel agencies and, 46, 62, 139; trust and cooperation, 330; vessel dangers, 175, 181, 185; victims, 78, 106–8; voluntary migrants, 113; waypoint countries, 140. *See also* Vienna Process

smuggling costs: acquiring funds, 202–4, 214; bribes, 201; cash allowances, 202; crowdfunding, 205; documents, 200–201; length of journey, 200; negotiations and, 199–201, 211–12; payment systems for, 216–17; premium for women, 200; services offered, 200, 233; three tries, 212; travel agencies and, 201; travel method, 200

smuggling networks, 134; communities of knowledge, 143; criminal networks, 136, 144; cross boarder networks, 229, 238; decentralized, 137; family members and, 139; high-end, 220, 232–33, 241; host country legality, 140; Libyan, 225; local and small scale networks, 161, 226, 229, 234, 258, 262, 425, 432; Maghreb states, 220, 223, 227–28; money transfer networks, 138; stereotypical image, 255–56, 275

smuggling payments: modes of payment, 207–8t; pay-as-you-go, 211; paying through kin, 210; postpayment, 210; sarafi system, 209, 212–13, 218n1

smuggling risks: money agents and, 198, 206, 209, 212–13, 215–17, 218n1; payment or nonpayment, 206, 209; performance or nonperformance, 206, 209, 212

snakehead, 20, 49

Social Hygiene Bureau, 95
Sontag, Susan, 335
Sook-jung (migrant), 284
Soon-chang (guide in China), 285
South America, 48, 109, 203, 345, 347, 355
Southeast Asian networks, 296
Spain: Algeria and, 229; border technology, 185; Morocco and, 224, 227, 229, 250; receiving state, 62, 223, 233, 347, 353, 417–18
Spener, David, 427
state–smuggler relationship, 18, 175
Stile, Wesley, 69
Stone-Cadena, Victoria, 136
Stop the Traffik, 117
straw (Panama) hat industry, 44–45
Sudan, 22, 205, 249–50, 258, 264–65, 362
Suu Kyi, Aung San, 50–51
Syria and Syrian refugees: asylum needs of, 190; avoiding arrest, 181; EU migration, 121, 250; EU migration crisis (2015), 162; from Gaza, 461; to Libya, 250; media and, 334; motivation of, 165, 251; northern Syria clashes and, 166; politically fragile state, 163; smuggling payments, 200, 204, 210–11; smuggling reputation, 332; trade with home country, 215–16; Turkey transit, 159–60, 328

Taft, William Howard, 92
Taleb, Nassim, 145–46
talents and talentism, 6–8, 11–12, 24–28, 31–32, 309, 372, 470
Taylor, J. Edward, 440
technology: border control and, 68, 74, 79; communication and, 26; density meters, 401; drones, 406–7; encrypted cellular phone networks, 407; international money transfers, 216; social media, 26, 31, 110, 237–38, 364; TikTok, 31. *See also under* US-Mexico border; US-Mexico border, technology of

terminology: coyotes or wolves, 20; *gosfand* (sheep), 20; *hajj* or *ammi* (paternal uncle), 331, 340nn2–3; pollos, 20; *shetou* (snakehead), 20; smuggling, 327

terrorism: in Afghanistan, 131; counterterrorism mission, 127, 131, 146; enabling networks, 131–32; GAO report, 39; military and social science theory, 131–33, 135; nonnefarious and nefarious networks, 128–30, 132–33, 135, 146–48; Salafi-jihadists to Europe, 454; September 11th and, 82; smuggling and, 81, 148, 427; smuggling threat, 130; special interest aliens (SIAs), 130–31, 135–36, 146–48; terrorist organizations, 130–31; World Trade Center bombing and, 39

Thailand: border of, 292; criminalization of smuggling, 293; destination state, 292; globalization and, 49; illegal aliens in, 49–50; immigration policy, 53–55; police and bribes, 52–53, 55; sex-work industry, 38, 49–50, 52–55

Thompson, Albert N., 426

Tijuana, Mexico, 81, 405

tourism, 48, 58, 96, 98, 102, 360, 420, 457

traffickers, 79–80, 88, 102, 108, 114, 293

Trafficking Victims Protection Act (2000), 116

Treaty of Guadalupe Hidalgo (1848), 66

Trump, Donald, 83, 119

Tucson, 76, 403

Tunisia, 29, 220, 224, 227, 229, 238–39, 242; enforcement, 244n1

Turkey: Directorate General for Migration Management, 158; EU relationship, 15, 167, 170, 225; immigration policies, 160; Iranian border, 160; law enforcement and, 162; Law on Foreigners and International Protection, 158; National Action Plan for Asylum and Migration, 158; "open border event of 2020," 168, 170; politicization of migrants, 168–69; smugglers and, 167–68; smuggling history, 153, 157–59, 169; transit migration, 153, 156–57, 159, 162, 225

UN Commission on Crime Prevention and Criminal Justice, 110

UN Convention against Transnational Organized Crime (UNTOC) (2000), ix, x, xi, xiii, xiv, xv, 102, 106–8, 110–12, 120, 329, 382

UN Convention for the Suppression of the Traffic in Persons and of the Exploitation of the Prostitution of Others (1949), 98–101

UN Convention on the Elimination of All Forms of Discrimination against Women (1979), 102

UN Convention on the Rights of the Child, 110

UN Convention Relating to the Status of Refugees, 293

Underground Railroad, 1, 288n2

UN Human Rights Council on Extrajudicial, Summary or Arbitrary Executions, xiii

Union of Soviet Social Republics (USSR), 89, 94, 100, 108–9, 415

United Nations: anti-trafficking efforts, 99, 101–2; prostitution debate, 101; slavery practices debate, 100; Temporary Subcommission on the Status of Women, 99–100; UN Convention, 98

United Nations High Commissioner for Refugees (UNHCR), 291, 293, 296, 301–2

United States: agribusiness, 70, 437–38; alien smuggling convictions, 310; anti-trafficking efforts, 98, 107; banned migrants, 68; border control agents, 311, 319; border security, 109, 348, 355, 365; criminalization of smuggling, 118; economics and immigration, 108;

employers and, 60; immigration policies, 59–60; legalization program, 72; national origin quotas, 68; trafficking control, 116; undocumented workers in, 60

United States v. Portale (1914), 92

Universal Declaration of Human Rights, 101

UN Office on Drugs and Crime, 4, 397

UN Panel of Experts on Libya, 258

UN Protocol against the Smuggling of Migrants by Land, Sea and Air: anti-smuggling regime, 119, 454; compromise position, 114–15; crime impetus, 106; definition of smuggling, 13, 19; human rights and, 112, 121–22; impact of, ix, xi, 116; parties to, x, 117–18; requirements of, xii, xiii, xiv, xviin1–n2; review mechanism, xv; smuggling definition, 310, 329

UN Protocol to Prevent, Suppress and Punish Trafficking in Persons, Especially Women and Children, 102, 106, 112, 114–16

UN Refugee Agency, 176

US Central Intelligence Agency, 354

US Citizenship and Immigration Services, 354

US Department of Defense, 127, 131, 401

US Department of Labor, 444

US Department of State, Office to Monitor and Combat Trafficking in Persons, 116

US General Accounting Office, 38

US Immigration and Customs Enforcement, 443

US Immigration and Naturalization Service: border control, 399; budget and staffing, 74–76, 82; deterrence by, 77–78; Homeland Security and, 395; limited border enforcement, 71; National Anti-smuggling Program, 72; Operation Blockade (Operation Hold-the-Line), 75–76; Operation Disruption, 80; Operation Gatekeeper, 76; Operation Safeguard, 76; professional smugglers, 38

US-Mexico border: assaults on agents, 402; backdoor, 68–69; California entry points, 68; Central Americans and, 427; chaos and clutter, 391, 398–99; Chinese smuggling, 67–68; complexity of, 18, 407–8, 427; corruption at the, 80; criminalization of smuggling, 312; cross-border traffic and trade, 393, 399; economic motivation, 320; geography of, 391–92; immigration policy, 155; interviews with women, 312–14; law enforcement and, 40, 65–66, 68, 71, 74–76, 391, 393; local networks, 425–26; Mexican farm workers, 69–70; migrant origin of residents, 311; narratives, 319; ports of entry, 392, 403; security personnel, 391; security technology, 392; smuggling and, 18, 65–66, 71; smuggling history, 28–29; threats and drug smuggling, 4, 397–98; threats and smugglers, 396; trek from Ecuador, 31; "undesirables" through, 68; Vietnam-era technology, 400; walls, 74–75, 83; women's smuggling role, 309–10, 319

US-Mexico border, security agencies: Drug Enforcement Agency (DEA), 396, 399; Federal Bureau of Investigation, 396, 401; Office of Field Operations (OFO), 395, 403–4; Office of National Drug Control Policy, 401; state and local law enforcement, 396; US Border Patrol, 6, 38, 69, 390, 395, 398, 402–3; US Customs and Border Protection (USCBP), 394, 396, 403, 405; US Customs Service, 394–95, 399, 401; US Department of Defense, 401; US Department of Homeland Security, 82, 394–96, 401, 404–6, 444; US Immigration and Customs Enforcement, 395–96, 440

US-Mexico border, technology of: aircraft, 400; American Shield Initiative, 400; Automated Biometric Identification System (IDENT), 74, 400–401; facial recognition software, 404; fiberscopes, 401; Integrated Automated Fingerprint Identification System, 401; Integrated Fixed Tower system, 403; remote video surveillance systems (RVSSs), 400, 403; surveillance equipment, 400; tightening of security, 28; unmanned aerial surveillance, 82; Vehicle and Cargo Inspection System (VACIS), 401, 404; Z Portal, 404
US Sentencing Commission, 310
US Special Operations Command, 16, 128
US Special Operations Forces (SOF), 127–29, 131, 133–36, 143–49

Vallina, Miguel, 77
Venezuelan migrant crisis, 345, 363
Vienna Process, 111–13
Vietnam, 102, 371
Vigh, Henrik, 455–56
violence: assaults on agents, 402; Ecuador-Mexico-US route and, 364, 367n4; gender-based, 102, 321; human smuggling and, 1; Malaysian smugglers, 300; men of violence, 445n3; migrant smuggling networks, 434; motivation for leaving, 7, 29, 58; narratives and, 5; Salafi-jihadists and, 148; solidarity and, 6, 20; Syrians and Greeks, 167; transiting migrants and, 62; voodoo rituals and fear, 417, 419
visas, 46–47, 69, 74, 116, 201, 223, 292, 348

visual social semiotics, 327–28, 337
Vogt, Wendy, 282, 318, 339
von Lampe, Klaus, 136

Wheat, Michael, 78
white slave trade: International Agreement for the Suppression of the White Slave Trade (1904), 87, 91, 92–94, 98, 122n3; International Convention for the Suppression of the White Slave Traffic (1910), 91–93; traffic in women, 94; *traite des blanches*, 89, 93
White Slave Traffic Act (Mann Act), 89, 92
Wilson, Kim, 21
women: Committee of Equal Status for Women, 97; domestic violence, 316; facilitators, 309; gendered services and, 89; motivation for smuggling, 313, 316, 319; passport requirements, 96; rape and torture of, 51; refugees, 5, 52; sexual exploitation, 38, 41, 49, 55, 95; sexual transactions, 315, 321; smuggling costs, 200; smuggling prosecution, 310–11, 319; smuggling roles, 23–24, 308–10, 312–17, 320; straw (Panama) hat industry, 43–44; trafficking history, 14; UN Temporary Subcommission on the Status of Women, 99–100
Workers Defense League, 100
World Trade Center, 39, 130

Young-Chul (Christian pastor), 286
Yúnez-Naude, Antonio, 440

Zhang, Sheldon, 330